Validated Practices for Teaching Students with Diverse Needs and Abilities

Susan Peterson Miller
University of Nevada, Las Vegas

D1314649

Allyn and Bacon

Boston • *Toronto* • *London* • *Sydney* • *Tokyo* • *Singapore*

Executive Editor: *Virginia Lanigan*
Series Editorial Assistant: *Erin Kathleen Liedel*
Marketing Managers: *Amy Cronin and Kathleen Morgan*
Production Editor: *Annette Pagliaro*
Editorial Production Serivce: *Innovation Publication Services*
Composition Buyer: *Linda Cox*
Manufacturing Buyer: *Julie McNeil*
Cover Administrator: *Kristina Mose-Libon*
Electronic Composition: *Innovation Publication Services*

A Pearson Education Company
75 Arlington Street
Boston, MA 02116

Internet: www.ablongman.com

Library of Congress Cataloging-in-Publication Data

Miller, Susan Peterson
    Validated practices for teaching students with diverse needs and abilities / Susan
Peterson Miller
        p. cm.
    Includes bibliographical references and index
    ISBN 0-205-30628-4 (pbk.)
    1. Special education—United States. 2. Mainstreaming in education—United States. I.
Title.

LC3981.M55 2002
371.9'0973—dc21   2001022422

Printed in the United States of America
10 9 8 7 6 5 4 3   05 04

This book is dedicated to my parents, Geraldine and Robert Peterson, for teaching me my first life lessons with kindness and love; to my sister, Terry Anne Findley, for teaching me how to play school and giving me a jump-start on first grade; and to my husband, Steven Michael Miller, for continuing to teach me about the funny and joyous sides of life. This book also is dedicated to the late Virginia Miller for taking me into her classroom and allowing me to absorb the work of an exemplary special education teacher.

CONTENTS

7 Modifying Curriculum and Instruction   287

PART THREE   EVALUATING STUDENT AND TEACHER PERFORMANCE

8 Monitoring Student Progress   331

) Preface

Society in general and schools in particular are experiencing monumental changes that have the potential to greatly improve the lives of students, including those with diverse needs and abilities. There exists a strong commitment among many educators to create learning environments that support the academic and social–emotional needs of all students. The tireless efforts of teachers, researchers, administrators, ancillary personnel, paraeducators, parents, teacher educators, employers, and students have resulted in new understandings about how to go about the business of teaching and learning. We know more now than ever about validated practices for students with diverse needs and abilities. This knowledge holds great promise for improved educational practice. It is critically important for educators, teacher educators, and other interested stakeholders to stay focused on educational practices that have validated support. The dynamic nature of schools, the increasing diversity among students, paradigm shifts with regard to delivery of support services, and the national agenda to increase academic standards accentuate the need to provide the best possible education to students with diverse needs and abilities.

One of the greatest challenges for anyone involved in the teaching and learning process is weeding through the voluminous amounts of available information to find "the right stuff." This book was written to assist in selecting the practices and methods that have the greatest potential for making significant and sustained improvements in the lives of students with diverse and special needs. In-depth discussions of practices that have been researched and/or field tested and subsequently found to be beneficial are included. Throughout the book, Validation Boxes are provided to share important information about the research or field testing that supports each practice. References also are provided to assist those who desire more detailed information about the validation procedures. The intent for including only validated practices and covering these practices in depth is to contribute to the important goal of moving our profession toward increased implementation of research-based educational practices.

This book is organized in three sections that model the most important components of the teaching and learning process: *(a)* Planning Instruction, *(b)* Delivering Instruction, and *(c)* Evaluating Student and Teacher Performance. Careful attention to each of these components increases the likelihood that students with diverse needs and abilities will receive the high-quality education they deserve. The chapters within these three sections are carefully crafted to model both the importance of selecting appropriate content (i.e., validated practices) and the importance of using appropriate processes for implementation of the content (i.e., advance organizers, clear explanations, many examples, visual representations, practice activities, post-organizers, and distributed reviews). This organizational structure, along with the content provided, helps reinforce the components that need to be in place for effective teaching and learning to take place.

Acknowledgments

Writing this book has been a challenging and rewarding journey. Numerous colleagues provided support along the way. Their willingness to share resources, knowledge, suggestions, smiles, laughs, and words of encouragement contributed to the successful completion of this book.

Thanks are extended to the faculty, staff, teachers on special assignment, and project coordinators who were members of the Department of Special Education at the University of Nevada, Las Vegas during the critical writing stages of this book. Special thanks to Beatrice Babbitt, Steve Baker, Monica Brown, Nancy Brown, Joe Crank, Karen Davis, Nasim Dil, John Filler, Jeff Gelfer, William Healey, Maggie Hierro, Edward Kelly, Marie Landwer, Connie Malin, Rebecca Nathanson, Nancy Sileo, Sherri Strawser, Colleen Thoma, and Lynnette Wilfling for their moral support, loaned materials, and content input. Special thanks to Kyle Higgins for her valuable content suggestions, moral support, and for taking on additional responsibilities during my sabbatical leave. Special thanks also are extended to Department Chairperson Thomas Pierce for being there during the highs and the lows, for providing both personal and professional support, and for candid reviews of important sections of this book. His humanness and gentleness helped keep me grounded during this three-year project.

Heartfelt thanks are extended to the conscientious graduate assistants who worked with me during the creation of this book. Special thanks to Michael Caulkins, Cynthia Lau, Laura Kaya, and Cathi Draper-Rodriquez for their ongoing support. Their ERIC searches, phone calls to professionals across the country, and tireless dedication contributed greatly to the quality of this book.

Many professionals provided support and information that contributed to the successful completion of this book as well. Thanks to Randy Boone; Kit-hung Lee, University of Nevada, Las Vegas; Candace Bos; Sharon Vaughn, University of Texas at Austin; Janis Bulgren; Donald Deshler; Keith Lenz; Suzanne Robinson; Janet Roth; Jean Schumaker; Jackie Schafer; James Sherman; and the SIM Network, University of Kansas; Pegi Denton, Overland Park, KS; Ed Ellis, University of Alabama; Ann Knackendoffel, Kansas State University; Carol Sue Englert, Michigan State University; Doug Fuchs, Lynne Fuchs; Kim Paulsen, Vanderbilt University; Leah Herner, California Lutheran University; Mel Hovell, San Diego University; Hal McGrady and the Executive Board of the Division for Learning Disabilities; Marilyn McKinney; Sandra Odell; Peggy Perkins; and Judy Pollak, UTP Leadership Team, University of Nevada, Las Vegas; Catherine Morocco, Educational Development Center, Newton, Massachusetts; Pam Hudson, Utah State University; Cecil Mercer, University of Florida; Victoria Morin, Troy State University; Jeanne Schumm, University of Miami; Tony Van Reusen, University of Texas at San Antonio. Thanks also to Christy Beaird, Jan Butz, Kathy Konold, Kyle Konold, Robin Stall, Ron Tamura, Barb Webb, and Michelle Dupree Wilson of Clark County School District—your support was appreciated. Special thanks to Frances Butler, Weber State University, for her positive attitude and diligent work on the Instructor's Manual for this book.

The hard-working individuals at Allyn & Bacon also deserve recognition for their contributions to this book. Thanks to Ray Short and Sean Wakely (formerly of Allyn & Bacon) for encouraging me to move forward with this book and for providing initial content ideas and suggestions. Special thanks to Virginia Lanigan, Executive Editor, for her support throughout the writing of this book. Her good thinking, patience, and responsiveness to my many e-mail questions were greatly appreciated. Thanks to Erin Liedel, Series Editorial Assistant, Annette Pagliaro, Production Editor, and John Cook, Project Editor, and Peg Markow, Managing Editor, with Innovation Publication Services, for their competence, efficiency and problem-solving abilities. Thanks also to Rori Carson and Judith J. Ivarie of Eastern Illinois University, Judy B. Engelhard of Radford University, and David A. Powers of East Carolina University for serving as reviewers of the book and to Diane Bryant, University of Texas at Austin, for her review of the technology section in Chapter 6. These reviewers' comments and suggestions were extremely helpful and greatly appreciated.

Support and love received from my family and "almost-family" members during the writing of this book reminded me that life is full of things for which I am grateful. Thank you, Mom, Dad, Terry, Neil, Jennie, Matt, Sydney, Pop, Betty, Ray, Janice, Lorena, Megan, Larry, Trisha, Jessica, Cindi, Gail, Susan, Jacky, Kim, Patty, and the Pams. Your calls, letters, e-mails, and visits were appreciated. And last, but certainly not least, thank you, Steve, for your daily support, encouraging words, and constant love. Your strength of character, wonderful sense of humor, and optimistic approach to life provide ongoing inspiration.

Understanding
School Context
and Student Diversity

*Nothing better defines what we are and what we will
become than the education of our children.*

—George Bush

ADVANCE ORGANIZER

The purpose of this chapter is to discuss the current context of schooling in the United States. Specifically, information about educational reform movements is presented. Noteworthy reports related to the reform effort are briefly discussed. Next, the diversity found among students in today's schools is discussed. Emphasis is placed on diversity related to disabilities, cultural and linguistic backgrounds, socioeconomic status, and sexual orientation. Increased student diversity coupled with current reform movements that emphasize higher expectations and standards for students provides a strong rationale for using validated teaching practices.

The context of schooling in the United States is dynamic and ever-changing. For more than a decade, the field of education has been in a state of transition. A national education reform movement emerged in the 1980s and continued through the 1990s into the twenty-first century. The major theme of this reform movement has been improving the quality of education to build a stronger nation. Raising standards and expectations for student performance in school to strengthen local economies and the nation's position in the global world market has been emphasized. Concurrent with the educational reform movement, significant demographic changes have occurred within U.S. society at large and are therefore reflected in school cultures as well. The combination of a national education reform movement and rapidly changing school demography presents unique challenges for general and special education professionals.

The Educational Reform Movement

Educational reform has received a significant amount of attention since the publication of *A Nation at Risk* (National Commission on Excellence in Education, 1983). This report challenged Americans to think about the importance of education and indicated the need to improve the current educational system in the United States. The report is credited with having significant influence on school districts, professional organizations, private-sector groups, and governmental agencies. Subsequently, additional reports emerged that helped set national and state agendas. Included among these were:

- AMERICA 2000: An Education Strategy, United States Department of Education, 1991
- What Work Requires of Schools: A SCANS Report for AMERICA 2000, Secretary's Commission on Achieving Necessary Skills, United States Department of Labor, 1991
- National Education Summit Policy Statement, Summit Participants, 1996

▶ The National Education Goals Report: Building a Nation of Learners, National Education Goals Panel, United States Government Printing Office, 1997

Each of these reports contributed to the emergence of a major educational reform movement.

AMERICA 2000: An Education Strategy

In 1991, President Bush announced AMERICA 2000: An Education Strategy. The strategy represented a bold, comprehensive, and long-range plan to encourage all school communities in the United States to meet six National Education goals that the president and governors adopted the previous year. The goals (United States Department of Education, 1991) were stated as follows:

By the year 2000:
1. All children in America will start school ready to learn.
2. The high school graduation rate will increase to at least 90 percent.
3. American students will leave grades four, eight, and twelve having demonstrated competency in challenging subject matter including English, mathematics, science, history, and geography; and every school in America will ensure that all students learn to use their minds well, so they may be prepared for responsible citizenship, further learning, and productive employment in our modern economy.
4. U.S. students will be first in the world in science and mathematics achievement.
5. Every adult American will be literate and will possess the knowledge and skills necessary to compete in a global economy and exercise the rights and responsibilities of citizenship.
6. Every school in America will be free of drugs and violence and will offer a disciplined environment conducive to learning. (p. 3)

The AMERICA 2000 plan was promoted as a national strategy that honors local control, relies on local initiative, affirms states' and localities' fiscal responsibilities for education, and recognizes the private sector as a partner in education. The federal government's role in this strategy was to assist in setting standards, contribute fiscal support, provide flexibility in exchange for accountability, and push states to begin their efforts to improve American schooling.

The SCANS Report for AMERICA 2000

The SCANS (Secretary's Commission on Achieving Necessary Skills, 1991) report addresses school curriculum that prepares students for the world of work. Specifically, this report outlines five competencies that individuals must master to be successful in the twenty-first century workplace:

▶ Identify, organize, plan, and allocate resources (e.g., time, money, material and facilities, human);

▶ Work on teams, teach others, serve clients, demonstrate leadership, negotiate, and work effectively with individuals from backgrounds different from their own;

▶ Acquire, organize, and interpret information;

▶ Understand, monitor, and improve social, organizational, and technological systems; and

▶ Work with a variety of technologies.

Thus, successful employment in the twenty-first century involves effective resource management, strong interpersonal skills, efficient information management through the use of computers, clear understanding of complex systems and interrelationships, and expertise in higher-level thinking skills such as problem solving and reasoning. These general competencies are generalizable across numerous work environments and are critical to employment success (Secretary's Commission on Achieving Necessary Skills, 1991).

National Education Summit Policy Statement

The 1996 National Education Summit was held March 26–27 in Palisades, New York. The governor from each state was invited to attend and bring one business leader from the state. Additionally, a limited number of resource personnel were invited (e.g., educators, state legislators, chief state school officers). Along with then President Bill Clinton, forty-one state governors, forty-nine business leaders, and thirty-four resource participants attended the summit. Together these individuals addressed two related issues: how to develop, implement, and measure high academic standards for K–12 public schools; and how to infuse new technologies into education to improve teaching, learning, and school administration.

The summit participants developed and unanimously adopted a policy statement encouraging all states to establish *(a)* internationally competitive academic standards, *(b)* assessments to measure academic achievement, and *(c)* accountability systems within the subsequent 2 years. The governors agreed to reallocate sufficient funds to support implementation of the standards (e.g., professional development, infrastructure, new technologies). The business leaders agreed to actively support the governors' efforts to improve student performance, develop other coalitions of business leaders to expand the support base, disseminate information related to the skills that students need to meet the workforce demands of the twenty-first century, and link hiring practices to school performance and achievement.

The summit participants also supported the establishment of a national resource center to assist states in raising academic standards, improving assessments, and increasing accountability. This support led to the development of a national information clearinghouse called ACHIEVE. The primary goals of ACHIEVE are to *(a)* provide national leadership on standards, assessments, accountability, and technology; *(b)* prepare annual reports that track the progress of states in meeting the commitments articulated at the 1996 National Education

Summit; *(c)* establish an electronic clearinghouse of pertinent information; *(d)* provide a system for comparing standards and assessment tools among states and also internationally; and *(e)* provide technical assistance to states seeking to establish higher academic standards.

National Education Goals Report

Congress passed the Goals 2000: Educate America Act in 1994. This act included the six original goals from AMERICA 2000: An Education Strategy and added two new goals, one related to professional development and the other to parental involvement. Thus, the eight national education goals (National Education Goals Panel, 1997) are as follows:

Goal 1: Ready to Learn
By the year 2000, all children in America will start school ready to learn.

Goal 2: School Completion
By the year 2000, the high school graduation rate will increase to at least 90 percent.

Goal 3: Student Achievement and Citizenship
By the year 2000, all students will leave grades 4, 8, and 12 having demonstrated competency over challenging subject matter including English, mathematics, science, foreign languages, civics and government, economics, arts, history, and geography, and every school in America will ensure that all students learn to use their minds well, so they may be prepared for responsible citizenship, further learning, and productive employment in our Nation's modern economy.

Goal 4: Teacher Education and Professional Development
By the year 2000, the Nation's teaching force will have access to programs for the continued improvement of their professional skills and the opportunity to acquire the knowledge and skills needed to instruct and prepare all American students for the next century.

Goal 5: Mathematics and Science
By the year 2000, United States students will be first in the world in mathematics and science achievement.

Goal 6: Adult Literacy and Lifelong Learning
By the year 2000, every adult American will be literate and will possess the knowledge and skills necessary to compete in a global economy and exercise the rights and responsibilities of citizenship.

Goal 7: Safe, Disciplined, and Alcohol- and Drug-free Schools
By the year 2000, every school in the United States will be free of drugs, violence, and the unauthorized presence of firearms and alcohol and will offer a disciplined environment conducive to learning.

Goal 8: Parental Participation
By the year 2000, every school will promote partnerships that will increase parental involvement and participation in promoting the social, emotional, and academic growth of children. (pp. xiv–xviii)

The National Education Goals Panel was created in July 1990 and consists of eight governors, four members of Congress, four state legislators, and two members appointed by the president. Each year the panel publishes a report documenting state and national progress toward achieving the eight national goals. The 1999 National Education Goals Report indicated that national performance improved (↑) significantly (from the previous year) in the following areas:

Goal 1: Ready to Learn
↑ The proportion of infants born with one or more of four health risks has decreased.
↑ The percentage of 2-year-olds who have been fully immunized against preventable childhood diseases has increased.
↑ The percentage of families who are reading and telling stories to their children on a regular basis has increased.
↑ The gap in preschool participation between 3- to 5-year-olds from high- and low-income families has decreased.

Goal 3: Student Achievement and Citizenship
The percentage of students who are proficient in reading has risen in:
↑ Grade 8.

The percentages of students who are proficient in mathematics have risen in:
↑ Grade 4;
↑ Grade 8; and
↑ Grade 12.

Goal 5: Mathematics and Science
The proportion of college degrees awarded in mathematics and science has increased. This is true for:
↑ all students;
↑ minority students; and
↑ female students.

Goal 7: Safe, Disciplined, and Alcohol- and Drug-free Schools
↑ The percentage of students who report that they have been threatened or injured at school has decreased (National Education Goals Panel, 1999, pp. 10–11).

According to this same 1999 report, significant declines in national performance (↓) were noted (from the previous year) in the following areas:

Goal 4: Teacher Education and Professional Development
↓ The percentage of secondary school teachers who hold a degree in their main teaching assignment has decreased.

Goal 7: Safe, Disciplined, and Alcohol- and Drug-free Schools
↓ The percentage of students reporting that they used an illicit drug has increased.
↓ The percentage of students reporting that someone offered to sell or give them drugs at school has increased.
↓ The percentage of public school teachers reporting that they were threatened or injured at school has increased.

↓   A higher percentage of secondary school teachers report that disruptions in their classrooms interfere with their teaching (National Education Goals Panel, 1999, p. 11).

Annual updates regarding national progress relative to national education goals may be obtained from the National Education Goals Panel, 1255 22nd Street, NW, Suite 502, Washington, DC 20037; telephone: (202) 724-0015; fax: (202) 632-0957; e-mail: negp@Ted.gov; Web site: www.negp.gov.

The Education Reform Movement, as evidenced by these various federal reports, has emphasized setting high goals and standards for public education. Many national associations have been involved in this standards-based reform movement. In 1989 the National Council of Teachers of Mathematics was the first professional association to issue curriculum standards. Since that time, standards for the arts, civics, foreign language, geography, health, history, music, physical education, science, social studies, and technology have been released. Some states are adopting these national standards and others are creating their own.

State standards are typically used for three purposes. First, they guide curriculum and instruction within local school districts. Second, they are used to design state- and district-level assessments. Finally, the state standards are used to establish graduation requirements (i.e., performance required to earn a high-school diploma).

The standards-based reform movement has had some opposition, but typically the opposition has resulted in modifying the content of the standards rather than stopping the reform efforts (Center for Policy Research on the Impact of General and Special Education Reform, 1996).

Standards-Based Reform and Special Education

Developers of national and state education goals and standards suggest that the goals and standards are appropriate for *all* students. The term *all* was used frequently in the educational reports generated during this reform movement. The emphasis on all students raises important issues and questions with regard to educating students with disabilities and other special needs. Foremost among these issues is whether it is appropriate and reasonable to have the same standards for all students regardless of abilities. One of the criticisms of the standards has been the lack of consideration for varying characteristics among students, particularly those with disabilities. Related concerns include how performance on the standards will be assessed and whether the instructional approaches advocated in the standards are appropriate for students with special learning needs. Initially, special educators had limited involvement in the standards-based reform movement. Consequently, little attention was given to students with disabilities. More recently, however, involvement of special educators in the reform process (e.g., reviewing standards; serving on state committees that develop content standards, developing standards-related instructional activities appropriate for students with disabilities) has increased.

The notion of increasing standards for students with disabilities is gaining momentum within the field of special education. For example, the 1997 Amendments to the Individuals with Disabilities Education Act (IDEA) clearly promote the concept of setting higher expectations for students with disabilities and holding school/agency personnel accountable for assessing and reporting student progress. The rules and regulations for implementing the amendments require states to *(a)* establish goals for the performance of students with disabilities that "are consistent, to the maximum extent appropriate, with other goals and standards for all children established by the state"; *(b)* establish "performance indicators that the State will use to assess progress toward achieving those goals that, at a minimum, address the performance of children with disabilities on assessments, drop-out rates, and graduation rates"; *(c)* every two years "report to the Secretary and the public on the progress of the State, and of children with disabilities in the State, toward meeting the goals established"; and *(d)* based on its assessment of progress, "revise its State improvement plan . . . as may be needed to improve its performance" (U.S. Department of Education, 1999, 34 CFR 300.137 (a) (2) (b) (c) (d)).

The rules and regulations for the 1997 Amendments to IDEA also require that states *(a)* have on file with the Secretary of Education information to demonstrate that students with disabilities are included in "general State and district-wide assessment programs, with appropriate accommodations and modifications in administration, if necessary"; and *(b)* develop alternate assessments and guidelines for the participation of children with disabilities who cannot participate in State and districtwide assessment programs (U.S. Department of Education, 1999, 34 CFR 300.138 (a) (b) (1) (2)). Additionally, the rules and regulations require that school personnel report to the public on the progress of students with disabilities as often and with the same amount of detail as they report on the progress of students without disabilities (U.S. Department of Education, 1999, 34 CFR 300.139 (a)).

Another important component of the 1997 IDEA amendments is the enhanced participation of students with disabilities in the general education curriculum through changes in the Individualized Education Program (IEP) process. Specifically, the rules and regulations state *(a)* IEPs must address "how the child's disability affects the child's involvement and progress in the general curriculum (i.e., the same curriculum as for nondisabled children)"; and *(b)* "The regular education teacher of a child with a disability, as a member of the IEP team, must, to the extent appropriate, participate in the development, review, and revision of the child's IEP, including assisting in the determination of appropriate positive behavioral interventions and strategies for the child, and supplementary aids and services, program modifications, or supports for school personnel that will be provided for the child" (U.S. Department of Education, 1999, 34 CFR 300.347 (a) (1) (i) and 300.346 (d) (1) (2)). The 1999 IDEA amendments reveal an "explicit obligation to explain how a student's disability affects involvement and progress in the general curriculum" (Huefner, 2000, p. 196). The standards-related message communicated through these amendments is that expectations for students with disabilities should be increased and students with disabilities should be included in the general education curriculum with appropriate supports. Additionally, IDEA amendments make it clear that most students with disabilities are expected to participate (at least partially) in the state's general education assessments and only a small percentage of students with disabilities should be allowed to participate in an alternate assessment system (Shriner, 2000). According to researchers at the National Center on Educational Outcomes, a majority of states reported that between 10 and 20 percent of students with disabilities in their states were permitted to participate in an alternate assessment system in 1999 (Thompson, Lehr, & Quenemoen, 2000).

The total effect of the standards-based reform movement and the IDEA amendments on students with disabilities has yet to be determined. One of the most visible outcomes resulting from the movement has been increased high-school graduation requirements. These include more overall credits required for graduation, more course work required in specific content areas such as math and science, initiation of minimum competency tests as a requirement for graduation, increased scores required to pass minimum competency tests, and more difficult content added to minimum competency tests. Little research has been conducted to evaluate the effects of these various endeavors, but in one study involving 8,748 students with learning disabilities and 78,757 students without learning disabilities, it was determined that the number of credits earned in math in high school was a better predictor of math scores on the American College Testing (ACT) entrance exam than high-school grade point average. For English and science, however, high-school grade point average was a better predictor of ACT English and science scores than the number of credits earned in these subjects (Shokoohi-Yekta & Kavale, 1994). Additional research is needed to further evaluate the effects of reform-based outcomes on students with disabilities.

Special Education Service Delivery Reform

Concurrent with the standards-based reform movement, a special education service-delivery reform movement emerged. Historically (i.e., prior to 1975), special education services were delivered primarily in classes composed only of students with disabilities. Once placed in these classes, students rarely returned to general education classes for any of their instruction. With the passage of the Education for All Handicapped Children Act of 1975, PL 94-142 (now Individuals with Disabilities Education Act), greater emphasis was placed on integrating or mainstreaming students with disabilities. According to the law, all children and youth with disabilities are guaranteed a free appropriate public education in the least restrictive environment. The general interpretation of the law has been that students with mild disabilities should be enrolled in general education classrooms and "pulled out" of these classes for a portion of the day to receive specialized instruction in special education classes.

Even after the passage of PL 94-142, students with more severe disabilities continued to receive instruction in special education classes for the entire school day. Throughout the 1990s, a more inclusive service-delivery model emerged. Consequently, increasing numbers of students with disabilities received instruction in general education classrooms without separate "pull-out" programs. Between the 1988–1989 school year and 1994–1995 school year, a 60 percent increase occurred in the number of students with disabilities who were placed in general education classes for at least 79 percent of the school day (McLeskey, Henry, & Hodges, 1998). Not surprisingly, the most significant movement toward general-education class placement involved students with mild disabilities (McLeskey, Henry, & Hodges, 1999). In inclusive educational models, special education teachers work collaboratively with general education teachers to provide effective instruction to all students. As a result of this special education reform movement, the diversity of students found in general education classes has increased significantly.

Student Diversity

Never before in the history of U.S. schooling has student diversity been so evident. Student diversity is seen across several dimensions: disabilities, gifts and talents, cultures and languages, socioeconomic levels, and sexual orientation. New thinking on the instruction of students with diverse needs has occurred concurrently with the increase in student diversity and the national education reform movement. Classrooms are viewed as communities of learners that include and value all students. As previously mentioned, there has been a significant reduction in instructional programs that require students to leave the general education classroom for special services. Instead, students are remaining in the general education classroom where services come to them and modifications and adaptations are made to accommodate their diverse needs. Thus, to effectively meet the vast array of student needs, teachers must be knowledgeable about student diversity and must learn to collaborate with professionals who have expertise in areas different from their own.

The purpose of the remainder of this chapter is to provide an overview of the types of diversity that teachers will likely encounter among the students in their classes. Student characteristics and educational recommendations are provided for consideration. More detailed explanations of validated methods and procedures that can be used when planning, delivering, and evaluating instruction for diverse groups of students are found in the remaining chapters of this book. A stronger emphasis is placed on *validated* practices because these are the practices that are likely to result in high rates of student and teacher success.

Students with Disabilities

The number of students who participated in federal programs for students with disabilities increased from 3.7 to 5.6 million between 1977 and 1996, representing a 51 percent increase (National Center for Education Statistics, 1998). From 1987 to 1997, the number of 6- to 11-year-olds who received special education services increased 25.3 percent, the number of 12- to 17-year-olds who received these services increased 30.7 percent, and the number of 18- to 20-year-olds who received them increased 14.7 percent (United States Department of Education Office of Special Education Programs, 1998).

During the 1996–1997 school year, students with learning disabilities accounted for more than half of all students with disabilities (51.1 percent). Students with speech or language impairments (20.1 percent), mental retardation (11.4 percent), and emotional disturbance (8.6 percent) constituted an additional 40.1 percent of all students with disabilities. Thus, 91.2 percent of students with disabilities had learning disabilities, speech or language impairments, mental retardation, or emotional disturbance. The remaining 8 to 9 percent had hearing impairments (1.3 percent), visual impairments (0.49 percent), deaf–blindness (0.02 percent), orthopedic impairments (1.2 percent), other health impairment (3.0 percent), autism (0.65 percent), traumatic brain injury (0.19 percent), or multiple disabilities (1.8 percent). The heterogeneity among students with disabilities is extensive even among students with the same disability label (United States Department of Education Office of Special Education Programs, 1998).

Students with Learning Disabilities

As previously noted, students with learning disabilities constitute a little more than half of all students with identified disabilities. The United States Department of Education (1999) provides the most widely accepted definition of specific learning disability:

> a disorder in one or more of the basic psychological processes involved in understanding or in using language, spoken or written, that may manifest itself in an imperfect ability to listen, think, speak, read, write, spell, or to do mathematical calculations, including conditions as perceptual disabilities, brain injury, minimal brain dysfunction, dyslexia, and developmental aphasia. The term does not include learning problems that are primarily the result of visual, hearing, or motor disabilities, of mental retardation, of emotional disturbance, or of environmental, cultural, or economic disadvantage. (34 CFR 300.7 (c)(10))

A wide range of characteristics are associated with students with learning disabilities. The most prominent characteristic is difficulty with academic learning. In spite of normal or above-normal intelligence, students with learning disabilities have difficulty completing academic tasks commensurate with their apparent ability. These difficulties are most frequently noted in the areas of reading, writing, spelling, and mathematics at the elementary level and in all content classes at the secondary level. Many students with learning disabilities have strengths in some academic areas and weaknesses in others. In addition to academic difficulties, students with learning disabilities also may have problems with language, perception, metacognition, memory, attention, motivation, generalization, and problem solving. Social-emotional and behavioral difficulties also are evident in some students. Thus, learning disabilities manifest themselves in a variety of ways and in varying degrees of severity (Mercer, 1997; Robinson & Deshler, 1995). Typically, individuals with learning disabilities need highly intensive instruction in both the process of learning and the content to be learned.

Students with Speech or Language Impairments

According to the previously cited figures, students with speech or language impairments constitute the second largest disability group. According to the United States Department of Education (1999), "Speech or language impairment means a communication disorder, such as stuttering, impaired articulation, a language impairment, or a voice impairment that adversely affects a child's educational performance" (34 CFR 300.7(c) (11)).

Many students who are identified as having a learning disability also have speech or language impairments as a secondary disability. Thus, speech and language impairments may actually represent the highest incidence of all the disability categories. Speech impairment typically involves voice, articulation, or fluency disorders. Voice disorders involve abnormal spoken language production (e.g., unusual pitch, loudness, or sound quality). Articulation disorders involve producing speech sounds incorrectly. Fluency disorders involve hesitations or repetitions of sounds or words (e.g., stuttering) that interrupt a person's flow of speech. Speech disorders rarely influence academic learning in negative ways. If, however, the disorder is severe, the student may have difficulty sustaining peer relationships and may withdraw from social situations.

Students with language impairment have difficulty with receptive or expressive language, or both. Receptive language refers to the ability to take in and understand what someone else says. Expressive language refers to the ability to express ideas in words and sentences. Difficulties with either receptive or expressive language undoubtedly affect students' abilities to perform in school. Receptive language is needed to understand verbal directions and information presented in lessons; expressive language is needed to participate in class and to complete many academic assignments. Thus, language abilities greatly influence student success in school (Smith & Luckasson, 1992). Students with speech and/or language impairments frequently need intensive therapy to improve their communication abilities.

Students with Mental Retardation

Although numerous definitions of *mental retardation* have emerged over the years, the United States Department of Education defines it as "significantly subaverage general intellectual functioning, existing concurrently with deficits in adaptive behavior and manifested during the developmental period, that adversely affects a child's educational performance" (United States Department of Education, 1999, 34 CFR 300.7 (c) (6)).

The American Association on Mental Retardation definition states, "Mental retardation refers to substantial limitations in present functioning. It is characterized by significantly subaverage intellectual functioning, existing concurrently with related limitations in two or more of the following applicable adaptive skill areas: communication, self-care, home living, social skills, community use, self-direction, health and safety, functional academics, leisure, and work. Mental retardation manifests before age 18" (Luckasson et al., 1992, p. 1). The authors of this definition (Luckasson et al., 1992) also identified four assumptions that are essential to the application of the definition. These are:

1. Valid assessment considers cultural and linguistic diversity as well as differences in communication and behavioral factors;
2. The existence of limitations in adaptive skills occurs within the context of community environments typical of the individual's age peers and is indexed to the person's individualized needs for supports;
3. Specific adaptive limitations often coexist with strengths in other adaptive skills or other personal capabilities; and
4. With appropriate supports over a sustained period, the life functioning of the person with mental retardation will generally improve. (p. 1)

Students with mental retardation display a wide variety of learning characteristics, but typically their academic profile is relatively consistent across academic areas. Rather than having pronounced strengths in some areas and weaknesses in others, individuals with mental retardation tend to perform similarly in all academic areas. Many students with mental retardation have difficulty with communication, attending, and memory skills. Moreover, they have difficulty with generalization and problem-solving activities. Poor social and behavioral skills are sometimes present and can hinder the development of peer relations. Finally, motivation can be a problem, particularly if there is a history of failure or if the student has learned to depend on others to have needs met (Morrison & Polloway, 1995; Smith & Luckasson, 1992). Students with mental retardation typically need intensive instruction in functional academic and daily living skills. Vocational education also is helpful.

Students with Emotional Disturbance

The United States Department of Education (1999) defines emotional disturbance as:

a condition exhibiting one or more of the following characteristics over a long period of time and to a marked degree that adversely affects a child's educational performance:
(A) An inability to learn that cannot be explained by intellectual, sensory, or health factors.
(B) An inability to build or maintain satisfactory interpersonal relationships with peers and teachers.
(C) Inappropriate types of behavior or feelings under normal circumstances.
(D) A general pervasive mood of unhappiness or depression.
(E) A tendency to develop physical symptoms or fears associated with personal or school problems.
The term includes schizophrenia. The term does not apply to children who are socially maladjusted, unless it is determined that they have an emotional disturbance. (34 CFR 300.7 (c) (4))

Emotional disturbance manifests itself in either externalizing or internalizing behaviors. Externalizing behaviors are typically aggressive and directed toward others. These behaviors include fighting, consistently irritating others, impulsivity, cursing, arson, stealing, or hurting others. Internalizing behaviors are those expressed in a socially withdrawn manner. These behaviors include social isolation, depression, eating disorders, fears and phobias, or elective mutism. Extremes in emotional and behavioral problems undoubtedly affect academic progress and the development of appropriate interpersonal skills (Kauffman, 1993; Smith, 1998; Whelan, 1995). Students with emotional disturbance typically need intensive educational programs that include behavioral training, social development, and/or counseling. When a student's behavior impedes his learning or that of others, the Individualized Education Program (IEP) team must consider the strategies and supports needed to address the behavior. The IEP must reflect programmatic application of positive behavior interventions (Warger, 1999).

As mentioned earlier, most students with disabilities (91.2 percent) are identified as having learning disabilities, speech/language impairment, mental retardation, or emotional disturbance. They are eligible for special education services under IDEA. Thus, most general and special education teachers will teach students with these particular disabilities. There are, however, numerous other disabilities that fewer numbers of students display. Included among these are hearing impairments, visual impairments, deaf–blindness, orthopedic impairments, other health impairments, autism, traumatic brain injury, and multiple disabilities.

Students with Hearing Impairment

Students with hearing impairment may be deaf or hard of hearing. The United States Department of Education (1999) defines deafness as "a hearing impairment that is so severe that the child is impaired in processing linguistic information through hearing, with or without amplification, that adversely affects a child's educational performance" (34 CFR 300.7 (c) (3)). Students who are hard of hearing, but not deaf, can process information from sound, usually with the help of a hearing aid.

There are two types of hearing loss: conductive and sensorineural. Conductive hearing losses involve problems with sound transmission from the outer or middle ear to the inner ear. Blockages or damage to the outer ear cause this problem and can sometimes be corrected through surgery or other medical treatments. Sensorineural losses occur when there is damage within the inner ear (specifically the cochlea) or to the auditory nerve that affects the conversion of sound waves into electrical impulses. Sensorineural losses usually are not amenable to correction through surgery, but some promising work is being done with multichannel cochlear implants that electronically bypass the defective cochlea (Lowenbraun, 1995). Moreover, hearing aids are sometimes helpful.

Students with hearing impairment may have difficulty with attending, following directions, and completing assignments. Consequently, their academic performance tends to be lower than that of their peers without disabilities. Speech and language difficulties also are common among students with hearing impairment and can impede students' ability to communicate with others. Thus, their ability to establish and maintain friendships can be affected (Salend, 1998; Smith & Luckasson, 1992). Educational programming for students with hearing impairment must include special attention to language and communication needs. Moreover, the bilingual (e.g., sign language and English) and bicultural (e.g., deaf culture and American culture) abilities of students with hearing impairment should be supported. Students with hearing impairment need opportunities for direct instruction in their language and communication mode, as well as opportunities for direct communication with peers and professional personnel.

Students with Visual Impairment

The United States Department of Education (1999) definition for visual impairment reads: "Visual impairment including blindness means an impairment in vision that, even with correction, adversely affects a child's educational performance. The term includes both partial sight and blindness" (34 CFR 300.7 (c) (13)). Some students are born with visual impairment while others acquire this disability. Students with visual impairment constitute a heterogeneous group. Most individuals with visual impairment have IQ scores that fall in the normal range; consequently, they learn to read and write and participate effectively in the general education curriculum. Many individuals with severe visual impairment display mannerisms that are sometimes called blindisms (rocking from the hips, poking at their eyes, rolling their heads).

It has been noted that visual impairments can affect psychosocial development. Much of social learning occurs as a result of watching others and modeling their behavior. Students with visual impairment are at a disadvantage when it comes to learning appropriate social interactions. Fewer social contacts can result in withdrawal or passive social behavior. Some students with visual impairment are overly dependent on others to solve their problems or meet their needs. Overprotection from family, friends, or teachers can contribute to student withdrawal and dependency (Smith, 1998; Tuttle & Ferrell, 1995). Various aids are available to assist students with visual impairments in their learning, such as glasses, computer technology, and machines that enlarge type. Recorded texts help students acquire important information. Some students with severe visual impairment read in Braille (a coded system of dots embossed on paper). IDEA requires the IEP team "to consider provision of instruction in Braille or the use of Braille" for any student who is blind or visually impaired (Warger, 1999, p. 2).

Students with Deaf–Blindness

A small number of students (in comparison to the number of students with other disabilities) are both deaf and blind. The United States Department of Education (1999) defines deaf–blindness as "concomitant hearing and visual impairments, the combination of which causes such severe communication and other developmental and educational needs that they cannot be accommodated in special education programs solely for children with deafness or children with blindness" (34 CFR 300.7 (c) (2)). A student who has deafness and blindness faces greater challenges than if only one of the disabilities were present. A compounding effect of one disability upon the other emerges. A child who is blind uses auditory clues to help with mobility. A child who is blind and deaf won't have the benefit of visual or auditory clues. Similarly, a child who is deaf relies on vision to assist with language development. Therefore, a child who is blind and deaf will face greater challenges in language development (Tuttle & Ferrell, 1995). Students with deaf–blindness need learning opportunities that facilitate purposeful movement. Specifically, orientation and mobility instruction, along with communication and daily living instruction, is needed. Such instruction provides a set of foundation skills that broaden students' awareness of the environment and frequently results in increased motivation, independence, and safety (Gense & Gense, 1999).

Students with Orthopedic Impairments and Students with Other Health Impairments

The United States Department of Education (1999) identifies two categories for students with physical and/or health-related needs: orthopedic impairment and other health impairment. Orthopedic impairment is defined as:

> a severe orthopedic impairment that adversely affects a child's educational performance. The term includes impairments caused by congenital anomaly (e.g., clubfoot, absence of some member), impairments caused by disease (e.g., poliomyelitis, bone tuberculosis, etc.), and impairments from other causes (e.g., cerebral palsy, amputations, and fractures or burns that cause contractures). (34 CFR 300.7 (c) (8))

According to the United States Department of Education (1999), other health impairment is defined as:

> having limited strength, vitality or alertness, including a heightened alertness to environmental stimuli, that results in limited alertness with respect to the educational environment, that is due to chronic or acute health problems such as asthma, attention deficit disorder or attention deficit hyperactivity disorder, diabetes, epilepsy, a heart condition, hemophilia, lead poisoning, leukemia, nephritis, rheumatic fever, and sickle cell anemia; and adversely affects a child's educational performance. (34 CFR 300.7 (c) (9))

Students with physical and/or health-related needs are a heterogeneous group with a variety of conditions. In addition to the conditions listed in the definitions of the U.S. Department of Education, students may qualify for services if they have muscular dystrophy, spina bifida, osteogenesis imperfecta (brittle bone disease), spinal cord injury, juvenile rheumatoid arthritis, Tourette's syndrome, seizure disorders, cancer, human immunodeficiency virus (HIV), or hepatitis or if they are considered to be medically fragile (i.e., students with chronic and progressive conditions that require special technological healthcare procedures for life support and/or health support during the school day). It is difficult to identify specific characteristics of students with physical and health needs because of the vast differences among conditions. On average, however, students with physical and health-related

Michael, a young man with physical and health-related needs, has access to the general education chemistry curriculum. He enjoys working in the lab and hopes to become a lab technician after completing high school.

needs have normal learning abilities, but academic progress is affected by absences from school related to their medical condition. These students also may have special social-emotional needs. Clearly, communication among teachers, school nurses, families, and healthcare providers is needed (Salend, 1998; Sirvis & Caldwell, 1995).

Students with Autism

Autism is a rare condition defined by the United States Department of Education (1999) as:

> a developmental disability significantly affecting verbal and nonverbal communication and social interaction, generally evident before age 3, that adversely affects a child's educational performance. Other characteristics often associated with autism are engagement in repetitive activities and stereotyped movements, resistance to environmental change or change in daily routines, and unusual responses to sensory experiences. The term does not apply if a child's educational performance is adversely affected primarily because the child has an emotional disturbance. (34 CFR 300.7 (c) (1))

Autism usually manifests itself as a severe disorder in communication and behavior and occurs within the first two and a half years of life. Some of the common characteristics of students with autism include *(a)* dysfunctional interpersonal skills (e.g., resist touch, seem aloof, avoid eye contact, act aggressively toward others), *(b)* self-stimulation or ritualistic behaviors (e.g., body rocking, staring at spinning objects, hand flapping, laughing at inappropriate times), *(c)* language difficulties (e.g., abnormal speech, no speech, limited verbalizations, echolalia), *(d)* behavioral difficulties (e.g., resistant to changes, no fear of common dangers, overactive, age inappropriateness, self-injurious), and *(e)* learning problems. Early intervention programs with behavior modification procedures are very important for these children (Lovaas, 1987).

Students with Traumatic Brain Injury

Another very rare condition is traumatic brain injury (TBI). The United States Department of Education (1999) defines TBI as:

> an acquired injury to the brain caused by an external force, resulting in total or partial functional disability or psychosocial impairment, or both, that adversely affects a child's educational performance. The term applies to open or closed head injuries resulting in impairments in one or more areas, such as cognition; language; memory; attention; reasoning; abstract thinking; judgment; problem-solving; sensory, perceptual, and motor abilities; psychosocial behavior; physical functions; information processing; and speech. The term does not apply to brain injuries that are congenital or degenerative, or to brain injuries induced by birth trauma. (34 CFR 300.7 (c) (12))

TBI is characterized by sudden onset; most frequently, it is the result of motor vehicle accidents. There are, however, a variety of other causes, including gunshot wounds, physical abuse, and accidental falls. Students with TBI experience physical, learning, or psychosocial difficulties well beyond their initial recovery and rehabilitation period. They lose previous levels of personal, academic, and social functioning. Cognitive deficits, memory losses, inability to focus, mental and physical fatigue, frequent headaches, organizational problems, up-and-down performance profiles, processing delays, language difficulties, emotional difficulties, loss of sensations, changes in behavior and self-management are common characteristics found in students with TBI. Social relationships and self-esteem also can be affected. Although these characteristics appear to be similar to those of students with learning disabilities or emotional disturbance, there is the added challenge of dealing with memories of how the student was prior to the injury. This recollection can be very painful for students with TBI, their families, friends, and teachers (Bergland & Hoffbauer, 1996; Salend, 1998). Thus, in addition to intensive academic instruction, students with TBI may need psychosocial intervention.

Students with Multiple Disabilities

Some students are identified as having more than one disability. The United States Department of Education (1999) defines students with multiple disabilities as those with:

concomitant impairments (such as mental retardation-blindness, mental retardation-orthopedic impairment, etc.), the combination of which causes such severe educational needs that they cannot be accommodated in special education programs solely for one of the impairments. The term does not include deaf–blindness. (34 CFR 300.7 (c) (7))

The characteristics of students with multiple disabilities vary widely from student to student, and therefore different levels of support are needed. Generally, students with multiple disabilities learn slowly, fail to demonstrate learned skills spontaneously, and have difficulty generalizing their learning to new situations (Noonan & Siegel-Causey, 1990). Delays in social, intellectual, language, and physical development are common. Students with multiple disabilities can learn a variety of skills with appropriate instructional programs. Current state-of-the-art practice involves teaching functional skills in natural environments (e.g., teaching life skills in settings where they normally occur), using technology to improve communication skills, providing opportunities for interactions and friendships with normally achieving peers, and coordinating needed services by using a team approach involving professionals from various disciplines (Siegel-Causey, Guy, & Guess, 1995).

Students Who Are Gifted and Talented

Another group of students who contribute to student diversity are those considered to be gifted and talented. Estimates suggest that between 3 and 5 percent of the school population is gifted (Sisk, 1987). These figures may actually be low due to limited methods for identifying students with giftedness, particularly those from culturally and linguistically diverse backgrounds (Cohen, 1994). Additionally, some states allocate more money for education and therefore more students receive specialized services (Swassing, 1992).

The Gifted and Talented Children's Education Act (1978) (PL 95-561) provided the following definition:

"Gifted and talented" means children, and whenever applicable, youth, who are identified at the preschool, elementary, or secondary level as possessing demonstrated or potential abilities that give evidence of high performance capability in areas such as intellectual, creative, specific academic, or leadership ability, or in the performing and visual arts, and who, by reason thereof, require services or activities not ordinarily provided by the school. (Sec. 902)

Although students with giftedness form a diverse group, they tend to display some common intellectual characteristics. Typically, students with giftedness reason abstractly, process information well, learn quickly, solve problems, demonstrate intellectual curiosity, generalize learning, remember great amounts of material, demonstrate high verbal abilities, show great depth in understanding topics, recognize relationships quickly, display long attention spans, see ambiguity in what appears to be factual information, and display interest in a wide range of topics.

With regard to social/emotional characteristics, students with giftedness may criticize themselves, expect perfectionism from themselves, play with older friends, demonstrate leadership, exhibit loner behavior, display empathy and sensitivity, exhibit individualism, and demonstrate strength of character (Silverman, 1995; Smith, 1998). Students with exceptional talents often excel in visual and performing arts (Turnbull et al., 1995). Talented individuals show natural aptitude in a specific area; they may also demonstrate superior intelligence.

A variety of approaches are used when providing services to students who are gifted and talented. Included among these are enrichment programs that allow students to explore topics in greater depth or topics not included in traditional curricula. Accelerated or honors programs that allow students to move through a curriculum or school grades at a quicker pace also are available. Mentor programs that pair students with adults who have expertise in areas of special interest, independent study to help students become self-directed in their learning, and hands-on experience in career fields of interest also are appropriate for students with giftedness (Smith & Luckasson, 1992). Historically, educational programs for students with giftedness involved "pull out" models similar to the service-delivery model for students with disabilities. In these programs, students with giftedness were enrolled in general education classes but spent a few hours each week in special classes for students who were gifted. More recently, support for providing services to gifted students within general education settings has increased, and some individuals are questioning the appropriateness of providing gifted education. Critics of gifted education believe it is elitist, morally incorrect, unfair to general education students who would benefit from more access to these peers, and potentially a way to disguise racial segregation in school settings (Smith, 1998). It is likely that these issues will continue to receive attention and consideration throughout the twenty-first century.

Students from Diverse Cultural and Linguistic Backgrounds

Cultural and linguistic diversity is increasing dramatically in American society; thus, demographic changes also are occurring within public schools. Students with non-European backgrounds make up an increasingly large segment of the school-age population. In 1976, non-European American students represented 24 percent of the total school population. In 1980, non-European American students represented 25 percent of the total school population. By 1985, this percentage increased to 29 percent; by 1994, it was 34 percent; and in 1995, 35 percent of students enrolled in grades 1 to 12 in public schools were from a non-European background. This 11 percentage point increase from 1976 to 1995 was primarily due to an increasing Hispanic student enrollment. The Hispanic population has increased more rapidly than any other ethnic group. In 1976, Hispanic students represented 6 percent of the student population in public elementary and secondary schools in the United States; this rose to 14 percent by 1995. Predictions indicate that more than 20 percent of the child population will be Hispanic by the year 2020. The num-

*Cultural and linguistic diversity among students adds a positive dimension to the class-
room and provides learning opportunities that extend beyond the prescribed curricula.*

ber of African American, Asian American, and Native American students is
expected to continue to increase over the next decade as well. Demographers predict that by the year 2020 students of color will constitute 46 percent of America's
school-age youth (National Center for Education Statistics, 1992, 1998; Pallas,
Natriello, & McDill, 1989). Currently, non-European American students make up or
approach the majority of students in many urban school districts (American Council on Education and Education Commission of the States, 1988; Quality Education
for Minorities Project, 1990).

Classrooms in today's schools are more diverse than ever. This diversity, however, is not limited to differences between ethnic groups. There also is a tremendous
amount of diversity within ethnic groups. Spanish-speaking students may come
from Mexico, Puerto Rico, Cuba, Central America, South America, or Spain. Cultural differences exist among students from these countries, and different variations
of Spanish are spoken depending on the original home location. The length of res-
idence in the United States also influences language. Similarly, considerable diversity is found among African American students. Socioeconomic status, geographic
location, acculturation of children and parents, and identification with African
American culture vary from student to student. There also exists much diversity

among Asians. Included among Asian Americans are students from Japan, China, Korea, Hong Kong, the Philippines, Cambodia, Laos, and Thailand. Pacific Islanders include students from Hawaii, Samoa, and Fiji. Asian Americans and Pacific Islanders are widely diverse in cultures, religions, and languages. Experiential and socioeconomic differences also exist. There are about one thousand Asian languages and dialects. Native Americans, another diverse group, include Indians, Alaskan natives, Native Hawaiians, and Aleuts. There are more than 500 different Native American groups, each with its own customs, languages, and traditions. The number of Native Americans living on reservations has declined in recent decades, but 40 percent of Native Americans still live on or near identified Native American areas. Many Native Americans believe it is important to maintain their own educational school system to reinforce the cultural identity of their children (Winzer & Mazurek, 1998).

Although certain characteristics are sometimes reported in connection with specific cultural groups (e.g., Latinos having fluid boundaries for time and space; Native Americans working together for the good of the group and maintaining a spiritual connection to the earth; Asian Americans maintaining close-knit extended, patrilineal, hierarchical families; African Americans valuing sense of community and viewing education as a way out of poor living conditions), these generalizations cannot be applied to all members of the respective ethnic group. Teachers must recognize that there are both similarities and differences among members within groups. To meet the needs of students from various cultural and linguistic groups, teachers must demonstrate cultural sensitivity and respect and must become knowledgeable about the particular students within their classes (Utley et al., 2000). It also is important to get to know the families of the students and to become familiar with their belief systems. This knowledge will help teachers avoid stereotyping, accurately interpret the behaviors of their students, distinguish cultural differences from deficits, and plan effective instructional programs that incorporate the richness of the various cultures represented in their classes.

Students from Diverse Socioeconomic Families

The United States is one of the wealthiest countries on earth, but the inequitable distribution of wealth is cause for concern. In 1989, the wealthiest 4 percent of Americans earned as much money as the bottom 51 percent of Americans (Barlett & Steele, 1992). In other words, the combined incomes of over half of all Americans equaled what the top 4 percent earned. Students who live in poverty and students who live in affluence bring very different life experiences and perspectives to their public school classrooms. Special needs can emerge for both students who live in poverty and those who live in affluence.

Students Who Live in Poverty

Throughout the 1980s and early 1990s, the disparity between the rich and the poor increased, and most Americans experienced real-wage reductions. The rich were getting richer and the poor were getting poorer (Bradsher as cited in Salend, 1998; Sleeter & Grant, 1999; Thurlow as cited in Salend, 1998). According to the United States Bureau of the Census, Current Population Reports (1998), this trend recently changed as United States households experienced significant annual increases in their income in 1995, 1996, and 1997. The overall poverty rate in the United States in 1997 was 13.3 percent, statistically lower than the 13.7 percent reported for 1996. This slight decline in overall poverty rate primarily resulted from reduced poverty among African Americans and Hispanic Americans. The poverty rate among African Americans dropped from 28.4 percent to 26.5 percent from 1996 to 1997. During the same year, the poverty rate among Hispanic Americans dropped from 29.4 percent to 27.1 percent. Although poverty rates dropped for these two groups, the rates are still significantly higher than the rates for European Americans (11 percent) and Asian and Pacific Islanders (14 percent) for the same year (Dalaker & Naifeh, 1998).

While the overall poverty rate in 1997 was 13.3 percent, the poverty rate for people under 18 years of age during the same year was 19.9 percent, significantly higher than the poverty rate for adults aged 18 to 64 (10.9 percent) and those aged 65 and over (10.5 percent). Children had the highest poverty rate; those under age six were particularly vulnerable (21.6 percent) (Dalaker & Naifeh, 1998).

Children who live in poverty need and deserve outstanding teachers who orchestrate educational experiences that result in high rates of student success. School success represents hope for a positive, productive, and decent future.

Children who live in poverty suffer numerous consequences. One of the most devastating consequences is poor literacy development. Research suggests that children who live in poverty have less access to books, a major factor in poor reading ability. In a study involving 40 public-school children from three economically diverse communities (i.e., Beverly Hills, an extremely affluent community; Compton, a working-class community; and Watts, a working and impoverished community), data were collected regarding access to books. The findings revealed that less affluent students not only had fewer books in their homes, but also had fewer books in their schools and public libraries than affluent students (Smith, Constantino, & Krashen, 1997). Children who live in poverty also are more likely to have disabilities. Longitudinal research involving annual data sets from 1983 to 1996 reveal a growing relationship between poverty and risk for disability (Fujiura & Yamaki, 2000). Students who live in poverty also are more likely to suffer adverse effects related to malnutrition and poor health care. They are more apt to encounter violence and crime. Recent research indicates that poverty harms children's health, education, and later earnings and that poverty is a stronger correlate of children's ability and achievement than maternal schooling, single parenthood, parental skills, family character, low parent IQ, or inadequate parenting ability (Sherman, 1997).

The harmful effects of poverty are compounded when individuals are both poor and members of non-European ethnic groups. In a study involving 66 less advantaged elementary students and 64 more advantaged elementary students, Schultz (1993) found that "minority elementary students who were more socioeconomically advantaged were more likely to achieve higher in mathematics and reading than peers with less socioeconomic advantage" (p. 228). Thus, teachers must put substantial energy into providing exemplary instruction that keeps students in school and promotes high levels of achievement. Martin Haberman (1995b) emphasized the importance of this by saying, "For the children and youth in poverty from diverse cultural backgrounds who attend urban schools, having effective teachers is a matter of life and death. These children have no life options for achieving decent lives other than by experiencing success in school. For them, the stakes involved in schooling are extremely high" (p. 1). He also said that students who live in poverty "have no other realistic options for 'making it' in American society. They lack the family resources, networks, and out-of-school experiences that could compensate for what they are not offered in schools. Without school success, they are doomed to lives of continued poverty and consigned to conditions that characterize a desperate existence: violence, inadequate health care, a lack of life options, and hopelessness" (Haberman, 1995a, p. 781).

Students Who Live in Affluence

Many high-income families have dual-income parents who are both pursuing "fast-track" professional careers. Throughout the late-twentieth century, there was an emphasis among many Americans on getting ahead professionally, obtaining material possessions, and living in the "fast lane." Parents who are involved in fast-paced, high-demand careers sometimes expect similar performance from their children.

Brooks (1990) interviewed 80 psychiatrists, psychologists, educators, and counselors. She also interviewed 60 parents and 100 youngsters. Her views about children of fast-track parents were formulated based on these combined interviews. Brooks's findings revealed that some fast-track parents validated their own success through high achievement of their children and therefore put enormous pressure on them. This pressure sometimes resulted in unintended negative consequences, such as stress-related disorders (e.g., headaches, stomachaches, facial tremors, aggressive behavior); cheating to obtain expected good grades; or giving up altogether, especially when the students believed the high expectations were unobtainable. Brooks also noted that involvement in highly competitive environments can cause difficulties with regard to establishing friendships, especially when peers are viewed as competitors.

Another conclusion drawn from Brooks's (1990) interviews was that self-esteem problems can arise when other adults are hired to rear children because of the parents' extensive work obligations. She noted there appeared to be a growing number of students coming to school from affluent environments seeking love, attention, and approval from their teachers. She further noted, in some cases, students from affluent backgrounds were highly demanding and expected others to fulfill their needs just as the hired caretakers in their homes had done for years. Some parents who felt guilty about spending little time with their children overcompensated by buying them costly possessions. Some of the interviewed students indicated they could get what they wanted because their parents were too tired to put up a fight. For some students, motivation and personal drive appeared to be low because they could get what they wanted without effort. Brooks also observed a seeming lack of accountability in certain youngsters that manifested itself in recklessness, disdain for rules, and an irritating arrogance.

Brantlinger and Guskin (1992) interviewed 20 high-income mothers to determine how they viewed their offspring and how they viewed children of lower income levels. The mothers were questioned with regard to how school personnel should accommodate for any perceived differences between the two groups of children. Most of the affluent mothers categorized high-income students as intelligent and talented and low-income students as less capable and less interested in school. Generally, they believed low-income parents didn't value education and didn't have high aspirations for their children. Moreover, they didn't think public schools were serving the needs of their children well. They believed public schools were satisfactory for low-income children, who in their opinion were less advanced, but that schools should provide greater rewards for their children. It is plausible, then, to assume that some children from affluent families are exposed to similar elitist attitudes. The influence of this exposure is not likely to be positive.

In another study, Brantlinger (1993) interviewed 34 adolescents from high-income families and 40 adolescents from low-income families about various aspects of schooling. Students from high-income families reported having much more successful school careers than students from low-income families. Students from high-income families admitted getting positive deferential treatment from teachers and felt entitled to the disproportionate school rewards they received. Moreover, these students believed that students from low-income families chose to be low achievers and chose to be bad.

Research related to students living in affluence is limited in quantity and methodology. Several educators, however, have offered opinions about students from wealthy families based on personal experience rather than empirical study. Baldwin (as cited in Salend, 1998) stated that many students from affluent families expected the best and most expensive, required much stimulation, and had difficulty finishing projects. Their relationships tended to be superficial and with little compassion. Moreover, they failed to take responsibility for personal property, misled others when convenient, and tended to be pleasure oriented. Metz (1993) noted that her "white and wealthy" students were particularly vulnerable to numerous risk factors, including depression and suicide, alcohol and substance abuse, pregnancy and abortion, AIDS and venereal disease, acquaintance/date rape, anxiety and stress, boredom and loneliness, cynicism, low self-esteem, and eating disorders.

After interviewing a psychiatrist with 11 years' experience counseling adolescents from affluent families and a psychologist with 25 years of counseling within an affluent community, Metz concluded that her "white and wealthy" students were at risk partly due to the lack of parental involvement needed to equip them with emotional support and sound moral values with which to guide their decisions and direct their lives. Metz also noted that other factors (e.g., friends, school, church, community, media, and the world at large) influence students and that teachers can play an important role in helping to meet the needs of students from affluent families.

Reinstein (1997/1998) discussed his experiences as a teacher in an affluent high school and compared them to his experiences as a teacher in an inner-city alternative school for dropouts and teenaged mothers. Both schools were in the same city. He noted that many of his affluent students recognized they were advantaged and tried to reach out to individuals who were less fortunate through charity fundraisers and volunteer work in soup kitchens and tutoring centers. He noted there were excellent as well as a few dysfunctional parents among his students living in affluence and excellent and a few dysfunctional parents among his students living in poverty. Parent-related problems in the affluent suburbs seemed to stem from an unreasonable sense of entitlement, whereas parent-related problems in the inner city seemed to come from a feeling of a lack of power and a lack of high expectations.

Clearly, there is great diversity among students who live in affluence, just as there is great diversity among students who live in poverty. It is important, however, for educators to realize that students from both environments may bring specific needs and challenges to school.

Students Who Are Gay or Lesbian

According to researchers and social scientists, 1 to 3 of every 10 students is either gay or lesbian, or has an immediate family member who is gay or lesbian. Thus, in an average class of 30 students, somewhere between 3 and 9 students have had direct

Students lead the way to promote respect and understanding within their diverse community.

experience with issues of homosexuality and homophobia (Youth Pride, Inc., 1997). Homophobia is defined as:

> the fear, dislike, and hatred of same-sex relationships or those who love and are sexually attracted to those of the same sex. Homophobia includes prejudice, discrimination, harassment, and acts of violence brought on by fear and hatred. It occurs in schools on personal, institutional, and societal levels (Youth Pride, Inc., 1997, p. 7).

It is not surprising that many youth who are gay or lesbian have trouble adjusting to their sexual orientation. They are brought up in a homophobic society with little access to information that portrays individuals who are gay or lesbian in positive ways (Grossman, 1995). Suspicion or knowledge that a student is gay or lesbian can lead to social ostracism, verbal abuse, physical attacks, or sexual assaults from homophobic peers or adults. A National Anti-Gay/Lesbian Victimization Report revealed that 45 percent of high-school males who were gay and 20 percent of high-school females who were lesbian reported verbal harassment and/or physical violence as a result of their sexual orientation (National Gay and Lesbian Task Force as cited in Youth Pride, Inc., 1997). In an attempt to avoid potential verbal and nonverbal attacks, many students who are gay or lesbian try to conceal their sexual orientation. Although this concealment may reduce direct attacks, it does not protect students from hearing gay-related jokes and other anti-gay/lesbian sentiments exchanged among some of their classmates. According to a report from the Massachusetts Governor's Commission on Gay and Lesbian Youth, "97% of students in public high schools report regularly hearing homophobic remarks from their peers" (Youth Pride, Inc., 1997, p. 5). Students also are subjected to anti-gay/lesbian sentiments from the media and from some politicians, church leaders, and entertainers.

Dealing with homophobia, especially during adolescence when peer recognition and friendships are extremely important, is quite a burden. If students are anxious about their sexual identity and the fear of discovery, they have less energy to devote to schoolwork. Thus, some students who are gay or lesbian have difficulty concentrating while they are in school, fall behind in their assignments, and receive failing grades (Children's Aid Society of Toronto, 1995). Additionally, a variety of emotional problems (e.g., depression, shame, guilt, low self-esteem, self-hatred) may emerge. These problems, along with strong feelings of isolation, lead some students who are gay or lesbian to drop out of school, abuse substances, and commit suicide (Grossman, 1995). Sadly, it has been reported that 28 percent of high-school students who are gay or lesbian drop out of school because of harassment resulting from their sexual orientation (Remafedi as cited in Youth Pride, Inc., 1997). Of adolescent males who identify themselves as gay, 68 percent use alcohol and 44 percent use other drugs, while 83 percent of females who are lesbian use alcohol and 56 percent use other drugs (Hunter as cited in Youth Pride, Inc., 1997). Youths who are gay or lesbian are two to three times more likely to attempt suicide than youths who are heterosexual, 30 percent of completed youth suicides each year are committed by youths who are lesbian or gay, and suicide is the leading cause of death among students who are gay or lesbian (Youth Pride, Inc., 1997).

Teachers and school personnel are responsible for providing a supportive and safe learning environment for all students. Some school district personnel have developed programs to assist students who are gay or lesbian and to reduce homophobia within the school environment. These programs, however, are rare. So, for the most part, students who are gay or lesbian rely on assistance and understanding from individual teachers and counselors. School personnel can assist in the following ways:

- Protect students from harassment. Respond to homophobia immediately and sincerely. Express disapproval of jokes about individuals who are gay. Adopt and enforce antidiscrimination policies that include race, sex, religion, and sexual orientation.
- Model acceptance of all individuals. Provide openly gay role models. Include issues and topics that affect students who are gay and lesbian in the curriculum (e.g., gay rights and contributions in social studies classes). Have something gay related (e.g., SAFE ZONE campaign stickers, poster,

flyer, book, button) visible to students. Oppose censorship of texts and library books that demonstrate respect for lesbian and gay rights.
▶ Learn about and refer students to community agencies and resources where they can obtain assistance and support (Grossman, 1995; Youth Pride, Inc., 1997).

Education in the Twenty-First Century

The context of public education is in a state of change. Current reform movements encourage the development and use of national standards, promote the idea of raising educational expectations for all students, and support the philosophy of increased inclusion of students with special needs. Simultaneously with these reform movements, student diversity in American schools is increasing. Quite simply, the portrait of public-school classrooms in the United States is quite different now than it was when most teachers were enrolled in elementary and high school. Thus, teachers must think differently about the process of teaching and learning. They must be willing to teach differently than how they were taught, because the school context has changed. Now, more than ever, it is critically important that teachers use validated practices in their daily rounds with students and colleagues. Instructional effectiveness and efficiency is critically important, given the diversity found in today's classrooms. Simply put, there is no time to waste on ineffective practices. To adequately meet the challenges in today's classrooms, teachers must be equipped with knowledge and skills that differ from those of their predecessors. Fortunately, research conducted over the past decade has substantially increased what is known about validated practices for teaching and learning. The present challenge is disseminating this information in organized ways that will result in high rates of implementation among teachers and other school personnel.

The purpose of this book is to provide information about these educational practices, with specific emphasis on successful implementation. The text is organized in three sections: planning, delivering, and evaluating instruction in diverse classrooms. Brief summaries of research and field tests that document the effectiveness of the practices included in this book are presented in Validation Boxes within each chapter. The boxes also include references for further study.

References

American Council on Education and Education Commission of the States. (1988). *One-third of a nation: A report by the Commission on Minority Participation in Education and American Life.* Washington, DC: Author.

Barlett, D. L., & Steele, J. B. (1992). *America: What went wrong?* Kansas City, MO: Andrews & McMeel.

Bergland, M., & Hoffbauer, D. (1996). New opportunities for students with traumatic brain injuries. *Teaching Exceptional Children, 28*(2), 54–56.

Brantlinger, E. (1993). Adolescents' interpretation of social class influences on schooling. *Journal of Classroom Interaction, 28*(1), 1–12.

Brantlinger, E., & Guskin, S. (1992, April). *Barriers to integrated schools and classrooms: Affluent parents' perceptions of their own and other people's children.* Paper presented at the Annual Meeting of the American Educational Research Association, San Francisco, CA.

Brooks, A. A. (1990). Educating the children of fast-track parents. *Phi Delta Kappan, 71*, 612–615.

Center for Policy Research on the Impact of General and Special Education Reform. (1996). *Standards-based school reform and students with disabilities* (Report No. EC 305 006). Alexandria, VA: Center for Policy Research on the Impact of General and Special Education Reform. (ERIC Document Reproduction Service No. ED 398 713).

Children's Aid Society of Toronto. (1995). *"We are children, too": Accessible child welfare services for lesbian, gay, and bisexual youth.* Reston, VA: Office of Diversity Affairs, Council for Exceptional Children. Also available online at: www.casmt.on.ca/lgby4.html.

Cohen, L. M. (1994). Meeting the needs of gifted and talented minority language students. *Teaching Exceptional Children, 26*(1), 70–71.

Dalaker, J., & Naifeh, M., United States Bureau of the Census, Current Population Reports, Series P60–201 (1998). *Poverty in the United States: 1997.* Washington, DC: U.S. Government Printing Office.

Fujiura, G. T., & Yamaki, K. (2000). Trends in demography of childhood poverty and disability. *Exceptional Children, 66*, 187–199.

Gense, D. J., & Gense, M. (1999). *The importance of orientation and mobility skills for students who are deaf-blind.* Available online at: www.tr.wou.edu/dblink/o&m2.htm.

Gifted and Talented Children's Education Act, Pub. L. No. 95–561. *Congressional Record.* H.R.H.-12179 95th Cong, 2d sess. (1978, October 10).

Grossman, H. (1995). *Special education in a diverse society.* Needham Heights, MA: Allyn and Bacon.

Haberman, M. (1995a). Selecting 'star' teachers for children and youth in urban poverty. *Phi Delta Kappan, 76*, 777–781.

Haberman, M. (1995b). *Star teachers of children in poverty.* West Lafayette, IN: Kappa Delta Pi.

Huefner, D. S. (2000). The risks and opportunities of the IEP requirements under IDEA '97. *The Journal of Special Education, 33*, 195–204.

Individuals with Disabilities Act Amendments of 1997, 20 U.S.C. §1400 *et seq.* (U.S. Government Printing Office, 1997).

Kauffman, J. M. (1993). *Characteristics of emotional and behavioral disorders of children and youth* (5th ed.). New York: Merrill, an imprint of Macmillan.

Lovaas, O. I. (1987). Behavioral treatment and normal educational and intellectual functioning in young autistic children. *Journal of Consulting and Clinical Psychology, 55*, 3–9.

Lowenbraun, S. (1995). Hearing impairment. In E. L. Meyen & T. M. Skrtic (Eds.), *Special education & student disability. An introduction: Traditional, emerging, and alternative perspectives* (4th ed., pp. 453–485). Denver: Love.

Luckasson, R., Coulter, D. L., Polloway, E. A., Reiss, S., Schalock, R. L., Snell, M. E., Spitalnik, D. M., & Stark, J. A. (1992). *Mental retardation: Definition, classification, and systems of supports.* Washington, DC: American Association on Mental Retardation.

McLesky, J., Henry, D., & Hodges, D. (1998). Inclusion: Where is it happening? *Teaching Exceptional Children, 31*(1), 4–10.

McLesky, J., Henry, D., & Hodges, D. (1999). Inclusion: What progress is being made across disability categories? *Teaching Exceptional Children, 31*(3), 60–64.

Mercer, C. D. (1997). *Students with learning disabilities* (5th ed.). Upper Saddle River, NJ: Merrill, an imprint of Prentice-Hall.

Metz, E. D. (1993). The camouflaged at-risk student: White and wealthy. *Momentum, 24*(2), 40–44.

Morrison, G. M., & Polloway, E. A. (1995). Mental retardation. In E. L. Meyen & T. M. Skrtic

(Eds.), *Special education & student disability. An introduction: Traditional, emerging, and alternative perspectives* (4th ed., pp. 213–269). Denver: Love.

National Center for Education Statistics. (1992). *Pocket projections: Projections of education statistics to 2002*. Washington, DC: U.S. Department of Education.

National Center for Education Statistics. (1998). *The condition of education 1998*. Washington, DC: U.S. Department of Education.

National Commission on Excellence in Education. (1983). *A nation at risk: The imperative for educational reform*. Washington, DC: U.S. Government Printing Office.

National Education Goals Panel. (1997). *The National Education Goals report: Building a nation of learners*. Washington, DC: U.S. Government Printing Office.

National Education Goals Panel. (1999). *The National Education Goals report: Building a nation of learners*. Washington, DC: U.S. Government Printing Office.

1996 National Education Summit Policy Statement. (1996). Available online at: http://www.summit96.ibm.com/index.html.

Noonan, M. & Siegel-Causey, E. (1990). Special needs of students with severe handicaps. In L. McCormick & R. L. Schiefelbusch (Eds.), *Early language intervention: An introduction* (2nd ed., pp. 383–435). Columbus, OH: Merrill.

Pallas, A. M., Natriello, G., & McDill, E. L. (1989). The changing nature of the disadvantaged population: Current dimensions and future trends. *Educational Researcher, 18*, 16–22.

Quality Education for Minorities Project. (1990). *Education that works: An action plan for the education of minorities*. Cambridge: Massachusetts Institute of Technology.

Reinstein, D. (1997/1998). Crossing the economic divide. *Educational Leadership, 55*(4), 28–33.

Robinson, S., & Deshler, D. D. (1995). Learning disabled. In E. L. Meyen & T. M. Skrtic (Eds.), *Special education & student disability. An introduction: Traditional, emerging, and alternative perspectives* (4th ed., pp. 171–211). Denver: Love.

Salend, S. J. (1998). *Effective mainstreaming: Creating inclusive classrooms* (3rd ed.). Upper Saddle River, NJ: Merrill, an imprint of Prentice-Hall.

Schultz, G. F. (1993). Socioeconomic advantage and achievement motivation: Important mediators of academic performance in minority children in urban schools. *Urban Review, 25*, 221–232.

Secretary's Commission on Achieving Necessary Skills. (1991). *What work requires of schools: A SCANS report for AMERICA 2000*. Washington, DC: U.S. Department of Labor.

Sherman, A. (1997). *Poverty matters: The cost of child poverty in America*. Washington, DC: Children's Defense Fund.

Shokoohi-Yekta, M., & Kavale, K. A. (1994). Effects of increased high school graduation standards on college entrance examination performance of students with learning disabilities. *Learning Disabilities Research & Practice, 9*, 213–218.

Shriner, J. G. (2000). Legal perspectives on school outcomes assessment for students with disabilities. *The Journal of Special Education, 33*, 232–239.

Siegel-Causey, E., Guy, B., & Guess, D. (1995). Severe and multiple disabilities. In E. L. Meyen & T. M. Skrtic (Eds.), *Special education & student disability. An introduction: Traditional, emerging, and alternative perspectives* (4th ed., pp. 415–450). Denver: Love.

Silverman, L. K. (1995). Gifted and talented students. In E. L. Meyen & T. M. Skrtic (Eds.), *Special education & student disability an introduction: Traditional, emerging, and alternative perspectives* (4th ed., pp. 377–413). Denver: Love.

Sirvis, B. P., & Caldwell, T. H. (1995). Physical disabilities and chronic health impairments. In E. L. Meyen & T. M. Skrtic (Eds.), *Special education & student disability. An introduction: Traditional, emerging, and alternative perspectives* (4th ed., pp. 533–564). Denver: Love.

Sisk, D. (1987). *Creative teaching of the gifted*. New York: McGraw-Hill.

Sleeter, C. E., & Grant, C. A. (1999). *Making choices for multicultural education: Five approaches to race, class, and gender*. Upper Saddle River, NJ: Merrill, an imprint of Prentice-Hall.

Smith, D. D. (1998). *Introduction to special education* (3rd ed.). Needham Heights, MA: Allyn & Bacon.

Smith, C., Constantino, R., & Krashen, S. (1997). Differences in print environment for children in Beverly Hills, Compton, and Watts. *Emergency Librarian, 24*(4), 8–9.

Smith, D. D., & Luckasson, R. (1992). *Introduction to special education.* Needham Heights, MA: Allyn & Bacon.

Swassing, R. H. (1992).Gifted and talented students. In W. L. Heward & M. D. Orlansky (Eds.), *Exceptional Children* (4th ed., pp. 451–487). New York: Merrill, an imprint of Macmillan Publishing Company.

Thompson, S., Lehr, C., & Quenemoen, R. F. (2000). *How are we doing across the nation? Current trends.* Paper presented at the Council for Exceptional Children Annual Convention and Expo, Vancouver, BC.

Turnbull, A. P., Turnbull, H. R., Shank, M., & Leal, D. (1995). *Exceptional lives: Special education in today's schools.* Upper Saddle River, NJ: Prentice-Hall.

Tuttle, D. W., & Ferrell, K. A. (1995). Visual impairment. In E. L. Meyen & T. M. Skrtic (Eds.), *Special education & student disability. An introduction: Traditional, emerging, and alternative perspectives* (4th ed., pp. 487–531). Denver: Love.

United States Bureau of the Census, Current Population Reports. (1998). *Money income in the United States: 1997 (with separate data on valuation of noncash benefits).* (P60–200). Washington, DC: U.S. Government Printing Office.

United States Department of Education. (1991). *AMERICA 2000: An education strategy* (Superintendent of Documents No. ED 1.310-2:332380). Washington, DC: U.S. Government Printing Office.

United States Department of Education (1999). Assistance to states for the education of children with disabilities and the early intervention program for infants and toddlers with disabilities; final regulations. *Federal Register, 34* CFR Part II.

United States Department of Education Office of Special Education Programs. (1998). *Twentieth annual report to congress on the implementation of the Individuals with Disabilities Education Act.* Washington, DC: Author.

Utley, C. A., Delquadri, J. C., Obiakor, F. E., & Mims, V. A. (2000). General and special educators' perceptions of teaching strategies for multicultural students. *Teacher Education and Special Education, 23,* 34–50.

Warger, C. (1999, August). New IDEA '97 requirements: Factors to consider in developing an IEP. *ERIC Digest, E578 EDO–99–6,* 1–2.

Whelan, R. J. (1995). Emotional disturbance. In E. L. Meyen & T. M. Skrtic (Eds.), *Special education & student disability an introduction: Traditional, emerging, and alternative perspectives* (4th ed., pp. 271–336). Denver: Love.

Winzer, M. A., & Mazurek, K. (1998). *Special education in multicultural contexts.* Upper Saddle River, NJ: Merrill, an imprint of Prentice-Hall.

Youth Pride, Inc. (1997). *Creating safe schools for lesbian and gay students: A resource guide for school staff.* Reston, VA: Office of Diversity Affairs, Council for Exceptional Children. Also available online at: http://members.tripod.com/~twood/guide.html.

Using Specific Planning Methods

If you fail to plan, you're planning to fail.
—Robert Schuller

A D V A N C E : ORGANIZER

Planning instruction that truly meets the needs of today's students is one of the most challenging and most important aspects of a teacher's job. The planning process, regardless of style or format, involves making critical decisions about teaching and learning. These decisions ultimately affect the futures of both students and teachers. Given the information presented in Chapter 1 related to school reform and increased student diversity, it is easy to understand why teachers must become masterful planners. Fortunately, planning models and routines are now available to assist teachers in making important educational decisions. The purpose of this chapter is to provide information regarding responsible planning processes that are likely to result in high student achievement.

Historically, the most typical planning process for a teacher has been developing specific lesson plans. According to a review of the literature on lesson planning models, Searcy and Maroney (1996) identified 14 frequently used lesson-plan components: objectives, materials required, time required, prerequisite skills, seating arrangements, anticipatory sets, instructional steps, checks for understanding, guided practice, independent practice, summary/closing, evaluation of student outcomes, follow-up activity, and self-evaluation of lesson presentation. Experienced special education teachers identified objectives, materials, instructional steps, checks for understanding, guided practice, independent practice, evaluation of student outcomes, and follow-up activity as the most important components for beginning teachers to include in their lesson plans. Planning that includes these components provides direction to teachers with regard to content to deliver and activities to implement during specific lessons.

Rosenshine (1983) reviewed seven experimental studies that investigated teaching behaviors that resulted in high levels of student achievement. From these studies, Rosenshine developed six instructional functions that can be used to develop lesson plans and subsequently deliver lesson content. These functions are:

1. Review (check student understanding of the previous day's work);
2. Presentation of new content and/or skills;
3. Initial student practice (with checks for understanding);
4. Feedback;
5. Independent practice; and
6. Weekly and monthly reviews.

Lesson planning using this approach involves thinking about the subject-matter content as well as the process for implementing each of these six functions. In other words, the teacher first considers what content needs to be reviewed and assessed and then determines how the review will be implemented and how student understanding will be assessed. Decisions also are made about how the reteaching will be done if it is needed. Next, the teacher plans what and how new content and/or skills will be taught. This type of thinking about *what to do* and *how to do it* continues throughout the six-function planning process.

In a similar approach, referred to as the Hunter Teacher Decision-Making Model, Madeline Hunter (1986,1991) indicated that teachers must consider three types of decisions when designing lesson plans. First, content decisions are made (i.e., What content is important to teach?). Specifically, teachers decide what to teach and then focus on maintaining the integrity of the content and related disciplines while simultaneously adjusting the level of difficulty for individual students. Second, decisions are made about learning behaviors (i.e., What will the students do to acquire the necessary skills and information? How will they demonstrate their learning?). Third, decisions are made about teaching behaviors (i.e., How will the teacher use research-based principles to promote and increase learning?). After making important content, learning, and teaching decisions, lesson plans are designed using the following elements:

1. Anticipatory set to prepare students for learning (acquiring students' attention, preparing them for upcoming lesson, motivating students);
2. Objective (stating what will be learned in the lesson and communicating why it is important);

Lesson planning requires deep thinking about curricular content, student needs, and teaching methodology.

3. Input (providing information and structuring the learning environment so students receive the material in a simple-to-complex sequence);
4. Modeling (showing students what is expected of them);
5. Checking for student understanding (asking questions in a variety of ways to ensure that students understand the content being taught);
6. Guided practice (monitoring student practice carefully, correcting and remediating errors soon after the initial instruction is provided);
7. Independent practice (providing opportunities for students to practice by themselves while doing homework or seatwork).

Although all seven elements typically are included in one lesson plan, this is not always the case. Also, the sequence of the elements may vary somewhat from one lesson plan to the next (Hunter, 1986). For example, it may be appropriate to design a lesson plan that includes an anticipatory set, objectives, input, modeling, and checking for understanding for only one day of instruction. The next day's lesson plan may include an anticipatory set, objectives, checking for understanding, and guided practice. In addition, teachers may plan to include checks for student understanding after each element in the lesson, especially when the lesson involves complex concepts. Hunter's process for lesson design is meant to be flexible to meet a variety of instructional needs (Batesky, 1987; see Validation Box 2.1).

Based on the standards and goals of the Education Reform Movement discussed in Chapter 1, many teachers use state, school district, and/or textbook curricula guidelines to determine the content of lesson plans and subsequent lessons (Vaughn & Schumm, 1994). Teachers should exercise caution and avoid writing prescribed lesson plans that involve undifferentiated, large-group instruction for all students. This type of planning and instructional implementation has been used in many classrooms (Baker & Zigmond, 1990; Ysseldyke, Thurlow, Wotruba, & Nanaia, 1990), and consequently, students with diverse learning needs sometimes are overlooked.

The increasing diversity among students enrolled in public school classrooms coupled with the rapid expansion of available content to teach necessitates compre-

VALIDATION BOX
2.1

Hunter Teacher Decision-Making Model

Data were gathered to assess a close derivation of the Hunter Teacher Decision-Making Model in Napa County California over 4 years. When teachers used the model, student achievement and time on task increased. Specifically, increases were noted in year 2 and year 3 of the project. These gains regressed a bit during year 4 of the project, when leadership from principals and project staff decreased and new teachers were hired. In spite of this regression, all scores were higher at the end of the project than at the beginning. For more information see: (Hunter, 1986).

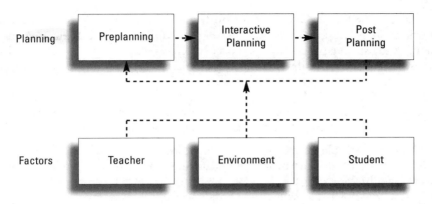

FIGURE 2.1

Flow of the Planning Process Model. (From "General Education Teacher Planning: What Can Students With Learning Disabilities Expect" by J. S. Schumm, S. Vaughn, D. Haager, J. McDowell, L. Rothlein, and L. S. Saumell, 1995, *Exceptional Children, 61*, p. 337. Copyright 1995 by The Council for Exceptional Children. Reprinted with permission.)

hensive planning processes that take into consideration a variety of factors (e.g., student interests, needs, and abilities; national, state, and district goals and standards). More than ever, instructional planning must focus first on the needs of the learners and then on the skills and content to be mastered within the various subject areas. Important decisions must be made regarding both content and pedagogy (i.e., what and how to teach) to adequately prepare increasingly diverse groups of students for a rapidly changing world.

Comprehensive Planning: Flow of the Planning Process Model

A teacher's lesson plans do not reflect all the decisionmaking that occurs when instruction is planned and delivered. The Flow of the Planning Process Model (Schumm, Vaughn, Haager, McDowell, Rothlein, & Saumell, 1995) illustrates the sequence and relationship among three types of planning: preplanning, interactive planning, and postplanning. The model also depicts the factors that influence planning: teacher, environment, and student (see Fig. 2.1).

Preplanning typically involves reading relevant background material, determining procedures, thinking about grouping, and considering ways to enhance the instruction. Preplanning also involves gathering materials, determining objectives, and deciding how to evaluate student learning. **Interactive planning** occurs as the teacher is delivering the instruction. Lessons are monitored and adjusted in response to student performance. Regardless of how thorough a teacher is during preplanning, inevitably things will occur during the lesson that necessitate immediate adaptations. For example, if students become confused with regard to a concept being taught, the teacher may spontaneously decide to reteach a portion of the lesson using different examples or materials. **Postplanning** involves reflecting on the teaching and learning process that just occurred. This reflection helps with planning the next lesson or unit of instruction. Student performance and students' reactions to the instruction assist teachers in planning for the future.

As mentioned earlier, the Flow of the Planning Process Model includes three factors that influence the effectiveness of the planning process: teacher, environment, and student. Included among the teacher-related factors are:

- teacher attitudes and beliefs about planning;
- teacher attitudes and beliefs about making adaptations for students with disabilities;
- teacher knowledge, skills, and confidence; and
- teacher motivation to plan and make accommodations for student differences.

Included among the environment-related factors are:

- demands for content coverage and accountability;
- materials available;
- class size; and
- availability of funds.

Included among the student-related factors are:

- engagement and interest in the subject matter;
- attention;
- use of effective learning strategies;
- motivation;
- behavior patterns;
- background knowledge; and
- response to adaptations.

Thus, the process of classroom planning requires thinking about numerous factors prior to, during, and after instruction. As classrooms grow in diversity and the breadth of needs increases, the planning process becomes more challenging. Fortunately, specific methods for planning instruction in diverse classrooms have emerged. These methods are designed to help teachers manage their planning activities in an effective and efficient manner. It may, however, be necessary for teachers to modify these planning methods to meet the specific needs that exist within their particular school settings. For example, if teachers are involved in team teaching arrangements or collaborative consultation, then the planning process can be modified to facilitate joint planning. Teachers can divide the planning responsibilities and then meet to provide one another feedback, or teachers can plan jointly from the beginning. These planning processes also can involve teachers and paraeducators who work together. A few experimental trials will provide the information needed to know what works best in specific teaching contexts.

Ms. Smith and Ms. Price explore their common beliefs about teaching second-language learners to facilitate the planning process for their team teaching endeavors.

Teacher Planning Processes

The Office of Special Education and Rehabilitative Services within the U.S. Department of Education supported four major research projects charged with the tasks of developing and field-testing innovative practices that would improve the ways teachers plan, individualize, and adapt curricula and instruction for students with disabilities in general education classrooms (Joint Committee on Teacher Planning for Students with Disabilities, 1995). These four projects were led by researchers at the University of Miami; University of Kansas; Education Development Center, Inc., in Massachusetts; and Vanderbilt University. From this work emerged new planning methods designed to help teachers meet the needs of all students within general education settings. Included among these methods are the Unit Planning Pyramid, the Lesson Planning Pyramid, the Course Planning Routine, the Unit Planning Routine, the Lesson Planning Routine, Planning with Thematic Units and Thinking Frames, Analogue Experiences, and Planning Around Focal Students.

The Planning Pyramid

Jeanne Shay Schumm and Sharon Vaughn developed the Planning Pyramid while working on the School-Based Research Project at the University of Miami. The Planning Pyramid is a tool that both special and general education teachers use to facilitate inclusion and collaboration. The pyramid is particularly helpful when planning instruction that involves concepts and vocabulary that are new to many of the students in the class (e.g., science, social studies). The Planning Pyramid is a flexible tool that teachers can adjust to complement their planning and teaching styles (Schumm, Vaughn, & Harris, 1997) and is used to plan units of instruction or individual lessons.

The Unit Planning Pyramid

Schumm, Vaughn, and Leavell (1994) developed the Unit Planning Pyramid to provide a framework for teachers to use when planning instructional units in subject-area classes (e.g., science, social studies). The Unit Planning Pyramid helps teachers plan for inclusionary instruction and meet the challenge of content coverage in classes that consist of students with a broad range of academic needs. The Unit Planning Pyramid provides a mental template for teachers to think about when planning a unit of instruction. A graphic device (i.e., the Planning Pyramid), self-questioning techniques, and a Unit Planning Pyramid Form are used to facilitate the planning process.

The Graphic Device   The Planning Pyramid is a graphic device designed to guide teachers' thinking about how to teach content to a group of diverse students who have a broad range of academic needs. Specifically, the Planning Pyramid helps teachers reflect on what needs to be taught so that all students in the class have the opportunity to learn at least a portion of the content. The pyramid is divided into three levels or degrees of learning (see Fig. 2.2).

The base or largest section of the pyramid represents the most important concepts in the unit. These are the concepts that the teacher wants *all* students in the class to learn. To ensure that this learning does indeed take place, the teacher plans lessons to explicitly teach these concepts to the students. Students will have ample opportunities to engage in the acquisition of these concepts. Extensive practice and ongoing monitoring of student progress with these concepts will occur. The next highest level of the pyramid (i.e., the middle) represents the content the teacher considers to be next in importance for understanding the content of the unit. Additional facts, extensions of the base or general concepts, related concepts, or more complex concepts are included in this portion of the pyramid. These are the concepts that the teacher wants *most* students in the class to learn. The top level of the Planning Pyramid represents information the teacher considers to be supplementary. This information is more complex or detailed and will be acquired by the fewest number of students in the class. This information may be mentioned in passing during various lessons, may be obtained through independent center activities,

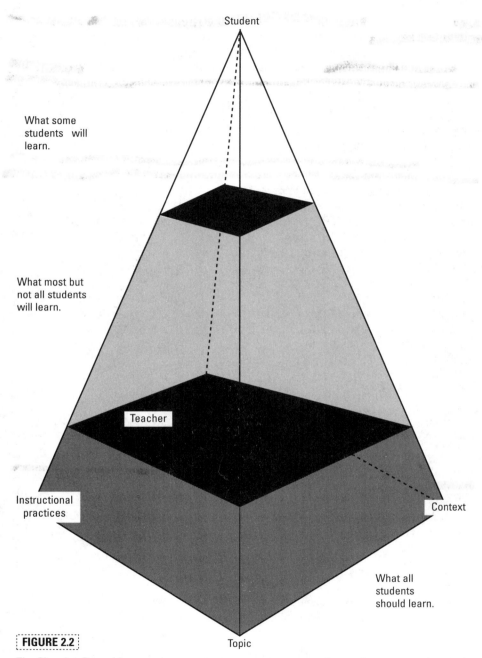

Student

What some
students   will
learn.

What most but
not all students
will learn.

Teacher

Instructional
practices

Context

What all
students
should learn.

FIGURE 2.2

The Planning Pyramid. (Source: Figure 1 from J. S. Schumm, S. Vaughn, and A. G. Leavell [1994, May]. Planning Pyramid: A framework for planning for diverse student needs during content area instruction. *The Reading Teacher, 47* [8], 608–615. Reprinted with permission of Jeanne S. Schumm and the International Reading Association.)

Topic

or may be acquired through student-directed learning experiences that occur outside the classroom. The information at the top level of the pyramid represents concepts the teacher wants *some* students in the class to learn.

An important principle related to using the Planning Pyramid is that student ability does not dictate which level of content the student experiences within a given unit. A student with learning difficulties, disabilities, and/or cultural differences has access to the higher level concepts in units of particular interest and/or in units in which the student has prior knowledge and/or experience. Thus, the amount of information a student learns varies from unit to unit and is not determined based on previous academic performance. Students who demonstrate a particular interest in or knowledge of the concepts presented at the base level should have opportunities to access more information.

Another important principle related to using the Planning Pyramid is that creative learning projects and motivating ways to practice should be included in the unit content at all three levels of the pyramid. Some students may require a significant amount of practice to master the base concepts. In such instances, a variety of practice activities should be used to maintain student interest.

In addition to the levels or degrees of learning represented in the Planning Pyramid, there also are five points of entry: topic, teacher, student, context, and instructional practices. Each axis of the pyramid represents one of these points. "They are called points of entry because no instructional episode should be entered without considering these factors" (Schumm, Vaughn, & Leavell, 1994, p. 612). Self-questioning is a helpful process to use when thinking about these points of entry and subsequently planning units of instruction.

Self-Questioning Techniques   One of the most important aspects of planning units of instruction is deciding what concepts to teach. Self-questioning is a valuable tool for teachers to use when planning units of instruction (Joint Committee on Teacher Planning for Students with Disabilities, 1995; Schumm, Vaughn, & Harris, 1997).

The following questions are designed to help teachers think about three of the five points of entry on the Planning Pyramid. Specifically, these questions help teachers make decisions related to the topic, themselves as teachers, and the students. The remaining two points of entry, instructional practices and context, are used for planning individual lessons rather than units of instruction and are discussed in the next section.

Questions pertaining to the topic:
- Is the material new or for review?
- What prior knowledge do students have of this topic?
- How interesting is the topic?
- How many new concepts are introduced?
- How clearly are concepts presented in the textbook?
- How important is this topic in the overall curriculum?

Questions pertaining to the teacher:
- What prior knowledge do I have of this topic?
- How interesting is the topic to me?
- How much time do I have to plan for the unit and individual lessons?
- What resources do I have available to me for this unit?

Questions pertaining to students:
- Will a language difference make comprehension of a particular concept difficult?
- Is there some way to relate this concept to the cultural and linguistic backgrounds of the students?
- Will students with reading difficulties be able to function independently in learning the concepts from text?
- Will students with behavior or attention problems be able to concentrate on this material?
- Will any students show high interest in or prior knowledge of these concepts?
- Will the students have the vocabulary they need to understand the concepts to be taught?
- What experiences have my students had that will relate to these concepts?

After reflecting on these questions, teachers can use The Unit Planning Form to record their best thinking about the upcoming unit (see Fig. 2.3 on p. 44).

Unit Planning Form   Teachers use the Unit Planning Form to record the concepts that will be learned by *all* students, *most* students, and *some* students within a given unit. Space also is provided for teachers to record the materials/resources, instructional strategies/adaptations, and evaluation/products that will be used during the unit. This form provides an overview or the "big picture" of what the teacher has planned.

In summary, the Unit Planning Pyramid provides a conceptual framework for teachers to use when planning units of instruction for diverse groups of students. Using this framework increases the likelihood that all students in the class will learn important content in meaningful and motivating ways.

The Lesson Planning Pyramid

Schumm, Vaughn, and Leavell (1994) developed the Lesson Planning Pyramid to provide a framework for teachers to use while reflecting on the content of their lessons. Similar to the Unit Planning Pyramid, the Lesson Planning Pyramid involves using a mental template or graphic device, self-questioning techniques, and a Lesson Planning Form. Teachers again use these tools to focus their attention on what content will be learned by *all* students, *most* students, and *some* students. Planning now focuses on each lesson within a larger unit. Thus, explicit detail about what will be taught and how it will be taught emerges when teachers use the Lesson Planning Pyramid.

UNIT PLANNING FORM

What some students will learn.	
What most students will learn.	
What all students should learn.	

Date: _____ Class Period: _____

Unit Title: _____

Materials / Resources:
_____
_____
_____
_____

Instructional Strategies / Adaptations:
_____
_____
_____
_____

Evaluation Products:
_____
_____
_____
_____

The Unit Planning Form. (From *Planning for Academic Diversity in America's Classrooms: Windows on Reality, Research, Change, and Practice* [p. 9] by S. Vaughn and J. S. Schumm—Joint Committee on Teacher Planning for Students with Disabilities, 1995, Lawrence, KS: Center for Research on Learning. Reprinted with permission.)

FIGURE 2.3

The Graphic Device   The teacher again uses the Planning Pyramid to plan lessons for a class of diverse students (see Fig. 2.2). The teacher identifies the lesson concepts that *all* students should learn, the lesson concepts that *most* students should learn, and the lesson concepts that *some* students should learn. This type of thinking assists teachers in developing appropriate lesson plans that will meet the varied needs of the students.

Self-Questioning Techniques

One of the most important aspects of planning individual lessons is to consider the context of the instruction. Included in the context of the instruction are the social aspects of the classroom (e.g., how well students work together), how the classroom is organized for instruction (e.g., content-related centers), and the school-based factors (e.g., special assembly) that affect the classroom environment. Another very important part of planning lessons involves the instructional practices that will be used (e.g., strategies, adaptations, assignments, assessment). Self-questioning is a valuable tool for teachers to use when planning lessons for diverse groups of students. The following questions are designed to help teachers think about the remaining points of entry on the Planning Pyramid: classroom context and instructional practices (Joint Committee on Teacher Planning for Students With Disabilities, 1995; Schumm, Vaughn, & Harris, 1997).

Questions pertaining to context:
- Are there any holidays or special events that are likely to distract the students or alter my instructional time?
- How will the class size affect my teaching of this concept?
- How well do the students work in small groups or pairs?

Questions pertaining to instructional strategies:
- What methods will I use to motivate students and set a purpose for learning?
- What grouping pattern is most appropriate?
- What instructional strategies can I implement to promote learning for all students?
- What learning strategies do my students know, or need to learn, that will help them master these concepts?
- What in-class and homework assignments are appropriate for this lesson?
- Do some assignments need to be adapted for students with special needs?
- How will I monitor student learning on an ongoing, informal basis?
- How will I assess student learning at the end of the lesson?

These questions prompt careful planning and increase the likelihood that teachers will consider the classroom context and instructional practices when designing lessons for diverse groups of students.

The Lesson Planning Form

The Lesson Planning Form (Fig. 2.4) is used to record the decisions made regarding what content will be covered and how it will be taught. Space is provided for teachers to write objectives, list materials needed, define how student learning will be evaluated, and identify class assignments, homework assignments, and the agenda for the lesson. Moreover, the form includes a pyramid to record the concepts that *all*, *most*, and *some* students will learn.

In summary, teachers who use the Unit and/or Lesson Planning Pyramid framework will be better prepared to meet the needs of their students. This type of planning takes into consideration that not all students need to learn the same information in the exact same way. Individual adaptations are considered during a planning process that focuses on the content to be taught *and* the needs of the students. Students' interests, abilities, and background knowledge are taken into consideration when using these planning processes. Clearly, *individual* teachers can use the Unit or Lesson Planning Pyramid processes, but special and general education teachers who collaboratively plan can also find these processes helpful (Schumm, Vaughn, & Harris, 1997; see Validation Box 2.2).

ReflActive Planning

ReflActive Planning is planning that incorporates the principles of both reflection and action (Lenz & Bulgren, 1994). The goal of ReflActive Planning is to plan group instruction that is sensitive to students with special needs without diminishing the integrity of the content. The basic premise of ReflActive Planning is that there are critical sets of important content that all students need to know. Planning time is spent determining what this critical content is and then focusing on how best to teach the critical content. Teachers who use ReflActive Planning involve themselves

---

VALIDATION BOX
2.2

The Planning Pyramid

Data were gathered over a period of 1 semester with 13 teachers. Data sources included teacher interviews, written plans, and videotaped teaching episodes. The Planning Pyramid was field tested with general education teachers at the elementary, middle, and high school levels. Teachers reported the process was easy to use and helped them include students with learning disabilities without sacrificing other students' progress. The planning process helped teachers become more explicit about what they wanted students to learn. The process also helped them become more proficient in planning lessons that promoted learning among all students. For more information see: (Schumm, Vaughn, & Harris, 1997; Schumm, Vaughn, & Leavell, 1994) or contact: University of Miami, School-Based Research Project, P.O. Box 248065, Coral Gables, FL 33124.

Date: _____ Class Period: _____ Unit: _____

Lesson Objective(s): _____

_____

_____

Materials	Evaluation

In-Class Assignments	Homework Assignments

LESSON PLANNING FORM

Pyramid	Agenda
What some students will learn.	1. _____
	2. _____
	3. _____
What most students will learn.	4. _____
	5. _____
What all students should learn.	6. _____
	7. _____

| FIGURE 2.4 |

The Lesson Planning Form. (From *Planning for Academic Diversity in America's Classrooms: Windows on Reality, Research, Change, and Practice* [p. 11] by S. Vaughn and J. S. Schumm—Joint Committee on Teacher Planning for Students with Disabilities, 1995, Lawrence, KS: Center for Research on Learning. Reprinted with permission.)

in three important processes. First, they develop content questions that all students in the group should be able to answer at the conclusion of the instruction. Second, they draw a graphic organizer to make the structure or organization of the content explicit. Third, they use the graphic organizer to share their plans with the students (Deshler, Ellis, & Lenz, 1996). The Course, Unit, and Lesson Planning Routines discussed in the following sections use ReflActive Planning. Specialized training is recommended prior to implementation of these planning routines. Individuals who are interested in obtaining such training should contact the Training Coordinator at the Center for Research on Learning, 521 Joseph R. Pearson Hall, 1122 West Campus Road, Lawrence, KS 66045; telephone: (785) 864-4780; fax: (785) 864-5728.

The Course Planning Routine

Keith Lenz and his colleagues at the University of Kansas Center for Research on Learning developed the Course Planning Routine to help teachers create courses for diverse groups of learners including students with disabilities, high achievers, average achievers, and low achievers (Lenz, Deshler, Schumaker, Bulgren, Kissam, Vance, Roth, & McKnight,1993; Joint Committee on Teacher Planning for Students With Disabilities, 1995). The routine involves reflecting on the most important content to include in the course being developed. Additionally, the routine involves creating a graphic device (i.e., the Course Organizer) depicting the important aspects of the course (see Fig. 2.5 on p. 49 and Fig. 2.6 on p. 50). This device is then used to introduce the course to the students.[1] Teachers use the graphic device to help students see the "big picture" of the course. Moreover, the routine provides a framework for making decisions related to launching the course, maintaining course themes throughout the course, and closing or concluding the course. The Course Planning Routine involves the following six stages.

Stage 1: Teachers begin thinking about the important course concepts and desired student outcomes. The desired student outcomes are then transposed into ten questions that everyone in the classroom will be able to answer at the end of the course. Teachers then create two visual devices that depict critical course information and also provide a place for students to plot their academic achievement throughout the course.

The first visual device, a Course Organizer, provides a place for teachers to record the name of the course, a place to describe the course and course standards (e.g., what content will be learned, what process for learning will be used, and how standards will be measured with accompanying point values), an area to list ten course questions, and a graph area for students to plot scores earned on daily work and quizzes (see Fig. 2.5).

[1]The content enhancement devices shown in Figures 2.5 to 2.8 are instructional tools developed and researched at the University of Kansas Center for Research on Learning. They represent a number of organizing and teaching devices designed for teachers to use as they teach content information to classes containing diverse student populations. They are data-based teaching instruments that have been found effective when used in instructional routines that combine cues about the instruction, specialized delivery of the content, involvement of the students in the cognitive processes, and a review of the learning process and content material (Bulgren, Deshler, & Schumaker, 1993). They have not been shown to be effective tools if they are simply distributed to students.

Teacher(s): Mr. Culbertson	**The**	Student: Jean Wojoski
Time: 10:05-10:57	**Course Organizer**	Course dates: 9/98-5/99

① THIS COURSE:

United States History to 1900

is about — How the United States was created, grew to be a nation, and led the world into a revolution based on technology.

②   COURSE QUESTIONS:

1. What ideas have shaped (are shaping) the destiny of the United States?
2. How has geography affected the creation and development of the United States?
3. How has conflict affected the destiny of the United States?
4. How do different sources help us understand the United States experience and how do we use these sources?
5. How have we protected our civil rights, and why has this been an important concern in the history of the people of the United States?
6. How have art and literature served as windows to United States history?
7. How has technology affected United States society and history?
8. How can learning and understanding history affect our decisions?
9. What is the culture of the United States?
10. How has the "American Dream" affected United States culture?

③ COURSE STANDARDS:

What?	How?	Value?
CONTENT:		
1. Understanding Big Ideas	Unit Tests	50 pts
2. Applying Big Ideas	Unit Projects	10 pts.
3. Providing Examples & Details	Daily Work	10 pts.
		70 pts.
PROCESS:		
1. Using Strategies	Class Demo	20 pts.
2. Participating	Class Demo	5 pts.
3. Following Rules	Class Demo	5 pts.
		30 pts.

COURSE PROGRESS GRAPH

[Graph: y-axis 0–100 in increments of 10; x-axis 1–10 Units]

○ Total points earned
● Content points earned
□ Process points earned

A = 100-90
B = 89-80
C = 79-70
D = 69-60
Less than 60 redo

FIGURE 2.5

The Course Organizer: Part One. (From *The Course Organizer* [p. 71] by B. K. Lenz [with J. B. Schumaker, D. D. Deshler, and J. A. Bulgren], 1998, Lawrence, KS: Edge Enterprises. Copyright 1998 by B. K. Lenz, J. B. Schumaker, D. D. Deshler, and J. A. Bulgren. Reprinted with permission. *Note:* This figure was taken from a book that is available through certified Strategic Instruction Model Trainers who conduct professional development workshops across the nation. To obtain information about this training and to identify trainers in your area, contact The University of Kansas Center for Research on Learning at http://www.ku-crl.org or [785] 864-4780.)

The second visual device, a Course Map, provides spaces to record critical course concepts, units that will be taught, community principles (i.e., words that represent the values, ideas, or general tone related to how students are to interact with both their peers and the teacher), learning rituals (i.e., teaching routines, learning strategies, social skill strategies, and/or communication systems that will be used throughout the course), and performance options (e.g., oral tests, project choices, extra credit, peer tutoring; see Fig. 2.6 on p. 50).

Stage 2: Teachers begin making decisions about how to ensure that the students enrolled in the course will feel they are part of a community of learners (Joint Committee on Teacher Planning for Students with Disabilities, 1995). The following questions are used to help teachers think about this important aspect of teaching and learning:

▶ How can I nurture the community of learners who are enrolled in this course so that connections among them are strengthened and students aid each other's learning?

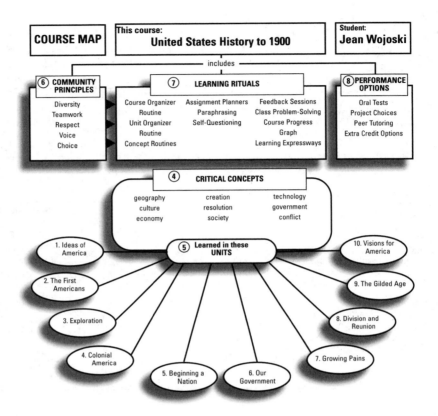

The Course Organizer: Part Two. (From *The Course Organizer* [p. 72] by B. K. Lenz [with J. B. Schumaker, D. D. Deshler, and J. A. Bulgren], 1998, Lawrence, KS: Edge Enterprises. Copyright 1998 by B. K. Lenz, J. B. Schumaker, D. D. Deshler, and J. A. Bulgren. Reprinted with permission. *Note:* This figure was taken from a book that is available through certified Strategic Instruction Model Trainers who conduct professional development workshops across the nation. To obtain information about this training and to identify trainers in your area, contact The University of Kansas Center for Research on Learning at http://www.ku-crl.org or [785] 864-4780.)

> ❱ How can I include everyone enrolled in the course in the learning process so that each person becomes an involved learner?
> ❱ How can I determine the strengths and resources of course participants to ensure they can be contributed to the community?
> ❱ How can I circumvent and compensate for the limitations of course participants? (p. 14)

These questions undoubtedly help teachers think about and plan for the diversity among students enrolled in their courses. Taking a bit of time to reflect on such matters sets the stage for classroom environments that include and value all students.

Stage 3: Teachers target students who represent high, average, and low achievers in the class as well as students with specific disabilities or needs. Teachers keep these selected target students in mind as they plan, implement, and reflect on their instruction throughout the school year. This selected group provides the teacher with a structure for thinking about the various needs that exist within diverse classrooms.

Stage 4: Teachers use the preceding planning ideas and the Course Organizer to assist in determining how to "launch" or begin the course. Teachers give students a blank copy of the Course Organizer and Course Map. Using blank overhead transparencies of these visual devices, the teacher facilitates a discussion among the students about the upcoming course. Together, the teacher and students fill in the various components on the visual devices (i.e., name of course, course questions, standards, etc.). Typically, the teacher uses the previously completed visual device as a cue sheet during this class discussion. Clearly, the course introduction sets the tone for the upcoming units and lessons. Attempts should be made to create interest and motivation among all the students. Moreover, students should understand the purpose, objectives, and teacher expectations related to the course. Stage 4 sets the stage for future learning success.

Stage 5: The Course Organizer is used throughout the course implementation. Teachers and students refer back to the visual devices and make changes when needed. Typically, the Course Map, course concepts, and ten questions are revisited at the beginning of each new unit. Student progress is plotted whenever appropriate (e.g., after unit tests or lesson quizzes). Thus, the visual devices serve as a reminder of the course goals and the progress being made by the students.

In addition to referring back to the visual devices, teachers evaluate student mastery of critical course content and related processes. Teachers reevaluate course decisions and revise plans for subsequent units while implementing the course. At the same time, decisions are being made regarding how to modify the course for the following year.

Stage 6: This stage concludes the course. During this stage, teachers assess student answers to the course questions, discuss the quality of the learning community with the students, and complete synthesis activities that help pull the course content together in meaningful ways.

In summary, these six stages provide an organized way for teachers to think about and plan for the courses they teach. The planning process begins prior to course implementation and then continues throughout the semester or year. This type of planning routine substantially affects how teachers attend to the needs of students within diverse classrooms. Decisions about the course are made keeping in mind the needs, interests, and abilities of the students who are in the class. Specifically, student diversity is taken into consideration when deciding what *all* students should know at the end of the course and when deciding what and how content should be taught. Planning various learning rituals and performance options maximizes the inclusiveness of students in the course. Discussing the performance options and reasons for the options at the beginning of a course reduces the misperception that certain students are being given "special rights" (Lenz, 1998). Moreover, monitoring individual student progress using graphs helps teachers identify students who need additional support to succeed in the course (see Validation Box 2.3 on p. 52).

The Unit Planning Routine

Keith Lenz and his colleagues at the University of Kansas Center for Research on Learning developed the Unit Planning Routine to assist teachers in planning units

VALIDATION BOX

2.3

The Course Planning Routine

Data were gathered over a period of 2 years with 16 teachers and over 400 students. Qualitative data sources included observations, planning interviews, journals, group discussions, and interviews with students. Quantitative data sources included teacher observations, student surveys, and student test scores. Findings revealed that teachers who used the Course Planning Routine integrated an average of 8 innovative practices throughout the school year to respond to academic diversity in their classes, whereas comparison teachers who didn't use the Course Planning Routine integrated an average of 1 innovative practice for addressing academic diversity among students. Secondary students with learning disabilities whose teachers used the routine answered 8 out of 10 course questions accurately at the end of the course; students with learning disabilities whose teachers did not use the routine answered only 4 out of 10 course questions accurately. For more information see: (Lenz, Deshler, Schumaker, Bulgren, Kissam, Vance, Roth, & McKnight, 1993; Lenz, 1998) or contact: The University of Kansas, Center for Research on Learning, 521 Joseph R. Pearson Hall, 1122 West Campus Road, Lawrence, KS 66045.

of instruction and subsequently teaching these units to diverse groups of learners including students with disabilities (Lenz, Schumaker, Deshler, Boudah, Vance, Kissam, Bulgren, and Roth, 1993; Joint Committee on Planning for Students With Disabilities, 1995). The Unit Planning Routine involves reflecting on the content and desired student outcomes of a unit. Additionally, the routine involves creating a graphic device (i.e., the Unit Organizer) depicting the important aspects of the unit (see Fig. 2.7). This device then is used to introduce the unit to the students. Teachers use the graphic device to help students see the "big picture" of the unit. Specifically, the students see where they have been in their learning, where they are, and where they are going. The Unit Planning Routine can be used in conjunction with the previously discussed Course Planning Routine or it can be used on its own.

The Unit Planning Routine has four stages:

Stage 1: Teachers reflect on the unit of instruction they are planning to teach. Specifically, teachers select desired content outcomes for the unit, think about the structure and organization of the content, analyze the content to identify difficult-to-learn material, and decide how to enhance the content to assist student understanding and retention of the material.

Stage 2: Teachers transfer the decisions made in Stage 1 into a graphic device called the Unit Organizer (see Fig. 2.7). "The Unit Organizer: *(a)* contains a paraphrase of the unit topic, *(b)* shows how the unit relates to previous and future units, *(c)* depicts the organization of the unit in seven or fewer graphic parts, *(d)* shows the relationships among the parts, *(e)* provides labels for the relationships, *(f)* depicts a timeline of activities and assignments for the unit, and *(g)* provides a space to record critical questions to be addressed during the unit instruction" (The Joint

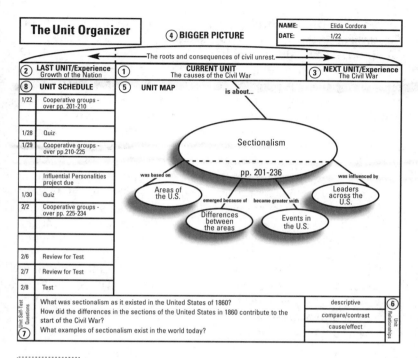

The Unit Organizer

④ BIGGER PICTURE

NAME: Elida Cordora
DATE: 1/22

←——— The roots and consequences of civil unrest. ———→

② LAST UNIT/Experience
Growth of the Nation

① CURRENT UNIT
The causes of the Civil War

③ NEXT UNIT/Experience
The Civil War

⑧ UNIT SCHEDULE

1/22	Cooperative groups - over pp. 201-210
1/28	Quiz
1/29	Cooperative groups - over pp.210-225
	Influential Personalities project due
1/30	Quiz
2/2	Cooperative groups - over pp. 225-234
2/6	Review for Test
2/7	Review for Test
2/8	Test

⑤ UNIT MAP

is about...

Sectionalism

pp. 201-236

was based on

Areas of the U.S.

emerged because of   became greater with

Differences between the areas

Events in the U.S.

was influenced by

Leaders across the U.S.

Unit Self-Test Questions

What was sectionalism as it existed in the United States of 1860?

How did the differences in the sections of the United States in 1860 contribute to the start of the Civil War?

⑦ What examples of sectionalism exist in the world today?

descriptive

compare/contrast

cause/effect

⑥ Unit Relationships

FIGURE 2.7

The Unit Organizer. (From *Planning for Academic Diversity in America's Classrooms: Windows on Reality, Research, Change, and Practice* [p. 17] by B. K. Lenz, J. Schumaker, and D. D. Deshler—Joint Committee on Teacher Planning for Students with Disabilities, 1995, Lawrence, KS: Center for Research on Learning. Reprinted with permission. *Note:* The book *The Content Enhancement Series: The Unit Organizer Routine* by B. K. Lenz [with J. A. Bulgren, J. B. Schumaker, D. D. Deshler, and D. A. Boudah] provides a thorough description of the Unit Organizer Routine and is available through certified Strategic Instruction Model Trainers who conduct professional development workshops across the nation. To obtain information about this training and to identify trainers in your area, contact The University of Kansas Center for Research on Learning at http://www.ku-crl.org or [785] 864-4780.)

Committee on Teacher Planning for Students with Disabilities, 1995, p. 16). The Unit Organizer is a tool that helps teachers make complex ideas more concrete and simple. It also helps teachers relate the unit to students' background knowledge. The Unit Organizer should be created to help students understand the relationships between the current unit and other units, the parts of the unit, the relationships between segments of the unit content, the tasks that need to be completed to learn the content in the unit, and the unit objectives (Lenz, 1994).

Stage 3: Teachers share the Unit Organizer with the students using an interactive process. Typically, teachers give students a blank copy of the Unit Organizer. Using an overhead transparency of the Unit Organizer, the teacher facilitates a discussion among the students about the upcoming unit. Together, the teacher and students fill in the various components on the visual device (i.e., name of current, last, and next unit; unit map, etc.). One of the most important aspects of introducing the unit is listing and discussing the Unit Self-Test Questions. Both the teacher and students participate in generating these questions and it should be understood that all students should be able to answer the questions at the end of the unit. Students can use these questions throughout the unit to ensure that they are learning the most important information in the unit. Typically, the teacher uses the visual device completed in Stage 2 as a cue sheet during this interactive process. Thus, the teacher has a clear idea about what should be included on the Unit Organizer, while simultaneously engaging students in the planning routine. This student involvement helps build a sense of community in the classroom.

Stage 4: The Unit Organizer is used throughout the instructional unit. Teachers and students revisit and expand the Unit Organizer when appropriate. For example, the organizer can be used at the beginning of each lesson within the unit to assess how much progress has been made. The organizer also can be used at the end of a lesson to remind students of assignments, to review the critical questions that now can be answered, and to review for an upcoming test. Using the Unit Organizer throughout the unit of instruction helps teachers focus their instruction and assessment activities on the most important concepts to be learned and helps students organize and understand important relationships among the content being taught.

In summary, the Unit Planning Routine helps teachers plan units of instruction and then communicate this plan to students in a way that ensures students will understand the "big picture." In other words, students will understand what information is important for them to learn and how this information relates to their previous and future learning. Low-achieving students, students with learning disabilities, and average-achieving students benefit from teacher instruction that also includes the Unit Planning Routine (see Validation Box 2.4).

The Lesson Planning Routine

Keith Lenz and his colleagues at the University of Kansas Center for Research on Learning developed the Lesson Planning Routine to assist teachers in planning lessons for diverse groups of learners including students with disabilities (Lenz,

---

VALIDATION BOX

2.4

The Unit Planning Routine

Data were gathered over an 8 month period of time with 6 secondary social studies and science teachers and their students. Qualitative data sources included interviews and group discussions. Quantitative data sources included teacher observations and student interviews. Results showed that teachers who used the Unit Planning Routine became more explicit with students about what they were to learn, the relationships among chunks of information, and the activities that would be completed to assist with learning. In addition, low-achieving students, students with learning disabilities, and average-achieving students understood and retained unit content better when their teachers used the routine. Students of teachers who used the routine regularly scored an average of 15 percentage points higher on unit tests than students of teachers who used the routine sporadically. For more information see: (Lenz, 1994; Lenz, Schumaker, Deshler, Boudah, Vance, Kissam, Bulgren, & Roth, 1993) or contact: The University of Kansas, Center for Research on Learning, 521 Joseph R. Pearson Hall, 1122 West Campus Road, Lawrence, KS 66045.

Boudah, Schumaker, and Deshler, 1993; Joint Committee on Teacher Planning for Students with Disabilities, 1995). The Lesson Planning Routine involves reflecting on the content and desired student outcomes of the lesson. Additionally, the routine involves creating a graphic device (i.e., The Lesson Organizer) depicting the important aspects of the lesson (see Fig. 2.8). This device then is used to introduce the lesson to the students. The Lesson Planning Routine allows teachers to "become explicit with students with regard to *(a)* what the lesson is about, *(b)* what students are expected to do and accomplish during the lesson, *(c)* the relationship of the current lesson to the rest of the unit, *(d)* the content parts of the lesson and the relationships among those parts, and *(e)* any background knowledge or vocabulary that might be useful during the lesson" (Joint Committee on Teacher Planning for Students with Disabilities, 1995, p. 19). The Lesson Planning Routine can be used on its own or in conjunction with the previously discussed Course Planning Routine and Unit Planning Routine. The Lesson Planning Routine involves four stages:

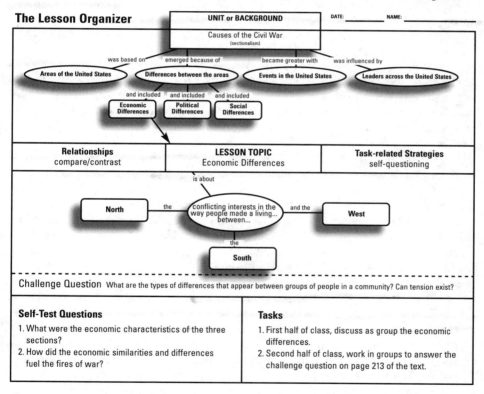

The Lesson Organizer. (From *Planning for Academic Diversity in America's Classrooms: Windows on Reality, Research, Change, and Practice* [p. 19] by B. K. Lenz, J. Schumaker, and D. D. Deshler—Joint Committee on Teacher Planning for Students with Disabilities, 1995, Lawrence, KS: Center for Research on Learning. Reprinted with permission. *Note:* The book *The Content Enhancement Series: The Lesson Organizer Routine* by B. K. Lenz, R. W. Marrs, J. B. Schumaker, and D. D. Deshler provides a thorough description of the Lesson Organizer Routine and is available through certified Strategic Instruction Model Trainers who conduct professional development workshops across the nation. To obtain information about this training and to identify trainers in your area, contact The University of Kansas Center for Research on Learning at http://www.ku-crl.org or [785] 864-4780.)

Stage 1: Teachers reflect on the lesson they are planning to teach. Specifically, teachers select desired content outcomes for the lesson, think about the structure and organization of the content, analyze the content to identify difficult-to-learn material, and decide how to enhance the content to assist student understanding and retention of the material.

Stage 2: Teachers transfer the decisions made in Stage 1 into a graphic device, the Lesson Organizer (see Fig. 2.8). "The Lesson Organizer: *(a)* contains the lesson topic, *(b)* shows how the lesson fits within the unit content, *(c)* depicts the organization of the lesson in seven or fewer graphic parts, *(d)* shows the relationships among the parts, *(e)* provides labels for the relationships, *(f)* displays expectations and assignments for the students, *(g)* names the strategies students should apply during the lesson, and *(h)* provides a space for self-test questions to be addressed during the lesson" (The Joint Committee on Teacher Planning for Students with Disabilities, 1995, p. 19) The Lesson Organizer is a tool that helps teachers make complex ideas more concrete and simple. It also helps teachers relate the information within the lesson to students' background knowledge. The Lesson Organizer helps students understand the relationships between lessons and segments of content within a given lesson (Lenz, Marrs, Schumaker, & Deshler, 1993).

Stage 3: Teachers use an interactive process to introduce the Lesson Organizer to the students. Typically, teachers give students a blank copy of the Lesson Organizer. Using an overhead transparency of the Lesson Organizer, the teacher facilitates a discussion with the students about the lesson. Together, the teacher and students fill in the various components on the visual device (i.e., lesson topic, relationships used in lesson, task-related strategies, etc.). One of the most important aspects of introducing the lesson is listing and discussing the Self-Test Questions. Both the teacher and students participate in generating these questions and it is understood that all students should be able to answer the questions at the end of the lesson. Students use these questions to ensure they are learning the most important information in the lesson. Typically, the teacher uses the visual device completed in Stage 2 as a cue sheet during this interactive process. Thus, the teacher has a framework with which to work, while simultaneously engaging students in the planning routine. As with the Course Planning Routine and Unit Planning Routine, this student involvement helps build a sense of community in the classroom.

Stage 4: The Lesson Organizer is reviewed to show students what they've learned, remind them of an assignment, and/or engage them in answering the Self-Test Questions. The Lesson Organizer also can be used to review for a test.

In summary, the Lesson Planning Routine helps teachers plan lessons and then communicate this plan to students in a way that helps students see the "big picture" of the lesson. In other words, students will understand what information is important for them to learn and how this information relates to their previous learning. Low-achieving students, students with learning disabilities, and average-achieving students benefit from teacher instruction that includes the Lesson Planning Routine (see Validation Box 2.5).

The Course, Unit, and Lesson Planning Routines help teachers identify the most important content to include in their instruction when teaching diverse

VALIDATION BOX

2.5

The Lesson Planning Routine

Three studies were conducted to evaluate the Lesson Planning Routine. Study 1 took place for 1 year in a middle school and involved 6 teachers. Study 2 took place for 1 year in a high school and involved 9 teachers. Study 3 was the 8-month Unit Planning study discussed in Validation Box 2.4. Qualitative data sources included planning interviews, planning "think aloud" sessions, and group discussions. Quantitative data sources included classroom observations and student interviews. Results from the first study revealed that low-achieving students and students with learning disabilities increased their identification of important lesson elements and increased verbal recall of lesson information when their general education teachers used the Lesson Planning Routine. Results from the second study revealed that students with learning disabilities whose teachers used the Lesson Planning Routine earned significantly higher test scores than students whose teachers did not use the routine. Results from the third study revealed that students of teachers who used the Lesson Organizer Routine in combination with the Unit Organizer Routine scored an average of 15 percentage points higher on unit tests than students of teachers who did not use the routine. For more information see: (Lenz, Boudah, Schumaker, & Deshler, 1993; Lenz, Marrs, Schumaker, & Deshler, 1993) or contact: The University of Kansas, Center for Research on Learning, 521 Joseph R. Pearson Hall, 1122 West Campus Road, Lawrence, KS 66045.

groups of students. The visual devices provide an organizational structure that helps students understand what they will be learning and how they will be learning it. The visual representation reinforces the verbal information as it is discussed. This helps students organize the content and distinguish important information from unimportant information and promotes content retention. Students review the visual devices periodically throughout the instructional process and before important assignments or tests. This type of structure is helpful for all students, but is particularly critical for students with learning difficulties.

Literacy Planning Processes

Cathy Morocco, Sue Gordon, and Maureen Riley at the Education Development Center in Newton, Massachusetts, developed the literacy planning processes described in this section to improve student writing and writing instruction. The basic premise involved in these planning processes is that dialogue plays a critical role in the construction of knowledge. Thus, teachers are encouraged to collaborate with fellow teachers when using the planning processes discussed in this section (i.e., Thematic Units and Thinking Frames, Analogue Experiences, and Planning around Focal Students). Structured workshops are sometimes helpful for facilitating collaboration.

Thematic Units and Thinking Frames

When teachers plan to integrate reading and writing instruction, it is helpful to use Thematic Units and Thinking Frames. A theme is selected for each instructional unit and a Thinking Frame is created to depict the type of thinking that is essential to the theme. The Thinking Frame is a schema or visual depiction of the kind of thinking that is essential to accomplish the writing assignment. The Thinking Frame (Fig. 2.9) identifies the components of writing (i.e., genre features) in expository writing and then identifies the thinking processes students will have to use when they complete an expository writing assignment that focuses on the theme "Making Hard Choices—Taking Sides." A Thinking Frame provides the framework for planning, teaching, and assessing reading and writing instruction (Riley, Morocco, Gordon, & Howard, 1993a; Joint Committee on Teacher Planning for Students with Disabilities, 1995). Teachers create and use a Thinking Frame to help plan for the diverse needs of their students while developing a Thematic Unit. Specifically, the following steps are used:

EXPOSITORY WRITING THEME
"REASON TO RIGHT — A REASON TO WRITE"
MAKING HARD CHOICES — TAKING SIDES

GENRE FEATURES	**THINKING PROCESSES**
Point of View	Perspective Taking
Explanation, Argument	Objective, Exocentric
Reasons, Facts, Details, Circumstances	*Causes* Comparing, Weighting, Reflecting, Analyzing
Consequences	*Effects* Comparing, Weighting, Reflecting, Analyzing
Values, Rules	Applying, Rejecting
Prediction	Hypothesizing, Inferencing
Resolution	Deciding, Judging
Clear, Cohesive, Audience Perspective	Interrelated, Logically Ordered

---

FIGURE 2.9

A Thinking Frame. (From C. C. Morocco, S. Gordon, and M. Riley [1995]. Planning with Thematic Units and Thinking Frames. *Planning for Academic Diversity in America's Classrooms: Windows on Reality, Research, Change, and Practice* [p. 25]. Lawrence, KS: University of Kansas Center for Research on Learning. Reprinted with permission.)

▶ Select a theme for each unit that is interesting and personally meaningful for students. Themes that encourage high-level thinking, that involve problem solving, and that provide opportunities for students to link new information to previous learning are appropriate.

▶ Select high-quality literature that reflects the selected theme. Literature that challenges students to think about new and different things is particularly useful.

▶ Construct a Thinking Frame. The Thinking Frame outlines or illustrates the kind of thinking (e.g., comparing, hypothesizing, inferencing, deciding, analyzing, weighing pros and cons) that students will engage in when completing their writing assignments. Webs and/or other visual devices are used to clearly reflect the type of thinking the students are expected to do in the unit.

▶ Use the information from the Thinking Frame to plan instruction. Think of activities that will result in the type of thinking that is depicted on the Thinking Frame and anticipate the kinds of individual support particular students may need to be successful in their reading and writing activities. Specifically, student background knowledge, writing skills, and learning strengths are considered when planning the instruction. Decide how to evaluate student performance within the reading and writing unit.

▶ Conduct ongoing assessment of students' thinking by asking stimulating questions during read-aloud and composing sessions. These questions are derived from the Thinking Frame. Assess students' thinking as it is expressed in their written products (Joint Committee on Teacher Planning for Students with Disabilities, 1995).

In summary, teachers who use a Thematic Unit and Thinking Frame plan their reading and writing instruction around a common theme emphasizing various ways of thinking about the content. This type of planning and instruction encourages students to integrate reading, writing, and thinking skills (see Validation Box 2.6).

VALIDATION BOX

2.6

Thematic Units and Thinking Frames

Data were gathered over a 2- to 3-month period with teachers and specialists in 7 classrooms. Data sources included interviews, classroom observations, and student writing samples. In a second study, data were collected for 2-1/2 years. Five specialists assisted 8 classroom teachers in their classrooms. Teachers experienced a high level of success with students who generally wrote very little. Thus, their expectations for these students increased. For more information see: (Joint Committee on Teacher Planning for Students with Disabilities, 1995; Riley, Morocco, Gordon, & Howard, 1993a; Riley & Morocco, 1999).

Analogue Experiences

Cathy Morocco, Sue Gordon, and Maureen Riley at the Education Development Center in Newton, Massachusetts, also developed the use of Analogue Experiences to assist with planning literacy instruction. Analogue Experiences are "adult learning experiences that replicate the specific thinking and social demands students face in the classroom" (Joint Committee on Teacher Planning for Students with Disabilities, 1995, p. 26). This method is used primarily for planning literacy instruction. Teachers participate in reading and writing experiences and focus on the thinking processes they must use to complete the assignments successfully. They use this experience to help plan similar experiences for their students. Awareness of one's own thinking processes helps in planning the activation of students' thinking processes. Analogue Experiences help teachers become more aware of why students become overwhelmed with reading and writing assignments. This knowledge helps teachers plan more effectively and anticipate the support that individual students will need to be successful. Analogue Experiences may involve specific reading and writing assignments, role-playing, assessment of memory and comprehension, or discussions. Each experience provides an opportunity for teachers to think about the demands placed on the students and ultimately leads to planning instruction that will activate higher level thinking on the students' parts. During and after Analogue Experiences, teachers reflect on three questions to assist in planning instruction. The three questions are:

> ▶ What kinds of thinking do I hope to activate in my students?
> ▶ What kinds of activities will engage all students in higher-level thinking?
> ▶ How can my interactions with students during writing encourage, rather than stifle, their thinking?

Analogue Experiences are most effective if they take place with a group of teachers who are planning instruction together. Teachers need time to reflect on their reading and writing experiences and discuss implications for planning similar instruction for their students. Since this type of introspection is not the customary method for planning instruction, it is helpful to have a person who is experienced with this type of planning serve as facilitator (see Validation Box 2.7).

Planning around Focal Students

Another literacy-based planning method that emerged from the work of Cathy Morocco, Sue Gordon, and Maureen Riley at the Education Development Center in Newton, Massachusetts, involves keeping a few focal students in mind when planning instruction. Using this method, teachers identify students functioning at high- and low-achievement levels and plan instruction so that the needs of these focal students are met. Teachers who use this planning process engage in the following steps:

> ▶ Teachers select one low-achieving student, usually with learning disabilities, and one student with high abilities.
> ▶ Teachers identify a theme for a reading–writing unit that broadly appeals to the class, including the two focal students.
> ▶ Teachers keep both students in mind when selecting literature and developing the assignment and specific writing activities related to the theme.

VALIDATION BOX
2.7

Analogue Experiences

Data were gathered over a 2-year period by 7 teachers and 6 specialists in 7 classrooms and 7 workshop sessions. Qualitative data sources included classroom observations, teacher interviews, student interviews, and student work samples. In a second study, data were collected for 2-1/2 years. Five specialists assisted 8 classroom teachers in their classrooms. Teachers involved in these projects were able to bridge theory and practice related to planning literacy instruction. Specifically, they acknowledged 4 principles that need to be considered when planning literacy instruction: *(a)* students need sufficient time to access prior knowledge, find a topic of interest, and develop their ideas; *(b)* students need to follow their own style of working; *(c)* students need prewriting support that provides a sense of structure; and *(d)* active learning is thwarted when teacher facilitation does not support students' interests and thinking. For more information see: (Riley, Morocco, Gordon, & Howard, 1993b; Riley & Morocco, 1999).

▶ Teachers think about background information and the instructional support that focal students will need to complete the assignments and participate in class discussions.

▶ Teachers test and revise their plans as they observe and interview individual students during the lesson and as they review students' work. They also think about whether the support they planned for the focal students was beneficial to other students as well (Joint Committee on Teacher Planning for Students with Disabilities, 1995).

In summary, this planning process gives teachers a method for meeting diverse student needs without having to plan for each individual student in the class. Teachers can use this planning approach on their own or in collaborative planning endeavors with other teachers (see Validation Box 2.8).

VALIDATION BOX
2.8

Planning around Focal Students

Data were gathered over a 2-year period with 7 teachers and 7 specialists in 7 classrooms. Data sources included transcripts of group planning, classroom observations, interviews with teachers, interviews with students, students' written work, and periodic written reviews involving participant knowledge of their focal students. In a second study, data were collected for 2-1/2 years. Five specialists assisted 8 classroom teachers in their classrooms. Teachers experienced a high level of success with students who wrote very little and for whom they had low expectations. For more information see: (Joint Committee on Teacher Planning for Students with Disabilities, 1995; Riley & Morocco, 1999).

Table 2.1 provides a brief summary of the steps involved in the teacher planning processes that have been described thus far in this chapter. This table may be useful when deciding which planning process to use for a particular teaching context.

Team Planning Processes

The planning processes discussed in the previous sections focus on planning for groups of diverse students who typically receive instruction within general education settings. Each of the planning methods included reflection on the varied needs of students within the context of the larger group. A slightly different approach to planning instruction for diverse classrooms involves the use of separate planning processes for students who have severe disabilities. The phrase "person-centered

TABLE 2.1

Teacher Planning Processes

Unit Planning Pyramid	Lesson Planning Pyramid	Course Planning Routine	Unit Planning Routine	Lesson Planning Routine	Thematic Units and Thinking Frames	Analogue Experiences	Planning Around Focal Students
Use self-questioning pertaining to topic, teacher, and student.	Use self-questioning pertaining to instructional context and strategies.	Identify 10 questions students should know at end of course.	Identify desired unit outcomes and ways to enhance content.	Identify lesson content and desired outcomes.	Select theme for literacy unit.	Participate in student literacy experiences.	Identify one low-achieving and one high-achieving student.
Complete Unit Planning Form.	Complete Lesson Planning Form.	Use self-questioning to plan.	Create Unit Organizer.	Create Lesson Organizer.	Create Thinking Frame.	Use self-questioning to plan.	Identify literacy unit theme.
		Identify high, average, low achiever to target.	Engage students in completing organizer.	Engage students in completing organizer.	Plan instructional activities.		Plan lessons keeping two students in mind.
		Create Course Organizer.			Conduct ongoing assessment.		Test and revise plans as needed.
		Engage students in completing organizer.					

planning" frequently is used to describe these planning processes. Person-centered planning is credited for shifting emphasis away from the disability label to a search for capacity in the person (O'Brien & Lovett, 1993; O'Brien, O'Brien, & Mount, 1997). This approach to planning emerged from earlier work designed to transition individuals with severe disabilities into greater community involvement, but now is used for a variety of purposes (e.g., teaching students with severe disabilities in general education classes, transitioning students to work settings). General and special education teachers have much to contribute to these team planning processes.

McGill Action Planning System

Marsha Forest (1987) developed the McGill Action Planning System (MAPS) at McGill University. MAPS is a systematic approach for developing plans for including students with disabilities into general education classrooms. Planning teams typically include family, friends, peers without disabilities, professionals, and the student. Planning teams are formed after the student with disabilities has been a member of the general education classroom so that friends without disabilities can be involved in the planning process. The members of the planning team meet, in one or two sessions for a minimum of 3 hours, to identify specific goals for the student with a disability and to identify the specific supports or resources needed to meet the goals. Team members sit in a half-circle and the team facilitator asks a prescribed set of questions. Included among these questions are the following:

1. What is the individual's history?
2. What is your dream for the individual?
3. What is your nightmare (fear) for the individual?
4. Who is the individual (i.e., adjectives that describe the individual)?
5. What are the individual's strengths, gifts, and abilities?
6. What are the individual's needs?
7. What would the individual's ideal day look like, and what must be done to make it happen?

The planning team facilitator ensures that all team members participate in the process of discussing and answering these questions. All answers to the questions are recorded on chart paper. Goals for the individual emerge based on the recorded responses. To end the planning process, the facilitator provides an opportunity for feedback specifically related to the planning process itself. Each person on the team is asked to describe, in one word, the MAPS process. Typically, adjectives describing the process are very positive and serve to affirm the time and effort that each member contributed (Vandercook, York, & Forest, 1989; see Validation Box 2.9 on p. 64).

Choosing Options and Accommodations for Children (COACH)

The COACH planning process originated in 1982 as an unnamed tool to assist in developing rehabilitation plans for adults with disabilities. In 1985, the tool was named COACH (Cayuga–Onondaga Assessment for Children with Handicaps) and was revised for use in public school programs serving students with disabilities. After numerous subsequent revisions, Michael Giangreco and his colleagues Chigee Cloninger and Virginia Iverson continued to improve the COACH planning process. COACH now stands for Choosing Options and Accommodations for Children to more accurately reflect the planning process that emerged over the years. COACH is designed to assist in developing educational programs that are implemented in general education settings with students who have disabilities. Six basic assumptions serve as the foundation for the COACH process: (a) pursuing valued life outcomes is an important aspect of education; (b) the family is the cornerstone of relevant and longitudinal educational planning; (c) collaborative team work is essential to quality education; (d) coordinated planning is dependent on shared, discipline-free goals; (e) using problem-solving methods improves the effectiveness of educational planning; and (f) special education is a service, not a place (Giangreco, Cloninger, & Iverson, 1993).

Family input is an integral and critical component of the COACH planning process. In fact, planning teams are encouraged to enter into the COACH process *only* if group members are willing to accept and use the priorities generated by the family. The COACH process is organized into three major components:

1. Family prioritization interview
2. Defining the educational program components
3. Addressing the educational program components in inclusive settings.

First, family members and school personnel come together to determine what the family's educational priorities are for the student with disabilities. Once these priorities are identified, the educational program components are defined. Annual goals and short-term objectives are identified based on the family's priorities and then learning outcomes that extend beyond the family-centered priorities are identified. Family and school personnel discuss the general supports and accommodations needed for the student to participate in his newly created educational program. These supports become part of the specific student's plan. Finally, the team determines options for addressing the student's educational program in the general education classroom. Collaborative teamwork among

---

VALIDATION BOX 2.9

McGill Action Planning System (MAPS)

The MAPS process was used with over 200 school-age students with moderate to profound disabilities in 50 school communities. Anecdotal outcomes have been positive. Specifically, the process capitalizes on the resources of classmates, family members, and educational personnel. Moreover, the process helps general and special educators merge resources needed to build integrated school communities. For more information see: (Vandercook, York, & Forest, 1989).

VALIDATION BOX
2.10

Choosing Options and Accommodations for Children (COACH)

Field-testing occurred over a 7-year period in collaboration with families and educators in settings where students with disabilities were taught in general education classes in their neighborhood schools. Major contributors to the development and field-testing of COACH included personnel affiliated with the Center for Developmental Disabilities at the University of Vermont in Burlington, members of the Vermont State Interdisciplinary Team for Intensive Special Education, and the staff of the Cayuga–Onondaga Board of Cooperative Educational Services in Auburn, NY. For more information see: (Giangreco, Cloninger, & Iverson, 1993).

school personnel and family members and goal commitment are emphasized throughout the COACH planning. The primary intention for using the COACH planning process is to increase the probability that students' lives will improve as a result of being educated in inclusive classrooms (Giangreco, Cloningen, & Iverson, 1993; see Validation Box 2.10).

Life-Style Planning

The Life-Style Planning Process was developed to facilitate planning for individuals with severe disabilities (O'Brien, 1987). The process guides family members, friends, and service providers through three essential planning activities:

1. describing a desirable future with the person,
2. developing a schedule of activities and supports that will organize available resources to move toward that future, and
3. accepting responsibility for using available opportunities and dealing with the lack of needed activities and supports. (p. 175)

Although the Life-Style Planning Process is, in some ways, similar to traditional IEP development, it differs in that it typically involves a more comprehensive effort and specifically relates to students with severe disabilities. The Life-Style Planning Process brings together people whose cooperation and involvement is important to the person with a disability (i.e., the focal person). Moreover, the process focuses attention on quality of life and results in a shared vision that guides the selection of curricular goals, training activities, and performance objectives. The process also facilitates reviewing progress and identifying new opportunities after periods of routine activity.

The basic assumptions that serve as the foundation for Life-Style Planning are:

1. *Everyday activities and relationships should be the focus of efforts on behalf of people with severe disabilities.* Planning should involve day-to-day

experiences that improve the quality of life in the *present*. Planning should not focus solely on the future.

2. *Services are not enough.* The connections of family and friends with potential employers can be a more effective route to employment than the most costly vocational service. Both informal and formal resources are important.

3. No single person or service can or should do everything. Effective life-style planning requires an interdependence among persons who provide support to the focal person.

These three assumptions guide the Life-Style Planning Process through four major activities: *(a)* convening the planning group, *(b)* reviewing the focal person's current quality of life, *(c)* conducting the planning meeting, and *(d)* following up on the implementation plan (O'Brien, 1987).

Convening the Planning Group

The planning group may include from 5 to 20 persons depending on how many persons' cooperation is important to the focal person's current quality of life and future quality of life. Family members, people who have an important connection to the focal person's family (e.g., friends, minister), direct service workers, and other individuals who have an important relationship with the person with a disability may be appropriate to invite to the planning meeting. The meeting should be scheduled at a convenient place and time. Roles should be assigned to the group members (e.g., arranging the meeting place, facilitating the meeting, summarizing current situation of the focal person, recording minutes for the meeting). Members of the planning group who have not recently spent time with the focal person are expected to do so prior to the meeting.

Reviewing the Individual's Current Quality of Life

Whoever agreed to summarize the current situation of the focal person prepares a summary describing the quality of the focal person's current life experiences. Consideration is given to the focal person's community presence and participation, opportunities to make choices, level of competence, and respect from others. It frequently is helpful to spend additional time with the focal person and his or her family prior to the meeting. After preparing the summary report, the focal person and those closest to him or her have an opportunity to review the report. These individuals may even want to participate in the presentation of the gathered information.

Conducting the Planning Meeting

The meeting begins with the summary of the focal person's current life-style and then moves to describing a desirable future. Then, the planning team negotiates responsibility for activities and supports that are consistent with the described future. O'Brien (1987) recommended the following questions to facilitate the meeting process:

1. What is the quality of the focal person's present life experiences?

2. What is changing for the focal person or in the surrounding environment that is likely to influence the quality of his or her life?
3. What are the most important threats and opportunities for improving the quality of life for the focal person?
4. What is the team's image of a desired life-style for the focal person?
5. What are the most critical barriers to the individual moving toward the desirable future the team has described?
6. How will the individual most effectively manage these critical barriers and move toward realizing the life-style the team has defined?
7. Based on the team's discussion, does the team want to make any statements about necessary changes in the capabilities of service systems?

The discussion and answers to these questions are recorded on large sheets of paper so that all participants can see and hear the suggestions being made. Addressing each of these questions enables the planning team to devise an implementation plan designed to improve the focal person's quality of life.

Following Up on the Implementation Plan

Someone copies the information recorded on the large sheets of paper and then disseminates them to each person on the planning team. This dissemination occurs shortly after the life-style planning meeting. If a more formal narrative is important for the record, it is prepared separately. A follow-up meeting is held two weeks after the life-style planning meeting with the people who are directly responsible for managing the activity schedule of the focal person. The purpose of this meeting is to review the last 2 weeks in light of the directions established at the previous meeting. Special consideration is given to the type, number, and balance of activities in which the focal person is now involved. One month after the life-style planning meeting, the individual who convened the planning process should review the commitments that were made at the meeting and then contact each person who accepted responsibility to find out how things are working out and what needs improvement. This Life-Style Planning Process provides an organized format for improving the quality of life for individuals with severe disabilities (see Validation Box 2.11).

VALIDATION BOX
2.11

Life-Style Planning

Data were gathered over a 6-month period. The study was conducted with 6 participants with mental retardation who ranged in age from 14 to 21 years. Qualitative data sources included observations, interviews, and document analysis. Life-style planning was evaluated within the context of person-centered planning. Most participants viewed the process as valuable and reported feeling "energized" by the increased sense of community, shared responsibility, and clearer focus that emerged from the process. For more information see: (Hagner, Helm, & Butterwork, 1996).

Student Planning Process

Bradley, King-Sears, and Tessier-Switlick (1997) discussed another team approach to planning that incorporates components from the previously discussed planning approaches (i.e., McGill Action Planning, COACH, Life-Style Planning). Their approach is called the Student Planning Process and involves six steps: *(a)* determine the desired long-range outcome, *(b)* identify the starting point, *(c)* determine steps to achieve the outcome, *(d)* establish a time line, *(e)* plan the details, and *(f)* evaluate the planning process.

Bradley, King-Sears, and Tessier-Switlick (1997) developed three forms (i.e., Profile Planning Worksheet, Programming at a Glance, and Follow-Up Form) to facilitate the Student Planning Process (see Fig. 2.10 on p. 69 and Figs 2.11 and 2.12 on pp. 70–71). Team members complete the Profile Planning Worksheet prior to the planning meeting. Each member records what he or she believes to be the student's strengths and needs related to listed curricular areas and then brings this completed form to the meeting. The Programming at a Glance form is used during the planning meeting to record the planning decisions made. The Follow-Up Form also is used during the meeting to record all necessary follow-up tasks to ensure successful implementation of the plan (see Validation Box 2.12 on p. 70).

Table 2.2 provides a brief summary of the steps involved in the team planning processes just discussed. This table may be useful when deciding which planning process to use for a particular student.

TABLE 2.2

Team Planning Processes

McGill Action Planning System	Choosing Options and Accommodations for Children	Life-Style Planning	Student Planning Process
Planning team meets.	Family priorities for student with disabilities are identified.	Planning team meets.	Profile Planning Worksheet is completed prior to planning meeting to identify person's strengths and weaknesses.
Prescribed questions are used to identify goals and supports for individual with disability.	Educational program is planned including general supports and accommodations.	Questions are used to facilitate planning.	Programming at a Glance and Follow-Up forms are completed during meeting to record planning decisions.
Meeting concludes with each person commenting on the planning process.	Options for implementing program in general education class are discussed.	Suggestions are recorded and disseminated to planning team.	
		Follow-up meetings are held to ensure plan implementation.	

Curriculum Areas	Strengths	Needs	Priority Areas
Academic *Reading:* Decoding, word recognition, comprehension *Writing:* Process, usage, grammar, punctuation, capitalization, size, spacing *Math:* Concepts, computation, application, problem solving *Science/Social Studies:* Content, participation			
Communication Speaking, adaptive technology needs, augmentative communication needs			
Social Skills Friendship skills, peer relations, expresses feelings, makes requests, takes risks			
Behavior Respect for others, attention span, activity level			
Work Study Skills Organization, on-task behavior, following directions, working with peers, task completion			
Motor Fine Motor: Writing—formation of letters, size, spacing, cutting Gross Motor: Trunk strength, ascending/descending stairs, age-appropriate physical skills			
Functional Survival language, travel training, money, shopping, daily living skills			
Recreation and Leisure Long-term age-appropriate hobbies, activities, or interests			
Vocational Job skills, positive work habits, on-site training			
Transition Services Adult services, job supports, social supports or community living supports			

Person Completing Form: Title: Date:

FIGURE 2.10

Profile Planning Worksheet. (From D. F. Bradley, M. E. King-Sears, and D. M. Tessier-Switlick, *Effective Practices for Diverse Classrooms.* © 1997 by Allyn & Bacon. Reprinted with permission.)

VALIDATION BOX

2.12

Student Planning Process

This planning process was field-tested over a period of 3 months with 18 teachers who also were enrolled in graduate course work at Johns Hopkins University. Informal feedback from these teachers indicated that the process was beneficial, flexible, and easy to use (D. M. Tessier-Switlick, personal communication, February 11 and March 3, 1998).

Physical Features		Priority Instruction Needs	Groupings
Regular classroom	%	Academic	Heterogeneous
Special education (in class)	%		Homogeneous
Special education (separate class)	%	Communication	Cooperative
Accessibility issues:		Social Skills	Peer tutoring
• ramps	Y/N		• same grade
• elevators	Y/N	Behavior	• cross grade
• class arrangement	Y/N	Work study skills	
• bathroom	Y/N	Motor skills	
• equipment	Y/N	Functional skills	
Services/Staffing		Recreation/leisure	**Preparation and Procedures**
Administrator		Vocational skills	Staff training
General educator		Transition skills	• staff
Special educator			• students
Speech/language pathologist			• community
Occupational/physical therapy			Behavior plans
Reading specialist			Medical/health plans
Psychologist/counselor			Emergency plans
Instructional assistants			
Nurse			
Long-Range Outcome:			

Student Self-Advocacy

To date, most research related to educational planning has involved either teacher-planning processes or team planning processes. Little emphasis, however, has been

Actions/Responses	Person Responsible	Time Lines

Follow-Up Form. (From D. F. Bradley, M. E. King-Sears, and D. M. Tessier-Switlick, *Effective Practices for Diverse Classrooms.* © 1997 by Allyn & Bacon. Reprinted with permission.)

placed on the student's self-advocacy role in many of these planning processes. If students with disabilities are to become independent and proactive in their approach to life, they must become involved in educational planning meetings. Their involvement needs to extend beyond simply attending these meetings. Instead, students need to become active participants in the planning process. Educators can and should teach students how to advocate for themselves.

Van Reusen, Bos, Schumaker, and Deshler (1994) developed the Self-Advocacy Strategy to help students gain a sense of control and influence over their own learning and development. The strategy is designed to get students actively involved in team planning meetings. Specifically, the strategy helps students prepare for and participate in Education or Transition Planning Conferences. There are five steps involved in the Self-Advocacy Strategy:

1. **I**nventory. Prior to the Education or Transition Planning Conference, students are taught to identify and list their perceived education and/or

When planning educational programs for students with disabilities, the student's goals, desires, and dreams should be recognized and valued. Thus, the student's participation in planning meetings is very helpful.

transition strengths, areas to improve or learn, goals, needed accommodations, and choices for learning. This information is recorded on an Education or Transition Inventory, a form that the students take to the conference (see Fig. 2.13 on pp. 73–74 and Fig. 2.14 on pp. 74–75).

2. **P**rovide your inventory information. Students are taught how to share their inventory information during the conference. Appropriate social skills (e.g., posture, voice tone, eye contact) are emphasized.

3. **L**isten and respond. Students are taught when and how to listen and respond. Emphasis is placed on active listening, using positive statements, and negotiating agreement.

4. **A**sk questions. Students are taught when and how to ask questions. Rationales for seeking information and clarifying information are emphasized. Students practice asking complete questions and asking one question at a time.

5. **N**ame your goals. Students are taught when and how to summarize their goals. They are taught to state what they want to do and when they want to complete it.

The Self-Advocacy Strategy

Student Name: _____

Date: _____   Updates: _____

EDUCATION INVENTORY

1. Strengths

Reading Skills: _____
_____
_____
_____

Writing Skills: _____
_____
_____
_____

Math Skills: _____
_____
_____
_____

Study Skills: _____
_____
_____
_____

Social Skills: _____
_____
_____

Career and Employment Skills: _____
_____
_____

EDUCATION INVENTORY (continued)

2. Areas to Improve or Learn

_____
_____
_____
_____
_____

3. Goals

School Goals:
Academic Goals: _____
_____
_____

Social Goals: _____
_____

Career/Employment Goals: _____
_____

Extracurricular Goals: _____
_____

Future Goals: _____
_____
_____

(continued)

FIGURE 2.13

Education Inventory. (From *The Self-Advocacy Strategy* [pp. 143–14] by A. K. Van Reusen, C. S. Bos, J. B. Schumaker, and D. D. Deshler, 1994, Lawrence, KS: Edge Enterprises. Copyright 1994 by A. K. Van Reusen, C. S. Bos, J. B. Schumaker, and D. D. Deshler. Reprinted with permission. *Note: The Self-Advocacy Strategy* may be ordered through Edge Enterprises, P. O. Box 1304, Lawrence, KS 66045; telephone: [785] 749-1473; fax: [785] 749-0207).

The Self-Advocacy Strategy

TRANSITION INVENTORY

Student Name: _____

Date: _____ Updates: _____

1. Strengths

Independent Living Skills:

_____
_____
_____
_____

Career and Employment Skills:

_____
_____
_____
_____

Financial and Consumer Skills:

_____
_____
_____
_____

Social and Family-Living Skills:

_____
_____
_____
_____

Citizenship and Legal Skills:

_____
_____
_____
_____

Health and Wellness Skills:

_____
_____
_____
_____

(continued)

FIGURE 2.14

Transition Inventory. (From *The Self-Advocacy Strategy* [pp. 159-161] by A. K. Van Reusen, C. S. Bos, J. B. Schumaker, and D. D. Deshler, 1994, Lawrence, KS: Edge Enterprises. Copyright 1994 by A. K. Van Reusen, C. S. Bos, J. B. Schumaker, and D. D. Deshler. Reprinted with permission. *Note: The Self-Advocacy Strategy* may be ordered through Edge Enterprises, P. O. Box 1304, Lawrence, KS 66045; telephone: [785] 749-1473; fax: [785] 749-0207)

EDUCATION INVENTORY (continued)

**4. Choices for Learning
Helpful Activities:**

_____
_____
_____
_____

Helpful Materials:

_____
_____
_____
_____

Learning Preferences:

_____
_____
_____
_____

Testing Preferences:

_____
_____
_____
_____

FIGURE 2.13

Education Inventory. (From *The Self-Advocacy Strategy* [pp. 143–14] by A. K. Van Reusen, C. S. Bos, J. B. Schumaker, and D. D. Deshler, 1994, Lawrence, KS: Edge Enterprises. Copyright 1994 by A. K. Van Reusen, C. S. Bos, J. B. Schumaker, and D. D. Deshler. Reprinted with permission. *Note: The Self-Advocacy Strategy* may be ordered through Edge Enterprises, P. O. Box 1304, Lawrence, KS 66045; telephone: [785] 749-1473; fax: [785] 749-0207).

TRANSITION INVENTORY (continued)

Goals	Skills Needed for Success	Skills to Improve or Learn
Independent Living		
Career and Employment		
Financial and Consumer		
Social and Family Living		
Citizenship and Legal		

TRANSITION INVENTORY (continued)

Goals	Skills Needed for Success	Skills to Improve or Learn
Health and Wellness		
Community Involvement		
Leisure and Recreation		
Further Education or Training		
Accommodations		
Potential Resources		

FIGURE 2.14

Transition Inventory. (From *The Self-Advocacy Strategy* [pp. 159-161] by A. K. Van Reusen, C. S. Bos, J. B. Schumaker, and D. D. Deshler, 1994, Lawrence, KS: Edge Enterprises. Copyright 1994 by A. K. Van Reusen, C. S. Bos, J. B. Schumaker, and D. D. Deshler. Reprinted with permission. *Note: The Self-Advocacy Strategy* may be ordered through Edge Enterprises, P. O. Box 1304, Lawrence, KS 66045; telephone: [785] 749-1473; fax: [785] 749-0207)

The acronym **I PLAN** helps the students remember the five steps. The Self-Advocacy Strategy is taught using an eight stage instructional sequence *(a)* orient and make commitments, *(b)* describe, *(c)* model and prepare, *(d)* verbal practice, *(e)* group practice and feedback, *(f)* individual practice and feedback, and (f) generalization. This sequence was adapted from the Strategies Instructional Model developed by Donald Deshler, Jean Schumaker, and their colleagues at the University of Kansas Center for Research on Learning (Deshler, Ellis, Lenz, 1996). Individuals who are interested in teaching the Self-Advocacy Strategy to students may order the Self-Advocacy Strategy instructional manual from Edge Enterprises, P.O. Box 1304, Lawrence, Kansas 66045; telephone: (785) 749-1473; fax: (785) 749-0207 (see Validation Box 2.13).

Selecting Planning Processes

As is evident from the content in this chapter, there are a variety of validated planning processes. Consequently, it can be challenging for teachers and other professionals to decide which process or processes to use. Perhaps the first step in selecting a particular process is to consider the purpose for the planning and then determine which of the planning processes most closely matches that purpose. For example, if the planning goal is to develop a systematic, effective skill-based lesson (e.g., solving multiplication facts) that requires structured practice and scaffolded support, then consideration should be given to the Rosenshine (1983) and Hunter (1986) models.

If the purpose for planning, however, is to select the most important information or content to teach groups of academically diverse students, then consideration should be given to the Planning Pyramid routines (i.e., Unit Planning Pyramid; Lesson Planning Pyramid) or the ReflActive Planning routines (i.e., Course Planning Routine, Unit Planning Routine, Lesson Planning Routine). These routines are particularly helpful for planning content-area instruction (e.g., science, social studies) that involves many important concepts. These routines can

VALIDATION BOX 2.13

Self-Advocacy Strategy: For Education and Transition Planning

This strategy was tested with middle- and high-school students with learning and behavior disabilities who participated in their annual IEP teacher conferences. The quality and quantity of students' verbal contributions during individual conferences increased substantially and were at higher levels than the contributions made by students who received a general overview of the content and format of IEP conferences. For more information see: (Bos & Van Reusen, 1987; Van Reusen & Bos, 1994; Van Reusen, Deshler, & Schumaker, 1989).

be used singly or in conjunction with one another. The Unit and Lesson Planning Pyramid routines work well together. Similarly, the Course, Unit, and Lesson Planning Routines work well together. Combining the planning routines in these ways enhances the effectiveness of the planning process (Lenz, 1998). If the purpose for the planning is to design literacy instruction, then consideration should be given to processes such as Thematic Units and Thinking Frames, Analogue Experiences, and Planning around Focal Students, since these deal specifically with facilitating and developing the writing process among students.

When the purpose of the planning is to meet the needs of students with severe disabilities who have more specialized needs than most students, then team planning processes (e.g., MAPS, COACH, Life-Style Planning, Student Planning) are very helpful. Each of these processes takes advantage of the expertise of numerous individuals and focuses on the strengths and abilities of the students involved. These planning processes are particularly appropriate when planning the inclusion of students with severe disabilities in general education classes.

Regardless of which process is selected, several factors seem to be important for meaningful planning to occur. These are: *(a)* consider student needs, interests, and abilities; *(b)* give students a voice in the planning process; *(c)* develop structured, systematic approaches to planning and use these approaches with consistency; *(d)* consider both content and pedagogy; and *(e)* recognize that planning is a fluid process that occurs before, during, and after instruction.

Becoming proficient in educational planning requires practice, reflection, and a willingness to refine or improve planning processes to ensure that student needs are being met. Select one or more of the following activities to gain experience with the important thinking that accompanies all planning processes. Experiment with a variety of processes to determine which ones seem most appropriate for your current or future teaching situations. Effective and efficient planning will, undoubtedly, result in higher student achievement.

Practice Activities

▶ Acquire copies of content standards and/or curriculum guidelines used in school districts near your home. Develop unit and/or lesson plans related to these standards.

▶ With a peer, collaboratively develop a lesson that would be appropriate for a group of diverse students. Within the context of the lesson, plan for differences in student reading abilities, interests, and/or various disabilities.

▶ Interview a teacher who teaches a class of diverse students. Ask the teacher to briefly describe the planning processes he or she uses to meet the students' varied needs.

▶ Create case studies involving students with disabilities and then role play several of the team planning processes.

P O S T ORGANIZER

Planning effective and efficient instruction for students with special needs who receive their instruction in diverse classrooms is indeed a challenge. Teachers who use specific planning processes are better equipped to meet this challenge. The teacher planning processes and the team planning processes described in this chapter have been field-tested and were found to be effective for students with special needs.

References

Baker, J. M., & Zigmond, N. (1990). Are regular education classes equipped to accommodate students with learning disabilities? *Exceptional Children, 56*, 515–526.

Batesky, J. (1987). Inservice education: Increasing teacher effectiveness using the Hunter lesson design. *Journal of Physical Education, Recreation, and Dance,* September, 89–93.

Bos, C. S., & Van Reusen, A. K. (1987). *Partner Project II: Final Report.* Tucson: University of Arizona.

Bradley, D. F., King-Sears, M. E., Tessier-Switlick, D. M. (1997). *Teaching students in inclusive settings: From theory to practice.* Needham Heights, MA: Allyn and Bacon.

Bulgren, J. A., Deshler, D. D., & Schumaker, J. B. (1993). *The content enhancement series: The concept mastery routine.* Lawrence, KS: Edge Enterprises.

Deshler, D. D., Ellis, E. S., & Lenz, K. (Eds.) (1996). *Teaching adolescents with learning disabilities* (2nd ed.). Denver: Love.

Forest, M. (1987). *More education integration: A further collection of readings on the integration of children with mental handicaps into regular school systems.* Downsville, ON: G. Allen Roeher Institute.

Giangreco, M. F., Cloninger, C. J., & Iverson, V. S. (1993). *Choosing options and accommodations for children: A guide to inclusive education.* Baltimore: Paul H. Brookes Publishing Co.

Hagner, D., Helm, D. T., & Butterworth, J. (1996). "This is your meeting": A qualitative study of person-centered planning. *Mental Retardation, 34*, 159–171.

Hunter, M. (1986). Comments on the Napa County, California, Follow-Through Project. *The Elementary School Journal, 87*, 173–179.

Hunter, M. (1991). Generic lesson design: The case for. *Science Teacher, 58*(7), 26–28.

Joint Committee on Teacher Planning for Students with Disabilities. (1995). *Planning for academic diversity in America's classrooms: Windows on reality, research, change, and practice.* Lawrence, KS: The University of Kansas Center for Research on Learning.

Lenz, B. K., Boudah, D. J., Schumaker, J. B., & Deshler, D. D. (1993). *The lesson planning routine: A guide for inclusive lesson planning* (Tech. Rep. No. 124). Lawrence, KS: University of Kansas Center for Research on Learning.

Lenz, B. K., & Bulgren, J. A. (1994). *ReflActive planning: Planning for diversity in secondary schools* (Tech. Rep. No. 128). Lawrence, KS: University of Kansas Center for Research on Learning.

Lenz, B. K. (with Bulgren, J. A., Schumaker, J. B., Deshler, D. D., & Boudah, D. A.) (1994). *The content enhancement series: The unit organizer routine.* Lawrence, KS: Edge Enterprises, Inc.

Lenz, B. K., Deshler, D., Schumaker, J., Bulgren, J., Kissam, B., Vance, M., Roth, J., & McKnight, M. (1993). *The course planning routine: A guide for inclusive course planning* (Tech. Rep. No. 125). Lawrence, KS: University of Kansas Center for Research on Learning.

Lenz, B. K., Marrs, R. W., Schumaker, J. B., & Deshler, D. D. (1993). *The content enhancement series: The lesson organizer routine.* Lawrence, KS: Edge Enterprises, Inc.

Lenz, B. K., Schumaker, J. B., Deshler, D. D., Boudah, D. J., Vance, M., Kissam, B., Bulgren, J. A., & Roth, J. (1993). *The unit planning routine: A guide for inclusive unit planning* (Tech. Rep. No. 126). Lawrence, KS: University of Kansas Center for Research on Learning.

Lenz, B. K. (with Schumaker, J. B., Deshler, D. D., & Bulgren, J. A.) (1998). *The content enhancement series: The course organizer.* Lawrence, KS: Edge Enterprises.

O'Brien, J. (1987). A guide to life-style planning. In B. Wilcox, & G. T. Bellamy (Eds.), *A comprehensive guide to the activities catalogue* (pp. 175–189). Baltimore: Paul H. Brookes Publishing Co.

O'Brien, J., & Lovett, H. (1993). *Finding a way toward everyday lives: The contribution of person centered planning* (Rep. No. H133B80048). Harrisburg, PA: Pennsylvania Office of Mental Retardation. (ERIC Document Reproduction Service No. ED 356 596.)

O'Brien, C. L., O'Brien, J., & Mount, B. (1997). Person-centered planning has arrived . . . or has it? *Mental Retardation, 35,* 480–483.

Riley, M. K., & Morocco, C. C. (1999). Talking in school: Constructive conversations for written language. In M. Z. Solomon (Ed.), *The diagnostic teacher: Revitalizing professional development* (pp. 104–132). New York: Teachers College Press.

Riley, M. K., Morocco, C. C., Gordon, S. M., & Howard, C. (1993a). *Using thinking frames to plan and assess writing* (Tech. Rep.). Newton, MA: Education Development Center, Inc.

Riley, M. K., Morocco, C. C., Gordon, S. M., & Howard, C. (1993b). Walking the talk: Putting constructivist thinking into practice in classrooms. *Educational Horizons, 71,* 187–196.

Rosenshine, B. (1983). Teaching functions in instructional programs. *Elementary School Journal, 83,* 335–351.

Searcy, S., & Maroney, S. A. (1996). Lesson planning practices of special education teachers. *Exceptionality, 6,* 171–187.

Schumm, J. S., Vaughn, S., Haager, D., McDowell, J., Rothlein, L., & Saumell, L. (1995). General education teacher planning: What can students with learning disabilities expect? *Exceptional Children, 61,* 335–352.

Schumm, J. S., Vaughn, S., & Harris, J. (1997). Pyramid power for collaborative planning. *Teaching Exceptional Children, 29*(6), 62–66.

Schumm, J. S., Vaughn, S., & Leavell, A. G. (1994). Planning pyramid: A framework for planning for diverse student needs during content area instruction. *The Reading Teacher, 47,* 608–615.

Vandercook, T., York, J., & Forest, M. (1989). The McGill action planning system (MAPS): A strategy for building the vision. *The Journal of the Association for Persons with Severe Handicaps, 14,* 205–215.

Van Reusen, A. K., & Bos, C. S. (1994). Facilitating student IEP participation through motivation strategy instruction. *Exceptional Children, 60,* 466–475.

Van Reusen, A. K., Bos, C. S., Schumaker, J. B., & Deshler, D. D. (1994). *The self-advocacy strategy.* Lawrence, KS: Edge Enterprises.

Van Reusen, A. K., Deshler, D. D., & Schumaker, J. B. (1989). Effects of a student participation in facilitating the involvement of adolescents in the IEP planning process. *Learning Disabilities: A Multidisciplinary Journal, 1*(2), 23–34.

Vaughn, S., & Schumm, J. S. (1994). Middle school teachers' planning for students with learning disabilities. *Remedial and Special Education, 15,* 152–161.

Ysseldyke, J. E., Thurlow, M. L., Wotruba, J. W., & Nanaia, P. A. (1990). Instructional arrangement: Perceptions from general education. *Teaching Exceptional Children, 22,* 4–8.

Organizing the Learning Environment

To affect the quality of the day, that is the highest of arts.
—Henry David Thoreau

A D V A N C E ORGANIZER

In the previous chapter, numerous planning methods were discussed. Included in these were routines that teachers can use to assist in making decisions about what and how to teach. The importance of selecting appropriate content and determining processes for teaching and learning the content were emphasized. In addition to thinking about content and process, teachers must also consider the learning environment itself. Clearly, there are numerous factors that affect the overall tone or atmosphere in any given classroom. The purpose of this chapter is to discuss four major dimensions of learning environments (i.e., psychosocial, procedural, physical, and personnel). Careful attention to these dimensions enhances the likelihood that students with differing needs will achieve success in diverse classroom settings.

Organizing the learning environment is a critical component of successful teaching and learning. Even the best content, taught with appropriate learning processes in mind, will be unsuccessful if the classroom environment is not conducive to learning. Thus, it is extremely important for teachers to think about the various dimensions within their classrooms that ultimately will influence the learning of their students. Included among these are the psychosocial, procedural, physical, and personnel dimensions. Attention to each of these plays an important role in establishing a learning environment that promotes quality teaching and learning (see Validation Box 3.1).

VALIDATION BOX

3.1

Classroom Dimensions Affect Learning

The influence of educational, psychological, and social factors on learning was evaluated using evidence collected from 61 research experts, 91 meta-analyses, and 179 handbook chapters and narrative reviews. Content analyses, expert ratings, and results from meta-analyses were the 3 methods used to quantify the importance and consistency of variables that affect learning. The results indicated that classroom management (e.g., use of time, transitions, minimizing behavioral disruptions, having materials ready for use, efficient handling of routine tasks) and positive student and teacher social Interactions were 2 of the top 5 categories that influence student learning. These categories, along with Metacognitive (ability to plan, monitor, revise, and evaluate learning strategies), Cognitive (level of academic knowledge) and Home Environment influenced learning more than Program Demographics, School Demographics, State and District Policies, School Policy and Organization, and District Demographics. For more information see: (Wang, Haertel, & Walberg, 1993).

Psychosocial Dimension

The psychosocial dimension of the learning environment involves the psychological and social aspects of the classroom. Characteristics of individuals within the classroom, characteristics of peer groups within the classroom, and characteristics of the class as a whole group interact to create a particular classroom atmosphere or "climate." Student attitudes, beliefs, expectations, previous learning experiences, family, and peer relationships in conjunction with teacher attitudes, beliefs, expectations, previous teaching/learning experiences, family, and peer relationships all influence the classroom climate. Fortunately, there are a number of things that teachers can do to organize and promote a healthy psychological and social atmosphere within the classroom.

Create a Positive Classroom Environment

A supportive, caring, and challenging classroom environment is conducive to effective teaching and learning. Teachers have the primary responsibility for creating positive learning environments in which students experience a sense of personal accomplishment. There is a strong relationship between self-esteem, self-efficacy, and students' academic and behavioral performance in school. Thus, it is very important for teachers and staff to provide many opportunities for students to succeed and then to recognize their successes (Elias et al., 1997). Verbal recognition of

Ms. Williams knows how to establish a positive learning environment in which students are anxious to participate. She provides specific academic praise related to student answers and also remembers to use intermittent praise for hand raises.

student accomplishments goes a long way toward establishing a positive classroom environment. Moreover, learning is greater and behavior is more appropriate in classrooms in which teachers verbally recognize more positive events than negative events. According to Sprick (1985), teachers who maintain a 3:1 ratio of attention to positive over negative events are likely to have a well-managed classroom of high-achieving students. Unfortunately, it is easy to notice and focus on negative rather than positive events and/or behaviors. Some teachers find their "natural reaction" is to reprimand students who aren't meeting classroom expectations rather than acknowledging those students who are. Thus, it takes practice and conscious effort to focus on the positive characteristics of the students. Some teachers find it helpful to tape record or videotape themselves teaching. Later these tapes can be played and teachers can hear or see how much attention they give to positive and negative events when interacting with their students. This awareness is frequently the first step toward creating a more positive teaching style and classroom environment. Another way for teachers to become informed about their attention toward positive and negative events is to invite someone, for example, a paraprofessional or another teacher, to observe and actually count or record positive and negative statements made to students during a lesson. Eventually, focusing on the positive events will become a habit and conscious attention to this particular teacher behavior will no longer be needed (see Validation Box 3.2).

Consider the Importance of Making Students Feel Accepted

Another important component of creating a healthy psychological and social environment within the classroom involves making sure all students feel a sense of acceptance from their teachers and peers. Undoubtedly, students perform better academically and behaviorally if they feel accepted and valued. Establishing rapport and communicating respect makes students feel valued. Students are more apt to feel accepted when their teachers demonstrate through words and actions a genuine concern for their well-being and a commitment to equitable treatment in the classroom. Inherent in the concept of equity is the principle that all students, regardless of gender, ethnicity, sexual orientation, or disability, must be given opportunities to receive high-quality instruction, participate in class discussions and class activities,

VALIDATION BOX
3.2

Positive Classroom Environment
Student perceptions related to how class time was spent revealed that teachers with positive styles spent about 10 percent of their time managing inappropriate behaviors, while teachers with negative styles spent 42 percent of their time doing the same. For more information see: (Goodlad, 1984).

achieve academic and social success, and receive teacher feedback regarding their learning and performance in the classroom.

Another important aspect involved in making students feel accepted within the school culture is to protect them from harassment. Teachers and other school personnel need to communicate that the purposeful intent to intimidate, exploit, scare, or hurt another individual will not be tolerated. It is important to have written policies that prohibit harassment. It also is important to have a formal complaint process to effectively and efficiently deal with cases of harassment, and students need to feel comfortable approaching adults in their school regarding harassment issues. They need to know that their complaints and/or concerns will be taken seriously and that action will be taken to ensure their safety. Educators are ethically and legally responsible for preventing and stopping harassment. The United States Supreme Court has determined that school districts can be held financially responsible if they are "deliberately indifferent" after learning that "severe, pervasive, and objectively offensive" harassment has taken place among students ("Protecting Students from Harrassment," 1999).

In addition to demonstrating concern and equitable practices and preventing or stopping harassment, teachers also can help students feel accepted in the classroom through behaviors that communicate positive messages, such as, "you're important," "your contributions are valued," "I see and recognize your strengths," and "you're an important person in this class." Some other ways to communicate these messages are:

- making eye contact with students;
- paying attention to students seated in all quadrants of the classroom (not just those who are closest in proximity);
- moving toward and staying close to students;
- acknowledging student accomplishments (e.g., verbal comments, high five, handshake, pat on the back);
- dignifying student responses or giving credit for the correct aspects of an incorrect response;
- providing wait time or pauses to provide students more time to process and answer questions rather than moving on to other students when an immediate response is not given; and
- providing prompts and cues to help students determine correct answers and/or display appropriate behaviors.

Teachers who use these behaviors on a regular basis are sending powerful messages of concern and acceptance to their students (Marzano, 1992). These messages help establish a healthy, positive psychological and social environment (see Validation Box 3.3 on p. 86).

Establish a Behavior-Management Program

Teachers who carefully plan their academic program to meet the diverse needs of their students, create positive classroom environments, and simultaneously pay careful

VALIDATION BOX

3.3

Teacher Caring and Acceptance

Student perceptions related to whether or not teachers were concerned about students appeared to be significantly related to student satisfaction with their classes. Students in classes where teachers were judged to be authoritarian were likely to feel less satisfied. Measures of student-to-teacher relationships had greater impact on student's satisfaction in the classroom than measures of student relations with their peers. For more information see: (Goodlad, 1984).

attention to the psychological and social needs of their students (e.g., feeling accepted, valued, and needed) prevent the emergence of many inappropriate classroom behaviors. Thus, the first steps involved in planning for successful behavior management focus on the academic and social needs of the students. Most students display appropriate behavior when academic expectations are clear; lessons are engaging and motivating with clear rationales; lessons are challenging, but within the students' capability; lessons are delivered effectively; and a positive, supportive atmosphere is evident. It is possible, however, for students to display behavioral difficulties in spite of the presence of strong academic and social programs. Thus, teachers must organize behavioral programs to address these difficulties should they emerge.

An effective behavior management program involves a continuum of options ranging from low-intensity techniques to high-intensity techniques. It makes sense for teachers to use low-intensity techniques first. These techniques generally require less time and effort to implement and thus take less time away from academic teaching and learning. If low-intensity techniques fail to manage inappropriate student behavior, then teachers can gradually increase the intensity of management techniques until successful management is achieved.

Low Intensity Techniques

Low-intensity techniques for managing student behavior include establishing class rules, providing specific praise, and ignoring inappropriate behaviors. These techniques are used to clearly communicate the expectations for appropriate behavior in the classroom. Teachers who use these techniques find many opportunities to integrate them into their daily interactions with students.

Establish class rules   Class rules help communicate teacher expectations. If the teacher involves the students in determining the class rules, then peer expectations also become evident to the students. Regardless of how the rules are determined, general guidelines for composing class rules exist (see Table 3.1). Following these guidelines increases the benefits associated with having class rules.

The concept of equity within the classroom is reinforced when rules are established and used with all students in a similar manner. Clearly stated and understood rules that apply to all students in the class communicate a sense of fairness and help

TABLE 3.1

Guidelines for Composing Class Rules

Guideline	Rationale
Limit the number of rules (e.g., 3 to 4 rules).	Facilitates student memory of the rules. Easier for teachers to remember for purposes of linking praise statements to the rules.
State rules positively.	Reinforces the creation of a positive classroom environment.
Align class rules with activity goals.	Ensures that rules are meaningful. For example, requiring students to raise their hand to speak won't make sense if the goal of a particular class activity is to get students to interact and share ideas with their peers in small groups. Thus, it may be helpful to establish a few global rules and then integrate special rules as needed. Global rules such as "Respect the property of others" or "Be kind to others" are appropriate for all situations, whereas special rules such as "Stay seated" or "Work quietly" may be appropriate during certain independent seatwork activities.
Post global class rules in a prominent location.	Provides visual reminder of the rules.

build a climate of trust. Thus, before deciding upon class rules, teachers must think about whether or not they will be comfortable using and enforcing the rules with every student in their class.

Class rules also help teachers remember what type of praise statements to use with students. Linking praise statements to the class rules is a good way to communicate that the rules are important and valued. This type of praise cues and reminds students who may not be thinking about the rules. Many students who have difficulty following class rules are influenced in positive ways when they see and hear the teacher commend students who remember to follow the rules.

Provide specific praise   Specific praise should be used when students are behaving appropriately. Praise statements should sound natural and genuine and directly relate to the student's behavior (e.g., "I sure like the way you're remembering to raise your hand." "You're so good at remembering to put your materials away before the bell rings.") It also is important to vary the praise statements so that they continue to have meaning to the students. Praise should be specific and immediately follow the desired behavior to ensure the student understands what he or she did correctly. Consider the following situation:

> Matt, a middle school student who does not participate in class, gets actively involved in his first period science class. He asks relevant questions and contributes excellent ideas during the class discussion. When the bell rings indicating that the class is over, Matt gathers his books and gets ready to leave for his next class. Matt's teacher walks over to him and says, " Matt, thanks for participating in class today. You had excellent ideas that really made the lesson more interesting for everyone." Matt leaves the science class feeling appreciated and good about his performance. Matt goes to his second period geography class and again participates more than usual. His teacher is impressed, but doesn't communicate this to Matt. After school, the geography teacher sees Matt waiting for the bus. The teacher walks by Matt and says, "Good job today, Matt."

Clearly, the science teacher's praise is more likely to affect Matt's future behavior in class. A lot has happened since second period that may interfere with Matt's memory about his specific performance in geography class. The general "good job" from the geography teacher didn't clearly communicate what Matt did well.

Ignore undesired behavior   Sometimes students' inappropriate behavior continues because of the attention received from others (teacher and/or other students). Some students enjoy the "notoriety" that results from being the student who knows how to "push the teacher's buttons," from being the student who doesn't let anyone tell him what to do, or from simply being the class clown. In such cases, the teacher's directions to stop the inappropriate behavior may stop it momentarily, but more than likely the behavior will reemerge later. When students misbehave to get attention, ignoring the inappropriate behavior is a powerful intervention. Planned ignoring involves making a conscious decision to ignore the behavior every time it occurs. Obviously, planned ignoring should not be used when someone's safety is in jeopardy. When planned ignoring is first used, the inappropriate behavior is likely to increase as the student struggles to get the attention he or she is used to receiving. It is very important to continue ignoring the behavior; otherwise, the student learns that increasing the inappropriate behavior results in getting what he or she wants. If the behavior is consistently ignored, however, it is likely to disappear. Consider the following situation.

> Bill comes to science class and asks his teacher for a pass to the media center to work on a report. His teacher says, "No, Bill. The report is meant to be homework. I want you to stay in class so you don't miss the new material we're going to cover." Bill argues, "Oh come on, Mr. Williams. I'll get someone's notes from class. I really need to go to the media center." Mr. Williams says, "No, Bill. I can't let you do that. It wouldn't be fair to the other students if I let you work on the report during class time when they have to do it for homework. So, go ahead and take your seat." Bill sits down, muttering under his breath. Bill frequently uses muttering and negative language to intimidate others and ultimately get what he wants. Mr. Williams decides to use planned ignoring, so he pretends not to hear Bill's comments and starts the lesson. The muttering continues, but Mr. Williams manages to keep the lesson going and keeps the other students actively involved in the new material. Bill's muttering gets a little louder and he doesn't participate in the lesson. He

slouches back in his chair, folds his arms across his chest, and maintains an "I'm-too-cool-for-school" look on his face as he continues to mutter. After about 20 minutes of this behavior, Mr. Williams finally says, "Oh, all right, Bill. You're not learning anything in here anyway, so go on to the media center. Here's the pass."

Bill, who enjoys getting out of classes to socialize with other students in the media center, has just learned that muttering long enough and loud enough will serve him well. He is likely to use this tactic again to get out of class. If Mr. Williams had maintained his planned ignoring, Bill may have learned that muttering long and loud wasn't an effective method for getting his way. The behavior would then decrease.

When using planned ignoring, it is helpful if both teacher and peers ignore the inappropriate behavior. It is sometimes challenging, but not impossible, to get the peers to ignore. Some techniques for getting peers to ignore inappropriate behaviors of their classmates include telling students to ignore the behaviors, verbally praising students who remember to ignore the inappropriate behavior (e.g., "Good ignoring, José. I appreciate that." "Thanks for continuing to work quietly, Jennifer."), or changing the pace of the lesson to increase student interest (e.g., "OK, put your books away, it's time to play science relay. The team who gets ready the quickest and quietest will get to go first.") These techniques will help prevent students from inadvertently reinforcing inappropriate classroom behaviors.

Combining low-intensity techniques (rules, praise, and ignoring)   These three low-intensity behavior management techniques (i.e., rules, praise, ignoring) are quite powerful when used concurrently. Class rules are established to communicate the major expectations for student behavior. Specific verbal praise is used to reinforce rule-following behavior; while ignoring is used to decrease rule-breaking behavior. For example, if one of the class rules is to raise your hand before talking, the teacher cues the students prior to asking a question (e.g., "Who can raise their hand and tell me how to solve the next problem?"). If Joey starts to yell out the answer, the teacher ignores Joey's response and finds a student sitting in close proximity to Joey whose hand is raised and says, "Nice hand raise, Steve. Tell us how to solve the problem." The next time Joey raises his hand to answer a question, the teacher praises him for remembering the hand-raising rule and calls on him to participate. Thus, the teacher has paid attention to appropriate rule-following behavior while simultaneously reshaping inappropriate behavior. The tone of the management procedure is positive and instructional momentum is maintained. At first teachers may find it challenging to ignore inappropriate student behavior. Thus, a conscious decision must be made to do so. This becomes easier with practice and the benefits of the technique become evident to the teacher and the student. It is important to remember that some students with more severe behavior problems will initially increase the inappropriate behavior when the teacher first uses planned ignoring. They appear to be trying even harder to get the teacher's attention. If, however, the teacher is consistent with the ignoring and consistent with praising the appropriate behaviors, even students with more severe behaviors can learn to follow class rules (see Validation Box 3.4 on p. 90).

VALIDATION BOX

3.4

Rules, Praise, and Ignoring

A study involving two classroom teachers was conducted to evaluate the effects of classroom rules, planned ignoring, and providing praise on student behavior. The results of this investigation revealed that classroom rules alone had no appreciable effect on inappropriate behavior. Simply ignoring inappropriate behavior produced inconsistent results, but the combination of rules, ignoring inappropriate behavior, and praising appropriate behavior was very effective in achieving improved classroom behavior. For more information see: (Madsen, Becker, & Thomas, 1968).

Medium-Intensity Techniques

If low-intensity techniques such as rules, praise, and ignoring are not sufficient for managing student behavior, teachers may need to supplement their behavioral program with medium-intensity techniques such as contingency contracting, token economy systems, and/or self-management strategies. These techniques require a bit more time and effort to implement, but are still quite reasonable to use within diverse classroom settings.

Contingency contracting   Contingency contracting involves establishing a verbal or written agreement between teacher and student(s) with regard to expected classroom behavior. This behavior management technique emerged from the work of David Premack who reported a series of studies that suggested using desirable or preferred activities to encourage participation in nonpreferred activities (Premack, 1959). Shortly thereafter, Homme, deBaca, Devine, Steinhorst, and Richert (1963) coined the term *Premack Principle* and applied Premack's theory to the classroom. They found that scheduling preferred activities (e.g., playing, puzzles) after nonpreferred activities (e.g., sitting and listening to the teacher) resulted in increasing appropriate behaviors of preschool students. The Premack Principle is affectionately referred to as "Grandma's Law" because grandmas frequently say things like "You can have ice cream as soon as you finish your vegetables." The Premack Principle or Grandma's Law gradually evolved into what is now referred to as contingency contracting.

Contingency contracting can be used with individual students or whole classes. The contract (usually written) clearly states an agreement between teacher and student. Parents may also be included in the contracting process when this is believed to be helpful. Contracts should include the following:

▶ a statement related to the desired student(s) behavior;
▶ terms or conditions of the agreement (e.g., time frame for demonstrating the desired behavior, amount of behavior required, amount of reinforcers, when the reinforcer will be available);

▶ a statement related to the activity or reinforcer that will be rewarded contingent on fulfilling the conditions of the contract;

▶ signatures of the student(s) and teacher.

These basic contract components are illustrated in Figure 3.1.

Contingency contracts are quite flexible. They can be adapted for use with a wide variety of students and behaviors within various settings. What appears to be most important is that both teacher and student clearly understand the conditions of the agreed-upon contract and that the identified reinforcer is delivered consistently and in a timely manner as specified in the contract (see Validation Box 3.5 on p. 92).

Token economy systems   Token economy systems are very effective for managing student behavior. These systems involve having students earn tokens (e.g., play money, plastic chips, checkmarks on a point card, stars) for exhibiting appropriate behaviors. These tokens are saved and later traded for something of value to the student (e.g., 10 minutes of computer time, instructional game time, media center time, small toys, sports trading cards). Thus, token systems operate much like economic money systems (i.e., work for money or tokens, receive payment, use money

---

Contingency Contract

Date contract begins: _____ Date contract ends: _____

I, _____ agree to _____
           (student's name)   (statement of the desired behavior)

_____

_____
                     (terms of the agreement)

If I do, then _____
              (statement of the preferred activity or reinforcer)

_____

_____
                     (terms of the agreement)

_____   _____
      (student signature)   (teacher signature)

FIGURE 3.1

Components of a Contingency Contract.

VALIDATION BOX

3.5

Contracts

The use of contingency contracts was validated in a variety of settings with a variety of students and behaviors. According to a review of 12 studies, data support the use of contracting for improving social behavior, school attendance, academic productivity, performance accuracy, and study skills of school-aged through college-level students. For more information see: (Murphy, 1988).

or tokens to obtain desired goods or services). There are many advantages to using token economy systems for managing student behavior. First, token systems promote positive student behavior in a short amount of time. Students learn there are advantages to following the rules and behaving appropriately. Second, one adult can realistically manage the system with either small or large groups of students. Third, the variety of potential reinforcers keeps students motivated; thus the effectiveness of the system is maintained over time. Fourth, the system can be individualized to meet specific student needs. For example, some students may earn tokens for staying on task, while others earn tokens for keeping their hands to themselves. Fifth, the frequency of administering tokens can easily be changed as behavior improves. Students with severe behavioral difficulties need more frequent administration of tokens when the system is first implemented. As the behavior improves, however, tokens are administered less frequently. The goal is to provide the fewest number of tokens required to maintain the appropriate student behavior, with the ultimate goal being maintenance of appropriate behavior without any tokens. With experience, teachers become adept at figuring out how much reinforcement is needed to maintain the desired behavior.

Prior to implementing a token economy system, teachers consider what procedures will work best in their particular classroom with their particular students. The following steps may be helpful in establishing a token economy system:

Step 1: Determine which behaviors will result in earning tokens (may want to focus on three or fewer behaviors per student).

Step 2: Decide what will be used as tokens taking into consideration durability, expense, safety, attractiveness, and ease of dispensing (e.g., plastic chips, play money, points on a point card). Plastic chips are usually colorful, durable, and reinforcing. Play money provides opportunities to combine behavior management with teaching money skills. Point cards are easy to manage and less apt to result in ownership debates since the student's name is written on the card (see Fig. 3.2).

Step 3: Identify reinforcers that students will be motivated to earn and determine how many tokens each reinforcer will cost (e.g., 100 tokens = 5 minutes of computer time or 1 baseball card or 1 pencil sharpener; 200 tokens = 10 minutes to play a game or 1 comic book or 2 arcade tokens to use after

Point Card

Student name: _____

Target behaviors: _____

FIGURE 3.2

Sample Point Card.

school; 300 tokens = pass to media center or 1 baseball cap or 1 poster). More valuable items cost more tokens. Thus, students have the opportunity to practice deferred gratification and the value of saving.

Step 4: Decide whether to display the reinforcers in a classroom "store" (e.g., special bookcase or cabinet) or whether to list the items on a poster board. In either case, the number of required tokens should be indicated so students know what they have to earn. The store and/or poster will serve as a visual reminder to demonstrate the behaviors that result in earning tokens.

Step 5: Decide when students will be permitted to trade in earned tokens (e.g., as soon as they have enough or at designated times throughout the day or at the end of the day/class period).

Step 6: Establish rules for the token economy system (e.g., students should not be given tokens if they ask for them; student's should not be allowed to take tokens from other students or give tokens to other students).

Step 7: Explain the token system and accompanying rules to students to ensure they understand what behaviors will result in earning tokens, how many tokens are needed for the various reinforcers, and when the trading may occur.

Successful token economy systems involve an emphasis on positive student behaviors. It is important to pair verbal praise with the administering of tokens. When misbehavior occurs, verbal cues can be used (e.g., "As soon as you . . . tokens can be earned again) or students in close proximity to the misbehaving students can be given tokens for their appropriate behaviors. These cues tend to redirect the inappropriate behavior while still maintaining a positive atmosphere in the class.

Some teachers link their token systems to life skills. Students in the class "apply" for various positions (e.g., banker, loan officer, stockbroker, bill collector, storekeeper) and then perform the related duties. Initially students receive a loan in play money. They are given a certain time period to pay off the loan without penalty. The students earn money for appropriate "job-related" behaviors and are "docked" money for certain "job errors." Interest-bearing checking and saving accounts are opened and used. Students spend money for goods and services (e.g., pencils, paper, computer time, hall pass, their seat) as well as luxury items from the class store. Token economy systems of this nature are used to manage behavior and teach important life skills (see Validation Box 3.6).

Self-management strategies   Clearly, one of the primary purposes of education is to teach students to manage their own behaviors independently so that they can live successful, happy lives. Although teacher-directed management strategies (e.g., contracting, token economy systems) are needed to teach some students appropriate classroom behaviors, once these behaviors are demonstrated on a consistent basis, it is important to decrease the students' dependency on these systems and increase their abilities to function independently. Self-management strategies help accomplish this important transition from teacher-directed behavior management to student-directed behavior management.

In the seventies and eighties, cognitive-behavioral modification approaches emerged in an attempt to connect the behavioral and cognitive aspect of learning. Meichenbaum (1977) discussed self-instructional training as a process whereby students can talk or whisper to themselves to encourage appropriate responses and discourage inappropriate responses. Meanwhile, Novaco (1975); Feindler and Fremouw (1983); Feindler, Marriott, & Iwata (1984); and Goldstein and Glick (1987) applied Meichenbaum's principles of self-instruction to anger-control strategies. Their work involved teaching students to become aware of their anger and then to use self-talk or instruction to diffuse the anger. The idea of teaching students techniques to manage their own behaviors caught on quickly (see Validation Box 3.7).

Self-management strategies have become very popular among teachers who teach diverse groups of students. Of particular interest are self-monitoring, self-evaluation, and self-reinforcement. Self-monitoring requires students to record the frequency of a particular behavior. Typically, students are given some type of recording form to use while monitoring their behavior (see Fig. 3.3 on p. 96 and Fig. 3.4 on p. 97). The students are taught to tally every time a behavior occurs or

VALIDATION BOX

3.6

Token Economy Systems

▶ In a review of literature, 18 studies were discussed related to the use of token economy systems. The findings suggest that token reinforcement programs in special education classrooms are effective for improving both academic and social behaviors. For more information see: (Axelrod, 1971).

▶ In another review of literature, 41 studies were identified related to interventions for students with behavioral disorders. A total of 8 different interventions emerged from the 41 studies. The intervention with the greatest effect was social and/or token reinforcement. The effect size (i.e., defined in this study as the number of standard deviations the experimental group improved relative to the control group) was 1.38. For more information see: (Skiba & Casey, 1985)

▶ In one study, a token economy system was used in a third-grade general education class of 18 boys who were identified as hyperactive and underachieving. Typical behaviors of the students were hitting, pencil throwing, chair throwing, shoving, and wandering around the room. The token system involved reinforcing students for reading behaviors that reduced time available for inappropriate behavior. Students who mastered specific reading words earned tokens and then helped a peer learn the same words. The peer earned tokens when he knew the words and then helped another student. Tokens were exchanged for 15 minutes of play on electrovideo games. Reading achievement, task completion, and appropriate behavior increased. For more information see: (Robinson, Newby, & Ganzell, 1981).

every time they hear an audible cue (e.g., tape-recorded beeps, timer with a bell). Another option is to provide students with wrist counters (typically used in playing golf) to click each time the target behavior occurs (e.g., student clicks every time he or she says something positive). The simple process of self-monitoring frequently results in an increase of the desired behavior. Self-evaluation requires students to compare their behavior to a preset standard to determine whether a particular criterion has been met. Thus, after monitoring a particular behavior,

VALIDATION BOX

3.7

Cognitive-Behavioral Modification

In a review of literature, 20 studies were located that investigated the effectiveness of cognitive-behavioral interventions for improving social skills and social problem-solving among students with behavioral disorders. Most of the interventions (95 percent) consisted of multicomponent packages that included modeling, coaching, role-play, social or token reinforcement, and discussion. The findings suggest that cognitive-behavioral interventions promote positive social behavior. For more information see: (Ager & Cole, 1991).

students evaluate or judge how well they did as indicated by the data they collected. In some cases, both teacher and students evaluate the performance and then compare ratings. Self-evaluation provides students opportunities to think about and reflect upon how well they are doing with their target behaviors. Self-reinforcement involves having students reinforce or reward themselves following appropriate behavior. The students select and administer the reward. To provide some structure to this process, it is helpful to provide a menu of potential reinforcers from which students may select.

Prior to implementing self-management strategies, teachers must consider which procedures will work best in their particular classrooms with their particular students. Teachers frequently decide to use self-monitoring, self-evaluation, and self-reinforcement concurrently rather than in isolation. The following steps may be helpful in establishing a self-management program that includes all three procedures. Modifications can be made to these steps if only one or two of the procedures are going to be used:

Step 1: Decide which behavior(s) will be monitored or recorded.

Step 2: Determine what recording method will be used (e.g., Will each occurrence be recorded? Will students be cued to record at particular times? If so,

---

Self-Recording Form

Student name: _____ Class: _____

Goal:_____

Put a tally mark in the space below each time you participate in a class discussion.

Monday
Tuesday
Wednesday
Thursday
Friday

Total for the week:

FIGURE 3.3

Self-Recording Form.

Self-Recording Form

Student name: _____ Date: _____

Goal:_____

Every time you hear a beep, record a smiley face if you are doing your work and a dash if you are not doing your work.

Total earned: _____   Total possible: _____   Percentage score: _____

FIGURE 3.4

Self-Recording Form.

how long will the intervals between recording be?). The more severe the behavior, the more frequent the recording needs to be.

Step 3: Create a form that students will use to record their behaviors.

Step 4: Determine criteria and a system for self-evaluation. It may be helpful to include the students in the development of these criteria since they will have to use the criteria to determine whether or not self-reinforcement should occur. A good rule of thumb with regard to setting criteria for reinforcement is to take the students' current levels of performance on the target behaviors and increase them by 20 to 25 percent. So, if a student currently pays attention 50 percent of the time during class lectures, an appropriate initial criterion may be 60 to 63 percent of the time.

Step 5: Determine what reinforcers will be available for the students. Again, consider involving the students in making these decisions.

Step 6: Teach the students how to self-monitor, self-evaluate, and self-reinforce. This instruction begins with discussing the rationale for using the procedures. Then, each procedure is demonstrated and modeled. Next, students are given opportunities to practice the recording and evaluating to ensure they understand how the system works. Finally, the teacher provides feedback on this practice.

Step 7: Begin the program. If needed, implement strategies to increase student accuracy with monitoring, evaluating, and reinforcing.

Step 8: Monitor the program's effectiveness and gradually increase criteria until students no longer need the system to perform the desired behaviors.

Self-management strategies have been successful for changing a wide variety of student behaviors. Self-management programs are time-efficient, inexpensive, easily adapted, and suitable for students with diverse abilities. Moreover, they promote generalization and increase student independence (McConnell, 1999; Schloss & Smith, 1994). Getting students actively involved in thinking about their behavior while learning to control it appears to have great merit (see Validation Box 3.8).

VALIDATION BOX

3.8

Self-Management Strategies

▶ In a review of literature, 37 studies were located that investigated the effectiveness of self-recording attention to task. These studies included students with learning disabilities, students with mental retardation, and students without an identified disability who ranged in age from 4 years to adolescence. A variety of settings were used in these studies including hospital classrooms, special education classrooms, and general education classrooms. The findings of these studies indicate that self-recording is effective for increasing attention to task. Researchers also noted beneficial effects on other measures (e.g., academic productivity, accuracy of academic performance, behavior). For more information see: (Lloyd & Landrum, 1990)

▶ In another review of literature, 16 studies were located that investigated the effectiveness of self-management systems (e.g., self-recording, self-instruction, self-evaluation) for students with behavior disorders. Overall, the results suggest that self-management procedures promote positive social and academic behaviors. Moreover, generalization occurs if systematically programmed. For more information see: (Nelson, Smith, Young, & Dodd, 1991).

▶ Twenty-seven studies related to the use of self-monitoring for behavior management revealed that self-monitoring can be used successfully with students of various ages, with various disabilities, and in various settings to increase attention to task, positive classroom behaviors, and social skills. Moreover, self-monitoring can reduce inappropriate behaviors. For more information see: (Webber, Scheuermann, McCall, & Coleman, 1993).

▶ Five case studies involving adolescents with learning disabilities revealed that self-monitoring procedures were effective for increasing on-task behavior. The procedures were effective in both special and general education classrooms regardless of whether classmates' percentages of on-task behavior were as high as or as low as the subject's on-task behavior. For more information see: (Prater, Joy, Chilman, Temple, & Miller, 1991).

High-Intensity Techniques

When low- and medium-intensity techniques are used and behavioral problems still exist, high-intensity techniques may be needed. These techniques typically require more planning and implementation time, but they are more powerful in terms of facilitating positive behavioral changes. Included among high-intensity techniques are highly structured behavioral programs that may require involvement of multiple individuals (e.g., other teachers, parents) and school-wide management systems.

Contingencies for Learning Academic and Social Skills (CLASS) program   The CLASS program (Hops & Walker, 1988) was designed to improve the classroom behavior of elementary students with acting-out problems. The primary objective of the program is to increase students' levels of academic and social achievement and to decrease the frequency of interfering or inappropriate acting-out behaviors. Thus, students who have a history of displaying acting-out behaviors can become productive, achieving members of the class. The program involves the use of a very structured token economy point system, teacher praise, systematic suspension (home or in-school) for behaviors such as fighting or destroying property, parent involvement, and daily monitoring of student progress. Specifically, a point card is used that is green on one side and red on the other. The card is used to let the student know if they are behaving appropriately. The green side is shown when the student is following the rules and therefore eligible to earn points. The red side is shown when the student should stop what he or she is doing. Points are not earned while the red side is showing. Points are recorded on a point card. These points result in home and school rewards.

The program requires at least 30 days and is organized in two phases. The first phase is the Consultant Phase and lasts for 5 days. Ideally, a consultant (i.e., someone familiar with the program) implements the program procedures within the classroom and gradually turns the responsibility for the program over to the teacher. If, however, a consultant is not available, the teacher may have to implement this first phase. In such cases, it is helpful to have two teachers teaming together. The second phase of the program is the Teacher Phase and lasts for at least 25 days. The first 20 days involve following specific procedures for awarding points, praise, and rewards. The last 5 days involve continuation of the praise, but tangible rewards are discontinued. The procedures used in the CLASS program may be extended beyond the classroom to other school settings (e.g., playground, hallway, cafeteria). The CLASS Program Manual may be obtained from Educational Achievement Systems, 319 Nickerson Street, Suite 112, Seattle, WA 98109; telephone: (425) 820-6111; Web site: www.edrearch.com (see Validation Box 3.9 on p. 100).

The Progress Program   The Progress Program (Schumaker, Hovell, & Sherman, 1992) was designed to help students improve their academic and social performance within classroom settings. The program can be used with elementary or secondary students and involves the use of a Daily Report Card that serves as a basis

VALIDATION BOX

3.9

Contingencies for Learning Academic and Social Skills (CLASS) Program

The CLASS program was developed and evaluated over a 4-year period of time using a three-stage process. The first research stage lasted 1 year and involved identifying economical and effective techniques (i.e., praise, tokens, rewards, response cost or losing earned points) for changing acting-out behaviors within an experimental classroom setting. The second research stage involved pilot testing the procedures within general education classrooms using 32 children with acting-out problems. During stage three, the revised program was field-tested in three school districts, which included both urban and rural settings. Children with acting-out behaviors made significantly greater gains in appropriate classroom behavior than did matched control subjects. For more information see: (Hops & Walker, 1988; Hops et al., 1978; Walker, Hops, & Greenwood, 1984).

for awarding home privileges. The student takes his or her Daily Report Card (see Fig. 3.5) to each class. At the end of each class period, the student's teachers indicate, through a checkmark system, whether that student obeyed specific class rules. Academic achievement (i.e., assignment and test grades) also is noted on the card. The Daily Report Card is taken home each day. The parents review the card, provide praise for improved performance, and award points based on the daily report. These points are saved and later traded for activities and privileges available in the home. Minimal privileges require fewer points than more significant activities such as going to a movie. The authors of the program recommend having a school representative (e.g., guidance counselor, teacher, principal, social worker) coordinate the activities of teachers, parents, and students involved in the program. This coordinator negotiates a basis for evaluating classroom behavior with the teachers as well as a basis for awarding privileges in the home. The coordinator also monitors the pro-

VALIDATION BOX

3.10

The Progress Program

The Progress Program was tested using parents, counselors, teachers, and adolescents with poor behavior and/or underachievement. Results indicated that students with histories of school problems can learn to attend school without disturbing others and can improve their academic advancement. Moreover, involving parents and counselors as part of the team to help these students worked well. For more information see: (Schumaker, Hovell, & Sherman, 1977).

Daily Report Card

Subjects:

Name: _____

Date: _____

Did the student . . .

	Yes	No	Yes	No	Yes	No	Yes	No	Yes	No	Yes	No
Come on time?												
Bring supplies?												
Stay in seat?												
Speak courteously?												
Not talk inappropriately?												
Follow directions?												
Raise hand?												
Not physically disturb others?												
Not chew gum?												
Clean up?												
Pay attention?												
Complete and hand in assignment on time?												
Points on today's classwork												
Grade on assignment or test												
Teacher's initials												

For parents only:

Points for rules

+ Points for classwork

+ Points for tests and assignments

= Total for each class   +   +   +   +   +   =

Total points earned   Total points lost   Daily point total   Total points earned

Total points earned   +   Total points lost   =   Daily point total

gram effectiveness and seeks solutions if problems emerge. The Progress Program may be obtained from Edge Enterprises, P.O. Box 1304, Lawrence KS 66045; telephone: (785) 749-1473; fax: (785) 749-0207 (see Validation Box 3.10).

School-Wide Management Systems   School-wide management systems are implemented to teach self-discipline while simultaneously managing student behavior. The primary purpose of school-wide management systems is to provide support and guidance for most of the students in the school (Todd, Horner, Sugai, & Sprague, 1999). In school-wide management systems all personnel within a given school adopt and use the same behavior-management program. School-wide rules, routines, and procedures are established and agreed upon (Scott & Nelson, 1999). Thus, everyone in the school building is "on the same page" and consistency is promoted. Most school-wide systems are found in elementary and middle schools, but there is a growing trend to move these programs into high-school settings as well. Developing school-wide management systems is a relatively new practice and several variations of the same theme have emerged. There are, however, common features that school-wide systems seem to need. Included among these are: (a) total staff commitment to the adopted program, (b) clearly defined and communicated expectations and/or rules for student behavior, (c) clearly stated procedures for handling rule-breaking behaviors, (d) an instructional component designed to teach students self-control and/or social skills, and (e) a support plan to meet the needs of students with chronic behavioral difficulties ("School-Wide Behavioral Management Systems," 1997). This last feature is important to remember. Although establishing school-wide rules, agreeing on the definitions of the rules, and using consistent feedback systems results in appropriate behavior among a majority of students, students with chronic behavioral difficulties will need additional support.

Developing a school-wide management system takes a significant amount of time initially and requires ongoing monitoring and training to work well. Long-term commitment from teachers and implementation consistency also are important for program success. Thus, teachers must agree with the system and willingly implement it. Moreover, as new teachers are hired, special effort must be made to ensure that they understand and implement the system correctly (see Validation Box 3.11)

Positive Behavioral Support for Students with Disabilities

The 1997 amendments to the Individuals with Disabilities Education Act (IDEA) includes requirements to follow when a student with a disability demonstrates behavior that impedes his or her learning and/or the learning of other students. Specifically, the student's IEP team must consider using Positive Behavioral Support (PBS). PBS provides one approach for understanding why the challenging behavior occurs (i.e., what function or purpose does it serve for the student?) and also examines the physical and social contexts of the behavior. The PBS approach avoids putting all the blame for the behavioral problem on the student and recognizes that things such as environment and lack of skill also contribute to the challenging or problematic behavior ("Positive Behavioral Support," 1999; Warger, 1999).

The 1997 amendments to IDEA also require that Functional Behavioral Assessments (FBAs) be conducted and that a Behavioral Intervention Plan (BIP) be developed "prior to a change in placement or suspension for more than 10 days based on inappropriate behavior(s) for students with disabilities" (Jolivette, Scott, & Nelson, 2000, p. 1). Both the FBA and BIP become a part of the student's IEP records. FBAs typically consist of five steps: (*a*) verifying the seriousness of the problem, (*b*) defin-

School-wide Management Systems

▶ A school-wide behavioral management system was implemented at John Fuller Elementary School in North Conway, NH. The primary goal of the system was to increase the inclusion of students with emotional disabilities. The staff developed a unified school-wide code of conduct that emphasized safety, respect, honesty, responsibility, and courtesy and developed a social, cognitive problem-solving component to address more severe behavior. Preliminary data, after 4 years of implementation, revealed that of all students, 80 percent were included in general education classrooms most of the day and 90 percent at least part of the day. Student gains on all subscales of the Walker-McConnell Behavioral Scale also were noted. For more information see: ("School-Wide Behavioral," 1997).

▶ A school-wide behavioral management system, Unified Discipline, was implemented at Windsor Park Elementary School in Charlotte, NC. The program emphasized unified attitudes, expectations, consequences, and team roles. Teachers reported positive attitudes toward the program and preliminary data revealed reductions in the nature and extent of office referrals. For more information see: ("School-Wide Behavioral," 1997).

▶ Preventing, Acting Upon, and Resolving Troubling Behaviors (PAR), a school-wide approach developed by Michael Rosenberg at Johns Hopkins University, leads school-based collaborative teams through a design process that results in a written discipline plan taking into consideration the unique needs of the particular school involved. The discipline plan includes a mission statement, rules/expectations, consequences for rule-breaking, crisis procedures, family involvement, ideas for adapting instruction, and implementation guidelines. In one middle school that used PAR, fights decreased 75 percent over 1 year. In 2 other middle schools, referrals out of classrooms for disruptiveness and suspensions decreased approximately 50 percent over a 2-year period. For more information see: ("School-Wide Behavioral," 1997).

▶ Project ACHIEVE, developed by Howard Knoff and George Batsche at the University of South Florida, is a school-wide program that targets the needs of at-risk and underachieving elementary students through school strategic planning and staff development, school-wide interventions to prevent and respond to school discipline and social skills, and parent involvement in school improvement. Over a 3-year period, data revealed a 75 percent decrease in student referrals to special education, 28 percent decrease in disciplinary referrals, and a decrease in school suspensions from 9 percent of the student population to 3 percent. For more information see: ("School-Wide Behavioral," 1997).

ing the challenging or problem behavior in concrete terms, *(c)* collecting data relevant to potential causes of the behavior, *(d)* analyzing the data, and *(e)* formulating and testing a hypothesis regarding the general conditions in which the behavior is most and least likely to occur (Fitzsimmons, 1998). Once the assessment process is complete, the resulting data are used to develop the BIP. A 10-step process has been developed to infuse FBA data into a BIP. (Scott & Nelson as cited in Jolivette, Scott, & Nelson, 2000) The steps are:

1. Determine the function of the undesired behavior.
2. Determine an appropriate replacement behavior.
3. Determine when the replacement behavior should occur.
4. Design a teaching sequence.
5. Manipulate the environment to increase the probability of success.
6. Manipulate the environment to decrease the probability of failure.
7. Determine how positive behavior will be reinforced.
8. Determine consequences for instances of problem behavior.
9. Develop a data-collection system.
10. Develop behavioral goals and objectives. (pp. 1–2).

The IDEA amendments related to positive behavioral support and subsequent functional behavioral assessments and behavioral intervention plans are designed to support students with serious behavioral concerns. The goal is to help students learn more responsible behavior and experience greater success in school. Initial research related to this approach for managing student behavior is promising (see Validation Box 3.12).

Procedural Dimension

In addition to thinking about the psychosocial dimension of the classroom (i.e., creating a positive classroom environment, making students feel accepted, and developing behavior-management systems), teachers must also think about the procedural dimension of the classroom. A classroom with organized procedures will undoubtedly run smoother than classrooms without well-established procedures. Of particular importance are procedures related to the management of time and paperwork.

Manage Time Effectively

The National Committee on Excellence in Education (1983) identified efficient use of time as one of its five major recommendations for improving schools in America. Several studies support the need for this committee's recommendation. Rich and Ross (1989) observed 230 elementary students with mild disabilities and found that almost 3 hours of each school day was spent in noninstructional activities such as transitions, wait time, free time, snacks, and housekeeping. Leinhardt, Zigmond, and Cooley (1981) observed 105 students with learning disabilities in 11 elementary schools and found that close to 1 hour of each student's day was spent on management chores or waiting. In another study, Rieth, Polsgrove, Okolo, Bahr, and Eckert (1987) observed 52 high-school students in resource rooms and found that 24 percent of their time was spent in nonacademic activities.

VALIDATION BOX

3.12

Positive Behavioral Support

▶ Case studies were conducted to investigate to effectiveness of implementing positive behavioral support including functional behavioral assessments within Head Start and Kindergarten classrooms. A total of 10 children, ages 4 to 6 years, participated in the study. Initially, the children displayed high rates of aggression, out of seat, and negative verbal statements, and low rates of social interaction with their classmates. After conducting a functional behavioral assessment, it was determined that improved teacher monitoring was needed during play, students needed to be taught social skills, students needed to be prompted to use the social skills, and reinforcement for appropriate behavior needed to increase. Subsequently, the children's compliance levels and peer interactions increased and inappropriate behaviors decreased for all 10 children. For more information see: (Kamps et al., 1995).

▶ In another study, office referral data were examined to determine the effectiveness of a school-wide behavioral support program. The behavioral support program was designed to define, teach, and reward appropriate student behavior in a middle school that had 530 students. Included in the program was a full-day behavioral training session for all students at the beginning of the year, ongoing reminders and precorrections, rewards for appropriate behavior, consistency, corrective consequences, periodic special rewards, and targeted support for students with chronic behavior problems. During the year prior to implementing the school-wide behavioral support program, there were 2628 office referrals. During the first year of implementing the program, there was a 42 percent reduction in office referrals. For more information see: (Taylor-Green et al., 1997).

Research related to the use of time in classrooms clearly indicates that Academic Learning Time (ALT) is a critical variable related to student achievement (Fisher et al., 1980; Gettinger, 1986; Good & Brophy, 1986; Greenwood, 1991; Wang, Haertel, & Walberg, 1993). ALT is defined as the amount of time that a student spends engaged in academic tasks that result in high rates of success (Gettinger, 1986). There are three important concepts associated with ALT: allocated time, engaged time, and student success. Allocated time refers to the time a teacher provides for students to work on particular academic tasks (scheduling of academics). Engaged time refers to the percentage of the allocated time that is actually spent working on the academic tasks (time on task) and student success rate relates to the appropriateness of the academic task (level of difficulty and relevance to student needs). Since student achievement increases as time spent on appropriate academic tasks increases, teachers must constantly look for ways to increase the amount of time spent on academic learning and reduce the amount of time spent on nonacademic matters (e.g., taking attendance, sharpening pencils, cleaning up, taking lunch counts).

Scheduling Academic Time

Decisions related to academic scheduling are very important. These decisions influence not only what will be taught, but also how much time will be spent teaching it. In essence, teachers' daily or class schedules serve as a blueprint for student learning. Schedules provide the structure or framework within which academic learning will take place. Thus, the challenge for educators is to devise a schedule that facilitates the greatest amount of learning in the limited amount of time available during each school day. Poor scheduling decisions can actually prevent students from learning. Consider Cal, a first-grade student who is extremely hyperactive. Cal prefers to run down the hallways rather than walk and his energy level increases whenever transitions occur. He enters the classroom so full of energy (i.e., moving quickly and talking incessantly) that it takes about 20 minutes to get him settled to the point that any instruction can begin. Cal qualifies for supplemental services from several different ancillary personnel. Review Cal's daily schedule outlined in Table 3.2. Clearly, Cal's academic needs cannot be met adequately with this schedule. Regardless of how skilled his teacher is, schooling will be unsuccessful for Cal if the current structure for delivering his instruction remains the same.

TABLE 3.2

Problematic Daily Schedule for Cal, a Student with Hyperactivity

Time	Activity and Location
9:00–9:30	General Education Classroom (Room 3)
9:30–10:00	Speech and Language Services (M, W, F) (Speech /Language Clinic Room 20)
	Friendship Group with Counselor (T, TH) (Counselor's office)
10:00–10:20	General Education Classroom (Room 3)
10:20–11:10	Recess with General Education Classroom (Playground)
11:10–11:20	Bathroom Break and Drink of Water
11:20–11:45	General Education Classroom (Room 3)
11:45–12:15	Lunch (Cafeteria)
12:15–1:10	General Education Classroom (Room 3)
1:10–1:40	Physical Therapy (T, TH) (Room 8)
	Resource Room (M, W, F) (Room 22)
1:40–2:10	General Education Classroom (Room 3)
2:10–2:40	Art or Music (Room 13 or 15)
2:40–3:15	General Education Classroom (Room 3)

Traditional scheduling Scheduling for elementary classrooms usually involves thinking about the sequence of instruction that will constitute an entire school day. Typically the same sequence will be followed each day of the week. Scheduling for secondary classrooms, on the other hand, usually involves thinking about smaller chunks of time (e.g., 50- to 60-minute class periods) that will be repeated throughout the day with different groups of students. Regardless of whether a schedule is being constructed for an entire day (i.e., elementary school) or a single class period (i.e., secondary school), making decisions in a thoughtful manner based on the needs of students contributes greatly to the amount of time students are engaged in academic learning and to the quality of the learning that takes place.

In Chapter 2, numerous planning routines were presented to help teachers select appropriate content and concepts when teaching students with diverse needs. Scheduling takes the planning process one step further. Decisions now are made regarding how much time will be allocated to teaching and learning the selected content. Although little research has been done with regard to establishing class schedules, the combined wisdom of numerous educators (Meier, 1992; Mercer & Mercer, 1998; Murdick & Petch-Hogan, 1996; Smith, 1985; Smith, Polloway, Patton, & Dowdy, 1995) suggests that teachers should consider the following guidelines.

When scheduling the whole school day:

▶ Teach difficult concepts when students are most alert.
▶ Review the IEP goals for students with disabilities to help decide how much time should be spent with particular content areas.
▶ Post the schedule in a prominent place using an age-appropriate format.
▶ Discuss the schedule with the students.
▶ Stick to the designated schedule.
▶ Provide time reminders (visual and audible).
▶ Share the daily schedule with parents (to assist in making decisions about class visits, scheduling dental appointments, scheduling doctor's appointments).
▶ Alternate highly preferred content with less-preferred content.
▶ Include opportunities for students to interact socially.
▶ Plan for transitions.

When scheduling chunks of instructional time (e.g., 60-minute class period)

▶ Schedule several short activities rather than one long activity to maintain student attention.
▶ Vary the types of activities to keep students interested and engaged in learning.
▶ Adjust the length of scheduled activities to meet the needs of the students.
▶ Begin the class with something that is motivating and interesting to the students.
▶ Schedule preferred activities after nonpreferred activities.

▶ Provide a variety of alternatives for students who complete assignments before their peers.
▶ Plan for transitions.

Daily and class schedules should reflect the instructional priorities for the students being taught keeping in mind that the amount of time allocated to academic instruction correlates highly with academic achievement (Paine et al., 1983). Once the schedule is developed, it's important to follow it. Naturally, there will be times when decisions are made to extend learning activities for very good reasons (e.g., high student interest). It must be remembered, however, that an extended activity means time is being taken away from another activity. Even deviations of 5 to 10 minutes add up quickly. If consistent deviations in the schedule begin to occur, it may be time to reevaluate and modify the schedule.

Block scheduling   The traditional scheduling model used in secondary schools is 6 to 7 classes that meet daily throughout an entire school year for approximately 50 minutes each. Block scheduling represents an alternative to this model. In block scheduling, fewer classes are taught each day, but each class lasts for an extended amount of time. Several variations of block scheduling have emerged. For example, some districts use a trimester approach that involves dividing the academic year into three terms rather than two and extending the length of individual classes in each trimester (e.g., 5 classes in each trimester with each class lasting 70 minutes) (Stumpf, 1995). Some districts use a 4-block semester (i.e., 4/4 Semester Plan). The students have 4 classes per day lasting 90 minutes each. These courses end after 1 semester rather than extending through an entire school year (Edwards, 1995; Shortt & Thayer, 1998–1999). Other districts use 8-block alternating-day schedules (i.e., A/B Day Schedule) whereby students have a total of 6 to 8 classes, but only half meet each day for 80 to 120 minutes each. The remaining half of the classes meet the subsequent day. The alternating of blocked classes continues throughout the school year (Hackmann, 1995; Santos & Rettig, 1999). Regardless of the configuration of block scheduling, the common goal is to address curriculum fragmentation and enhance the quality of instructional time. The use of block scheduling is becoming increasingly common in both middle and high schools. In a nationwide survey, Cawelti (1994) found that 39 percent of high schools had fully implemented block schedules or intended to do so by 1994. Interviews with 18 special-education teachers revealed that they preferred block scheduling over traditional single-period schedules. There seemed to be a preference for the 4/4 Semester Plan over the A/B Day Schedule, but teachers in both types of block scheduling reported having better relationships with their students (Santos & Rettig, 1999). In another survey study (Shortt & Thayer, 1998–1999), findings revealed that both principals and teachers were satisfied with block scheduling and believed this type of scheduling promoted positive school climates (see Validation Box 3.13).

VALIDATION BOX
3.13

Block Scheduling

The 4-block schedule was implemented at Orange County High School in Orange, VA. After 2 years, students, on average, completed 18 percent more English classes, 43 percent more math, 10 percent more social studies, 11 percent more science, and 30 percent more foreign language. The percentage of "A" grades earned by students rose from 21 to 32 percent. Moreover, more students took and passed Advance Placement Exams under the 4-block schedule. The four-block schedule was also implemented in Champlin Park High School in Champlin, MN. Evaluators from the University of Minnesota found that both teachers and students favored the 4-block schedule. They also found that student engagement was higher in the four-block schedule than in a traditional 7-period high-school day. For more information see: (Edwards, 1995; O'Neil, 1995).

Managing Transitions Effectively

In addition to thinking about instructional scheduling, plans must be made for transitioning from one component of the schedule to the next. Numerous transitions (i.e., movement from one activity to the next; movement from one part of the room to another; movement from one room to another) will be necessary during each school day. Unfortunately, these transitions represent one of the major detractors from academic learning time. Observations in typical classrooms reveal that transition time adds up to 70 to 80 minutes per day. In other words, up to 20 percent of a school day, or the equivalent of 1 day each week, is lost to transition time (Fisher et al., 1980; Paine, Radicchi, Rosellini, Deutchman, & Darch, 1983).

It is not uncommon for students to have difficulties making transitions. The typically unstructured nature of transitions is troublesome for students who lack adequate self-control. Other students experience difficulty with transitions because they resist change and don't want to stop what they're doing. Thus, it is important for teachers to develop specific procedures for managing transitions.

Activity transitions   Several techniques can be used to facilitate transitions from one activity to the next. For example, it helps to have a written schedule posted in the classroom that clearly indicates the "beginning" and "ending" times of class activities. Teachers should discuss the schedule with the students so they know what to expect. Sticking to the schedule reduces lost academic time while clearly communicating to students that time is important and transitions will occur in a predictable manner. Another technique that teachers can use to assist with activity transitions is to clearly state at the beginning of the activity how much time will be spent before moving on (e.g., "You will have 10 minutes to work on your journals, then we're going to begin our math lesson"). It may also be helpful to cue students shortly before the transition is to occur (e.g., "You have 5 more minutes to try to solve the mystery, then we're going to discuss our ideas") and then praise them after a successful transition has occurred (e.g., "Wow, that was a quick and quiet transition! Thank you.").

Timing and feedback procedures also assist in transitioning from one activity to another. For example, some teachers tell students they will be timed to see if they can stop one activity and get ready for another in less than 2 minutes. A stopwatch is used to time the students. When the last student finishes the transition, the watch is stopped and the students are told how long the switch took. If the class meets or exceeds the criterion, verbal praise or some type of reward is provided (e.g., bonus points if a point system is used for behavior management or a note informing the principal or a sticker for each student). In one study, this simple procedure resulted in consistently short transition times (between 30 seconds and 2 minutes). The students always met the predetermined criterion goal (Paine, Radichi, Rosellini, Deutchman, & Darch, 1983).

Within-class transitions   Movement from one part of the room to the next can be facilitated with specific procedures that are explained to the students and practiced. Timing devices such as kitchen timers or watches that beep can be useful. For example, if the teacher sets up a variety of academic learning centers and wants students to spend 15 minutes in each center, the timer is set for 15 minutes. When the timer sounds, students stand quietly next to their center. When the teacher signals, one student designated as the counter begins counting backward from 10 to 1. When the counting begins, all students move quickly and quietly to their next center. The goal for the students is to get to their next center before the counter reaches "1." Thus, the whole transition process is accomplished in less than 15 seconds.

Within-school transitions   Transitions from one room to another in the school are a bit more challenging, especially when the transitions occur without adult supervision. In some schools, schoolwide procedures for walking in the halls are established. For example, lines are painted on the hallways and students walk on a particular colored line when walking in one direction and a different colored line when walking in the opposite direction (much like designated lanes for cars on a road). This reduces the likelihood that students will run into each other when moving from one place to another. Another schoolwide procedure, especially appropriate for elementary students, involves having students walk with their arms folded in front of them when moving from one location to another. This reduces student pushing and hitting and also reduces opportunities to flash gang signs in schools where this is a concern. The walking procedure is presented to students in a positive manner, for example, "This is our proud Bear walk" (assuming the school mascot is a bear).

Another possibility for facilitating within-school transitions is to include appropriate transition behavior in whatever behavior management program is being used. For example, contingency contracts can include agreements regarding transitions that result in arriving to class before the bell rings or, if a token economy system is being used, students can earn tokens for being in their seats when the tardy bell rings. Even self-monitoring systems can be used to reinforce appropriate transitions. Students can be taught to use timing devices to reduce the time traveling between classes (Miner, 1990) or they can be taught self-monitoring techniques, including self-recording and graphing of performance, to reduce time between classes (Stecker, Whinnery, & Fuchs, 1996).

Regardless of what method is used to facilitate movement from one part of the school to another, it is first important to ensure that students know their way around the school. They must be familiar with the physical layout of the school and know how to get from one part of the school to another in an efficient manner. Richard Lavoie (1994), in his videotape "Last One Picked—First One Picked On," tells a story about a young man with learning disabilities who was always late to his classes in spite of his diligent efforts to arrive on time. He didn't stop and talk to anyone or get distracted along the way. In fact, he walked as fast as his legs would permit and still never made it to class on time. He couldn't figure out how everyone else did it. It seemed he was the only one who couldn't get to class before the tardy bell rang. Finally, one of the adults in the school realized this young man didn't take a direct route to his next class. Instead, he always went back to his homeroom and then progressed to the next class. He only knew his way around the school starting from his homeroom. A simple tour of the school and a lesson on how the school was laid out solved this young man's tardiness problem and prevented the potential for many negative consequences. It is not uncommon for persistent tardiness to result in various disciplinary measures (e.g., referrals to the dean's office, loss of behavioral points, calls home). How many negative consequences would a student subject himself or herself to before making the decision to avoid school altogether?

Manage Instructional Materials and Paperwork

Managing instructional materials and paperwork is a critical component of organizing the learning environment. Teachers must select appropriate materials and then manage their storage and use. Additionally, teachers must manage student and administrative paperwork. Establishing procedures for managing materials and paperwork helps establish an organized classroom and increases student learning.

Selecting Appropriate Materials

Kameenui and Carnine (1998) recommend selecting educational materials that have six validated instructional design features: big ideas, conspicuous strategies, mediated scaffolding, strategic integration, primed background knowledge, and judicious review. Materials that include these features are particularly important when teaching groups of students with diverse learning abilities.

Big ideas   Big ideas are the really important ideas, concepts, or principles that facilitate efficient acquisition of knowledge. In other words, big ideas are the most important aspects of a particular content area (e.g., reading, math, social studies, science) that all students from the brightest to the most challenged are likely to benefit from knowing. Kameenui and Carnine (1998) identify big ideas for reading, writing, math, science, and social studies. (See Table 3.3 for a sample listing.) Once the big ideas have been identified, educational materials that provide the most extensive coverage of the big ideas may be selected.

Conspicuous strategies Strategies are step-by-step processes that individuals use to approach and solve problems. Although some individuals develop strategies on their own, evidence suggests that many students, particularly those with diverse learning needs, benefit from having strategies made conspicuous or from being taught specific strategies. Thus, selecting materials that include strategy instruction is particularly helpful when teaching students with various ability levels.

Mediated scaffolding Mediated scaffolding involves providing support to students to ensure success in learning new content. Typically, more support is needed when new concepts are first introduced. As students become proficient in their understanding of the content, the support is reduced. Materials that offer evidence of using demonstrations and modeling, guided practice (i.e., practice with prompts and cues), systematic feedback procedures, and transitions from teacher directedness to student independence are incorporating the idea of scaffolding.

TABLE 3.3

Big Ideas for Various Content Areas

Content Area	Sample Big Ideas
Reading	Phonemic awareness (i.e., a sequence of sounds makes up words); alphabetic understanding (i.e., words are formed by groups of letters); automaticity with code (i.e., transfer letters to sounds to words fluently).
Writing	Writing process (i.e., plan, draft, and revise); text structures (i.e., explanations and compare/contrast).
Math	Number families or relationships between basic operations such as addition/subtraction and multiplication/division (i.e., $2 + 4 = 6$; $6 - 4 = 2$; $6 - 2 = 4$ or $3 \times 4 = 12$; $12 \div 4 = 3$; $12 \div 4 = 3$); estimation; proportions.
Science	Science inquiry or scientific method (i.e., form hypotheses, control and manipulate variables, plan investigation to test hypotheses, interpret resulting data).
Social Studies	Problem–solution–effect structure (i.e., common problems in social studies relate to economic or human rights issues; recurring solutions to problems categorized as move, invent, dominate, tolerate, or accommodate; effect of solution may be that problem disappears or that a new problem emerges).

Strategic integration   Strategic integration refers to the process of combining essential information in ways that result in new, more complex knowledge. For example, when learning to read, the combination of phonemic awareness (awareness that words are sequences of sounds), and knowledge of letter-sound correspondence (the phonetic sounds that each letter makes), results in being able to read words. In social studies, students can integrate their understanding of problem–solution–effect and historical events such as getting the U.S. Constitution ratified or ending the Civil War. Effective educational materials first present concepts in isolation, then provide opportunities for students to apply newly learned content to what was learned previously.

Primed background knowledge   Prior to teaching new content, it is important to determine whether students have the necessary background knowledge to benefit from the new instruction. Educational materials that include assessment tools for making this determination are needed. In addition to having the prerequisite knowledge, students must be able to readily access and apply the knowledge to the new content being taught. Teachers can help students remember important background knowledge by reminding them verbally or planning an activity that will cause the background knowledge to emerge again. The goal is to help the student retrieve and use information that he or she already knows. For example, before writing a story about a Pueblo girl who lives on a reservation, students' background knowledge can be primed (or prompted) using pictures from a social studies text that relate to the Pueblo way of life. The pictures help students remember what they know about the Pueblo people and thus help in coming up with good ideas for writing the story.

Judicious review   Educational materials that contain many opportunities for review are very helpful to students. Reviews that are well distributed throughout the content presented are more effective than reviews that occur in one massed format at the end of the program, unit, or text. Built-in cumulative reviews and various types of review help promote strategic integration of content and generalization. Effective reviews greatly enhance the learning and remembering of important content. Moreover, reviews are important for building fluency with new information.

Thus, materials that are organized around and include big ideas and contain evidence of conspicuous strategies, scaffolding, strategic integration, background knowledge assessments, and judicious reviews are helpful when teaching groups of diverse students. These instructional design components promote effective and efficient learning (see Validation Box 3.14 on p. 114).

In addition to looking for materials that include these validated design variables, it is wise to select materials that have been field-tested with students prior to being published. Unfortunately, limited field testing has been done on educational materials. According to Sprick (1987), only 3 percent of published curriculum materials are field-tested and validated prior to being marketed. Thus, the impor-

Selecting Appropriate Materials

Researchers at the University of Oregon National Center to Improve the Tools of Educators (funded by the U.S. Office of Special Education Programs) investigated and validated the benefits of using curriculum materials that include big ideas, conspicuous strategies, mediated scaffolding, primed background knowledge, strategic integration, and judicious review when teaching students with diverse learning needs. Their studies involved junior and senior high students with and without disabilities. The combined findings from their programmatic research clearly show that curricular materials with the specified design variables resulted in higher student achievement than materials without these features. For more information see: (Carnine, Caros, Crawford, Hollenbeck, & Harniss, 1997; Fischer & Tarver, 1997; Grossen, Lee, & Johnston, 1997, or write to The National Center to Improve the Tools of Educators, Institute for the Development of Educational Achievement, College of Education, University of Oregon, Eugene, OR 97403-1211).

tance of looking for materials that contain the design variables described in this section cannot be overemphasized.

After selecting the major curricular materials, teachers select a variety of supplemental materials. These materials provide variety and extended practice for those students who need additional support. Teachers accumulate many supplemental materials over the course of their careers and therefore need to develop a system for organizing and storing them.

Organizing and Storing Materials

There does not appear to be a right or wrong way for organizing and storing classroom materials. Rather, teachers must consider what will work best in their classrooms. Some teachers, who use a learning center approach, will opt to store materials on shelves or bookcases near the centers in which the materials will be used. Other teachers prefer to have one central location (e.g., a closet) in the classroom to organize and store their materials. Still others prefer to store materials in file cabinets organized according to content areas. Using clear containers such as plastic bags that seal shut makes it easy to locate desired materials quickly. Regardless of what system a teacher uses, it is helpful to keep a log, electronic file, or index card file with a listing and/or brief description of the materials available. Thus, as teachers plan lessons, they can quickly see what materials are available to incorporate into the lessons. Without such a listing or file, it's easy to forget about materials that are stored out of sight.

Managing Student Paperwork

Another challenge related to classroom organization is managing student paperwork. Decisions must be made with regard to how papers are collected, distributed, and graded. Decisions also need to be made with regard to managing paperwork when students are absent.

Collecting and distributing student papers

Involving students in the collection and distribution of papers and/or other instructional materials saves time and allows the teacher to monitor the class during sometimes troublesome transition periods (Evertson, Anderson, Anderson, & Brophy, 1980). Another benefit that emerges when students are selected to assist with material distribution is that the student feels important and valued and usually enjoys being called on to help the teacher. One method for involving students in material distribution is to have several students identified as zone leaders. Each zone leader is assigned a particular area within the classroom for which he or she is responsible. Whenever papers or materials need to be passed out, the zone leaders pass them out in their designated areas. Having several zone leaders involved in paper management, rather than a single student, is efficient because it reduces the amount of time spent in transition and therefore increases the amount of time available for instruction. It may be helpful to practice the passing and collecting procedures with the class to ensure that everyone understands how these tasks will be accomplished.

Grading student papers

Decisions also need to be made with regard to when student work is graded. Prompt feedback is important for improving academic achievement (Barringer & Gholson, 1979; Hughes, 1973). Thus, it is important to manage the checking of student work in expeditious ways. One option is to circulate as students are working on independent assignments and conduct some on-the-spot checking rather than waiting for students to finish the whole assignment. There are several advantages to checking student work in this manner. For example, teachers reduce the amount of time needed to grade papers if the checking begins while the students are working. When students see that they are doing well, they're motivated to complete the assignment. Finally, on-the-spot checking provides immediate feedback to students who are having problems with the work. The teacher can redemonstrate what the student should be doing and thus prevent the student from practicing errors (Emmer, Evertson, Sanford, Clements, & Worsham, 1989; Paine et al., 1983).

Another option for managing the amount of grading is to get the students involved in checking their own work. Answer keys can be provided to students after they complete their assignments. Self-correcting materials that include immediate feedback for students also can be used to facilitate practice. Research suggests that students are quite capable of scoring their own work accurately and that doing so doesn't have a negative effect on future test performance (Farnum & Brigham, 1978). Moreover, accurate student scoring may be maintained through random checks or awarding bonus points for accuracy (Hundert & Bucher, 1978).

Managing paperwork for students who are absent

Student absences result in additional paper management issues for teachers. When students return to school and ask "Did I miss anything important?" it's difficult for teachers (who are now thinking about today's lessons) to automatically remember all the missed assignments and class handouts that were provided while the student was absent. This becomes particularly challenging when several students are absent for varying lengths of time. Creating a classroom notebook is an excellent way to address this challenge and place the responsibility for make-up work on students ("Creating a Classroom Notebook," 1996). The classroom notebook contains copies of all class notes (a student in the class may be appointed class notetaker), handouts (one original and one for each absent student), and homework assignments. The materials are organized by date so students can find the materials they need for the days they were absent. It may also be helpful to include a table of contents or notebook dividers to assist students in finding what they need. Students who have been absent use the notebook to get caught up with their assignments. Other students use the notebook to compare their notes with the notes in the book to ensure that their information is thorough and correct. This is particularly helpful when preparing for tests (see Validation Box 3.15).

Managing Administrative Paper Work

In addition to managing students' paperwork, teachers must manage significant amounts of administrative-related paperwork. The initial development of paperwork systems saves precious time in the long run. The following suggestions are designed to help teachers organize the necessary "administrivia" of teaching.

▶ Use a word processor and save written products that will likely be needed again (e.g., letters to parents, permission forms, reimbursement requests, district reports). It's much easier to edit an existing document that to create a new one from scratch.

▶ Make up a phone-conversation log and keep notes (e.g., date, time, key points discussed) of all school-related phone conversations with parents, teachers, support staff, and administrators.

▶ Purchase a yearlong calendar and make notes related to due dates of necessary paperwork (e.g., IEPs, reports, forms for ordering materials). Make these notations one week before the paperwork is actually due to ensure that deadlines are met.

VALIDATION BOX
3.15

Managing Paperwork

Kay Younginger, a special education teacher/inclusion specialist at Wachusett Regional High School in Holden, Massachusetts organized a classroom notebook for her students. The notebook turned out to be such a successful tool that Kay shared the idea with other teachers. Now, at least 30 additional teachers are using classroom notebooks to help with paperwork organization. Kay reports that the teachers love the system. For more information see: ("Creating a Classroom Notebook," 1996).

▶ Organize one file drawer for important administrative paperwork (e.g., letters from parents, policy memos from the district office, media request forms, school calendar, meeting agenda and minutes).

▶ Prepare master copies of forms that are used on a regular basis (e.g., lunch forms, attendance forms, certificates, good-day notes for parents, IEP forms).

Taking time to organize administrative paperwork results in increased time to spend on more preferred activities such as collaborating with other teachers, creating new instructional materials, previewing software, and planning creative lessons. Spending time on these activities is much more rewarding than searching for a needed form or lost memo.

Physical Dimension

In addition to thinking about the psychosocial and procedural dimensions of the classroom, teachers must also consider the physical dimension. Decisions related to the design of the classroom environment are very important because they affect student learning and behavior (Cegelka & Berdine, 1995; Hood-Smith & Leffingwell, 1983; Rieth & Polsgrove, 1994; Soldier, 1988).

Seating Arrangements

Perhaps the most important aspect of physically arranging the classroom is deciding how to arrange the student desks. When making this decision it is helpful to consider instructional goals and characteristics of the students.

Instructional Goals

Research related to seating arrangements indicates that different arrangements promote different student and teacher behaviors. For example, circular and cluster arrangements promote discussion and interaction among students (Rosenfield, Lambert, & Black, 1985). Similarly, split-half and semicircular arrangements promote more frequent interactions between teacher and students and among students themselves (Ridling, 1994; see Fig. 3.6 on p. 118). Thus, these arrangements are appropriate when students are expected to work together and/or discuss their ideas with others. If, however, the expectation is for students to work independently without interacting with others, then arranging the desks in rows is more appropriate (Wheldall & Lam, 1987). Thus, prior to determining how to arrange students' desks, teachers should think about their instructional goals and then select the arrangement that is most conducive to meeting those goals (Wengel, 1992).

Characteristics of Students

In addition to thinking about the instructional goals and desk arrangements that help achieve those goals, teachers also need to consider the characteristics of their

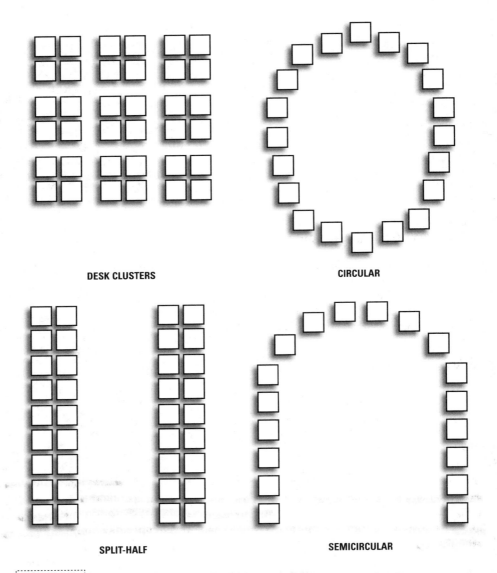

DESK CLUSTERS   CIRCULAR

SPLIT-HALF   SEMICIRCULAR

FIGURE 3.6

Seating Arrangements.

students. Cultural diversity as well as specific disabilities among students influence decisions about desk arrangement. Thinking about the special needs of these students undoubtedly prevents problems in the classroom and helps students feel they belong to the classroom community.

Cultural diversity and classroom arrangement   The cultural background of students influences the type of classroom arrangement in which the students are most comfortable. Students from Native American tribes that endorse working together for the good of the group are accustomed to a culture that emphasizes cooperation and group achievement (Lewis & Doorlag, 1991). Thus, students from these cultures may be most comfortable and perform best when the class is arranged to promote interaction and collaboration (e.g., desk clusters, semicircle, circular, split-halves). Students from Latino families experience more fluid boundaries between spaces and activities in the home than do Anglo students. In Latino homes many activities occur simultaneously in the same area. For example, the television may be on while children are doing homework. Other children may be playing nearby and moving from activity to activity. Multiple conversations may be taking place among family members while music is playing, neighbors are dropping by, and business transactions are taking place at the kitchen table (Gallimore & Goldberg, 1993; Vasquez, Pease-Alvarez, & Shannon, 1994; Wortham, Contreras, & Davis, 1997). Individuals successfully attend to several different activities simultaneously. They communicate and help each other with various tasks and feel a strong sense of togetherness. Thus, in the classroom, students from Latino environments may be most comfortable with arrangements that facilitate extensive interaction and collaboration (e.g., clusters, semicircular, circular, split-halfs).

Disability and classroom arrangement   In addition to considering cultural needs and preferences, thought should be given to the academic and behavioral needs resulting from student disabilities. These needs also have implications for classroom seating arrangements. Students with hearing impairments who depend on lipreading need to be seated so they have clear visual access to the teacher's lips. It may be helpful to seat these students in the center of the room and provide a chair that swivels on casters so they can follow class discussions with greater ease. During small-group academic instruction, a semicircular arrangement works well for students who depend on lipreading. It may also be helpful to seat students with hearing impairments next to a competent, alert peer who can assist with cueing during fire drills and conveying messages received via the school intercom system (Salend, 1998).

Students with visual impairments need to be seated in areas that have bright light without distracting glares. Positioning a student's desk so that the light comes over the shoulder of the student's nondominant hand helps reduce glare. It also is important to think about the walking paths from the students' desks to other important places in the classroom (e.g., the pencil sharpener, the homework basket, learning centers). Unobstructed pathways are important. Additionally, the desks should be placed away from potential danger (e.g., doorways, heavy objects, furniture with sharp corners), and near the auditory stimuli that the students depend on for their learning (e.g. teacher's voice, cassette tapes). When the room arrangement changes, it is important for students with visual impairments to have the opportunities to practice maneuvering in the new environment (Salend, 1998). This practice enhances student confidence and lets the teacher evaluate the accessibility of the classroom, given the new arrangement.

Special consideration with regard to room arrangement must also occur to meet the needs of students with physical disabilities. Students who use wheelchairs, walkers, or crutches need aisles or pathways at least 32 inches wide to maneuver easily and safely in the classroom. Thus, paths from the students' desks to other important places in the classroom should be at least this width. Students who have electrically charged wheelchairs need to be near a wall outlet. In addition to thinking about the placement of the desks, consideration must be given to the height of the desk and surrounding furniture that the students need to use (e.g., bookshelves, center tables). Furniture that allows for height adjustments, has rounded edges, and lacks protrusions is appropriate for many students with physical disabilities (Knight & Wadsworth, 1993; Salend, 1998).

Students with learning disabilities may not have special sensory or physical needs that influence seating arrangements, but their learning and social needs are important to consider. Students with learning disabilities sometimes have difficulty with environmental distractions. Thus, it may be helpful to position their desks away from doorways, windows, and cluttered areas of the classroom. It may also be helpful to position their desks in the quieter areas of the classroom during independent seat work activities. This positioning should not, however, result in the student feeling isolated or separated from the other students in the room. Since students with learning disabilities sometimes have difficulty with social skills, attempts should be made to provide opportunities for these students to interact with their peers. In such cases, desk arrangements that promote interaction are desirable.

Students with behavioral difficulties benefit from sitting near the teacher so that frequent reinforcement and monitoring are available. Sitting near the teacher does not mean being separated from the other students. It just means that the teacher's presence is obvious to the student. Students with behavioral difficulties also benefit from sitting near students who model appropriate classroom behavior. Students are less apt to engage in inappropriate behavior when the peers around them are actively engaged in the lesson and are behaving appropriately. Moreover, this provides opportunities for the teacher to cue students with behavior difficulties by praising students in close proximity. Keeping some distance between student desks is helpful when teaching students with acting-out behaviors (Wheldall and Lam, 1987).

So, there is much to think about when deciding how to arrange the classroom. Teachers can expect positive outcomes when the class is arranged to meet the instructional objectives, while simultaneously taking into consideration cultural preferences and disability-related needs (see Validation Box 3.16).

Special Activity Areas

Depending on the size of the classroom and the number of students, special activity areas may be desired. Special activity areas include computer stations, audiovisual centers, free time areas, and/or learning centers. Research appears to be lacking with regard to organizing special activity areas within the classroom, so applying the

Classroom Arrangement

▸ In one study, during discussion-based lessons, circular arrangements and clusters of desks produced more on-task comments, more on-task behaviors, and more hand-raising in students' participation than when the desks were arranged in rows. For more information see: (Rosenfield, Lambert, & Black, 1985)

▸ Observations conducted in 90 junior high-school classrooms revealed that teachers using either semicircular or split-half seating engaged in more inter-active verbal behaviors than those who used row seating arrangements. Semicircular and split-half seating enabled teachers to use discussions in ways that made their lesson presentation more active and collaborative among students. These seating arrangements resulted in increased student interaction. Teachers who used row seating demonstrated higher frequencies of lecturing and giving directions than teachers who used semicircular or split-half seating. For more information see: (Ridling, 1994).

▸ Another study involved 3 classes in a special school. A total of 34 students with behavioral and learning problems participated in the study. Data were collected during 39 observations over a 4-month period. During independent seat work, the on-task behavior of the students doubled (i.e., from 35 to 70 percent) when their seats were changed from table clusters to row formation. Additionally, the rate of disruptive behavior was 3 times higher when the cluster seating arrangement was used. Teacher behavior also changed depending on the seating arrangement. During the row arrangement, teachers increased their positive comments and decreased their negative comments. For more information see: (Wheldall and Lam, 1987).

same principles that are used to determine students' seating arrangements seems appropriate. The goals associated with the activity area should be matched (to the degree possible) with student characteristics and needs. Accessibility, safety, and the potential for learning should be at the forefront of the teacher's thinking when organizing special activity areas.

There does not appear to be one best way to organize the physical dimension of classrooms. Rather, it seems that flexibility is needed in order to address the various needs of diverse groups of students. This becomes somewhat of a balancing act for teachers and likely results in the need to change the physical environment from time to time rather than simply selecting and using only one format. A periodic review of the classroom arrangement and noting arrangements used by other teachers is helpful.

Personnel Dimension

Classroom personnel undoubtedly have a tremendous effect on the learning environment. Of particular importance are teachers and paraprofessionals. Inclusive models for serving diverse groups of students in one classroom have necessitated a close examination of the roles of general education teachers, special education teachers, and paraprofessionals. Roles have changed to meet the demands of these new models and collaboration among the adults in these classrooms has increased.

Coteaching Models for General and Special Education Teachers

Coteaching has emerged as a model to address the educational needs of both general and special education students within inclusive classroom settings. Coteaching involves "two or more professionals delivering substantive instruction to a diverse, or blended, group of students in a single physical space" (Cook & Friend, 1995, p. 2).

A variety of coteaching approaches has emerged. Cook and Friend (1995) identified five distinct approaches. They are *(a)* one teaching, one assisting (one teacher is in charge and the other observes students or serves as a teaching assistant); *(b)* station teaching (teachers divide students into smaller groups and also divide content so that each teacher is responsible for a part of the material); *(c)* parallel teaching (students are divided into heterogeneous groups and each teacher works with one group to deliver the same content in the same amount of time); *(d)* alternative teaching (one teacher provides a different approach to a smaller group of students); and *(e)* team teaching (teachers teach lessons together taking on different roles and responsibilities). According to Cook and Friend, no one approach is best or worst. Instead, each has a place in a cotaught classroom. These five approaches or similar variations can be used alone or together to meet the needs of the students. There appears to be a relationship between the amount of joint planning, trust, and comfort teachers have for one another and the approach they select to use. Team teaching seems to require the highest level of trust.

Bauwens, Hourcade, and Friend (1989) described three approaches to cooperative teaching in which both general and special education teachers work together: *(a)* complementary instruction, *(b)* team teaching, and *(c)* supportive learning activities. Complementary instruction involves having the general education teacher primarily responsible for content instruction, while the special education teacher accepts responsibility for teaching strategies and skills for mastering the content. In team teaching, general and special education teachers jointly plan and teach lessons, but they assume different levels of responsibility for different parts of the curriculum. In the supportive learning activities approach, the general education teacher is responsible for teaching the curricular content and the special education teacher is responsible for providing supplementary and supportive learning activities. Both teachers are present in the classroom and they cooperatively monitor both types of learning activities.

Pugach and Johnson (1995) described an approach to team teaching that emphasizes that teachers who team teach need to agree that their primary goal is to improve the teaching/learning process. They recommended that teachers challenge themselves to improve their teaching, share the responsibility for all students, share responsibility for instruction, communicate regularly, support one another, and work to include all students.

Although various models for coteaching have emerged, the rationales for engaging in coteaching seem to be clear. Coteaching relationships are used to reduce stigma for students with special needs, improve program intensity and continuity, provide another service option in general education classes, improve instructional options for all students, and increase support for teachers. A review of research (Reinhiller, 1996) revealed challenges and barriers as well as benefits for implementing coteaching models. Included among the challenges and barriers were dealing with ethical and professional issues (e.g., maintaining a continuum of services; not enough special education teachers to get around to all the general education classrooms; increasing the use of peers, paraprofessionals, and parents who are less qualified to teach), funding constraints, achieving cooperation between teachers (e.g., different beliefs about teaching; personality differences); and increased workloads (e.g., dealing with scheduling problems). Included among the benefits for teachers were improved instruction, renewed enthusiasm and energy, and efficient communication, and the benefits for students were additional services for students who didn't qualify for special services, but needed additional assistance, and increased generalization (e.g., less fragmented learning, students learn skills in settings where they use them, fewer transitions, exposure to two teaching styles).

Successful coteaching requires careful planning. Cook and Friend (1995) suggested a seven-step process for planning a coteaching program. These steps are listed and briefly discussed in Table 3.4 (see Validation Box 3.17 on p. 125).

| TABLE 3.4 |

Steps for Planning Coteaching Programs

Step 1: Establish a planning structure.
Determine whether the program will be planned through a school-wide effort, a committee or task force of teachers, or simply two teachers. The appeal of a small planning team is that it is logistically easier and perhaps quicker. The appeal of a larger schoolwide effort is that more stakeholders will be involved and thus greater "buy in" or commitment to the program is likely.

Step 2: Describe the program.
Name the program (e.g., coteaching, team teaching, teaching partners) and describe the program in writing (i.e., several sentences). Writing a brief description helps establish commitment. Moreover, points of confusion may emerge that result in productive discussion. This sets the tone for clear communication throughout the development of the program.

Step 3: Specify goals and objectives.
Develop realistic goals taking into consideration student needs, staff receptivity, and available time for planning. The program goals and objectives indicate expected outcomes and provide a basis for program evaluation.

Step 4: Determine who is eligible.
Decide who should receive services in a cotaught classroom. The criteria for selecting students to participate should be written down and discussed so that everyone is clear with regard to eligibility for the program.

(continued)

TABLE 3.4

Steps for Planning Coteaching Programs (*continued*)

Step 5:   Specify responsibilities.
Determine roles and responsibilities of personnel involved in the program. Again, it is helpful to put this information in writing. This helps clarify the nature of the program and related expectations.

Step 6:   Outline the types of service.
Clarify the nature of the services that will be included in the program. For example, will the program include services for language development? Will the speech therapist deliver these services in the general education classroom?

Step 7:   Design evaluation strategies/measures.
Create formative and summative evaluation procedures. Ongoing formative evaluation assists in making changes in goals, objectives, or strategies as the program is actually taking place. Summative evaluation occurs after the program has been in operation long enough to produce some results (e.g., end of the first year) and is designed to assess progress toward program objectives and desired outcomes.

Paraeducators

Nationwide, school districts are hiring increased numbers of paraeducators. In 1965, fewer than 10,000 paraeducators were employed nationally, whereas in 1995 there were almost 500,000. Of these 500,000, approximately one-half were working in special education programs (Pickett, 1996). Several factors have contributed to the increased reliance on paraeducators. These factors are:

1. More students are receiving their education in general education classrooms. Thus, there is a need to provide special education services in multiple locations at the same time (Blalock, 1991; Kauffman & Hallahan, 1995).
2. More students whose first language is something other than English are attending schools. Recruiting enough teachers from diverse backgrounds has been difficult in some places, thus paraeducators from diverse backgrounds have been hired to bridge the gap between teachers and students who are culturally and linguistically diverse (Miramontes, 1990; Salend, 1998).
3. The continuing shortage of special education teachers and related professionals has resulted in higher student caseloads and an increased need for assistance (American Speech-Language-Hearing Association, 1995; Augenblick & Myers, as cited in French & Pickett, 1997; Miramontes, 1990).

In addition to influencing the number of paraeducators who are hired, these factors influence the role that paraeducators play in educating students. Increased inclusion and diversity among students has resulted in paraeducators taking an active role in supporting the instructional and behavioral programs of students with disabilities. Thus, it is essential for paraeducators to acquire the knowledge and skills for the responsibilities they have. Per IDEA 97, paraeducators must be appropriately trained

Coteaching

▶ A review of literature was conducted and 10 articles published between 1988 and 1995 were located that discussed studies involving coteaching programs. The teachers in all of the studies generally had positive feelings about their participation in coteaching activities. The teachers agreed that the advantages outweighed the disadvantages. Of the 10 coteaching arrangements discussed in this review, 8 reported quantitative and/or qualitative evidence that supported coteaching. For more information see: (Reinhiller, 1996).

▶ In another review of literature, 40 articles that were published between 1980 and 1997 on team teaching were found. Of these articles, 19 (47.5 percent) reported positive outcomes, while 16 (40 percent) were position papers or technical guides and therefore did not report specific outcomes. The remaining 5 (12.5 percent) articles reported mixed results related to team teaching. None of the studies resulted in only negative outcomes. For more information see: (Welch, Brownell, & Sheridan, 1999).

▶ In a review of literature designed to explore the impact of inclusion on students with and without disabilities and their educators, four studies related to coteaching were examined. Findings from these studies revealed that general and special education teachers enjoyed coteaching relationships. They reported that coteaching enriched their professional and personal lives, helped make teaching more enjoyable and stimulating, encouraged experimentation in new methodologies, and prevented feelings of isolation. They also reported challenges including: communicating with each other, resolving differences in teaching styles, scheduling planning and instructional time, determining various responsibilities, maintaining appropriate caseloads, eliciting support from administrators, and obtaining staff development. For more information see: (Salend, & Duhaney, 1999).

▶ In a study involving 70 students with disabilities and 53 students without disabilities, interviews were conducted to evaluate how students felt about coteaching. The students were selected from 4 elementary, 4 middle, and 2 high schools. Some of the parents of these students (i.e., 37 parents of the students with disabilities and 32 parents of the students without disabilities) also were interviewed. Results of the interviews revealed that the students with disabilities liked the coteaching model and felt it helped them get better grades and receive more teacher help. They noted positive effects in their organizational skills and their use of learning strategies. Students without disabilities also liked the coteaching model. They reported positive effects on grades and self-esteem. They identified behavioral and academic advantages of the model. Parents of students with disabilities believed the model helped their children and promoted positive self-esteem. Parents of students without disabilities believed the model enabled their children to gain an understanding of diversity among students, especially students with disabilities. For more information see: (Gerber & Popp, 1999).

Ms. Gonzoles, the paraeducator in this class of predominantly Latino students, assists with instructional activities and provides expertise in promoting positive communication and friendships among English and Spanish-speaking students. Her understanding of Latino families is helpful for students, parents, and the classroom teacher.

and supervised if they provide special education and related services to students with disabilities ("CEC Approves Standards for Paraeducators," 1998). Consequently, the Council for Exceptional Children and the National Resource Center for Paraprofessionals in Education and Related Services developed international standards for paraeducators. These standards address multiple aspects of education and instruction (see Table 3.5). Additionally, national standards for professional educators now include skills related to working with paraeducators. It is the responsibility of the classroom teacher to coordinate the activities of paraeducators. This includes determining and communicating their roles and responsibilities (i.e., matching their skills to program needs), providing orientation and training, communicating regularly, and acknowledging their accomplishments.

Teachers also are responsible for supervising and evaluating the performance of paraeducators. It is the teacher's responsibility to provide frequent modeling, coaching, and mentoring to guide the paraeducator toward increased competency. As the paraeducator becomes more proficient in his or her assigned tasks, the nature and extent of the supervision may change (National Joint Committee on Learning Disabilities, 1998). Four guiding principles assist teachers in supervising paraeducators (French, 1999). The first principle is to actively involve the paraeducator in developing a personalized "job description." This helps clarify what the paraeducator's responsibilities will be. To the degree possible, the paraeducator's skills should be matched to programmatic needs within the classroom. This increases the likelihood

TABLE 3.5

National Standards for Paraeducators (From *CEC Knowledge and Skills for Beginning Special Education Paraeducators* [pp. 93–96] by The Council for Exceptional Children, 1998, Reston, VA: Council for Exceptional Children, Copyright 1998 by the Council for Exceptional Children. Reprinted with permission.)

CEC Knowledge and Skills for
Beginning Special Education Paraeducators:
Knowledge and Skills Statements

PE: Paraeducator Common Core
1. Philosophical, Historical, and Legal Foundations of Special Education

Knowledge:

K1 Purposes of programs for individuals with exceptionalities.

K2 Beliefs, traditions, and values across cultures and their effect on the relationships among children, families and schooling.

K3 Rights and responsibilities of parents and children/youth as they relate to individual learning needs.

K4 The distinctions between roles and responsibilities of professionals, paraeducators, and support personnel.

Skills:

S1 Perform responsibilities under the supervision of a certified/licensed professional in a manner consistent with the requirements of law, rules and regulations, and local district policies and procedures.

PE: Paraeducator Common Core
2. Characteristics of Learners

Knowledge:

K1 Impact of different characteristics of individuals with exceptionalities on the individual's life and family in the home, school, and community.

K2 Indicators of abuse and neglect that put students at risk.

Skills:

PE: Paraeducator Common Core
3. Assessment, Diagnosis, and Evaluation

Knowledge:

K1 Rationale for assessment.

Skills:

S1 Demonstrate basic data collection techniques.

S2 With direction from a professional, make and document objective observations appropriate to the individual with exceptional learning needs.

PE: Paraeducator Common Core
4. Instructional Content and Practice

Knowledge:

K1 Demands of various learning environments on individuals with exceptional learning needs.

K2 Basic instructional and remedial methods, techniques, and materials.

K3 Basic technologies appropriate to individuals with exceptional learning needs.

Skills:

S1 Establish and maintain rapport with learners.

S2 Use developmentally and age-appropriate strategies, equipment, materials, and technologies, as directed, to accomplish instructional objectives.

S3 Assist in adapting instructional strategies and materials according to the needs of the learner.

S4 Follow written plans, seeking clarification as needed.

(*continued*)

TABLE 3.5

National Standards for Paraeducators (*continued*)

PE: Paraeducator Common Core
5. Supporting the Teaching and Learning Environment

Knowledge:	Skills:
	S1 Assist in maintaining a safe, healthy learning environment that includes following prescribed policy and procedures.
	S2 Use basic strategies and techniques for facilitating the integration of individuals with exceptional learning needs in various settings.
	S3 As directed by a certified/licensed professional, prepare and organize materials to support teaching and learning.
	S4 Use strategies that promote the learner's independence.

PE: Paraeducator Common Core
6. Managing Student Behavior and Social Interaction Skills

Knowledge:	Skills:
K1 Rules and procedural safeguards regarding the management of behaviors of individuals with exceptional learning needs.	S1 Demonstrate effective strategies for the management of behavior.
	S2 Use appropriate strategies and techniques to increase the individual's self-esteem, self-awareness, self-control, self-reliance, and self-advocacy.
	S3 Assist in modifying the learning environment to manage behavior.
	S4 Collect and provide objective, accurate information to professionals, as appropriate.
	S5 Use appropriate strategies and techniques in a variety of settings to assist in the development of social skills.

PE: Paraeducator Common Core
7. Communication and Collaborative Partnerships

Knowledge:	Skills:
K1 Characteristics of effective communication with children, youth, families, and school and community personnel.	S1 Under the direction of a certified/licensed professional, use constructive strategies in working with individuals with exceptional learning needs, parents, and school and community personnel in various learning environments.
K2 Common concerns of parents of individuals with exceptionalities.	S2 Follow the instructions of the professional.
K3 Roles of individuals with exceptionalities, parents, teachers, paraeducators, and other school and community personnel in planning an individualized program.	S3 Foster respectful and beneficial relationships between families and other school and community personnel.
K4 Ethical practices for confidential communication about individuals with exceptionalities.	S4 Participate as requested in conferences with families or primary caregivers as members of the educational team.
	S5 Use appropriate basic educational terminology regarding students, programs, roles, and instructional activities.

TABLE 3.5

National Standards for Paraeducators (*continued*)

PE: Paraeducator Common Core
7. Communication and Collaborative Partnerships

Skills:

S6 Demonstrate sensitivity to diversity in cultural heritages, lifestyles, and value systems among children, youth, and families.

S7 Function in a manner that demonstrates the ability to use effective problem solving, engage in flexible thinking, employ appropriate conflict management techniques, and analyze one's own personal strengths and preferences.

PE: Paraeducator Common Core
8. Professional and Ethical Practices

Knowledge:

K1 Personal cultural biases and differences that affect one's ability to work effectively with children, youth, families, and other team members.

K2 The paraeducator as a role model for individuals with exceptional learning needs.

Skills:

S1 Demonstrate commitment to assisting learners in achieving their highest potential.

S2 Function in a manner that demonstrates a positive regard for the distinctions among roles and responsibilities of paraeducators, professionals, and other support personnel.

S3 Function in a manner that demonstrates the ability to separate personal issues from one's responsibilities as a paraeducator.

S4 Demonstrate respect for the culture, religion, gender, and sexual orientation of individual students.

S5 Promote and maintain a high level of competence and integrity.

S6 Exercise objective and prudent judgment.

S7 Demonstrate proficiency in academic skills including oral and written communication.

S8 Engage in activities that promote paraeducator's knowledge and skill development.

S9 Engage in self-assessment activities.

S10 Accept and use constructive feedback.

S11 Practice within the context of the CEC Code of Ethics and other written standards and policies of the school or agency where they are employed.

---

of successful performance. The second guiding principle for supervising paraeducators is to conduct firsthand observations rather than relying on hearsay regarding the paraeducator's performance. Short (e.g., 5 minutes), but frequent (e.g., 2 times a week) observations are helpful. The third guiding principle is to focus the observations on tasks assigned to the paraeducator in his or her personalized job description. "The tasks on which a person's performance will be evaluated should never be a surprise" (French, 1999, p. 12). The final principle for supervising paraeducators is to use written data to provide feedback. Written data should be collected during observations and then shared. A variety of data collection procedures may be used (e.g., scripting exact words used while giving directions to students; counting how many times specific academic praise is used).

Careful attention related to the best ways to involve paraeducators in the classroom coupled with clear communication results in positive professional relationships and enhanced instructional programming for students, especially students who need additional support (see Validation Box 3.18).

Organizing the learning environment requires careful planning. The uniqueness of each classroom (e.g., student characteristics, teacher characteristics, subject matter demands, school context) makes it impossible to prescribe one specific method or technique for organizing the environment (Evertson, 1996). Instead, teachers must take into consideration the needs of their particular students, available resources, research findings related to classroom organization and then orchestrate the creation of an environment that results in positive learning experiences for all students. Although much time is spent making organizational decisions prior to the initiation of the school year, the organizational process is ongoing and continues

---

VALIDATION BOX
3.18

Paraeducators

An Instructional Assistant Program was created in Columbus, OH, to provide instructional service to underachieving pupils in kindergarten and Grade 1. The kindergarten program took place in 61 schools with an equivalent of 94.5 paraprofessionals serving 1668 students and 107 teachers. The Grade 1 program took place in 15 schools with an equivalent of 23.5 assistants serving 455 students and 50 teachers. The program included 9 inservice training sessions and emphasized activities designed to increase the language and reading skills of students. It was reported that 78.8 percent of the kindergarten students successfully completed 12 of 17 items on a locally constructed test that measured concepts about print (12 out of 17 was the preestablished criterion used to distinguish readiness for Grade 1). Moreover, 81 percent of the teacher ratings indicated that pupil success was attributable to the services of the paraprofessionals. In the Grade 1 program, 50 percent of the students gained 3.0 Normal Curve Equivalent in Total Reading on a nationally standardized achievement test (i.e., Comprehensive Test of Basic Skills). Data indicated that 80.7 percent of the first graders were promoted to second grade and 71.4 percent of the teacher ratings indicated that pupil success was attributable to the paraprofessionals. Ninety percent of the paraprofessionals in this study rated the inservice meetings as informative and helpful for classroom use. Results indicated that the Instructional Assistant Program should be continued. For more information see: (Johnson, 1993).

throughout the entire year. The dynamics within classrooms rarely stay constant. Thus, changes and refinements to the organizational structure are needed routinely.

Practice Activities

▶ Conduct classroom observations to identify ways teachers create positive environments, make students feel accepted, and manage student behavior.

▶ Select one of the medium-intensity behavior techniques discussed in this chapter and develop a specific plan for using the technique in an elementary or secondary setting. Develop the plan using greater detail than what is presented in the chapter (e.g., determine criteria for reinforcement, develop the materials needed, develop procedures for implementing the system).

▶ Review the problematic daily schedule outlined in Table 3.2. Develop a schedule that would be more appropriate for Cal.

▶ Develop a daily schedule to be used in an elementary setting.

▶ Develop a class schedule to be used in a secondary setting.

▶ Create/draw a plan that illustrates the physical arrangement for a classroom that consists of 30 students. Of these students, 4 have learning disabilities, 1 has severe behavioral difficulties, 1 has a hearing impairment, and 2 are Mexican Americans whose primary language is Spanish.

▶ Interview teachers who have participated in coteaching models. Based on these interviews, identify advantages for coteaching, disadvantages for coteaching, and methods for promoting effective coteaching.

▶ Develop interview questions or a questionnaire that could be given to paraprofessionals to help decide how to use their services.

POST ORGANIZER

Organizing the learning environment for students with special needs who receive their instruction in classrooms of diverse students is indeed a challenge. Attention must be given to psychosocial, procedural, physical, and personnel dimensions of the classroom. Teachers who take the time to organize their learning environments based on student needs and validated practices, such as those discussed in this chapter, are better equipped to meet this challenge.

References

Ager, C. L., & Cole, C. L. (1991). A review of cognitive-behavioral interventions for children and adolescents with behavioral disorders. *Behavioral Disorders, 16,* 276–287.

American Speech-Language-Hearing Association (1995). *Guidelines for the training, credentializing, use and supervision of speech-language pathology assistants.* Rockville, MD: American Speech-Language-Hearing Association.

Axelrod, S. (1971). Token reinforcement programs in special classes. *Exceptional Children, 37,* 371–379.

Barringer, C. & Gholson, B. (1979). Effects of type and combination of feedback upon conceptual learning by children: Implications for research in academic learning. *Review of Educational Research, 49,* 459–78.

Bauwens, J., Hourcade, J. J., & Friend, M. (1989). Cooperative teaching: A model for general and special education integration. *Remedial and Special Education, 10*(2), 17–22.

Blalock, G. (1991). Paraprofessionals: Critical team members in our special education programs. *Intervention in School and Clinic, 26,* 200–214.

Carnine, D., Caros, J., Crawford, D., Hollenbeck, K., & Harniss, M. (1997). Five intervention studies evaluating "understanding U.S. history." *Effective School Practices, 16*(1), 36–54.

Cawelti, G. (1994). *High school restructuring: A National Study.* Arlington, VA: Educational Research Service.

CEC approves standards for paraeducators. (1998, August/September). *CEC Today, 5*(2), 2.

Cegelka, P. T., & Berdine, W. H. (1995). *Effective instruction for students with learning difficulties.* Needham Heights, MA: Allyn & Bacon.

Cook, L., & Friend, M. (1995). Co-teaching: Guidelines for creating effective practices. *Focus on exceptional Children, 28*(3), 1–16.

Creating a Classroom Notebook. (1996, December). *Strategram, 9*(2), 5.

Edwards, C. M. (1995). The 4 × 4 plan. *Educational Leadership, 53*(3), 16–19.

Elias, M. J., Zins, J. E., Wessberg, R. P., Frey, K. S., Greenberg, M. T., Haynes, N. M., Kessler, R., Schwab-Stone, M. E., & Shriver, T. P. (1997). *Promoting social and emotional learning: Guidelines for educators.* Alexandria, VA: Association for Supervision and Curriculum Development.

Emmer, E. T., Everson, C. M., Sanford, J. P., Clements, B. S., & Worsham, M. E. (1989). *Classroom management for secondary teachers* (2nd ed.). Upper Saddle River, NJ: Prentice-Hall.

Evertson, C. M. (1996). Who's in charge here?: Learning about classroom management. In G. G. Brannigan (Ed.), *The enlightened educator: Research adventures in the schools* (pp. 126–153). NY: McGraw-Hill.

Evertson, C., Anderson, C., Anderson, L., & Brophy, J. (1980). Relationship between classroom behaviors and student outcomes in junior high school mathematics and English classes. *American Educational Research Journal, 17,* 43–65.

Farnum, M., & Brigham, T. (1978). The use and evaluation of study guides with middle school students. *Journal of Applied Behavior Analysis, 11,* 137–144.

Feindler, E. L., & Fremouw, W. J. (1983). Stress inoculation training for adolescent anger problems. In D. Meichenbaum & M. E. Jaremko (Eds.), *Stress reduction and prevention.* (pp. 451–485). New York: Plenum.

Feindler, E. L., Marriott, S. A., & Iwata, M. (1984). Group anger control training for junior high school delinquents. *Cognitive Therapy and Research, 8,* 299–311.

Fisher, C. W., Berliner, D. C., Filby, N. N., Marliave, R., Cahen, L. S., & Dishaw, M. M. (1980). Teaching behaviors, academic learning time, and student achievement: An overview. In C. Denham & A. Lieberman (Eds.), *Time to learn* (pp. 7–32). Washington, DC: National Institute of Education.

Fischer, T. A., & Tarver, S. G. (1997). Meta-analysis of studies of mathematics curricula designed around big ideas. *Effective School Practices, 16*(1), 71–79.

Fitzsimmons, M. K. (1998, November). Functional behavior assessment and behavior intervention plans. ERIC EC Digest, E571. Also available online at http://ericec.org.

French, N. (1999). Supervising paraeducators—What every teacher should know. *CEC Today, 6*(2), 12.

French, N. K., & Picket, A. L. (1997). Paraprofessionals in special education: Issues for teacher educators. *Teacher Education and Special Education, 20,* 61–73.

Gallimore, R. & Goldenberg, C. (1993). Activity settings of early literacy. In E. Forman, N. Minick, C. Stone (Eds.), *Contexts for learning* (pp. 315–335). NY: Oxford.

Gerber, P. J., & Popp, P. A. (1999). Consumer perspectives on the collaborative teaching model. *Remedial and Special Education, 20,* 288–296.

Gettinger, M. (1986). Issues and trends in academic engaged time of students. *Special Services in the Schools, 2*(4), 1–17.

Goldstein, A. P., & Glick, B. (1987). *Aggression replacement training: A comprehensive intervention for aggressive youth.* Champaign, IL: Research Press.

Good, T. L., & Brophy, J. E. (1986). School effects. In M. C. Wittrock (Ed.), *Handbook of research on teaching* (3rd ed.). New York: Macmillan.

Goodlad, J. I. (1984). *A place called school.* New York: McGraw-Hill.

Greenwood, C. R. (1991). Longitudinal analysis of time, engagement, and achievement in at-risk versus non-risk students. *Exceptional Children, 57,* 521–535.

Grossen, B., Lee, C., & Johnston, D. (1997). A comparison of "big idea" design in reasoning and writing with constructivist methods. *Effective School Practices, 16*(1), 55–70.

Hackmann, D. G. (1995). Ten guidelines for implementing block scheduling. *Educational Leadership, 53*(3), 24–27.

Homme, L. E., deBaca, P. C., Devine, J. V., Steinhorst, R., & Richert, E. J. (1963). Use of the Premack Principle in controlling the behavior of nursery school children. *Journal of the Experimental Analysis of Behavior, 6,* 544–548.

Hood-Smith, N. E., & Leffingwell, R. J. (1983). The impact of physical space alteration on disruptive classroom behavior: A case study. *Education, 104,* 224–230.

Hops, H., & Walker, H. M. (1988). *Contingencies for learning academic and social skills: A classroom behavior management program for children with acting-out behaviors.* Delray Beach, FL: Educational Achievement Systems.

Hops, H., Walker, H. M., Fleischman, D. H., Nagoshi, J. T., Omura, R. T., Skindrud, K., & Taylor, J. (1978). CLASS: A standardized in-class program for acting-out children. II. Field test evaluations. *Journal of Educational Psychology, 70,* 636–644.

Hughes, D. C. (1973). An experimental investigation of the effects of pupil responding and teacher reacting on pupil achievement. *American Educational Research Journal, 10,* 21–37.

Hundert, J., & Bucher, B. (1978). Pupils' self-scored arithmetic performance: A practical procedure for maintaining accuracy. *Journal of Applied Behavior Analysis, 11,* 304.

Johnson, J. (1993). *Adaptation of curriculum, instructional methods, and materials component, instructional assistant program.* (Rep. No. CS 011 342). Columbus, OH: Columbus Ohio Public Schools Department of Program Evaluation. (ERIC Document Reproduction Service No. ED 358 442)

Jolivette, K., Scott, T. M., & Nelson, C. M. (2000, January). The link between functional behavioral assessments (FBAs) and behavioral intervention plans (BIPs). *ERIC Digest, E592 EDO-00-1,* 1–2.

Kameenui, E. J., & Carnine, D. W. (1998). *Effective teaching strategies that accommodate diverse learners.* Upper Saddle River, NJ: Merrill, an imprint of Prentice-Hall.

Kamps, D. M., Ellis, C., Mancina, C., Wyble, J., Greene, L., & Harvey, D. (1995). Case studies using functional analysis for young children with behavior risks. *Education and Treatment of Children, 18,* 243–260.

Kauffman, J. M., & Hallahan, D. P. (Eds.). (1995). *The illusion of full inclusion.* Austin, TX: PRO-ED.

Knight, D., & Wadsworth, D. (1993). Physically challenged students. *Childhood Education, 69*(4), 211–215.

Lavoie, R. D. (Speaker). (1994). *Last one picked—first one picked on* (Videorecording). Alexandria, VA: PBS Video.

Leinhardt, G., Zigmond, N., & Cooley, W. W. (1981). Reading instruction and its effects. *American Educational Research Journal, 18,* 343–361.

Lewis, R. B., & Doorlag, D. H. (1991). *Teaching special students in the mainstream* (3rd ed.). New York: Merrill.

Lloyd, J. W., & Landrum, T. (1990). Self-recording of attending to task: Treatment components and generalization of effects. In T. E. Scruggs & B. Y. L. Wong (Eds.), *Intervention research in learning disabilities* (pp. 235–262). New York: Springer-Verlag.

Madsen, C. H., Jr., Becker, W. C., & Thomas, D. R. (1968). Rules, praise, and ignoring: Elements of elementary classroom control. *Journal of Applied Behavior Analysis, 1,* 139–150.

Marzano, R. J. (1992). *A different kind of classroom: Teaching with dimensions of learning.* Alexandria, VA: Association for Supervision and Curriculum Development.

McConnell, M. E. (1999). Self-monitoring, cueing, recording, and managing: Teaching students to manage their own behavior. *Teaching Exceptional Children, 32*(2), 14–21.

Meichenbaum, D. (1977). *Cognitive behavior-modification: An integrative approach.* New York: Plenum.

Meier, F. E. (1992). *Competency-based instruction for teachers of students with special learning needs.* Needham Heights, MA: Allyn & Bacon.

Mercer, C. D., & Mercer, A. R. (1998). *Teaching students with learning problems* (5th ed.). Columbus, OH: Merrill, an imprint of Prentice-Hall.

Miner, S. (1990). Use of a self-recording procedure to decrease the time taken by behaviorally disordered students to walk to special classes. *Behavioral Disorders, 15,* 210–216.

Miramontes, O. B. (1990). Organizing for effective paraprofessional services in special education: A multilingual/multiethnic instructional service team model. *Remedial and Special Education, 11,* 248–256.

Murdick, N. L., & Petch-Hogan, B. (1996). Inclusive classroom management: Using preintervention strategies. *Intervention in School and Clinic, 31,* 172–176.

Murphy, J. J. (1988). Contingency contracting in schools: A review. *Education & Treatment of Children, 11,* 257–269.

National Committee on Excellence in Education. (1983). *A nation at risk: The imperative for educational reform.* Washington, DC: U.S. Government Printing Office.

National Joint Committee on Learning Disabilities. (1998, February 1) *Learning disabilities: Use of paraprofessionals.* American Speech-Language-Hearing Association, Rockville, MD.

Nelson, J. R., Smith, D. J., Young, R. K., & Dodd, J. M. (1991). A review of self-management outcome research conducted with students who exhibit behavioral disorders. *Behavioral Disorders, 16,* 169–179.

Novaco, R. W. (1975). *Anger control: The development and evaluation of an experimental treatment.* Lexington, MA: Lexington.

O'Neil, J. (1995). Finding the time. *Educational Leadership, 53*(3), 11–15.

Paine, S. C., Radicchi, J., Rosellini, L. C., Deutchman, L., & Darch, C. B. (1983). *Structuring your classroom for academic success.* Champaign, IL: Research Press Company.

Pickett, A. L. (1996). *A state of the art report on paraeducators in education and related services.* New York: National Resource Center for Paraprofessionals.

Positive behavioral support. (1999, Winter). *Research Connections in Special Education, 4,* 1–2.

Prater, M. A., Joy, R., Chilman, B., Temple, J., & Miller, S. R. (1991). Self-monitoring of on-task behavior by adolescents with learning disabilities. *Learning Disability Quarterly, 14,* 164–177.

Premack, D. (1959). Toward empirical behavior laws: Vol. I. Positive reinforcement. *Psychological Review, 66,* 219–223.

Protecting students from harassment: It's the law—and then some. (1999, Fall). *Association for Supervision and Curriculum Development Curriculum Update,* 2–3.

Pugach, M. C., & Johnson, L. J. (1995). *Collaborative practitioners collaborative schools.* Denver: Love.

Reinhiller, N. (1996). Coteaching: New variations on a not-so-new practice. *Teacher Education and Special Education, 19,* 34–38.

Rich, H. L., & Ross, S. M. (1989). Student's time on learning tasks in special education. *Exceptional Child, 55,* 508–515.

Ridling, Z. (1994, April). *The effects of three seating arrangements on teachers' use of selective interactive verbal behaviors.* Paper presented at the annual meeting of the American Educational Research Association, New Orleans, LA.

Rieth, H. J., & Polsgrove, L. (1994). Curriculum and instructional issues in teaching secondary students with learning disabilities. *Learning Disabilities Research and Practice, 9,* 118–126.

Rieth, H. J., Polsgrove, L., Okolo, C., Bahr, C., & Eckert, R. (1987). An analysis of the secondary special education classroom ecology with implications for teacher training. *Teacher Education and Special Education, 10,* 113–119.

Robinson, P. W., Newby, T. J., & Ganzell, S. L. (1981). A token system for a class of underachieving hyperactive children. *Journal of Applied Behavior Analysis, 14,* 307–315.

Rosenfield, P., Lambert, N. M., & Black, A. (1985). Desk arrangement effects on pupil classroom behavior. *Journal of Educational Psychology, 77,* 101–198.

Salend, S. J. (1998). *Effective mainstreaming: Creating inclusive classrooms* (3rd ed.). Upper Saddle River, NJ: Merrill, an imprint of Prentice-Hall.

Salend, S. J., & Duhaney, L. M. G. (1999). The impact of inclusion on students with and without disabilities and their educators. *Remedial and Special Education, 20,* 114–126.

Santos, K. E., & Rettig, M. D. (1999). Going on the block: Meeting the needs of students with disabilities in high schools with block scheduling. *Teaching Exceptional Children, 31*(3), 54–59.

Schloss, P. J., & Smith, M. A. (1994). *Applied behavior analysis in the classroom.* Needham Heights, MA: Allyn and Bacon.

School-wide behavioral management systems. (1997). *Research Connections in Special Education, 1*(1), 1–8.

Schumaker, J. B., Hovell, M. F., & Sherman, J. A. (1992). *The progress program: A teaming technique.* Lawrence, KS: Edge Enterprises.

Schumaker, J. B., Hovell, M. F., & Sherman, J. A. (1977). An analysis of daily report cards and parent-managed privileges in the improvement of adolescents' classroom performance. *Journal of Applied Behavior Analysis, 10,* 449–464.

Scott, T. M., & Nelson, C. M. (1999). Universal school discipline strategies: Facilitating positive learning environments. *Effective School Practices, 17*(4), 54–64.

Shortt, T. L., & Thayer, Y. V. (1998–1999). Block scheduling can enhance school climate. *Educational Leadership, 56*(4), 76–84.

Skiba, R., & Casey, S. (1985). Interventions for behaviorally disordered students: A quantitative review and methodological critique. *Behavioral Disorders, 10,* 239–252.

Smith, M. A. (1985). Scheduling for success. *Perspectives for Teachers of the Hearing Impaired, 3*(3), 354–371.

Smith, T. E. C., Polloway, E. A., Patton, J. R., & Dowdy, C. A. (1995). *Teaching students with special needs in inclusive settings.* Needham Heights, MA: Allyn and Bacon.

Soldier, L. L. (1988). *Sociocultural context and language learning of native American pupils.* Paper presented at the annual meeting of the National Association for Bilingual Education, Houston, TX.

Sprick, R. S. (1985). *Discipline in the secondary classroom: A problem-by-problem survival guide.* West Nyack, NY: The Center for Applied Research in Education.

Sprick, R. S. (1987). *Solutions to elementary discipline problems* (audiocassette tapes). Eugene, OR: Teaching Strategies.

Stecker, P. M., Whinnery, K. W., & Fuchs, L. S. (1996). Self-recording during unsupervised academic activity: Effects on time spent out of class. *Exceptionality, 6,* 133–147.

Stumpf, T. (1995). A Colorado school's un-rocky road to trimesters. *Educational Leadership, 53*(3), 20–22.

Taylor-Greene, S., Brown, D., Nelson, L., Longton, J., Gassman, T., Cohen, J., Swartz, J., Horner, R. H., Sugai, G., & Hall, S. (1997). School-wide behavioral support: Starting the year off right. *Journal of Behavioral Education, 7*(1), 99–112.

Todd, A. W., Horner, R. H., Sugai, G., & Sprague, J. R. (1999). Effective behavior support: Strengthening school-wide systems through a team-based approach. *Effective School Practices, 17*(4), 23–33.

Vasquez, O., Pease-Alvarez, L., & Shannon, S. (1994). *Pushing boundaries.* NY: Cambridge.

Walker, H. M., Hops, H., & Greenwood, C. R. (1984). The CORBEH research and development model: Programmatic issues and strategies. In S. Paine, T. Bellamy, & B. Wilcox (Eds.), *Human services that work.* Baltimore: Paul H. Brookes.

Wang, M. C., Haertel, G. D., & Walberg, H. J. (1993). Toward a knowledge base for school learning. *Review of Educational Research, 63,* 249–294.

Warger, C. (1999, September). Positive behavior support and functional assessment. *ERIC Digest, E580 EDO-99-8,* 1–2.

Webber, J., Scheuermann, B., McCall, C., & Coleman, M. (1993). Research on self-monitoring as a behavior management technique in special education classrooms: A descriptive review. *Remedial and Special Education, 14*(2), 38–56.

Welch, M., Brownell, K., & Sheridan, S. M. (1999). What's the score and game plan on teaming in schools?: A review of the literature on team teaching and school-based problem-solving teams. *Remedial and Special Education, 20*(1), 36–49.

Wengel, M. (1992). *Seating arrangements: Changing with the times.* (Rep. No. PS 020 682). Washington, DC: U.S. Department of Education, Office of Educational Research and Improvement. (ERIC Document Reproduction Service No. ED 348 153)

Wheldall, K., & Lam, Y. Y. (1987). Rows vs. tables, II. The effects of two classroom seating arrangements on classroom disruption rate, on-task behaviour and teacher behaviour in three special school classes. *Educational Psychology, 7,* 303–312.

Wortham, S., Contreras, M., & Davis, L. (1997). *The organization of space and activities among Latinos: A strategy for making school more culturally familiar.* Paper presented at the annual meeting of the American Educational Research Association, Chicago, IL.

Selecting
Instructional Models

*Quality is never an accident; it is always the result of high
intention, sincere effort, intelligent direction, and skillful
execution; it represents the wise choice of many alternatives.*
—Willa A. Foster

Review of Chapters 1 to 3

The first three chapters in this text addressed issues related to instructional prepa-ration. The importance of understanding school contexts including student charac-teristics and the demands they face, using specific planning routines, and organizing the learning environment were emphasized. The following questions are designed to provide review and promote integration of information presented thus far. While reviewing, it's important to remember that the processes described in these initial chapters do not have precise beginning and ending points. Understanding school contexts, planning instruction, and organizing classrooms begins in August or Sep-tember and continues throughout the school year. These are ongoing processes that clearly represent the saying, "A teacher's work is never done." Before preceding with Chapter 4, consider the following questions:

1. What potential good and what potential harm can emerge from national education goals and standards?
2. How have school demographics changed over the past couple of decades? How do these changes affect teaching?
3. How do learner characteristics influence instructional decisions?
4. What common characteristics exist among students with various disabilities? What common characteristics exist among students with disabilities and students without disabilities?
5. What are some of the possible challenges involved in teaching students who live in poverty? What are some of the possible challenges involved in teaching students who live in affluence?
6. What can teachers do to promote acceptance of all students regardless of gender, disability, cultural background, and sexual orientation?
7. What validated planning methods are appropriate for creating lessons that include diverse groups of students?
8. What validated planning methods are appropriate when planning for an individual student?
9. What are the benefits of using systematic planning procedures?
10. Why should students be involved in instructional, educational, and/or transition planning?
11. What should be done if parents, school personnel, and a student with disabilities fail to agree on an appropriate educational program? How should the disagreements be resolved?
12. What can be done if one member of an educational planning team consistently fails to follow through on the agreed-on plan?
13. What dimensions should teachers consider when organizing their classrooms? Within each dimension, what are the important concepts or principles to think about?
14. What are some of the common components found among the behavior management techniques discussed in Chapter 3?

15. What are some of the optional approaches for coteaching? What do you perceive to be the strengths and weaknesses of these approaches?
16. What can teachers do to establish positive working relationships with the paraeducators who are assigned to work in their classes?

A D V A N C E ORGANIZER

In Chapter 3, various dimensions of classroom organization were discussed. Included in the discussion were specific suggestions for enhancing the psychosocial, procedural, physical, and personnel dimensions of the learning environment. Classroom organization undoubtedly plays a major role in setting the stage for effective and efficient teaching and learning. It was noted, however, that numerous differences exist from one class to the next. Consequently, organizational structures will vary as well. Teachers must consider their instructional goals, the students they teach, and the current knowledge base regarding effective classroom organization. Thinking about these three variables enhances teachers' abilities to make good organizational decisions. This same type of thinking must occur when teachers select instructional models to use with their students. It is unlikely that one model will meet the needs of all of the students all of the time in a particular class. Therefore, the integration of several validated models may be the best solution for teaching in diverse learning environments. The purpose of this chapter is to discuss validated instructional models—explicit instruction, Direct Instruction, and strategy instruction—and to provide direction regarding when to use the various approaches.

Selecting and integrating instructional models is very important when teaching diverse groups of students. To date, several models have been developed and used extensively to promote student learning. Included among these are explicit instruction, Direct Instruction, and strategy instruction.

The Explicit Instruction Model

Explicit instruction (sometimes referred to as direct instruction with lowercase "d" and "i" and sometimes referred to as systematic instruction) refers to teacher-directed instruction that is highly organized and task-oriented. Academic skills and concepts are presented in a clear, direct manner to promote student understanding and mastery. Clear goals are established for lessons, student performance toward the goals is monitored, and feedback is provided. A typical instructional sequence used during explicit instruction is: (*a*) provide advance organizer, (*b*) describe and

Mr. Washington provides an advance organizer that includes a review of content from the previous day.

demonstrate, *(c)* provide guided practice, *(d)* provide independent practice, and *(e)* provide post-organizer.

Provide Advance Organizer

The concept of advance organizers originated in the early sixties through the work of Ausubel and his colleagues (as cited in Williams & Butterfield, 1992). Ausubel described an advance organizer as material introduced in advance of learning that links specific, new information to a broader, more general concept that is already known. Advance organizers were developed specifically to bridge the gap between what someone already knows and what is to be learned.

Advance organizers occur immediately before an instructional lesson begins. They set the stage for the upcoming lesson and engage students' attention. Advance organizers can be delivered through a variety of formats (i.e., verbal, written text, and/or graphic organizer). Typical components included in an advance organizer are stating the purpose and benefits of the advance organizer, identifying the major topics and subtopics of the lesson, clarifying actions that teacher and students will take, providing background information, reviewing previous content and linking it to the new material, stating lesson objectives and clarifying concepts to be learned, providing rationales to personalize learning and motivate students, introducing new vocabulary, and stating desired outcomes and/or performance expectations (Hudson, 1996; Lenz, 1983; Lenz, Alley, & Schumaker, 1987; Lenz, Ellis, & Scanlon, 1996). Not every advance organizer will have all of these components. Teachers select the components that are appropriate for the lesson they are preparing to teach. See Table 4.1 for several samples of verbal advance organizers.

Since the inception of advance organizers in the early sixties, hundreds of studies have demonstrated the effectiveness of advance organizers for teaching students without disabilities. More recently, studies have demonstrated the effectiveness of advance organizers for teaching students with disabilities and have contributed to the refinement of how advance organizers are used. Findings from these more recent studies indicate:

▶ Using an outline/overview of reading assignments to preteach important facts and concepts to students with learning disabilities is more effective than simply introducing the topics and encouraging students to discuss the topics and relate them to personal experiences (Darch & Gersten, 1986);

TABLE 4.1

Sample Verbal Advance Organizers

Yesterday, we learned how to multiply counting cups and counting bears. Who can tell me how to find the answer to 7 × 9 using cups and bears? . . . Good remembering! Today, we are going to practice multiplication again, but we're going to use drawings instead of cups and bears. Who can think of some advantages of using pictures rather than cups and bears? . . . Those are good ideas. I expect you to pay close attention while I demonstrate how to use drawings to solve multiplication problems. After the demonstration, I'm going to give you a chance to show me that you can use drawings to solve similar problems. Then we'll play a game to practice what we've learned so far about multiplication.

Yesterday, we began our unit on conflict resolution. Who remembers the definition of conflict resolution? . . . That's correct, good remembering. Today, I'm going to tell you about one method for resolving conflicts. I'd like you to take notes. Then you're going to work in small groups to identify examples of how you might apply this method to real-life events. I know you are very creative thinkers, so I expect each group to come up with at least three examples. A spokesperson from each group will share the examples with the class. Remember to follow our class rules for working in small groups.

Today is going to be a great class. I've been looking forward to this all week. Now that we've finished writing our play and selecting characters, we can begin practicing our lines. Today, you can use your script. I want you to focus on reading with expression. Don't forget to follow along even when it's not your turn to speak. Why do you think this is important? . . . Right, so you know when it's your turn to speak again. Let's review some of the important vocabulary words that we included in our play. . . .

▶ Having students with learning disabilities identify and record information from advance organizers results in increased understanding of the lesson content (Lenz, Alley, & Schumaker, 1987);

▶ Graphic organizers promote learning and recall among students with disabilities in content subject areas (e.g., science, social studies) (Bergerud, Lovitt, & Horton, 1988; Griffin, Simmons, & Kameenui, 1991; Horton, Lovitt, & Bergerud, 1990; Kooy, Skok, & McLaughlin, 1992);

▶ Verbal organizers that include a review component are more effective than having students silently review headings and subheadings from note-taking guides (Hudson, 1996).

Thus, advance organizers promote success with the lesson content. They provide a meaningful context for learning, help students compensate for lack of prior knowledge, and benefit both high- and low-achieving students (Williams & Butterfield, 1992). Advance organizers are easy to implement in large or small group instruction, making them especially appropriate for students receiving their instruction in diverse educational settings (see Validation Box 4.1).

VALIDATION BOX
4.1

Advance Organizers

▶ Several meta-analyses have been conducted to investigate the effect of advance organizers on learning and retention. The first included 135 published and unpublished studies. The second included 99 published and unpublished studies, and the third included 29 published and unpublished studies. All 3 analyses revealed that advance organizers facilitate both learning and retention. For more information see: (Luiten, Ames, & Ackerman, 1980; Kozlow, 1978; Stone 1983).

▶ Two studies were conducted at Warwood Junior High in Wheeling, WV. The first study involved 30 students who were at least 1 year behind grade level in reading. The second study involved 90 students who were categorized as either above or below grade level in reading. Both studies revealed that advance organizers read aloud by teachers and followed with class discussion were more effective than organizers read aloud by teachers without discussion, organizers read silently by students with discussion, and organizers read silently by students without discussion. For more information see: (Rinehart, Barksdale-Ladd, & Welker, 1991; Rinehart & Welker, 1992).

▶ Seven studies involving students with disabilities in upper elementary (i.e., fifth grade) through high school indicate that advance organizers facilitate learning and recall of content subject areas including English, geography, history, math, science, and social studies. For more information see: (Bergerud, Lovitt, & Horton, 1988; Darch & Gersten, 1986; Griffin, Simmons, & Kameenui, 1991; Horton, Lovitt, Bergerud, 1990; Hudson, 1996; Kooy, Skok, & McLaughlin, 1992; Lenz, Alley, & Schumaker, 1987).

Describe and Demonstrate (modeling)

After delivering an advance organizer, teachers describe and demonstrate whatever they are teaching. Students with learning difficulties benefit from short demonstrations that are explicit, repetitive, and focused on the lesson objectives (Ysseldyke, Christenson, & Thurlow, 1987). Therefore, teachers create concise, well-organized, step-by-step explanations using language that the students understand. For example, when Ms. Lee demonstrates how to use tallies to determine the answer to addition problems she says, "I can draw tallies to solve this problem. I will use three steps. First, I look at the top number and draw that many tallies. Second, I look at the bottom number and draw that many tallies. Third, I count all the tallies together and write the answer in the answer space." Ms. Lee physically demonstrates the steps as she verbalizes each one. After describing and demonstrating a few more problems in this manner, Ms. Lee begins to involve the students in the demonstration process through prompts and questioning. She says, "OK, I'm going to solve this problem using tallies. First, I look at the top number and do what?" "Yes, I draw that many tallies. Then I look at the second number and do what? . . . Now, who remembers what I need to do to figure out the answer?" Thus, Ms. Lee begins to get the students actively involved in the learning process. Questioning is an excellent way to maintain student attention while simultaneously checking their understanding of the skill or concept being taught.

Step-by-step demonstrations along with verbal explanations are critical to the learning process. Consider learning a new dance. Is it easier to learn if someone describes the dance, demonstrates the dance, or describes *and* demonstrates the dance? Think about learning how to cook. Is it easier to learn if someone describes how to cook, demonstrates how to cook, or describes *and* demonstrates how to cook? How about learning to throw a football? How about learning to program a VCR? Classroom learning is no different. Explanations paired with physical step-by-step demonstrations work well when teaching discrete skills such as addition, telling time, counting money, hitting a softball, writing a sentence, looking up words in a dictionary, using a word processor. This approach works well when teaching material that has a clear *sequential* process.

When teaching concepts (e.g., fruit, discrimination, balance of governmental powers, sharing), different types of descriptions and demonstration processes are needed. First, the concept is defined and related attributes are described. Then, the concept is demonstrated through the use of examples and nonexamples. For instance, Ms. Lee might say, "I've got a dictionary here and I just looked up the word *fruit*. It says that a fruit contains seeds and is a product of a plant or a tree. It also says that a fruit is frequently used as food." Then Ms. Lee holds up a bag and says, "I've got some examples of fruit in this bag. I'm going to pick one out and hold it up so everyone can see. If you know what the name of the fruit is, raise your hand and I'll call on someone to say the name aloud. . . . OK, let's look at another fruit. When I pull this fruit out of the bag, everyone say the name together. . . . Now, I'm going to show you something that's food, but it's not a fruit because it doesn't come from a plant or tree and it doesn't have seeds. . . ." After continuing to show the students examples of fruit and examples of non-fruit, Ms. Lee gets the students involved in learning the concept by asking them to repeat the definition of fruit and getting them to provide additional examples of fruit and examples of non-fruit.

In addition to describing and demonstrating step-by-step procedures for completing academic tasks and describing and demonstrating concepts through the use of examples and nonexamples, teachers also demonstrate metacognitive and cognitive processes involved in learning. Many students have difficulty in school because they don't know what they should be thinking when completing their assignments. Teacher "think alouds" are very helpful for demonstrating effective ways of thinking. During "think alouds," teachers say out loud what the students should be thinking when they attempt to complete whatever task they're being taught. In other words, the teacher demonstrates or role-plays the thinking that accompanies the physical action. Mr. Smith just finished describing and demonstrating the parts of a business letter and now he's going to demonstrate the thinking process that students can use when trying to write a business letter. Mr. Smith says aloud, "Let's see, first I've got to open Microsoft[1] Word. So, how do I do that? Oh yes, I click on the program icon. OK, so far, so good. Now, that the program is up and ready, I need to remember the parts to a business letter. I've got to type in today's date . . . oh, and now I've got to type in the name and address of the person I'm sending the letter to . . . so let me do that. OK, I'd better check to be sure I've spelled the name correctly and that I typed the right address. It looks good, so now I'm ready for the salutation . . . *Dear Mr. Greenjeans* . . . oh, and I have to remember the colon. OK, now I'm ready to start the main part of the letter. . . . *It is with* . . . oops, I don't know how to spell *pleasure*, so I can either look it up in a dictionary or I can try to get close and then use the spell-checker. " Mr. Smith continues to say aloud what he would actually be thinking. He tries to sound authentic, as if he were thinking rather than talking aloud. Teacher "think alouds" help students activate their own thinking (see Validation Box 4.2).

Provide Guided Practice

After the describe-and-demonstrate portion of the lesson, guided practice is provided. Students now have the opportunity to practice what was demonstrated, with teacher support still available. Initial success when attempting new tasks is very important for motivation. Students who experience failure when trying something new are more likely to give up than students who experience success. Thus, it is quite appropriate for teachers to look for ways to ensure student success during initial practice attempts. Guided practice typically begins with a significant amount of teacher support. Let's consider the previously discussed example of Mr. Smith teaching students how to write a business letter using a word processor. To provide guided practice, Mr. Smith says, "OK, what is the first thing we do when we want to write a business letter? . . . Right, and what do we do next? . . . Right, and what can

[1]Microsoft is a registered trademark of Microsoft Corporation.

VALIDATION BOX

4.2

Demonstration

▶ In a review of literature related to applied behavior analysis interventions, six studies involving the effects of demonstration and modeling procedures were identified. Students with learning disabilities who had difficulties with arithmetic and letter/numeral reversals were the participants in these studies. Demonstration and modeling procedures coupled with feedback were effective for reducing letter and numeral reversals. For more information see: (Rose, Koorland, & Epstein, 1982).

▶ In 3 studies, demonstration and modeling were used to teach 17 students with learning disabilities (Grade 5 to Grade 9) math computation skills. Demonstration and modeling increased student accuracy and resulted in efficient learning. Moreover, students were able to generalize their learning to similar, uninstructed problem types. For more information see: (Rivera & Smith, 1987).

we do if we want to use a word that we can't spell?" Questioning is an excellent technique to use during guided practice. The questions lead the students through the task. A variety of techniques are used during guided practice. For example, teachers use prompts, partial answers, hints, and feedback with additional opportunities to model the new learning. Guided practice sometimes involves students working together to help one another with the new learning. Additionally, self-correcting materials (i.e., materials that provide immediate feedback to students with regard to their accuracy) and computer software with feedback components provide guided practice opportunities to students. It is, however, important that students receive feedback beyond simply knowing whether they got something correct or not. So, if self-correcting materials are used, teachers still need to be available to provide further explanation and support.

When teaching concepts that don't have a distinct sequence, guided practice takes a different form. In such cases, guided practice involves periodic pauses to provide students with opportunities to process and integrate what they're learning (Hudson, 1997). If, for example, the lesson involves presenting information about mammals in North America, the teacher might use overhead transparencies to list important information related to the topic. The students copy the information and listen as the teacher discusses each item on the list. Periodically, throughout the lecture (after natural chunks of information have been presented), the teacher stops and asks questions related to the content just covered. These periodic pauses are designed to give students opportunities to process, understand, and use their new learning. Teacher feedback and clarification is provided as needed to ensure that students understand the important content.

Thus, guided practice is an interactive process involving the teacher and students. Guided practice is designed to keep students actively involved with new content while simultaneously ensuring their success. As students become more proficient with the new content, teachers decrease the amount of support provided. The number of leading questions, prompts, and cues decrease as students become more competent. The teacher's goal is to provide enough support to promote student understanding while challenging students to develop their own abilities. Ultimately, new learning benefits students when they can take and use what they've learned without teacher assistance. So, guided practice gradually moves students away from teacher dependency toward self-dependency (see Validation Box 4.3).

Provide Independent Practice

Once students demonstrate a high level of understanding during guided practice, opportunities for independent practice are provided. Independent practice serves four important functions. First, it gives students opportunities to demonstrate that they understand what has been taught. Second, it gives students opportunities to become more proficient (i.e., faster and more accurate) with the newly learned content or skills. Third, it provides a means for teachers to evaluate the effectiveness of their teaching. Finally, it helps students retain what they've learned. Thus, independent practice is critical to the learning process. The goals for success during independent practice should be set high. Accuracy levels on independent work should range from 90 to 100 percent (Christenson, Ysseldyke, & Thurlow, 1989; Rosenshine, 1983). Once students achieve high levels of accuracy, the goals for independent practice may expand to include an emphasis on fluency or speed. Many skills that students learn in school need to be performed with automaticity to be beneficial in their lives (e.g., math facts, reading, money skills, keyboarding). Thus, both accuracy and automaticity are important measures for independent work.

Independent-practice tasks frequently occur in the form of seat work. To be effective, the seat-work task should directly relate to the lesson objective and require responses similar to those that were used during the describe-and-demonstrate and guided-practice phases of instruction (Meese, 1994). For example, if the demonstration and guided practice in a math lesson involves teaching the concept of multiplication using paper plates to represent groups and manipulative devices to

VALIDATION BOX

4.3

Guided Practice

Teacher-guided practice was more effective than individual study time in an investigation involving 18 middle-school students with mild to moderate disabilities. The students were taught social studies content via lecture format. Periodic pauses occurred throughout the lectures to promote practice with the content. Students who practiced via teacher questioning and feedback performed significantly better on unit and maintenance tests than students who practiced via individual silent reviews of the content. For more information see: (Hudson, 1997).

represent objects in the group, then the independent practice phase of the lesson should involve students using paper plates and manipulative devices to solve the same type of multiplication problems. The independent practice should match (except with different problems) what was done earlier in the lesson. Independent seat work is assigned to reinforce the lesson content, not to keep students occupied.

Although independent practice frequently involves completing written work, other options are available. For example, teachers and paraeducators can alternate working with students to provide opportunities for verbal independent practice. Moreover, learning centers with hands-on activities and computer-assisted practice provide alternatives to written practice. Varying the types of independent practice helps maintain student interest. Again, the important thing to remember regardless of which format independent practice takes, is to match the practice to the demonstration and guided-practice phases of the lesson.

Provide Post-Organizer

Post-organizers are used to bring closure to a lesson. Post-organizers provide a signal to students that a transition is about to occur (e.g., transition to new lesson, transition to new class, transition home). Typical components included in post-organizers are reviews related to the content, statements about what was accomplished during the lesson, reminders related to the importance of the newly learned material, feedback regarding student performance during the lesson, and previews of upcoming lessons. The post-organizer may also include a review of homework assignments related to the lesson and discussion to foster generalization of the content learned. Teachers select post-organizer components that are most appropriate for the lesson taught. Sometimes post-organizers are delivered after guided practice and before independent practice. Teachers select the sequence that will meet the needs of the students and facilitate smooth transitions.

The Explicit Instruction Model represents an organized way to orchestrate learning opportunities and is particularly beneficial for students with learning challenges. The approach used in this model is systematic and teacher directed with high levels of student involvement in the learning process. Clear, organized lessons promote student learning and increase the likelihood of academic success. The gradual transition from teacher directedness to student independence also promotes academic success and helps students recognize their capabilities. Unfortunately, students with learning challenges frequently have extensive histories of failure in school and consequently develop patterns of learned helplessness. Thus, it is very important to promote feelings of success and independence and to reduce feelings of dependence. Explicit instruction represents a structured approach to teaching, but simultaneously provides teachers with flexibility to make decisions based on the varying needs of students (e.g., whether to use graphic organizers, how many demonstrations to provide, what format to use for guided and independent practice, content of the post-organizer). Thus, the model is particularly relevant for teaching diverse groups of students (see Validation Box 4.4 on p. 148).

VALIDATION BOX

4.4

Explicit Instruction

In a study involving 59 fourth- and fifth-grade students with learning disabilities, academic achievement and classroom ecobehavioral processes were measured over a 5-month period. The Metropolitan Achievement Test was used to measure student achievement; class observations and teacher interviews were conducted to determine the types of teaching practices the teachers used. Results of this study revealed that students who made high-achievement gains received direct (explicit) instruction that was fast-paced with complex, immediate, and highly structured feedback. Students with low-achievement gains received instruction that was characterized by lecture and discussion with only verbal or social forms of feedback such as a pat on the back. The high-achieving students also had more opportunities to respond during instruction than the low-achieving students. For more information see: (Greenwood, Arreaga-Mayer, & Carta, 1994).

The Direct Instruction Model

The Direct Instruction Model emerged from the work of Siegfried Engelmann and his colleagues in the mid 1960s. Direct Instruction is guided by two major rules: *(a)* teach more in less time, and *(b)* control the details of what happens (Engelmann, Becker, Carnine, & Gersten, 1988). The underlying assumptions of the model are "*(a)* all children can be taught; *(b)* the learning of basic skills and their application in higher-order skills is essential to intelligent behavior and should be the main focus of a compensatory education program; *(c)* the disadvantaged must be taught at a faster rate than typically occurs if they are to catch up with their middle-class peers" (Engelmann, Becker, Carnine, & Gersten, 1988, p. 303). Specifically, the model emphasizes the importance of three teaching components: instructional design, presentation techniques, and instructional organization. Each of these is considered essential for successful teaching and learning. A well-designed program with a good teacher won't result in high levels of student achievement if the instructional time is too limited. Moreover, a well-designed program with adequate instructional time won't result in high student achievement if the teacher is unskilled. Finally, a skilled teacher with adequate time won't produce optimum results if the curricular materials are poorly designed (Stein, Silbert, & Carnine, 1997). Thus, instructional design, presentation techniques, and instructional organization must all receive careful attention.

Instructional Design

The Direct Instruction Model uses carefully designed curricular materials that specify long- and short-term objectives and provide systems for monitoring student progress toward the objectives. The content and skills presented in the Direct Instruction materials are sequenced carefully. Necessary preskills are taught first, easy skills are taught before more difficult skills, and skills or pieces of information that are likely to be confused are not introduced consecutively. Explicit and generalizable strategies that students can apply to a broad set of examples are directly taught. Teacher scripts are provided for the lessons. These scripts promote clear explanations and allow teachers to focus on the students rather than thinking about what comes next in the lesson. The scripts present numerous examples that relate to the new content being taught. Also included are examples that relate to previously learned material. Thus, students learn to discriminate between the two. Direct Instruction programs provide extensive practice and review to promote skill retention (Stein, Silbert, & Carnine, 1997; Tarver, 1999). Direct Instruction commercial materials are available for instruction in reading, writing, language, spelling, mathematics, and world facts (see Table 4.2)

TABLE 4.2

Commercial Direct Instruction Programs (Adapted from Research on Direct Instruction: 25 Years Beyond DISTAR [pp. 113–119] by G. L. Adams and S. Engelmann, 1996, Seattle, WA: Educational Achievement Systems. Copyright 1996 by Educational Achievement Systems. Adapted with permission.)

Program	Placement Level	Brief Content Summary
Reading Mastery I	Students placed in K or Grade 1	Decoding; comprehension (words, sentences, stories)
Reading Mastery II	Students who completed Reading I	Strategies for decoding and comprehension; basic reasoning skills
Reading Mastery: Fast Cycle	High-performing K or Grade-1 students	Skills covered in Reading I and II covered more rapidly
Reading Mastery III	Students who read at 3rd-grade level	Apply rules in variety of contexts, interpret maps, graphs, and timelines; complex sentence forms
Reading Mastery IV	Students who read at 4th-grade level	Skills for reading content-area textbooks; problem solving, research projects, many stories about science
Reading Mastery V	Students who read at 5th-grade level	Classical literature; analyze character, setting, plots, themes; deduce meanings from context; daily writing
Reading Mastery VI	Students who read at 6th-grade level	Classical literature and poetry; interpret figurative language, identify contradictions; write stories and poems
Corrective Reading: Decoding	Grades 3 to 12 remedial education	Word attack, decoding strategies, skill application (to textbook-type materials)
Corrective Reading: Comprehension	Grades 4 to 12 remedial education	Thinking basics, comprehension skills, concept applications

(*continued*)

TABLE 4.2

Commercial Direct Instruction Programs (*continued*)

Program	Placement Level	Brief Content Summary
Reading and Writing: Level A	Students in K or grade 1	Higher-order thinking skills; create endings to stories; group writing projects; act out plays
Reasoning and Writing: Level B	Students who complete Level A or pass placement test	Story grammar; thinking skills needed to comprehend different content areas; write simple stories
Reasoning and Writing: Level C	Students who complete Level B or pass placement test	Emphasize clear communication; write clear, unambiguous passages; grammar and mechanics
Reasoning and Writing: Level D	Students who complete Level C or pass placement test	Identify problems and propaganda in advertising; read, analyze, and objectively summarize articles
Reasoning and Writing: Level E	Students who complete Level D or pass placement test	Continue to build logical analysis skills; reasoning skills using cause and effect; take notes and reconstruct passages
Reasoning and Writing: Level F	Students who complete Level E or pass placement test	Expands on grammar, retelling, logical analysis, and summarizing; new formats for handling different types of writing
DISTAR Language I	Lower performing students in K to Grade 1, including ESL students	Understanding language of classroom instruction; practice using complete sentences, answering questions, and following verbal directions
DISTAR Language II	Average K students or students who complete DISTAR I	Word and sentence skills; thinking skills; questioning and reasoning skills
Cursive Writing Program	Grades 3 to 4	Structured approach to cursive writing; form letters, create words, write sentences, improve speed/accuracy
Expressive Writing 1	Grades 4 to 6 and secondary students with special needs	Sentence and paragraph writing; editing skills
Expressive Writing 2	Grades 4 to 6 and secondary students with special needs	More sophisticated conversational writing (compound sentences, dependent clauses, direct quotations)
Spelling Mastery	Grades 1 to 6	Progress from sound-symbol principles and general strategies to advanced morphemic guidelines
Corrective Spelling through Morphographs	Grades 4 to Adult	Analytic techniques; predictable highly generalizable rules; 500 morphographs and 12,000 words are learned
Connecting Math Concepts: Level A	Grade 1	Counting; more or less; addition and subtraction; place value, estimation, money, measurement

TABLE 4.2

Commercial Direct Instruction Programs (*continued*)

Program	Placement Level	Brief Content Summary
Connecting Math Concepts: Level B	Students who complete Level A or pass placement test	Number families for addition and subtraction; translating story problems; measurement, time, money, geometry, estimation, mental arithmetic
Connecting Math Concepts: Level C	Students who complete Level B or pass placement test	Mapping techniques for relating problem solving to real life; measurement, money, time
Connecting Math Concepts: Level D	Students who complete Level C or pass placement test	Multiplication and division; fractions, mixed numbers, and decimals; extensive problem solving
Connecting Math Concepts: Level E	Students who complete Level D or pass placement test	Relationship between fractions, decimals, percents, and the whole-number system; long division; fraction operations
Connecting Math Concepts: Level F	Students who complete Level E or pass placement test	Property or multiplication statements, algebra, probability, interpret pie graphs, geometry
DISTAR Arithmetic I	Students in K or low-performing students	Counting strategies for analyzing and solving addition, subtraction, and algebra addition problems
DISTAR Arithmetic II	Students who complete DISTAR I or pass placement test	Multiplication, operations with fractions; and problems in columns; broaden knowledge of basic facts
Corrective Mathematics	Grades 4 to 12	Addition, subtraction, multiplication, division; number manipulation, story problems, and application
Mathematics Modules	Grades 4 to Adult	Adding, subtracting, multiplying, and dividing fractions, decimals, percentages; ratios, and equations
Your World of Facts I and II	Grades 3 to 6	Key facts and relationships related to world (geography, plants, climate, animals, human body, machines)

These Direct Instruction programs are available through Science Research Associates (SRA), telephone: 800 843-8855.

Presentation Techniques

The presentation techniques used in Direct Instruction lessons are designed to maintain a high level of student attention while simultaneously allowing teachers to monitor student performance. Included among these techniques are unison responding with signals, rapid pacing, and correction techniques.

Unison Responding with Signals

One of the most distinctive features of the presentation techniques is unison responding to teacher questions. The teacher uses hand signals (e.g., finger snap, hand drop, clap, touching the board or presentation materials) to cue students to make a unison response. Typically, the teacher gives directions or asks a question, provides a thinking pause, and then cues the response. Unison responding gives all students an opportunity to participate. Using a signal to cue the response gives slower students in the group extra time (i.e., 5 to 10 seconds) to think about the answer. Without this cue, quicker students tend to dominate lesson participation (Stein, Silbert, & Carnine, 1997). Another advantage of using a signal for unison responding is when students say the answer together on cue, it is more intelligible than each student responding at slightly different times. Thus, the students hear the correct response as they say it and learning is reinforced.

Rapid Pacing

The overall pacing of Direct Instruction lessons is relatively quick. The idea is to present numerous examples in rapid succession so students can see how the examples are similar to and different from one another. If the presentation of examples is too slow, students may forget the earlier examples and therefore won't be able to compare them to later examples. This interferes with learning the concept being taught (Adams & Engelmann, 1996).

Correction Techniques

Another important component of the presentation techniques used in Direct Instruction is monitoring and correcting student errors. Clearly, having students respond individually allows teachers to monitor student understanding. Monitoring can also occur, however, with unison responding. It is relatively easy to hear a response that differs from the group, especially if students who need more support are seated near the front of the class. When error responses occur, a variety of correction procedures are used depending on the instructional task. Stein, Silbert, and Carnine (1997) outline three distinct correction procedures for motor, labeling, and strategy tasks.

If the student error results from a motor deficit (e.g., writing a symbol), the teacher models the task, leads students until they can respond accurately, and then tests them (i.e., model-lead-test). This correction technique is used repeatedly until the student responds correctly several times in a row. The repetition helps promote retention.

If the student error involves an inability to label (e.g., saying a word that correctly labels an object or symbol), a slightly different correction procedure is used (i.e., model-alternating pattern-delayed test). First, the teacher models the correct label (e.g., "This is 9"). Second, the teacher provides alternating pattern practice. In other words, the teacher has the student practice labeling whatever was initially missed along with other items (e.g., if 9 was initially missed, practice might include labeling numbers in the sequence of 9, 4, 9, 1, 3, 9, 2, 4, 3, 9). The third part of this correction procedure involves a delayed test. For example, at the end of the lesson, the teacher again asks the student to label whatever was missed (e.g., the teacher points to 9 and asks, "What is this number?").

If the student error occurs during strategy-related tasks (e.g., tasks that involve a series of sequential steps), a two-step correction procedure occurs. First, the teacher corrects the specific error either through modeling or prompting the student with questions. Second, the teacher returns to the beginning of the sequential steps and presents the entire process again. Going back to the beginning of the steps and starting over helps prevent students from losing track of how all the steps are integrated and necessary to complete the task.

These correction procedures are designed to give immediate feedback that will enhance student learning. They should be used in a positive, supportive manner so students feel good about ultimately "getting it right." Correction procedures accompanied by negative voice tone or facial expressions reduce the likelihood that students will continue to take risks when learning new or challenging material.

Instructional Organization

In addition to instructional design and presentation techniques, the Direct Instruction Model also emphasizes the importance of instructional organization. This involves the effective use of classroom and school resources with a special emphasis on the use of time. Teachers must first decide which Direct Instruction programs will be used to teach their students.

Once the materials have been selected and obtained, teachers conduct initial assessments (provided with the programs) to help make decisions related to the grouping of students for instruction. In some instances, whole-class grouping is possible. If, however, there is a wide variance in student abilities within the class, several smaller groups may be needed, in which case the teacher must decide how to best juggle instructional time to ensure that all groups receive quality instruction. The arrangements for providing the instruction vary depending on whether students are in elementary (all day in one class) or secondary schools (limited time for each class). The personnel available to teach (coteaching, paraeducators) also affects the organization of instruction. The overall goal is to organize the instruction in ways that allow students to progress through the programs at an optimal rate, demonstrating mastery as they go (see Validation Box 4.5 on p. 154).

Direct Instruction and Videodisc Technology

Extensive research exists which documents the effectiveness of the Direct Instruction Model. Since the 1960s, researchers at the University of Oregon have provided leadership in the development and refinement of Direct Instruction methodology. Over the past decade, videodisc programs have emerged to expand the application

┌─────────────────┐
VALIDATION BOX
4.5
└─────────────────┘

Direct Instruction

▶ Project Follow Through involved over 10,000 students in 180 communities and was designed to evaluate 9 different models for educating children from low-income families. Students involved in the Direct Instruction Model outperformed those in the other 8 models on the 3 areas measured in the study: basic skills, cognitive, and affective achievement. For more information see the original evaluation report (Stebbins, St. Pierre, Proper, Anderson, & Cerva, 1977) or subsequent analyses of the data (Bereiter & Kurland, 1981–1982; House, Glass, & McLean, 1978). These and other Project Follow Through studies including positive longitudinal data are summarized in Adams & Engelmann (1996) and the Winter 1996 issue of *Effective School Practices, 15*(1).

▶ A total of 34 research studies were included in a meta-analysis of Direct Instruction. An overall effect size of 0.97 was calculated based on the effect size of each individual variable compared in all the studies. An overall effect size of 0.87 was calculated based on average effect size per study. For more information see: (Adams & Engelmann, 1996).

▶ These findings were consistent with an earlier meta-analysis in which 25 studies revealed an average effect size of 0.84. In this analysis none of the 25 studies showed results favoring the comparison groups, and 53 percent of the outcomes significantly favored Direct Instruction. For more information see: (White, 1988).

Effect sizes approaching the range of 0.40 or greater are considered significant (Forness, Kavale, Blum, & Lloyd, 1997) and therefore effective.

of the Direct Instruction Model. Specifically, the use of videodisc technology that incorporates the instructional design features used in Direct Instruction has been explored (Gersten & Kelly, 1992; Hofmeister, Engelmann, & Carnine, 1989; Kelly, Carnine, Gersten, & Grossen, 1986). Videodisc technology involves the use of a videodisc player, television monitor, and videodiscs (8- or 12-inch formats) that contain full-motion video, sound, text, and/or still images. The technology is similar to videotapes, with a couple of important distinctions. First, videodiscs can store significantly more content than videotapes. Second, videodisc technology provides easy access to any frame on the disc at any time during the lesson. Pausing and rewinding or fast forwarding are not required. Instead, the teacher uses a standard remote or bar code scanner to quickly and easily access specific frames on the disc in any desired order. The integration of videodisc technology and Direct Instruction design variables has resulted in positive student outcomes. Consequently, a variety of videodisc programs have been developed (see Table 4.3 and Validation Box 4.6).

Doug Carnine and his colleagues at the University of Oregon Center to Improve the Tools of Educators have studied ways to teach higher-order thinking

Direct Instruction and Videodisc Technology

Direct Instruction videodisc fraction instruction was compared to traditional basal fraction instruction in a study involving 34 ninth-, tenth-, and eleventh-grade low-achieving students including 17 with identified learning disabilities. The Direct Instruction videodisc instruction was significantly more effective than the basal instruction. Moreover, the videodisc instruction was equally effective for students with learning disabilities and those who were low achieving. For more information see: (Kelly, Gersten, & Carnine, 1990).

TABLE 4.3

Direct Instruction Videodisc Programs (Adapted from Research on Direct Instruction: 25 Years Beyond DISTAR [pp. 120–121] by G. L. Adams and S. Engelmann, 1996, Seattle, WA: Educational Achievement Systems. Copyright 1996 by Educational Achievement Systems. Adapted with permission.)

Program	Placement Level	Brief Content Summary
Mastering Fractions	Grade 4 to Adult	Addition, subtraction, multiplication of fractions
Mastering Decimals and Percents	Grade 5 to Adult	Reading and writing decimals; converting decimals, percents, whole numbers; word problems
Mastering Ratios and Word Problem Strategies	Grade 5 to Adult	Estimating ratio numbers, rewriting equations, unit conversions; word problems
Mastering Equations, Roots, and Exponents: Signed Numbers to Operations	Grade 7 to Adult	Signed number operations; combining like terms; solving equations using exponents; square roots; word problems
Mastering Informal Geometry	Grade 7 to Adult	Perimeter and circumference; area; volume; line and angle relationships; graphic figures
Problem Solving with Addition and Subtraction	Grade 3 to Adult	Addition with carrying; subtraction with borrowing; word problems
Problem Solving with Multiplication and Division	Grade 4 to Adult	Column multiplication; long division; problem-solving strategies for word problems
Problem Solving with Tables, Graphs, and Statistics	Grade 5 to Adult	Data interpretation and organization; real-world applications
Understanding Chemistry and Energy	Grade 7 to Adult	Atomic and molecular structure; common forms of energy; organic compounds; energy of activation and catalysts
Earth Science	Grade 5 to Adult	Phases of matter; density and mass; facts about the earth; forces of gravity

These videodisc programs are available from BFA Educational Media, 2349 Chaffee Drive, St. Louis, MO 63146, telephone: 800 221-1274.

(e.g., reasoning, analysis, problem solving) to students with and without learning difficulties (Carnine, 1989, 1990, 1991; Collins, Carnine, & Gersten, 1987; Grossen & Carnine, 1990). Findings from investigations related to higher-order skills indicate that specific instruction in relevant facts and concepts is needed before learning cognitively complex skills. Findings also indicate that clear models of successful solutions, a range of examples, and specific corrective feedback are needed when teaching higher-order skills (i.e., skills with open-ended processes in which a range of responses is appropriate) (Gersten, Carnine, & Woodward, 1987). A curriculum called the BIG Accommodations Program incorporates these features and helps students understand the big ideas, principles, and/or concepts that underlie subject-area content and thus enhance students' higher-order thinking skills (Carnine, 1994; Carnine, Crawford, Harniss, & Hollenbeck, 1995; Carnine & Kameenui, 1992). The curriculum consists of textbook and videodisc units of study.

Thus, although the Direct Instruction Model has been around for some time, new applications and improvements continue to emerge. The model has been refined and expanded to better meet the needs of today's students. Direct Instruction programs may be used with all students from whom high levels of academic achievement are expected and desired (Tarver, 1999). The repetition, reinforcement, careful sequencing of skills, and correction procedures are helpful for all students, but are critical for students with disabilities. This instructional model sets students up for success and ensures mastery-level learning prior to moving on to new content.

The Strategy Instruction Model

Over the past 20 years, much work has been done related to the development of cognitive strategies for students with learning difficulties. The most comprehensive model is the Strategy Instruction Model (SIM) developed through the work of Donald Deshler, Jean Schumaker, and their colleagues at the University of Kansas Center for Research on Learning. In 1978, the Center for Research on Learning was originally funded as an Institute for Research on Learning Disabilities through the Office of Special Education Programs. Since that time, more than $20 million has been secured to develop and validate the various components of the Strategy Instruction Model, create and disseminate instructional materials, provide teacher training, and infuse the model into education programs (Deshler, Ellis, & Lenz, 1996; Lenz, Ellis, & Scanlon, 1996).

The Learning Strategy Curriculum

The importance of teaching students *how* to learn and perform is emphasized in the Learning Strategy Curriculum. This is one of several curricula that compose the Strategy Instruction Model. A primary goal of the Learning Strategy Curriculum is to help students become independent learners. The curriculum consists of three strands: Acquisition Strand, Storage Strand, and Demonstration and Expression of Competence Strand. The Acquisition Strand consists of learning strategies that help students acquire or take in new information from written text. The Storage Strand consists of learning strategies that help students organize, store, and retrieve newly learned information; and the Expression and Demonstration of Competence Strand consists of learning strategies that help students complete assignments, take tests, and express themselves in writing (see Table 4.4). Each of the strategies in these three strands are taught using the same eight-stage instructional sequence.

The Eight-Stage Instructional Sequence

The eight-stage instructional sequence in the Strategy Instruction Model is designed to promote acquisition and generalization of the strategy being taught (see Fig. 4.1 on p. 158). The stages are identified to denote different emphases in the instructional process (Deshler, Ellis, & Lenz, 1996).

TABLE 4.4

Strategy Instruction Model: Learning Strategies Curriculum

Acquisition Strand	Storage Strand	Demonstration and Expression of Competence Strand
Word Identification (decoding unknown words)	First-Letter Mnemonic (remembering lists of important information)	Assignment Completion (completing and turning in assignments on time)
Visual Imagery (reading comprehension)	Paired Associates (remembering pairs of information)	Test Taking (taking tests effectively and efficiently)
Self-questioning (reading comprehension)	Vocabulary (remembering new vocabulary words)	Fundamentals in the Sentence-Writing Strategy (writing four types of simple sentences)
		Proficiency in the Sentence-Writing Strategy (writing simple, compound, complex, and compound-complex sentences)
Paraphrasing (reading comprehension)		Paragraph Writing (writing organized paragraphs)
		Error Monitoring (correcting errors in written work)
		InSPECT: A Strategy for Detecting and Correcting Spelling Errors (using a computerized spell checker or hand-held spelling device)

Training is required to obtain these materials. To obtain information about this training and to identify trainers in your area, contact The University of Kansas Center for Research on Learning; Website: www.ku-crl.org; telephone: (785) 864-4780; fax: (785) 864-5728.

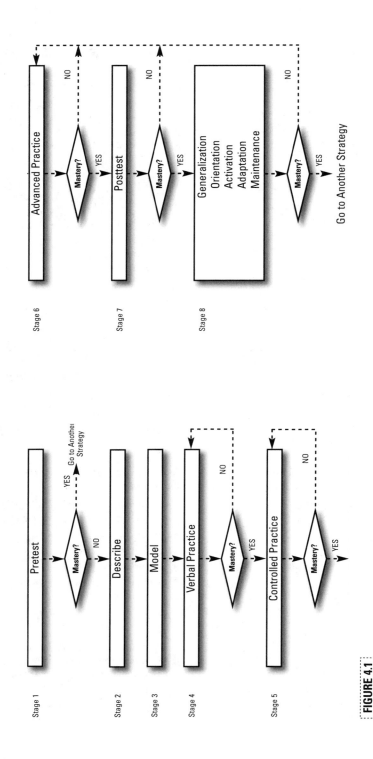

FIGURE 4.1

Eight Instructional Stages in the Learning Strategies Curriculum. (From *The Learning Strategy Curriculum: The Paraphrasing Strategy* [p. 4] by J. B. Schumaker, P. H. Denton, and D. D. Deshler, 1984, Lawrence, KS: University of Kansas, Institute for Research in Learning Disabilities, Copyright 1984 by J. B. Schumaker, P. H. Denton, and D. D. Deshler. Reprinted with permission. *Note:* This figure was taken from a book that is available through certified Strategic Instruction Model Trainers who conduct professional development workshops across the nation. To obtain information about this training and to identify trainers in your area, contact The University of Kansas Center for Research on Learning at http://www.ku-crl.org or (785) 864-4780.)

Stage I: Pretest and Make Commitments   The purpose of the Pretest Stage is to determine the students' current abilities related to the strategy and to establish the students' willingness to learn the strategy. An appropriate pretest is administered to determine whether the students will benefit from learning a particular strategy. Students' prerequisite skills also are considered at this time. Next, the pretest is evaluated and the outcomes are shared with each student. Discussions are used to help students realize the benefits of learning the strategy. Specifically, attempts are made to connect the strategy to real-world setting demands (e.g., taking tests, understanding written text, writing paragraphs). Finally, a commitment is obtained from the student to learn the strategy and the teacher expresses a commitment to help the students learn the strategy.

Stage 2: Describe   The purpose of the Describe Stage is to provide students with a detailed description of the strategy. Specifically, the students are introduced to the step-by-step process used in the strategy. Each strategy in the curriculum consists of several steps that are cued through the use of a mnemonic device. For example, in the Paraphrasing Strategy (Schumaker, Denton, & Deshler, 1984) students are cued to *R*ead a paragraph, *A*sk themselves what the main idea and details were, and *P*ut the main idea and details in their own words (RAP). During the Describe Stage, the teacher discusses each step and attempts to "paint a picture" for the students that illustrates what the new strategy is about. An emphasis is placed on self-regulation and helping students realize how the strategy will help improve their learning and performing. Goals are established related to learning the strategy and progressing through the eight stages.

Stage 3: Model   The purpose of the Model Stage is to demonstrate the cognitive thinking involved in progressing through the strategy steps, and to demonstrate the physical action used in the strategy. Teacher "think alouds" are used to demonstrate the cognitive aspect of the strategy. In other words, the teacher says aloud what the students should be thinking when they use the strategy steps. The teacher models the covert thinking and the overt action simultaneously. After the initial teacher model, students are prompted to gradually get involved in using the covert and overt processes of the strategy. Getting the students involved in the modeling process allows the teacher to check the students' initial understandings of the strategy. Moreover, teachers can elaborate on student understanding and clarify any points of confusion. This stage of the strategy instruction is very important as it provides the foundation for future success with the strategy.

Stage 4: Verbal Practice   The purpose of the Verbal Practice Stage is to promote students' comprehension and retention of strategy procedures. There are two phases of instruction during stage 4: verbal elaboration and rehearsal of the strategy steps. During verbal elaboration, students are asked to describe the purpose of the strategy, how the strategy will help them, and the process involved in using the strategy. The students should be able to describe each step in the strategy and tell why it's important. This discussion ensures that students understand the "big picture" with regard to the strategy and its use. During the rehearsal phase, students memorize the steps of the strategy (i.e., the steps of the mnemonic device). Students must be able to say the steps of the strategy quickly with 100 percent accuracy. Fluency with the strategy steps is important so that when students begin to use the strategy, they don't get bogged down trying to remember the steps. Instead, they can focus on the application of the strategy.

A procedure called "rapid-fire rehearsal" frequently is used to help students with the rote memorization of strategy steps. The teacher points to a student or tosses a beanbag to the student and the student says the first step in the strategy (e.g., R—Read a paragraph). Then the teacher points to or tosses the beanbag to another student who then says the second step in the strategy (e.g., A—Ask myself, "What were the main idea and details in the paragraph?"). Then the teacher points to or tosses the beanbag to another student who says the next step in the strategy (e.g., P—Put the main idea and details in my own words). Initially, the strategy steps are listed on the board, posted in the room, or written on cue cards on the students' desks. Students are encouraged to look at the steps, as needed. As the students become more proficient, these visual cues are removed and students rely totally on memory to say the steps. The rapid-fire rehearsal gradually gets faster as students become more fluent. To add variety to the Verbal Practice Stage, instructional games are played to supplement rapid-fire rehearsal. Students progress to Stage 5 when they can discuss the strategy process and accurately name all the strategy steps.

Stage 5: Controlled Practice and Feedback   The purpose of the Controlled Practice Stage is to provide students with opportunities to practice the strategy with materials or assignments that lack some of the higher-level demands found in grade-level materials and assignments. Thus, students focus on the procedural techniques of the strategy and gain confidence and fluency in applying the various steps. As students become fluent in applying the strategy steps, the complexity of the practice materials increases. Teacher feedback to students is very important during Controlled Practice. This involves telling students what they are doing well and then providing corrective feedback related to areas with which they are experiencing difficulty. The feedback is specific to student performance. Additional descriptions and demonstrations are helpful and prepare students for improved performance in the future. Criteria for mastery in controlled practice vary from one strategy to another, but once mastery is achieved the student progresses to more advanced practice.

Stage 6: Advanced Practice and Feedback   The purpose of the Advanced Practice Stage is to provide opportunities for students to apply the strategy to grade-level materials or assignments (e.g., seventh-grade students use the strategy while reading an assigned chapter in their seventh-grade geography textbook). A variety of grade-appropriate materials and/or assignments may be used. It is helpful to provide practice opportunities with challenging materials and assignments that resemble real assignments the students are expected to complete. Thus, the practice is

Learning Strategy Instruction prepares students with learning difficulties to succeed within the general education curriculum.

meaningful and directly relates to students' needs. During this stage, the emphasis shifts from learning how to perform the strategy to applying the strategy to meet real-world, grade-level demands. Students learn when to use the strategy and how to adapt the strategy to meet the expectations in the criterion environment. Support, however, is still provided to the students. Although teacher feedback is provided, students are now encouraged to evaluate their own performance as well. As with Controlled Practice, criteria for mastery in Advanced Practice varies from one strategy to another. When mastery is achieved students progress to stage 7.

Stage 7: Posttest and Commitment to Generalize   The purpose of the Posttest and Commitment Stage is to confirm that the student has mastered the strategy and to establish the student's willingness to use the strategy in novel situations. During this stage, a posttest is administered and scored. Feedback is provided to the student. If mastery is achieved, student and teacher reflect on and celebrate the success. If mastery is not achieved, additional practice occurs and then the posttest is readministered. Next, students and teacher make the commitment to generalize to ensure use of the strategy across settings, situations, and time. The importance of generalization is emphasized to help students recognize the value of using what they've learned.

Stage 8: Generalization   The purpose of the Generalization Stage is to get students to apply the strategy to real-world situations that extend beyond the classroom where the strategy was learned. There are four phases within the Generalization Stage: orientation, activation, adaptation, and maintenance. The orientation phase involves introducing the concept of generalization and making students aware of the importance of using the strategy to meet relevant setting demands. Through discussion, students determine where, when, how, and why they can use the newly learned strategy. The activation phase involves giving the students assignments that require generalization and then monitoring their performance. Prompts and cues are provided, if needed. The adaptation phase involves having the students think about the various cognitive strategies they are using when engaged in the strategy just learned. Students are encouraged to change or adapt the strategy to meet new and different setting demands. The maintenance phase involves periodic checks to ensure continued, long-term use of the strategy.

Instructional Principles

The Strategy Instruction Model adheres to seven important instructional principles that enable students to acquire strategies in an effective and efficient manner (Deshler, Ellis, & Lenz, 1996). The principles are:

1. Teach prerequisite skills before formal strategy instruction begins.
2. Teach learning strategies regularly and intensely (on a daily basis, if possible).
3. Emphasize personal effort to ensure that students realize that the strategy combined with their own effort will result in success.
4. Require mastery in correct performance of the strategy and in fluent use of the strategy.
5. Integrate instruction throughout the eight stages (e.g., references to generalization are included in all stages; modeling is included in controlled and advanced practice as needed; verbal practice of strategy steps is included as review in controlled and advance practice).
6. Emphasize covert processing throughout the instructional process (e.g., cognitive processes such as paraphrasing, visual imagery, and metacognitive processes such as decision making, goal setting, self-monitoring).
7. Emphasize generalization in a broad sense so that students learn to adapt the processes involved in a task-specific strategy to meet the demands of other problems they face (see Validation Box 4.7).

The initial work of researchers at the University of Kansas Center for Research on Learning focused primarily on the Learning Strategy Curriculum just discussed. More recently, the Strategy Instruction Model has been expanded to include a Content Enhancement Series and a Strategic Math Series. Each of these series consist of

Strategy Instruction Model

Extensive field testing related to the Strategy Instruction Model (SIM) supports its use with students who have academic difficulties in school. Findings of field tests revealed that students can learn to use the strategies effectively and efficiently. Moreover, students can apply and adapt the strategies to new settings and circumstances. Most of the original field tests took place in resource-room settings. All strategies included in SIM are field-tested and validated prior to publication in manual form. Research reports for individual strategies are available through the University of Kansas, Center for Research on Learning, 521 Joseph R. Pearson Hall, 1122 West Campus Road, Lawrence, KS 66045. Additionally, several studies document the effectiveness of SIM strategies (i.e., LINCS Vocabulary Strategy, Paraphrasing Strategy, Self-Questioning Strategy, Sentence-Writing Strategy, Error Monitoring Strategy) in general education classrooms. For more information see: (Beals, 1983; Fisher, Schumaker, & Deshler, 1996; Deshler & Schumaker, 1993; Wedel, Deshler, & Schumaker, 1988).

a group of strategies designed to meet needs that differ from those met through the Learning Strategy Curriculum.

Content Enhancement Series

The Content Enhancement Series consists of routines for teachers to use in academically diverse classes when delivering content-area instruction (e.g., science, social studies, math, English). Table 4.5 on page 164 lists the guidebooks included in the series. The routines are particularly appropriate for general education classes that include students with learning disabilities. Specifically, the teaching routines are designed to help teachers:

▶ Identify critical components of the content;
▶ Organize and deliver critical content in meaningful ways;
▶ Address group and individual student needs;
▶ Maintain the integrity of the academic content;
▶ Involve students in the learning process; and
▶ Promote student learning (Fisher, Schumaker, & Deshler, 1996; Lenz & Bulgren, 1995).

Each teaching routine in the Content Enhancement Series uses instructional devices (e.g., graphic organizers) to enhance the content being taught. These instructional devices assist with planning and delivering instruction (see Lesson,

TABLE 4.5

Guidebooks Included in the Content Enhancement Series

Teaching Routine	Purpose of Routine
Course Organizer	Plan and introduce the big ideas of a course.
Unit Organizer	Plan and introduce the big ideas of a unit.
Lesson Organizer	Plan and introduce important information in lesson.
Concept Mastery	Explain concept and how it fits within a particular body of knowledge.
Concept Anchoring	Link new concept to an already familiar concept.
Concept Comparison	Compare and contrast key concepts.
Clarifying	Teach meaning of important vocabulary terms.
Survey	Provide overview of reading assignment.
Framing	Transform abstract main ideas into concrete representation.
Quality Assignment	Plan, present, and engage students in quality assignments.

Training is required to obtain these materials. To obtain information about this training and to identify trainers in your area, contact The University of Kansas Center for Research on Learning; Website: www.ku-crl.org; telephone: (785) 864-4780; fax: (785) 864-5728.

Unit, and Course Organizers in Chapter 2). The teaching routines in the Content Enhancement Series are based on validated instructional principles. Specifically, the series is based on research that shows "students learn more when they are actively involved in the learning process, when abstract and complex concepts are presented in concrete forms, when information is organized for them, when new information is tied to previously learned information, when important information is distinguished from unimportant information, when relationships among pieces of information are made explicit, and when students are involved in apprenticeships with their teachers whereby they are shown how to learn specific types of content" (Rademacher, Deshler, Schumaker, & Lenz, 1998, p. 1). Several routines (i.e., Concept Mastery, Concept Anchoring, Concept Comparison) from the Content Enhancement Series are discussed in greater detail in Chapter 5 (see Validation Box 4.8).

Strategic Math Series

The Strategic Math Series, another component of the Strategy Instruction Model, consists of strategies for teaching basic math facts, initial place value concepts, and related problem solving (e.g., word problems). Table 4.6 lists the seven guidebooks that are included in the series.

Content Enhancement Series

A review of literature related to the Content Enhancement Series suggests these routines are beneficial for secondary students with and without disabilities who receive instruction in inclusive general education settings. The routines helped students organize, understand, and recall important information in their content-area classes. Moreover, teachers and students rated the routines positively and indicated they would continue using them even though the studies were complete. For more information see: (Bulgren, Deshler, & Schumaker, 1997; Bulgren, Schumaker, & Deshler, 1988, 1994; Fisher, Schumaker, Deshler, 1996).

The Strategic Math Series promotes conceptual understanding of math using the concrete–representational–abstract teaching sequence in a systematic and explicit manner (Mercer & Miller, 1998). Lessons at the concrete level involve the use of manipulative devices (i.e., three-dimensional objects); lessons at the representational level involve the use of drawings and tallies; and lessons

TABLE 4.6

Guidebooks Included in the Strategic Math Series

Skills	Purpose of Strategy
Addition Facts 0 to 9	Teach computation and problem solving involving problems with sums up to 9 (e.g., $6 + 2 =$ ____; $5 + 4 =$ ____).
Subtraction Facts 0 to 9	Teach computation and problem solving involving problems with minuends up to 9 (e.g., $9 - 3 =$ ____; $5 - 4 =$ ____).
Place Value: Discovering Tens and Ones	Teach place value and related problem solving involving double-digit numbers (e.g., 47, 86).
Addition Facts 10 to 18	Teach computation and problem solving involving problems with sums up to 18 (e.g., $5 + 9 =$ ____; $7 + 7 =$ ____).
Subtraction Facts 10 to 18	Teach computation and problem solving involving problems with minuends up to 18 (e.g., $17 - 6 =$ ____; $13 - 4 =$ ____).
Multiplication Facts 0 to 81	Teach computation and problem solving involving problems with products up to 81 (e.g., $7 \times 8 =$ ____; $3 \times 4 =$ ____).
Division Facts 0 to 81	Teach computation and problem solving involving problems with quotients up to 9 (e.g., $81 \div 9 =$ ____; $12 \div 6 =$ ____).

These books are available through Edge Enterprises, P.O. Box 1304, Lawrence, KS 66045; telephone: (785) 749-1473; fax: (785) 749-0207.

at the abstract level involve the use of number symbols without objects or drawings. Mnemonic devices (i.e., FIND, DRAW, FAST DRAW) are used to cue specific cognitive strategies for attacking difficult problems and solving advanced word problems (see Figs. 4.2 to 4.4). Additionally, a graduated word problem sequence is used that progresses from basic word problems to more complex problems (Miller & Mercer, 1993). Initially word problems contain only a few words, then phrases, then sentences, then paragraphs without extraneous information, and finally paragraphs with extraneous information, and ultimately students learn to create their own word problems (see Table 4.7 on p. 168). Instructional procedures used in the lessons include advance organizers, describe and model, guided practice, independent practice, problem-solving practice, timed probes (i.e., one-minute timings on newly learned facts), facts review probes (i.e., one-minute timings on newly learned and previously learned facts), instructional games, and feedback routines. Mastery learning is emphasized in the program. Specific performance criteria are established for students to progress from one lesson to the next and fluency criteria are established to ensure mastery-level performance prior to initiating new skills (see Validation Box 4.9 on p. 169).

The University of Kansas Strategy Instruction Model currently represents the most comprehensive model for strategy instruction. Research is translated to practice through field-tested curricular materials designed to help students become more successful learners and performers both in and outside of school settings.

The FIND Place Value Strategy

Problem: How many tens are there in 58?

Step 1: **F**ind the columns.

5 8 — Student puts pencil point in between the numbers.

Step 2: **I**nsert the T.

5 | 8 — Student draws T.

Step 3: **N**ame the columns.

T | O
5 | 8 — Student names the columns T and O for Tens and Ones.

Step 4: **D**etermine the answer.

Since the 5 is under the T, the student now knows there are 5 tens in 58.

FIGURE 4.2

FIND Place Value Mnemonic Device. (Adapted from *Strategic Math Series: Place Value: Discovering Tens and Ones*, by S. P. Miller and C. D. Mercer, 1993, Lawrence, KS: Edge Enterprises. Copyright 1993 by S. P. Miller and C. D. Mercer. Reprinted by permission. *Note: The Strategic Math Series* may be ordered through Edge Enterprises, P.O. Box 1304, Lawrence, KS 66045; telephone: [785] 749-1473; fax: [785] 749-0207.)

The DRAW Computation Strategy

Problem: 4 × 6 = _____

Step 1: **D**iscover the sign. ————————▸ Student looks at operation sign × and knows to multiply.

Step 2: **R**ead the problem. ————————▸ Student says the problem, "Four times six equals ____ ."

Step 3: **A**nswer, or draw and check. ▸ If the student can think of the answer, the student proceeds to Step 4.
If the student doesn't know the answer, the student draws 4 horizontal
lines to represent groups and 6 vertical tallies to represent objects per
group, then all tallies are counted and recounted to check for accuracy.

Step 4: **W**rite the answer. ————————▸ Student writes answer in answer space: 4 × 6 = <u>24</u>

FIGURE 4.3

DRAW Computation Mnemonic Device. (Adapted from *Strategic Math Series: Multiplication Facts 0 to 81*, by C. D. Mercer and S. P.
Miller, 1992, Lawrence, KS: Edge Enterprises. Copyright 1992 by C. D. Mercer and S. P. Miller. Reprinted by permission. *Note: The Strategic Math Series*
may be ordered through Edge Enterprises, P.O. Box 1304, Lawrence, KS 66045; telephone: [785] 749-1473; fax: [785] 749-0207.)

The FAST DRAW Word Problem Strategy

Problem: Bob had 5 bags. There were 9 golf balls in each bag.

Geraldine had 3 cookies. How many golf balls were there altogether?

Step 1: **F**ind what you're solving for. ————▸ Student looks for questions in the problem.

Step 2: **A**sk yourself, "What are the parts ▸ Student identifies bags as the "group" because the bags are
of the problem?" "people or things that have something in common." Student
identifies golf balls as "objects per group" because ther are 9
in each bag or group. Since "groups" and "objects per group"
are provided and the question asks for a total, the student
now knows to multiply.

Step 3: **S**et up the numbers. ————————▸ Student writes numbers.

5 bags
of 9 golf balls
golf balls

Step 4: **T**ie down the sign. ————————▸ Student writes problem with operation sign.

5 bags
× 9 golf balls
golf balls

Step 5: **D**iscover the sign.

Step 6: **R**ead the problem.

Step 7: **A**nswer, or draw and check

Student then solves the problem from memory or by using
the DRAW strategy.

Step 8: **W**rite the answer.

FIGURE 4.4

FAST DRAW Problem-Solving Mnemonic Device. (Adapted from *Strategic Math Series: Multiplication Facts 0 to 81*, by C. D. Mercer
and S. P. Miller, 1992, Lawrence, KS: Edge Enterprises. Copyright 1992 by C. D. Mercer and S. P. Miller. Reprinted by permission. *Note: The Strategic
Math Series* may be ordered through Edge Enterprises, P.O. Box 1304, Lawrence, KS 66045; telephone: [785] 749-1473; fax: [785] 749-0207.)

TABLE 4.7

Graduated Word-Problem Sequence

3 ___clips___ + 2 ___clips___	During concrete level instruction, students write the name of the manipulative device used in the lesson in each blank.
4 ___boxes___ ☐ + 3 ___boxes___ ☐ ___boxes___	During representational instruction, students write the name of the drawing used in the lesson in each blank.
7 balls + 2 balls	During abstract instruction, word problems progress from single words, to phrases, to sentences with the numbers still aligned, to traditional paragraph formats.
4 brown dogs + 5 brown dogs brown dogs	
Steve has 3 backpacks. Susan has 2 backpacks. They have ___ backpacks in all.	
Terry has 4 books. Neil has 5 books. How many books do Terry and Neil have altogether?	Traditional paragraph format without extraneous information
Jennie has 3 games. Matt has 3 games. Sydney has 5 dolls. How many games are there altogether?	Traditional paragraph format with extraneous information
	Finally, students create and solve their own word problems.

Strategic Written Expression Models

Carol Englert with her colleagues and Steve Graham, Karen Harris, and their colleagues have developed strategy approaches to promote the development of expository writing skills (De La Paz & Graham; 1997; Englert, 1990; Englert et al., 1991; Graham & Harris, 1989; Graham, MacArthur, Schwartz, & Page-Voth, 1992; Harris & Graham, 1992). From these researchers, two primary lines of research involving strategy instruction and the writing process have emerged: the Cognitive Strategy Instruction Writing (CSIW) Program and the Self-Regulated Strategy Development (SRSD) Model.

VALIDATION BOX

4.9

Strategic Math Series

▶ Field-testing of the Strategic Math Series involved 56 teachers and 248 students who were experiencing difficulties in math. The program was field tested in self-contained, resource, and general education classes in 7 school districts. Students demonstrated significant improvements on skill acquisition and fluency measures. For more information see: (Miller & Mercer, 1998).

▶ The Multiplication Facts 0 to 81 was taught to 123 second graders in general education classrooms using whole-group instruction. Students with identified learning disabilities, students who were identified as low achievers, and students who were achieving normally all improved significantly from pre- to posttest. There were no significant differences between the students with disabilities and the students who were low achievers on 6 dependent measures of acquisition and proficiency. When these two groups were combined and contrasted with the students who were considered to be normal achievers, the combined lower performing group performed statistically similarly to the normal achievers on 4 of the 6 dependent measures. Again, both groups improved significantly from pre- to posttest. For more information see: (Miller, Harris, Strawser, Jones, & Mercer, 1998).

▶ Additional studies validate various components of the Strategic Math Series and provide earlier field-test results. For more information see: (Peterson, Mercer, & O'Shea, 1988; Mercer & Miller, 1992; Miller & Mercer, 1993; Morin & Miller, 1998).

Cognitive Strategy Instruction Writing Program

Carol Englert and her colleagues developed and evaluated the Cognitive Strategy Instruction Writing (CSIW) program. The purpose of the program is to foster self-regulation and internalization of the subprocesses involved in expository writing. In this program, students learn to use the mnemonic device POWER, which stands for Plan, Organize, Write, Edit/Editor, and Revise. The steps in this mnemonic device guide students as they write explanation or comparison/contrast papers. "Think-sheets" are used during each step of the strategy to make cognitive strategies visible to the students (see Fig. 4.5 on p. 170, Fig. 4.6 on p. 171, Figs. 4.7 and 4.8 on p. 172, and Fig. 4.9 on p. 173). The think-sheets include questions that students ask themselves to facilitate or prompt their performance in the various writing steps. Modeling and guided practice are used to teach students how to use "think-sheets" to complete each step in the writing process. Teachers also model making adaptations to the sheets. This promotes strategic rather than mechanistic use of the think-sheets. The CSIW enhances students' expository writing performance and their metacognitive knowledge. Consequently, they acquire skills that help throughout their school career and beyond (Englert, 1990; Englert & Raphael, 1989; see Validation Box 4.10 on p. 174).

PLAN

Name: *Carrie*   Date: *3 - 9*

Topic: *How to take care of fish*

WHO: Who am I writing for?

_____
for people who have some fish

WHY: Why am I writing this?

_____
So people know how to care for fish

WHAT: What do I know? (Brainstorm)   *203*
1.   *I now you need*
2.   _____
3.   _____
4.   _____
5.   _____
6.   _____
7.   _____
8.   _____

HOW: How can I group my ideas?

Materials	Setting

A fish Bole, fish, food   *a*
gravel, Plans, and little   *bathroom*
                stuff

Steps	Care

Get materials   *food*
Set up tank ^{1st put in gravel}   *Protect fish*
            ^{2nd put in plants}

FIGURE 4.5

Plan Think-Sheet. (From "Unraveling the Mysteries of Writing Through Strategy Instruction" by C. S. Englert. In T. E. Scruggs and B. Y. L. Wong [Eds.], *Intervention Research in Learning Disabilities* [pp. 202–203],1990, New York: Springer-Verlag New York. Copyright 1990 by Springer-Verlag New York. Reprinted with permission.)

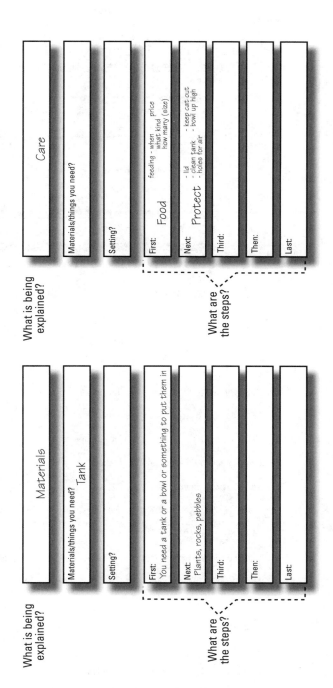

FIGURE 4.6

Explanation Organize Think-Sheet. (From "'Unraveling the Mysteries of Writing Through Strategy Instruction" by C. S. Englert. In T. E. Scruggs and B. Y. L. Wong [Eds.], *Intervention Research in Learning Disabilities* [pp. 206–207],1990, New York: Springer-Verlag New York. Copyright 1990 by Springer-Verlag New York. Reprinted with permission.)

What is being compared/contrasted?
Grand Canyon & Yosemite National Parks

On what?
Location

Alike?	Different?
United States	Grand Canyon—Arizona Yosemite—California

On what?
Wildlife

Alike?	Different?
deer, rabbits, birds	Grand Canyon—Big Horn Sheep Yosemite—Bear

On what?
Activities

Alike?	Different?
Ranger-led walks, fishing, cross country skiing	Grand Canyon—Mule Trip Yosemite—Stage Coach Rides

FIGURE 4.7

Compare/Contrast Organize Think-Sheet. (Adapted from "Developing Successful Writers Through Cognitive Strategy Instruction" by C. S. Englert and T. E. Raphael. In J. Brophy [Ed.], *Advances in Research on Teaching* [1989], p. 128, with permission from Elsevier Science.)

EDIT

Name: _____   **Date:** _____

Read to check your information. Reread my paper.

What do I like best? (Put a • by the parts I like best)

What parts are not clear? (Put a ? by unclear parts)

Question yourself to check organization. Did I

Tell what was being explained?	YES	sort of	NO
Tell what things you need?	YES	sort of	NO
Make the steps clear?	YES	sort of	NO
Use keywords (first, second)?	YES	sort of	NO
Make it interesting?	YES	sort of	NO

Plan revision. Look back.

What parts do I want to change?
1. _____
2. _____

Write two or more questions for my editor.
1. _____
2. _____

FIGURE 4.8

Explanation Edit Think-Sheet. (From C. S. Englert, T. E. Raphael, and L. M. Anderson. *Cognitive Strategy Instruction in Writing Project.* East Lansing, MI: Institute for Research on Teaching. Reprinted with permission.)

Revision Think Sheet

Name: _____ Date: _____

1.   What revision do you plan to make? Put a √ next to the
      suggestions on the Edit and Editor sheet that you will use.

2.   How will you make your paper more interesting?

      _____
      _____
      _____
      _____

3.   Go back to your first paper and make your revisions
      directly on the paper.

Revision Symbols

Type	Symbol	Example
Add words.	∧	The girl is my sister. *(little)*
Take words out.		The woman ~~has~~ tried to give
Change order.	∩∪	He had (go to) home
Add ideas here.	✓_____	The ✓dog is friendly. *Tell which dog*

FIGURE 4.9

Revision Think-Sheet. (From C. S. Englert, T. E. Raphael, and L. M. Anderson. *Cognitive Strategy Instruction in Writing Project.*
East Lansing, MI: Institute for Research on Teaching. Reprinted with permission.)

Self-Regulated Strategy Development Model

Steve Graham, Karen Harris, and their colleagues created the Self-Regulated Strategy Development (SRSD) Model to facilitate the use of specific strategies during the writing process (Graham, Harris, MacArthur, & Schuartz, 1991a). The model includes eight basic stages: *(a)* preskill development to ensure readiness to learn the strategy, *(b)* initial conference with student to set instructional goals and obtain student commitment to learn the strategy, *(c)* discussion of the strategy including information about how and why each strategy step is used, *(d)* modeling of the strategy and self-instructions, *(e)* collaborative practice (teacher and student) of the strategy and self-instruction, *(f)* independent performance to ensure students can use the strategy on their own, *(g)* generalization and maintenance of the strategy to other tasks and settings (Graham, Harris, MacArthur, & Schwartz, 1991b). With this model, students learn strategies along with procedures to regulate strategy use. Specifically, students learn self-regulatory procedures such as goal setting, self-

VALIDATION BOX
4.10

Cognitive Strategy Instruction Writing Program (CSIW)

▶ The Cognitive Strategy in Writing program was implemented in a year-long study with seven secondary students with learning disabilities who had difficulties in writing. Prior to using CSIW, the students had difficulty selecting topics and generating ideas. Written products tended to be about one paragraph in length. Students had to be coaxed to edit their work and editing tended to focus on spelling, punctuation, and sentence structure rather than content and organization. Pre- and posttest papers revealed dramatic improvement for all seven students in areas such as length, organization, paragraph structure, and development of their voices as writers. For more information see: (Hallenbeck, 1996).

▶ In a study involving 63 upper-elementary students (32 with learning disabilities), the CSIW was implemented 3 times per week for 1 year. Results indicated that students both with and without disabilities revealed more metacognitive knowledge about writing after using the CSIW program. Moreover, the quality of students' metacognitive knowledge was positively related to measures of academic performance in writing and reading. For more information see: (Englert, Raphael, & Anderson, 1992).

▶ In a study involving 183 fourth- and fifth-grade students (including low-achieving students, high-achieving students, and students with learning disabilities), the CSIW was implemented for 7 months. Students who received the CSIW instruction outperformed control group students in their knowledge of the writing process and their expository writing abilities. Moreover, students with learning disabilities performed similarly to their peers without disabilities on all five posttest writing variables. For more information see: (Englert, Raphael, Anderson, Anthony, & Stevens, 1991).

instruction, and self-monitoring. These procedures help students coordinate the writing process and cognitive strategies, while simultaneously managing behaviors that interfere with effective writing (e.g., impulsivity). In one SRSD procedure, students are taught three prompts: think, plan, and write/say more. The students also learn a mnemonic device, TREE, to generate ideas for their opinion essays: note *Topic* sentence, note *Reasons* to support their premise, *Examine* reasons (Are they convincing?), and note an *Ending* for the paper (Harris & Graham, 1992). This approach to writing encourages students to spend more time preparing to write, which ultimately results in a better product (see Validation Box 4.11).

Keyword, Pegword, and Symbolic Representation Strategies

Another group of researchers, Margo Mastropieri, Thomas Scruggs, and their colleagues, conducted over a decade of research on mnemonic strategy instruction

┌─────────────────┐
│ **VALIDATION BOX** │
│ **4.11** │
└─────────────────┘

Self-Regulated Strategy Development Model (SRSD)

The SRSD model has been validated with more than 15 studies involving elementary and secondary students. These studies revealed that students with and without learning disabilities who learn to self-regulate their writing performance display substantial improvements in the quantity and quality of their writing. Specifically, students use webbing, brainstorming, text structures, goal setting, revising, and editing strategies for various types of expository writing. For more information see: (Danoff, Harris, & Graham, 1993; De La Paz, 1997; De La Paz & Graham, 1997; Graham, Harris, MacArthur, & Schwartz, 1991a; Graham, MacArthur, & Schwartz, 1995; Graham, MacArthur, Schwartz, & Page-Voth, 1992; MacArthur, Schwartz, Graham, Molloy, & Harris, 1996).

designed to help students with disabilities recall important content-related information (Fulk, 1994; Mastropieri & Fulk, 1990; Mastropieri & Scruggs, 1998; Mastropieri, Scruggs, Whittaker, & Bakken, 1994; Scruggs & Mastropieri, 1990; Scruggs & Mastropieri, 1992). The keyword cognitive strategy approach has been central to their research. The keyword method is a mnemonic memory tool that uses auditory and visual cues to help students build vocabulary, increase factual learning, acquire information from texts, and make information more meaningful. Specifically, students are taught vocabulary words and their related definitions or content information using teacher-provided or student-generated illustrations. These pictures link students' prior knowledge to new information that needs to be learned. For example, if the student needs to remember that the earth's mantle is made of solid rock, the key word could be "man" because students already know what a man is, and because "man" sounds similar to the word "mantle." A picture of a man who is made out of rocks links the term *mantle* with the information to be learned (i.e., made of solid rock) (see Fig. 4.10 on p. 176). Teacher-directed practice occurs using the picture cues. Specifically, students are taught to think of the keyword (man) and then remember the picture. Remembering the key word and the related picture facilitates memory of the newly learned information (mantle is made of solid rock) (Mastropieri et al., 1994).

Mastropieri, Scruggs, and their colleagues also explored the use of keyword/pegword combinations to help students learn information that contained multiple attributes, rather than single definitions or single pieces of information. Pegwords are used for remembering ordered or numbered information. Pegwords are words that rhyme with the numbers one, two, three and so forth. So, a pegword for one is *bun*. A pegword for two is *shoe*. A pegword for three is a *tree*. Similar to a keyword, a pegword has to be a word that can be represented with a picture. So, if a student needs to remember that the hardness level for the mineral bauxite is 1, the keyword/pegword method can be used. A keyword such as "box" can be used to remember bauxite and a pegword "bun" can be used to remember that the hardness level is 1.

Mantle
(Man)

made of solid rock

Thus, the keyword/pegword illustration is a box of buns. When the student sees the box of buns, he remembers bauxite, 1, or the hardness level of bauxite is 1 (Mastropieri, Scruggs, & Levin, 1986).

The vocabulary studies using keywords and the multiple-attributes studies using keywords and pegwords have been extended and applied to complex history and science textbook content. Simple keyword constructions using words that sound like what needs to be learned (e.g., man of rocks representing that the earth's mantle is made of solid rock) are not sufficient for learning the many complex concepts found in content texts. Abstract concepts such as justice, religion, or U.S. policy are better represented with *symbolic* pictures that get at the meaning of the concepts rather than simple irrelevant retrieval links. Appropriate pictures might be scales to illustrate the concept of justice, a church to represent religion, and a picture of Uncle Sam to represent U.S. policy (Scruggs & Mastropieri, 1990). These symbolic representations are used to help students understand the most important concepts in the textbooks.

Teachers who use mnemonic instruction involving keywords, pegwords, or symbolic representations must develop materials with pictures that clearly illustrate the mnemonic. In addition to having appropriate pictures, teachers must implement the strategy instruction in a systematic way. Fulk (1994) recommends a seven-phase instructional sequence for teachers to use when teaching students to use keyword strategies (see Table 4.8). This sequence helps promote acquisition and generalization of strategies.

Mnemonic strategy approaches are beneficial for students with learning disabilities or mental retardation. Specifically, these approaches help students develop language skills, acquire and retain content vocabulary, and understand important science and social-studies concepts. In a review of meta-analyses involving various special education interventions, mnemonic strategies were identified as most effective (Forness, Kavale, Blum, Lloyd, 1997; see Validation Box 4.12 on p. 178).

Synthesis and Integration of the Models

The teaching models discussed in this chapter are not necessarily mutually exclusive. It is possible for teachers to use one teaching model for one part of the curriculum and a different model for another part. Similarly, certain models may be appropriate for particular students, but not others. Educators and researchers have begun to explore ways to integrate various components of these teaching models to meet the needs of diverse groups of students (Bulgren & Lenz, 1996; Darch, 1989; Ellis, 1993; Ellis, 1994; Fisher, Schumaker, Deshler, 1996; Gersten & Baker, 1998; Scanlon, Deshler, & Schumaker, 1996).

TABLE 4.8

Seven-Phase Instructional Plan for Teaching Keyword Strategies

Phase 1:	Provide a purpose/rationale for using the strategy.
Phase 2:	Provide explicit strategy-attribution instruction; tell the student about the strategy and emphasize the importance of effort.
Phase 3:	Model how to use the strategy with teacher think-alouds.
Phase 4:	Provide verbal practice until students are fluent with the strategy steps.
Phase 5:	Provide guided practice with feedback.
Phase 6:	Provide explicit instruction to transfer; instruct students to use the strategy in other classes.
Phase 7:	Incorporate attribution training, prompting students to reinforce themselves for improved strategy and attributional performance.

VALIDATION BOX

4.12

Keyword and Pegword Strategies

▶ A meta-analysis of 24 studies involving keyword and keyword-pegword mnemonics revealed an overall mean effect size of 1.62 (one of the highest, if not the highest average effect size of any synthesis of special education research). For more information see: (Mastropieri & Scruggs, 1989).

▶ Several reviews of literature related to keyword mnemonic strategy instruction reveal extensive support for using this type of instruction with elementary and secondary students who are experiencing learning difficulties. Keyword mnemonic strategies improve academic performance on immediate and delayed recall measures. Specifically, keyword mnemonic strategies have been validated with vocabulary terms, history content, science content, and state capitols. Both teacher-generated and student-generated keyword mnemonics result in positive learner outcomes. Moreover, teacher and student satisfaction with the strategies is high. For more information see: (Fulk, 1994; Mastropieri & Fulk, 1990; Scruggs & Mastropieri, 1990).

Similarities and Differences among the Models

The three models discussed in this chapter (i.e., Explicit Instruction, Direct Instruction, and Strategy Instruction) have some common features. For example, all three models emphasize the importance of:

▶ Using a continuum of support for student learning (increased teacher-directedness or support is provided during initial learning stages, and reduced support is provided as students increase in competence);
▶ Presenting academic skills and concepts in a clear, direct manner;
▶ Providing adequate practice with teacher feedback;
▶ Using systematic instructional procedures; and
▶ Monitoring student progress.

The primary differences among the three models involve instructional goals and teacher presentation style. The Explicit Instruction and Direct Instruction models are used primarily to teach basic skills and content-area instruction. The primary goal of the Strategy Instruction Model, however, is to teach students *how* to learn, so the emphasis is on the *processes* for learning the academic content. Clearly, students with disabilities need both content knowledge and process-for-learning knowledge.

With regard to teacher presentation style, Direct Instruction is the most structured and prescriptive of the three models (e.g., scripted lessons, hand signals for choral responding, immediate correction procedures). Suggested scripts are frequently used in the Explicit Instruction Model and the Strategy Instruction Model, but strict adherence to the script is emphasized less than in the Direct Instruction

Model. Moreover, class discussions are frequently used in Explicit Instruction and Strategy Instruction, whereas Direct Instruction is virtually discussion- and lecture-free (Ellis & Fouts, 1997).

Situated Cognition and Explicit Instruction

Gersten and Baker (1998) proposed a framework for refining instruction in content areas such as science and math. Their framework involves integrating Explicit Instruction with cognitively based approaches (e.g., Strategy Instruction) that emphasize problem-solving skills on real-world tasks. Specifically, they recommend first using Explicit Instruction to teach key concepts or essential factual information (e.g., vocabulary, computation) that students need for meaningful involvement in problem-solving activities. Once this initial information is mastered, students engage in problem solving using *situated cognition* (i.e., conceptual learning that is "situated" or based in real-life scenarios or contexts). This framework increases students' knowledge of basic concepts in math and science and then promotes transfer of this knowledge which results in deeper understandings of the content being taught. Graphic organizers, "think-sheets," or semantic maps are used to help students identify options, strategies, and questions to use during the complex problem-solving activities (see Validation Box 4.13).

Advance Organizers and Direct Instruction

The integration of advance organizers and Direct Instruction is another viable teaching approach for students with disabilities (Darch, 1989). A written advance organizer in the form of an outline is given to the students. The outline contains key concepts that help students process information in the upcoming lesson. The teacher presents the content included on the advance organizer using the Direct Instruction approach (i.e., brisk-paced, scripted teacher questions that require short, direct, choral responses from students). Thus, students are more apt to remember and understand the newly learned information. Another option for combining

VALIDATION BOX

4.13

Situated Cognition and Explicit Instruction

The combination of situated cognition and explicit instruction was validated in three studies involving adolescents with learning difficulties. All three studies investigated the effectiveness of situated cognition and explicit instruction on students' ability to solve real-world problems. One study focused on mathematics and two focused on biology concepts. Results from these studies indicate that situated cognition and explicit instruction facilitate the transfer of learning to real-world problems. For more information see: (Gersten & Baker, 1998).

advance organizers and Direct Instruction involves the use of visual displays instead of a written outline. Visual displays help students see the relationships of main concepts within the unit of study. Again, Direct Instruction procedures can be used to practice the content illustrated in the visual displays (see Validation Box 4.14).

Strategy and Content Instruction

Content instruction (e.g., science, social studies, math, English) is undoubtedly important for all students who attend school. Unfortunately, many students struggle with content instruction because they lack necessary cognitive strategies for acquiring, retaining, and generalizing the information they are taught. Since most students with special learning needs now receive some or all of their content instruction in general education settings, it is very important to combine strategy and content instruction. The Integrated Strategies Instruction Model (Ellis, 1993) and the Strategies Integration Approach (Scanlon, Deshler, & Schumaker, 1996) are two methods for accomplishing this important integration process.

Integrated Strategies Instruction

The Integrated Strategies Instruction (ISI) model involves teaching students how to be strategic learners while simultaneously teaching content-area instruction (e.g., science, social studies, English, math). "The ISI model focuses on how teachers can facilitate student understanding and intentional use of effective thinking and problem-solving cognitive processes, or 'cognitive literacy,' in the context of facilitating acquisition and mastery of content-area subjects" (Ellis, 1994, p. 169). In other words, teachers teach students how to think effectively and efficiency while learning content-area subjects. Students are taught cognitive strategies to use as teachers provide content instruction using analogies and/or graphic organizers. The strategies are generally taught using four phases: orienting, framing, applying and extending. During the orienting phase, teachers teach content using strategies that help students learn (e.g., graphic organizers). The emphasis in on the content, not the strategy. During the framing phase, teachers describe and model how the strategy is used

VALIDATION BOX

4.14

Advance Organizers and Direct Instruction

The combination of advance organizers and Direct Instruction was validated in two science studies involving high-school students with learning disabilities. In both studies, the students who received this integrated instructional approach outscored control-group students who received traditional textbook instruction. For more information see: (Darch, 1989).

when learning content. How and when to use the strategy is emphasized in this phase. During the applying phase, students independently practice using the strategy to acquire content knowledge. Ideally, students apply the strategy in multiple contexts within and across content areas. During the extending phase, students learn to extend their understanding of the strategy by using it with additional academic content and problem-solving situations (Bulgren & Lenz, 1996; Ellis, 1993; Ellis, 1994).

Strategies Integration Approach

The Strategies Integration Approach is designed to integrate instruction in learning strategies with instruction in classroom content. There are three phases in this integration approach. First, teachers introduce their students to the idea of strategic learning. Second, teachers describe and model the strategy using classroom content and, third, students practice using the strategy to learn the classroom content. This approach is particularly appropriate for instruction that takes place in general education settings. Students with and without disabilities benefit from combined strategy and content instruction (Fisher, Schumaker, & Deshler, 1996; Scanlon, Deshler, & Schumaker, 1996; see Validation Box 4.15).

It is promising to note that researchers and educators appear to be moving away from dogmatic allegiances to specific teaching models. Instead, there is increased emphasis on identifying instructional components that have validated support and thus result in positive achievement for students with and without special instructional needs. An openness exists for integrating best practices from various models to meet the diverse needs of both elementary and secondary students.

Direct Instruction and Strategy Instruction

Historically, Direct Instruction (DI) and Strategy Instruction (SI) have been distinguished from one another based on several characteristics. DI focuses on individual

---

VALIDATION BOX

4.15

Strategies Integration Approach

The efficacy of the Strategies Integration Approach was examined in a study involving 204 middle-school students. Of these students, 17 had learning disabilities. Over the course of a semester, general education teachers taught a learning strategy in conjunction with social studies content. The strategy was designed to help students identify key content information, create a graphic organizer, and use the graphic organizer to study for a test or complete written assignments. Students involved in the strategies integration approach outscored students in the control group in their ability to create content organizers. No significant differences were found between students with and without learning disabilities. For more information see: (Scanlon, Deshler, & Schumaker, 1996).

skills, whereas SI focuses on process-type thinking. DI emphasizes fast-paced, well-sequenced, and highly focused lessons with many opportunities for students to respond and receive feedback, and SI emphasizes the thinking processes involved in learning new information (e.g., advance organizers used as a mental scaffolding on which to build new understanding, directing students to assess their understanding, thinking about how new information relates to previously learned information, general study strategies) (Swanson, 1999). In spite of the distinctly different theoretical orientations of these two models, they share some important instructional characteristics. In both models, effective methods of instruction include daily reviews, statements of objectives, teacher presentations of new material, guided practice, independent practice, and formative assessments. Additionally, instruction in both models follows a sequence of events similar to the following:

1. State the learning objectives and orient the students to what they will be learning and what performance will be expected of them.
2. Review the skills necessary to understand the concept.
3. Present the information, give examples, and demonstrate the concepts/materials.
4. Pose questions (probes) to students, assess their level of understanding, and correct misconceptions.
5. Provide group instruction and independent practice. Give students an opportunity to demonstrate new skills and learn the new information on their own.
6. Assess performance and provide feedback. Review the independent work and give a quiz. Give feedback for correct answers and reteach skills if answers are incorrect.
7. Provide distributed practice and review. (Swanson, 1999, p. 130)

In an extensive review of intervention studies, both DI and SI models were found to be effective for students with learning disabilities. Interventions that combined DI and SI models were found to be even more effective. Students need and benefit from both skill-based and strategy-based instruction (Swanson, 1999; see Validation Box 4.16).

Practice Activities

▶ Write a lesson script that would follow the Explicit Instruction Model.
▶ Observe several classroom teachers and identify the models or components of models they use.
▶ Review a curricular material that is used in one of the models described in this chapter.
▶ Read and critique a journal article that describes Explicit, Direct, or Strategy Instruction.
▶ Develop keyword mnemonic illustrations for a science or social studies lesson.
▶ Develop a plan for integrating the models or model components discussed in this chapter.

VALIDATION BOX
4.16

Direct Instruction and Strategy Instruction

In a comprehensive review of literature involving 180 intervention studies, interventions were categorized as direct instruction alone, strategy instruction alone, combined direct and strategy instruction, or nondirect instruction and nonstrategy instruction. All of the intervention studies used an experimental design in which individuals with learning disabilities received treatment to enhance academic, social, and cognitive performance. Effect sizes were determined for the four categories of interventions and then compared. The effect size for direct instruction alone was 0.68 and the effect size for strategy instruction alone was 0.72. Thus, both approaches were viable for individuals with learning disabilities. The effect size for the interventions that combined direct and strategy instruction was 84. This effect size was significantly higher than direct instruction alone, strategy instruction alone, and nondirect instruction and nonstrategy instruction. For more information see: (Swanson, 1999).

P O S T ORGANIZER

Explicit instruction, Direct Instruction, and strategy instruction models have validated support for teaching students with and without learning difficulties. These models are particularly appropriate for teaching diverse groups of students. It should not be assumed, however, that one model will meet all of the needs of all of the students all of the time. There is no one "right" model; teachers must, therefore, think about the content to be learned and the students they teach and then select from among these validated approaches.

References

Adams, G. L., & Engelmann, S. (1996). *Research on Direct Instruction: 25 years beyond DISTAR.* Seattle: Educational Achievement Systems.

Beals, V. L. (1983). *The effects of large group instruction on the acquisition of specific learning strategies by learning disabled adolescents.* Unpublished doctoral dissertation, University of Kansas, Lawrence.

Bergerud, D., Lovitt, T. C., & Horton, S. V. (1988). The effectiveness of textbook adaptations in life science for high school students with learning disabilities. *Journal of Learning Disabilities, 21,* 70–76.

Bereiter, C., & Kurland, M. (1981–1982). A constructive look at Follow Through results. *Interchange, 12,* 1–22.

Bulgren, J. A., Deshler, D. D., & Schumaker, J. B. (1997). Use of a recall enhancement routine and strategies in inclusive secondary classes. *Learning Disabilities Research & Practice, 12,* 198–208.

Bulgren, J., & Lenz, K. (1996). Strategic instruction in the content areas. In D. D. Deshler, E. S. Ellis, & B. K. Lenz (Eds.), *Teaching adolescents with learning disabilities* (2nd ed., pp. 409–473). Denver: Love.

Bulgren, J. A., Schumaker, J. B., & Deshler, D. D. (1988). Effectiveness of a concept teaching routine in enhancing the performance of LD students in secondary-level mainstream classes. *Learning Disability Quarterly, 11,* 3–17.

Bulgren, J. A., Schumaker, J. B., & Deshler, D. D. (1994). The effects of a recall enhancement routine on the test performance of secondary students with and without learning disabilities. *Learning Disabilities Research & Practice, 9,* 2–11.

Carnine, D. (1989). Teaching complex content to learning disabled students: The role of technology. *Exceptional Children, 55,* 524–533.

Carnine, D. (1990). Beyond technique—Direct instruction and higher-order skills. *Direct Instruction News, 9*(3), 1–13.

Carnine, D. (1991). Curricular interventions for teaching higher order thinking to all students: Introduction to the special series. *Journal of Learning Disabilities, 24,* 261–269.

Carnine, D. (1994). The BIG Accommodations Program. *Educational Leadership, 51,* 87–88.

Carnine, D., Crawford, D., Harniss, M., & Hollenbeck, K. (1995). *Understanding U.S. History* (Vol. 1). Eugene, OR: Considerate Publishing.

Carnine, D., & Kameenui, E. (1992). *Higher order thinking: Designing curriculum for mainstreamed students.* Austin, TX: Pro-Ed.

Christenson, S. L., Ysseldyke, J. E., & Thurlow, M. L. (1989). Critical instructional factors for students with mild handicaps: An integrative review. *Remedial and Special Education, 10*(5), 21–31.

Collins, M., Carnine, D., & Gersten, R. (1987). Elaborated corrective feedback and the acquisition of reasoning skills: A study of computer-assisted instruction. *Exceptional Children, 51,* 254–262.

Danoff, B., Harris, K. R., & Graham, S. (1993). Incorporating strategy instruction within the writing process in the regular classroom: Effects on normally achieving and learning disabled students' writing. *Journal of Reading Behavior, 25,* 295–322.

Darch, C. (1989). Comprehension instruction for high school learning disabled students. *Research in Rural Education, 5*(3), 43–49.

Darch, C., & Gersten, R. (1986). Direction-setting activities in reading comprehension: A comparison of two approaches. *Learning Disabilities Quarterly, 9,* 235–243.

De La Paz, S. (1997). Strategy instruction in planning: Teaching students with learning and writing disabilities to compose persuasive and expository essays. *Learning Disability Quarterly, 20,* 227–248.

De La Paz, S., & Graham, S. (1997). Strategy instruction in planning: Effects on the writing performance and behavior of students with learning difficulties. *Exceptional Children, 63,* 167–181.

Deshler, D. D., Ellis, E. S., & Lenz, B. K. (1996). *Teaching adolescents with learning disabilities* (2nd ed.). Denver, CO: Love.

Deshler, D. D., & Schumaker, J. B. (1993). Strategy mastery by at-risk students: Not a simple matter. *The Elementary School Journal, 94,* 154–167.

Ellis, A. K., & Fouts, J. T. (1997). *Research on educational innovations* (2nd ed.). Larchmont, NY: Eye On Education.

Ellis, E. S. (1993). Integrative strategy instruction: A potential model for teaching content area subjects to adolescents with learning disabilities. *Journal of Learning Disabilities, 26,* 358–383.

Ellis, E. S. (1994). Integrating writing strategy instruction with content-area instruction: Part I. Orienting students to organizational devices. *Intervention in School and Clinic, 29,* 169–179.

Engelmann, S., Becker, W. C., Carnine, D., and Gersten, R. (1988). The Direct Instruction Follow Through model: Design and outcomes. *Education and Treatment of Children, 11*(4), 303–317.

Englert, C. S. (1990). Unraveling the mysteries of writing through strategy instruction. In T. E. Scruggs, & B. Y. L. Wong (Eds.), *Intervention research in learning disabilities* (pp. 186–223). New York: Springer-Verlag.

Englert, C. S., & Raphael, T. E. (1989). Developing successful writers through cognitive strategy instruction. In J. Brophy (Ed.), *Advances in research on teaching* (pp. 105–151). Greenwich, CT: JAI Press.

Englert, C. S., Raphael, T. E., & Anderson, L. M. (1992). Socially mediated instruction: Improving students' knowledge and talk about writing. *The Elementary School Journal, 92,* 411–449.

Englert, C. S., Raphael, T. , Anderson, L., Anthony, H., & Stevens, D. (1991). Making writing strategies and self-talk visible: Cognitive strategy instruction in writing in regular and special education classrooms. *American Educational Research Journal 28,* 337–373.

Fisher, J. B., Schumaker, J. B., & Deshler, D. D. (1996). Searching for validated inclusive practices: A review of the literature. In E. L. Meyen, G. A. Vergason, & R. J. Whelan (Eds.), *Strategies for teaching exceptional children in inclusive settings* (pp. 123–154). Denver: Love.

Forness, S. R., Kavale, K. A., Blum, I. M., & Lloyd, J. W. (1997). Mega-analysis of meta-analyses. *Teaching Exceptional Children, 29*(6), 4–9.

Fulk, B. M. (1994). Mnemonic keyword strategy training for students with learning disabilities. *Learning Disabilities Research & Practice, 9,* 179–195.

Gersten, R., & Baker, S. (1998). Real world use of scientific concepts: Integrating situated cognition with explicit instruction. *Exceptional Children, 65,* 23–35.

Gersten, R., Carnine, D., & Woodward, J. (1987). Direct instruction research: The third decade. *Remedial and Special Education, 8*(6), 48–56.

Gersten, R., & Kelly, B. (1992). Coaching secondary special education teachers in implementation of an innovative videodisc mathematics curriculum. *Remedial and Special Education, 13,* 40–51.

Graham, S., & Harris, K. R. (1989). Improving learning disabled students' skills at composing essays: Self-instructional strategy training. *Exceptional Children, 56,* 201–214.

Graham, S., Harris, K., MacArthur, C., & Schwartz, S. (1991a). Writing and writing instruction with students with learning disabilities: A review of a program of research. *Learning Disability Quarterly, 14,* 89–114.

Graham, S., Harris, K., MacArthur, C., & Schwartz, S. (1991b). Writing instruction. In B. Y. L. Wong (Ed.), *Learning about learning disabilities* (pp. 309–343). San Diego: Academic Press

Graham, S., MacArthur, C., & Schwartz, S. (1995). Effects of goal setting and procedural facilitation on the revising behavior and writing performance of students with writing and learning problems. *Journal of Educational Psychology, 87,* 230–240.

Graham, S., MacArthur, C., Schwartz, S., & Page-Voth, V. (1992). Improving the compositions of students with learning disabilities using a strategy involving product and process goal setting. *Exceptional Children, 58,* 322–335.

Greenwood, C. R., Arreaga-Mayer, C., & Carta, J. J. (1994). Identification and translation of effective teacher-developed instructional procedures for general practice. *Remedial and Special Education, 15,* 140–151.

Griffin, C. C., Simmons, D. C., Kameenui, E. J. (1991). Investigating the effectiveness of graphic organizer instruction on the comprehension and recall of science content by students with learning disabilities. *Reading, Writing, and Learning Disabilities, 7,* 355–376.

Grossen, B., & Carnine, D. (1990). Diagramming a logical strategy: Effects in difficult problem types and transfer. *Learning Disability Quarterly, 13,* 168–182.

Hallenbeck, M. J. (1996). The cognitive strategy in writing: Welcome relief for adolescents with learning disabilities. *Learning Disabilities Research & Practice, 11,* 107–119.

Harris, K. R., & Graham, S. (1992). *Helping young writers master the craft: Strategy instruction and self-regulation in the writing process.* Cambridge, MA: Brookline.

Hofmeister, A., Engelmann, S., & Carnine, D. (1989). Developing and validating science education videodisks. *Journal of Research in Science Teaching, 26,* 665–677.

Horton, S. V., Lovitt, T. C., & Bergerud, D. (1990). The effectiveness of graphic organizers for three classifications of secondary students in content area classes. *Journal of Learning Disabilities, 23,* 12–22, 29.

House, E. R., Glass, G. V., McLean, L. D. (1978). No simple answer: Critique of the Follow Through evaluation. *Harvard Educational Review, 48*, 128–160.

Hudson, P. (1996). Using a learning set to increase the test performance of students with learning disabilities in social studies classes. *Learning Disabilities Research & Practice, 11*, 78–85.

Hudson, P. (1997). Using teacher-guided practice to help students with learning disabilities acquire and retain social studies content. *Learning Disability Quarterly, 20*, 23–32.

Kelly, B., Carnine, D., Gersten, R., & Grossen, B. (1986). Effectiveness of videodisc instruction in teaching fractions to learning-disabled and remedial high school students. *Journal of Special Education Technology, 8*, 5–17.

Kelly, B., Gersten, R., & Carnine, D. (1990). Student error patterns as a function of curriculum design: Teaching fractions to remedial high school students and high school students with learning disabilities. *Journal of Learning Disabilities, 23*(1), 23–29.

Kooy, T., Skok, R. L., & McLaughlin, T. F. (1992). The effect of graphic advance organizers on the math and science comprehension with high school special education students. *B. C. Journal of Special Education, 16*, 101–111.

Kozlow, M. J. (1978). *A meta-analysis of selected advance organizer research reports from 1960–1977.* Unpublished doctoral dissertation, Ohio State University, Columbus.

Lenz, B. K. (1983). Using advance organizers. *The Pointer, 27*(2), 11–13.

Lenz, B. K., Alley, G. R., & Schumaker, J. B. (1987). Activating the inactive learner: Advance organizers in the secondary content classroom. *Learning Disability Quarterly, 10*, 53–67.

Lenz, B. K., & Bulgren, J. A. (1995). Promoting learning in content classes. In P. A. Celgelka & W. H. Berdine (Eds.), *Effective instruction for students with learning problems* (pp. 385–417). Boston: Allyn & Bacon.

Lenz, B. K., Ellis, E. S., & Scanlon, D. (1996). *Teaching learning strategies to adolescents and adults with learning disabilities.* Austin: PRO-ED.

Luiten, J., Ames, W., & Ackerman, G. (1980). A meta-analysis of the effects of advance organizers on learning and retention. *American Educational Research Journal, 17*, 211–218.

MacArthur, C., Schwartz, S., Graham, S., Molloy, D., & Harris, K. (1996). Integration of strategy instruction into a whole language classroom: A case study. *Learning Disabilities Research & Practice, 11*, 168–176.

Mastropieri, M. A., & Fulk, B. J. M. (1990). Enhancing academic performance with mnemonic instruction. In T. E. Scruggs, & B. Y. L. Wong (Eds.), *Intervention research in learning disabilities* (pp. 102–121). New York: Springer-Verlag.

Mastropieri, M. A., & Scruggs, T. E. (1989). Constructing more meaningful relationships: Mnemonic instruction for special populations. *Educational Psychology Review, 1*(2), 83–111.

Mastropieri, M. A., & Scruggs, T. E. (1998). Constructing more meaningful relationships in the classroom: Mnemonic research into practice. *Learning Disabilities Research & Practice, 13*, 138–145.

Mastropieri, M. A., Scruggs, T. E., & Levin, J. R. (1986). Direct vs. mnemonic instruction: Relative benefits for exceptional learners. *The Journal of Special Education, 20*, 299–308.

Mastropieri, M. A., Scruggs, T. E., Whittaker, M. E. S., & Bakken, J. P. (1994). Applications of mnemonic strategies with students with mild mental disabilities. *Remedial and Special Education, 15*(1), 34–43.

Meese, R. L. (1994). *Teaching learners with mild disabilities: Integrating research & practice.* Pacific Grove, CA: Brooks/Cole.

Mercer, C. D., & Miller, S. P. (1992). Strategic math series: Instructional procedures and field test results. *Strategram, 4*(3), 1–3.

Mercer, C. D., & Miller, S. P. (1998). Teaching students with learning problems in math to acquire, understand, and apply basic math facts. In E. L. Meyen, G. A. Vergason, & R. J. Whelan (Eds.), *Educating students with mild disabilities* (pp. 177–205). Denver: Love.

Miller, S. P., Harris, C. A., Strawser, S., Jones, W. P., & Mercer, C. D. (1998). Teaching multiplication to second graders in inclusive settings. *Focus on Learning Problems in Mathematics, 29*(4), 49–69.

Miller, S. P., & Mercer, C. D. (1993). Using a graduated word problem sequence to promote problem solving skills. *Learning Disabilities Research & Practice, 8,* 169–174.

Miller, S. P., & Mercer, C. D. (1998). *Strategic math series trainer's guide.* Lawrence, KS: Edge Enterprises.

Morin, V. A., & Miller, S. P. (1998). Teaching multiplication to middle school students with mental retardation. *Education and Treatment of Children, 21*(1), 22–36.

Peterson, S. K., Mercer, C. D., & O'Shea, L. (1988). Teaching learning disabled students place value using the concrete to abstract sequence. *Learning Disabilities Research, 4*(1), 52–56.

Rademacher, J. A., Deshler, D. D., Schumaker, J. B., & Lenz, B. K. (1998). *The content enhancement series: The quality assignment routine.* Lawrence, KS: Edge Enterprises.

Rinehart, S. D., Barksdale-Ladd, M. A., & Welker, W. A. (1991). Effects of advance organizers on text recall by poor readers. *Reading, Writing, and Learning Disabilities, 7,* 321–335.

Rinehart, S. D., & Welker, W. A. (1992). Effects of advance organizers on level and time of text recall. *Reading Research and Instruction, 32*(1), 77–86.

Rivera, D. M., & Smith, D. D. (1987). Influence of modeling on acquisition and generalization of computational skills: A summary of research findings from three sites. *Learning Disability Quarterly, 10,* 69–80.

Rose, R. L., Koorland, M. A., Epstein, M. H. (1982). A review of applied behavior analysis interventions with learning disabled children. *Education and Treatment of Children, 5,* 41–58.

Rosenshine, B. V. (1983). Teaching functions in instructional programs. *Elementary School Journal, 83,* 335–352.

Scanlon, D., Deshler, D. D., & Schumaker, J. B. (1996). Can a strategy be taught and learned in secondary-inclusive classrooms? *Learning Disabilities Research & Practice, 11,* 41–57.

Schumaker, J. B., Denton, P. & Deshler, D. D. (1984). *The learning strategies curriculum: The paraphrasing strategy.* Lawrence: University of Kansas.

Scruggs, T. E., & Mastropieri, M. A. (1990). The case for mnemonic instruction: From laboratory research to classroom applications. *The Journal of Special Education, 24*(1), 7–32.

Scruggs, T. E., & Mastropieri, M. A. (1992). Classroom applications of mnemonic instruction: Acquisition, maintenance, and generalization. *Exceptional Children, 58,* 219–229.

Stebbins, L. B., St. Pierre, R. G., Proper, E. C., Anderson, R. B., & Cerva, T. R. (1977). *Education as experimentation: A planned variation model* (Vol. IV-A). Cambridge, MA: Abt Associates.

Stein, M., Silbert, J., & Carnine, D. (1997). *Designing effective mathematics instruction: A direct instruction approach* (3rd ed.). Upper Saddle River, NJ: Merrill, an Imprint of Prentice-Hall.

Stone, C. L. (1983). A meta-analysis of advance organizer studies. *Journal of Experimental Education, 51,* 194–199.

Swanson, H. L. (1999). Instructional components that predict treatment outcomes for students with learning disabilities: Support for a combined strategy and direct instruction model. *Learning Disabilities Research & Practice, 14* 129–140.

Tarver, S. (with the Division for Learning Disabilities and Division for Research Alerts Editorial Committee). (1999, Summer). Focusing on Direct Instruction. *Current Practice Alerts, 2,* 1–4.

Wedel, M., Deshler, D. D., & Schumaker, J. B. (1988). *Effects of instruction of a vocabulary strategy in a mainstream class.* Unpublished masters thesis, University of Kansas: Lawrence.

White, W. A. T. (1988). A meta-analysis of the effects of Direct Instruction in special education. *Education and Treatment of Children, 11,* 364–374.

Williams, T. R., & Butterfield, E. C. (1992). Advance organizers: A review of the research, Part I. *Journal of Technical Writing and Communication, 22,* 259–272.

Ysseldyke, J. E., Christenson, S. L., & Thurlow, M. L. (1987). *Instructional factors that influence student achievement: An integrative review* (Monograph No. 7). Minneapolis: University of Minnesota.

Using Effective Teaching Behaviors

*Tell me, I'll forget. Show me, I may remember. But
involve me and I'll understand.*

—Chinese proverb

ADVANCE ORGANIZER

Several models for teaching were discussed in Chapter 4. These models provide frameworks for teaching diverse groups of students. Regardless of which model or models teachers use, there are numerous effective teaching behaviors that enhance the effectiveness of instruction. Use of effective teaching behaviors is absolutely critical when teaching groups of diverse students. Teachers who use and master the behaviors described in this chapter increase the likelihood of academic success for their students.

There is a lot more to teaching than simply telling students information that someone has determined they should know. The orchestration and implementation of daily lessons is both an art and a science. Each teacher brings his or her unique personality, creative ability, knowledge, and experience to the teaching/ learning process. These qualities represent the artistry of teaching. To facilitate the greatest amount of student learning, however, this artistry must be combined with the science of effective teaching practices. Over the past several decades, many studies have been conducted and much has been learned about what effective teachers do to promote student understanding. In this chapter, for the sake of organization, this body of research is presented within the context of beginning a lesson, continuing the lesson, and ending the lesson. It is important to note, however, that the teaching behaviors discussed are not restricted to only one part of the lesson. They may be used throughout the lesson as appropriate.

Teacher Effectiveness for Beginning the Lesson

The manner in which teachers begin their lessons is extremely important. The beginning of the lesson sets the tone for everything that follows. Thus, it is important for teachers to be organized (e.g., have materials ready, start on time) and have a clear understanding of the lesson goals.

Obtain Students' Attention

To get the lesson off to a good start, teachers must first ensure that they have the students' attention. There is little benefit to beginning a lesson if students are talking or otherwise preoccupied. It is better to take a few extra seconds to help students focus and prepare for learning than to forge ahead without having their attention. Teachers frequently use positive verbal and/or nonverbal cues to gain students' attention. Sample verbal cues include statements such as:

- All eyes up here.
- One, two, three, look at me.

▶ As soon as everyone is quiet, I'll know you're ready.
▶ We can begin as soon as everyone is ready.
▶ Listen up.
▶ Put your thinking caps on.
▶ It' s time to get in our thinking positions.
▶ Let's get started.
▶ Eyes on me.

Sample nonverbal cues include signals such as:

▶ Flipping the light switch on and off;
▶ Raising a hand (when students see the teacher's hand raised, they raise their hands and keep them raised until all students have noticed and responded to the signal);
▶ Clapping a rhythmic pattern that students imitate;
▶ Holding up a red card that indicates it's time to stop and listen;
▶ Looking at the students, but saying nothing until everyone is quiet and listening; and
▶ Ringing a bell.

When verbal and nonverbal cues are used consistently, students learn to recognize them quickly and little instructional time is wasted.

Spark Student Interest through Teacher Enthusiasm

Once the teacher has the students' attention, it is important to get the students interested and engaged in the lesson topic. There are, of course, a variety of options for sparking student interest (e.g., telling stories that relate the topic to student interests, using visual displays, role playing, posing provocative questions, using humor). Perhaps one of the best ways to get students interested in an upcoming lesson is to display high levels of teacher enthusiasm. Research suggests that teacher enthusiasm influences student interest and achievement in positive ways (Brigham, Scruggs, & Mastropieri, 1992; Brophy & Good, 1986; Collins, 1978; Rosenshine, 1970). Included among the attributes that represent teacher enthusiasm are rapid, uplifting vocal expression; varied voice inflection and vocabulary; expressive, wide-open eyes; frequent hand gestures; animated facial expressions; animated acceptance of student ideas and feelings, and an overall high energy level (Collins, 1978; Brigham et al., 1992). Teachers who lack enthusiasm are more apt to speak in monotone voices without much variance in facial expressions. They tend to sit or stand in one spot and their interactions with students are sparse. Teacher enthusiasm tends to be contagious. Students are more apt to get interested and respond favorably to lessons when teachers demonstrate sincere enthusiasm. Although enthusiasm is especially important when first beginning a lesson, it continues to be important throughout the instructional process (see Validation Box 5.1 on p. 192).

: VALIDATION BOX :
5.1

Teacher Enthusiasm

The effects of teacher enthusiasm were explored in a study involving 16 seventh- and eighth-grade students with learning disabilities and two special education teachers in an urban school setting. Science units were taught with and without teacher enthusiasm. Statistically significant differences favoring enthusiastic teaching were found with regard to student interest, degree to which students appeared to be learning, unit test scores, and time on-task. For more information see: (Brigham, Scruggs, & Mastropieri, 1992).

Communicate Expectations for Participation

In addition to getting students' attention and sparking their interest in the lesson, it's also important to communicate clear expectations with regard to student participation. Active participation in lessons (e.g., taking part in class discussions, answering questions, following directions, taking notes) is important because it increases students' understanding and retention of the content, reduces the amount of independent study time needed prior to taking tests, and enables students to practice cognitive actions (e.g., monitoring comprehension of the material, asking relevant questions, using prior knowledge). Active participation also is beneficial to students because it has a positive effect on their teachers. When students participate in class, teachers perceive that the students are interested. Teachers respond positively and even improve the quality of their instruction when students appear to be interested. Conversely, if students don't participate in class, teachers may assume they are less knowledgeable or less capable and not able to respond. Teachers tend to interact less with low-participating students and in some cases "give up" on them (Ellis, 1991). Since class participation or lack thereof ultimately results in either positive or negative learning cycles (see Fig. 5.1), it is very important for teachers to communicate to students that participation is expected. Simply telling students to participate, however, may not be enough to get them to do so. Unfortunately, many students avoid class participation because they don't recognize the benefits of participation, and/or they don't recognize the negative consequences of low participation.

Ellis (1991) developed the SLANT Strategy to help students participate in class in appropriate and productive ways. The strategy also helps students recognize the social (i.e., increased reciprocal interactions; teacher approval) and cognitive (i.e., increased comprehension and memory of lesson content) benefits of participation. The steps in the SLANT Strategy are:

▶ **Sit up**   Sit upright to communicate readiness to learn.
▶ **Lean forward**   Lean forward slightly to communicate interest.

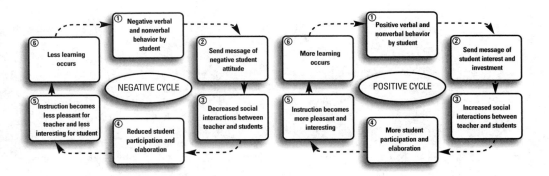

Positive and Negative Learning Cycles Based on Student Participation. (From *SLANT: A Starter Strategy for Class Partici-pation* [p. 2] by E. Ellis, 1991, Lawrence, KS: Edge Enterprises. Copyright 1991 by E. Ellis. Reprinted with permission. *Note: SLANT: A Starter Strategy for Class Participation* may be ordered through Edge Enterprises, P.O. Box 1304, Lawrence, KS 66045; telephone: [785] 749-1473; fax: [785] 749-0207.)

▌ **Activate your thinking**   Ask yourself questions such as "What is this about?" "What should I remember?"; try to answer your questions; ask the teacher questions when you don't understand.

▌ **Name key information**   Answer teacher questions; share ideas or comments; add to others' statements.

▌ **Track the talker**   Keep your eyes on the teacher when he or she is talking; look at other students when they are talking.

Ellis (1991) recommends teaching this strategy using a slightly modified version of the Strategy Instruction Model (SIM) stages: pretest, describe, model, verbal practice, practice the strategy, posttest, and generalization (discussed in Chapter 4). A variety of motivating practice activities can be used when teaching the SLANT Strategy. For example, students can: *(a)* role play examples and nonexamples of the SLANT behaviors (the nonexamples add a bit of humor to the lesson while reinforcing what the SLANT steps mean, *(b)* participate in team activities that involve observing SLANT behaviors among peers, *(c)* create and play instructional games involving the SLANT steps, and/or *(d)* self-record (discussed in Chapter 3) their own use of SLANT behaviors. An 8-page booklet describing this strategy and how to teach it, is available through Edge Enterprises, P.O. Box 1304, Lawrence, KS 66044, telephone: (785) 749-1473; fax: (785) 749-0207 (see Validation Box 5.2 on p. 194).

Consider Necessary Prerequisite Skills

Teachers need to consider necessary prerequisite skills and prior knowledge of the students when beginning to teach a lesson. Getting the students' attention, sparking their interest, and communicating expectations for active participation are mean-

The SLANT Strategy

The SLANT Strategy was field-tested in elementary and secondary special education and general education content-area classes. Included in the field tests were students with learning disabilities, emotional disabilities, and low achievement. Significant gains were realized in behaviors associated with listening and participating in class. Gains were noted in both the quality and quantity of verbal contributions. Students with mild disabilities who learned participation strategies outperformed normally achieving students who had not learned participation strategies. For more information see: (Ellis, 1989).

ingless if they don't have the required skills and knowledge to become engaged in the lesson. Recognizing lack of readiness for a lesson prior to beginning the lesson prevents a variety of problems (e.g., student frustration, teacher frustration, behavior problems). Several options are available for making sure students will be able to participate in the lesson: review the critical prerequisite information, change the lesson in some way, or teach mini-preparation lessons. Prerequisite practice ensures that students who are attentive, motivated, and willing to participate and learn are able to do so. Consider what happens to students when this goal is not met. For example, if Mr. Brake comes into his classroom dressed up like a pirate and says, "Ahoy mates! Today we are going to experience an adventure. We're going to go on a treasure hunt that will lead us to new discoveries. These discoveries are going to help you understand important information about some of the early American explorers. Raise your hands if you are ready to join me on this grand adventure." Let's assume that Mr. Brake now has the students' attention and interest in the lesson. He proceeds, saying, "First, I'll show you how the treasure hunt works. Then you'll have a chance to get involved." Mr. Brake opens a treasure chest and pulls out a slip of paper. Mr. Brake reads the clue on the slip of paper and then uses the clue to answer one of the questions on his worksheet about early explorers. This lesson works well for students who can read and understand the clues. Dave, however, can't read the clues. Stephanie can read the clues, but the vocabulary in the clues is unfamiliar. She doesn't know what most of the words mean. What are the likely learner outcomes for Dave and Stephanie, who, by the way, were very attentive and interested when Mr. Brake introduced the lesson? When students are interested and willing to participate in lessons, but are unable to do so successfully, their motivation quickly vanishes. Considering the prerequisite skills and knowledge that are needed for student success prevents negative learning experiences.

Teacher Effectiveness for Continuing the Lesson

A variety of teaching behaviors contribute to the success of a lesson. Of critical importance are the things that teachers do that increase the likelihood of high student achievement. Review of effective teaching literature reveals that providing clear and focused instruction, using content enhancements, and keeping students actively engaged are especially important for effective learning to occur (Benner, 1987; Bickel & Bickel, 1986; Brophy & Good, 1986; Christenson, Ysseldyke, & Thurlow, 1989; Cotton, 1995; Hudson, Lignugaris-Kraft, & Miller, 1993; Phillips, Fuchs, Fuchs, & Hamlett, 1996; Zigmond, Sansone, Miller, Donahoe, & Kohnke, 1986).

Provide Clear and Focused Instruction

Undoubtedly, clear and focused instruction enhances student learning. To provide clarity in lessons, teachers use multiple examples; signal transitions; and eliminate irrelevant information. They also avoid vague language (e.g., "sort of," "maybe," "probably"), discontinuities (e.g., losing one's place, losing one's train of thought, forgetting what comes next in a lesson), saying "uh," and digressing from the lesson topic (Brophy & Good, 1986; Chilcoat, 1989; Zigmond et al., 1986). Lesson clarity also is enhanced when systematic instructional procedures are followed. Examples of systematic instructional procedures were provided in the three teaching models discussed in Chapter 4. The basic idea is to present well-organized, step-by-step lessons without a lot of unnecessary and distracting verbiage. Chilcoat (1989) reported findings from a large body of research related to the effects of highly-organized, structured teacher presentations. Specifically these findings suggest clear, precise oral presentations:

- ▶ Increase the rate of learning new concepts;
- ▶ Facilitate long-term retention;
- ▶ Help students organize lesson content;
- ▶ Promote on-task behavior;
- ▶ Reduce errors in daily tasks; and
- ▶ Facilitate student achievement.

Chilcoat also found several studies that indicated lower-ability students learn better under structured instructional conditions, whereas higher-ability students learn well in both structured and unstructured conditions. Thus, when teaching in classes with a wide range of student abilities, it seems that structured, clearly focused instructional lessons will benefit the greatest number of students.

Clarity also is very important when providing directions. Students need to understand what they're supposed to do and how they're supposed to do it. In an attempt to assess whether students understand directions, one might ask, "Does anyone have any questions?" Posing this question, however, does not ensure student understanding. Some students think they understand, but don't, and others know they are confused, but don't want to admit it. A better way to check student understanding of directions is to have several students repeat the directions in their own words. Even students who aren't called on to repeat the directions benefit because they are hearing the directions several times.

Clarity of teacher presentations is one of the most important aspects of teaching. In fact, research suggests that clarity of presentation is one of the most consistent correlates of student achievement (Brophy & Good, 1986). Thus, teachers must continually evaluate the clarity of their teaching and seek ways to improve their instructional delivery.

Use Content Enhancements

Many students, especially those with disabilities, have difficulty acquiring and retaining important content information. They especially have trouble distinguishing important information from unimportant information, which makes it difficult to know what to concentrate on when learning new material. The inability to distinguish important information also makes it difficult to take good notes and to study the right information for tests. A variety of teaching behaviors, referred to as content enhancements, can help students who have these problems. Specifically, content enhancements are techniques that teachers use to help students identify, organize, understand, and remember critical information (Hudson, Lignugaris-Kraft, & Miller, 1993; Lenz, Bulgren, & Hudson, 1990). The content enhancements discussed in this section are instructional cues, visual displays, concept-teaching routines, and study guides. These enhancements are quite beneficial during the interactive teaching portion of group lessons.

Instructional Cues

Teachers can highlight important pieces of information through overt language and/or action. Verbal cues such as, "This is important, hint-hint," or "You need to know this," or "Be sure to get this in your notes" are helpful. Verbal repetitions of important information also cue students. When teachers say the same thing several times, perhaps using slightly different language, students are more apt to realize the information is important than if the teacher states the information only once. When information is presented on the board, an overhead transparency, or presentation software (e.g., Microsoft PowerPoint[1]) teachers can highlight what's important by circling, underlining, labeling, color-coding, pointing, or increasing print size. Having students repeat back (verbally rehearse) important information also is helpful. Finally, teachers can emphasize important points through stories, analogies, or pictures that help students remember the content.

Visual Displays

Another way teachers can emphasize important information during a lesson is to use visual displays. Visual displays are illustrations or diagrams that depict the relationship between two or more pieces of information. They are used to help students organize and understand the critical content being taught (Crank & Bulgren, 1993; Dye, 2000; Hudson et al., 1993; Lenz et al., 1990). There are five frequently used formats for displaying important information in a lesson: central, hierarchical, directional, comparative, and representative (see Fig. 5.2).

---

[1]Microsoft PowerPoint is a registered trademark of Microsoft Corporation.

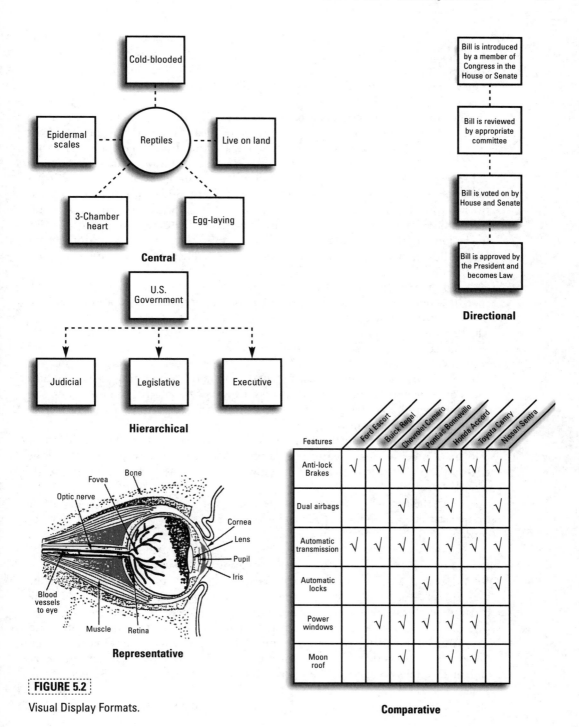

Central

Directional

Hierarchical

Representative

Comparative

The central format is used when there is one central idea with all other information extending from that one idea. For example, if Ms. Webb wants to activate students' thinking about attributes of reptiles, she writes "reptiles" in the center and then writes information about reptiles (e.g., cold-blooded, live on land) in the boxes that extend from the center.

The hierarchical format is used when the information being taught has a main topic with several subtopics. The main topic or idea is presented at the top of the visual display, indicating that it is the big idea or most important idea. The subtopics are subsumed under the main topic. For example, if Mr. Roberts is teaching government, he writes "U.S. Government" at the top of his display and then writes the three branches of the United States Government (Judicial, Legislative, Executive) in three equal-sized and level boxes below the "U.S. Government" box (indicating there are three equally important branches of the U.S. Government. During the lesson, Mr. Roberts could add extensions from each branch of government containing information specific to that branch. The visual display helps students organize and understand the relationships of the content presented.

The directional display format is used when items of information occur in a specific sequence. For example, when Mr. Roberts presents information related to the steps involved in getting a bill passed in Congress, he uses a directional display. The first step is listed in the first box, the second step in the second box, and so forth.

The comparative display format is used when two pieces of information are compared and contrasted. A matrix format helps display comparative data. For example, if Ms. Ford wants to teach students methods for selecting an automobile, she writes the names of several cars across the top of the matrix and the features of the cars down the side of the matrix. Checks are then placed in the boxes to display which cars have which features.

The representative display form is used when pictures are needed to illustrate information being taught. For example, when Mr. Lenz teaches students about the anatomy of the human eye, he uses a picture of the eye with the various parts clearly labeled.

Thus, the format or structure of the visual display is determined based on the information being taught. Particular formats lend themselves to particular types of content.

In addition to creating visual displays by hand, computer software also may be used to develop displays. For example, Inspiration (Inspiration Version 6.0 Software, 1988–1999)[2] is an easy-to-use program that allows teachers and students to create meaningful visual displays to illustrate ideas or concepts being taught. This software program also provides an integrated outlining environment. In some cases, it is helpful to create outlines first and then create visual displays to represent the content in the outline. Thus, this program combines visual and linear thinking to deepen understanding of concepts, increase memory retention, develop organizational skills, and tap creativity (Inspiration Version 6.0 Software Manual, 1988–1999). Students in

---

[2]Inspiration and Inspiration Software are registered trademarks of Inspiration Software, Inc.

VALIDATION BOX

5.3

Visual Displays

In a review of literature, eight studies were located that investigated the use of visual displays for teaching secondary students with learning disabilities. In these studies, visual displays were used in science, social studies, English, and health classes. The findings from this review were positive with regard to student achievement in seven of the eight studies. It was noted that it is important for the display to match lesson objectives and that effective teaching practices must accompany the use of the displays. For more information see: (Hudson, Lignugaris-Kraft, & Miller, 1993).

all grades (elementary through high school) can learn to use Inspiration for a variety of purposes. Specifically, the software can be used to develop concept maps (i.e., hierarchical diagram used to illustrate concepts beginning with a general concept and becoming more detailed), idea maps (i.e., visual brainstorming technique used to explore ideas and thoughts), web (i.e., visual display that shows how various bits of information are related to one another), storyboards (i.e., visual method to organize multimedia presentation or to design a Web page or site), and outlines for a variety of purposes (e.g., written reports, stories, class notes). One of the advantages of using software to create displays is that the final product is neat and easy to read. This is particularly helpful for students with fine motor and/or organizational difficulties who have trouble drawing the displays, but who benefit from the visual structures (see Validation Box 5.3).

Specific teaching routines (Concept Mastery Routine, Concept Anchoring Routine, and Concept Comparison Routine) that use visual displays for concept instruction have been developed at the University of Kansas Center for Research on Learning. In these routines, blank visual displays are provided to the students and they fill in information as the lesson progresses. These routines are effective for teaching classes with diverse groups of students.

Concept Teaching Routines

Much instructional time is spent teaching students concepts. A concept is a broad category or class into which events, ideas, or objects can be grouped (*The Concept Anchoring Routine Trainer's Guide*, 1994). Three teaching routines (Concept Mastery Routine, Concept Anchoring Routine, Concept Comparison Routine) have been developed to assist with concept teaching. Each of these routines involves using visual displays and a step-by-step process when teaching important concepts or concepts that students find confusing, but are expected to remember. The displays help students focus on the most important pieces of information in a lesson. They also help students understand the relationships between various pieces of content information.

The Concept Mastery Routine (Bulgren, Deshler, & Schumaker, 1993) is designed to help students understand and master key concepts. When using this routine, teachers engage students in discussion about the concept being taught. A visual display is used to guide the discussion (see Fig. 5.3).[3] The teacher and each student have a blank copy of the display. In addition to the blank display, the teacher also has a previously completed display to use as a reference during the lesson. The teacher's blank copy can be in the form of a transparency and used with an over-

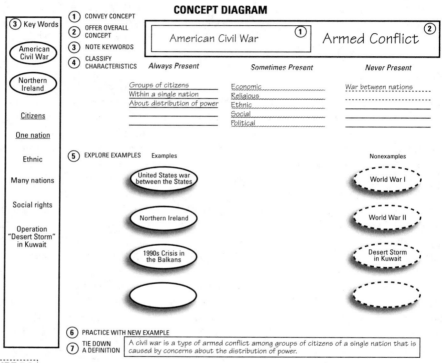

Visual Display for Concept Mastery Routine. (From *The Content Enhancement Series: The Concept Mastery Routine* [p. 15] by J. A. Bulgren, J. B. Schumaker, and D. D. Deshler, 1993, Lawrence, KS: Edge Enterprises. Copyright 1993 by J. A. Bulgren, J. B. Schumaker, and D. D. Deshler. Reprinted with permission. *Note:* This figure was taken from a book that is available through certified Strategic Instruction Model Trainers who conduct professional development workshops across the nation. To obtain information about this training and to identify trainers in your area, contact The University of Kansas Center for Research on Learning at http://www.ku-crl.org or [785] 864-4780.)

[3]The Content Enhancement devices shown in Figures 5.3 to 5.5 are instructional tools developed and researched at the University of Kansas Center for Research on Learning. They represent a number of organizing and teaching devices designed for teachers to use as they teach content information to classes containing diverse student populations. They are data-based teaching instruments that have been found effective when used in instructional routines that combine cues about the instruction, specialized delivery of the content, involvement of the students in the cognitive processes, and a review of the learning process and content material (Bulgren, Deshler, & Schumaker, 1993). They have not been shown to be effective tools if they are simply distributed to students.

head projector to ensure that all students can see how the display is used. Together, teachers and students fill in the appropriate information as the lesson progresses. After the teacher introduces the visual display explaining why and how it will be used, a seven-step routine is used to discuss the important concept in the lesson. Specifically, the teacher and students:

1. Identify and write the target concept on the visual display (e.g., American Civil War).
2. Identify a word or phrase that represents the overall or larger concept in which the target concept and similar concepts can be grouped, and write it on the visual display (e.g., armed conflict).
3. Identify key words, based on student background knowledge, that are associated with the target concept and write these words on the visual display.
4. Discuss characteristics that are always present, sometimes present, and never present in the concept and write them on the display.
5. Discuss examples and nonexamples of the concept and write them on the display.
6. Think of another possible example of the concept and test it using the identified characteristics.
7. Identify a definition for the newly learned concept. Include the concept name, the overall larger concept category, characteristics that are always present, and any additional information or rules that are needed to clarify relationships between or among characteristics. Write the definition on the display.

After completing the routine, teachers ask questions about the new concept and discuss the process of analyzing a concept (e.g., identifying broader, overall concept; thinking of characteristics and examples; defining concept) to ensure student understanding (Bulgren, Deshler, & Schumaker, 1993; see Validation Box 5.4).

The Concept Anchoring Routine (Bulgren, Schumaker, & Deshler, 1994a) is another teaching routine designed to help students understand new concepts by linking or anchoring characteristics of the new concept to characteristics of an

---

VALIDATION BOX

5.4

Concept Mastery Routine

The effectiveness of the Concept Mastery Routine was evaluated in a study involving 9 secondary teachers and 475 students. Of these students, 32 had learning disabilities. Results indicated that teachers could implement the routine after attending a 4-hour workshop. Students with and without learning disabilities showed significant improvements on concept acquisition tests and regularly scheduled class tests when the Concept Mastery Routine was used. They also took better class notes. For more information see: (Bulgren, 1987; Bulgren, Schumaker, & Deshler, 1988; Bulgren, Deshler, & Schumaker, 1993).

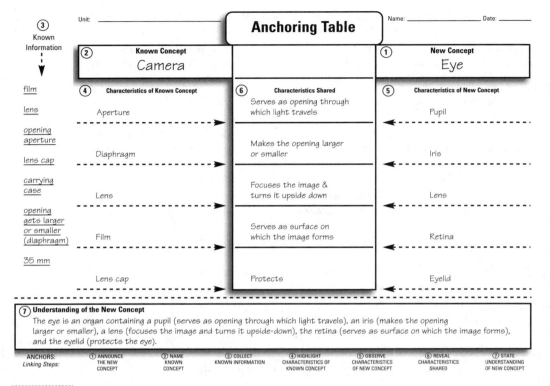

FIGURE 5.4

Visual Display for Concept Anchoring Routine. (From *The Content Enhancement Series: The Concept Anchoring Routine* [p. 42] by J. A. Bulgren, J. B. Schumaker, and D. D. Deshler, 1994, Lawrence, KS: Edge Enterprises. Copyright 1994 by J. A. Bulgren, J. B. Schumaker, and D. D. Deshler. Reprinted with permission. *Note:* This figure was taken from a book that is available through certified Strategic Instruction Model Trainers who conduct professional development workshops across the nation. To obtain information about this training and to identify trainers in your area, contact The University of Kansas Center for Research on Learning at http://www.ku-crl.org or [785] 864-4780.)

already-known concept. Similar to the Concept Mastery Routine, teacher and students use a visual display to facilitate discussion and illustrate relationships between the new and already-known concept (see Fig. 5.4). As the lesson progresses, the visual display is filled in. This routine involves six important steps. Specifically, the teacher and students:

1. Identify and write the New Concept on the visual display.
2. Identify a familiar or already-known concept that is similar in critical ways to the new concept being taught. Write the Known Concept on the visual display.
3. Explore the critical characteristics in the Known Concept that are similar to those in the New Concept and write these on the display.
4. Identify the critical characteristics of the New Concept that are analogous to those of the Known Concept and write them on the display.

Concept Anchoring Routine

The effectiveness of the Concept Anchoring Routine was evaluated in general education science and social studies classes that consisted of diverse groups of students (i.e., low-achieving, average-achieving, high-achieving, and students with learning disabilities). A total of 83 secondary students participated in the validation study. All four groups of students correctly answered substantially more test questions when the Concept Anchoring Routine was used than when traditional teaching methods were used. For more information see: (Bulgren & Schumaker, & Deshler, 1994a; Bulgren, Schumaker, & Deshler, 1994b).

5. Explore a more general way to describe how each critical characteristic pair of the Known Concept and New Concept are related and record this information in the center of the display.
6. Write a summary statement about the New Concept on the display.

After completing the routine, teachers ask students questions related to the new concept. The questions prompt students to connect the New Concept to the Known Concept and facilitate student thinking about the process of creating analogies to assist in understanding new information (Bulgren et al., 1994a; see Validation Box 5.5).

The Concept Comparison Routine (Bulgren, Lenz, Deshler, & Schumaker, 1995) is another teaching routine designed to help students understand two or more related concepts by analyzing similarities and differences among them. As with the other teaching routines, a visual display is used along with interactive discourse between the teacher and students (see Fig. 5.5 on p. 204). In this nine-step routine, the teacher and students:

1. Identify the concepts to be compared and write them on the visual display (e.g., cooperation and competition).
2. Identify the overall concept group within which both concepts fit and write this overall concept on the display (e.g., ways to do work).
3. Review the major characteristics of the two concepts being compared and list them on the display.
4. Identify the characteristics that both concepts share and record them on the display (i.e., like characteristics).
5. Identify the characteristics that are unique to each of the concepts and record them on the display (i.e., unlike characteristics).
6. Create and record names for the categories that describe the shared or like characteristics (i.e., like categories).
7. Create and record names for the categories that describe the unique or unlike characteristics (i.e., unlike characteristics).
8. Create a summary statement describing how the concepts are similar, and different from one another. Write the summary on the visual display.

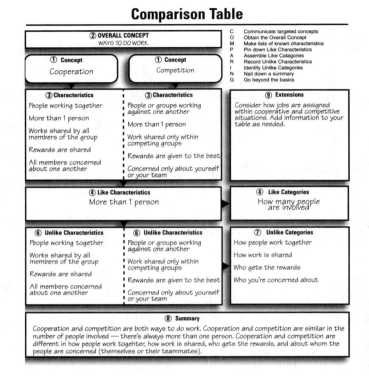

Comparison Table

② OVERALL CONCEPT WAYS TO DO WORK		C Communicate targeted concepts O Obtain the Overall Concept M Make lists of known characteristics P Pin down Like Characteristics A Assemble Like Categories R Record Unlike Characteristics I Identify Unlike Categories N Nail down a summary G Go beyond the basics
① Concept *Cooperation*	**① Concept** *Competition*	
③ Characteristics People working together More than 1 person Works shared by all members of the group Rewards are shared All members concerned about one another	**③ Characteristics** People or groups working against one another More than 1 person Work shared only within competing groups Rewards are given to the best Concerned only about yourself or your team	**⑨ Extensions** Consider how jobs are assigned within cooperative and competitive situations. Add information to your table as needed.
④ Like Characteristics More than 1 person		**④ Like Categories** How many people are involved
⑥ Unlike Characteristics People working together Works shared by all members of the group Rewards are shared All members concerned about one another	**⑥ Unlike Characteristics** People or groups working against one another Work shared only within competing groups Rewards are given to the best Concerned only about yourself or your team	**⑦ Unlike Categories** How people work together How work is shared Who gets the rewards Who you're concerned about
⑧ Summary Cooperation and competition are both ways to do work. Cooperation and competition are similar in the number of people involved — there's always more than one person. Cooperation and competition are different in how people work togehter, how work is shared, who gets the rewards, and about whom the people are concerned (themselves or their teammates).		

FIGURE 5.5

Visual Display for Concept Comparison Routine. (From *The Content Enhancement Series: The Concept Comparison Routine* [p. 54] by J. A. Bulgren, B. K. Lenz, J. B. Schumaker, and D. D. Deshler, 1995, Lawrence, KS: Edge Enterprises. Copyright 1995 by J. A. Bulgren, B. K. Lenz, J. B. Schumaker, and D. D. Deshler. Reprinted with permission. *Note:* This figure was taken from a book that is available through certified Strategic Instruction Model Trainers who conduct professional development workshops across the nation. To obtain information about this training and to identify trainers in your area, contact The University of Kansas Center for Research on Learning at http://www.ku-crl.org or [785] 864-4780.)

9. Extend understanding of the concepts in some way (e.g., explore one of the characteristics in greater detail; research an unanswered question; explore a new characteristic). Write the extension task on the visual display.

After completing the routine, the teacher asks a variety of questions to review the new learning. The questions relate to concept characteristics, concept categories, and the similarities and differences among the concepts. Finally, the benefits for identifying like and unlike characteristics are discussed (e.g., helps with remembering; helps with learning new information). Students are encouraged to refer back to their visual displays when preparing for exams or completing other content-related assignments (Bulgren et al., 1995; see Validation Box 5.6).

Study Guides

Another technique to enhance student learning during lessons is to provide study guides (sometimes referred to as "guided notes") for students to use while a lesson

VALIDATION BOX

5.6

Concept Comparison Routine

The effectiveness of the Concept Comparison Routine was evaluated in general education science and social studies classes that consisted of diverse groups of students including low-achieving students and students with learning disabilities. A total of 107 secondary students participated in the validation study. Test questions that were related to content covered using the Concept Comparison Routine were answered with a higher accuracy rate than questions related to content taught using traditional methods. For more information see: (Bulgren, Lenz, Deshler, & Schumaker, 1995; Bulgren, Lenz, Schumaker, & Deshler, 1995).

is in progress. Study guides consist of partial outlines of the lesson content, a list of questions related to the content, or diagrams (see Fig. 5.6 on p. 206). These various study guide formats help students organize the information they're learning. The students fill in missing information or answer the questions on the study guide as the lesson progresses. Study guides are easy to individualize to meet varying student needs. For example, students who need a great deal of support with their notetaking can receive study guides that contain more information than those for students who are capable of entering the information themselves. Teacher verbalizations also can be used to provide varying degrees of support. When students first begin to use study guides, teachers may want to remind them to fill in information as it is discussed (e.g., "Let's write the six states of Australia on our study guides."). As students become more proficient in using the guides, these verbal cues are reduced. In addition to helping students focus on critical information during a lesson, study guides can be used later to prepare for tests or class assignments. Study guides also can be used to facilitate student understanding of independent reading assignments. The students fill in the missing information on their study guides as they read the assigned text. When study guides are used in this manner, Horton and Lovitt (1989) found that students performed better with guides than they did with self-study. The versatility of study guides makes them especially appropriate when teaching groups of diverse students (see Validation Box 5.7 on p. 207).

Keep Students Actively Engaged in the Lesson

In addition to providing clear and focused instruction that includes content enhancements, it is very important to keep students actively engaged in the lesson. Students who experience learning difficulties frequently display passive learning characteristics (e.g., avoid active participation, let attention wander) that can hinder their learning. Thus, teachers must use numerous techniques to keep students involved in the learning process. Included among these techniques are maintaining instructional momentum, using effective questioning, providing feedback, and using lecture pauses.

Partial Outline Format

Australia

I. Geography

   A. Six States/Capitals

      1. _____

      2. _____

      3. _____

      4. _____

      5. _____

      6. _____

   B. Two Territories

      1. _____

      2. _____

II. Land of Diversity

   A. People

      1. _Aboriginal_____

      2. _____

   B. Places

      1. _Great Barrier Reef_____

      2. _____

      3. _____

   C. Wildlife

      1. _____

      2. _____

      3. _____

Question Format

1. What are the states and territories that make up Australia?

   _____

   _____

2. Who were the native people of Australia? What contributions have they made?

   _____

   _____

3. What geographical diversity exists in Australia?

   _____

   _____

4. What animals are native to Australia that are not native to the United States?

   _____

   _____

Diagram Format

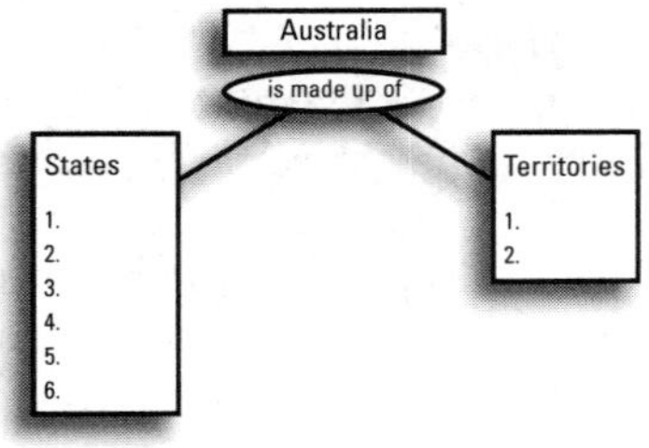

FIGURE 5.6

Study Guide Formats.

Study Guides

▶ In two studies, study guides were used to enhance lectures for students with diverse abilities in seventh grade science classes. In the first study, 42 high-, medium-, and low-achieving students used outline format study guides and precision teaching drills (i.e., 1-minute timings). When the performance of these students was compared with that of 124 control group students, findings revealed that medium- and low-achieving students performed significantly better than control-group students. No differences were found between the high-achieving groups. In the second study, the same intervention was used with 20 students with learning disabilities and 172 students without disabilities. Students with and without learning disabilities who used study guides outperformed the students who didn't use the guides. For more information see: (Lovitt, Rudsit, Jenkins, Pious, & Benedetti, 1985; Lovitt, Rudsit, Jenkins, Pious, Benedetti, 1986).

▶ The effects of using guided notes (i.e., study guides) were assessed in a study involving 6 students with learning disabilities who ranged in age from 9.2 to 11.8 years. The intervention was used in a general education science class with all students in the class. Results indicated that students with and without disabilities produced greater gains on tests when they used guided notes rather than their own personal, idiosyncratic notetaking. Results also suggested that reviews immediately following class lectures are helpful. For more information see: (Lazarus, 1991).

▶ In a follow-up study, the effects of using guided notes (i.e., study guides) and in-class reviews were assessed with four high school students with learning disabilities and one high school student with behavior disorders. The intervention was used in general education history classes with all students enrolled in the courses. The use of guided notes without review and of guided notes with review were both effective for improving student performance on chapter tests. The gains obtained by students who received both guided notes and in-class reviews were greater and more immediate than the gains obtained by students who received guided notes without in-class reviews. For more information see: (Lazarus, 1993).

▶ In a second follow-up study, the effects of using guided notes with three post-secondary students in a general psychology course were investigated. Again, the intervention resulted in increased performance on course quizzes and excellent performance on the final examination for the course. For more information see: (Lazarus, 1993).

▶ In another study, the effects of guided notes on the academic performance of 7 students with learning and behavioral difficulties were investigated. The students, aged 13 to 18, were enrolled in a juvenile detention center. Six of the 7 students improved their quiz performance when guided notes were used. All 7 students reported that they learned more when they used guided notes. For more information see: (Hamilton, Seibert, Garner III, Talbert-Johnson, 2000).

Instructional Momentum

When teaching a lesson to a group of students, it is important to maintain instructional momentum. In other words, the lesson needs to progress without lulls that result in nonproductive time. This means teachers need to be prepared for the lesson prior to its initiation. They need to know the sequence of events in the lesson. Using commercial programs with scripted lessons is one way to maintain instructional momentum. Some teachers use note cards, lesson outlines, or their actual lesson plan to maintain the flow of their lessons. Highlighting key points on these cards, outlines, or plans is helpful because teachers can glance down and quickly cue themselves with regard to the next part of the lesson. Diagrams, overhead transparencies, and/or multimedia presentations also can be used to help teachers maintain the momentum of the lesson. These instructional tools help keep the lesson focused and on track without unnecessary delays. If a variety of instructional materials are being used in a lesson, it is helpful to have all needed materials organized and ready. The flow of the lesson is obviously disrupted if the teacher has to stop to look for or retrieve a material that he or she forgot to get prior to beginning the lesson. Simply put, one of the best ways for teachers to maintain instructional momentum is to be prepared and organized. This includes knowing what the specific components of the lesson are and the sequence in which they will be presented.

Another important aspect of maintaining instructional momentum relates to the pacing of the lesson. Even when teachers are well prepared and organized, decisions must be made regarding how quickly to move through the lesson. General consensus from research on effective teaching indicates that quick-paced lessons facilitate student involvement (Benner, 1987; Brophy & Good, 1986; Brophy & Alleman, 1991; Englert, 1984; Phillips et. al., 1996; Rosenshine, 1983). Quick-paced lessons help keep students on-task while simultaneously providing more opportunities for student involvement than slower-paced lessons. Additionally, maintaining a quick pace promotes the completion of planned activities. It is important to note that the recommendation for quick-paced lessons refers to the presentation rate that the teacher uses during individual lessons. It does not refer to the total amount of instructional time spent on learning a particular skill or content. The amount of time needed for content mastery varies from student to student. Lower-achieving students may need more instructional lessons to acquire and retain information being taught. It is important for students to master instructional material before moving on to new lessons.

Effective Questioning

Teacher questioning is an important aspect of lesson implementation. The primary purposes for asking questions are to assess student understanding and facilitate further learning. Specifically, questioning provides opportunities for students to practice previously learned or newly obtained knowledge, focuses students' attention on important information in a lesson, helps students and teachers assess whether learning is taking place, keeps students actively involved in the lesson (Gall, 1984), and perhaps most importantly, facilitates student achievement (Brophy &

Good, 1986; Sindelar, Smith, Harriman, Hale, & Wilson, 1986; Stallings, Cory, Fairweather, & Needels, 1977; see Validation Box 5.8).

A variety of recommendations related to teacher questioning have emerged from research. Following these recommendations enhances the likelihood that students will benefit from teacher questioning:

1. Ask one question at a time. In other words, avoid asking a second or third question prior to receiving a response to the first question. Asking multiple questions in sequence without related responses is confusing to students (Brophy & Good, 1986).
2. Provide 3 to 5 seconds of wait time (i.e., the length of time a teacher waits for an answer from a student after asking a question and the length of time a teacher waits for further comments or questions after receiving a response from the student). The wait time allows students to process the question, formulate their responses, and extend their thinking about the content (Rowe, 1974, 1986; Tobin, 1980) (see Validation Box 5.9 on p. 210).
3. State questions clearly using language that students understand. Care should be taken to avoid ambiguous or vague questions (Brophy & Good, 1986).
4. Ask questions students can answer. Most questions (i.e., 75 percent) should elicit correct answers; the remaining questions should elicit incorrect or incomplete answers rather than complete failures to respond (Brophy & Good, 1986).
5. Use response cards (i.e., cards, signs, or items such as lap white boards that are simultaneously held up by all students in the class to indicate their answers/responses to teacher questions). Response cards provide opportunities for every student to answer every question and to learn from watching peers (Gardner III, Heward, Grossi, 1994; Heward, Gardner III, Cavanaugh, & Courson, 1996).

**VALIDATION BOX
5.8**

Teacher Questioning

The effects of teacher instructional behaviors on student reading achievement were investigated in a study involving 30 teachers; 15 teachers predominantly served students with learning disabilities and 15 teachers predominantly served students with mental retardation. A total of five 80-minute observations were conducted in each classroom over a period of 4 months. The use of teacher questioning (i.e., asking questions and monitoring responses) was the single best predictor of reading achievement gain for both students with learning disabilities and mental retardation. Moreover, the achievement of students with learning disabilities was strongly related to watching other students engaged in answering teacher questions. For more information see: (Sindelar, Smith, Harriman, Hale, & Wilson, 1986).

VALIDATION BOX

5.9

Wait Time

▶ A review of literature related to the use of wait time revealed that the quality of discourse is markedly improved when wait time is increased to 3 or more seconds. This finding was consistent across a variety of instructional situations and levels ranging from first grade to university-level instruction. Moreover, these studies revealed that wait time is effective with high-achieving students and students with disabilities. For more information see: (Rowe, 1986).

▶ The relationship between wait time and student achievement was investigated in a study involving 733 students in 23 intact middle-school classes in Australia. Findings revealed that extended wait time of approximately 3 seconds resulted in higher student achievement in science than wait time lasting for shorter periods of time. For more information see: (Tobin, 1980).

6. Acknowledge student responses to questions (Albers & Greer, 1991; Brophy & Good, 1986) and encourage or prompt students to provide additional information (Mariage, 1995).

Research findings related to how difficult questions should be and whether higher-level questioning (e.g., questions that require interpretation and synthesis of information) results in higher student achievement than lower-level factual questioning (e.g., simple recall of information presented) are inconsistent. Thus, further study is needed in these areas (Brophy & Good, 1986; Johnston, Markle, & Haley-Oliphant, 1987).

Feedback

Providing feedback to students is an important aspect of the teaching/learning process. The primary purpose for feedback is to let students know how they are doing and to extend the opportunity for learning beyond the initial question, assignment, or activity. High-quality feedback is timely, direct, accurate, substantive, constructive, prescriptive, specific, outcome-focused, encouraging, and positive (Baechle & Lian, 1990; Danielson, 1996; Larrivee, 1986; Mastropieri & Scruggs, 1994; Silverman, 1992). Several types of feedback can be used when teaching interactive lessons to groups of diverse students.

Consequating student responses   Consequating student responses simply involves letting students know whether their answer is correct or incorrect. In other words, the teacher asks a question and the student responds. The teacher then consequates the response with statements such as "Right!" and "That's correct!" or "No, let me show you." This three-step process (i.e., teacher asking question, student answering question, teacher consequating) is referred to as a three-term contingency trial and serves as a basic unit of instruction. Research shows that increasing the number of three-term contingency trials increases the rate of correct student responses while simultaneously maintaining low rates of incorrect responses (Albers & Greer, 1991).

Ms. Butler's students enjoy using their lap boards to answer math questions. This procedure gives each student a chance to answer all questions. The students are actively engaged and Ms. Butler can easily identify students who need additional instruction and practice.

Differentiated feedback During verbal questioning, four types of student responses can be identified: *(a)* correct, quick, and firm; *(b)* correct but hesitant; *(c)* incorrect but a careless error; or *(d)* incorrect, suggesting lack of knowledge of facts or a process (Rosenshine & Stevens, 1986). Each of these four responses necessitates a different type of feedback response from the teacher. If the student's response to the teacher's question is correct, quick, and firm, then a short statement of acknowledgment (e.g., "That's correct.") is appropriate because it doesn't disrupt the flow of the lesson. If the student's response is correct, but hesitant, indicating some uncertainty, the teacher response again includes a short statement of acknowledgment (e.g., "That's the correct answer to this word problem") and then includes moderate amounts of process feedback (e.g., "We know that Michael can purchase all three items because when we add up the individual costs, the total is $4.45 and he has $5.00."). If the student's response is incorrect, but the teacher knows it was just a careless mistake, then it is best to simply correct the student and continue with the lesson. If, however, a student's response is incorrect due to lack of knowledge or understanding, then the teacher provides prompts or hints to lead the student to the correct answer or reteaches the material. Typically, hints, prompts, or rephrased questions are posed when the error response is initially made and reteaching occurs at a later time when students who have mastered the material are engaged in something else (Rosenshine & Stevens, 1986). It is best to avoid dwelling on incorrect student responses during an interactive group lesson. The correction procedure (e.g., prompts or rephrased questions) should be positive and quick. If the student doesn't respond to the prompt, the teacher can provide the answer and then immediately ask the question again. Thus, the teacher-student interaction ends with the student responding correctly. The following example illustrates this process:

Teacher: "What is the capital of Florida?" (teacher pauses 3 to 5 seconds)
Student: (doesn't respond)
Teacher: "It's a city in the northern part of Florida that begins with a *T*."
    (teacher pauses 3 to 5 seconds)
Student: (still doesn't respond)
Teacher: "Tallahassee. What's the capital of Florida?"
Student: "Tallahassee."
Teacher: "That's correct."

Instructive feedback   Instructive feedback is a procedure designed to increase the efficiency of instruction (i.e., to allow students to acquire additional information in the same amount of instructional time). The procedure involves consistently adding additional information to students' responses. For example, if, during a lesson on the bones in the human body, the teacher asks, "What is the radius?" and the student says, " It's the bone in our arms," the teacher could provide instructive feedback by saying, "That's right. It's the thicker and shorter bone in our forearm." Instructive feedback is "instructive" because new or additional information is provided; it is "feedback" because the information is provided after students respond. The primary value of instructive feedback is that students learn more in about the same amount of time it takes to simply recognize that the response was correct (Werts, Wolery, Gast, & Holcombe, 1996).

There are three types of instructive feedback: expansion of the target skill, parallel instructive feedback, and novel instructive feedback (Werts et al., 1996). Expansion feedback involves presenting information that relates to the topic, but is somewhat different. For example, when learning the definition of photosynthesis, the teacher tells the student an additional fact about photosynthesis that isn't included in the dictionary definition. Another example of expansion feedback is telling students the definition of words when the target skill is simply reading the words. Parallel feedback involves giving the students a different form of the stimulus material that requires the same response. For example, after presenting the math fact 4 + 4, the teacher shows multiple facts (e.g., 2 + 6, 3 + 5, 7 + 1) that result in the same answer as the target fact. Another example of parallel feedback is numerals and corresponding number words (i.e., 1 and one; 3 and three). Novel feedback involves presenting information that is unrelated to the target skill and from a different curricular area. For example, when students are learning to solve multiplication word problems, the teacher points out that sentences begin with a capital letter and end with a punctuation mark or when learning shapes, the teacher names the colors of the shapes. Students are not expected to respond to instructive

In this math class, students work in triads during the intentional 2- to 4-minute lecture pauses. They compare their notes and work a problem together to be sure they understand what the teacher just explained.

feedback. It's simply provided as supplemental information. Students with disabilities learn most of the supplemental information when instructive feedback is used (Werts et al., 1996) and the procedure seems to be appropriate for any classroom setting (Latham, 1997; see Validation Box 5.10 on p. 214).

Lecture Pauses

Another teaching behavior that helps facilitate student acquisition and retention of lesson content is the use of structured pauses when covering large amounts of information through lecture format (Rowe, 1976, 1980, 1983; Hawkins, 1988; Hughes, Hendrickson, & Hudson, 1986). Typically, the lecture-pause procedure involves lecturing for a short period of time (e.g., 4 to 10 minutes) and then pausing for 2 to 4 minutes. During the pauses, students form dyads or triads and discuss the content just covered, compare their notes for completeness and accuracy, or practice using the newly acquired information (e.g., problem solving, naming lists of information). Several variations of this procedure can be used. For example, instead of forming dyads or triads, students can use the pause time to independently review their notes and think about the content (Hawkins, Brady, Hamilton, Williams, & Taylor, 1994) or teachers can conduct a quick question-answer review of the mate-

VALIDATION BOX

5.10

Instructive Feedback

A review of 23 research studies containing 113 participants (94.6 percent with disabilities) revealed that instructive feedback is an effective teaching strategy. Students acquire and maintain most of the instructive feedback information without requiring additional instructional time (i.e., less than 1 minute increase was noted). Studies revealed that instructive feedback is effective in a variety of instructional arrangements (i.e., one-to-one, small group, group, and computer-assisted) with a variety of presentation modes (i.e., verbal, visual, and combinations of the two). Findings also revealed this procedure is effective with pre-school through secondary-aged students. For more information see: (Werts, Wolery, Holcombe, & Gast, 1995).

rial just covered (Hudson, 1997). Depending on the students in the class, teachers decide how much structure is needed during the pause time. For example, some students may be quite capable of deciding how to best use the pause time, but other students benefit from having an index card that specifically lists what should be done during the pause (e.g., 1. Ask your partner two questions about the material just covered; 2. Work two additional problems together; and 3. Thank your partner for his or her help). Regardless of the amount of imposed structure, the purpose of the lecture-pause procedure is to help students retrieve missed information, process the lesson content, and focus their attention on important details (see Validation Box 5.11).

Teacher Effectiveness for Ending the Lesson

Post-organizers are used to bring closure to the interactive portion of a lesson. A variety of components may be included in post-organizers. Included among the possible components are verbal summary of the content covered in the lesson, a question-answer review of the key concepts in the lesson, review of visual displays used in the lesson, discussion with regard to generalizing what has been learned, feedback regarding student performance during the interactive portion of the lesson, predictions regarding future learning, review of rationale for learning and using the information, and statements related to upcoming lesson.

Provide Practice Opportunities

After an interactive lesson, students need opportunities to practice what they've learned. In-class assignments and homework assignments are typically used to provide this practice. Students with and without disabilities benefit from high-quality, independent practice assignments and related feedback (Brophy & Good, 1986; Jenson, Sheridan, Olympia, & Andrews, 1994; Mims, Harper, Armstrong, & Savage, 1991; Paschal, Weinstein, & Walberg, 1984; Rosenshine & Stevens, 1986). Many stu-

Lecture-Pause Procedures

▶ Eight ninth-grade students with mild disabilities participated in a study evaluating the effectiveness of two types of lecture pause procedures (i.e., pauses that involved independent review and pauses that involved peer dyad review). The procedures involved a repeated sequence of 2 minutes of teacher-directed review, 4 minutes of lecture, and 4 minutes of pause. Both independent and peer pauses were effective for increasing student performance in decimal computation and fluency in addition, subtraction, and multiplication. For more information see: (Hawkins, Brady, Hamilton, Williams, & Taylor, 1994).

▶ The lecture pause procedure was implemented with 8 junior high students with emotional disturbance in a private psychiatric hospital. The procedure was used during English class. Lecture occurred for 4 minutes; then student dyads paused for 3 minutes and followed a 5-step process that was written on index cards (i.e., Check understanding with peer; Discuss the point of grammar shown on care; Work on the examples on the card with your peer; Write new examples; Thank peer for help.). Seven of the 8 students improved on their worksheets when the pause procedure was used. For more information see: (Hawkins, 1988).

▶ In another study, the lecture pause procedure was used with 16 seventh graders (8 low achievers and 8 high achievers) in their science class. Lecture occurred for 6 to 8 minutes; then students discussed the covered content in small groups for 2 minutes. Seven of the 8 low-achieving students improved their factual recall, and all 8 of the high-achieving students improved their factual recall. For more information see: (Hughes, Hendrickson, & Hudson, 1986).

dents with disabilities have difficulty completing independent assignments (Gajria & Salend, 1995; Lenz, Ehren, & Smiley, 1991; Polloway, Foley, & Epstein, 1992). Thus, it is important for teachers to provide high-quality assignments and the necessary support to promote content mastery and meaningful learning experiences.

In an attempt to better understand and meet the needs of students with disabilities, several studies have been conducted to explore student and teacher views about homework and/or in-class assignments (Bryan, Nelson, & Mathur, 1995; Nelson, Epstein, Bursuck, Jayanthi, & Sawyer, 1998; Rademacher, Schumaker, & Deshler, 1996; Sawyer, Nelson, Jayanthi, Bursuck, & Epstein, 1996). These studies reveal important ideas for providing quality assignments to both elementary and secondary students.

Student and Teacher Perceptions about Homework and Class Assignments

Bryan, Nelson, and Mathur (1995) studied the views of 701 elementary students receiving instruction in general education classrooms, 91 elementary students with disabilities receiving instruction in resource room settings, and 17 elementary students with disabilities receiving instruction in self-contained special education classrooms. Students with disabilities were experiencing the greatest amount of difficulty with homework. When compared to students in general education, students in resource settings believed homework was dull and boring, too hard, and a waste of time. When compared to students in general education, students in self-contained classes believed they were less likely to complete their homework, wouldn't do well on the homework, and that homework was too hard. All three groups of elementary students viewed parents as knowledgeable and helpful in doing homework.

In another study, middle-school students (17 with high incidence disabilities and 194 without disabilities) voiced their opinions about homework in general education classes (Nelson et al., 1998). They indicated a preference for: *(a)* giving assignments that can be finished in school, *(b)* allowing extra-credit assignments, *(c)* starting assignments in class to ensure understanding, *(d)* giving assignments that can be completed without any help, and *(d)* allowing small groups of students to work on assignments together. They didn't like differential treatment regarding assignments (i.e., giving different students different assignments, grading assignments differently, giving shorter assignments to some students, giving fewer assignments to some students). All students felt strongly about this including those with disabilities.

Teacher and student focus groups in two middle schools identified twelve characteristics of quality assignments (Rademacher, Schumaker, & Deshler, 1996). Teachers and students reported that quality assignments include *(a)* clear, well-organized instructions; *(b)* an understood purpose so students see how completing the work will benefit their learning; *(c)* evaluation criteria so students know how their work will be judged or graded; *(d)* optimal challenge to avoid boredom and frustration; *(e)* personal relevance to students' lives; *(f)* feedback so students know what they did well and how they can improve their work; *(g)* format variety that differs from traditional worksheets; *(h)* available resource lists needed to complete the work; *(i)* opportunities for creative expression; *(j)* opportunities to work with others; *(k)* completion time considerations, including time to work in class; and *(l)* student choices and options within the general parameters of the assignment.

When asked what teachers should do when giving assignments, students indicated that teachers should incorporate nine factors: (1) offer challenge, (2) consider amount of work/time, (3) offer help, (4) give clear directions, (5) offer variety, (6) promote understanding, (7) provide feedback, (8) provide opportunities to redo work, and (9) demonstrate enthusiasm (Rademacher, Deshler, Schumaker, & Lenz, 1998).

To follow up the work of the focus groups, 71 middle- and high-school teachers, 71 middle-school students with learning disabilities, and 102 middle-school students without learning disabilities completed surveys that involved ranking the importance of the 12 characteristics of quality assignments and the 9 factors teachers should use. All of the characteristics and factors were deemed important. There were a couple of noteworthy similarities and differences among the teacher and student responses. Teachers and students with learning disabilities identified clear, well-organized directions as the most important characteristic, while students without disabilities ranked this as the second-most-important characteristic. An interesting difference between teacher and student rankings was noted with regard to giving students choices within their assignments. Of the important characteristics, teachers ranked student choice last. Students without learning disabilities ranked student choice as most important and students with learning disabilities ranked it second in importance (Rademacher et al., 1996).

In another study, high school students with learning disabilities who received their instruction in general education classes were individually interviewed (Sawyer et al., 1996). Results of the interviews revealed seven factors that make homework easy or difficult for these students. The seven factors were: *(a)* methods of assigning homework, *(b)* assistance for students, *(c)* student ability, *(d)* attitude and effort, *(e)* routine and structure, *(f)* traits, and *(g)* sense of future. Specifically, students noted that teachers should: *(a)* assign homework early in the class period to allow time for questions; *(b)* explain the task and provide examples; *(c)* provide assistance that includes explanations, demonstrations, or checking for accuracy (assistance from teachers or families); *(d)* provide routine and structure (self-managed routines such as keeping homework assignments in one place, recording due dates, and using assignment books were noted as most helpful); and *(d)* demonstrate patience. Students also noted that thinking about their future after high school improved their homework performance. With regard to what makes homework difficult, the students specifically noted the following: *(a)* not understanding the content; *(b)* understanding the homework in class, but not remembering how to do it later (at home); and *(c)* not liking the subject, teacher, or homework in general.

The combined findings from these studies suggest that teachers should:

▶ Make assignments meaningful (related to student interest and needs);
▶ Ensure appropriate level of difficulty;
▶ Provide clear instructions including examples;
▶ Devote time to answering questions about the assignment;
▶ Check student understanding of the assignment;
▶ Give students opportunities to make choices;
▶ Involve parents in the homework process; and
▶ Provide assistance and feedback.

Review of Recommended Homework Practices

Patton (1994) conducted an extensive review of literature related to homework practices. He organized his findings into four categories: management considerations, assignment considerations, student competencies, and parent involvement. Management considerations refer to teacher-initiated procedures used to improve the homework process. Assignment considerations relate to the assignment itself (e.g., purpose of the assignment, demands on the students, possible adaptations). Recommendations related to student competencies focus on skills and information that students need to be successful with their homework, as well as skills that can be developed through the homework process. Finally, recommendations related to parent involvement focus on effective ways for parents to participate in the homework process. Within each of these four categories, Patton identified homework practices that have research-based support.

Management practices with validated support include assessing students' homework skills to prevent problems, involving the parents, communicating the consequences for not completing assignments, implementing incentive programs for completing homework, having parents sign and date homework, and evaluating assignments. Assignment practices with validated support include using homework for proficiency, generalization, or maintenance of skills rather than initial learning; ensuring reasonable chance of completion and high rate of success; and providing assistance to students who need additional support. Validated practices related to student competence include ensuring that students have the knowledge and skills required to complete the assignment, promoting the use of resources to help with homework, and helping students with self-management skills. Validated practices related to parent involvement include providing parent training on homework assistance and maintaining ongoing communication and involvement between parents and teachers. Following these recommendations enhances the likelihood that homework assignments will result in positive student outcomes.

Strategies for Improving Independent Practice Assignments

A variety of strategies are available for teachers to use related to student assignments. Included among these are the Quality Assignment Routine (Rademacher, Deshler, Schumaker, & Lenz, 1998), cooperative homework teams (O'Melia & Rosenberg, 1994), and parent communication strategies (Jayanthi, Bursuck, Epstein, & Polloway, 1997). The Quality Assignment Routine is appropriate for either in-class or homework assignments. Cooperative homework teams and parent communication strategies are specifically designed for homework assignments.

The Quality Assignment Routine

The Quality Assignment Routine (Rademacher, Deshler, Schumaker, & Lenz, 1998) is a teaching routine that helps with planning and delivering quality assignments to diverse groups of students. The routine consists of three phases: planning, presenting, and evaluating.

During the Planning Phase, teachers create motivating assignments taking into consideration the students' interests, needs, abilities, background knowledge, and potential difficulties with the assignment. Specifically, teachers use four steps to plan quality assignments for students. The steps are remembered using the acronym PLAN. The four steps are *(a)* **P**lan the purpose of the assignment, *(b)* **L**ink assignment to student needs and interests, *(c)* **A**rrange clear student directions, and (*d*) **N**ote evaluation date and results. Three questions are used to help teachers plan the purpose of the assignment:

1. What will the students accomplish?
2. How will they do this?
3. Why is this important? What are the benefits?

Four questions are used to help teachers link the assignment to student needs and interests:

1. How can the assignment be made personally relevant for students?
2. What options or choices can be given to the students?
3. What are the pitfalls for successful completion of the work?
4. What are the solutions to these pitfalls?

Next, teachers identify the action steps required to complete the assignment, the supplies and resources students can use, and the grading criteria (e.g., accuracy, neatness, timeliness) along with the due date and total possible points for the assignment. Thinking about this information helps teachers arrange clear directions. The final step in PLAN, note evaluation date and results, involves identifying a date that the teacher will evaluate the assignment outcomes and consider ways to improve the assignment if it is given again in the future.

During the Presenting Phase of the routine, teachers explain the assignment in such a way that all students understand what they are supposed to do. During this phase, teachers communicate what constitutes "quality" for the assignment. Students are taught to listen to and record assignment directions. Assignment Sheets are used to facilitate this process. The teacher demonstrates and students model filling in the Assignment Sheet with important information about the assignment (e.g., due date, step-by-step directions, options available, grading criteria, supplies/resources, number of study sessions needed). After completing the Assignment Sheets, students are given an opportunity to review the information, ask questions, think about how they'll approach the assignment, and set some goals related to the assignment. Teachers then ask questions about the assignment to ensure student understanding. Students are given time in class to begin the assignment so that teachers can circulate and further monitor their understanding of the assignment. Assistance can be provided to any student who seems confused or who proceeds incorrectly.

The final phase in the Quality Assignment Routine is the Evaluating Phase. During this phase, teachers ensure that students receive feedback about their performance on the assignment. The primary goal for this feedback is to motivate students to complete more assignments and to improve the quality of their work. After evaluating students' assignments, feedback is provided to the whole class, identifying the primary strengths noted and any error patterns that emerged among the group. Feedback to individual students is provided when deemed necessary. Students also are taught to self-evaluate their assignments related to promptness, neat-

VALIDATION BOX

5.12

Quality Assignment Routine

Twelve middle-school social studies teachers and 262 students participated in a study to determine whether the Quality Assignment Routine could be implemented in general education classes. The study also examined teacher and student satisfaction with the routine. The routine was taught to six teachers; the remaining six served as the control group. The six teachers who learned the routine demonstrated significantly more of the effective planning, explanation, and evaluation behaviors involved in providing quality assignments than the six teachers who were not taught the strategy. Follow-up questionnaires revealed that teachers who learned the routine and their students were more satisfied with the assignment completion process in their classes than the control group teachers and students. For more information see: (Rademacher, Deshler, Schumaker, & Lenz, 1998; Rademacher, Schumaker, & Deshler, 1996).

ness, completeness, and editing (i.e. spelling, grammar, punctuation, clarity of ideas, and accuracy of content).

Students benefit from active involvement in the Quality Assignment Routine (Rademacher et al., 1998). In addition to the previously discussed involvement, the authors of the routine recommend including students in the planning of class assignments. Moreover, students can help make decisions about the requirements for a quality assignment. If students help create assignments, they are more motivated to complete them. [Information regarding training in this routine is available through the University of Kansas Center for Research on Learning, 521 Joseph R. Pearson Hall, 1122 West Campus Road, Lawrence, KS 66045; telephone: (785) 864-4780; fax: (785) 864-5728] (see Validation Box 5.12).

Cooperative Homework Teams

The use of cooperative homework teams is another strategy for improving independent practice (O'Melia & Rosenberg, 1994). Using this strategy, students with varying ability levels are assigned to three- or four-member cooperative homework teams. Homework assignments that take between 15 and 20 minutes are assigned each night. The next day, the homework teams meet for approximately 10 minutes. One team member is designated as the checker for that particular day. The checker uses an answer key to grade the students' papers and the teacher records the individual grades. Then the checker returns each student's paper. Errors are corrected and team members are encouraged to work together to make all the needed corrections. The corrected papers are then turned in to the teacher. Individual student scores are averaged together to come up with a team score. Points are awarded for completing the assignment and for percentage correct on the assignment. At the end of the week, certificates are awarded to members of the teams who met or exceeded a preselected criteria. When O'Melia and Rosenberg used this strategy,

VALIDATION BOX

5.13

Cooperative Homework Teams

One hundred seventy-one middle-school students and 10 teachers participated in a study involving the use of cooperative homework teams. The students who were a part of cooperative homework teams completed significantly more homework assignments than students who were in a control group and therefore not a part of a team. Students in the cooperative homework teams also earned significantly higher percentage scores on the homework assignments than the control group students. For more information see: (O'Melia & Rosenberg, 1994).

they provided differentiated math practice depending on student needs. Answer keys were provided to the checker, students were encouraged to work together, and points were awarded equally regardless of the level of difficulty of the assignments (see Validation Box 5.13).

Parent Communication Strategies

Focus groups consisting of parents of students with disabilities, general education teachers, and special education teachers identified six problems related to communication about student homework that is assigned in general education classes (Jayanthi, Bursuck, Epstein, & Polloway, 1997). The six problems were that parents and teachers do not: (1) initiate communication, (2) communicate often enough, (3) communicate regularly enough with each other, (4) communicate when problems first occur, (5) follow through with what they say, and/or (6) communicate clearly. Although parents and teachers agreed on these problems, not surprisingly they didn't agree on who was responsible for the problems. The focus groups identified a variety of strategies that teachers, administrators, parents, and students can use to overcome communication difficulties related to homework assignments. A list of the identified strategies is presented in Table 5.1 on page 222. The listed strategies can be used as a springboard for additional ideas. Clearly, the feasibility and effectiveness of the identified strategies will vary from school to school and from classroom to classroom. What appears to be particularly important, however, is that some type of systematic communication occurs on a continuous basis. Moreover, the communication system needs to begin early in the school year or when problems are first noticed (Epstein et al., 1997; see Validation Boxes 5.14 and 5.15 on p. 223).

Provide Feedback on In-Class and Homework Assignments

Earlier in this chapter, the importance of providing feedback during the interactive portion of lessons was discussed. Feedback also is important with regard to students' performance on in-class and homework assignments. These assign-

TABLE 5.1

Homework Communication Strategies for Teachers, Administrators, Parents, and Students

Teachers	Administrators	Parents	Students
Provide written progress reports using brightly colored paper.	Establish homework hotlines.	Call teachers early in the morning so call can be returned same day.	Keep track of homework assignments and seek needed assistance.
Give parents information about homework assignments and policies at beginning of semester.	Facilitate communication among teachers (e.g., change teacher schedules, room assignments).	State expectations regarding homework and communication to teachers and students.	Act as liaison between home and school (e.g., deliver messages).
Communicate with other teachers to avoid too many assignments on one night.	Provide release time for teachers to communicate with parents, students, and each other.	Try to attend face-to-face meetings. Ask students about homework every night.	Record assignments in an assignment book and have the book available at school and home.
Have face-to-face communication with parents and other teachers.	Create schoolwide or districtwide policies on homework and communication.	Establish and follow through with consequences when students do not complete homework.	
Realize that homework may not always be the first priority.	Encourage students to use assignment notebooks.	Provide phone numbers and schedules to teachers.	
Help students complete and turn homework in on time.	Facilitate opportunities for communication (e.g., evening conferences, phone lists of teachers and when they are available, host family nights, phone in every classroom).		
	Ask teachers who are good communicators to mentor other teachers.		
	Provide opportunities for students to do homework while at school.		
	Place assignments in public libraries that stay open in evenings.		
	Avoid giving homework to students whose family situation interferes with possible completion.		

VALIDATION BOX

5.14

Parent and Teacher Homework Communication

▶ A national survey involving 502 elementary-, middle-, and high-school general education teachers indicated a perception that communication problems among teachers and parents are serious impediments to the effective use of homework with special education students who receive instruction in general education classes. Specifically, these teachers indicated that serious communication problems exist related to frequency and quality of communications with parents, parent attitudes about homework, the role of the special education teacher, availability of teachers to communicate with parents, and teacher knowledge about learning disabilities and homework strategies; therefore specific communication strategies regarding homework are needed. For more information see: (Epstein et al., 1997).

▶ In another national survey involving 673 special education teachers in elementary, middle-, and high-school settings, teachers were asked to rank-order recommendations for improving communication between parents and teachers regarding homework for students with disabilities. Among the top-ranked recommendations were: (a) general education teachers should require students to keep a daily assignment book, (b) parents should check with their child about homework each day, (c) administrators should provide release time for teachers to communicate with parents, (d) school personnel should provide telephone homework hotlines for parents to call with homework-related questions, (e) students should maintain their daily assignment book, (f) school personnel should schedule after-school homework sessions for students who need extra help, and (g) special education teachers should provide general education teachers with information about the strengths and weaknesses of students with disabilities. For more information see: (Bursuck et al., 1999).

VALIDATION BOX

5.15

Homework and Student Achievement

▶ The results of a review of literature that included 120 studies indicate that homework has a positive effect on achievement, but the effect varies depending on grade level. Homework had substantial positive effects on high-school students and also benefited junior-high-school students, but only half as much. The effect of homework on elementary-school students was trivial. In-class assignments were found to be more effective than homework in elementary classes. In junior-high and high-school classes, homework was superior to in-class study. This review did not differentiate between students in general or special education programs. For more information see: (Cooper, 1989).

▶ In a review of literature, eight studies were located that involved homework and students with learning disabilities. The results of these studies suggest that homework practices for students with learning disabilities should emphasize (a) simple, short assignments; (b) careful monitoring and rewards for completing homework; and (c) parental involvement. For more information see: (Cooper & Nye, 1994).

ments provide students with the practice that is needed to master lesson content. Providing students with feedback helps them reach mastery faster. Two types of feedback have support for increasing student achievement: personally designed, written comments and verbal feedback routines.

Personally Designed, Written Comments

One method teachers can use to provide feedback to students is to write performance-related comments. If the practice activity involves turning in a written product, comments can be put right on the assignments and then returned to the students. If the assignment doesn't involve a written product, but instead involves a presentation or hands-on project, written comments can be recorded on an evaluation form that is designed specifically for the assignment (see Fig. 5.7). When measuring the effects of written comments on student achievement, research suggests that personally designed comments (i.e., comments that teachers write based on knowledge of the student and details of their work) are more beneficial than prespecified comments based on the assignment grade (i.e., A = Excellent!; B = Good Work; C = Perhaps try to do still better?; D = Let's bring this up; F = Let's raise this grade!), but prespecified comments are better than no comments at all (Page, 1992).

SCIENCE PROJECT EVALUATION FORM

Student name: _____   Date: _____

Points Earned:

Thoroughness (25 points possible)   _____

Creativity (25 points possible)   _____

Appearance (25 points possible)   _____

Accuracy (25 points possible)   _____

Total Points Earned out of 100   _____

Comments: _____

_____

_____

Strengths: _____

_____

_____

Suggestions for improvement: _____

_____

_____

FIGURE 5.7

Written Evaluation Form.

Elaborated Feedback Routines

Elaborated feedback involves providing verbal feedback that extends beyond "knowledge of results." First, the teacher evaluates the students' work by analyzing the types of errors the student is making. Then, the teacher meets with the student and provides specific feedback about what the student is doing well and what needs improvement. Kline's (1989) Feedback Routine involves the following steps:

1. Teacher grades student product and makes note of the types of errors the student is making.
2. Teacher gives product back to the student and asks student to correct the work.
3. Teacher checks student corrections and notes any changes in the types of errors made.
4. Teacher and student meet for feedback conference.
5. Teacher elicits from student positive statements about the work. If the student is unable to identify any positives, the teacher makes at least three positive statements about the work.
6. Teacher describes one type of error the student made and shows examples (e.g., "In each problem that required regrouping, the number in the tens place was one more than it should have been. Let's find out why.").
7. Teacher describes a method for avoiding the error, models the method, and asks the student to practice the method. The teacher watches and

Ms. Jones is using a systematic feedback routine with Sarah. She knows that this type of feedback will help Sarah master the content in an efficient manner.

provides assistance until the student independently completes at least one example.

8. Teacher describes another type of error that the student made and repeats the process described in Step 7. This continues until all the error types are addressed.

9. Teacher summarizes the content of the feedback conference and indicates what the student should do in the future. Finally, a statement of high expectation for the next trial is made (e.g., "I bet you will reach mastery tomorrow.").

Another elaborated feedback routine (i.e., Feedback-Plus-Assistance Routine) involves these same nine steps, with a few additional steps at the end of the conference. Specifically, the student makes a summary statement about what he or she learned in the feedback conference and then writes this statement in the form of a goal to be reviewed before and after the next similar assignment. Information about how to accept feedback appropriately is also included in this second routine. (Kline, Schumaker, & Deshler, 1991). Both the Feedback Routine and the Feedback-Plus-Assistance Routine offer a systematic method for providing detailed information to students about their performance. Elaborated feedback takes more time than written feedback, especially in classes with large groups of students. The overall instructional time needed for students to master the content, however, will be reduced if this type of feedback is provided. Elaborated feedback is especially helpful when students first begin to practice new and challenging material (see Validation Box 5.16).

Clearly, teachers must monitor student performance carefully to give appropriate written or verbal feedback. Many experts indicate that high rates of success are important when students are involved in practice activities. Recommendations for appropriate levels of student performance on independent practice activities range from 80 to 100 percent (Brophy, 1980; Christensen, Ysseldyke, & Thurlow, 1989; Gersten, Carnine, & Williams, 1981; Rosenshine, 1983).

VALIDATION BOX 5.16

Feedback Routines

The Feedback Routine and the Feedback-Plus-Assistance Routine were validated in a study involving 27 teachers and 54 students with learning disabilities. Results indicated that the teachers effectively integrated the feedback routines into their teaching. Moreover, use of the routines significantly reduced the number of student trials to mastery and the number of student errors in subsequent practice trials. The two routines seemed to be equally powerful in terms of teacher and student learning. For more information see: (Kline, Schumaker, & Deshler, 1991).

Teacher Effectiveness and Personal Belief Systems

The material presented in this chapter, thus far, has emphasized the technical aspects of effective teaching. Research-based information related to the orchestration of effective instructional lessons has been shared. Teachers who master the technical aspects of teaching and simultaneously integrate their own creative "touch" into the instructional process will undoubtedly be more successful with students than those who don't. There is, however, an additional dimension that correlates to teacher effectiveness and student success. This additional dimension involves the personal belief systems of teachers.

Research suggests that three types of teacher beliefs (i.e., teacher efficacy, teacher locus of control, and pupil-control ideology) are highly correlated to student achievement (Agne, Greenwood, & Miller, 1994). Teacher efficacy is defined as teachers' beliefs that their skills and abilities can influence student learning regardless of external factors such as home environment or family background (Gibson & Dembo, 1984). Locus of control is defined as the belief that specific behaviors will produce certain outcomes (Bandura, 1977). According to Bandura, teachers may believe that certain teacher behaviors result in student achievement (locus of control) while simultaneously believing they are not personally capable of executing those particular behaviors (self-efficacy). Pupil-control ideology refers to teacher beliefs about how to best control the behavior of their students. There appears to be a continuum of teacher beliefs related to student control. On one end of the continuum, teachers demonstrate high control needs, punitive sanctions, impersonal relationships with students, lack of trust, moralistic perceptions, and a priority for maintaining order. On the other end of the continuum, teachers demonstrate a humanistic orientation with high levels of communication and interaction in the classroom, close relationships with students, mutual respect, positive attitudes, flexibility while promoting self-discipline, self-determination, and independence (Willower, Eidell, & Hoy as cited in Agne et al., 1994).

Although all three types of teacher beliefs are interconnected and appear to influence teacher effectiveness, the pupil-control ideology appears to be the most powerful. Teachers who display strong humanistic pupil-control beliefs (i.e., a belief system whose fundamental orientation is characterized as "caring") are more likely to be recognized as outstanding teachers with significant expertise than teachers who display a highly controlling belief structure (Agne et al., 1994; see Validation Box 5.17 on p. 228).

Thus, in addition to being technically sound, teachers need to focus on the humanistic aspects of teaching. It is critically important for teachers to conscientiously develop behaviors that demonstrate caring. Teachers need to model respectful, supportive interactions with others and promote this type of behavior among all students in the class. The likelihood of academic success increases when students form an emotional attachment to teachers, peers, and their school (Solomon, Watson, Battistich, Schaps, & Delucchi, 1992). Educators can help facilitate these emotional attachments by communicating that they care and fostering healthy relationships among their students. The significance of caring and demonstrating that concern on a daily basis is very important:

VALIDATION BOX

5.17

Teacher Belief Systems

Differences between the Teacher of the Year award winners and other practicing teachers were investigated using four instruments designed to measure teacher beliefs. There were 180 teachers who participated in this study. The award-winning teachers were significantly more humanistic in their beliefs regarding pupil-control issues and they held a significantly greater number of degrees at the graduate level than other teachers with nearly identical school settings, grade levels, subjects taught, and teaching experience. These two variables were the strongest predictors for receiving "Teacher of the Year" recognition. More internal locus of control and higher efficacy beliefs also were noted among the recognized teachers. No differences were noted between the two groups of teachers with regard to job-related stress, gender, years of teaching experience, or grade level taught. For more information see: (Agne, Greenwood, & Miller, 1994).

Caring is central to the shaping of relationships that are meaningful, supportive, rewarding, and productive. Caring happens when children sense that the adults in their lives think they are important and when they understand that they will be accepted and respected, regardless of any particular talents they have. Caring is a product of a community that deems all of its members to be important, believes everyone has something to contribute, and acknowledges that everyone counts. We work better when we care and when we are cared about, and so do students. Caring is a spoken or an unspoken part of every interaction that takes place in classrooms, lunchrooms, hallways, and playgrounds. Children are emotionally attuned to be on the lookout for caring, or a lack thereof, and they seek out and thrive in places where it is present. The more emotionally troubled the student, the more attuned he or she is to caring in the school environment. At-risk kids are most vulnerable for growing up without caring. It is caring that plays a critical role in overcoming the narrowness, selfishness, and mean-spiritedness that too many of our children cannot avoid being exposed to, and that replaces these attitudes with a culture of welcome (Elias et al., 1997, p. 6).

Practice Activities

▶ Select a lesson topic and write the prelesson teacher dialogue. The dialogue should reflect obtaining the students' attention, getting students interested in the topic, communicating expectations, and considering prerequisite skills or prior knowledge.

▶ Select a specific school level (i.e., elementary, middle, or high). Next, select a lesson topic and write the teacher dialogue. Focus on using clear, concise language.

▶ Create visual displays using five formats (central, hierarchical, directional, comparative, and representative). Include the relevant content information on the displays.

▶ Select a lesson topic and create a study guide.

▶ Role-play teaching scenarios that include asking questions and providing various types of verbal feedback (consequating, differentiated, instructive).

▶ Practice using the lecture-pause procedure.

▶ Observe an interactive lesson and create potential assignments that would provide in-class or homework practice related to the lesson.

▶ Role-play elaborated feedback routines.

▶ Identify twenty things teachers can do to demonstrate caring and/or promote caring among their students.

P O S T ORGANIZER

The things that teachers do when providing instruction greatly influence how much students will learn. Thus, it is very important to use effective teaching behaviors that enhance students' abilities to understand, remember, and generalize their learning. Additionally, it is important for teacher belief systems to reflect genuine caring that results in the orchestration of a caring classroom environment. The validated practices described in this chapter are appropriate for providing instruction to groups of diverse students within various educational settings.

References

Agne, K. J., Greenwood, G. E., & Miller, L. D. (1994). Relationships between teacher belief systems and teacher effectiveness. *The Journal of Research and Development in Education, 27*, 141–152.

Albers, A. E., & Greer, R. D. (1991). Is the three-term contingency trial a predictor of effective instruction? *Journal of Behavioral Education, 1*, 337–354.

Baechle, C. L., & Lian, M. J. (1990). The effects of direct feedback and practice on metaphor performances in children with learning disabilities. *Journal of Learning Disabilities, 23*, 451–455.

Bandura, A. (1977). Self-efficacy: Toward a unifying theory of behavioral change. *Psychological Review, 84*, 191–215.

Benner, S. M. (1987). Using effective teaching practices in the special education classroom. *European Journal of Special Needs Education, 2*, 191–201.

Bickel, W. E., & Bickel, D. D. (1986). Effective schools, classrooms, and instruction: Implications for special education. *Exceptional Children, 52*, 489–500.

Brigham, F. J., Scruggs, T. E., & Mastropieri, M. A. (1992). Teacher enthusiasm in learning disabilities classrooms: Effects on learning and behavior. *Learning Disabilities Research & Practice, 7*, 68–73.

Brophy, J. E. (1980). *Recent research on teaching.* East Lansing, MI: Institute for Research on Teaching, Michigan State University.

Brophy, J. E., & Alleman, J. (1991). Activities as instructional tools: A framework for analysis and evaluation. *Educational Researcher, 20*(4), 9–23.

Brophy, J. E., & Good, T. L. (1986). Teacher behavior and student achievement. In M. C. Wittrock (Ed.), *Handbook of research on teaching* (3rd ed., pp. 328–375). New York: MacMillan.

Bryan, T., Nelson, C., & Mathur, S. (1995). Homework: A survey of primary students in regular, resource, and self-contained special education classrooms. *Learning Disabilities Research & Practice, 10,* 85–90.

Bulgren, J. A. (1987). *The development and validation of instructional procedures to teach concepts in secondary mainstream classes which contain students with learning disabilities.* Unpublished doctoral dissertation, University of Kansas.

Bulgren, J. A., Deshler, D. D., & Schumaker, J. B. (1993). *The content enhancement series: The concept mastery routine.* Lawrence, KS: Edge Enterprises.

Bulgren, J. A., Lenz, B. K., Deshler, D. D., & Schumaker, J. B. (1995). *The content enhancement series: The concept comparison routine.* Lawrence, KS: Edge Enterprises.

Bulgren, J. A., Lenz, B. K., Schumaker, J. B., & Deshler, D. D. (1995). *Use and effectiveness of a concept comparison routine in secondary-level mainstream classes.* Lawrence, KS: University of Kansas Center for Research on Learning.

Bulgren, J. A., Schumaker, J. B., & Deshler, D. D. (1988). Effectiveness of a concept teaching routine in enhancing the performance of LD students in secondary-level mainstream classes. *Learning Disability Quarterly, 11,* 3–17.

Bulgren, J. A., Schumaker, J. B., & Deshler, D. D. (1994a). *The content enhancement series: The concept anchoring routine.* Lawrence, KS: Edge Enterprises.

Bulgren, J. A., Schumaker, J. B., & Deshler, D. D. (1994b). *Use and effectiveness of a concept anchoring routine in secondary-level mainstream classes.* Lawrence, KS: University of Kansas Center for Research on Learning.

Bursuck, W. D., Harniss, M. K., Epstein, M. H., Polloway, E. A., Jayanthi, M., & Wissinger, L. M. (1999). Solving communication problems about homework: Recommendations of special education teachers. *Learning Disabilities Research & Practice, 15,* 149–158.

Chilcoat, G. W. (1989). Instructional behaviors for clearer presentations in the classroom. *Instructional Science, 18,* 289–314.

Christenson, S. L., Ysseldyke, J. E., & Thurlow, M. L. (1989). Critical instructional factors for students with mild handicaps: An integrative review. *Remedial and Special Education, 10*(5), 21–31.

Collins, M. L. (1978). Effects of enthusiasm training on preservice elementary teachers. *Journal of Teacher Education, 29,* 53–57.

The concept anchoring routine trainer's guide. (1994). Lawrence, KS: Edge Enterprises.

Cooper, H. (1989). Synthesis of research on homework. *Educational Leadership, 47*(3), 85–91.

Cooper, H., & Nye, B. (1994). Homework for students with learning disabilities: The implications of research for policy and practice. *Journal of Learning Disabilities, 27,* 470–479.

Cotton, K. (1995). *Effective schooling practices: A research synthesis 1995 update.* Portland, OR: Northwest Regional Educational Laboratory.

Crank, J. N., & Bulgren, J. A. (1993). Visual depictions as information organizers for enhancing achievement of students with learning disabilities. *Learning Disabilities Research & Practice, 8,* 140–147.

Danielson, C. (1996). *Enhancing professional practice: A framework for teaching.* Alexandria, VA: ASCD.

Dye, G. A. (2000). Graphic organizers to the rescue! *Teaching Exceptional Children, 32*(3), 72–76.

Elias, M. J., Zins, J. E., Weissberg, R. P., Frey, K. S., Greenberg, M. T., Haynes, N. M., Kessler, R., Schwab-Stone, M. E., & Shriver, T. P. (1997). *Promoting social and emotional learning: Guidelines for educators.* Alexandria, VA: Association for Supervision and Curriculum Development.

Ellis, E. E. (1989). A metacognitive intervention for increasing class participation. *Learning Disabilities Focus, 5*(1), 36–46.

Ellis, E. E. (1991). *SLANT: A starter strategy for class participation.* Lawrence, KS: Edge Enterprises.

Englert, C. S. (1984). Effective direct instruction practices in special education settings. *Remedial and Special Education, 5*(2), 38–47.

Epstein, M. H., Polloway, E. A., Buck, G. H., Bursuck, W. D., Wissinger, L. M., Whitehouse, F., Jayanthi, M. (1997). Homework-related communication problems: Perspectives of general education teachers. *Learning Disabilities Research & Practice, 12,* 221–227.

Gajria, M., & Salend, S. J. (1995). Homework practices of students with and without learning disabilities: A comparison. *Journal of Learning Disabilities, 28,* 291–296.

Gall, M. (1984). Synthesis of research on teachers' questioning. *Educational Leadership, 42,* 40–47.

Gardner, R., III, Heward, W. L., & Grossi, T. A. (1994). Effects of response cards on student participation and academic achievement: A systematic replication with inner-city students during whole-class science instruction. *Journal of Applied Behavior Analysis, 27,* 63–71.

Gersten, R. M., Carnine, D. W., & Williams, P. B. (1981). Measuring implementation of a structured educational model in an urban school district. *Educational Evaluation and Policy Analysis, 4,* 56–63.

Gibson, S., & Dembo, M. (1984). Teacher efficacy: A construct validity. *Journal of Educational Psychology, 76,* 569–582.

Hamilton, S. L., Seibert, M. A., Gardner III, R., & Talbert-Johnson, C. (2000). Using guided notes to improve the academic achievement of incarcerated adolescents with learning and behavior problems. *Remedial and Special Education, 21,* 133–140, 170.

Hawkins, J. (1988). Antecedent pausing as a direct instruction tactic for adolescents with severe behavioral disorders. *Behavioral Disorders, 13,* 263–272.

Hawkins, J., Brady, M . P., Hamilton, R., Williams, R. E., & Taylor, R. D. (1994). The effects of independent and peer guided practice during instructional pauses on the academic performance of students with mild handicaps. *Education and Treatment of Children, 17,* 1–28.

Heward, W. L., Gardner III, R., Cavanaugh, R. A., & Courson, F. H. (1996). Everyone participates in this class. *Teaching Exceptional Children, 28*(2), 4–10.

Horton, S. V., & Lovitt, T. C. (1989). Using study guides with three classifications of secondary students. *The Journal of Special Education, 22,* 447–462.

Hudson, P. (1997). Using teacher-guided practice to help students with learning disabilities acquire and retain social studies content. *Learning Disability Quarterly, 20,* 23–32.

Hudson, P., Lignugaris-Kraft, B., & Miller, T. (1993). Using content enhancements to improve the performance of adolescents with learning disabilities in content classes. *Learning Disabilities Research & Practice, 8,* 106–126.

Hughes, C. A., Hendrickson, J. M., & Hudson, P. J. (1986). The pause procedure: Improving factual recall from lectures by low and high achieving middle school students. *International Journal of Instructional Media, 13,* 217–226.

Inspiration Version 6 [Computer Software]. (1988–1999). Portland, OR: Inspiration Software.

Inspiration Version 6 [Software Manual]. (1988–1999). Portland, OR : Inspiration Software.

Jayanthi, M., Bursuck, W., Epstein, M. H., Polloway, E. A. (1997). Strategies for successful homework. *Teaching Exceptional Children, 30*(1), 4–7.

Jenson, W. R., Sheridan, S. M., Olympia, D. E., & Andrews, D. (1994). Homework and students with learning disabilities and behavior disorders: A practical, parent-based approach. *Journal of Learning Disabilities, 27,* 538–548.

Johnston, J. H., Markle, G. C., & Haley-Oliphant, A. (1987). About questioning in the classroom: Questions about questions are difficult to answer. *Middle School Journal, 18*(4), 29–33.

Kline, F. M. (1989). *The development and validation of feedback routines for use in special education settings.* Unpublished dissertation, University of Kansas, Lawrence.

Kline, F. M., Schumaker, J. B., & Deshler, D. D. (1991). Development and validation of feedback routines for instructing students with learning disabilities. *Learning Disability Quarterly, 14,* 191–207.

Larrivee, B. (1986). Effective teaching for mainstreamed students is effective teaching for all students. *Teacher Education and Special Education, 9*(4), 173–179.

Latham, A. S. (1997). Learning through feedback. *Educational Leadership, 54*(8), 86–87.

Lazarus, B. D. (1991). Guided notes, review, and achievement of secondary students with learning disabilities in mainstream content classes. *Education and Treatment of Children, 14,* 112–127.

Lazarus, B. D. (1993). Guided notes: Effects with secondary and post secondary students with mild disabilities. *Education and Treatment of Children, 16,* 272–289.

Lenz, B. K., Bulgren, J., & Hudson, P. (1990). Content enhancement: A model for promoting the acquisition of content by individuals with learning disabilities. In T. E. Scruggs & B. Y. L. Wong (Eds.), *Intervention research in learning disabilities* (pp. 122–165). New York: Springer-Verlag.

Lenz, B. K., Ehren, B. J., Smiley, L. R. (1991). A goal attainment approach to improve completion of project-type assignments by adolescents with learning disabilities. *Learning Disabilities Research & Practice, 6,* 166–176.

Lovitt, T., Rudsit, J., Jenkins, J., Pious, C., & Benedetti, D. (1985). Two methods for adapting science materials for learning disabled and regular seventh graders. *Learning Disabilities Quarterly, 8,* 275–285.

Lovitt, T., Rudsit, J., Jenkins, J., Pious, C., & Benedetti, D. (1986). Adapting science materials for regular and learning disabled seventh graders. *Remedial and Special Education, 7*(1), 31–39.

Mariage, T. V. (1995). Why students learn: The nature of teacher talk during reading. *Learning Disability Quarterly, 18,* 214–234.

Mastropieri, M. A., & Scruggs, T. E. (1994). *Effective instruction for special education* (2nd ed.). Austin: PRO-ED.

Mims, A., Harper, C., Armstrong, S. W., & Savage, S. (1991). Effective instruction in homework for students with disabilities. *Teaching Exceptional Children, 24*(1), 42–44.

Nelson, J. S., Epstein, M. H., Bursuck, W. D., Jayanthi, M., Sawyer, V. (1998). The preferences of middle school students for homework adaptations made by general education teachers. *Learning Disabilities Research & Practice, 13,* 109–117.

O'Melia, M. C., & Rosenberg, M. S. (1994). Effects of cooperative homework teams on the acquisition of mathematics skills by secondary students with mild disabilities. *Exceptional Children, 60,* 538–548.

Page, E. B. (1992). Is the world an orderly place? A review of teacher comments and student achievement. *Journal of Experimental Education, 20,* 161–181.

Paschal, R. A., Weinstein, T., & Walberg, H. J. (1984). The effects of homework on learning: A quantitative synthesis. *Journal of Educational Research, 78,* 97–104.

Patton, J. R. (1994). Practical recommendations for using homework with students with learning disabilities. *Journal of Learning Disabilities, 27,* 570–578.

Phillips, N. B., Fuchs, L. S., Fuchs, D., & Hamlett, C. L. (1996). Instructional variables affecting student achievement: Case studies of two contrasting teachers. *Learning Disabilities Research & Practice, 11,* 24–33.

Polloway, E. A., Foley, R. M., & Epstein, M. H. (1992). A comparison of the homework problems of students with learning disabilities and nonhandicapped students. *Learning Disabilities Research & Practice, 7,* 203–209.

Rademacher, J. A., Deshler, D. D., Schumaker, & Lenz, B. K. (1998). *The quality assignment routine.* Lawrence, KS: Edge Enterprises.

Rademacher, J. A., Schumaker, J. B., & Deshler, D. D. (1996). Development and validation of a classroom assignment routine for inclusive settings. *Learning Disability Quarterly, 19,* 163–177.

Rosenshine, B. (1970). Enthusiastic teaching: A research review. *School Review, 78,* 499–514.

Rosenshine, B. (1983). Teaching functions in instructional programs. *Elementary School Journal, 83,* 335–352.

Rosenshine, B., & Stevens, R. (1986). Teaching functions. In M. C. Wittrock (Ed.) *Handbook of research on teaching* (3rd ed., pp. 376–391). New York: MacMillan.

Rowe, M. B. (1974). Wait-time and rewards as instructional variables, their influence on language, logic, and fate control: Part one-wait-time. *Journal of Research in Science Teaching, 11,* 81–94.

Rowe, M. B. (1976). The pausing principle—two invitations to inquiry. *Research on College Science Teaching, 5,* 258–259.

Rowe, M. B. (1980). Pausing principles and their effects on reasoning in science. *New Directions in Community Colleges, 31,* 27–34.

Rowe, M. B. (1983). Getting chemistry off the killer course list. *Journal of Chemical Education, 60,* 954–956.

Rowe, M. B. (1986). Wait time: Slowing down may be a way of speeding up!. *Journal of Teacher Education, 37,* 43–50.

Sawyer, V., Nelson, J. S., Jayanthi, M., Bursuck, W. D., & Epstein, M. H. (1996). Views of students with learning disabilities of their homework in general education classes: Student interviews. *Learning Disability Quarterly, 19,* 70–85.

Silverman, S. (1992). Teacher feedback and achievement in physical education: Interaction with student practice. *Teaching and Teacher Education, 8,* 333–344.

Sindelar, P. T., Smith, M. A., Harriman, N. E., Hale, R. L., & Wilson, R. J. (1986). Teacher effectiveness in special education programs. *The Journal of Special Education, 20,* 195–207.

Solomon, D., Watson, M., Battistich, V., Schaps, E., & Delucchi, K. (1992). Creating a caring community: A school-based program to promote children's prosocial competence. In E. Oser, J. Patty, & A. Dick (Eds.), *Effective and Responsible Teaching* (pp. 383–396). San Francisco: Jossey-Bass.

Stallings, J., Cory, R., Fairweather, J., & Needels, M. (1977). *Early childhood education classroom evaluation.* Menlo Park, CA: SRI International.

Tobin, K. G. (1980). The effect of an extended wait time on science achievement. *Journal of Research in Science Teaching, 17,* 469–475.

Werts, M. G., Wolery, M., Gast, D. L., Holcombe, A. (1996). Sneak in some extra learning by using instructive feedback. *Teaching Exceptional Children, 28*(3), 70–71.

Werts, M. G., Wolery, M., Holcombe, A., & Gast, D. L. (1995). Instructive feedback: Review of parameters and effects. *Journal of Behavioral Education, 5,* 55–75.

Zigmond, N., Sansone, J., Miller, S. E., Donahoe, K. A., & Kohnke, R. (1986). Teaching learning disabled students at the secondary school level: What research says to teachers. *Learning Disabilities Focus, 1,* 108–115.

Facilitating Various Instructional Arrangements

Usefulness and value can come in many forms.
—Po-Lung Yu

A D V A N C E ORGANIZER

Groups of students with diverse learning needs benefit from the use of various instructional arrangements. As learned in previous chapters, there is strong literature support for teacher-directed instruction for students with diverse learning needs. There are, however, other instructional arrangements that also result in high rates of student learning and achievement. Included among these are peer tutoring, cooperative learning, and computer-based instruction. In each of these arrangements, the teacher's role is largely to serve as a facilitator rather than the direct disseminator of instructional content. The teacher is still responsible for planning and monitoring the instructional process.

Teachers of diverse groups of students find that using a variety of instructional arrangements helps address the differing needs and learning preferences of the students in their classes. Rather than selecting one teaching approach (e.g., large-group, teacher-directed lectures) and using that approach with every lesson, creative teachers find ways to facilitate student learning using various approaches (e.g., small-group work; one-to-one instruction). This provides variety to the instructional program and gives students structured ways to interact and learn from one another and other mediums (e.g., technology).

Three instructional arrangements that have validated support for teaching elementary and secondary students with diverse learning needs are peer tutoring, cooperative learning, and computer-based instruction. These arrangements can be used to supplement the teaching models discussed in Chapter 4.

Peer Tutoring Arrangements

Peer tutoring is an instructional arrangement that involves students mediating instruction for other students. The teacher pairs students and identifies one student as the tutor and the other as the tutee. The tutor assists the tutee in learning and retaining academic content. A variety of peer tutoring configurations are used depending on students' needs, instructional goals, the teaching environment, and teacher preference. Variations of tutoring arrangements involve manipulating three key variables: age, delivery model, and ability level. With regard to age, teachers must decide whether to use same-age tutoring or cross-age tutoring. In same-age tutoring, the tutor and tutee are peers according to their chronological age and typically are enrolled in the same class. In cross-age tutoring, the tutor is older than the tutee and frequently comes from another class to do the tutoring. With regard to delivery model, teachers must decide whether to use classwide tutoring or individual tutoring. In classwide tutoring models, all students in the class participate in peer tutoring sessions at the same time. In individual tutoring models, just a few students are paired for tutoring sessions while most the class is engaged in other learning activities. With regard to ability level, teachers must decide whether to use tutor-as-expert, reverse-role tutoring, or reciprocal teaching. In tutor-as-expert, the tutor is functioning at a higher ability level or has already mastered the content being taught. In reverse-role tutoring, the student who typically has learning difficulties serves as the tutor. In some peer tutoring arrangements, reciprocal teaching occurs whereby both students, regardless of ability level, have a chance to be the tutor and the tutee. Each of these peer tutoring arrangements has research support.

Rationale for Using Peer Tutoring

Numerous studies confirm that peer tutoring is an effective instructional arrangement for students with and without learning difficulties (see Validation Box 6.1 on p. 238). Perhaps the most compelling reasons to include peer tutoring in students' instructional programs are: (a) the positive effects on student achievement, and (b) the responsiveness of this arrangement to student diversity. Both of these benefits are important given the current context of most elementary and secondary classrooms.

Increased Student Achievement

Research on effective instruction repeatedly shows that active student engagement is a critical factor in academic achievement (Warger, 1991). Achievement is higher when students are given many opportunities to respond and participate in lessons. Opportunity to respond is a core principle of peer tutoring. Unlike large-group instruction that allows students to spend large portions of time waiting to respond, peer tutoring arrangements promote constant participation with immediate feedback. The interactive, one-to-one nature of peer tutoring increases the amount of practice students receive and keeps them actively involved in academic tasks. This is particularly helpful for students who have difficulty staying on task during large group instruction. It also is helpful for students who have difficulty working independently. The immediate feedback received during tutoring sessions is beneficial in that it serves as a motivator while simultaneously preventing the practice of errors. Although one would expect tutees' achievement to increase, it is interesting to note that tutors also benefit academically from the tutoring process (Eiserman, Shisler, & Osguthorpe, 1987; Osguthorpe & Scruggs, 1986; Scruggs & Richter, 1988).

Responsiveness to Diversity

As public school classrooms become more ethnically and linguistically diverse and as policy initiatives continue to support teaching most or all students, including those with disabilities, in general education settings, it is not uncommon to find classrooms of students with levels of achievement that span more than five grades (Fuchs, Fuchs, Mathes, & Simmons, 1996; Jenkins, Jewell, Leceister, & Troutner, 1990). Teachers must therefore find ways to accommodate this diversity. Peer tutoring arrangements help teachers manage the vast differences among students' abilities. The tutoring activities

VALIDATION BOX

6.1

Peer Tutoring

▶ The effectiveness of peer tutoring for students with disabilities in reading was examined in a review of literature. A total of 11 studies were included in the review. The results indicated that peer tutoring in reading can be effective for students with disabilities. Studies that paired students with disabilities with normally achieving peers and allowed the students with disabilities to serve as tutor some of the time consistently produced strong effect sizes and significant outcomes. For more information see: (Mathes & Fuchs, 1991).

▶ The effectiveness of students with disabilities serving as peer tutors was investigated through a review of literature. A total of 19 studies were included in this review. Findings revealed that tutoring programs were effective for increasing academic achievement. Effect sizes on academic measures were very similar for tutors (0.59) and tutees (0.65). For more information see: (Cook, Scruggs, Mastropieri, & Casto, 1985–86).

▶ In a review of literature that included three review articles, six essays, and nine empirical studies on peer tutoring, results indicated that peer tutoring is a viable technique for providing instruction in diverse general education classrooms. Students with learning disabilities obtained positive outcomes in both the tutor and tutee roles as long as training and supervision were adequate. For more information see: (Byrd, 1990).

▶ The academic performance of students with mild disabilities who were involved in classwide peer tutoring programs in general-education classes was investigated in a review of literature on validated inclusive practices. Four experimentally controlled studies were reviewed. Results of the studies support the use of classwide tutoring programs for improving the academic performance of students with mild disabilities. Similar positive effects were found for students without disabilities. In three of the studies, students with disabilities were failing content tests prior to the peer tutoring intervention. After involvement in the peer tutoring programs, the students earned passing test scores. For more information see: (Fisher, Schumaker, & Deshler, 1996).

▶ The effectiveness of classwide peer tutoring was investigated in two general education elementary classes that included students with mental retardation. Specifically, the study compared classwide peer tutoring to teacher-led instruction for improving spelling performance among four students with mental retardation and four students without disabilities (i.e., two high achievers, two low achievers). Findings revealed that spelling accuracy and levels of academic engagement were better during classwide peer tutoring than teacher-led instruction for both students with mental retardation and students without disabilities. For more information see: (Mortweet et al., 1999).

can vary among student pairs and therefore the amount of appropriate-level practice that each student receives is increased. In fact, research suggests that peer tutoring can double or triple the amount of practice students receive on instructional tasks (Greenwood, Delquadri, & Hall, 1989; Mathes & Fuchs, 1993). Peer tutoring relationships also can foster friendships among students from different ethnic backgrounds. As students work together and get to know one another, their comfort level increases and cross-cultural friendships are likely to occur. Moreover, students from cultures who value working together to accomplish important goals are apt to respond positively to peer tutoring arrangements. Peer tutoring relationships also promote positive interactions between students with disabilities and those without disabilities. Attitudes toward students with disabilities improve and interactions that extend beyond the tutoring sessions increase (Haring, Breen, Pitts-Conway, Lee & Gaylord-Ross, 1987; Kamps, Barbetta, Leonard, & Delquadri, 1994; Shisler, Osguthorpe, & Eiserman, 1987; Osguthorpe, Eiserman, & Shisler, 1985).

Classwide Peer Tutoring Programs

Although many variations of peer tutoring are effective for students with and without disabilities, classwide peer tutoring programs seem to work especially well in diverse classroom settings. Two classwide tutoring programs that have been validated for use with elementary and secondary students are *Together We Can! Class-Wide Peer Tutoring to Improve Basic Academic Skills* (CWPT) (Greenwood, Delquadri, & Carta, 1997) and Peer-Assisted Learning Strategies (PALS) for reading and math instruction (Fuchs, Mathes, & Fuchs, 1996; Fuchs, Fuchs, Karns, & Phillips, 1996). Both programs have been used successfully in general education classrooms that include students with disabilities.

The Classwide Peer Tutoring Program (CWPT)

Joseph Delquadri, Charles Greenwood, Judith Carta, and their colleagues at Juniper Garden Children's Project in Kansas City, KS, developed, field-tested, and refined the CWPT from 1981 to 1989 (Greenwood, Terry, Arreaga-Mayer, & Finney, 1992). Since that time, educators and researchers have continued to validate the use of CWPT. Specifically, research data indicate that CWPT improves students' engagement in academic tasks, increases academic achievement, enhances cooperative peer relations, and has long-term positive effects on academic performance (Bell, Young, Blair, Nelson, 1990; DuPaul & Henningson, 1993; Fuchs, Fuchs, Mathes, & Simmons, 1997; Greenwood et al., 1984; Greenwood, Terry, Utley, Montagna, Walker, 1993; Kamps, Barbetta, Leonard, & Delquadri, 1994; Maheady, Harper, & Mallette, 1991; Reddy et al., 1999; Simmons, Fuchs, Fuchs, Hodge, & Mathes, 1994).

To implement the CWPT program, teachers typically:

1. Schedule time for the tutoring sessions and assessment. The tutoring sessions are designed to last approximately 30 minutes and occur Monday through Thursday of each week. Assessment time is scheduled for Friday of each week.
2. Plan the content that will be practiced during the tutoring sessions (e.g., orally spelling and writing words, reciting and writing math facts) and

create lists for students to use while tutoring. Lists containing 10 to 30 items for students to practice in a given week are appropriate. Each item on the list should require an overt student response. Items may be acquired from existing class materials that correspond to instruction students have received.

3. Designate CWPT pairs and weekly teams. Tutor–tutee pairs can be on different instructional levels as long as answer keys are available (e.g., spelling and math). If answer keys are not available (e.g., reading), then students need to be paired based on similar skill levels. Triads may be formed if there is an odd number of students in the class. Once the tutoring pairs are established, each pair is assigned to one of two class teams. Thus, in a class of 28 students, there would be two teams with 7 tutoring pairs each. Tutoring pairs and teams change each week to add variety to the program. One student in each tutoring pair is designated as the "mover."

4. Teach students how to make a smooth transition to the tutoring session. A 6-step process is used. First, obtain students' attention. Second, tell the "movers" to stand. Third, provide a signal for the "movers" to go stand next to their tutoring partner. Fourth, praise the movers for quick and quiet moving and praise their partners for waiting quietly. Fifth, check to be sure each student has a partner and chair. Finally, have the "movers" sit down. It may be helpful to have students practice this transition routine several times prior to initiating the tutoring program.

5. Teach students how the tutoring program works. If, for example, the instructional activity is spelling, the tutor reads the spelling words from the tutoring list. The tutee writes the word and at the same time spells the word out loud. The tutor checks it against the word on the tutoring list. If the word is correct, the tutor awards two points. If the word is incorrect, the tutor spells it slowly for the tutee. The tutee can then earn 1 point by spelling the word out loud and writing the word correctly three times. No points are awarded if any of the three practice attempts are misspelled. If an error occurs, the tutor repeats the correct spelling and moves on to the next word. If the tutor goes through the entire list of words before 10 minutes are up, he or she starts again at the top of the list and the tutee continues to earn points. When 10 minutes are up, the students switch roles. The tutee now becomes the tutor and the tutor becomes the tutee and the tutoring process is repeated. If a tutor is unable to pronounce any of the words on the list, he or she can raise a help sign (i.e., the word *help* written on a piece of paper) and the teacher comes to assist.

   Throughout the tutoring session, the teacher moves among the students and awards bonus points for correct tutoring behaviors (e.g., saying spelling words clearly, correcting mistakes, awarding correct number of points, remembering to start the list over again). Verbal praise from the teacher accompanies the bonus points. After 10 minutes, both students in the tutoring pair add their points together. Then, the scores from all pairs on the team are added together to determine the team total. Finally, one of the two teams is declared the winner and receives applause from the other team.

On Fridays, the teacher conducts an assessment of each student's progress on the skills practiced that week. Daily point totals are summed up at the end of the week and a weekly team winner is announced.

6. Implement the tutoring program after students have been trained and clearly understand what to do.
7. Evaluate the program periodically to determine whether modifications are needed.

Although the CWPT program was originally designed to provide practice in reading, spelling, and math, researchers successfully extended the program's application to science and social studies in general education settings (Maheady, Sacca, & Harper, 1988; Pomerantz, Windell, & Smith, 1994). Students with and without disabilities improved test scores in both science and social studies after using modified CWPT procedures.

For additional information on this program, contact Sopris West Publishers at 4093 Specialty Place, Longmont, CO 80504; e-mail: www.sopriswest.com; telephone: (800) 547-6747; fax: (303) 776-5934.

Peer-Assisted Learning Strategies (PALS) for Instruction in Reading and Math

Douglas Fuchs, Lynn Fuchs, and their colleagues at Peabody College at Vanderbilt University developed the Peer-Assisted Learning Strategies (PALS) program to provide intensive reading and math practice (Vanderbilt University Publications and Design, 1996). The PALS program (formally known as the Peabody Classwide Peer Tutoring Program) was validated through a series of efficacy studies that were conducted for two successive years in general education classes in which students with learning disabilities were enrolled for reading and math instruction. More than 150 teachers and 3500 students participated in these studies. The results of these studies clearly support the effectiveness of the program (Joint Committee on Teacher Planning for Students with Disabilities, 1995).

PALS Reading (Fuchs, Mathes, & Fuchs, 1996) typically involves three 35-minute tutoring sessions per week. In this program, each tutoring pair consists of a higher- and a lower-performing student. Teachers list all their students from highest performer to lowest performer and then divide the list in half. The highest student in the high group is paired with the highest student in the low group. This matching process continues until all students have a partner. Each tutoring pair is then assigned to one of two teams; the ability levels of the two class teams is closely matched.

PALS Reading engages students in three strategic reading processes: partner reading, paragraph shrinking, and prediction relay. A total of 10 minutes is spent on each of these processes during the 35-minute tutoring session. The remaining five minutes is divided between a 2-minute retelling activity and 3 minutes of organiza-

Peer tutoring is used to provide additional practice on important academic skills. In classwide peer tutoring programs, all students have an opportunity to be both the tutor and tutee.

tional time (i.e., getting materials ready, putting materials away, transitioning between partners). Each tutoring session begins with partner reading. The higher-performing reader in each pair reads connected text for 5 minutes while the lower-performing peer acts as tutor. Then, the lower-performing student reads the same text for 5 minutes while the higher-performing student acts as tutor. Thus, the higher-performing student actually serves as a model for the lower-performing student while simultaneously gaining reading fluency practice.

Tutors are trained to use a standard correction procedure as errors are made. First, the tutor points to the missed word and says, "You missed this word. Can you figure it out?" The tutee is given 4 seconds to say the word correctly. Then, the tutee rereads the sentence and continues on. If the tutee does not say the word correctly in 4 seconds, the tutor says the word. The tutee repeats the word and then rereads the sentence and continues on. After both students have had their turn to read aloud for 5 minutes, the lower-performing student retells, in sequence, what has been read. The higher-performing student prompts with questions such as "What happened first?" and "Then what happened?" Both students are allowed to skim the text again. This retelling activity lasts for 2 minutes.

The next 10 minutes of the tutoring session involves paragraph shrinking. As with partner reading, the stronger reader first serves as the tutee. The tutee reads one paragraph aloud and then stops. The tutor asks the tutee two questions to help determine the main idea of the paragraph (i.e., "Who or what was the paragraph mainly about?" "What was the most important thing about the who or what?"). If an error is made, the tutor tells the tutee to skim the paragraph and try again. If the tutee is still incorrect, the tutor provides the answer. Next, the tutee must state the main idea in 10 words or less. Tutees are allowed multiple attempts to "shrink" their answer. These procedures are repeated with the next paragraph. After 5 minutes, the student roles reverse and the weaker reader becomes the tutee. The new tutee begins reading where his or her partner left off rather than repeating the same paragraphs.

The next 10 minutes of the tutoring session involve prediction relay, which extends paragraph shrinking to larger chunks of the connected text. Subsequent paragraphs of the same text are used in this activity. Prediction relay involves five steps: (1) higher-performing tutee makes prediction about what will be learned on the next half page of text, (2) tutee reads the half page of text aloud, (3) tutee confirms or disconfirms the prediction, (4) tutee states the main idea of the half page in 10 words or less, and (5) tutee predicts what will happen in the next half page of text. The tutor's job is to ensure that the tutee's predictions are reasonable, that the reading is accurate, and that the tutee follows the five steps. After 5 minutes the roles reverse.

Student prompt cards are used throughout the tutoring sessions to remind students what to do. The prompt card includes the questions the higher-performing student asks the lower-performing student during the retell phase of the tutoring session (e.g., "What happened first?" "Then what happened?"). The prompt card also includes things the tutor can say to facilitate the paragraph shrinking phase of the session (e.g., "Name the who or what"; "Tell the most important thing about the who or what"; "Say the main idea in 10 words or less"). Finally, the prompt card lists the four steps that are completed during the prediction relay phase of the tutoring session (i.e., predict, read, check, and summarize). Points are awarded for good performance during all phases of the tutoring session. During partner reading, 1 point is awarded after each correctly read sentence. After the retell activity, 10 points are awarded if the partners believe they worked hard and did their best. During paragraph shrinking, students can earn 3 points per paragraph: 1 for correctly identifying the subject, 1 for the main idea, and 1 for shrinking the main idea to 10 words or less. During prediction relay, students can earn 1 point for each step in the process: make reasonable prediction, read half a page aloud, check prediction, state main idea in 10 words or less (Mathes, Fuchs, Fuchs, Henley, & Sanders, 1994).

It is important to ensure that students understand all aspects of the tutoring process prior to initiating the PALS Reading program. It is a good idea to practice the process several times before actually beginning the first tutoring session. The program authors recommend spending 45 minutes teaching students how to set up materials, award points, and be a helpful partner. They also recommend practicing the three processes (partner reading, paragraph shrinking, prediction relay) for about 45 minutes each to prevent problems once the program begins.

PALS Math (Fuchs, Fuchs, Karns, & Phillips, 1996) involves 40-minute sessions that are conducted at least twice a week. A computer program is used to identify which students need help on particular math skills and to decide which students should be paired together based on their math needs. Similar to PALS Reading, each tutoring session is reciprocal (i.e., both students have an opportunity to be the tutor and both students have an opportunity to be the tutee).

PALS Math uses two primary procedures: coaching and practice. During coaching, the tutor asks a series of scripted questions that guide the tutee through the process needed to solve the first three math problems on his or her worksheet. The tutor has an answer key and uses correction procedures as needed. The tutee completes the next three problems without question guidance from the tutor. The tutee must explain what he or she is doing as these problems are solved. The tutor corrects any misunderstandings. Students switch roles halfway through the problem sheet. The total coaching process lasts 15 to 20 minutes.

Next, the students receive a mixed-problem worksheet containing the types of problems used during the coaching procedure and easier types of problems. Students work independently and then exchange papers and score each other's work. This practice lasts 5 to 10 minutes.

Each PALS pair works together to earn points. Specifically, points are earned for cooperating and constructing good explanations during coaching and for solving problems correctly during practice. The pair with the most points receives applause from the class and gets to collect the PALS tutoring materials (i.e., folders containing worksheets and pointsheets).

Prior to initiating PALS Math, the authors recommend that students receive training in how to conduct the tutoring sessions. Specifically, students need to know how to give and receive help, how to provide satisfactory explanations to their partners, and how the tutoring process is organized. In the commercial materials available for this program, there are seven 45-minute lessons that prepare students for the tutoring.

The PALS Reading program is available in four levels: kindergarten, beginning (1st grade), grades 2 to 6, and high school. There is one commercially available PALS Math program (grades 2 to 6). For additional information on these programs, contact the Kennedy Center Institute on Education and Learning, Box 328 Peabody, Vanderbilt University, Nashville, TN 37203-5701; telephone: (615) 343-4782; fax: (615) 343-1570; www.peerassistedlearningstrategies.net.

Individualized Peer Tutoring Programs

Peer tutoring also can be used with one pair or a few pairs of students while the majority of students in the class are engaged in some other activity. This type of peer tutoring provides opportunities for the teacher to simultaneously provide teacher-directed, small-group instruction or to monitor students involved in independent practice activities. Peer tutoring that doesn't involve the entire class still needs to be organized with a structured plan. The teacher identifies the goals for tutoring and determines the specific activities that will be used to meet the goals. The teacher selects the instructional materials and frequently develops materials to facilitate the tutoring process as well. For example, the teacher may design a tutoring folder that includes directions for the tutor and some type of monitoring sheet to record the tutee's progress (see Fig. 6.1). It is the teacher's responsibility to ensure that students' understand the tutoring procedures prior to implementing them. Clear expectations and opportunities to practice the tutoring procedures increase the likelihood that successful tutoring will occur. Another important factor related to the success of peer tutoring is the assignment of tutoring pairs. The teacher must think about which students will work well together and must decide whether to use cross-age tutoring involving older students tutoring younger students, same-age tutoring, or reciprocal tutoring in which students take turns serving as tutor and tutee. These decisions typically are based on the needs of the students and logistical issues. Finally, the teacher is responsible for monitoring the peer tutoring process to ensure that productive learning is taking place. Program adjustments and refinements are made as needed.

Guidelines for Implementing Peer Tutoring

Regardless of whether teachers implement one of the prescribed classwide peer tutoring programs or a tutoring program that involves select students rather than the whole class, certain implementation guidelines seem to result in positive student outcomes. Included among these are:

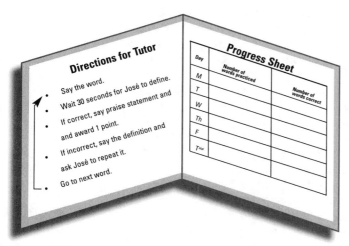

Peer Tutoring Folder

FIGURE 6.1

Peer Tutoring Folder.

▶ Train the tutors and tutees in a structured peer tutoring process (Fantuzzo, King, & Heller, 1992; Lazerson, Foster, Brown, Hummel, 1988).

▶ Provide training and practice in how to ask for and provide helping behaviors (Bentz & Fuchs, 1996; Niedermeyer, 1970).

▶ Provide rewards, performance contingencies, and structure to guide peer tutoring sessions (Fantuzzo, King, & Heller, 1992; Greenwood, Carta, & Hall, 1988; Maheady, Sacca, & Harper, 1988).

▶ Avoid assigning peer tutoring tasks that are too easy for the tutee (Greenwood, Terry, Arreaga-Mayer, & Finney, 1992).

▶ Implement peer tutoring sessions at least three to four times per week (Greenwood, Terry, Areaga-Mayer, & Finney, 1992).

Following these guidelines increases the positive outcomes from peer tutoring programs. In addition to academic achievement and responsiveness to diversity, peer tutoring programs promote interdependence and collaboration among students. Social relationships improve and students seem to prefer peer tutoring over teacher-led and independent work activities (Maheady, 1996).

Cooperative Learning Arrangements

Cooperative learning is an instructional arrangement whereby small groups of students with mixed abilities work together toward shared academic goals rather than competing against one another or working individually. Putting students in small groups and asking them to work together on an assignment doesn't necessarily result in cooperation among the students. The learning environment must be structured in such a way that the essential components of cooperation are integrated into the lesson and thus become a part of the group process. There are five essential components of cooperative learning that need to be included in each lesson: positive interdependence, promotive interaction, individual accountability, interpersonal and small-group skills, and group processing (Johnson & Johnson, 1994).

Positive interdependence, the first essential component of cooperative learning, is extremely important. Students need to understand that they are working as a team and that each member's individual effort helps both the individual and the team. This realization promotes interest in each other's achievement and encourages students to share ideas, share resources, provide assistance and support, and celebrate successes. The feeling of connectedness between students serves as the heart of cooperative learning activities.

Promotive interaction, the second essential component of cooperative learning, involves students promoting their peers' learning through praise, assistance, support, and/or encouragement. These face-to-face interactions are positive in nature and facilitate solving problems, understanding new concepts, and sharing one's knowledge with others.

Individual accountability, the third essential component of cooperative learning, is very important. One of the goals of cooperative learning is for students to

These students are using cooperative learning to complete an important class project. Each student contributes his or her talents to the project and feels like a valued member of the group.

learn together so they can become stronger as individuals. To achieve this goal, students must contribute to the group and do their fair share of the work. Individual accountability is needed to ensure that: *(a)* the group goal is met and *(b)* individual growth is taking place as well. Therefore, each student is assessed and results are reported to both the individual and the group. This assessment helps determine who needs additional assistance while simultaneously ensuring that no one takes a "free ride," allowing others in the group to do all the work.

Teaching students necessary interpersonal and small-group skills is the fourth essential component of cooperative learning. To be successful in cooperative learning groups, students must understand and use certain social skills; otherwise, the group process is likely to disintegrate. It is important to teach students these skills prior to expecting them to participate in cooperative learning groups. In addition to social skills, decision-making, communication, and conflict-management skills must be taught directly. The SCORE and Teamwork Strategies, discussed later in this chapter, are excellent tools for preparing students to function appropriately in cooperative learning groups.

Group processing, the fifth essential component of cooperative learning, involves group members discussing and assessing their accomplishments. Specifically, group members discuss whether goals are being met and whether effective working relationships are being maintained. In essence the team assesses its group behavior to determine whether changes need to occur.

Teachers who integrate these five essential components into their cooperative learning activities are likely to experience high rates of success. These components facilitate cooperation and encourage students to value the process.

Rationale for Using Cooperative Learning

There are several compelling reasons to include cooperative learning activities in students' instructional programs. A significant amount of research has documented positive outcomes for students involved in cooperative learning arrangements. Hundreds of published individual studies as well as numerous reviews, syntheses, and meta-analyses support the use of cooperative learning (Ellis & Fouts, 1997; Johnson & Johnson, 1989; Slavin, 1996; Vermette, 1998). Specifically, research indicates that cooperative learning increases student achievement, responds to student diversity, and increases self-esteem (see Validation Box 6.2).

Increased Student Achievement

Cooperative learning can be used to increase student achievement in academic subjects such math, reading, language arts, science, and social studies. In a synthesis of research related to cooperative learning, Slavin (1991) reported that using cooperative learning arrangements increased achievement for students in grades 2 through 12 regardless of school settings (i.e., rural, suburban, urban). He also noted that cooperative learning arrangements were equally positive for students who were high, average, and low achieving. Several studies that compared cooperative learning arrangements with more traditional (e.g., competitive or individualistic) teaching approaches revealed higher achievement gains with cooperative learning (Mesch, Johnson, & Johnson, 1987; Nichols & Miller, 1994; Slavin, 1989; Slavin, 1991).

In addition to increased academic skills, cooperative learning has been used to increase problem-solving abilities (e.g., reasoning, comparing, analyzing data and making decisions, categorizing) among elementary and secondary students (Johnson, Skon, & Johnson, 1980; Johnson, Johnson, & Stanne, 1985; Skon, Johnson, & Johnson, 1981; Qin, Johnson, & Johnson, 1995). Research in this area is quite promising given the current emphasis on including higher-level problem solving in school curricula.

Research related to cooperative learning and academic achievement among students with disabilities has been mixed. In one review of 12 studies, Tateyama-Sniezek (1990) concluded that cooperative learning was sometimes effective for students with disabilities and sometimes not. She surmised that certain variables related to how the cooperative learning was implemented may account for the mixed findings regarding its effectiveness with students with disabilities. She stated that further research was needed to determine which specific variables resulted in increased achievement. Other researchers have reported that reading and language

┌─────────────────────┐
│ **VALIDATION BOX** │
│ 6.2 │
└─────────────────────┘

Cooperative Learning

▶ Studies related to the use of cooperative learning in elementary and secondary schools were synthesized and positive outcomes were noted in academic achievement, intergroup relations, teaching students with disabilities in general education classes, and self-esteem. It was noted that 37 out of 44 studies (84 percent) involving cooperative learning methods, such as Student Teams-Achievement Divisions (STAD), Teams-Games-Tournament (TGT), Team Assisted Individualization (TAI), and Cooperative Integrated Reading and Composition (CIRC), reported significant positive achievement outcomes. It also was noted that 8 studies revealed positive effects of cooperative learning on intergroup relations and 6 revealed positive effects related to teaching students with disabilities in general education classes. Finally, studies involving TGT, STAD, Jigsaw, and TAI revealed improved self-esteem. For more information see: (Slavin, 1991).

▶ In a 2-year study, the long-term effects of CIRC were investigated with 635 second through sixth grade students. These students were compared to 664 students who were not involved in the CIRC program. The CIRC students had significantly higher achievement in vocabulary, comprehension, and language expression. These findings also were true for students with academic disabilities. CIRC students displayed better cognitive awareness than students not involved in CIRC. For more information see: (Stevens & Slavin, 1995a).

▶ In a meta-analysis including 46 studies, it was determined that members of cooperative teams (preschool through adults) outperformed individuals competing with each other on 4 types of problem solving: effect sizes were 0.37 on linguistic problems (i.e., solved through written and oral language), 0.72 on nonlinguistic problems (i.e., solved through math, symbols, motor activities, actions), 0.52 on well-defined problems (i.e., having clearly defined operations and solutions), and 0.60 on ill-defined problems (i.e., lacking clear definitions, operations, and solutions). For more information see: (Qin, Johnson, & Johnson, 1995).

achievement was improved when students with disabilities participated in interventions that had cooperative learning components (Jenkins et al., 1994; Slavin, Madden, & Leavey, 1984; Stevens, Madden, Slavin, & Farnish, 1987).

Responsiveness to Diversity

Cooperative learning arrangements are particularly appropriate for groups of diverse students. The small groups in cooperative learning arrangements consist of students with varied achievement levels. Given the diversity of student ability in most classrooms, forming such groups is not a problem. Teachers can easily identify students with varying academic levels to work together. Cooperative learning arrangements also are well suited for students from diverse cultures. Students from cultures and families that emphasize interdependent behavior (i.e., working with others to accomplish established goals) will feel quite comfortable in cooperative learning arrangements. Specifically, African Americans, Asian Americans, Hawaiian Americans, Latinos, and Native Americans seem to display values that align nicely with cooperative learning (Winzer & Mazurek, 1998). The extensive opportunities for verbal interaction among peers in cooperative learning groups promotes language development and is therefore especially helpful for students whose first language is something other than English.

Cooperative learning arrangements promote friendships among students who otherwise may not get to know one another. Students with and without disabilities (Johnson & Johnson, 1981a; Slavin, Madden, & Leavey, 1984), students from ethnically diverse backgrounds (Johnson & Johnson, 1981b), and students of different gender (Johnson, Johnson, Scott, & Ramolae, 1985) seem to form positive attitudes about one another and develop friendships as a result of working together in cooperative groups.

Increased Self-Esteem

Much research (i.e., over 80 studies) has been done comparing the effects of cooperative, competitive, and individualistic experiences on self-esteem. Findings from these studies reveal that cooperative arrangements have a stronger effect on self-esteem than the other two arrangements (Johnson & Johnson, 1994). Cooperative interactions with peers tend to result in promoting one another's successes, giving and receiving accurate feedback, and formulating realistic impressions of one another's competencies. This promotes self-acceptance and helps students recognize their own competence (Johnson & Johnson, 1994). Self-esteem is less likely to improve when students compete with one another. Competition means there is a winner and a loser and losing can trigger feelings of inadequacy. When students work individually, there is less opportunity for positive feedback from peers.

Cooperative Learning Models

Various cooperative learning models have emerged over the years, but they all involve students working in groups or teams to achieve certain educational goals. Interdependence among students is stressed in each model. Teachers select, adapt, and modify cooperative learning programs to fit the needs of their students and to maximize positive program outcomes. This is sometimes necessary given the unique nature of classrooms. It is important, however, to avoid making drastic changes that threaten the program's integrity and effectiveness. Included among the major cooperative learning models are Student Team Learning, Jigsaw, Learning Together, Group Investigation, and Schoolwide Cooperative Learning.

Student Team Learning

Robert Slavin of Johns Hopkins University developed the Student Team Learning Model. Within this model, Slavin emphasizes learning activities that require students to work cooperatively, but he also includes limited amounts of competition and individualized learning. There are four different learning configurations within the Student Team Learning Model: Student Teams-Achievement Divisions (STAD), Teams-Games-Tournament (TGT), Team Assisted Individualization (TAI), and Cooperative Integrated Reading and Composition (CIRC).

The Student Teams-Achievement Divisions (STAD) (Slavin, 1978, 1983, 1986, 1995) is adaptable across subject areas and grade levels. The teacher presents a lesson and, after the lesson, students work in four- to five-member teams to ensure that all students mastered the information in the lesson. Then, each student takes a quiz on the material without peer assistance. Each student earns points based on the degree of individual improvement over previous scores. These individual points are totaled to yield a team score. Teams with high scores are rewarded with certificates or recognition in class newsletters. STAD works best with academic tasks that have single correct answers.

The Teams-Games-Tournament (TGT) (DeVries and Slavin, 1978; Slavin, 1986) is similar to STAD. The teacher presents a lesson and students meet in four- to five-member teams to help one another learn the material. Instead of taking individual quizzes, students compete at three-member tournament tables with peers of similar achievement levels, but from other teams. The winner from each tournament table earns the same number of points for his or her team. So, although TGT is primarily a cooperative approach, there also exists this competitive component. Low-achieving students compete against other low achievers, but they can earn as many points as high-achieving students who compete against other high achievers. This equalizes the opportunities for success among all students in the class. Teams with high point totals receive public recognition.

Team Assisted Individualization (TAI) (Slavin, Madden, & Stevens, 1990) is a math curriculum for students in elementary or middle school. Students complete math assignments using self-instructional curriculum materials (Slavin, as cited in Johnson & Johnson, 1994). Students are assigned to heterogeneous four- or five-member teams. They try to complete their work on their own, but can ask team members for help when needed. The teacher works with homogeneous groups of students who are at the same place in the curriculum. While the teacher works with these students, the rest of the class works on their own assignments. Team members check one another's work and administer tests. Students who reach mastery (typically 80 percent) move on to a new unit. Those who don't achieve mastery receive individualized attention from the teacher (Putnam, 1997). Students receive grades based on their own individual work, but team scores are computed on a weekly basis and team members receive certificates based on how much work each member completed (Johnson & Johnson, 1994).

Cooperative Integrated Reading and Composition (CIRC) (Slavin, Stevens, & Madden, 1988) is designed to supplement basal reading programs. CIRC is appropriate for students in elementary and middle school grades. This program combines mixed-ability cooperative learning teams and same-ability reading groups to teach reading, writing, and language arts to diverse groups of students. The class is divided into two or three groups (8 to 15 students per group) based on reading ability. Students are then assigned to pairs or triads within their reading groups. These pairs or triads are combined with pairs or triads from the other reading groups to form a team. Thus, the teams are composed of mixed-ability students. Students participate in a wide range of cooperative activities within their team arrangements. For example, students read aloud to their partners; identify structural components of stories (e.g., characters, setting, problem in story) and make predictions; practice vocabulary, decoding, and spelling; and write compositions in response to stories. Students receive direct instruction from the teacher in reading comprehension and then practice with their teammates. Related to language arts and writing, students work with teammates to plan, draft, revise, edit, and publish compositions.

Commercial materials (i. e., packages that include teacher scripts, lessons, and activities) are available for individuals who wish to use the Student Team Learning Model. For additional information about these materials and training opportunities, contact: Success for All Foundation, 200 W. Towsontown Blvd., Baltimore, MD 21204-5200; telephone: (800) 548 4998; fax: (410) 616-2300; e-mail: www.successforall.net.

Jigsaw

The Jigsaw Cooperative Learning Model is used to help students learn new academic material (Aronson, Blaney, Stephan, Sikes, & Snapp, 1978). Students are assigned to a five- or six-member team to learn about a particular topic (e.g., cactus). Each individual in the team is given a unique assignment related to the topic (e.g., one student explores the various types of cacti; one student learns how to take care of cacti; one student learns methods for growing new cacti; one student researches the origin of cacti; and one student creates visuals of cacti). These same assignments are used in the other five- or six-member teams in the class. After students have worked individually on their particular assignment, "expert groups" are formed. Individuals from each team who have the same assignment come together to form an expert group. The expert group members work together to finish the assignment and master the material. Then, members of the expert group go back to their original teams and share their knowledge and expertise with their teammates.

Learning Together

David and Roger Johnson of the University of Minnesota developed the Learning Together Model. In the Learning Together Model, students are assigned to small groups and each group is given an assignment. Together the group members decide how to go about completing the assignment. They must decide whether to divide the assignment into subparts with various group members taking on certain tasks or whether to approach the assignment as a whole group. All group members are involved in the decision-making process and each is expected to offer his or her knowledge and skills and seek help and assistance from fellow group members. Teachers nurture and promote a philosophy of cooperation emphasizing the five essential elements of cooperative learning discussed earlier: positive interdependence, promotive face-to-face interaction, individual accountability, small-group skills, and group processing. In the Learning Together Model, every group produces one product that represents the combined effort of the individual group members. Students are typically rewarded for both individual performance and the overall performance of the group, but neither individuals nor groups compete against each other (Johnson & Johnson, 1994).

The Learning Together model is sometimes referred to as the "conceptual" approach to cooperative learning because it is based on the assumption that teachers can learn the key principles involved in cooperative learning and then apply them in various ways to meet the needs of their particular students. In other words, teachers can experiment with various cooperative learning procedures to determine which ones are compatible with their teaching philosophies and styles (Putnam, 1997).

Group Investigation

Shlomo Sharan of Tel Aviv University in Israel and Yael Sharan of the Israel Educational Television Center developed the Group Investigation Model of cooperative learning. Like other models, Group Investigation consists of students working together in small groups. The teacher typically identifies a general problem area or question to be explored. The problem should be interesting to the students and relevant to their lives both in and out of school. After the problem is posed, six stages of group investigation are followed. *Stage 1:* The class determines subtopics to be explored. Students then decide which subtopic they want to explore and small groups are formed based on these student interests. *Stage 2:* Members of the small groups plan their investigations, deciding what information is needed, how to organize the information, and how to present the information to their fellow classmates. Thus, students take an active role in what they study and how they study it. *Stage 3:* The students carry out the plan. Group members, working alone or in pairs, find information from a variety of sources. They share what they find with their group members. They interpret and integrate the findings. *Stage 4:* Each group plans a presentation for the whole class. Groups are encouraged to follow six guidelines: *(a)* emphasize the main ideas and conclusions of the inquiry, *(b)* make sure everyone in the group participates in the presentation, *(c)* adhere to time limits, *(d)* involve the audience as much as possible, *(e)* allow time for questions, and *(f)* acquire needed equipment and materials. *Stage 5:* The groups make their presentations. *Stage 6:* Both students and teacher evaluate the work. A variety of evaluation methods can be used (e.g., tests, group reflection on how to improve next time) (Sharan & Sharan, 1976; Sharan & Sharan, 1992; Sharan & Sharan, 1994).

Schoolwide Cooperative Learning Model

In schoolwide cooperative learning models, cooperation is used as a philosophical and practical approach to create a supportive social environment for students and teachers in an entire school. Cooperation and working together become a schoolwide theme rather than an individual classroom theme. An emphasis is placed on equal access to learning for all students. Typical components found in schoolwide cooperative learning models include:

1. Using cooperative learning in many subjects and grade levels.
2. Teaching students with learning disabilities in general education classes.
3. Providing opportunities for teachers to visit one another's classes to provide support and feedback.
4. Promoting collaborative planning and decision making among teachers and the principal.
5. Encouraging active involvement of parents to develop a joint sense of responsibility for students' success in school. (Stevens & Slavin, 1995b)

Initial research related to the implementation and effectiveness of schoolwide cooperative learning models appears promising (see Validation Box 6.3).

Preparing Students to Succeed in Cooperative Learning Arrangements

Regardless of which cooperative learning models are used, students need to have specific interpersonal skills to perform appropriately in small groups. Students need to be taught how to contribute to the group and how to accept contributions from others. In other words, students need to be taught the social skills that are needed for group work. This is important not only for success with cooperative learning activities, but also for success in school and extracurricular activities. Thus, it is worth the time and energy to teach group social skills prior to implementing a cooperative learning program. Two strategies are specifically designed to prepare students for cooperative learning activities: The SCORE Skills: Social Skills for

VALIDATION BOX
6.3

Schoolwide Cooperative Learning

A 2-year study was conducted to investigate the effects of a schoolwide cooperative learning elementary model. There were 5 elementary schools and 1,012 students in second through sixth grades in the study. The findings revealed that after 1 year of implementation, students in cooperative schools performed significantly better on reading vocabulary than students in traditional schools. After 2 years of implementation, students in cooperative schools performed significantly better in reading vocabulary, reading comprehension, language expression, and math computation than students in traditional schools. Students with disabilities in cooperative schools outperformed their peers in traditional schools in the previously mentioned academic areas and math application. Moreover, students with giftedness in heterogeneous cooperative learning classes outperformed their peers in enrichment programs without cooperative learning. For more information see: (Stevens & Slavin, 1995b).

TABLE 6.1

Instructional Sequence for Lessons in the SCORE Skills

- Give an advance organizer.
- Introduce the targeted skill.
- Model the targeted skill.
- Analyze and discuss the targeted skill.
- Conduct verbal practice.
- Provide a second model of the skill.
- Conduct role-play practice.
- Give a post-organizer.
- Conduct generalization activities.

Cooperative Groups (Vernon, Schumaker, & Deshler, 1993) and the Teamwork Strategy (Vernon, Deshler, & Schumaker, 1993).

The SCORE Skills: Social Skills for Cooperative Groups

The SCORE Skills program (Vernon, Schumaker, & Deshler, 1993) consists of seven lessons that each take 30 to 60 minutes to teach. The lessons are designed to teach five basic social skills using the mnemonic device SCORE: (a) **S**hare ideas, (b) **C**ompliment others, (c) **O**ffer help or encouragement, (d) **R**ecommend changes nicely, and (e) **E**xercise self-control. These skills provide the foundation for students to work together in a pleasant, cooperative, and effective manner.

The instructional sequence for each lesson is the same (see Table 6.1). The teacher begins with an advance organizer that includes a review of the previous lesson, includes a discussion of the assignment from the previous lesson, identifies the new social skill to be learned, and specifies what students are expected to do during the lesson. Next, the social skill to be learned in the lesson (e.g., compliment others) is introduced. The skill is defined and discussion regarding why the skill is important occurs. Next, the teacher models the skill and students watch. Then the teacher leads the students to identify the steps required in the skill (e.g., "Say the person's name" "Say something nice"). Each step is clearly defined and students are taught why each step is important. Students memorize the steps for each skill so they can instruct themselves in what comes next when practicing the social skills. Verbal practice is used to help students remember the steps. Next, the teacher models the skill again to solidify student understanding. After seeing this second model, students practice the social skill through role playing. The lessons conclude with a post-organizer to review what was learned, to give students an assignment related to the lesson, and to identify what will be learned in the next lesson. The assignments given at the end of the lesson are designed to help students generalize their social skill use. The assignments include activities such as identifying situations in which the social skill can be used or identifying instances when the teacher or other students used the social skill. Also included in the SCORE Skills program is instruction on body language including voice tone, facial expressions, and use of eye contact.

The Teamwork Strategy

The Teamwork Strategy (Vernon, Deshler, & Schumaker, 1993) is an excellent strategy to teach after teaching The SCORE Skills. The purpose of the Teamwork Strategy is to provide a framework for organizing and completing assignments in small-group arrangements. Specifically, the strategy is designed to teach students to analyze an assignment and divide it into equitable subtasks among members of the group. The strategy also helps students learn how to offer and request help, ask for and give feedback, assemble individual subtasks into one product or presentation, evaluate the group process, and evaluate the interpersonal skills used during the group process.

The mnemonic device TEAMS is used to cue students to the steps in the strategy. The steps in TEAMS are: (a) **T**alk about tasks, (b) **E**xecute your job or jobs, (c) **A**sk and share, (d) **M**ake it great, and (e) **S**urvey your team's SCORE. When using these strategy steps, students first learn to discuss the group assignment and decide who is going to do what. Then they complete their jobs, help their teammates, and/or ask for help if needed. Next, they show their teammates what they've done and ask for constructive feedback. After getting feedback, students follow the suggestions of others to improve the quality of the assignment. Finally, the team discusses how well they performed as a group and reviews the social skills they used. Team members also try to identify ways to improve the group effort in the future.

The instructional sequence for each lesson in the Teamwork Strategy is similar to the sequence used in the SCORE Skills strategy (see Table 6.2). The teacher begins the lessons with an advance organizer that includes: (a) review of previous learning, (b) discussion of the previous lesson's assignment, (c) statement about content to be learned in lesson, and (d) statement about what students are expected to do during the lesson. The next part of the lesson involves a verbal description of the concepts to be covered (e.g., the strategy step to be learned). Then the teacher models the strategy step so students see how it should be done. After seeing the step modeled, students practice the step. The lesson concludes with a post-organizer that includes a review of what was just learned and a statement about what the students will learn in the next lesson. Activities and assignments are provided to help students generalize what they've learned to other settings, situations, and people.

TABLE 6.2

Instructional Sequence for Lession in the Teamwork Strategy

- ▶ Give an advance organizer.
- ▶ Introduce and describe.
- ▶ Provide a model.
- ▶ Conduct the practice activity.
- ▶ Give a post-organizer.
- ▶ Take it a step further.

Teaching the SCORE Skills and the Teamwork Strategy strengthens students' abilities to participate successfully in cooperative learning arrangements. Students who master the social and cooperative skills taught in these programs are ready to obtain maximum benefit from cooperative learning activities. Instructor manuals for both the SCORE Skills and the Teamwork Strategy are available from Edge Enterprises, P.O. Box 1304, Lawrence, KS 66045; telephone: (785) 749-1473; fax: (785) 749-0207.

Guidelines for Implementing Cooperative Learning

Research- and field-based guidelines for implementing cooperative learning arrangements include the following:

- Give special consideration to group assignment; put students with disabilities in groups with students who are willing and able to help (O'Connor & Jenkins, 1996);
- Ensure that group goals and individual accountability are clear (Slavin, 1991);
- Provide students with specific training in interpersonal, social, and/or cooperative skills (O'Connor & Jenkins, 1996; Pomplun, 1997; Schultz, 1989/1990);
- Monitor group functioning (O'Connor & Jenkins, 1996; Schultz, 1989/1990);
- Resist temptation to interrupt groups to help students with disabilities (O'Connor & Jenkins, 1996);
- Keep assignments similar in length for all students (O'Connor & Jenkins, 1996); and
- Establish an ethic of cooperation in the class (O'Connor & Jenkins, 1996).

Teachers who follow these guidelines will undoubtedly experience greater success with cooperative learning arrangements than those who do not.

Computer-Based Arrangements

Computer-based instruction refers to the use of computers with the intention of improving students' skills, knowledge, or academic performance (Okolo, Bahr, Rieth, 1993). Computer-based instruction is common in today's schools. In 1997, the average public school had 75 computers and 79 percent of the students in first through eighth grades and 70 percent of the students in high school grades used computers at school. The proportion of schools with Internet access increased from 35 percent in 1994 to 89 percent in 1998 (U.S. Department of Education, 1999). In 1998, 78.4 percent of grades 1 to 12 students used the Internet at school (U.S. Department of Education, 2000). The percentage of *instructional classrooms* with Internet access was approximately 51 percent in 1998 (U.S. Department of Education, 1999). The usage of computer-based instruction is likely to increase further throughout the next decade.

Two primary models for integrating computers into schools have emerged: classroom-based and lab-based. In the classroom-based model, computers are placed in individual classrooms. There typically are one or two computers per class; therefore, one or two students engage in computer-based instruction (e.g., practicing math facts, writing a story) while the rest of the class is involved in something else (e.g., independent seat work, peer tutoring, learning centers). In the classroom model, the teacher is responsible for planning and implementing the computer-based instruction. The teacher selects the software that will be used, teaches the students how to use the software, and monitors their progress throughout the instructional process. Different software programs are used with different students depending on their instructional needs. Since the teacher is in the classroom where the computer is located, he or she provides feedback and assistance as needed.

In the lab-based model, enough computers for an entire class are available in a single room usually called the computer lab. Thus, a whole class of students simultaneously engages in computer-based instruction. In this arrangement, the instruction sometimes involves teaching the class how to use a particular software program. The instructor's computer screen is projected on a large screen in front of the class. Thus, the entire class learns to use the software by watching the teacher demonstrate what to do. As the teacher demonstrates, the students model the process with their computers. It also is possible for students to work on individualized assignments during computer lab time (e.g., some students work on math, some work on a science report, some work on reading). Lab-based models usually are organized in one of three ways: *(a)* teacher-supervised, *(b)* computer specialist and teacher cooperation, or *(c)* computer specialist-supervised (Cosden & Abernathy, 1990).

In the *teacher-supervised approach*, the classroom teacher is directly responsible for the computer activities of his or her class during their scheduled lab period. The teacher determines the instructional objectives and develops lesson plans to meet the objectives. Computer usage is integrated into the lesson. For example, the teacher may demonstrate a new math algorithm (i.e., step-by-step process for solving a particular type of problem) and then have students practice the algorithm using a related software program. One of the advantages of this approach is the high likelihood that the computer will be used to support and reinforce the students' curricula. There will be a good match between the programs used in the lab and the students' instructional needs. For this approach to work, the teacher must have strong computer skills as well as time and interest in learning new computer technologies as they emerge.

In the *computer specialist* and *teacher cooperation approach*, the responsibilities for the computer-based instruction are shared between the specialist and teacher. Typically, the teacher has primary responsibility for planning the instructional content and the specialist has primary responsibility for implementing the content using computer capabilities. The specialist role varies somewhat depending on the particular expertise of the individual who assumes that position. Some specialists assist with curricular issues; others restrict their involvement to teaching students how to use specific software programs. The primary advantage of this approach is that the teacher and the specialist combine their expertise. This has the potential to result in greater benefits for the students. For this approach to work, the teacher and specialist need to communicate well and establish regular planning times. Agreements must be reached regarding who will select software, who will deliver and supervise instruction, and who will prepare the lessons.

In the *computer specialist–supervised approach*, the specialist is responsible for the instruction that occurs in the lab. Computer instruction is viewed as a self-contained course with few attempts to integrate computer instruction with content the student is learning in other classes. Instead, the instruction emphasizes computer literacy, computer art, or computer simulations. Ideally, the computer specialist has expertise in both educational and computer technologies. In reality, however, the specialist may have limited knowledge related to students' specific instructional needs (e.g., readability level). Communication between the specialist and the teacher increases the likelihood that efficient student learning will occur.

Rationale for Using Computer-Based Instructional Arrangements

There are several compelling reasons to include computer-based instructional arrangements in students' educational experiences. As with peer tutoring and cooperative learning arrangements, there are several benefits related to computer-based instruction. Included among these are: *(a)* academic achievement, *(b)* responsiveness to student diversity, and *(c)* preparation for postsecondary settings.

Academic Achievement

Computer-based instruction that provides individualized (e.g., appropriate readability level, appropriate pacing, appropriate skill level) and appropriately designed instruction (e.g., advance organizers, clear explanations, small "chunks" of information, adequate practice opportunities, ongoing feedback) increases the academic performance of students (Collins, Carnine, & Gersten, 1987; Gleason, Carnine, Vala, 1991; Kenny, 1994). It is important to remember that the instructional design of the software and accompanying lessons play a major role in the amount of learning that takes place during computer-based instruction. Additionally, researchers tend to agree that computer-based instruction should be integrated into the curricula to strengthen the instructional process rather than to replace traditional curricula and instruction (Hammill & Bartel, 1995). One of the limitations of many commercially available curricula is the absence of an adequate number of practice opportunities to ensure that students achieve mastery before moving on to more complex skills. Thus, computer-based instruction can be used to provide the additional practice that many students need. Computer-based instruction also can be used to supplement traditional curricula for students who have particular interests or talents in a given subject area. In such cases, students use the computer to access information that extends beyond what the teacher presents during structured group lessons.

Computer-based instruction is highly motivating to students and therefore keeps them actively engaged in the instructional process. Increased time-on-task results in higher rates of learning. Because students enjoy using computers, they sometimes are more willing to focus on computer-based assignments than assignments that are presented in a different format (e.g., paper-and-pencil tasks). It is important, however, to consider student characteristics when making specific decisions about how to organize computer-based instruction. For example, teachers must decide whether students will work independently or with peers at the computer. Students with hyperactivity may have difficulty staying engaged with the program when working with peers especially when the peer is operating the keyboard. These same students may remain highly engaged in the program when it is their turn to use the keyboard or when they work independently (D. Bryant, personal communication, August 16, 2000). Students in the process of learning English may benefit from working at the computer with peers who can assist with the reading demands that accompany many software programs.

Students who have difficulty meeting particular academic demands because of specific disabilities also benefit from the use of computers. For example, students with fine-motor difficulties who have difficulty with writing may find that using a keyboard is more efficient and results in a higher-quality product. Thus, the students' written expression skills are not stifled due to a fine-motor problem.

There appears to be a growing body of literature related to the academic benefits of using computers. Specifically, research indicates that computer-based instruction improves student performance in mathematics computation, word recognition, spelling, vocabulary knowledge, and reasoning skills (Okolo, Barr, & Rieth, 1993; Okolo, Cavalier, Ferretti, & MacArthur, 2000). Additionally, word processing programs improve written expression skills (MacArthur, 1998; MacArthur, Graham, Schwartz, & Schafer, 1995; McNaughton, Hughes, & Ofiesh, 1997).

Responsiveness to Student Diversity

The versatility of computer software makes computer-based instructional arrangements particularly responsive to student diversity. Many software programs have features that allow teachers to make adjustments based on student needs (e.g., pacing, level of difficulty, amount of practice, feedback options). Additionally, there are software programs available for almost any topic included in the curriculum. Thus, computer-based instruction is easily linked to specific student goals and objectives.

Computer technology and assistive devices (discussed in more detail in Chapter 7) are used to integrate students with disabilities into general education classes and to enhance their success in these classes. For example, students who are unable to write or speak use computers to write, problem solve, and communicate. Individualized pacing is possible for initial instruction, review, remediation, and enrichment. Thus, computers can be used to facilitate mastery learning among groups of students who are performing at very different academic levels.

Computer-based instruction also is useful for students from culturally or linguistically diverse backgrounds. Bilingual word processing programs, for example, provide assistance with vocabulary, spelling, and grammar. Moreover, access to the Internet enables students to learn about various parts of the world and helps students develop more global understandings of cultures that differ from their own. Access to this information also helps teachers better understand the needs of students whose first language is not English.

Finally, computer technology has been used to promote communication between students from economically diverse backgrounds. Specifically, interactive technology has been used to link diverse schools (e.g., urban, suburban). Farley (1999) discussed a successful linkage between two New Jersey schools: Hunterdon Central Regional High School, a technologically advanced, suburban school that received national and state awards for technology innovation and Asbury Park High School, an urban school that suffered from problems typical of urban areas including low test scores, poverty, white flight, and a diminishing tax base. With the assistance of Rider University faculty, a grant from AT&T, and computer donations from Compaq Computer, these two schools collaborated in many interdisciplinary online projects (e.g., celebrating Black History Month, debating controversial topics, writing poetry and manuscripts for online publishing, videoconferencing with university professors, e-mailing position statements to political delegates in their state). Students from both schools benefited from their collaborative projects. Students from Asbury Park had access to the same academic rigor available to their suburban counterparts. Students from Hunterdon Central gained new awareness and appreciation of their urban neighbors, shared in their cultural diversity, and recognized the socioeconomic differences that influence equality and equity. Students from both schools learned a great deal about the cultures, values, and feelings of peers whose life experiences differed from their own (Farley, 1999).

Preparation for Postsecondary Settings

Economists have noted a dramatic shift in the types of jobs that are available for individuals who plan to enter the work force during the twenty-first century. Specifically, they see a shift away from jobs that involve production services and movement toward jobs that involve "symbolic analysts" (Kozma & Schank, 1998). Symbolic analysts identify and solve problems. They use:

> a variety of tools and resources, including computers and scientific and creative instruments, to generate and examine words, numbers, and images. They often have partners and associates and work in small teams. Their work schedules may vary, depending on a particular project. Their work products range from plans, designs, sketches, and scripts to reports, models, and multimedia productions that are judged on such criteria as originality, cleverness, and the degree to which they solve a problem. (p. 4)

The new demands being placed on students when they leave the school environment and enter the world of work necessitate a new set of job skills. Students need to be able to use various tools to locate and organize large amounts of information. They need to generate, analyze, and interpret data and then transform the data to create something new. They must understand how their work fits with others' work to accomplish specific goals. "They must develop the capacity to work with others to develop plans, broker consensus, communicate ideas, seek and accept criticism, give credit to others, solicit help, and generate joint products" (Kozma & Schank, p. 4). Included among the expectations for twenty-first century employees are technological knowledge and strong computer skills (Churma, 1999).

Clearly, computer literacy is becoming increasingly important in terms of student performance after high school. In the late 1990s, projections indicated that only 22 percent of the work force had the necessary technology skills for 60 percent of the jobs in 2000 (Hancock, 1997). Thus, students who graduate from high school with a strong understanding of computer technology are at a distinct advantage when it comes to transitioning to post–high school settings. The use of computer-based arrangements in public school settings is, therefore, necessary to prepare students for the job market that awaits them. Additionally, computer knowledge may be helpful to students who seek part-time jobs while still enrolled in school. Such knowledge enhances students' employability and frequently results in increased pay.

Students who plan to enroll in higher education also need computer skills. Many universities and colleges across the country are adopting policies that require students to own their own computer while attending school. Computer-based assignments and related research are requirements in many university courses. Some instructors develop Web sites for their courses and communicate with their students using e-mail. Many universities now offer online applications for financial aid and campus work experience programs. Moreover, campus information and news frequently are reported online.

Thus, the use of computer-based instructional arrangements in elementary and secondary schools is needed to prepare students for their futures. Within these arrangements, the computer can be used for instructional purposes (i.e., to teach academic content) and/or the computer can be used as a tool (i.e., to assist students in accomplishing specific tasks more effectively and efficiently). Both of these applications have been used successfully to help students with special learning needs.

Using the Computer for Instruction

Computer-assisted instruction (CAI) refers to using commercially available software programs to supplement instruction and provide practice on academic skills. CAI takes on a variety of forms depending on the needs of the students and availability of software. Included among the various types of CAI software are: *(a)* tutorial, *(b)* drill and practice, *(c)* educational games, *(d)* simulations, and *(e)* problem-solving programs. Additionally, classwide groupware systems are available that link students' computers to the teacher's computer.

Tutorial Programs

Tutorial programs are designed to provide instruction and guided practice on new concepts and skills. Therefore, tutorial programs are appropriate to use when students are in the acquisition stage of learning (i.e., new learning that is not yet mastered) (Hasselbring & Goin, 1993). Material is presented in small sequential steps with frequent reinforcement and specific, corrective feedback. Tutorial programs may be simple or complex in design (Mathews, Pracek, & Olson, 2000). Simple tutorial programs tend to be linear (i.e., all students progress through the same step-by-step process dictated by the software), but with different pacing capabilities. More complex tutorial software contains *branching* capabilities. In other words, the program progresses to various alternatives based on student responses. If the student is responding accurately, the program advances to more challenging material. If, however, the student is struggling with the content, the program moves to easier material that reviews prerequisite skills or concepts. Although not foolproof, branching capabilities help individualize instruction based on student performance.

Hasselbring and Goin (1993) identified five characteristics that should be evident within tutorial software. Specifically, effective tutorial software should:

1. Require a response that resembles the skill being taught;
2. Limit the amount of new information presented at one time;
3. Provide review of recently learned information;
4. Provide corrective feedback; and
5. Provide a management component that monitors student progress through the learning stages. (p. 153)

Drill-and-Practice Programs

Drill-and-practice programs provide numerous opportunities to practice previously taught skills and concepts. These programs typically present questions or problems in a timed format and the student types in appropriate answers. Drill-and-practice programs are particularly useful for building skill fluency or automaticity (e.g., math facts or oral reading). The purpose of fluency building is to increase the rate at which the student can perform the skill. Fluency is important because it promotes skill retention and generalization. To prevent student frustration, fluency building should be used only *after* a skill has been taught and critical concepts are understood. Well-designed drill-and-practice programs provide prompts when needed and immediate feedback to prevent students from practicing errors. According to Hasselbring and Goin (1993) software that is used for developing skill fluency should:

1. Provide practice on acquired skills only;
2. Provide practice on the desired terminal skill;
3. Provide ample opportunities for practice;
4. Emphasize speed of responding; and
5. Provide a management component that monitors student progress. (p. 154)

Drill-and-practice programs provide students with disabilities the additional practice they need to reach skill mastery in a more novel format than traditional paper-and-pencil tasks. In many cases, this increases students' willingness to continue the practice. Drill-and-practice programs also are appropriate to help students maintain skills they previously mastered. In fact, the same program that was used to develop fluency can be reintroduced periodically to ensure the student still performs the skill with automaticity. Another option that provides variety for the student is to find a different program that emphasizes the same skill and then allow the student to select the program he or she prefers to use for maintenance practice (Hasselbring & Goin, 1993).

Educational Game Programs

Similar to drill-and-practice software, educational game programs are designed to provide students with opportunities to practice previously taught skills and assist in developing skill fluency and/or skill maintenance. These programs combine video arcade–style graphics and audio effects with academic skill practice (Bos & Vaughn, 1994). Educational game programs are designed to be fun and therefore motivate students to practice. They are, of course, more motivating to some students than to others. For students who enjoy educational game programs, it is possible to use the games as reinforcers for completing less-preferred instructional tasks or for demonstrating appropriate classroom behavior. It is important for teachers to monitor student practice when educational game programs are used to ensure that the student is practicing the skill and not simply activating various game stimuli.

Simulation Programs

Simulation programs are designed to replicate real-life or imaginary situations so that students vicariously experience complex circumstances or events. The software enables students to feel as though they actually are experiencing the situation or event. Well-designed simulation programs provide authentic experiences to promote student learning. Simulation programs are appropriate to use when:

1. Safety is a concern (e.g., initial driver's education training, dangerous science experiments) (Hammill & Bartel, 1995; Hasselbring & Goin, 1993);
2. Students need to see the consequences of their decisions (Mathews, Pracek, & Olson, 2000);
3. The real-life event cannot be carried out in the classroom (e.g., voting) (Hasselbring & Goin);
4. The time involved in the real-life event is too long to allow efficient learning (e.g., money management) (Hasselbring & Goin);
5. Decision-making abilities are being taught (e.g., survival activities) (Bos & Vaughn, 1994; Hasselbring & Goin); and
6. Generalization to out-of-school activities is important (e.g., vocational training). (Mathews, Pracek, & Olson, 2000)

Emerging advances in simulation technology have resulted in virtual reality learning experiences and distributed simulations that create an illusion of three-dimensional space. Special glasses, displays, and hand-held wands enhance the life-like effect of the environment and allow students to interact with the simulation (Kozma & Schank, 1998).

Problem-Solving Programs

Problem-solving programs are designed to give students practice in identifying problems, finding plausible solutions, selecting appropriate strategies, and evaluating the results of important decisions (Mathews, Pracek, & Olson, 2000). There is a great deal of diversity among various problem-solving programs. Some use adventure or game formats that are motivating for students. Within the context of the games, students are taught analytic reasoning, sequencing, risk taking, perseverance, logical reasoning, prediction, strategic planning, evaluation, or decision making (Hammill & Bartel, 1995). Other problem-solving programs involve collecting information, taking notes, discovering patterns, making generalizations, charting data, or creating a product (Mathews, Pracek, & Olson, 2000).

Several problem-solving programs that reinforce concepts in particular content areas (e.g., math, science, literacy) are available. For example, the *Jasper Woodbury Problem Solving Series* engages students in the use of important math concepts to solve authentic challenges and problems (Williams et al., 1998). The program was designed

Students enjoy and benefit from computer-based instructional arrangements.

for students in grade 5 or higher and consists of 12 interactive video environments that last approximately 17 minutes each. Students work together in small groups. They watch a video that presents a challenge or problem within the context of a story. Then they review and discuss the important aspects of the story to ensure understanding of the problem. The students work together to set up the necessary calculations to solve the problem. When all the small groups have a solution, they share and compare their work with one another and select the best solution for the problem. The Jasper series is available through LEARNING, Inc., a division of Lawrence Erlbaum Associates, 10 Industrial Avenue, Mahwah, NJ 07430-2262; telephone: (800) 9-BOOKS-9; Web site: www.erlbaum.com/. For additional information and data on the Jasper series, see Cognition and Technology Group at Vanderbilt (1992, 1993, 1997).

In Scientists in Action, another video-based problem-solving program, students become engaged in challenges that require them to learn about important science concepts (Williams et al., 1998). Scientific processes such as data collection, analysis, problem formulation, and hypothesis testing are emphasized. In one episode, students explore a polluted river, determine the source of the pollution, and propose a method for cleaning it up. The Scientists in Action program is designed for students in middle grades. For additional information see Goldman et al. (1996); Sherwood, Petrosino, Lin, Lamon, and Cognition and Technology Group at Vanderbilt (1995); Web site: peabody.vanderbilt.edu/projects/funded/sia/sia.html; or contact the Learning Technology Center of Vanderbilt University, Peabody College, Nashville, TN 37203 (see Validation Box 6.4).

VALIDATION BOX 6.4

Computer-Based Instruction

▶ In a review of literature published between 1982 and 1992, the effects of computer-based instruction for students with mild disabilities were explored. The results of this review indicated that computer-based instruction had a positive effect on academic achievement (i.e., basic and higher-order skills), motivation, and time-on-task when quality instructional design and teacher mediation were used. For more information see: (Okolo, Bahr, & Rieth, 1993).

▶ In another extensive review of literature, the effects of technology for developing literacy skills was evaluated. The studies included in this review were published from 1984 to 1999 and involved school-age learners with cognitive disabilities (i.e., learning disabilities, reading disabilities, mild mental retardation, students considered at risk for reading disabilities, and students with severe cognitive disabilities). The reviewers reported cautious optimism regarding the potential of technology to improve the literacy skills of students with disabilities. Moreover, they concluded that the effects of using technology depend on software design characteristics, the instruction that accompanies the technology, the way in which the technology is used, and the characteristics of the students who use the technology. For more information see: (Okolo, Cavalier, Ferretti, & MacArthur, 2000).

Classwide Groupware Systems

When using computers for instructional purposes (e.g., tutorials, drill and practice, games, simulations, problem solving) it is important to monitor student performance and progress. Many software programs provide a computer-generated report that documents how well a student did on a particular computer-assisted assignment (e.g., number or percentage of correct responses). These reports are provided *after* the student completes the entire assignment. Classwide groupware systems (e.g., Discourse GroupWare Classroom) enable teachers to monitor the participation and performance of all students in the class in real time (Shin, Deno, Robinson, & Marston, 2000). In groupware systems, the teacher's computer is linked to each of the students' computers. The teacher presents spontaneous or previously programmed instructional content. The students respond to the instruction using their computer terminals. The student responses are displayed on the teacher's monitor. Thus, the teacher monitors all students' responses simultaneously as they are being emitted. The system also has the capability to score, save, and publicly display student responses on a classroom video monitor. Additionally, light and sound at each student's computer terminal is used to provide feedback regarding response accuracy. Classwide groupware systems are designed to promote frequent student-teacher interaction, elicit many responses from students, provide ongoing feedback related to student responses, and assess student progress (Robinson, DePascale, & Roberts, 1989; Shin, Deno, Robinson, & Marson, 2000). Thus, students are actively engaged in the lessons and teachers closely monitor their performance.

Using the Computer as a Tool

In addition to using computers for instructional purposes, they also are useful as tools that help students accomplish specific tasks more effectively and efficiently. Included among the various tool-based applications for computer usage are: *(a)* word processing, *(b)* writing assistance programs, *(c)* hypertext and hypermedia, *(d)* the Internet, *(e)* spreadsheets, and *(f)* database management.

Word Processing

Specific computer tools are available to help students improve their writing performance. One of the most widely used tools is the word processor. Word processors help students improve their writing in numerous ways. The "delete," "move," and "copy" functions of word processors, as well as the thesaurus and spell checker facilitate editing and reduce student frustration while writing. The ability to produce neat, error-free printed copies enhances student motivation and positively influences judgments that others make about the overall writing quality. Word processing also promotes the fluent production of text (MacArthur, Graham, Schwartz, & Schafer, 1995). Some word-processing programs have *speech synthesis capabilities* in which typed-in letters and words are translated into speech. Thus, students can hear what they've written and sometimes detect errors in their writing as a result. Speech synthesis also assists students in reading and editing other students' writing.

Another helpful feature found in some word processing programs is *word prediction*. As the student begins to type a word, the software predicts the intended word and provides a list of words from which the student chooses. Typically, speech synthesis is available to read the word choices. Word processing programs vary in complexity and in the number of features offered (e.g., spell checker, grammar checker, speech synthesis, word prediction), but the quality of these programs continues to improve as software revisions occur and new versions are released.

Word processors and their added features help students with disabilities improve their writing, provided they are taught how to use the program and features accurately (MacArthur & Graham, 1987). For example, spell checkers help students with spelling disabilities produce written products that others can read. If a student's inability to spell is too severe to use a spell checker (i.e., the student's estimate of the correct spelling isn't close enough for the spell checker to identify the attempted word), then word prediction software can be used. Students with physical disabilities and fine-motor problems, who are taught to type can use word processors to remove the burden involved in mechanically forming each printed or manuscripted letter by hand (MacArthur, 1998; see Validation Box 6.5).

Writing Assistance Programs

Several researchers (Daiute, 1986; Zellermayer, Salomon, Globerson, & Givon, 1991) have explored the use of writing assistance programs to help students improve their written expression skills. Typically, these programs provide prompts that help students adopt metacognitve strategies that assist with writing. Some programs include a series of questions designed to help students generate ideas prior to writing. The questions frequently relate to specific text structures. For example, for a newspaper article, the prompt questions involve *who*, *where*, *why*, and *when*; for a story, the questions relate to *characters*, *problem*, *action*, and *resolution* (MacArthur, 1997). Question prompts related to completeness, clarity, organization, coherence, sentence structure, and punctuation also are common. Some word-processing programs have question-insertion capabilities that allow teachers to insert specific prompting questions to help students as they complete their writing assignments (e.g., Terry, did you remember to capitalize all proper nouns?). In addition to question prompts, outlining features and writer's aids also are available to help students think about and improve their writing.

Writer's Helper (1990) is a writing assistance program that contains structured questions and other writing supports for brainstorming, categorizing ideas, and free writing. This program is useful for planning and writing stories or other narrative texts. The Inspiration (1988–1999) software program (discussed in Chapter 5 as a tool for creating visual displays) also can be used to assist students who struggle with written expression. Specifically, students who have difficulty getting started with writing projects use this software to brainstorm writing ideas, organize their thoughts, outline the content, and identify appropriate vocabulary to use. Thus, Inspiration is used to help students during the planning stage of the writing process. Other programs are available to help young students who have difficulty with writ-

VALIDATION BOX

6.5

Word Processing

▶ The effectiveness of word processing with speech synthesis and word prediction features was investigated with five elementary students who had learning disabilities and severe writing problems. The students used the word processing program for dialogue journal writing activities (i.e., dialogue writing involved the teacher and students writing back and forth to one another). The results revealed that the combination of speech synthesis and word prediction had a strong positive effect on the legibility and spelling of journal entries for four of the five students. For more information see: (MacArthur, 1998).

▶ In another study, the effectiveness of word processing and strategy instruction was investigated with 113 elementary students with learning disabilities. Students in the experimental classes who received word processing and strategy instruction made greater gains in the quality of their narrative and informative writing than students in the control group. For more information see: (MacArthur, Graham, Schwartz, & Shafer, 1995).

▶ In another study, three high school students with learning disabilities were taught a proofreading strategy that incorporated the use of a word processor spell checker. All three students demonstrated substantial improvement in correcting their errors and reducing their final error rate. For more information see: (McNaughton, Hughes, & Ofiesh, 1997).

ing. These programs typically combine drawing with writing. For example, in Kid Works 2 (1992), students create pictures using a variety of drawing tools and then write stories to accompany their pictures. The program has the capability to display the student's pictures and read their stories using synthesized speech. In other programs, such as Storybook Weaver (1992), background scenes, objects, and animated figures are provided for students to create pictures. Then, the students create stories to go with the pictures. Using this program, sounds and music can be added to the stories. To benefit from writing assistance programs, students must take advantage of the prompting, coaching, and/or pictorial features (e.g., answer the question prompts, make revisions, draw pictures) (Okolo, Barr, & Rieth, 1993).

Hypertext and Hypermedia

Hypertext is an educational tool that differs from traditional software programs by offering students immediate access to supplemental text in a nonlinear manner. Higgins and Boone (1990) describe hypertext as follows:

A screen or page in a hypertext document might be thought of as a composite of several sheets of transparency film overlaying one another, the top layer not only providing the original text to be read but also serving as a menu for accessing additional information, such as getting help with unknown words, or following tutorial strategies for building comprehension. Words, parts of words, graphics, or parts of graphics provide more information than what first appears on the surface layer of the screen. Positioning the cursor on specific areas of the top-layer hypertext page makes the appropriate layers beneath accessible. (p. 529)

So, hypertext stories or textbooks provide easy access to information that extends beyond the original text. Parts of text on one screen are linked to related content on another screen. This tool is particularly helpful to students with learning difficulties because it provides a method to independently clarify confusing concepts and/or define challenging vocabulary. Hypertext also represents a means for students who are particularly interested in the topic about which they are reading to acquire additional information and therefore learn more (see Validation Box 6.6).

Hypermedia tools include hypertext, but also include other media (e.g., video, sound) that are accessed in a nonlinear manner. Hypermedia tools allow for the integration of digital video clips, animated presentations, computer-produced speech and sound effects, and photo-quality pictures. Thus, the presented content is enhanced beyond simple text. For example, a student reads about a famous person, sees a picture of the person, and hears a famous speech that the person delivered. Hypermedia materials offer experiential and direct instruction formats and

---

VALIDATION BOX

6.6

Hypertext

▶ Two studies were conducted to explore the use of hypertext study guides. In Study 1, the effectiveness of using hypertext study guides for social studies instruction was investigated with 40 ninth-grade students (10 with learning disabilities, 15 remedial students, and 15 general education students). Findings from this study revealed that hypertext study guides with or without an accompanying lecture were just as effective as well-prepared lectures alone. In Study 2, the five students from Study 1 who received the lowest unit test scores used hypertext study guides as a follow-up to teacher-presented instruction. All five students improved from pre- to posttest, and four of the five met the criteria for a passing grade. For more information on these studies see: (Higgins & Boone, 1990).

▶ The effectiveness of using hypertext study guides for social studies instruction was investigated with 25 ninth-grade students. Of these students, 13 had learning disabilities and 12 were remedial students. Students who had access to hypertext study guides demonstrated better information retention than students who did not have access to these guides. For more information see: (Higgins, Boone, & Lovitt, 1996).

▶ In a 3-year longitudinal study, the effectiveness of adapting basal readers to computer hypertext formats was explored. Eight classes of kindergarten to third-grade students participated in this study. Students who received hypertext instruction during all three years significantly outperformed control group students who received traditional basal instruction for three years. For more information see: (Higgins & Boone, 1991).

appear to be particularly helpful for students whose primary language is something other than English (Bermudez & Palumbo, 1994). The additional context tools (e.g., pictures, speech) facilitate increased comprehension of the academic content. Hypermedia materials are available commercially or teachers can create their own using authoring software (Boone, Higgins, Falba, & Langley, 1993; Higgins, Boone, & Lovitt, 1996). Authoring software provides teachers with tools to create hypermedia lessons without having to learn a complete programming language. Several authoring programs are available. Hyperstudio,[1] available from Roger Wagner Publishing, Inc., 1050 Pioneer Way, Suite P, El Cajon, CA 92020; telephone: (800) 497-3778, and Hypermedia!Now, available from Randall Boone, University of Nevada, Las Vegas, Box 453005, Las Vegas, NV 89154; telephone: (702) 895-3241, are appropriate for beginners; whereas AuthorWare and Director,[2] available from Macromedia, Inc., 600 Townsend Street, San Francisco, CA 94103; telephone: (800) 457-1774, are appropriate for intermediate or advanced users. Web authoring programs also are available for teachers who want to create hypermedia environments online. Included among these are DreamWeaver,[3] available from Macromedia, Inc., 600 Townsend Street, San Francisco, CA 94103; telephone: (800) 457-1774, and FrontPage,[4] available from Microsoft Corporation, One Microsoft Way, Redmond, WA 98052; telephone: (800) 426-9400 (K. Higgins & R. Boone, personal communication, September 18, 2000).

The Internet

As was mentioned earlier, most students now have access to the Internet in their public school settings. Through the Internet, students and teachers explore an enormous electronic library of resources, pictorials, and databases that contain information about almost any topic of interest. Access to the Internet motivates many students to become active in their own learning process (Doyle, 1999). The Internet also is used to facilitate communication between students and other individuals. Bulletin-board folders, electronic mail, and chat rooms are used to establish communication networks. Bulletin-board folders on the Internet allow students to locate and meet others with whom they may want to interact. Electronic mail systems allow students to send and receive messages from other individuals who have access to such systems regardless of where they live. Communication with individuals in other countries is just as easy as communication with individuals who live in the same city; the process for sending and receiving mail is the same. Thus, students send messages and when the receivers check their electronic mail, they read the messages and send responses. Chat rooms allow students to communicate via computer with other people in what is referred to as "real time." This means that both parties are online at the same time and communicating via typed messages.

[1]Hyperstudio is a registered trademark of Roger Wagner Publishing, Inc.
[2]AuthorWare and Director are registered trademarks of Macromedia, Inc.
[3]DreamWeaver is a registered trademark of Macromedia.
[4]FrontPage is a registered trademark of Microsoft Corporation.

Through the Internet, students have computer pals from other schools, cities, states, and countries. Thus, the opportunities for learning are extensive.

Web-based curricula (i.e., curricula accessed through Internet Web sites) also are available. Carol Sue Englert of Michigan State University developed a site called TELE-Web (i.e., Technology-Enhanced Learning Environments on the Web) that is designed to promote literacy development. Through the tools associated with the Web site, teachers develop, manage, and share multimedia literacy materials. They create and manage collaborative learning projects for students. Students create, revise, and complete assignments; read other students' stories; and write comments about the stories. The students' reading and writing responses are archived (saved and later retrieved). Within the Web site environment, students explore, experiment, receive feedback from teacher and peers, and consequently develop stronger reading and writing skills ("Integrating Technology into the Standard Curriculum," 1998).

In another project, four inclusive classes consisting of students with and without disabilities, their teachers, and a development team from Western Illinois University created Web sites called TEChPLACEs (http://www.techplaces.wiu.edu) (Hutinger & Clark, 2000). The four classes were located in different school districts in Illinois. Each TEChPLACE Web site included four components: *(a)* all about us; *(b)* our community; *(c)* resource links to carefully screened web sites related to teachers, families, products, and children; and *(d)* e-mail (Hutinger & Clark, 2000). The first two components were planned and developed by each individual class. The students included animation, photographs, music, sounds, their voices, and real-time video in their sites. The third component, resource links, facilitated access to professional organizations, magazines, software publishers, and a variety of child-oriented web sites (e.g., Winnie the Pooh site, Disney site, Dr. Seuss[5]). These resource links were helpful to teachers and parents. The e-mail component of TEChPLACE allowed students to communicate with one another across sites. It also provided a forum for communication among teachers, administrators, and parents. Involvement in TEChPLACE sites resulted in student learning and improved behavior. Both students with and without disabilities surpassed teacher expectations as they participated in the Web site activities (Hutinger & Clark, 2000).

When using Internet instructional activities with students with disabilities, it is helpful to structure the environment to prevent information overload and the potential frustration that results from navigating through complex, multistep Web sites in search of useful information. Bernie Dodge of San Diego State University created the WebQuest lesson design to help provide the structure that many students with disabilities need when participating in Internet lessons (http://edweb.sdsu.edu/webquest/webquest.html) (Kelly, 2000). The WebQuest is a teacher-created lesson plan in the form of a simple World Wide Web page that includes sequenced steps and preselected Web site links to guide students through the lesson. Thus, students avoid aimless searching without clearly specified goals. WebQuest lessons fre-

---

[5]Winnie the Pooh and Disney are registered trademarks of Walt Disney Productions Corporation. Dr. Seuss is a registered trademark of Dr. Seuss Enterprises L.P. Corporation.

quently involve research, problem solving, and application of basic skills. They include instructional supports (e.g., controlled readability level, larger text, easier directions) as needed to help students succeed with the general education curriculum. WebQuest lessons are easily linked to students' individualized education programs (IEPs) and can be used independently or in small groups. Moreover, they can be used for a variety of instructional purposes (i.e., introducing a new unit, extending ideas presented in a unit, providing a culminating project at the end of a unit) (Kelly, 2000).

Research findings related to the use of the Internet typically show that "the integration of the Internet into the classroom leads to *(a)* increased access to information, *(b)* opportunities to communicate with experts, *(c)* access to external resources, and *(a)* motivating opportunities for teachers and students to learn (Birman, Kirshenstein, Levin, Matheson, & Stephenson and Center for Applied Special Technologies as cited in Castellani, 2000, p. 297). As Internet usage increases, additional investigations regarding its effectiveness are likely to emerge (see Validation Box 6.7).

Spreadsheets

Computer-based spreadsheet programs frequently are used in math education (e.g., Microsoft Excel[6] published by Microsoft Corporation, One Microsoft Way,

---

VALIDATION BOX 6.7

Internet

- Preliminary data collected in three elementary classrooms suggest that students with access to TELE-Web improved their writing skills. Students wrote longer and more descriptive stories. Also, motivation to write increased. For more information see: ("Integrating Technology Into the Standard Curriculum," 1998).
- Eighth grade students with disabilities who were enrolled in inclusive general education classes participated in a preliminary investigation of the effects of WebQuests. Students with disabilities who used technological approaches (i.e., WebQuests and PowerPoint) showed an average increase of 2.3 grade levels in reading, whereas students with disabilities who received instruction without technology increased 1.2 grade levels. Both groups of students received instruction over the same period of time with the same general education teachers. For more information see: (Kelly, 2000).
- In a yearlong qualitative study involving five high school teachers, the effects of using the Internet with students with emotional and learning disabilities were explored. Findings revealed that the Internet was a useful tool for enhancing transition and career-development skills, increasing basic skills for spelling and word recognition, and improving student motivation. One of the challenges involved in using the Internet was the amount of planning time needed to locate appropriate sites to meet the needs of individual students. For more information see: (Castellani, 2000).

---

[6]Microsoft Excel is a registered trademark of Microsoft Corporation.

Redmond, WA 98052; telephone: [800] 426-9400). Spreadsheets consist of columns and rows of numerical data. Students are taught to enter data into the spreadsheet and then use the data to solve mathematical problems (e.g., finding the mean age of all students in the class; determining the sum of money obtained in a class fundraising event; setting up a budget; evaluating numerical results of a survey). Spreadsheets are particularly helpful for performing calculations involving large sets of data. Spreadsheets also are used to explore mathematical relationships. For example, students can explore the relationship between area and perimeter. The formula for area and perimeter is entered into the spreadsheet by the teacher. Then the students use the premade spreadsheet to enter various values for the length and width of objects. The effects of doubling, tripling, and otherwise changing values are explored. Relationships between area and perimeter and the length and width of objects or shapes are studied (Churma, 1999). Some spreadsheet programs have the capability of converting the numerical values of entered data into charts and graphs. Thus, students gain an understanding of various ways to represent and display data.

Database Management

Database management software is designed to help students organize and maintain large amounts of information. Students develop databases that are useful in various content areas (Bos & Vaughn, 1994). A science database may include information related to plants that grow in a particular region of the United States, a social studies database may include information on world continents, and an English database may consist of information related to famous authors. Database software provides a means for students to enter bits of information (e.g., plant name, geographical zone best suited for the plant, average size, amount of water needed, type of soil needed) into individual data records. The entered information may be in the form of narrative text or numerical values. Once the information has been entered, students sort and retrieve it in various ways (e.g., list plants that grow in zone 11; list plants that are drought tolerant). They modify or delete individual data records as needed. Moreover, new data records are added as information is obtained. Thus, database projects frequently extend over a period of time (e.g., semester or school year).

In addition to creating databases, students benefit from learning how to use previously established databases. To retrieve important information from databases that contain large amounts of information, students must develop several skills. First, students must know the technical aspects involved in using the database program (e.g., which buttons to push for various functions). Second, students must know exactly what information they want to obtain. Keywords frequently are used to search for and obtain relevant information from the database. Thus, students must be able to identify and enter the keywords that most closely relate to the topic of interest. Third, students must be able to sort through large amounts of information and determine what relates to their particular topic, especially when using online databases (Hammill & Bartel, 1995).

Clearly, computer-based instruction has a variety of applications. Using the computer for instruction or using the computer as a tool provides students with opportunities to improve their academic skills, solve problems, organize and manipulate data, explore mathematical concepts, and develop logical thinking. These opportunities can be individualized to meet specific students' goals and objectives or integrated into large-group instruction in which all students are learning the same applications simultaneously. When group instruction is provided, data from the computer screen can be projected on a larger screen in front of the class (Drier, Dawson, & Garofalo, 1999). Additionally, cooperative learning and peer tutoring arrangements may be used in conjunction with computer-based activities to provide additional supports for students who benefit from involvement with their peers.

Guidelines for Implementing Computer-Based Instructional Arrangements

Researchers and educators offer several recommendations related to implementing computer-based instructional arrangements. These recommendations focus on software selection and technology integration.

Software Selection

Regardless of the type of software being used, software selection is very important. Computer-assisted instruction is effective when high-quality, pedagogically sound software programs are used. Thus, teachers need to evaluate software programs carefully before using them with students. A variety of factors must be taken into consideration when selecting software. Included among these are: *(a)* appropriateness of content, *(b)* screen design, *(c)* effective teaching and learning principles, *(d)* options for individualization, and *(e)* publisher agreement. Table 6.3 on page 276 lists specific characteristics and features to consider when thinking about these factors (Male, 1997; Okolo, Bahr, & Rieth, 1993; Mathews, Pracek, & Olson, 2000). It is helpful to create a checklist or evaluation form to use when evaluating and/or comparing software programs. The items listed in Table 6.3 are easily transformed into yes-or-no questions or questions with rating scale. Using one of these formats, an evaluation tool can be developed and used to select appropriate software programs (see Table 6.4 on p. 277).

In addition to previewing and evaluating software, useful information also can be obtained from software reviews published in professional journals and from talking with other teachers who have used the software. Additionally, teachers join listservs on the Internet and post questions to other teachers about software. When soliciting information through software reviews or other teachers, it is important to remember that different programs are needed for different purposes. It also is important to remember that certain software programs may be appropriate and successful with some students, but not others. Thus, field-testing and monitoring student progress while using the program is particularly helpful and provides meaningful information.

Technology Integration

Researchers from Johns Hopkins Education Development Center and Technical Education Research Center and Macro Systems, Inc. conducted three studies related

TABLE 6.3

Characteristics and Features to Consider When Evaluating and Selecting Software

Appropriateness of Content
▶ Addresses curricular and IEP goals
▶ Supports national and district content standards
▶ Uses age-appropriate examples and graphics
▶ Presents content at students' instructional levels
▶ Addresses students' interests and needs
▶ Presents accurate and useful information
▶ Avoids bias and stereotypes

Screen Design
▶ Provides clear and uncluttered displays
▶ Presents adequate spacing between words and lines to facilitate easy reading
▶ Provides consistent commands from one screen to the next
▶ Emphasizes important details (bold type, color coding, underlining, arrow cues, highlighting)
▶ Provides logical labels
▶ Provides on-screen instructions with visual and/or auditory cues
▶ Avoids unnecessary distracters

Effective Teaching and Learning Principles
▶ Follows hierarchy of skills (i.e., logical sequence)
▶ Models accurate punctuation, capitalization, grammar, and spelling
▶ Provides thorough and clear directions
▶ Provides full range of examples
▶ Administers frequent and informative feedback
▶ Provides many practice opportunities
▶ Includes branching features to provide further concept development when student responses reflect a need for additional instruction
▶ Integrates distributed or intermittent review opportunities
▶ Promotes fluency through decreased response time
▶ Maintains records of student performance
▶ Limits opportunities to avoid or skip critical segments of the program
▶ Avoids prolonged transition periods
▶ Provides activities specifically related to program goals.

Options for Individualization
▶ Provides adjustable sound levels
▶ Provides adjustable difficulty levels
▶ Offers various practice formats
▶ Features adjustable pacing
▶ Provides mouse and keyboard access
▶ Provides authoring capabilities (i.e., teacher can add new content)
▶ Includes supplemental materials
▶ Offers adaptation suggestions in accompanying manual

Publisher Agreements
▶ Offers prepurchase samples or copies of software for evaluation purposes
▶ Provides clearly stated and fair policy governing replacement of defective or damaged software

TABLE 6.4

Sample Formats for Developing Software Evaluation Form

Yes–No Format

	YES	NO
1. Does the software address curricular/IEP goals?		
2. Does the software support national and/or district standards?		
3. Are the examples/graphics in the program age-appropriate?		
4. Does the content match my students' instructional levels?		

Rating Format
Rate this program in the following areas:

	GOOD	FAIR	POOR
1. Match to curricular/IEP goals			
2. Allignment with national/district standards			
3. Age-appropriateness of examples/graphics			
4. Instructional level of content			

to technology integration at the elementary-, middle-, and high-school levels. The researchers (Anderson, 1990–91) defined successful technology integration as:

- teachers' applications of technology in a sustained way to promote and support all students' participation and progress in learning; and
- technology application occurring across a number of classrooms and content areas over time, and a school-based effort rather than the special interest of an individual teacher. (p. 6)

The findings from these three studies suggested that successful technology integration occurs when *entire* school systems commit to using technology to deliver the curriculum and develop academic skills at successive grade levels. Results also indicated that when teachers integrate computer technology, they should:

- Consider both curriculum objectives and individual student needs;
- Introduce the computer lesson (e.g., explain the purpose of the activity, state expectations for the students, outline student roles related to the software, explain how the program generalizes to situations in real life);

▶ Participate in computer-based lessons;

▶ Provide opportunities for students to work together in groups;

▶ Discuss the computer lesson after the student finishes;

▶ Monitor student progress and software effectiveness;

▶ Preview software prior to using it;

▶ Attend inservice opportunities related to technology; and

▶ Collaborate with other teachers to generate or improve lesson ideas (Anderson, 1990–1991).

The three instructional arrangements discussed in this chapter (peer tutoring, cooperative learning, computer-based instruction) are particularly adept at getting students actively involved in the learning process. The teacher plans, facilitates, and monitors student learning, but steps out of the traditional teacher role of standing in front of the class delivering content. Thus, students have opportunities to learn from one another and computer-based materials as well as from the teacher. Using a variety of instructional arrangements keeps the educational experience interesting and provides a forum for addressing the needs of diverse groups of students.

Practice Activities

▶ Outline a peer tutoring system for students at the elementary or secondary level. Develop the needed materials.

▶ Implement a peer tutoring session. Identify what worked well and what needs to be improved.

▶ Create a cooperative learning assignment to be used in a class of diverse students.

▶ Implement the cooperative learning assignment and then improve it based on the implementation experience.

▶ Create a resource file for available computer software.

▶ Review and evaluate software designed for elementary or secondary students.

▶ Identify Internet Web sites with potential instructional applications.

P O S T ORGANIZER

Using a variety of instructional arrangements increases the likelihood that the needs of diverse groups of students will be met. It is important, however, to select instructional arrangements that have validated support. The three arrangements discussed in this chapter (i.e., peer tutoring, cooperative learning, and computer-based instruction) have support for increasing achievement among students with and without disabilities. In each of these instructional arrangements, the teacher's role is to plan the instructional activities carefully, communicate directions and expectations to the students, monitor student performance, and provide feedback. The students' role is to actively engage in the learning process and to demonstrate acquired knowledge.

References

Anderson, M. A. (1990–1991). Technology integration for mainstreamed students. *The computing teacher, 18*(4), 6–8.

Aronson, E., Blaney, N., Stephan, C., Sikes, J., & Snapp, M. (1978). *The jigsaw classroom.* Beverly Hills, CA: Sage.

Bell, K., Young, K. R., Blair, M., & Nelson, R. (1990). Facilitating mainstreaming of students with behavioral disorders using classwide peer tutoring. *School Psychology Review, 19,* 564–573.

Bentz, J. L., & Fuchs, L. S. (1996). Improving peers' helping behavior to students with learning disabilities during mathematics peer tutoring. *Learning Disability Quarterly, 19,* 202–215.

Bermudez, A. B., & Palumbo, D. B. (1994). Bridging the gap between literacy and technology: Hypermedia as a learning tool for limited English proficient students. *The Journal of Educational Issues of Language Minority Students, 14,* 165–184.

Boone, R., Higgins, K., Falba, C., Langley, W. (1993). Cooperative text: Reading and writing in a hypermedia environment. *LD Forum, 19*(1), 28–37.

Bos, C. S., & Vaughn, S. (1994). *Strategies for teaching students with learning and behavior problems* (3rd ed.). Boston: Allyn and Bacon.

Byrd, D. E. (1990). Peer tutoring with the learning disabled: A critical review. *Journal of Educational Research, 84,* 115–118.

Castellani, J. D. (2000). Strategies for integrating the Internet into classrooms for high school students with emotional and learning disabilities. *Intervention in School and Clinic, 35,* 297–305.

Churma, M. (1999). *A guide to integrating technology standards into the curriculum.* Upper Saddle River, NJ: Merrill, an imprint of Prentice-Hall.

Cognition and Technology Group at Vanderbilt. (1992). The Jasper Series and assessment data. *Educational Psychologist 27*(4), 291–315.

Cognition and Technology Group at Vanderbilt. (1993). The Jasper experiment: Using video to furnish real-world problem-solving contexts. *Arithmetic Teacher 40,* 474–478.

Cognition and Technology Group at Vanderbilt. (1997). THE JASPER PROJECT: *Lessons in curriculum, instruction, assessment, and professional development.* Mahwah, NJ: Erlbaum.

Collins, M., Carnine, D., & Gersten, R. (1987). Elaborated corrective feedback and the acquisition of reasoning skills: A study of computer-assisted instruction. *Exceptional Children, 54,* 254–262.

Cook, S. B., Scruggs, T. E., Mastropieri, M. A., & Casto, G. C. (1985–86). Handicapped students as tutors. *The Journal of Special Education, 19,* 483–492.

Cosden, M. A., & Abernathy, T. V. (1990). Microcomputer use in the schools: Teacher roles and instructional options. *Remedial and Special Education, 11,* 31–38.

Daiute, C. (1986). Physical and cognitive factors in revising: Insights from studies with computers. *Research in Teaching of English, 20,* 141–159.

DeVries, D. L., & Slavin, R. E. (1978). Teams-games-tournament (TGT): Review of ten classroom experiments. *Journal of Research and Development in Education, 12,* 28–38.

Doyle, A. (1999). A practitioner's guide to snaring the net. *Educational Leadership, 56*(5), 12–15.

Drier, H. S., Dawson, K. M., & Garofalo, J. (1999). Not your typical math class. *Educational Leadership, 56*(5), 21–25.

DuPaul, G. J., & Henningson, P. N. (1993). Peer tutoring effects on the classroom performance of children with attention deficit hyperactivity disorder. *School Psychology Review, 22*, 134–143.

Eiserman, W. D., Shisler, L., & Osguthorpe, R. T. (1987). Handicapped students as tutors: A description and integration of three years of research findings. *B. C. Journal of Special Education, 11*, 215–231.

Ellis, A. K., & Fouts, J. T. (1997). *Research on educational innovations* (2nd ed.). Larchmont, NY: Eye on Education.

Fantuzzo, J. W., King, J. A., & Heller, L. R. (1992). Effects of reciprocal peer tutoring on mathematics and school adjustment: A component analysis. *Journal of Educational Psychology, 84*, 331–339.

Farley, R. P. (1999). A tale of two schools. *Educational Leadership, 56*(5), 39–42.

Fisher, J. B., Schumaker, J. B., & Deshler, D. D. (1996). Searching for validated inclusive practices: A review of the literature. In E. L. Meyen, G. A. Vergason, & R. J. Whelan (Eds.), *Strategies for teaching exceptional children in inclusive settings* (pp. 123–154). Denver, CO: Love.

Fuchs, L. S., Fuchs, D., Karns, K., & Phillips, N. (1996). *Peabody peer-assisted learning strategies in math.* Nashville, TN: Peabody College.

Fuchs, D., Fuchs, L. S., Mathes, P. G., & Simmons, D. C. (1996). *Peer-assisted learning strategies: Making classrooms more responsive to diversity* (Report No. EC 304 716). Bethesda, MD: National Institute of Child Health and Human Development. (ERIC Document Reproduction Service No. ED 393 269).

Fuchs, D., Fuchs, L. S., Mathes, P. G., & Simmons, D. C. (1997). Peer-assisted learning strategies: Making classrooms more responsive to diversity. *American Educational Research Journal, 34*, 174–206.

Fuchs, D., Mathes, P. G., & Fuchs, L. S. (1996). *Peabody peer-assisted learning strategies reading methods.* Nashville, TN: Peabody College.

Gleason, M., Carnine, D., & Vala, N. (1991). Cumulative versus rapid introduction of new information. *Exceptional Children, 57*, 353–358.

Goldman, S. R., Petrosino, A., Sherwood, R. D., Garrison, S., Hickey, D., Bransford, J. D., & Pellegrino, J. (1996). Anchoring science instruction in multimedia learning environments. In S. Vosniadou, E. De Corte, R. Glaser, & H. Mandl (Eds.), *International perspectives on the design of technology-supported learning environments* (pp. 257–284). Hilsdale, NJ: Lawrence Erlbaum Associates.

Greenwood, C. R, Carta, J. J., & Hall, R. V. (1988). The use of peer tutoring strategies in classroom management and educational instruction. *School Psychology Review, 17*(2), 258–275.

Greenwood, C. R., Delquadri, J. C., & Carta, J. J. (1997). *Together we can! Classwide peer tutoring to improve basic academic skills.* Longmont, CO: Sopris West.

Greenwood, C. R., Delquadri, J. C., & Hall, R. V. (1989). Longitudinal effects of classwide peer tutoring. *Journal of Educational Psychology, 81*, 371–383.

Greenwood, C. R., Dinwiddie, G., Terry, B., Wade, L., Stanley, S. O., Thibadeau, S., & Delquadri, J. C. (1984). Teacher- versus peer-mediated instructions: An eco-behavioral analysis of achievement outcomes. *Journal of Applied Behavior Analysis, 17*, 521–538.

Greenwood, C. R., Terry, B., Arreaga-Mayer, C. & Finney, R. (1992). The classwide peer tutoring program: Implementation factors moderating students' achievement. *Journal of Applied Behavior Analysis, 25*, 101–116.

Greenwood, C. R., Terry, B., Utley, C. A., Montagna, D., Walker, D. (1993). Achievement, placement, and services: Middle school benefits of classwide peer tutoring used at the elementary school. *School Psychology Review, 22*, 497–516.

Hammill, D. D., & Bartel, N. R. (1995). *Teaching students with learning and behavior problems* (6th ed.). Austin, TX: PRO-ED.

Hancock, V. (1997). Creating the information age school. *Educational Leadership, 55*(3), 60–63.

Haring, T. G., Breen, C., Pitts-Conway, V., Lee, M., & Gaylord-Ross, R. (1987). Adolescent peer tutoring and special friend experiences. *Journal of the Association for Individuals with Severe Handicaps, 12*, 280–286.

Hasselbring, T. S., & Goin, L. I. (1993). Integrated technology and media. In E. A. Polloway & J. R. Patton (Eds.), *Strategies for Teaching Learners With Special Needs* (pp. 145–162). New York: Merrill, an imprint of Macmillan.

Higgins, K., & Boone, R. (1990). Hypertext computer study guides and the social studies achievement of students with learning disabilities, remedial students, and regular education students. *Journal of Learning Disabilities, 23,* 529–540.

Higgins, K. & Boone, R. (1991). *Hypertext CAI: Maintaining handicapped students in a regular classroom reading program.* (Report No. CFDA 84.024J). Seattle, WA: University of Washington Experimental Education Unit. (ERIC Document Reproduction Service No. ED 387 949)

Higgins, K., Boone, R., & Lovitt, T. C. (1996). Hypertext support for remedial students and students with learning disabilities. *Journal of Learning Disabilities, 29,* 402–412.

Hutinger, P. L., & Clark, L. (2000). TEChPLACES an Internet community for young children, their teachers, and their families. *Teaching Exceptional Children, 32*(4), 56–63.

Inspiration Version 6 [Computer Software]. (1988–1999). Portland, OR: Inspiration Software.

Integrating technology into the standard curriculum. (1998, Fall). *Research Connections in Special Education, 3,* 1–6.

Jenkins, J. R., Jewell, M., Leceister, N., O'Connor, R., Jenkins, L., & Troutner, N. (1994). Accommodations for individual differences without classroom ability groups: An experiment in school restructuring. *Exceptional Children, 60,* 344–358.

Jenkins, J. R., Jewell, M., Leceister, L., & Troutner, N. (1990, April). *Development of a school building model for educating handicapped and at-risk students in general education classrooms.* Paper presented at the meeting of the American Educational Association, Boston, MA.

Johnson, R. T, & Johnson, D. W. (1981a). Building friendships between handicapped and nonhandicapped students: Effects of cooperative and individualistic instruction. *American Educational Research Journal, 18,* 415–423.

Johnson, D. W., & Johnson, R. T. (1981b). Effects of cooperative and individualistic learning experiences on interethnic interaction. *Journal of Educational Psychology, 73,* 444–449.

Johnson, D. W., & Johnson, R. T. (1989). *Cooperation and competition: Theory and research.* Edina, MN: Interaction Book Company.

Johnson, D. W., & Johnson, R. T. (1994). *Learning together and alone: Cooperative, competitive, and individualistic learning* (4th ed.). Boston: Allyn and Bacon.

Johnson, R. T., Johnson, D. W., Scott, L. E., & Ramolae, B. A. (1985). Effects of single-sex and mixed-sex cooperative interaction on science achievement and attitudes and cross-handicap and cross-sex relationships. *Journal of Research in Science Teaching, 2,* 207–220.

Johnson, R. T., Johnson, D. W., & Stanne, M. B. (1985). Effects of cooperative, competitive, and individualistic goal structures on computer-assisted instruction. *Journal of Educational Psychology, 77,* 668–677.

Johnson, D. W., Skon, L., & Johnson, R. T. (1980). Effects of cooperative, competitive and individualistic conditions on children's problem-solving performance. *American Educational Research Journal, 17,* 83–93.

Joint Committee on Teacher Planning for Students with Disabilities. (1995). *Planning for academic diversity in America's classrooms: Windows on reality, research, change, and practice.* Lawrence, KS: The University of Kansas Center for Research on Learning.

Kamps, D. M., Barbetta, P. M., Leonard, B. R., & Delquadri, J. (1994). Classwide peer tutoring: An integration strategy to improve reading skills and promote peer interactions among students with autism and general education peers. *Journal of Applied Behavior Analysis, 27,* 49–61.

Kelly, R. (2000). Working with WebQuests: Making the Web accessible to students with disabilities. *Teaching Exceptional Children, 32*(6), 4–13.

Kenny, R. F. (1994). The effectiveness of instructional orienting activities in computer-based instruction. *Canadian Journal of Educational Communication, 23*(3), 161–188.

Kid Works 2 [Computer software]. (1992). Torrance, CA: Davidson & Associates.

Kozma, R., & Schank, P. (1998). Connecting with the 21st century: Technology in support of educational reform. In C. Dede (Ed.), *ASCD Year Book 1998 Learning With Technology* (pp. 3–27). Alexandria, VA: Association for Supervision and Curriculum Development.

Lazerson, D. B., Foster, H. L., Brown, S. I., & Hummel, J. W. (1988). The effectiveness of cross-age tutoring with truant junior high school students with learning disabilities. *Journal of Learning Disabilities, 21,* 253–255.

MacArthur, C. A. (1997). Using technology to enhance the writing processes of students with learning disabilities. In K. Higgins & R. Boone (Eds.), *Technology for students with learning disabilities* (pp. 7–23). Austin, TX: Pro-Ed.

MacArthur, C. A. (1998). Word processing with speech synthesis and word prediction: Effects on the dialogue journal writing of students with learning disabilities. *Learning Disability Quarterly, 21,* 151–166.

MacArthur, C., & Graham, S. (1987). Learning disabled students composing under three methods of text production: Handwriting, word processing, and dictation. *Journal of Special Education, 21,* 22–42.

MacArthur, C. A., Graham, S., Schwartz, S. S., & Schafer, W. D. (1995). Evaluation of a writing instruction model that integrated a process approach, strategy instruction, and word processing. *Learning Disability Quarterly, 18,* 278–291.

Maheady, L. (1996). Peer-mediated instruction: I'll get by with a little help from my friends. In G. G. Brannigan (Ed.), *The enlightened educator: Research adventures in the schools* (pp. 206–225). New York: McGraw-Hill.

Maheady, L., Harper, G. F., & Mallette, B. (1991). Peer-mediated instruction: A review of potential applications for special education. *Reading, Writing, and Learning Disabilities International, 7,* 75–103.

Maheady, L., Sacca, M. K., & Harper, G. F. (1988). Classwide peer tutoring with mildly handicapped high school students. *Exceptional Children, 55,* 52–59.

Male, M. (1997). *Technology for inclusion: Meeting the special needs of all students* (3rd ed.). Boston: Allyn and Bacon.

Mathes, P. G., & Fuchs, L. S. (1991). The efficacy of peer tutoring in reading for students with disabilities: A best-evidence synthesis. (Report No. EC 301 078). Washington, DC: Special Education Programs. (ERIC Document Reproduction Service No. ED 344 352)

Mathes, P. G., & Fuchs, L. S. (1993). Peer-mediated reading instruction in special education resource rooms. *Learning Disabilities Research & Practice, 8,* 233–243.

Mathes, P. G., Fuchs, D., Fuchs, L. S., Henley, A. M., & Sanders, A. (1994). Increasing strategic reading practice with Peabody Classwide Peer Tutoring. *Learning Disabilities Research & Practice, 9,* 44–48.

Mathews, D. M., Pracek, E., & Olson, J. (2000). Technology for teaching and learning. In J. L. Olson & J. M. Platt, *Teaching children and adolescents with special needs* (3rd ed.) (pp. 322–346). Upper Saddle River, NJ: Merrill, an imprint of Prentice-Hall.

McNaughton, D., Hughes, C., & Ofiesh, N. (1997). Proofreading for students with learning disabilities: Integrating computer and strategy use. *Learning Disabilities Research & Practice, 12,* 16–28.

Mesch, D., Johnson, D. W., & Johnson, R. (1987). Impact of positive interdependence and academic group contingencies on achievement. *Journal of Social Psychology, 128,* 345–352.

Mortweet, S. L., Utley, C. A., Walker, D., Dawson, H. L., Delquadri, J. C., Reddy, S. S., Greenwood, C. R., Hamilton, S., Ledford, D. (1999). Classwide peer tutoring: Teaching students with mild mental retardation in inclusive classrooms. *Exceptional Children, 65,* 524–536.

Nichols, J. D., & Miller, R. B. (1994). Cooperative learning and student motivation. *Contemporary Educational Psychology, 19,* 167–178.

Niedermeyer, F. C. (1970). Effects of training on the instructional behaviors of student tutors. *Journal of Educational Research, 64,* 119–123.

O'Connor, R. E., & Jenkins, J. R. (1996). Cooperative learning as an inclusion strategy: A closer look. *Exceptionality, 6,* 29–51.

Okolo, C. M., Bahr, C. M., & Rieth, H. J. (1993). A retrospective view of computer-based instruction. *Journal of Special Education Technology, XII*(1), 1–27.

Okolo, C. M., Cavalier, A. R., Ferretti, R. P., & MacArthur, C. A. (2000). Technology, literacy, and disabilities: A review of the research. In R. Gersten, E. P. Schiller, & S. Vaughn (Eds.), *Contemporary special education research: Synthesis of the knowledge base on critical instructional issues* (pp. 179–250). Mahwah, NJ: Erlbaum.

Osguthorpe, R. T., Eiserman, W. D., & Shisler, L. (1985). Increasing social acceptance: Mentally retarded students tutoring regular class peers. *Education and Training of the Mentally Retarded, 20,* 235–240.

Osguthorpe, R. T., & Scruggs, T. E. (1986). Special education students as tutors: A review and analysis. *Remedial and Special Education, 7*(4), 15–26.

Pomerantz, D. J., Windell, I. J., & Smith, M. A. (1994). The effects of classwide peer tutoring and accommodations on the acquisition of content area knowledge by elementary students with learning disabilities. *LD Forum, 19*(2), 28–32.

Pomplun, M. (1997). When students with disabilities participate in cooperative groups. *Exceptional Children, 64,* 49–58.

Putnam, J. (1997). *Cooperative learning in diverse classrooms.* Upper Saddle River, NJ: Merrill, an imprint of Prentice-Hall.

Qin, Z., Johnson, D. W., & Johnson, R. T. (1995). Cooperative versus competitive efforts and problem solving. *Review of Educational Research, 65,* 129–143.

Reddy, S. S., Utley, C. A., Delquadri, J. C., Mortweet, S. L., Greenwood, C. R., & Bowman, V. (1999). Peer tutoring for health and safety. *Teaching Exceptional Children, 31*(3), 44–52.

Robinson, S. L., DePascale, C., & Roberts, F. (1989). Computer-delivered feedback in group-based instruction: Effects for learning disabled students in mathematics. *Learning Disabilities Focus, 5,* 28–35.

Schultz, J. L. (1989/1990). Cooperative Learning: Refining the process. *Educational Leadership, 47*(4), 43–45.

Scruggs, T. E., & Richter, L. (1988). Tutoring learning disabled students: A critical review. *Learning Disabilities Quarterly, 2,* 274–286.

Sharan, S., & Sharan, Y. (1976). Small group teaching. Englewood Cliffs, NJ: Prentice-Hall.

Sharan, Y., & Sharan, S. (1992). Expanding cooperative learning through group investigation. New York: Teachers College Press.

Sharan, Y., & Sharan, S. (1994). Group investigation in the cooperative classroom. In S. Sharan (Ed.), *Handbook of cooperative learning methods* (pp. 97–114). Westport, CT: Greenwood Press.

Sherwood, R. D., Petrosino, A. J., Lin, X., Lamon, M., & Cognition and Technology Group at Vanderbilt. (1995). Problem-based macro contexts in science instruction: Theoretical basis, design issues, and the development of applications. In D. Lavoie (Ed.), *Towards a cognitive-science perspective for scientific problem solving* (pp. 191–214). Manhattan, KS: National Association for Research in Science Teaching.

Shin, J., Deno, S. L., Robinson, S. L., & Marson, D. (2000). Predicting classroom achievement from active responding on a computer-based groupware system. *Remedial and Special Education, 21,* 53–60.

Shisler, L., Osguthorpe, R. T., & Eiserman, W. D. (1987). The effects of reverse-role tutoring on the social acceptance of students with behavioral disorders. *Behavioral Disorders, 13*(1), 35–44.

Simmons, D. C., Fuchs, D., Fuchs, L., Hodge, J. P., & Mathes, P. G. (1994). Importance of instructional complexity and role reciprocity to classwide peer tutoring. *Learning Disabilities Research & Practice, 9,* 203–212.

Skon, L., Johnson, D. W., & Johnson, R. T. (1981). Cooperative peer interaction versus individual competition and individualistic efforts: Effects on the acquisition of cognitive reasoning strategies. *Journal of Educational Psychology, 73,* 83–92.

Slavin, R. E. (1978). Student teams and achievement divisions. *Journal of Research and Development in Education, 12,* 39–49.

Slavin, R. E. (1983). *Cooperative learning*. New York: Longman.

Slavin, R. E. (1986). *Using student team learning* (3rd ed.). Baltimore, MD: Center for Research on Elementary and Middle Schools, Johns Hopkins University.

Slavin, R. E. (1989). Comprehensive cooperative learning models for heterogeneous classrooms. *Pointer, 32,* 12–19.

Slavin, R. E. (1991). Synthesis of research on cooperative learning. *Educational Leadership, 48(5),* 71–82.

Slavin, R. E. (1995). Cooperative learning: Theory, research, and practice (2nd ed.). Boston: Allyn and Bacon.

Slavin, R. E. (1996). Research on cooperative learning and achievement: What we know, what we need to know. *Contemporary Educational Psychology, 21,* 43–69.

Slavin, R. E., Madden, N. A., & Leavey, M. (1984). Effects of cooperative learning and individualized instruction on mainstreamed students. *Exceptional Children, 50,* 434–442.

Slavin, R. E., Madden, N. A., & Stevens, R. J. (1990). Cooperative learning models for the 3 R's. *Educational Leadership, 47*(4), 22–28.

Slavin, R. E., Stevens, R. J., & Madden, N. A. (1988). Accommodating student diversity in reading and writing instruction: A cooperative learning approach. *Remedial and Special Education, 9*(1), 60–66.

Stevens, R., Madden, N., Slavin, R., & Farnish, A. (1987). Cooperative integrated reading and composition: Two field experiments. *Reading Research Quarterly, 22,* 433–454.

Stevens, R. J., & Slavin, R. E. (1995a). Effects of a cooperative learning approach in reading and writing on academically handicapped and nonhandicapped students. *The Elementary School Journal, 95,* 241–262.

Stevens, R. J., & Slavin, R. E. (1995b). The cooperative elementary school: Effects on students' achievement, attitudes, and social relations. *American Educational Research Journal, 32,* 321–351.

Storybook Weaver [Computer software]. (1992). Minneapolis, MN: MECC.

Tateyama-Sniezek, K. M. (1990). Cooperative learning: Does it improve the academic achievement of students with handicaps? *Exceptional Children, 56,* 426–437.

United States Department of Education, National Center for Education Statistics (1999). *Digest of education statistics 1999* [On-line]. Washington DC: U.S. Government Printing Office. Available: http://nces.ed.gov.

United States Department of Education, National Center for Education Statistics (2000). *The condition of education 2000* [On-line], NCES 2000–602. Washington DC: U.S. Government Printing Office. Available: http://nces.ed.gov.

Vanderbilt University Publications and Design. (1996). *PALS: Peer-assisted learning strategies for instruction in reading and math* [Brochure]. Nashville, TN: Author.

Vermette, P. J. (1998). *Making cooperative learning work: Student teams in K–12 classrooms*. Upper Saddle River, NJ: Merrill, an imprint of Prentice-Hall.

Vernon, D. S., Deshler, D. D., & Schumaker, J. B. (1993). *The teamwork strategy*. Lawrence, KS: Edge Enterprises.

Vernon, D. S., Schumaker, J. B., & Deshler, D. D. (1993). *The SCORE skills: Social skills for cooperative groups*. Lawrence, KS: Edge Enterprises.

Warger, C. L. (1991). Peer tutoring: When working together is better than working alone. *Research & Resources on Special Education, 30,* 1–6. (ERIC Clearinghouse on Handicapped and Gifted Children under contract No. R188062007 with the Office of Special Education Programs, U.S. Department of Education)

Williams, S. M., Burgess, K. L., Bray, M. H., Bransford, J. D., Goldman, S. R., & The Cognition and Technology Group at Vanderbilt. (1998). Technology and learning in schools for thought classrooms. In C. Dede (Ed.), *ASCD Year Book 1998 Learning With Technology* (pp. 97–119). Alexandria, VA: Association for Supervision and Curriculum Development.

Winzer, M. A., & Mazurek, K. (1998). *Special education in multicultural contexts*. Upper Saddle River, NJ: Merrill, an imprint of Prentice-Hall.

Writer's Helper [Computer software]. (1990). Iowa City, IO: CONDUIT, University of Iowa.

Zellermayer, M., Salomon, G., Globerson, T., & Givon, H. (1991) Enhancing writing-related metacognitions through a computerized writing partner. *American Educational Research Journal, 28*, 373–391.

Modifying Curriculum and Instruction

All students can learn and succeed, but not on the same day in the same way.

—Spady

A D V A N C E ORGANIZER

In addition to using a variety of instructional arrangements, teachers can use a variety of curricular and instructional modifications to enhance student learning and performance. The purpose of this chapter is to discuss the use of accommodations, adaptations, and assistive technology to help students with special learning needs. Discussion and guidelines related to teaching students with various cultural and linguistic backgrounds also are presented. The chapter concludes with a discussion related to the use of universally designed curricula. The need for curricular and instructional modifications is becoming increasingly evident as student diversity increases in classrooms throughout the United States.

Curricular and instructional modifications are necessary when teaching groups of diverse students. Not all students respond to the curriculum or to the instructional practices in the same way. What works for one student won't necessarily work for another. In fact, what works for one student on one day may not work for the same student on a different day. This means that teachers must constantly consider alternative ways to present and improve their instructional practices. They must continually ask themselves, "What can I try next if this doesn't work?"

When any student fails to succeed in the classroom, it is appropriate to make curricular and/or instructional modifications. For students with disabilities, legislation guarantees the right to supplemental services and modified instructional practices. The 1997 Individuals with Disabilities Education Act (IDEA) (PL 105-17) maintains that each student with a disability is entitled to a free, appropriate public education that includes a carefully designed program of special education and related services that meets the student's unique learning needs. The law also requires that the student be given an opportunity to participate in the same general curriculum taught to other students in the public educational system. Moreover, related documentation must be included in the student's Individualized Education Program (IEP). Specifically, the IEP must include statements related to (a) how the student's disability affects his or her involvement and progress in the general curriculum, (b) annual goals for enabling the student to be involved in and progress in the general curriculum, and (c) the education, services, program modifications, and supports needed for the student to be involved in and progress in the general curriculum, including whether the student requires assistive technology devices and services. Furthermore, the March 12, 1999, Final Regulations for IDEA state that students with disabilities may not be removed from "age-appropriate regular classrooms solely because of needed modifications in the general curriculum" (U.S. Department of Education, 1999, 34 CFR 300.552(e)). Thus, IDEA clearly entitles students with disabilities to instructional modifications that enhance their learning experiences.

Similarly, Section 504 of the 1973 Rehabilitation Act (PL 93-112) offers protection to students with disabilities. Section 504 is a civil rights law that forbids all institutions receiving federal financial assistance from discriminating against individuals with disabilities with regard to employment, housing, and access to public programs and facilities. In the public school arena, Section 504 applies to students with special needs who are ineligible for services under IDEA (Conderman & Katsiyannis, 1995). This law defines disability more broadly than IDEA; therefore, far more students are eligible for services under 504 than IDEA. Under 504, students qualify for services if they *(a)* have a physical or mental impairment that substantially limits one or more major life activities (i.e., walking, seeing, hearing, speaking, breathing, learning, working, caring for oneself, and performing manual tasks), *(b)* have a record of such impairment, or *(c)* are regarded as having such an impairment by others (Henderson, 1995). Potential recipients of 504 services include students with attention-deficit disorder, communicable diseases, medical conditions, temporary conditions due to illness or accident, arthritis, cancer, acquired immune deficiency syndrome (AIDS), AIDS-related complex, or human immunodeficiency virus (HIV) (Council of Administrators in Special Education, 1991). Students who are deemed eligible for 504 services are guaranteed a free, appropriate education that includes the delivery of related services and reasonable accommodations to meet their unique learning needs. Thus, although modifying instructional practices is an ethical responsibility related to teaching any student, with regard to teaching students with disabilities it also is a legal responsibility as evidenced through IDEA and Section 504.

Modifications

Ebeling, Deschenes, and Sprague (1994) identified nine types of modifications that teachers can use to meet the needs of diverse groups of students: size, time, input, output, difficulty, participation, level of support, goals, and substitute curriculum. Typically, these modifications involve reducing the amount of content, providing additional time for learning, and changing the way something is taught or the way students demonstrate understanding. It may be appropriate to change the difficulty level, expectations for student participation, or the learning goals. It might also be beneficial to increase the amount of support and/or change the curriculum. As special needs emerge among students, teachers can use these nine types of modifications as a framework for thinking about ways to change their instructional program. Then, modifications that seem appropriate can be implemented in a systematic manner until success is achieved. Combining several modifications also may be appropriate. Table 7.1 on page 290 provides further descriptions and examples of these nine modifications.

Another approach for modifying instructional practices is to consider student needs based on a continuum of teaching that ranges from explicit instruction to implicit instruction (Mercer, Jordan, & Miller, 1996; Mercer, Lane, Jordan, Allsopp,

TABLE 7.1

Nine Types of Modifications

Type of Modification	Description	Examples
Size	Change the amount or number of items the student is expected to learn or complete.	Have student complete the even-numbered problems in their math text.
		Have student learn 10 rather than 20 vocabulary terms.
Time	Change the amount of time allowed for learning; change amount of time for completing assignments or tests.	Give student extra week to complete science project.
		Give student 1-1/2 hours instead of 1 hour to complete unit exam.
Input	Change the way instruction is presented.	Use cooperative learning.
		Use visual displays.
		Use computer-assisted instruction.
Output	Change the way students respond.	Allow student to say answers into a tape recorder rather than writing responses.
		Allow students to complete projects rather than take tests.
Difficulty	Change the skill level required for task completion.	Allow open-book test.
		Allow students to use spell checker.
Participation	Allow for various levels of student involvement.	One student counts and distributes 20 manipulative devices to each student; other students use the devices to solve subtraction problems.
		One student writes report; another student draws accompanying illustrations.
Level of Support	Change the amount of individual assistance.	Have paraeducator work one-to-one with student needing additional help with assignment.
		Arrange peer tutoring.
Alternative Goals	Use same materials, but change the expected outcomes.	Given a diagram of the parts of the eye, one student labels the parts; others label the parts and their function.
		One student identifies the ingredients in a recipe; other students identify, measure, and mix the ingredients.
Substitute Curriculum	Change the materials and instruction.	Some students read and discuss novel; some students participate in Reading Mastery lessons.

*A variety of learning activities and instructional modifications
are used in this elementary classroom to ensure that the diverse
needs of all class members are met.*

& Eisele, 1996). Explicit instruction involves teaching skills and concepts in a clear
and direct fashion. The teacher serves as the disseminator of knowledge and typically demonstrates skills, involves students in modeling the skills, provides many
opportunities for practice, and places an emphasis on mastery of the skill. Implicit
instruction, on the opposite end of the continuum, emphasizes creating situations
in which students can discover and construct their own new knowledge. The teacher
creates meaningful contexts for students to experience and then serves as a facilitator of learning. Students' needs for explicit or implicit instruction seem to depend
on the depth and breadth of their background knowledge and whether or not they
have specific learning difficulties. Students who have problems learning, limited
background knowledge about a particular topic, initial failure with learning the
content, and limited intrinsic motivation to learn benefit from *explicit* instruction
for mastering new skills and concepts, whereas students with positive learning experiences, rich background knowledge, initial success with the content, and intrinsic
motivation to learn benefit from *implicit* instruction (Howell, Fox, & Morehead,
1993). Students who have limited success with academic tasks need the greatest
amount of teacher-directed support. As students become more proficient in their

learning, implicit instruction can be increased. The challenge is to provide only the amount of support that students actually need to succeed, because the ultimate goal is to promote independent rather than dependent learning behavior. Using the idea of a continuum from explicit to implicit instruction (i.e., teacher-directed to student-directed; greater support to lesser support) provides a way for teachers to think about meeting the various learning needs that exist within a class of diverse students.

In addition to thinking about students' learning abilities and needs related to the explicit to implicit continuum, it also is important to think about the academic task itself. Explicit instruction may be more appropriate for some academic tasks, and implicit instruction may be more appropriate for others. Explicit instruction is appropriate when the task is complex, factual, necessary for subsequent learning, or potentially hazardous (e.g., chemistry experiment). It also is appropriate to use explicit instruction when teaching task-specific strategies and aspects of the curriculum that need to be mastered with high rates of fluency (e.g., basic math facts; word recognition). Implicit instruction is appropriate when the task is conceptual and requires problem-solving strategies (e.g., math problems involving estimation; reading comprehension) (Howell, Fox & Morehead, 1993; Stanovich, 1994). Thus, it is important for teachers to consider both their students and the academic task when determining how explicit or implicit the instruction should be. Considering these factors will help teachers make appropriate instructional modifications for students who are experiencing limited success in their learning.

As is already evident, there are many modifications that teachers can make to improve their instructional practices when teaching students with special learning needs. Among the most frequently used modifications are accommodations, adaptations, and assistive technology. These modifications are becoming more prevalent as the diversity within public school classrooms increases.

Accommodations

Accommodations are changes to the delivery of instruction, method of student performance, or method of assessment that do not significantly change the content or conceptual difficulty level of the curriculum. Accommodations frequently involve alternative strategies that help students reach the curricular objectives (Bradley, King-Sears, & Tessier-Switlick, 1997; Wood, 1998). Accommodations are generally helpful for many students in the class. Because of the differences among students, accommodations may be absolutely necessary for some students, somewhat helpful for others, and totally unnecessary for still others. Thus, teachers must consider student characteristics and needs when selecting accommodations to use in the classroom.

Delivery of Instruction

A variety of accommodations can be made to enhance the delivery of instruction and therefore increase the likelihood that students with special learning needs will experience success in school. Several of the methods discussed earlier in this text represent examples of validated accommodations (e.g., instructional cues, visual displays, study guides, lecture-pause procedures, concept teaching routines, peer tutoring, cooperative learning, computer-based instruction). From these examples, it is evident that accommodations designed to improve instruction may involve either changes in teaching style or changes in instructional arrangements. The overall goal, in both instances, is to help students succeed in the selected curriculum without significantly changing the content or making it much easier (i.e., "watering down" the curriculum). Instead, the emphasis is on enhancing the instructional process so that students can learn more efficiently and effectively (see Validation Box 7.1).

Educators and researchers have identified numerous accommodations that teachers can use to modify their delivery of instruction (Bradley, King-Sears, & Tessier-Switlick, 1997; Hammeken, 1995; Conderman & Katsiyannis, 1995; Hudson, Lignugaris-Kraft, & Miller, 1993; "Effective Accommodations," 1997; Salend, 1998; Wood, 1998). Most teachers find that accommodations are needed to help students understand and remember the content being taught. Accommodations for these purposes are summarized in Table 7.2 on page 294.

Method of Student Performance

In addition to making accommodations to the way instruction is delivered, teachers facilitate accommodations related to how students perform. Clearly, students demonstrate differences in their abilities to perform typical school-related tasks. Consequently, a variety of accommodations are needed. Most teachers have students in their class whose rate of voluntary participation can be increased with carefully selected accommodations. Increased participation results in increased learning. Students who have difficulty using their textbooks or taking notes during lectures and class discussions benefit from accommodations that allow them to

VALIDATION BOX

7.1

Instructional Enhancements

Seven methods for modifying or enhancing instruction for students with learning disabilities were investigated in an extensive literature review of 33 studies. The seven enhancements were advance organizers, visual displays, study guides, mnemonic devices, audio recording, computer-assisted instruction, and peer mediation. Findings from this review of literature suggest that each of these instructional enhancements can be used in a variety of ways to increase the performance of low-achieving and normal-achieving students in secondary-level content classes. For more information see: (Hudson, Lignugaris-Kraft, & Miller, 1993).

TABLE 7.2

Sample Accommodations for Instructional Delivery

To accommodate for student difficulties related to acquiring and remembering academic information:

▶ Integrate several short learning activities rather than a single long one into the lesson.
▶ Use visual displays or graphic organizers (see Chapter 5).
▶ Use study guides (see Chapter 5).
▶ Provide analogies, stories, examples, nonexamples.
▶ Teach mnemonic devices.
▶ Provide many opportunities for review (before, during, and after lessons).
▶ Use advance organizers and post-organizers to introduce and summarize lesson content.
▶ Provide hands-on experiences.

---

compensate for these challenges. Similarly, students who have difficulties with written or verbal expression benefit from accommodations because so much of the school experience involves these two modes of communication.

Educators and researchers have identified numerous accommodations that teachers can use to modify methods for student performance (Bradley, King-Sears, & Tessier-Switlick, 1997; Hammeken, 1995; "Effective Accommodations," 1997; Sacca & Raimondi, 1997; Salend, 1998; Schumm & Vaughn, 1995; Wood, 1998). Specific accommodations for difficulties with participation, textbook usage, note-taking, verbal expression, and writing are summarized in Table 7.3.

TABLE 7.3

Sample Accommodations for Student Performance

To accommodate for low rates of voluntary student participation:

▶ Integrate choral responding into lessons (provide a signal for students to respond verbally in unison).
▶ Use cooperative learning activities (see Chapter 6).
▶ Use Free-Write or Free-Tell (stop an activity or lesson for about 5 minutes and have students write or talk about what they've learned, allow them to write or ask questions about things that seem confusing).
▶ Use instructional games (practice important information using game formats).
▶ Use KWL (At beginning of unit, students write what they already know and what they want to know about the topic on large charts posted in the room. After completing the unit, students record what they learned.
▶ Use lecture-pause procedures (see Chapter 5).
▶ Establish peer tutoring programs (see Chapter 6).
▶ Use response card formats (after posing a question, students simultaneously respond using cards, signs, or lap boards).
▶ Use Think-Pair-Share strategy (after posing a question, have students think about their response, find a peer to share their ideas, and then share with another pair).
▶ Follow Three-Statement Rule (for every three statements made by the teacher, get response from students).

(continued)

TABLE 7.3

Sample Accommodations for Student Performance (*continued*)

▶ Use Turn-to-Your-Neighbor strategy (periodically throughout a lesson, have students turn to a student sitting next to them and discuss key concepts, answer a question together, or solve a posed problem together).
▶ Use Names-in-a-Can (write student names on separate Popsicle sticks and put in a can, then randomly draw names to answer questions).

To accommodate for difficulties with textbooks:
▶ Use alternative instructional materials.
▶ Highlight, underline, or color-code main ideas, important vocabulary, and/or key concepts.
▶ Let students listen to taped versions of texts or paraphrased versions of the text.
▶ Provide students with a list of discussion questions before reading the material.
▶ Introduce key vocabulary before students read.
▶ Structure postreading activities to increase retention.
▶ Develop study guides for students to complete as they read.
▶ Provide chapter outlines.
▶ Read sections of the text aloud or have students volunteer to read aloud.
▶ Teach students how to interpret graphs, charts, and illustrations.
▶ Teach textbook organization and structure (e.g., headings, varied print).
▶ Permit students to work in small groups to master textbook content.
▶ Use video tapes, recordings, and/or computer programs to supplement textbook.
▶ Teach reading comprehension strategies.

To accommodate for poor note-taking performance:
▶ Assign a note-taking buddy.
▶ Make photocopies of a proficient note-taker's notes.
▶ Provide study guides/partial outlines (see Chapter 5).
▶ Let students tape record lectures/discussions.
▶ Provide handouts summarizing important information.
▶ Provide copy of lecture notes.
▶ Provide visuals (e.g., multimedia presentations, transparencies, flip charts) to list important concepts.

To accommodate for difficulties with verbal expression:
▶ Give extra time to respond.
▶ Provide cues or hints.
▶ Let students read silently before reading aloud.
▶ Encourage students to use outlines when giving an oral report.
▶ Tell students a day ahead of time what they'll be asked to read aloud in class.
▶ Let students tape oral reports instead of doing them live in class.
▶ Provide extra "wait time" after asking a question.

To accommodate for poor writing abilities:
▶ Allow students to use word processor and related tools (see Chapter 6).
▶ Provide additional space for students to record written responses.
▶ Give students the option of a verbal assignment.
▶ Provide students with models.
▶ Provide "story starters" (i.e., beginning of a story) that students must finish.
▶ Post frequently misspelled words.
▶ Reduce amount of required writing.
▶ Provide extra time for completing written assignments.
▶ Allow alternatives to writing lengthy sentences (e.g., single-word responses; multiple choice; taped responses).
▶ Allow students to use either manuscript or cursive writing.
▶ Allow students to use pencil grips or large pencils.

Method of Assessment

Assessing student knowledge and understanding of the curriculum is one of the most important aspects of teaching. The most frequently used method for assessing student learning is the administration of tests (e.g., weekly quizzes, unit tests, district-wide standardized achievement tests). There are, however, a number of students who have great difficulty demonstrating what they know through tests and therefore benefit from special accommodations. These accommodations address poor test-taking abilities and/or low reading abilities. Accommodations related to test construction also enhance student performance (see Validation Box 7.2 on pp. 298–299).

Educators and researchers have identified numerous testing accommodations that teachers can use when assessing student progress (Beattie, Grise, & Algozzine, 1983; "Effective Accommodations," 1997; Gajria, Salend, & Hemrick, 1994; Hughes, 1996; Jayanthi, Epstein, Polloway, & Bursuck, 1996; Thurlow, Ysseldyke, & Silverstein, 1993; Tindal, Heath, Hollenbeck, Almond, Harniss, 1998). Accommodations related to poor test-taking abilities, low reading abilities, and test construction are summarized in Table 7.4.

A variety of accommodations may be made for students with disabilities who have difficulty taking standardized tests. Administering fewer subsections of the test per testing session, providing an example for each different set of items on the test, and orally reading test items are a few examples of possible accommodations.

There is little debate with regard to the appropriateness of using accommodations to facilitate student learning. Changing instructional strategies to meet the needs of students is one of the cornerstones of quality teaching. Exemplary teachers routinely think about potential accommodations for their students. This type of thinking becomes a natural part of the instructional planning process. At times, it is helpful for groups of teachers to get together to devise accommodations for students who are experiencing learning difficulties. Collaborative efforts between teachers result in greater consistency in terms of implementing the accommodations. Students benefit from such consistency.

TABLE 7.4

Sample Accommodations for Student Assessment

To accommodate for poor test-taking abilities:
- Provide extended time to take tests or extend testing over several days.
- Provide breaks during the testing session.
- Teach test-taking strategies.
- Provide clear directions (written and verbal).
- Emphasize important words in written directions through underlining, color-coding, bolding, enlarging print.
- Emphasize important words in verbal directions through voice emphasis and repetition.
- Give individual help with directions during tests.
- Seek alternative ways to assess student understanding (projects, papers, homework, in-class assignments).
- Provide in-class reviews for tests.
- Arrange for students to take tests alone or in small groups rather than in large groups.
- Vary response format (e.g., mark in test booklet, point to response, respond orally, sign language, computers).
- Provide a scribe.
- Allow students to practice with the accommodations prior to taking the test.

To accommodate for low reading abilities:
- Read test directions to student.
- Read test questions to student.
- Record questions on tape recorder for student.
- Simplify the wording on tests.

To accommodate for difficulties related to test construction:
- Order items from easy to difficult.
- Avoid hyphenating words at the end of lines.
- Include example items and responses.
- Provide plenty of space for answers.
- Provide clear, readable, uncluttered test formats.
- Vary test format (e.g., Braille, large type, cassette).
- Vary item format of tests (e.g., multiple choice instead of essay).
- Provide typed rather than handwritten tests.
- Match the test to information taught.
- List multiple choice options in vertical rather than horizontal format.

Test Modifications

▸ A survey study was conducted to assess general education teachers' perceptions with regard to 32 test modifications. Sixty-four secondary general education teachers from two New York suburban school districts participated in this study. The findings revealed that a majority of the teachers were aware of 30 of the 32 test modifications identified on the survey. More than 90 percent of the teachers reported using modifications that pertained to the design or construction of the test (e.g., typewritten, ample space) because these modifications were easy to make, could be used with all students, and maintained academic integrity. Teachers also indicated a willingness to provide students with disabilities more time to complete their tests. For more information see: (Gajria, Salend, & Hemrick, 1994).

▸ In a national survey study, 401 general education teachers expressed their opinions regarding testing modifications for students with disabilities. The modifications that were rated as being most helpful were giving individual help with directions, reading test questions to students, and simplifying wording of test questions. Modifications that were rated as being easiest to make were using black-and-white copies, providing extra space, giving study guides, allowing students to use notes or their books, and giving help with directions. Of the surveyed teachers, 66.6 percent indicated that it was not fair to make testing modifications only for students with disabilities. For more information see: (Jayanthi, Epstein, Polloway, & Bursuck, 1996).

▸ A review of literature examined policies for state assessment programs and empirical studies conducted by the Educational Testing Service (ETS) and the American College Testing (ACT) Program. Written state policies revealed there is variance among states with regard to the testing modifications (e.g., alternate presentation, response, setting, scheduling/time) allowed. The most common modification is to allow alternate presentations (Braille, oral reading of questions), and the least common is partial exclusion of some subtests. ETS and ACT studies revealed that nonstandard versions of tests (i.e., Braille, cassette recorded, large-type editions) and standard versions were equivalent in reliability. When supplemented with grade point averages, nonstandardized versions of tests did not consistently over- or underpredict academic performance for students with disabilities. For more information see: (Thurlow, Ysseldyke, & Silverstein, 1993).

▸ A study was implemented to investigate two testing accommodations involving response condition (i.e., writing in test booklet rather than bubbling in answers on a separate answer sheet) and test administration (i.e., orally reading the test to students rather than having them read it themselves). There were 481 fourth-grade students in this study. Of these, 403 were students without disabilities and 78 were students with disabilities. Findings revealed that students without disabilities outperformed students with disabilities on reading and math subtests. Bubbling in answers and writing in the test booklet were equally effective for both groups of students. Orally reading the test to students with reading disabilities resulted in more valid measures of math proficiency. For more information see: (Tindal, Heath, Hollenbeck, Almond, & Harniss, 1998).

▶ A study involving 345 third-grade students with learning disabilities was conducted to evaluate the effects of several test modifications. The modifications were used when students took the Grade 3 State Student Assessment Test (SSAT). Students with learning disabilities performed similarly on regular- and large-print versions of the SSAT. Modifications that enhanced student competence on the test included *(a)* administering fewer subsections (30 to 40 items) of the test per testing session, *(b)* providing at least one example for each different set of items on the test, *(c)* grouping items that measure similar skills in progressive order of difficulty, *(d)* placing answer options in a vertical format with answer bubbles to the right, *(e)* using unjustified formats for reading comprehension passages and placing them in separate boxes set off from the comprehension questions, and (f) using continuation arrows and stop signs to organize the flow of items on the test. For more information see: (Beattie, Grise, & Algozzine, 1983).

Once accommodations are implemented, it is important for teachers to evaluate their effectiveness. Accommodations that do not result in improved student learning or performance are unnecessary and should be discontinued. Teachers can use the following questions to help evaluate the appropriateness of accommodations:

▶ Does the accommodation increase the student's interactions with peers?
▶ Does the accommodation increase the student's involvement with the lesson?
▶ Does the accommodation increase skills over time?
▶ Does the accommodation help relate the curriculum to the student's current or future life?
▶ Does the accommodation reduce the abstraction of the material and increase the student's ability to handle complex material?
▶ Does the accommodation match the educator's teaching style to the student's learning preferences? ("Effective Accommodations," 1997)

Adaptations

Adaptations involve changes to the curricular content, changes to the conceptual difficulty level of the curriculum, or changes to the instructional objectives and methodology (Bradley et al., 1997). Adaptations typically involve more significant changes or modifications to the instructional process than accommodations. Instructional adaptations can be categorized as either *routine* or *specialized*

(Fuchs, Fuchs, Hamlett, Phillips, & Karns, 1995). *Routine adaptations* are the instructional variations that teachers plan for at the beginning of the year because they anticipate the need for ongoing differentiated instruction. An example of routine adaptation is the use of ability-determined reading groups. Students within a given class are grouped according to their reading levels. Each of these smaller reading groups use different reading materials and receive different instruction based on their learning needs. *Specialized adaptations* are instructional variations that extend beyond routine adaptations. Specialized adaptations are created and used when unique difficulties emerge among individual students. For example, if a student demonstrates confusion within a lesson or performs poorly on an assignment, specialized adaptations to enhance the student's understanding may be needed. Reteaching the material in a different way can be very helpful.

Many teachers find it challenging to provide adaptations, especially those that are specialized and based on difficulties that individual students display. Thus, research has been conducted to explore the types of adaptations teachers use and to find ways to help teachers implement needed adaptations (see Validation Box 7.3). Fuchs and Fuchs (1998) report that the combination of ongoing assessment and peer-mediated instructional arrangements helps teachers determine when adaptations are needed and provides a structure for integrating the modifications. Consequently, achievement of lower performing students who typically need adaptations is enhanced.

Adaptations may be appropriate for several students in a class, but not all of them. For example, some students may work on math word problems, while other students solve computation problems using a calculator. In this example, different students have different curricular objectives with different cognitive expectations. Differentiating lesson plans to meet the varied needs of students is a time-consuming and challenging process. The increased diversity found among students in today's classrooms, however, necessitates that adaptations be made. Adaptations should be designed to increase the likelihood that students will experience success rather than failure in their school endeavors.

Many of the teacher-planning processes discussed in Chapter 2 (e.g., Planning Pyramid, ReflActive Planning, Planning around Focal Students) can be used to help teachers plan for needed adaptations and differentiated instruction. Additionally, teachers may use multilevel instruction, curriculum overlapping, and/or tiered assignments to help address student needs.

Multilevel Instruction

Multilevel instruction is an approach to teaching that engages all students in the class in the same curricular areas, but with differing goals and varying levels of difficulty (Giangreco, Baumgart, & Doyle, 1995). For example, in the curricular area of mathematics, a teacher may write math problems on the board. Some students may need counting practice, so their task is to look at the first number in each problem

Adaptations

▶ A study designed to explore the use of routine and specialized adaptations when teaching students with learning disabilities was conducted in general education classrooms. The participants in this study included 110 elementary and middle school general education teachers from 25 schools. Each teacher taught reading or math to at least one student with learning disabilities. Results revealed that teachers make more routine and specialized adaptations in reading than in math. Most of the reading adaptations involved increasing goal ambitiousness, changing students' ability groups, modifying instructional materials, or altering instructional strategies. The few math adaptations that were made involved deleting the objectives or giving students more time to reach objectives, moving students into special education classes, or decreasing expected criterion levels. Adaptations in reading were likely to occur when students displayed academic difficulties, whereas adaptations in math were likely to occur when students displayed behavioral difficulties. For more information see: (Fuchs, Fuchs, & Bishop, 1992).

▶ In a follow-up study, 40 teachers were assigned to 1 of 2 treatments to explore general education teachers' use of adaptations when providing math instruction to students with learning disabilities. The first treatment involved the implementation of routine adaptations (i.e., curriculum-based measurement and peer-mediated instruction). The second treatment involved the implementation of routine and specialized adaptations (i.e., curriculum-based measurement, peer-mediated instruction, prompting, and special support to implement adjustments in response to students' difficulties). Findings revealed that general educators engaged in specialized adaptations when they were prompted and supported to do so. Specifically, they adapted goals and teaching strategies, differentiated skills taught, retaught more lessons, deviated from the teacher's manual more frequently, and relied more on curriculum-based measurement than criterion-referenced tests. It was noted, however, that the teachers selected adaptations that they perceived to be easiest to implement. For more information see: (Fuchs, Fuchs, Hamlett, Phillips, & Karns, 1995).

and count out that many manipulative devices. Other students may need practice with computation, so their task is to copy and solve the problems.

Multilevel instruction is based on the assumption that one lesson is taught to the whole class and that all students engage in the lesson, but in different ways. The teacher plans for all students within the context of this single lesson. To facilitate this type of planning, a four-step process is recommended for developing lessons (Collicott, 1991).

Step 1. Identify underlying concepts to be taught (i.e., the broad ideas that all students in the class need to understand).

Step 2. Identify various methods that can be used to present the identified concepts, for example, integrating visual, auditory, and hands-on activities into the lesson. Additionally, differing levels of questioning can be used (e.g., knowledge recall questions; application/analysis/synthesis questions).

Step 3. Provide a variety of methods for student practice. Different instructional materials and methods of practice can be used to facilitate student learning. The learning objectives and difficulty level of the practice can vary depending on student interests, needs, and abilities.

Step 4. Make decisions about evaluation methods. The methods of evaluation should be based on individual ability levels and should closely match the method used for practice. For example, if a student is asked only knowledge recall questions during practice, it is not appropriate to expect him or her to address application/analysis/synthesis questions on an exam.

Thus, multilevel teaching involves thinking about adaptations in four areas: concepts to be taught, methods for teaching the concepts, methods for student practice, and methods of evaluation.

When using differentiated objectives and instructional practices, care must be taken to avoid alienation of students who receive the adapted assignments (Stainback, Stainback, & Stefanich, 1996). To help ensure that all students are viewed as part of the class, teachers can integrate activities that address differing ability levels while still maintaining a group context. For example, a group of students working on a science experiment can have different roles and tasks based on their abilities, but all of the roles and tasks can contribute to completing the experiment. One student may have to read the step-by-step directions in the experiment, another student may have to complete each step as it is read, and another student may have to describe the findings to the class. An additional tactic for preventing alienation of students who receive instructional adaptations is to involve numerous students in different tasks rather than just one or two (Stainback et al.).

Curriculum Overlapping

Another approach for adapting instruction is to use *curriculum overlapping*. Curriculum overlapping provides opportunities for students to pursue individually appropriate learning outcomes from different curriculum areas within the context of a shared activity. Students may be engaged with the same instructional materials, but the instructional objectives or curricular goals are totally different for some of the students. Thus, curriculum overlapping is particularly helpful when teaching a diverse group of students within the same classroom setting (Ayres, Belle, Greene, O'Connor, & Meyer, 1992; Giangreco, 1993; Giangreco, Baumgart, & Doyle, 1995). For example, when Ms. Smith, an elementary school teacher, is teaching cursive writing, special writing tablets may be placed on the wheelchair tray of a student named Debbie. As students in the class come to get their writing tablets, Debbie's curricular goal is to give eye contact to her peers and provide a verbal greeting such as "Hi" or "How are you?" Debbie's disability prevents her from writing. So, while most students practice cursive writing, she practices one of her curricular goals (i.e., appropriate greeting behavior). Mr. Price, a high school teacher, uses curriculum overlapping when engaging four students in a science board game. The objective for Steve, Ray, and Larry is to learn specific science facts, while the objective for Todd is to learn how to take turns. Curriculum overlapping primarily is used to imbed functional, practical skills into learning activities across the curriculum (Salend, 1998).

Tiered Assignments

Tiered assignments is an adaptation whereby teachers identify concepts that need to be learned and then provide diverse assignments to students in the class. The assignments differ in difficulty level based on student needs. The goal is to ensure that all students are challenged appropriately. The assignments also are designed to match student learning preferences. For example, after the teacher reads a story to the class, some students may be asked to write a report, others may be asked to compose a play, others may be asked to illustrate the story or make a video about the story (Salend, 1998). Diversification based on students' abilities and interests increases engagement in and commitment to academic tasks and ultimately results in increased learning.

Student Opinions about Instructional Accommodations and Adaptations

Schumm & Vaughn (1994) discussed a series of six studies that were conducted over a four-year period of time to assess students' views about teacher practices. Over 3,000 students participated in these studies by completing questionnaires and in some cases participating in structured interviews. Findings revealed that students at all grade levels (i.e., elementary, middle school, and high school) preferred teachers who made appropriate instructional accommodations and adaptations over teachers who did not. The students involved in the research had distinct opinions, however, with regard to the types of accommodations and adaptations that teachers should use. Generally, students believed that some students really *needed* adaptations and accommodations, and that other students benefited from them as well. Additionally, students preferred adaptations and accommodations that did not single them out and make them feel less capable. Students had strong opinions about modifications that involved the pacing of instruction, homework and assignments, textbooks, instructional grouping, and tests. Specifically, Schumm and Vaughn found that students:

▶ Appreciated teachers who changed the pacing of assignments (e.g., slowed down) to ensure that all students understood what was being taught;

▶ Preferred uniform homework and class assignments for all students in the class;

> Preferred a balance between textbook learning and hands-on active learning;
> Liked flexible grouping practices that included opportunities to work with and learn from peers; and
> Preferred that everyone in class received the same tests.

In another study, Nelson, Jayanthi, Epstein, and Bursuck (2000) investigated middle school students' opinions about testing accommodations and adaptations. A total of 158 students completed a questionnaire that involved rating 23 testing modifications. The most preferred modifications were:

> Open-notes tests;
> Open-book tests;
> Practice questions for study;
> Multiple-choice instead of short-answer/essay tests;
> Use of dictionary/calculator;
> Provision of a copy of the test for study; and
> Provision of extra answer space. (p. 45)

The least preferred modifications were:

> Teacher reading questions to students;
> Tests with fewer questions than tests given other students;
> Tests covering less material than tests given other students;
> Tests written in larger print;
> Oral responses instead of writing;
> Use of computer to write answers;
> Individual help with directions during the test; and
> Teaching test-taking skills (p. 45). (*Note:* Researchers indicated that students didn't seem to understand what "test-taking skills" meant and speculated that they were unable to envision test-taking skills and therefore indicated low preference for this accommodation.)

Not surprisingly, students with disabilities and those with low achievement expressed a stronger preference for testing accommodations and adaptations than did students of average or high achievement. Overall, students with and without disabilities generally favored testing accommodations and adaptations.

Both groups of researchers (Schumm & Vaughn, 1994 and Nelson et al., 2000) found that students' preferred unobtrusive accommodations and adaptations. Generally, overt differential treatment from the teacher was preferred less than the provision of assistive materials or equipment (see Validation Box 7.4).

It is important to consider students' opinions regarding potential accommodations and adaptations. Students' views about receiving accommodations or adaptations and their views about other students receiving accommodations and adaptations undoubtedly will affect the efficacy of instructional modifications as well as the overall classroom climate. Knowledge about students' views can help teachers select appropriate modifications and provide insight into how to present these modifications to students. The focus, of course, should be on helping students experience higher levels of success while simultaneously preserving their dignity.

Student Opinions about Adaptations and Accommodations

Student opinions about instructional procedures used in general education classrooms that included students with high-incidence disabilities were obtained in 20 studies. There were a total of 4,659 students in these 20 studies; 760 had high-incidence disabilities. The students ranged from kindergarten through 12th grade. The combined findings revealed that most students, with and without disabilities, believed that adaptations and accommodations could facilitate their learning. Specifically, students with and without disabilities valued teachers who slowed instruction down when needed, explained concepts and assignments clearly, and taught the same material in various ways to ensure that everyone learned. Both groups of students indicated that students with learning disabilities should *(a)* be involved in the same activities, *(b)* read the same books, *(c)* have the same homework, *(d)* be evaluated with the same grading criteria, and *(e)* be a part of the same groups as their peers. Fairness was the rationale given for these beliefs. For more information see: (Klinger & Vaughn, 1999).

Assistive Technology

Advances in technology have really benefited students with disabilities. Specifically, the use of assistive technology provides many students with opportunities to engage in the general education curriculum. In 1988, The Technology-Related Assistance for Individuals with Disabilities Act (Tech Act) (P. L. 100-407) was passed to enhance the availability and quality of assistive technology devices and services to all individuals with disabilities and their families throughout the United States (Behrmann, 1995). In this law, *assistive technology* was defined as "any item, piece of equipment, or product system, whether acquired commercially off the shelf, modified, or customized, that is used to increase, maintain, or improve functional capabilities of an individual with disabilities." *Assistive technology service* was defined as "any service that directly assists an individual with a disability in the selection, acquisition, or use of an assistive technology device" (Technology-Related Assistance for Individuals with Disabilities Act, 1988, 3, 102 Stat. 1046). The Tech Act legislated state grants for developing and implementing statewide programs of technology-related assistance to individuals with disabilities.

In 1991, the Individuals with Disabilities Education Act (IDEA) (P. L. 101-476) also included support for assistive technology. The Tech Act definitions for *assistive technology* and *assistive technology service* were included in the 1991 IDEA and the 1997 reauthorization of IDEA with minor, nonsubstantive word changes (e.g., "a child" instead of "individuals"). According to the U.S. Department of Education (1999), assistive technology service includes:

A. The evaluation of the needs of a child with a disability, including a functional evaluation of the child in the child's customary environment;

B. Purchasing, leasing, or otherwise providing for the acquisition of assistive technology devices by children with disabilities;

C. Selecting, designing, fitting, customizing, adapting, applying, maintaining, repairing, or replacing assistive technology devices;

D. Coordinating and using other therapies, interventions, or services with assistive technology devices, such as those associated with existing education and rehabilitation plans and programs;

E. Training or technical assistance for a child with a disability or, if appropriate, that child's family; and

F. Training or technical assistance for professionals (including individuals providing education or rehabilitation services), employers, or other individuals who provide services to, employ, or are otherwise substantially involved in the major life functions of that child. (34 CFR 300.6 (a–f))

Use of assistive technology is viewed as a viable modification for expanding student access to the general education curriculum. Furthermore, the March 12, 1999, Final Regulations for IDEA state that "on a case-by-case basis, the use of school-purchased assistive technology devices in a child's home or in other settings is required if the child's IEP team determines that the child needs access to those devices in order to receive FAPE [Free Appropriate Public Education]" (United States Department of Education, 1999, 34 CFR 300-308 (b)). Assistive technology devices and services must be considered for all students who qualify for special education services ("Integrating Technology into the Standard Curriculum," 1998).

Types of Assistive Technology

There are many types of assistive technology that range from simple, inexpensive, sometimes home-made tools (low-tech) to complex, expensive, electronic or computer-based systems (high-tech) that are purchased through specialized manufacturers (Behrmann, 1998). Naturally, it makes sense to select low-tech options when they adequately meet students' needs. Assistive devices such as pencil grips, tape recorders, blocks of wood to raise the height of a desk, or picture boards (boards with pictures that students point to in order to communicate with others) are easy for teachers to access and use and may be all that a student needs. There are, however, numerous tools available to meet more complex student needs.

Organizational Tools

Students with learning disabilities and/or poor organizational skills, memory deficits, and/or illegible handwriting may benefit from using personal digital assistants (PDAs) (e.g., Apple's Newton). PDAs are small hand-held organizers that students can easily carry. PDAs include calendars and can be used to keep track of homework assignments, due dates for projects, and testing dates. PDAs allow students to take notes that include illustrations. They also allow students to create to-do lists. Additionally, PDAs include alarms or paging systems that allow students to cue themselves to perform a particular task (e.g., stop reading and check for understanding), access and remember correct sequence of tasks and routines, or organize important information (Mathews, Pracek, & Olson, 2000; Salend, 1998).

Although PDAs are helpful for organizing academic tasks (e.g., keeping track of important course requirements). Tools also are available to help students organize the academic content they are learning. As was mentioned in Chapter 5, software programs such as Inspiration (Inspiration, Inc.) allow students to create visual displays related to academic content. Such displays help students remember important content and help students understand how various concepts are connected.

Academic Tools

Numerous hand-held devices are available to assist students with various academic difficulties. For example, students with spelling disabilities can use hand-held spellers (e.g., Bookman Speaking Merriam Webster Dictionary and Thesaurus from Franklin Learning Resources). With this tool, students type in a word as close as possible to the correct spelling. The device then displays the correct spelling for the word. The student sees the correct spelling and hears the pronunciation of the word displayed. Hearing the word is important to ensure that the intended word has been provided. Spellers also allow students to store lists of words for future spelling practice.

Students with math disabilities frequently find calculators helpful. Calculators are appropriate tools for students who are working on higher-order problem-solving or thinking skills without having mastered computation skills. Thus, the opportunity to participate in higher-level problem-solving instruction is available even though computation skills may be weak. Calculators with speech capabilities (e.g., Speech Plus Calculator by Telesensory Systems) are available to assist students in addition, subtraction, multiplication, division, square roots, and percentages. As a calculator key is pressed, the number name or function is stated. Graphing calculators also are helpful for students with math difficulties, and particularly those who benefit from visual representations when learning abstract algebraic concepts.

A primary benefit of these hand-held academic tools is their portability. Students can carry them from class to class and/or from home to school. Moreover, the devices are easy to access and use.

Orthopedic Tools

Students with physical disabilities sometimes need orthopedic tools. There are three categories of orthopedic devices: mobility, environmental adaptation, and computer access. The most frequently used mobility tool is a wheelchair. Many improvements have been made to wheelchairs over the years. Lightweight, titanium-framed chairs are available that enhance speed and maneuverability. Motorized chairs with lightweight batteries, infrared or radio interfaces to computers, and cellular phones now exist. Additionally, four-wheel-drive chairs are available that allow individuals to handle rough terrain (Behrmann, 1998).

Included among the assistive tools for environmental adaptation are ramps, grab bars, remote controls, and robotic systems. Ramps offer an alternative to stairs for students who cannot use stairs safely. Grab bars mounted on walls assist students who need to hold on to something in order to move within the environment. Remote controls with large buttons allow students to operate televisions, stereos, and VCRs. Similarly, infrared remote control systems allow individuals to operate appliances and computerized controls. Remote control systems and special switches can be used to operate robotic devices. These devices (e.g., robotic arms) allow students to initiate and exert control over their environment while simultaneously advancing cognitive and language development (Cook & Cavalier, 1999). Perhaps the most exciting advancement with regard to accessing the environment is the development of "smart environments." Smart environments are emerging whereby voice commands, movements, and/or computerized systems are "smart" enough to anticipate requests and needs and are used to adapt environments (e.g., turning on lights, cooking, adjusting sound of television) (Behrmann, 1998; Salend, 1998). As this technology advances, increased applications within the school environment are likely to occur.

A variety of devices are available to increase access to computers. Included among these are keyboard adaptations, alternative keyboards, touch screen monitors, tools for inputting information when range of motion is limited, and switches. Potential keyboard adaptations include the following:

▶ Place a piece of Plexiglas with holes over a standard keyboard so that the student can rest his or her hand on the plexiglass and stick one finger or a touch stick through the holes to activate individual keys;

▶ Add stickers to identify keys that should be used;

▶ Cover keys that are not to be used;

▶ Use key guards to change the size and spacing of keys and to lock certain keys;

▶ Use a keyboard alteration program that delays the responsiveness of the keys (i.e., key must be held down longer to activate); and

▶ Rearrange the order of the keys (e.g., alphabetical order). (Behrmann, 1998; Male, 1997; Salend, 1998)

If adaptations to standard keyboards are not sufficient to meet the students' needs, then alternative keyboards may be necessary. Some of the available options include keyboards with only a few keys, small keyboards in which all keys are accessible with one hand, touch-sensitive keyboards, keyboards that are designed to motivate young children, and enlarged keyboards.

In some cases, adapted keyboards and/or alternative keyboards may not meet an individual's needs. Touch-screen monitors may be a more appropriate option. Touch screens allow students to activate the computer by touching the screen rather than pushing keys on the keyboard. Light pens are used in a similar manner; the computer is activated when the student writes on the screen with a special light pen (Salend, 1998).

A variety of tools (e.g., joystick, mouthstick, headband, eyegaze system) are available for inputting information when range of motion is limited. A joystick is a stick that is moved in different directions to control the movement of the cursor. A mouthstick is a stick that is placed in the mouth and used to press buttons and activate switches that control various computer functions. A headband is a device worn on the head that allows students to control the computer through head or eye movements. Eyegaze systems allow students to select stimuli on the computer screen using eye gazes. These tools are particularly helpful for students who are unable to use their hands to operate the computer (Salend, 1998).

A variety of specialized switches are available to provide greater access to computers and software programs. Different types of switches are activated through different means (e.g., very light touch; tilted head movement; sipping or puffing on tubing; downward pressure from hand, foot, arm, leg). In addition to providing greater access to computers, switches can be used to activate other electrical or battery-operated devices with single movements (Male, 1997).

Communication Tools

Students with expressive language difficulties sometimes need augmentative communication tools to assist in their ability to interact with others. Sign language, lip reading, or a combination of the two is helpful for some students. Communication boards that use pictures, objects, symbols, and words also are helpful. Communication boards range from very basic, low-technology boards (e.g., simple yes/no option) to very complex, high-technology boards (e.g., many options provided through layering of "pages" for different environments). Students typically begin with basic communication boards and advance to more complex boards as their abilities increase. To meet differing student needs, communication boards can include graphic or spoken features. Moreover, a variety of input methods are possible with different communication boards (e.g., pointing, eye gaze, moving cursor or pointer to highlight selection) (Behrmann, 1998).

Vision and Reading Tools

Students who are blind, who have visual impairments, or who have significant reading difficulties benefit from a variety of vision and reading tools. For example, reading machines can transpose written text into speech. Printed material is placed on the glass top of the machine (similar to a photocopying machine). The machine records and stores the printed text in its memory and then uses a speech synthesizer to transpose the text into speech (Salend, 1998).

Numerous technological adaptations enable students with vision or reading disabilities to access computer-based information. Text-to-speech software translates computer-based text to spoken language, and when combined with other tools such as scanners the software also translates hard-copy text into spoken language. Voice-activated software programs as well as books and dictionaries with digitized speech are very helpful for some students. For students who have only vision difficulties, large computer screens, screen-magnification programs, and large-font

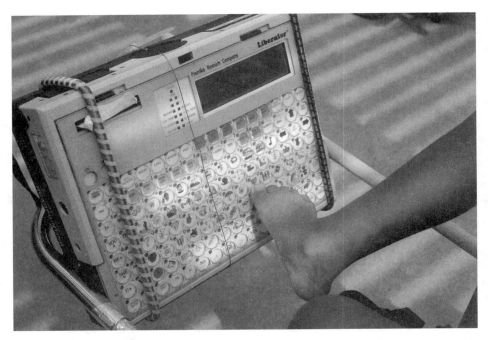

Billy has become quite proficient with his communication board. He uses this assistive technology to communicate with friends, teachers, and family members.

options make reading computer-based text easier (Behrmann, 1998; Male, 1997; Salend, 1998; Vanderheiden, 1996).

Hearing Tools

Technology is having a tremendous effect on the tools that are available for individuals with hearing disabilities. The quality of hearing aids continues to improve. Digital hearing aids use powerful computer chips that filter out background noise, cause sound to be realistic and tailor amplification to meet individual hearing needs (Holusha, as cited in Salend, 1998). FM radio loops can be installed in classrooms. These loops along with special hearing aid receivers allow students to hear microphone speech. Another option is for teachers to wear a microphone transmitter and for students to wear receivers that allow them to hear what the teacher says.

Sensor devices also help students with hearing disabilities. Lights coming on or blinking can alert students to changes in the environment (e.g., someone approaching, fire alarm sounding). Similarly, vibrating pagers can be used to signal specific messages.

Computer technology also is helpful for students with hearing disabilities. Multimedia computer software is available to assist sign-language users. Text and/or graphics appear on the monitor along with a video clip of someone signing supplemental information. For students with partial hearing, digitized speech can occur along with the signing (Behrmann, 1998; Salend, 1998).

Another very exciting technology involves cochlear implants. A cochlear implant is a sensory aid with an electronic microprocessor. It is implanted in the ear and replaces the cochlea. A cochlear implant takes on the function of cochlear hairs and translates auditory vibrations into nerve impulses. This technology has enabled some individuals who have been deaf since birth to hear for the first time (Behrmann, 1998; Smith & Luckasson, 1992; see Validation Box 7.5 on p. 312).

Assistive Technology Assessment

The assessment process used to identify and access assistive technology is very important. The combination of rapidly advancing technological capabilities and an increased emphasis on considering assistive technology for all learners with disabilities makes the assessment process even more critical. A team approach should be used when making decisions about assistive technology because no one individual has all the information needed to make informed decisions. The team should include the student, the student's family, individuals who know the student and understand his or her goals and needs, individuals with knowledge about assistive technology, and individuals who will work with the student using the technology (see Validation Box 7.6 on p. 313).

A culturally sensitive, family-centered approach is recommended for assistive-technology assessments (Parette, 1997). In this approach, five domains are considered during the assessment process: child, technology, service system, family, and culture. The child's needs, capabilities, interests, and goals are considered and appropriate technology is identified. The team considers new opportunities as well as new demands that the technology will place on the student and family. Finally, service systems and related resources for acquiring and supporting the use of the assistive technology are explored. Consideration of these factors occurs within the context of the family and cultural factors. Family involvement is critical when making assistive-technology decisions because the decisions made will affect family functioning. Additionally, abandonment of assistive technology is less likely to occur when family members are a part of the decision-making team and when cultural customs, values, and beliefs are taken into consideration (Hourcade, Parette, & Huer, 1997; Parette & Brotherson, 1996; Parette, Brotherson, Hourcade, & Bradley, 1996) (see Validation Box 7.6 on p. 313).

Several guiding principles are helpful when working with parents to identify appropriate assistive devices for their children. First, professionals should recognize and respond to family needs for information about assistive technology. Providing opportunities for parents to see how the technology works is especially helpful. Second, professionals need to recognize how the assistive technology will change family routines. Family members and the student may need specialized training to use the assistive technology, which may result in additional stress being placed on the

Assistive Technology

▶ In a survey study, the use of assistive technology in special education classrooms in Indiana, Kentucky, and Tennessee was explored. Surveys were sent to 1,266 teachers and 405 were returned (i.e., 32 percent return rate). Results suggested that respondents used assistive technology with approximately 34 percent of their students. The most commonly used assistive device was computer technology for academic purposes. Of the respondents, 69 percent reported they had received some type of training in assistive technology, 20 percent reported receiving no training, and the rest did not answer the question related to training. Only 19 percent thought all of their training needs were being met. Results also indicated that 41 percent of the respondents felt they lacked adequate skills to use assistive technology in the classroom. For more information see: (Derer, Polsgrove, & Rieth, 1996).

▶ In another study, 366 teachers in Pennsylvania who had educational responsibility for one or more students who used assistive technology were surveyed. Most of these students had physical disabilities and used some type of augmentative communication device. The teachers in this survey study rated themselves as highly proficient in using assistive technology and computers. Even though the teachers felt highly proficient, they were substantially less satisfied with their ability to use technology in their teaching due to several barriers. Barriers related to equipment complexity and lack of support emerged as the teachers' greatest concerns. Specifically, teachers reported needing fiscal resources, training, and assistance to set up and program equipment. For more information see: (McGregor & Pachuski, 1996).

▶ A 2-year qualitative study involving 13 students ranging in age from 4 to 20 years was conducted to explore issues related to using assistive technology. The students had a variety of physical disabilities and demonstrated a range of cognitive abilities. The most common high-tech devices used in this study included motorized and nonmotorized wheelchairs, personal computers, and communication devices with voice output. Some of the students also used low-tech positioning, mobility, and communication devices. Several variables emerged as being important for successful use of assistive technology. Included among these were (a) student and family values formed the basis of the educational program, (b) acquisition and use of assistive technology was linked directly to academic, social, and personal goals, (c) a team approach (i.e., student, family, educators, assistive technology specialists) was used to select, obtain, implement, and monitor the assistive technology, (d) frequent and honest communication about student's school program occurred, (e) devices and equipment were replaced, modified, or abandoned as needed, and (f) major and minor glitches were viewed as solvable. For more information see: (Todis, 1996).

VALIDATION BOX

7.6

Assistive Technology Assessment

A survey study was conducted to determine current assessment practices used to prescribe augmentative and/or alternative communication (AAC) devices for young children with disabilities. A survey was sent to each of the 50 states and to 8 territories; of these, 28 questionnaires were returned in usable form. The findings revealed an apparent lack of training for children and their families and a lack of consideration toward family factors that influence the success of AAC devices. Less than half of the respondents indicated that child preferences were considered highly. Exploration of financial resources and availability of support personnel were considered frequently during AAC decision-making processes and most respondents reported that cultural issues were taken into consideration during AAC decision making. For more information see: (Parette & Hourcade, 1997).

family (e.g., time, transportation to training sites, insecurity about learning new things). Some assistive devices may be large, bulky, or heavy and difficult for family members to manage. Third, professionals must be sensitive to family needs for acceptance in community settings. Some families prefer to blend in when out in public places and may feel uncomfortable using assistive technology outside the home. In such cases, the assessment team should consider the least conspicuous options. The assessment process, for determining whether students would benefit from assistive technology and then identifying the appropriate technology, must take into consideration all of these important issues. Careful and comprehensive assessment is needed to increase the likelihood that students' needs will be met.

Cultural Sensitivity and Assistive Technology

It is critically important to demonstrate cultural sensitivity when working with families to identify appropriate assistive-technology devices. School personnel must realize that traditional Euro-American values of future-oriented achievement, independence, and self-sufficiency are not necessarily valued by family members from all cultures. In some cultures (e.g., Asian Pacific Islander, Native American), children are viewed less as individuals in their own right and more as parts of a collectivist family or community. Dependence on family members throughout life is expected and valued and, therefore, somewhat in conflict with the notion of using assistive technology to increase individual independence (Hourcade et al., 1997).

Some families demonstrate strong cultural identifications and others do not. Regardless of how strong or weak a family's cultural association appears to be, it is important to realize that not everyone will be comfortable with the use of assistive technology. Moreover, unique background experiences and cultural influences will affect the nature and extent of family participation in making decisions regarding assistive technology. A variety of specific factors will influence families' attitudes toward assistive technology. Included among these are:

▶ Involvement with the technology;
▶ Goals for the family member who may benefit from assistive technology;
▶ Level of trust of school personnel;
▶ Perceptions about disabilities;
▶ Family priorities;
▶ Communication styles; and
▶ Roles, responsibilities, and restrictions dictated by culture (Hourcade et al., 1997; Parette, 1997).

Thus, when making decisions about students and assistive technology is it important to understand and respect the family attitudes and values. The cultural context in which the student lives must be an integral part of evaluating student needs as well as evaluating appropriate ways to respond to those needs.

Further Consideration of Cultural and Linguistic Diversity

In addition to considering cultural attitudes and values when selecting assistive devices, it is important for teachers to demonstrate cultural competence in their classrooms (Craig, Hull, Haggart & Perez-Selles, 2000). Cultural competence involves the ability to respond to all students in ways that acknowledge and respect their cultural and linguistic diversity. The development of cultural competence involves taking risks and practicing behaviors that may feel unfamiliar and uncomfortable. According to Lynch and Hanson (1998), cultural competence requires "a flexible mind, an open heart and a willingness to accept alternative perspectives" (p. 48).

It is important for teachers to consider students' cultural and linguistic backgrounds when providing classroom instruction. Students benefit from instructional modifications that include culturally relevant explanations and examples that specifically relate the school curriculum to specific life experiences. Thus, knowledge about students' cultures is helpful in terms of making instruction meaningful and facilitating the greatest amount of learning. Curricular materials (e.g., books, media) that integrate multiculturalism into the content also are helpful. Such materials help teachers promote increased understanding about various cultures and instill a sense of belonging among all students.

Researchers have explored effective instructional practices for students from various cultural and linguistic backgrounds. In spite of these efforts, few practices have emerged as being specifically appropriate for students based solely on their cultural or linguistic backgrounds. Lomawaima (1995) sums this up by saying, "The search for the single teaching method or learning style that best serves or typifies a racially, linguistically, ethnically, or economically defined subgroup of U.S. society is like the search for the Holy Grail. It risks becoming a sacred calling that consumes resources in the search for an illusory panacea for complex social and educational ills" (p. 342). Clearly, there is extensive heterogeneity within individual cultural groups, as well as homogeneity across cultural groups, so caution must be exercised when prescribing specific instructional modifications based primarily on ethnicity. There are, however, some suggestions found in the literature for making instruction appropriate for African American, Asian Pacific American, Mexican American, Native American, and Puerto Rican students (see Table 7.5). It is interesting to note the similarities among the recommendations across cultures. It also is interesting to note the large number of suggestions that have already been discussed in this book as validated practices without being linked to particular ethnic groups. This might lead one to conclude that effective teaching practices are effective with a wide range of diverse students and that ineffective teaching practices are detrimental to students regardless of ethnicity. While there is some truth to this, there is more to the picture.

Students' cultural life experiences provide the context in which learning takes place. Thus, teachers whose ethnicity differs from those of students in their classes must learn as much as possible about their students' cultures. Involvement with students, families, and their communities can help facilitate this learning. Knowledge about the culture is then used to modify the curriculum and provide meaningful learning experiences.

It is important to recognize that classroom practices may be in direct conflict with students' cultural experiences and consequently affect students' learning and performance in school. For example, many teachers expect students to complete

---

TABLE 7.5

Suggestions for Teaching Culturally Diverse Students

African American Students (Byrd, 1995; Ewing, 1995; Boykin as cited in Lee & Slaughter-Defoe, 1995).

▶ Use cooperative learning instructional strategies.
▶ Use mnemonic activities (e.g., acronyms; pictures as memory aids).
▶ Use interactive activities (e.g., computer-assisted instruction; peer tutoring; group work; use manipulative devices).
▶ Include movement-for-learning activities (e.g., theatrics/role-playing; rhythmics/beating, clapping, stepping to a pattern with recitation; creative construction/songs, rap).

Asian Pacific American Students (Pang, 1995)

▶ Secure and maintain positive relationships with parents.
▶ Provide bilingual education.
▶ Provide a culturally affirming learning environment.
▶ Provide programs to help students and parents understand and cope with anxiety related to high-achievement expectations and pressure.

(*continued*)

TABLE 7.5

Suggestions for Teaching Culturally Diverse Students (*continued*)

Asian Pacific American Students (Pang, 1995) (*continued*)

▶ Provide positive role models that have struck a balance among the diverse ethnic, religious, peer, family, ⬤ borhood, and school expectations.
▶ Select and use literature with positive Asian role models.
▶ Provide opportunities for students to work collaboratively.

Mexican American Students (Garcia, 1995)

▶ Emphasize functional communication between teacher and students and among students themselves.
▶ Conduct many comprehension checks to ensure that students understand assignments and their roles re⬤ the assignments.
▶ Emphasize student collaboration on small-group projects organized around "learning centers."
▶ Limit worksheet exercises.
▶ Use thematic units to organize basic skill and content instruction.
▶ Provide many opportunities for students to assist one another with learning activities (e.g., cooperative le⬤
▶ Allow students to use either English or Spanish.
▶ Use English and Spanish for language instruction in lower grades; use primarily English for language instr⬤ in upper grades.

Native American Students (Bradley, 1984; Lomawaima, 1995; Sawyer, 1991)

▶ Integrate Native American cultural values into the curriculum.
▶ Avoid discrediting or marginalizing Native Americans when teaching American history.
▶ Deemphasize competition.
▶ Reduce lecturing.
▶ Use visual, motor, tactile, or auditory games and activities.
▶ Allow longer pauses after questioning.
▶ Use peer learning.
▶ Acknowledge the diversity of native cultures and experiences, and work locally to develop relevant curric⬤ and methods.

Puerto Rican Students (Nieto, 1995)

▶ Establish links to the community.
▶ Develop strong parent involvement in schools.
▶ Maintain high expectations for all students.
▶ Provide Latino role models.
▶ Provide bilingual/bicultural programs.
▶ Acknowledge and affirm Latino diversity and shared values.
▶ Use student-experience approach to organize curriculum and validate students as learners.
▶ Promote students' use of native and second language.

tasks one at a time in sequence. This approach works for many students. Students from families with a more flexible, interactive style that involves doing several things at one time, though, may have difficulties performing academic tasks in a traditional linear-sequential manner. Cultural influences also may result in some students frequently commenting on what the teacher or other speaker says rather than listening passively. Additionally, some students may "swarm" around the teacher and enthusiastically interact in an apparently random manner, rather than interacting in a more linear fashion in which each student takes a turn to speak (Craig et al., 2000).

Cultural influences also affect styles of verbal communication between teachers and students. For example, many teachers expect students to ask questions and use critical-thinking skills. They want students to become independent thinkers and problem solvers and to debate issues rather than simply accepting what they're told by others. This expectation may be difficult for students who have been taught that questioning or challenging what the teacher says is disrespectful. Additionally, engaging some students in discourse with school personnel (e.g., teachers, speech therapists, school counselors, principal) is difficult because at home they are expected to interact with siblings, similar-age cousins, or friends their own age rather than the adults in the environment (Craig et al., 2000). Awareness of potential conflicts between classroom practices and students' cultural experiences helps teachers understand student behaviors and make appropriate instructional modifications.

If, in addition to cultural differences, students have specified disabilities, then further modifications to the curriculum may be necessary. Winzer and Mazurek (1998) recommend establishing a collaborative team (general education teacher, bilingual teacher, special education teacher, parents) to work on appropriate modifications. Specifically, they recommend the following steps for developing and implementing a curriculum for nonwhite students (with or without limited English) who also have disabilities.

1. Discuss students' current levels of performance and identify discrepancies between students' skill levels and class requirements in the general education classroom.
2. Explore students' learning preferences and learning needs.
3. Know the language abilities of the students.
4. Become familiar with students' backgrounds, cultures, and languages.
5. Plan and adapt curriculum (i.e., specify goals; establish clear performance expectations; consider content, scope and sequence, instructional pacing, and materials to use).
6. Decide how to infuse multicultural perspectives throughout the curriculum. Consider the background information, vocabulary, and cultural assumptions that must be addressed for students to understand the content.
7. Develop the lessons and materials for the curriculum.
8. Review the instructional activities and materials to ensure that they are age and culturally appropriate.
9. Seek assistance from other resources (e.g., individuals in the community).
10. Develop systems for monitoring student progress that are culturally and linguistically relevant.

Positive outcomes are likely to occur when professionals with different areas of expertise combine their knowledge and experience to develop appropriate instructional modifications for non-Euro-American students with special needs. Parents and students also can contribute a great deal to the planning process. Thus, a team approach is beneficial to everyone involved.

Research involving the examination of *successful* school programs for students from diverse cultural backgrounds reveals similar characteristics among the teachers. Specifically, the teachers in these programs demonstrate high levels of commitment to the educational success of all students. They believe it is their responsibility to find ways to engage students in meaningful learning. They persist in their search for methods that work. They demonstrate strong commitment toward establishing positive school-family communication networks. Moreover, successful teachers view themselves as strong instructional innovators with the autonomy to change the curriculum and instruction in their classrooms even if the changes deviate from district guidelines. They focus on doing what is best for their students. They get involved in professional development activities including small-group support networks. They are strong advocates for their students and reject the notion that their students are intellectually or academically disadvantaged (Garcia, 1995; Haberman, 1995).

Second-Language Instructional Models

Bilingual educators and researchers have debated the issue of how to best teach students whose first language is not English. Consequently, two primary instructional models have emerged for second-language learners: Native Language Emphasis and Sheltered English. Although these models differ with regard to which language should be used under what conditions, a common goal exists: to build competence in English without causing students unnecessary frustration (Gersten & Woodward, 1994).

The Native Language Emphasis Model involves providing instruction on complex academic content in students' native languages until their English skills are relatively strong. Not surprisingly, there are differences of opinion with regard to how long instruction in the students' native languages should continue. Greater consensus exists, however, regarding the rationales for using the Native Language Emphasis Model (Gersten & Woodward, 1994; Grossman, 1995). Supporters of this model believe that:

▶ Students have a right to learn the typical school curriculum without "watering it down" due to limited understanding of English;
▶ Students will learn more if their native language is emphasized;
▶ Students will feel less alienation if they perceive acceptance of their native languages;
▶ Students who transition from their native language to English too soon may experience difficulties with both languages;
▶ Students who master content in their native language find that transferring the knowledge to English is easier than transferring knowledge from English to their native language; and

▶ Students experience stress when new content and a new language are taught simultaneously.

The Sheltered English Model, on the other hand, involves teaching students academic content using English vocabulary that is controlled at their level of comprehension. Teachers omit difficult words and use various techniques to make lessons easier for students to understand. Included among these techniques are: *(a)* slowing speech rate to promote understanding, *(b)* teaching concepts within the context in which they are used, *(c)* using hands-on activities, and *(d)* adapting the curriculum (Echevarria, 1995). English is used for most of the instructional school day. The student's primary language is used for a limited amount of time (e.g., 30 to 90 minutes each day). Teachers use cues, gestures, media, manipulative devices, drama, and visual aids to assist in teaching new vocabulary and concepts. Special emphasis is placed on teaching vocabulary so students can acquire and understand the academic content taught. Teachers also look for opportunities to connect the curriculum to students' cultural and experiential backgrounds (Gersten & Woodward, 1994; Grossman, 1995). The typical instructional sequence used in the Sheltered English approach includes the following steps (Salend, 1998):

1. Preteach the vocabulary needed to understand the lesson content. A variety of strategies are used (e.g., visual cues, cue cards, word banks) to help students understand the definitions of important words.
2. Select and explain important concepts using a context that is rich in visual aids, objects, physical gestures, facial expressions, hands-on activities, and interactions with peers.
3. Relate the concepts to students' personal experiences.
4. Check students' understanding of content and provide feedback.

Longitudinal studies comparing Native Language Emphasis programs to Sheltered English programs have shown little or no difference in student achievement. It appears that the quality of instruction is more closely related to student achievement than the particular model used (Gersten & Woodward, 1994; Moran & Hakuta, 1995; see Validation Box 7.7).

VALIDATION BOX 7.7

Instructional Models for Second-Language Learners

In a 4-year longitudinal study, three second-language instructional programs (i.e., Sheltered English [immersion], Native Language Emphasis [Early-Exit K to fourth grade bilingual], Native Language Emphasis [Late-Exit K to sixth grade bilingual]) were compared. The academic progress of more than 2000 students for whom English was a second language was evaluated. Academic progress from kindergarten to fourth grade revealed no significant differences in math, English language, and English reading skills among students enrolled in the three instructional programs. Findings also suggest that learning a second language takes 6 or more years. For more information see: (Ramirez, 1992).

Second-Language Instructional Methods

A variety of instructional methods have been developed to facilitate language acquisition among second-language students. Included among these are: Cognitive Acquisition Language Learning Approach, Optimal Learning Environment, Instructional Conversations, and Total Physical Response.

Cognitive Acquisition Language Learning (CALLA)

The CALLA approach is intended to help students make the transition from a bilingual program to the general education classroom. The program is designed to assist students in obtaining English language specifically related to science, math, and social studies. CALLA lessons include both language and content objectives and can be adapted for elementary-, middle-, or high-school students with or without disabilities. The lessons used in CALLA include five phases: preparation, presentation, practice, evaluation, and expansion. During the preparation phase, teachers provide advance organizers related to the lesson and students share what they already know about the topic. During the presentation phase, teachers provide new information. Students are encouraged to use a variety of strategies (e.g., self-monitoring, summarizing) to help in understanding the new content. During the practice phase, students engage in application activities related to their new learning. Cooperative learning activities frequently are used to facilitate practice. During the evaluation phase, students reflect on their own learning successes and review the content. During the expansion phase of the lessons, students relate the newly learned information to their own lives and use higher-level thinking skills to anticipate extensions of the information they've learned (O'Malley, 1988; Winzer & Mazurek, 1998).

Optimal Learning Environment (OLE)

The Optimal Learning Environment (OLE) is a curriculum designed to provide language arts instruction to students with learning disabilities whose primary language is Spanish. The curriculum includes language activities that require peers to interact and work together to solve problems. The activities promote English proficiency because students must use specific and precise language to clarify meaning and messages for successful completion of the activities. The guiding principles of the program suggest that when teaching language to non-native English speakers with disabilities it is important to:

1. Take into account the effects of sociocultural backgrounds and specific learning disabilities when teaching oral language, reading, writing, and second-language learning.
2. Consider developmental processes involved in literacy acquisition.
3. Use curriculum in a meaningful context with a clear communicative purpose.
4. Connect the curriculum to students' personal experiences.

5. Integrate children's literature in reading, writing, and language lessons.
6. Involve parents in the instruction of their children.
7. Use collaborative learning activities on a regular basis. (Winzer & Mazurek, 1998; Ruiz, 1989)

Instructional Conversations

Instructional conversations foster learning through verbal dialogues between students and teachers and among students. These dialogues are used to supplement the direct teaching of specific skills and are particularly appropriate for second-language students who are learning English. Instructional conversations are used to help students develop their language abilities and to help them understand the content being taught. Specifically, students are engaged in interactions that promote analysis, reflection, and critical thinking. Instructional conversations activate background knowledge, promote the use of complex language in a supportive environment, provide an authentic context for learning, and increase student achievement. Theme-based instruction is particularly helpful for facilitating instructional conversations. When using instructional conversations with students who also have learning disabilities, accommodations or adaptations may be necessary. For example, the level of questioning used must match the students' conceptual levels. Students with disabilities may also need more prompting and encouragement to feel comfortable expressing their ideas. Finally, behavior-management strategies may need to be used to help students learn when to speak and when to listen (Echevarria & McDonough, 1995).

Total Physical Response

Total Physical Response is an approach for teaching second-language students vocabulary and language using modeling, practice, and movement (Asher, as cited in Salend, 1998). The teacher states a command and then physically demonstrates movements related to the command. Next, the class as a whole group models the appropriate response to the teacher's command. Finally, individual students are called on to respond to commands provided by either the teacher or their peers. For example, the teacher may say, "Take out a sheet of notebook paper." The teacher then demonstrates opening a notebook and taking out a sheet of paper. The teacher repeats the command and the students model taking out a sheet of paper. Finally, individual students are called on to demonstrate the command. The complexity of the commands increases as students' language skills improve.

Infusing Multicultural Content

In addition to thinking about how to teach language and academic content to students from diverse cultural and linguistic backgrounds, teachers must also think about ways to help students learn about and develop positive attitudes toward individuals' whose cultures differ from their own. Perhaps one of the best ways to accomplish this is to infuse multicultural content throughout the various curricular areas rather than simply including units within social studies classes. Multicultural infusion also means that concepts are presented throughout the school year rather than during one condensed time period. It may be helpful first to identify the overarching themes or strands that need to be infused throughout the curriculum. Potential strands (adapted from Winzer & Mazurek, 1998) for infusing multicultural perspectives include:

- Appreciation for common cultural values (e.g., justice, equality, human dignity);
- Exploring one's own culture;
- Exploring other cultures;
- Understanding and respecting similarities and differences among people;
- Exploring diversity in the United States and other countries; and
- Eliminating stereotypes and biases.

Once the strands or themes have been identified, learning activities that relate to these strands are planned and integrated throughout the curricula (e.g., social studies, English, science, music, art). This comprehensive approach to multicultural education is more apt to result in positive outcomes than isolated lessons within the social studies curricula.

Multicultural education is used to help students understand and value the differing cultures of their classmates and to promote new understandings of the world in which they live.

Guidelines for Addressing Cultural and Linguistic Diversity

Given the increased diversity among students in today's schools, teachers undoubtedly must develop skillful ways to address the learning and emotional needs of students from various cultural and linguistic backgrounds. There appear to be two important aspects to consider: how to teach students from diverse backgrounds and how to promote understanding, appreciation, and respect for cultural and linguistic differences among students. Common guidelines for addressing cultural and linguistic diversity have emerged from various educators and researchers (Banks & Banks, 1995; Burnette, 1999; Craig et al., 2000; Gersten & Woodward, 1994; Grossman, 1995; Echevarria & McDonough, 1995; Ford, Obiakor, & Patton, 1995; Winzer & Mazurek, 1998). Included among these guidelines are:

- Learn about students' cultural backgrounds;
- Model appreciation and respect for the similarities and differences among students' cultures;
- Build relationships with students;
- Develop strong partnerships with families;
- Link academic content to students' knowledge and life experiences;
- Use a team approach for planning and implementing meaningful instruction;
- Become familiar with students' learning preferences;
- Create activities that take into account students' learning preferences;
- Provide opportunities for students to communicate and work with their peers;
- Establish high expectations for all students;
- Communicate expectations;
- Use effective teaching behaviors (discussed in Chapter 5);
- Promote an atmosphere of caring, acceptance, and respect; and
- Infuse multicultural education through the curriculum.

In addition to the accommodations, adaptations, assistive technology, and instructional considerations for culturally and linguistically diverse students that have been discussed thus far in this chapter, the use of universally designed materials and activities also can help teachers meet the diverse needs within their classrooms.

Universal Design for Curricula and Instruction

Universal design is defined as "the design of instructional materials and activities that allows the learning goals to be achievable by individuals with wide differences in their abilities to see, hear, speak, move, read, write, understand English, attend, organize, engage, and remember" (Orkwis & McLane, 1998, p. 9). Curricular materials that use universal design are very flexible and provide many built-in accommodations for students with differing educational needs. Thus, the same curriculum can be used with a wide range of different students (e.g., students with visual, hearing, language, or learning difficulties, as well as students with limited English proficiency). The built-in supports greatly reduce the amount of teacher time spent on developing needed add-on modifications. Currently, digital media are the most efficient tool for providing universal design to curricular materials. Technological capabilities (e.g., hypertext, hypermedia) allow students to access a variety of supports in a quick and productive manner.

There are three essential qualities of universally designed curricula (see Fig. 7.1). The first quality is to provide *multiple means of representation* to reduce perceptual and cognitive barriers to the curriculum. For example, to reduce perceptual barriers, content is presented in written text, audio forms, and graphic or pictorial forms. This variety allows students with learning disabilities, low vision, blindness, and deafness to benefit from the same curriculum. To reduce cognitive barriers, summaries of the "Big Ideas" are included to assist students who struggle with the linguistic or conceptual complexity of the content. Similarly, supports related to background knowledge that are needed to understand the content are provided. The second essential quality of universal design is to provide *multiple means of expression* to reduce motor and cognitive barriers to the curriculum. For example, to reduce motor barriers, students who have difficulty with writing and drawing use on-screen scanning keyboards, enlarged keyboards, word prediction, spell checkers, or digital graphics programs or provide oral presentations. Students who have difficulty with speaking create multimedia presentations. To reduce cognitive barriers to expression, step-by-step strategies and scaffolding (i.e., temporary supports that are gradually removed) are provided. The third essential quality of universal design is to provide *multiple means of engagement* to ensure that everyone is motivated to participate. Flexible alternatives are needed related to *(a)* the amount of support and challenge provided, *(b)* novelty and familiarity of activities, and *(c)* developmental and cultural interests. Additionally, students benefit from opportunities to add to the curriculum based on their interests and needs (Orkwis & McLane, 1998).

One example of an early literacy program that uses universal design is Wiggleworks.[1] The program provides opportunities for students to read stories and participate in various reading activities. The text can be enlarged, changed in color, or highlighted. An audio version of the text also is available. Students can use either a mouse or keyboard to navigate through the activities. A built-in scanning feature can be activated with a single switch. The Wiggleworks program offers a variety of options for expression including writing, drawing, and recording. For example, when beginning a composition, students can type, record themselves talking, draw, or place words from a word list into their text. More information about this program is available through the Scholastic Web site: www.scholastic.com /wiggle works/index.htm, or through Scholastic, Inc., telephone: (800) WIGGLE1 (Orkwis & McLane, 1998; "Universal Design," 1999).

Another example of a program that uses universal design is Microsoft's Encarta.[2] In this program, written text is supplemented with video and audio to make many concepts

---

[1]Wiggleworks is a registered trademark of Scholastic Inc.
[2]Encarta is a registered trademark of Microsoft Corporation.

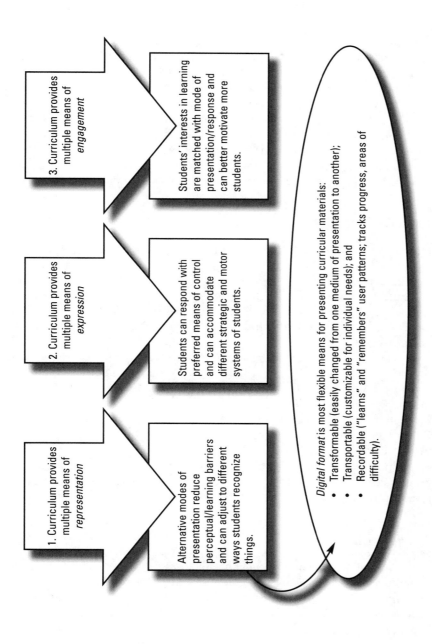

The diagram contains the following elements:

1. Curriculum provides multiple means of *representation*

Alternative modes of presentation reduce perceptual/learning barriers and can adjust to different ways students recognize things.

2. Curriculum provides multiple means of *expression*

Students can respond with preferred means of control and can accommodate different strategic and motor systems of students.

3. Curriculum provides multiple means of *engagement*

Students' interests in learning are matched with mode of presentation/response and can better motivate more students.

Digital format is most flexible means for presenting curricular materials:

• Transformable (easily changed from one medium of presentation to another);
• Transportable (customizable for individual needs); and
• Recordable ("learns" and "remembers" user patterns; tracks progress, areas of difficulty).

Source: Center for Applied Special Technology.
For the neurological foundations on which this diagram is based, and for examples of its application, see www.cast.org.

FIGURE 7.1

The Essential Qualities of Universal Design for Learning. (From "A Curriculum Every Student Can Use: Design Principles for Student Access" by R. Orkwis and K. McLane, *ERIC/OSEP Topical Brief,* Fall 1998, p. 11 by The Council for Exceptional Children. Reprinted with permission.)

clearer and easier to understand. Every video and audio is captioned for students who are deaf. More information about this program is available through Microsoft's Web site: www.microsoft.com/encarta/; or telephone: (800) 426-9400 (Orkwis & McLane, 1998).

The number of students needing modifications to gain access to and benefit from the general curriculum has increased as American classrooms have become more inclusive and more diverse. Thus, teachers are challenged to find effective and efficient ways to meet the varying needs of all their students while simultaneously striving to meet national standards, state standards, and the legal requirements of IDEA and Section 504. Implementing ideas from this chapter takes practice and dedication, but ultimately the educational experiences for many students will be improved.

Practice Activities

▶ Observe in classrooms that include students with diverse learning needs and identify accommodations and adaptations that are used to improve student performance.

▶ Plan and teach a demonstration lesson that involves multilevel instruction.

▶ Plan and teach a demonstration lesson that involves curriculum overlapping.

▶ Develop a lesson plan that includes tiered assignments to meet various students' needs.

▶ Explore resources to learn more about assistive technology.

▶ Identify ways to establish partnerships with parents from cultures that differ from your own.

▶ Develop examples of how teachers can infuse multicultural concepts throughout the school curricula.

▶ Prepare a bibliography of children's books that speak to the experiences of various cultural groups.

▶ Spend time in classrooms with teachers and students whose cultural background differs from your own. Write a summary of what you learned as a result of this experience.

POST ORGANIZER

Students with special needs benefit greatly from appropriate modifications to curricula and/or instruction. Thus, teachers are encouraged to become familiar with accommodations and adaptations that promote academic and social success among their students. Care must be taken, however, to avoid *over-adapting*. Providing accommodations or adaptations that are not really needed deprives students of challenges that ultimately result in additional learning and quality education (Stainback et al., 1996). Thus, it is important for teachers to set high expectations for their students, monitor student progress closely, and provide the necessary support for continuous achievement.

References

Ayres, B., Belle, C., Greene, K., O'Connor, J., & Meyer, L. H. (1992). *Examples of curricular adaptations for students with severe disabilities in the elementary classroom. Study Group Series, No. 3.* (Report No. EC 301 147). Syracuse, NY: Division of Special Education, Syracuse University. (ERIC Document Reproduction Service No. ED 344 418)

Banks, J. A., & Banks, C. A. M. (Eds.). (1995). *Handbook of research on multicultural education.* New York: Macmillan.

Beattie, S., Grise, P., & Algozzine, B. (1983). Effects of test modifications on the minimum competency performance of learning disabled students. *Learning Disability Quarterly, 6,* 75–77.

Behrmann, M. M. (1995, January). Assistive technology for students with mild disabilities. *ERIC Digest,* E529, EDO-EC-93-12.

Behrmann, M. M. (1998). Assistive technology for young children in special education. In C. Dede (Ed.), *Learning with technology* (pp. 73–93). Alexandria, VA: Association for Supervision and Curriculum Development.

Bradley, C. (1984). Issues in mathematics education for Native Americans and directions for research. *Journal for Research in Mathematics Education, 15*(2), 96–106.

Bradley, D. F., King-Sears, M. E., & Tessier-Switlick, D. M. (1997). *Teaching students in inclusive settings: From theory to practice.* Boston: Allyn and Bacon.

Burnette, J. (1999, November). Critical behaviors and strategies for teaching culturally diverse students. *ERIC Digest,* E 584, EDO-99-12.

Byrd, H. B. (1995). Curricular and pedagogical procedures for African American learners with academic and cognitive disabilities. In B. A. Ford, F. E. Obiakor, & J. M. Patton (Eds.), *Effective education of African American exceptional learners: New perspectives* (pp. 123–150). Austin, TX: PRO-ED.

Collicott, J. (1991). Implementing multi-level teaching: Strategies for classroom teachers. In G. L. Porter & D. Richler (Eds.), *Changing Canadian schools: Perspectives on disability and inclusion* (pp. 191–218). Toronto: Roeher Institute.

Conderman, G., & Katsiyannis, A. (1995). Section 504 accommodation plans. *Intervention in School and Clinic, 31,* 42–45.

Cook, A. M., & Cavalier, A. R. (1999). Young children using assistive robotics for discovery and control. *Teaching Exceptional Children, 31*(5), 72–78.

Council of Administrators in Special Education. (1991). *Student access: Section 504 of the Rehabilitation Act of 1973.* Reston, VA: Author.

Craig, S., Hull, K., Haggart, A. G., Perez-Selles, M. (2000). Promoting cultural competence through teacher assistance teams. *Teaching Exceptional Children, 32* (3), 6–12.

Derer, K., Polsgrove, L., & Rieth, H. (1996). A survey of assistive technology applications in schools and recommendations for practice. *Journal of Special Education Technology, XIII* (2), 62–80.

Ebeling, D. G., Deschenes, C., & Sprague, J. (1994). *Adapting curriculum and instruction in inclusive classrooms: Staff development kit.* Bloomington, IN: The Center for School and Community Integration Institute for the Study of Development Disabilities, Indiana University.

Echevarria, J. (1995). Sheltered instruction for students with learning disabilities who have limited English proficiency. *Intervention in School and Clinic, 30,* 302–305.

Echevarria, J., & McDonough, R. (1995). An alternative reading approach: Instructional conversations in a bilingual special education setting. *Learning Disabilities Research & Practice, 10,* 108–119.

Effective accommodations for students with exceptionalities. (1997, September). *CEC Today, 4*(3), 1, 9, 15.

Ewing, N. J. (1995). Restructured teacher education for inclusiveness: A dream deferred for African American children. In B. A. Ford, F. E. Obiakor, & J. M. Patton (Eds.), *Effective education of African American exceptional learners: New perspectives* (pp. 189–207). Austin, TX: PRO-ED.

Ford, B. A., Obiakor, F. E., & Patton, J. M. (Eds.) (1995). *Effective education of African American exceptional learners: New perspectives.* Austin, TX: PRO-ED.

Fuchs, L. S., & Fuchs, D. (1998). General educators' instructional adaptation for students with learning disabilities. *Learning Disability Quarterly, 21,* 23–33.

Fuchs, L. S., Fuchs, D., & Bishop, N. (1992). Instructional adaptation for students at risk. *Journal of Educational Research, 86,* 70–84.

Fuchs, L. S., Fuchs, D., Hamlet, C. L., Phillips, N. B., & Karns, K. (1995). General educators' specialized adaptation for students with learning disabilities. *Exceptional Children, 61,* 440–459.

Gajria, M., Salend, S. J., & Hemrick, M. A. (1994). Teacher accountability of testing modifications for mainstreamed students. *Learning Disabilities Research & Practice, 9,* 236–243.

Garcia, E. E. (1995). Educating Mexican American students: Past treatment and recent developments in theory, research, policy, and practice. In J. A. Banks & C. A. M. Banks (Eds.), *Handbook of research on multicultural education* (pp. 372–387). New York: Macmillan.

Gersten, R., & Woodward, J. (1994). The language-minority student and special education: Issues, trends, and paradoxes. *Exceptional Children, 60,* 310–322.

Giangreco, M. F. (1993). Using creative problem-solving methods to include students with severe disabilities in general education classroom activities. *Journal of Educational and Psychological Consultation, 4,* 113–135.

Giangreco, M. F., Baumgart, M. J., & Doyle, M. B. (1995). How inclusion can facilitate teaching and learning. *Intervention in School and Clinic, 30,* 273–278.

Grossman, H. (1995). *Special education in a diverse society.* Boston: Allyn and Bacon.

Haberman, M. (1995). *Star teachers of children in poverty.* West Lafayette, IN: Kappa Delta Pi.

Hammeken, P. A. (1995). *Inclusion: 450 strategies for success.* Minnetonka, MN: Peytral Publications.

Henderson, K. (1995). Overview of ADA, IDEA, and Section 504. *ERIC Digest,* EDO-EC-94-8.

Hourcade, J. J., Parette, H. P., & Huer, M. B. (1997). Family and cultural alert! Considerations in assistive technology assessment. *Teaching Exceptional Children, 30*(1), 40–44.

Howell, K. W., Fox, S. L., & Morehead, M. K. (1993). *Curriculum-based evaluation: Teaching and decision-making* (2nd ed.). Pacific Grove, CA: Brooks/Cole.

Hudson, P., Lignugaris-Kraft, B., Miller, T. (1993). Using content enhancements to improve the performance of adolescents with learning disabilities in content classes. *Learning Disabilities Research & Practice, 8,* 106–126.

Hughes, C. A. (1996). Memory and test-taking strategies. In D. D. Deshler, E. S. Ellis, & B. K. Lenz (Eds.), *Teaching adolescents with learning disabilities* (2nd ed.) (pp. 209–266). Denver: Love.

Integrating technology into the standard curriculum. (1998, Fall). *Research Connections in Special Education, 3,* 1–6.

Jayanthi, M., Epstein, M. H., Polloway, E. A., & Bursuck, W. D. (1996). A national survey of general education teachers' perceptions of testing adaptations. *The Journal of Special Education, 30,* 99–115.

Klinger, J. K., & Vaughn, S. (1999). Students' perceptions of instruction in inclusion classrooms: Implications for students with learning disabilities. *Exceptional Children, 66,* 23–37.

Lee, C. D., & Slaughter-Defoe, D. T. (1995). Historical and sociocultural influences on African American education. In J. A. Banks & C. A. M. Banks (Eds.), *Handbook of research on multicultural education.* (pp. 348–371). New York: Macmillan.

Lomawaima, K. T. (1995). Educating Native Americans. In J. A. Banks & C. A. M. Banks (Eds.), *Handbook of research on multicultural education* (pp. 331–347). New York: Macmillan.

Lynch, E., & Hanson, M. (1998). *Developing cross-cultural competency: A guide for working with young children and their families.* Baltimore: Paul H. Brookes.

Male, M. (1997). *Technology for inclusion: Meeting the special needs of all students* (3rd ed.). Boston: Allyn & Bacon.

Mathews, D. M., Pracek, E., & Olson, J. (2000). Technology for teaching and learning. In J. L. Olson & J. M. Platt, *Teaching children and adolescents with special needs* (3rd ed.) (pp. 322–346). Upper Saddle River, NJ: Merrill, an imprint of Prentice-Hall.

McGregor, G., & Pachuski, P. (1996). Assistive technology in schools: Are teachers ready, able, and supported? *Journal of Special Education Technology, XIII*(1), 4–15.

Mercer, C. D., Jordan, L., & Miller, S. P. (1996). Constructivistic math instruction for diverse learners. *Learning Disabilities Research & Practice, 11*, 147–156.

Mercer, C. D., Lane, H. B., Jordan, L., Allsopp, D. H., Eisele, M. R. (1996). Empowering teachers and students with instructional choices in inclusive settings. *Remedial and Special Education, 17*(4), 226–236.

Moran, C. E., & Hakuta, K. (1995). Bilingual education: Broadening research perspectives. In J. A. Banks & C. A. M. Banks (Eds.), *Handbook of research on multicultural education* (pp. 445–462). New York: Macmillan.

Nelson, J. S., Jayanthi, M., Epstein, M. H., & Bursuck, W. D. (2000). Student preferences for adaptations in classroom testing. *Remedial and Special Education, 21*, 41–52.

Nieto, S. (1995). A history of the education of Puerto Rican students in U. S. mainland schools: "Losers," "outsiders," or "leaders"? In J. A. Banks & C. A. M. Banks (Eds.), *Handbook of research on multicultural education* (pp. 388–411). New York: Macmillan.

O'Malley, J. M. (1988). The cognitive academic language learning approach (CALLA). *Journal of Multilingual and Multicultural Development, 9*, 43–58.

Orkwis, R., & McLane, K. (1998, Fall). A curriculum every student can use: Design principles for student access. *ERIC OSEP Topical Brief*, 1–20.

Pang, V. O. (1995). Asian Pacific American students: A diverse and complex population. In J. A. Banks & C. A. M. Banks (Eds.), *Handbook of research on multicultural education* (pp. 412–423). New York: Macmillan.

Parette, H. P. (1997). Assistive technology devices and services. *Education and Training in Mental Retardation and Developmental Disabilities, 32*, 267–280.

Parette, H. P., & Brotherson, M. J. (1996). Family participation in assistive technology assessment for young children with mental retardation and developmental disabilities. *Education and Training in Mental Retardation and Developmental Disabilities, 31*, 29–43.

Parette, H. P., Brotherson, M. J., Hourcade, J. J., & Bradley, R. H. (1996). Family-centered assistive technology assessment. *Intervention in School and Clinic, 32*, 104–112.

Parette, H. P., & Hourcade, J. J. (1997). Family issues and assistive technology needs: A sampling of state practices. *Journal of Special Education Technology, 13*(3), 27–43.

Ramirez, J. D. (1992). Executive summary. *Bilingual Research Journal, 16* (1&2), 1–62.

Ruiz, N. T. (1989). An optimal learning environment for Rosemary. *Exceptional Children, 56*, 130–144.

Sacca, K. C., & Raimondi, S. L. (1997). *7 superb strategies for active engagement.* Paper presented at the Council for Exceptional Children International Conference, Salt Lake City, UT.

Salend, S. J. (1998). *Effective mainstreaming: Creating inclusive classrooms* (3rd ed.). Upper Saddle River, NJ: Merrill, an imprint of Prentice-Hall.

Sawyer, D. (1991). Native learning styles: Shorthand for instructional adaptations? *Canadian Journal of Native Education, 18*(1), 99–104.

Schumm, J. S., & Vaughn, S. (1994). Students' thinking about teachers' practices. In T. E. Scruggs & M. A. Mastropieri (Eds.), *Advances in learning and behavioral disabilities* (Volume 8, pp. 105–119). Greenwich, CT: JAI Press.

Schumm, J. S., & Vaughn, S. (1995). Getting ready for inclusion: Is the stage set? *Learning Disabilities Research & Practice, 10*, 169–179.

Smith, D. D., & Luckasson, R. (1992). *Introduction to special education.* Boston: Allyn & Bacon.

Stainback, W., Stainback, S., & Stefanich, G. (1996). Learning together in inclusive classrooms. *Teaching Exceptional Children, 28*(3), 14–19.

Stanovich, K. E. (1994). Constructivism in reading education. *The Journal of Special Education, 28*, 259–274.

Technology-Related Assistance for Individuals with Disabilities Act of 1988, Pub. L. No. 100–407, 29 U.S.C. 2201 (1988).

Thurlow, M. L., Ysseldyke, J. E., & Silverstein, B. (1993). Testing accommodations for students with disabilities: A review of the literature (Report No. EC 302 220). Minneapolis, MN: National Center on Educational Outcomes. (ERIC Document Reproduction Service No. ED 358 656)

Tindal, G., Heath, B., Hollenbeck, K., Almond, P., & Harniss, M. (1998). Accommodating students with disabilities on large-scale tests: An experimental study. *Exceptional Children, 64,* 439–450.

Todis, B. (1996). Tools for the task? Perspectives on assistive technology in educational settings. *Journal of Special Education Technology, XIII* (2), 49–61.

United States Department of Education (1999). Assistance to states for the education of children with disabilities and the early intervention program for infants and toddlers with disabilities; Final regulations. *Federal Register,* 34 CFR Part II.

Universal design: Ensuring access to the general education curriculum. (1999, fall). *Research Connections in Special Education, 5,* 1–2.

Vanderheiden, G. C. (1996). Computer access and use by people with disabilities. In J. C. Galvin & M. J. Scherer (Eds.), *Evaluating, selecting, and using appropriate assistive technology* (pp. 237–276). Gaithersburg, MD: Aspen.

Winzer, M. A., & Mazurek, K. (1998). *Special education in multicultural contexts.* Upper Saddle River, NJ: Merrill, an imprint of Prentice-Hall.

Wood, J. W. (1998). *Adapting instruction to accommodate students in inclusive settings.* Upper Saddle River, NJ: Merrill, an imprint of Prentice-Hall.

Monitoring
Student Progress

*It is good to have an end to journey towards, but it is
the journey that matters in the end.*

—Ursula Le Guin

Review of Chapters 4 to 7

The previous four chapters addressed issues relating to instructional delivery. Research-based instructional models, effective teaching behaviors, the importance of using various instructional arrangements, and methods for modifying curriculum and instruction were emphasized. The following questions are designed to provide review and promote integration of information from Chapters 4 to 7. While reviewing, it is important to remember that instructional delivery represents the heart and soul of teaching. Student learning is dependent on teachers' abilities to orchestrate positive learning environments and provide instructional experiences in organized and meaningful ways. Before proceeding with Chapter 8, consider the following questions:

1. How are Explicit, Direct, and Strategy Instructional models similar? How are they different?
2. What instructional purposes are each of these models designed to meet?
3. What are the most important things to remember when beginning a lesson, continuing a lesson, and ending a lesson? Why are these things important?
4. What are some options for increasing the likelihood that students will complete and turn in homework assignments?
5. Why should feedback extend beyond identifying correct and error responses on written classwork?
6. What are the potential benefits of using peer-tutoring programs?
7. What are the potential benefits of using cooperative-learning activities?
8. What are the potential benefits of using computer-based instruction?
9. What are the advantages of using a variety of instructional arrangements rather than implementing one arrangement on a consistent basis?
10. How do student characteristics influence decisions about instructional arrangements?
11. How can the instructional needs of students who perform on various academic and social levels be met within the same classroom setting?
12. Is it fair to modify instruction and/or expectations for performance within heterogeneous groups of students? Why or why not?
13. What types of modifications might be needed for students whose cultural and linguistic backgrounds differ from the backgrounds of Anglo American students?
14. How does cultural diversity enrich the classroom environment?
15. Who should pay for assistive technology?

ORGANIZER

The validated practices addressed in the previous chapters of this text are very important because they have contributed to student learning and success. When teachers implement these practices in their own classrooms, judgments must be made regarding the value of the practices within the new context. Thus, it is very important for teachers to monitor student progress and continuously improve their instructional programs. The purpose of this chapter is to review various methodologies for monitoring student progress. Included in this chapter is a discussion of grading practices, curriculum-based measurement, portfolio assessment, and technology-assisted assessments.

Monitoring and reporting student progress is one of the most important responsibilities of teachers. Student learning represents the bottom line when it comes to teaching. Regardless of what teaching methodology is used, if students aren't learning, changes need to be made. It is, therefore, very important for teachers to develop methods for monitoring and reporting student progress. Traditionally, educators have used grading systems to indicate student success or failure within the school curriculum. Grading continues to be common practice, but limitations with traditional grading systems have resulted in the development of alternative grading practices and specific monitoring procedures.

Grading Practices

Assigning grades is an integral part of educational practice and serves several purposes. The primary purpose for assigning grades is to provide feedback to students, parents, teachers, and other community stakeholders (e.g., prospective employers, post–secondary school personnel). High grades reflect appropriate progress and learning, and low grades reflect lack of appropriate performance or learning and signal a need for additional supports. Another purpose for assigning grades is to facilitate administrative functions within the school. For example, grades are used to (a) determine promotion from one grade to the next, (b) transmit information when students transfer from one school to another, (c) communicate accountability to the public, and (d) determine eligibility for extracurricular activities. Another important purpose for assigning grades is to provide guidance with regard to future planning. Grades are used to predict future performance and to screen students for specialized programming (e.g., vocational programs, college preparation programs).

Typically, student grades are determined based on individual performance on tests and quizzes, class assignments, homework, and projects. Letter grades (i.e., A, B, C, D, F) or percentage scores (i.e., 0 percent to 100 percent) are recorded for each individual assignment and then at the end of a designated period of time (i.e., grading period), the scores are averaged and a final grade determined. Determining and assigning grades is relatively straightforward when teaching homogeneous groups of students who all work on the same tasks at the same instructional levels. As the diversity within public school classrooms increases, however, there are simultaneous increases in differentiated instructional activities. This raises important questions with regard to traditional grading practices. Educators and researchers have noted the need for alternative grading systems, particularly for students with disabilities (Polloway et al., 1994; Rojewski, Pollard, & Meers, 1990, 1992; Salend, 1998a; Wood, 1998) (see Validation Box 8.1).

VALIDATION BOX

8.1

Grading Systems

▸ A qualitative study involving 10 secondary-school vocational teachers was conducted to explore grading practices used with students with disabilities who participated in general education vocational classes. Semistructured interviews were used to collect data for this study. The most commonly used grading system among these teachers combined normative and criterion-referenced evaluation procedures. This was believed to be favorable for both general and special education students. Included among the practices that these teachers believed to be successful for grading students with special needs were *(a)* individualization and modification of evaluation based on student abilities; *(b)* flexibility in evaluation methods; *(c)* collaboration between general and special education teachers and support staff; *(d)* use of predetermined objectives, competencies, and standards; *(e)* multiple evaluation methods; and *(f)* always emphasizing the positive aspects of student performance when communicating with students and parents. For more information see: (Rojewski, Pollard, & Meers, 1990).

▸ A total of 19 studies related to grading practices among K to 12 teachers were included in a review of literature. The findings from this review indicated that *(a)* teachers try hard to be fair to students, including informing them up front about their grading practices; *(b)* achievement measures, particularly tests, are the main determinant of student grades, but that effort and ability also are commonly considered; *(c)* elementary teachers use more informal evidence and observation for assigning grades than secondary teachers; *(d)* written achievement measures make up a much larger portion of a student's grade in secondary school than in elementary school; and *(e)* there is individual variation among teachers' grading practices. For more information see: (Brookhart, 1994).

VALIDATION BOX

8.1

▶ A national survey study involving 225 school districts was conducted to explore the grading policies used and to determine whether the policies addressed guidelines for grading students with disabilities. Of these 225 districts, 206 were larger school districts with one superintendent and 19 were smaller districts that shared a superintendent. The survey results revealed that 146 (64.9 percent) of the districts had formal grading policies. Of the 146 school districts that had a formal grading policy, 88 (60.3 percent) also stipulated a grading policy for students with disabilities. The most common policies for students with disabilities involved recording grading modifications on the IEP, making team decisions regarding grading, and noting accommodations on report cards. Letter grades were used most frequently with designated percentage cutoffs. Criterion-referenced and individually referenced systems were cited frequently, as well as the use of multiple grades. For more information see: (Polloway et al., 1994).

▶ In another national survey study, involving 368 school districts, the grading practices of elementary and secondary general education teachers were explored. Results of the survey indicated that letter and number grades were rated more useful for students without disabilities and that pass–fail and checklist grades were rated more useful for students with disabilities. Teachers believed grading modifications (e.g., grading for effort) were appropriate for students with and without disabilities. Only one-fourth of the teachers believed it was fair to limit modifications to students with diagnosed disabilities. Findings also revealed that a majority of elementary-, middle-, and high-school students' grades were determined based on tests/quizzes and in-class work/homework. For more information see: (Bursuck et al., 1996).

Alternative Grading Systems

The development of alternative grading systems is not *always* needed for students with disabilities. In some cases, instructional accommodations allow students to acquire and retain information and subsequently demonstrate new knowledge similarly to peers without disabilities. In other cases, however, it is appropriate to modify grading systems to maintain student motivation, decrease student stress and anxiety, increase the likelihood of continued student progress, provide greater detail regarding student progress, and/or establish congruence between modified instructional programs and reported outcomes. There are a variety of alternative grading systems available to school district personnel. When making decisions about alternative grading systems it is helpful and important to keep the purposes for grading in mind (e.g., feedback and communication, accountability, access to extracurricular activities, future planning). Alternative grading systems may be more appropriate for some students than traditional grading systems and may be designed so that the purposes of grading are still met. Alternative grading systems typically involve changing the criteria used for grading, supplementing traditional grades, or using alternatives to letter and number grades (Munk & Bursuck, 1998). Numerous educators and researchers have provided information related to the alternative grading systems discussed in this section. Included among these are Afflerbach, 1993; Bursuck et al., 1996; Cohen, 1983; Colby, 1999; Mercer and Mercer, 1998; Polloway et al., 1994; Rojewski et al., 1990; Salend, 1998a; Vasa, 1981; Wood, 1998.

Individual Education Program (IEP) Grading

Alternative grading systems may be created that specifically link grades to the goals and objectives stated in the students' IEPs. One method for doing this is to translate the competency levels specified in the IEP into the school's grading scale. If the school's percentage grading scale is 90 to 100 = A, 80 to 89 = B, 70 to 79 = C, then a student who mastered an IEP objective that specified a minimum acceptable performance level of 80 percent accuracy would earn a "B." If the student exceeded the 80 percent criterion and demonstrated 95 percent accuracy, he or she would receive an "A" since 95 on the grading scale is an "A."

Another way to link grades to a student's IEP is to assign grades based on progress toward meeting the specified IEP goals. Since the goals are based on the student's abilities and needs, assigning grades based on accomplishment of the goals makes sense. With this system, grades may be assigned based on the number of goals mastered during a predetermined amount of time. For example, if 10 goals are designated for a student to master during the first 6-week grading period and the student masters 7, representing 70 percent, his grade would be a "C" assuming the school grading scale identifies 70 to 79 percent as "C" work.

One of the challenges related to linking grades to IEP objectives is ensuring that the objectives are challenging but obtainable. Establishing objectives that are too challenging will frustrate students, prevent them from experiencing success, and result in low grades. Perhaps the more likely scenario is establishing objectives that aren't challenging enough in an attempt to ensure good grades. The grades may be high, but the student won't learn as much as he or she should over the course of the year. Thus, care must be taken to establish appropriate objectives. Ongoing assessment of student learning assists with setting appropriate goals and mastery criteria.

Multiple-Source Grading

In multiple-source grading systems, teachers base student grades on several different dimensions. Included among the possible dimensions are tests, homework, projects, behavior, and extra-credit assignments. The primary advantage of using multiple-source grading is that it allows students to take advantage of their strengths. For example, a student who typically performs poorly on tests has an opportunity to offset test scores with homework assignments or class projects. Sometimes attendance is figured into student grades. In fact, in some school districts a predetermined number of absences automatically translates to a failing grade.

Another very common example of multiple-source grading involves considering both achievement and effort when determining student grades. One way to do this is to average achievement grades (i.e., accuracy, quality) and effort grades (i.e., amount of time and energy expended) to determine a final grade. For example, if a student uses independent work time wisely, follows directions, and demonstrates persistence, then an "A" may be assigned for effort. The accuracy grade may be a "C," so the final grade would be a "B." An alternative to averaging the grades is simply to record two separate grades, indicating which is achievement and which is effort. A potential advantage of considering effort in addition to achievement when assigning grades is increased student motivation. Additionally, this helps communicate that "doing your best" is important and that both "process" and "product" are important.

Contract Grading

In contract grading systems, the teacher and student agree on what has to be done to obtain a particular grade. Specifically, a contract is a written agreement that addresses the quantity, quality, and time lines required to earn a specific grade. The student and teacher agree on the content to be learned; the activities, strategies, and resources to be used; specific assignments to be turned in; and how the assignments will be evaluated. The language used to write the contract must be appropriate for the student's level of understanding. A well-written contract clearly articulates what is required to earn a passing grade. This helps prevent misunderstandings with regard to teacher expectations.

Criterion Grading

Another alternative grading system involves establishing mastery-level criteria for a hierarchy of specific skills that students need to learn. A pretest is given to identify the skills to include in the hierarchy. The skills are listed according to level of difficulty from easy to more complex. Instruction is provided on the first skill. After instruction, the student takes a posttest. If the student achieves the predetermined mastery level criteria on the posttest, he or she progresses to the next skill. If mastery is not achieved on the posttest, more instruction and practice occurs until the criterion is met. This process continues until all skills in the hierarchy are mastered. A grade of pass or fail or a letter grade can be assigned based on the individual posttests or based on an overall posttest that assesses all the skills in the hierarchy.

Level Grading

Level-grading systems include information related to the level of difficulty of student work. Students are not penalized or rewarded gradewise for working on lower-level or higher-level material, but a notation is made that indicates the grade level that is different from the grade in which the student is enrolled. In other words, if a student in the sixth grade is working on third-grade math skills and earns an average of 95 percent on all math assignments during the grading period, the student would receive an A with a subscript 3 next to it. This indicates the student is doing A work on third-grade math materials. An alternative to writing an exact grade level is to use a 1, 2, 3 numbering system to indicate levels of difficulty (i.e., 1 = above grade-level material; 2 = grade-level material; 3 = below grade-level material.

With this option, "A1" for a seventh-grade student means the student did A work on material above the seventh-grade level.

Checklist Grading

Report card grades can be supplemented with checklists that provide more specific information related to student performance. For example, checklists related to the use of reading strategies might include statements such as "adjusts rate of reading to reflect the reading task," "summarizes text effectively," or "predicts meaning." Checks are placed by items the student performs correctly on a regular basis. Thus, the unchecked items indicate areas that still need improvement. It also is possible to develop checklists with multiple options for each statement such as "in progress" and "achieved mastery." Additionally, rating scales can be used whereby the teacher indicates the level of development related to each item on the list (e.g., "not yet evident," "beginning," "developing," "independent"). Clearly, checklists can be used to provide beneficial information that extends beyond a single letter or number grade.

Narrative Grading

Another alternative grading option is to abandon percentage and letter grades and instead write narrative reports that communicate student progress. With this approach, teachers describe the student's performance related to skill achievement, attitude, effort, and learning preferences. Descriptive comments have the potential to provide more useful information than letter grades and can be used to assist in establishing or adjusting student educational goals.

Pass–Fail Grading

In pass–fail grading systems, minimum criteria for passing are established. Students who meet or surpass the minimum criteria receive a grade of pass; those who do not meet the preestablished criteria receive a grade of fail. No letter or percentage grades are assigned. In an attempt to motivate students to surpass the minimum criteria, additional levels of pass may be added (e.g., pass with distinction; honors pass; high pass). Potential advantages of pass–fail grading systems include reduced student anxiety, limited pressure to compete, and the establishment of clear expectations for satisfactory performance.

Standards-Based Grading

Many states and school districts have developed subject-area standards in an attempt to meet the national education goals (discussed in Chapter 1). Another alternative approach to grading involves monitoring student progress toward mastery of the standards. A four-step process can be used to develop standard-based grading systems (Colby, 1999).

> *Step 1:* Design student grade sheets that are user-friendly. One option is to list the standards on the left-hand side of the paper. Boxes are included

next to each standard to record coded information related to student progress.

Step 2: Develop a coding system. It's helpful to code the type of assessment used to measure student progress (e.g., performance, assignment, test, direct observation); the levels of student performance (e.g., "has demonstrated proficiency" or "in progress" or actual test scores can be recorded); and the time period in which the assessment took place (e.g., first grading period).

Step 3: Create a grade book. Three-ring notebooks work well. The standard-based grade sheets of all students in the class can be kept in one notebook.

Step 4: Revise and refine the standards-based grading system, as needed.

Student Opinions about the Fairness of Report Card Adaptations

Student opinions regarding the fairness of report card adaptations may influence teachers' decisions about alternative grading systems. Teachers want students to feel as though they are treated fairly. Bursuck, Munk, & Olson (1999) conducted a study involving 275 high-school students who were low, average, above average, and high achieving. Students with and without learning disabilities were included in the study. They were asked to determine whether the following grading modifications were "fair" or "not fair" for *some* students:

- Giving higher report card grades for improvement;
- Giving two grades (effort and achievement);
- Changing how much certain things count toward the report card grade (e.g., assignments worth more points than tests);
- Giving a higher grade for working up to potential;
- Reducing the amount of material to be learned without grade penalty;
- Using a different grading scale;
- Giving a passing report card grade no matter what;
- Giving a passing report card grade as long as they try hard; and
- Assigning pass–fail rather than letter grades.

A majority of the students rated all nine of these modifications as unfair. The adaptations rated as unfair by the greatest margin were giving students a passing grade no matter what, grading some students using a different scale, and giving higher grades for showing improvement. The adaptation rated unfair by the smallest margin was giving two grades, one for effort and one for achievement. Low-achieving students were much more accepting of pass–fail grading than the other students. Similarly, students with learning disabilities were much more accepting of giving higher grades for demonstrating improvement, changing how much certain assignments count toward report card grades, and using different grading scales than for students without disabilities.

Grading Responsibility

Ultimately, the responsibility for assigning grades belongs to the teacher. It is, however, the teacher's responsibility to determine whether specific grading policies must be followed in his or her particular teaching environment. District-wide or school-wide grading policies may exist. If policies do exist, it is important to find out whether exceptions to the policies are allowed for students with disabilities or students whose first language is not English.

For students who have more than one teacher, decisions must be made with regard to how grades will be assigned. Results from a national survey revealed that general education teachers assumed complete responsibility for grading about half of the time and that the responsibility was shared between general and special education teachers about 40 percent of the time (Bursuck et al., 1996). When teachers work collaboratively to provide instruction to students, a process needs to be established whereby both teachers provide input into grading so that student progress is communicated with others in an effective and fair manner.

Christiansen and Vogel (1998) developed a four-step decision model that general and special education teachers can use when grading students with disabilities.

Step 1 in this model is to determine district, state, and federal policies and guidelines regarding grading. Knowledge of these policies helps teachers set parameters for their grading systems. Clearly, it is important for teachers to establish grading practices that are in line with policies, regulations, and the law.

Step 2 in this model is for each teacher to identify his or her own theoretical approaches to grading. Individual belief systems influence the type of grading that one prefers. For example, some teachers believe grades should be based on the mastery of designated objectives; other teachers believe grades should be based on how much improvement a student demonstrates; and some teachers believe that grades should be based on comparisons with other students in the class (Rojewski, Pollard, & Meers, 1990). It is helpful for teachers to understand their basic beliefs about grading prior to developing a collaborative grading system.

Step 3 in Christiansen and Vogel's decision model is for each teacher to identify their colleagues' theoretical approaches to grading. This can be accomplished through teachers meeting one-on-one or through a group forum such as a faculty meeting or staff development meeting. Understanding each other's views and beliefs will help in developing a mutually agreeable grading system.

Step 4 in this model is to cooperatively determine the grading practices for individual students. A good time to discuss and agree on grading practices for individual students is during the development of the individualized education plan (IEP). Since the IEP is a tool for establishing goals, objectives, services, and appropriate modifications, it is certainly reasonable to discuss the implications of these modifications on the grading process. When disagreements exist regarding grading practices, redirecting the discussion to the needs of the student rather than the needs of the teachers is helpful. Moreover, it may be helpful to ask someone else to facilitate the decision-making process.

Grading guidelines should be established prior to the time of actual evaluation. Ideally, grading systems and related criteria are agreed on at the beginning of the year and revisited if problems emerge.

Students also can be involved in the grading process. They can conduct self-evaluations related to their individual performance on assignments. Self-evaluation helps students *(a)* realize they have strengths, *(b)* recognize that progress is being made, and *(c)* notice error patterns to avoid in the future. If a decision is made to involve students in the grading process, teachers must accept the students' evaluation even if it differs from their perceptions. In most cases, when a discrepancy exists between the teacher's evaluation and the student's evaluation, it is because the student is underestimating his or her own merits (Wood, 1998).

Recommendations for Grading Practices

Grading student performance has been an integral educational practice for many years. Issues surrounding grading practices have been somewhat controversial. Much debate has taken place regarding the advantages and disadvantages of various grading procedures and in some instances, the debate has progressed to pros and cons for assigning *any* grades. Differing opinions related to grading practices are likely to continue as the diversity among students increases. As teachers move further and further away from "one-size-fits-all" instruction, issues related to grading will need to be reexamined and modified. Empirical validation of appropriate grading practices is limited, but suggestions based on these limited data and "best judgment" have emerged (Brookhart, 1994; Bursuck et al., 1996; Duke, 1989; Ellett, 1993; Gersten, Vaughn, & Brengelman, 1996; Guskey, 1994; Ornstein, 1994; Polloway et al., 1994; Rojewski et al., 1990). Included among these suggestions are:

- Provide multiple methods for students to demonstrate competence;
- Provide corrective feedback and additional opportunities for students to demonstrate their competence (e.g., retake tests or extra credit assignments);
- Explain grading system to students when introducing assignments rather than after the grading has taken place;
- Base grades on a predetermined set of standards;
- Include an academic/cognitive component in grading (avoid assigning a grade solely on behaviors such as percentage of assignments turned in);
- Become familiar with school and school district grading policies;
- Consider alternative grading systems for students with disabilities;
- Establish collaborative grading practices when multiple teachers provide instruction in the same content area to the same students (e.g., teacher A and teacher B both teach math to Johnny); and
- Emphasize the positive aspects of student performance.

Specific Monitoring Procedures

In addition to using grading systems to report student progress, specific monitoring procedures such as curriculum-based measurement and portfolio assessments provide important data and feedback that help both students and teachers. Both of these monitoring procedures involve frequent measures that highlight student progress or lack thereof. Typically, these procedures provide more in-depth information regarding student performance than grading systems. Thus, teachers can make data-based instructional decisions in a timely manner.

Curriculum-Based Measurement

Curriculum-based measurement (CBM) is a system for monitoring student progress using classroom curricular materials and repeated, timed tests. There are five basic steps involved in CBM:

Step 1: Planning the assessment procedures.
Step 2: Identifying performance goals.
Step 3: Measuring student performance in time-limited format.
Step 4: Graphing the data.
Step 5: Analyzing the data to make instructional decisions. Careful attention must be given to each of these steps when implementing a successful CBM program.

Step 1: Planning the Assessment Procedures

Before initiating a CBM program, a variety of decisions must be made. First, teachers must decide which parts of the curriculum are appropriate for CBM. To make these decisions, teachers should think about the content being taught and consider the following questions:

1. What content from the curriculum is most important for students to master?
2. What content from the curriculum will be difficult for students to understand?
3. What skills from the curriculum need to be performed fluently with a high rate of accuracy before moving on to more challenging skills?
4. What long- and short-term goals have been included in the IEPs of students with disabilities?

Reflecting on these questions helps determine what content should be used in CBM.

Second, teachers must determine the duration of the timed tests. Typically, one-minute timings are used. With some skills, however, longer timings are more appropriate. For example, if students are learning to write introductions to stories, five-minute timings result in more meaningful writing samples.

Third, teachers must select or develop the materials that will be used during the timed assessments. In some cases, the teacher uses books that are part of the class curriculum for the timings (e.g., to assess oral reading). In other cases, the teacher creates an assessment or probe sheet that contains items from the curriculum (see Fig. 8.1). Regardless of whether commercial materials or teacher-developed materi-

---

Subtraction Probe

Name: _____   Date: _____

16	10	14	15	13	16	18	17	11	12
−7	−2	−8	−8	−7	−9	−9	−9	−4	−9

13	18	14	12	11	14	15	13	10	11
−9	−9	−7	−9	−5	−6	−6	−4	−6	−2

15	11	14	17	10	15	13	16	11	10
−9	−9	−7	−9	−5	−6	−6	−4	−6	−2

15	12	14	14	11	12	10	17	16	11
−9	−9	−7	−9	−5	−6	−6	−4	−6	−2

15	10	13	11	13	12	10	17	14	10
−8	−9	−5	−8	−6	−3	−5	−8	−7	−8

18	11	14	13	12	12	11	15	17	10
−9	−6	−5	−8	−5	−9	−9	−7	−8	−4

16	14	12	18	10	13	15	17	11	11
−9	−9	−7	−9	−2	−5	−6	−8	−2	−4

Number correct digits: _____
Number incorrect digits: _____

FIGURE 8.1

Sample Probe Sheet.

als are used, a decision must be made with regard to the type of measurement that will be used. There are two types from which to choose: performance and progress. Performance measurement involves assessing student progress on a specific task with the same level of material over time (e.g., oral reading from a 4th-grade text). The task stays the same throughout the CBM and the goal is to improve the students' performance on the same level material. Progress measurement, on the other hand, involves assessing students' progress on sequentially ordered skills or objectives from the curriculum. The goal is to track the students' progress on increasingly more difficult material over time. The teacher identifies a hierarchy of skills or objectives and then assesses student mastery of each one. The assessment task changes each time a student reaches mastery (Gliszczinski & Wesson, 1989). With both types of assessment, the assessment instrument (book or probe sheet) must contain more items than a student can complete in the allotted assessment time (e.g., one minute).

Finally, teachers must decide how frequently to administer the CBM. Clearly, students achieve mastery quicker when CBM is used on a daily basis. Depending on the students' needs and available time, teachers may decide to implement CBM three times a week rather than daily. It should be remembered that although CBM is an assessment process, the timings actually serve as additional practice for the students. Thus, CBM is both an instructional and assessment process.

Step 2: Identifying Performance Goals

Once the CBM planning decisions have been made, teachers must identify measurable performance goals for the students. With most academic tasks, the goal is to have the students perform the task without hesitation and with a high rate of accuracy. For example, in reading, a typical goal is to have students read grade-level material fluently with few errors. Fluent readers understand or comprehend the material better and also retain or remember the material better. Thus, reading fluency is very important. Determining what is meant by *fluent* or just how fast a student should be able to read to be considered fluent is the first step in establishing appropriate performance goals for oral reading.

There are several methods available for making this determination. One method involves taking a percentage of a student's speaking rate. To determine the student's speaking rate, the student repeats a simple sentence as many times as possible in one minute (e.g., "My name is Joey.") If the student says "My name is Joey" 50 times in 1 minute, then he actually spoke 200 words (i.e., 50 × 4 words in the sentence = 200 words). For students in upper elementary grades or higher, 75 percent of their speaking rate is an appropriate goal for reading fluency. For younger students, 50 percent of their speaking rate is an appropriate goal for reading fluency. So, if Joey is in the second grade, his reading performance goal would be 100 words per minute. This same principle is applied to other academic tasks. For example, to establish a performance goal for solving multiplication facts, a percentage of the student's writing rate is used. To determine the student's writing rate, he writes numbers that he has mastered for one minute. If the student writes the numbers 0 to 9 eight times in one minute, then his writing rate is 80 numbers per minute (i.e., 10 numbers $\times$ 8 times in a minute = 80 numbers per minute). Again 75 percent of the writing rate is used for upper elementary and older students and 50 percent is used for younger students (Mercer & Miller, 1991–1994). If Stevie is in the 8th grade and writes 80 numbers per minute, then 60 digits per minute would be a reasonable goal for computing multiplication facts. In both of these examples (i.e., oral reading and solving multiplication facts), reasonable goals were determined based on a percentage of the students' performance on related tasks (i.e., speaking and writing) that were performed easily without hesitations. The same method can be used to establish goals for other academic tasks. Table 8.1 lists sample skills and related tasks that can be used to establish students' speaking and writing rates (i.e., tool skills). The speaking or writing rates then are used to determine appropriate fluency goals for curriculum-based assessments.

Another method for determining performance goals for a student is to use the adult/student proportional formula (Koorland, Keel, & Ueberhorst, 1990). This formula uses the speaking or writing rates (i.e., tool skills) of both the student for whom the goal is being established and a competent adult. The formula also uses

> **TABLE 8.1**

Sample Skills and Related Tasks for Establishing Fluency Goals for Curriculum-Based Assessments

Sample Skills (to be timed for 1 minute)	Related Tasks to Establish Fluency Goals (to be timed for 1 minute)
Writing numbers 0 to 9	Writing number 1
Writing answers to addition, subtraction, multiplication, or division facts	Writing numbers 0 to 9
Writing time shown on clock faces	Writing numbers 0 to 9
Writing amount of pictured coins	Writing numbers 0 to 9
Writing the alphabet in sequence	Writing the letter "A"
Writing spelling words as they are dictated	Writing the alphabet
Reading from instructional level book	Saying easy sentence
Reading sight words	Saying easy sentence
Saying answers to math facts on flashcards	Saying numbers 0 to 9

the adult's task-performance rate. With these three scores, a performance goal for the student is determined. The formula is:

$$\frac{\text{Student goal (to be determined)}}{\text{Student tool skill rate}} = \frac{\text{Adult task-performance rate}}{\text{Adult tool skill rate}}$$

Examples:

Student says "My name is Joey" 40 times in 1 minute or 160 words per minute (student tool skill rate).
Adult reads 200 words per minute (adult task performance rate).
Adult says "My name is Gail" 88 times in 1 minute or 352 words per minute (adult tool skill rate).

$$\frac{x}{160} = \frac{200}{352}$$

$$x = (160 \times 200) \div 352; x = 32{,}000 \div 352 = 90.9$$

Therefore, the student's reading goal is 91 words per minute.

Another method for determining performance goals is to establish local norms. Average-performing students (as determined by student grades and standardized achievement test scores) complete one-minute timings on a variety of tasks to determine mean performance rates. These mean rates then are used to establish standards or goals for other students. Another approach to establishing local norms is to administer one-minute timings to *all* of the students in a given class or school rather than just the average-performing students. After the scores are obtained (e.g., how many addition facts are computed in one minute), the following procedure is used:

▶ List the individual student scores from highest to lowest.
▶ Determine the median score (i.e., 50th percentile) by finding the score in the middle of the list. If there are 13 scores in the list, the seventh score is the median. If there is an even number of scores in the list, the two scores in the middle are averaged together. For example, if there are 14 scores, the median is determined by averaging the seventh and eighth scores.

Sample 1 (odd-number scores)	Sample 2 (even-number scores)
75	75
72	72
68	68
65	65
50	50
45	45

<u>40 = Median (50th percentile)</u> <u>40</u> 40 + 36 = 76 ÷ 2 = 38
36   <u>36</u> The median or 50th percentile is 38.
35   35
25   25
20   20
15   15
14   14
                                        14

▶ Establish student goals based on their current performance relative to the median score. Students performing below the median need additional instructional support. Students performing at or above the median would benefit from higher goals or enrichment learning activities.

A final method for determining performance goals for CBM is to use goals reported in the educational literature. Although individual students may need modifications of these goals, it is helpful to consider the standards that other educators and researchers have established (see Table 8.2).

TABLE 8.2

Curriculum-Based Measurement Goals Reported in Educational Literature

Skill	Goal for Mastery	Source
Oral Reading (student reads aloud for 1 minute)	50 to 70 wpm for 1st to 2nd graders	Marston, Dement, Allen, and Allen (1992)
	70 to 100 wpm for 3rd to 6th graders	Marston, Dement, Allen, and Allen (1992)
	53 to 94 wpm for 2nd graders	Hasbrouck and Tindal (1992)
	79 to 114 wpm for 3rd graders	Hasbrouck and Tindal (1992)
	99 to 118 wpm for 4th graders	Hasbrouck and Tindal (1992)
	105 to 128 wpm for 5th graders	Hasbrouck and Tindal (1992)
Spelling (teacher dictates words with 10 seconds in between each word)	60 to 80 correct letter sequences in 2 minutes for 1st to 2nd graders	Deno, Mirkin, and Wesson (1984)
	80 to 140 correct letter sequences in 2 minutes for 3rd to 4th graders	Deno, Mirkin, and Wesson (1984)
Written Expression (student writes story starter or topic sentence)	14.7 words in 3 minutes for 1st graders	Deno, Mirkin, and Wesson (1984)
	27.8 words in 3 minutes for 2nd graders	Deno, Mirkin, and Wesson (1984)
	36.6 words in 3 minutes for 3rd graders	Deno, Mirkin, and Wesson (1984)
	40.9 words in 3 minutes for 4th graders	Deno, Mirkin, and Wesson (1984)
	49.1 words in 3 minutes for 5th graders	Deno, Mirkin, and Wesson (1984)
	53.3 words in 3 minutes for 6th graders	Deno, Mirkin, and Wesson (1984)
Basic Math Facts (+, −, ×, ÷) (student writes answers to problems)	45 to 50 digits per minute	Smith and Lovitt (1982)
	30 digits per minute	Mercer and Miller (1991–1994)

Step 3: Measuring Student Performance in Time-Limited Format

Once the assessment procedures are planned and performance goals are established, measurement of student performance begins. Student performance on the identified assessment task is measured in a timed format. Typically, students are given one minute to complete as much as possible of the given task. Timings are administered either to an entire class or to individual students.

If all of the students in a class are learning the same skill and performance of the skill is measured through writing, then group administration is quite easy. Probe sheets are given to each student. The teacher then provides directions for completing the task (e.g., "Today we're going to practice writing the letters of the alphabet using cursive writing. I want you to write the lowercase letters as many times as you can in one minute, but remember that for you to get credit for the letter I must be able to read it. If you forget how to make any of the letters, it's OK to look at the letter strip model that is taped to your desk. Who can tell me what we're going to do? . . . That's correct, you listened to my directions! Now everyone get ready, please begin . . . [after one minute] Please stop."). The teacher then collects the papers to be graded later. Grading involves counting the number of correct letters and the number of incorrect letters that the student wrote.

Group administration also is possible if students in the class are working on different skills, as long as the task requires writing. For example, some students may be working on addition while others are working on subtraction. Each student has a probe sheet with the type of problems that are appropriate for him or her. The teacher provides directions (e.g., "Today I want you to begin with the second row of problems on your sheet [to prevent practicing the same problems with each timing] and answer as many problems as you can until I tell you to stop. Remember, if you skip a problem and leave the answer space blank, I have to count it as an error. So, try to answer each problem as you come to it. Let's see if you can beat your score from yesterday. Who remembers what row we're going to start on today? . . . Good, you remembered. And what happens if you leave a problem blank? . . . That's right, it counts as an error. Everyone get ready, please begin . . . [after one minute] Please stop."). The papers are collected and graded later or answer keys may be provided so students can do their own scoring. Another option for scoring CBM probes is to have the class score their work as a group. The students who had the addition probe sheet can say the problems and answers together in unison responding (e.g., three plus two equals five, four plus four equals eight). Students check their own work as the unison responding occurs. Then the students who had the subtraction probe sheet would score their work using the same unison responding format. This type of scoring gives the students extra practice with the problems, offers immediate feedback, and simultaneously gets the task of scoring accomplished.

When CBM is used to measure oral performance such as reading, individual timings are needed that involve the student and one other individual. These one-to-one timings can be managed in a variety of ways. The teacher and other adults (e.g., paraeducators, parent volunteers) can rotate among the students and listen to each one read for one minute. The adult has a copy of the student's reading passage. The adult provides directions and then begins the timing (e.g., "Today I'd like you to read as many words as you can in one minute. If you come to a word that you don't know, just skip it and continue reading. We'll practice any unknown words later. What is it you're supposed to do today? . . . That's correct. Get ready, please begin . . . [after one minute] Please stop."). As the student reads, the adult follows along with his or her copy of the passage and makes a mark next to any incorrect or unknown words. At the conclusion of the timing, the number of correct words read and the number of incorrect words are counted and recorded. Another option for administering individual timings is to teach students to time one another. Even if students are not entirely accurate with their scoring, the additional reading practice is helpful and reading skills improve.

Step 4: Graphing the Data

It is easier to interpret and monitor CBM data if the students' scores are displayed on a graph rather than simply recorded on a record sheet or in a grade book. The visual display of data helps teachers monitor student progress in a quick and effi- cient manner. Line graphs such as the one in Figure 8.2 on page 350 are particularly conducive to CBM data. In addition to being helpful to teachers, graphing student performance also serves as a motivator to students and helps increase academic achievement (Fuchs & Fuchs, 1986). Graphing student data also is helpful in terms of communicating student progress to parents and other teachers. So, although graphing student performance requires a little extra time, the benefits obtained make the extra time worthwhile. Moreover, students can be taught to do the graph- ing. Getting them involved reinforces awareness of their progress while simultane- ously giving them practice with graphing skills.

CBM graphs typically involve a vertical axis that reports the number, frequency, or rate of student performance and a horizontal axis that reports the days or ses- sions of data collection. Data are plotted by finding the intersection of the value on the vertical axis that represents the student's performance and the day or session on the horizontal axis. A dot is drawn at that intersection point. It is usually helpful to graph both the number of correct student responses and the number of incorrect student responses. These two measures are plotted on the same day or session line since they occur during the same timing. Therefore, two different symbols are needed, one to represent the number of corrects and one to represent the number of incorrects (e.g., dot [•] for corrects and X for incorrects). It is important to use two different symbols rather than assuming that a student will always have more corrects than errors.

It is helpful to indicate student performance goals on the graph (see Fig. 8.2 on p. 350). This serves as a visual reminder for the student and teacher. Much satisfac- tion is felt when the goal is met!

Step 5: Analyzing the Data to Make Instructional Decisions

Student data that are plotted on a graph provide a "learning picture." This picture is analyzed to determine whether the student's performance is improving, staying the

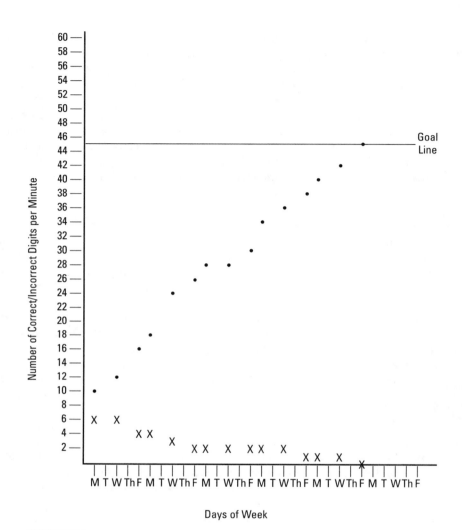

FIGURE 8.2

Curriculum-Based Line Graph.

same, or getting worse. If the trend of the student data reflects an increase in correct responses and a decrease in incorrect responses, then the student's performance is improving. If the trend of the student data is stable (i.e., neither an increase nor decrease in correct or incorrect responses), then the student's performance is staying the same. If the trend of the student's data reflects a decrease in correct responses and/or an increase in incorrect responses, then the student's performance is getting worse (see Fig. 8.3). Typically, visual inspection of a student's data clearly depicts

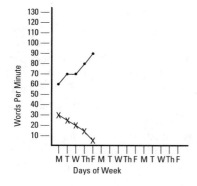

Improving

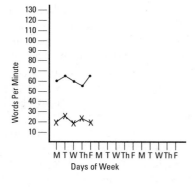

Staying the Same

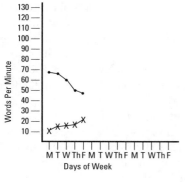

Getting Worse

• = Correct words read
X = Incorrect words read

FIGURE 8.3

Student-Learning Pictures.

one of these three trends. If the student's data are staying the same or getting worse for three or more days in a row, the teacher needs to modify the instructional process in some way to improve the student's performance. In some instances, however, it may be difficult to interpret the trend. Moreover, it may be apparent that student performance is increasing but at a very slow rate, perhaps at an unacceptably slow rate. It is difficult to judge how slow is too slow through simple visual inspection. Thus, in cases like these, with data trends that are difficult to analyze, a celeration value can be calculated to help teachers make instructional decisions.

The celeration value indicates the extent or magnitude of student learning over time (Evans, Evans, & Mercer, 1986). To calculate the celeration value, two weeks of student data are needed. The median score for each week is found. The smaller median is then divided into the larger median. The answer (i.e., the quotient) is the celeration value. If the first week's median score for correct responses is less than the second week's median score for correct responses, then the student's performance is improving and a multiplication sign ($\times$) is put in front of the quotient (i.e., the answer after dividing the median scores). The multiplication sign indicates that student performance is increasing or accelerating. If the second week's median score for correct responses is less than the first week's median score for correct responses, then the student's performance is getting worse and a division sign ($\div$) is put in front of the quotient. The division sign indicates that student performance is decreasing or decelerating. If the quotient of the two median scores is $\times$ 1.50 or greater, then acceptable progress is being made (Salvia & Hughes, 1990). If the quotient is less than $\times$ 1.50, the teacher should consider altering the instructional procedures in some way so that student learning can occur in a more efficient manner. For example, if Ms. Price, a third grade teacher, has been using worksheets to provide practice on multiplication facts and Larry's celeration rate on these facts is $\times$ 1.11, Ms. Price might want to try an alternative practice format such as computer-assisted programs, peer tutoring, or instructional games. Larry may enjoy one of these practice formats more than worksheets and consequently reach mastery with the facts more quickly (see Fig. 8.4).

Graphing and analyzing student data helps teachers make wise and timely decisions that ultimately result in better student performance. Suggestions regarding how often teachers should analyze student data and make decisions about continuing the instruction "as is" or changing the instruction range from three days to two weeks (Salvia & Hughes, 1990). Thus, teachers can use their best judgment depending on the content and objectives, the intervention, and both prior and present student performance (see Validation Box 8.2 on p. 354).

Other Purposes for Curriculum-Based Measurement

In addition to using curriculum-based measurement to monitor student progress, educators and researchers also have used CBM for other purposes. For example, CBM has been used to help reintegrate students with disabilities into general-education classrooms for math instruction using a case-by-case process (Fuchs, Fuchs, & Fernstrom, 1992; Fuchs, Roberts, Fuchs, & Bowers, 1996). Specifically, the process involves using CBM and transenvironmental programming. CBM is used to

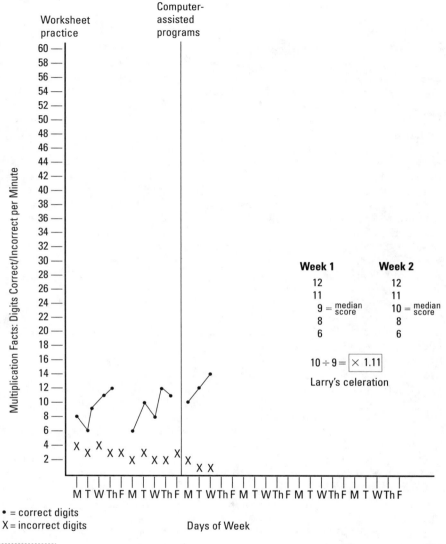

FIGURE 8.4

Using Celeration Values to Make Instructional Decisions.

improve students' math skills and transenvironmental programming is used to facilitate the transition from special to general education settings.

Transenvironmental programming involves four phases: (a) environmental assessment, (b) intervention and preparation, (c) promoting transfer across set-

VALIDATION BOX

8.2

Curriculum-Based Measurement

▶ Curriculum-based measurement (CBM) was compared to conventional special education evaluation (i.e., teacher-made tests, nonsystematic observation, and workbook exercises to assess goal mastery) in an 18-week study involving 39 special education teachers. Each teacher selected three to four students to participate in the study. Findings revealed that student achievement was higher among the teachers who used CBM. Moreover, the CBM teachers' decisions reflected greater realism and responsiveness to student progress. Additionally, students of the CBM teachers were more aware of goals and progress. For more information see: (Fuchs, Deno, & Mirkin, 1984).

▶ In another study, teacher-developed goals and monitoring systems were compared to curriculum-based measurement goals and monitoring systems. Additionally, this study compared the effectiveness of follow-up consultation provided by a university staff member to group consultation that involved three teachers getting together to help one another make instructional decisions. The participants in this study were 55 elementary students with mild or moderate disabilities and 55 special education teachers. CBM and group consultation were more effective than teacher-developed monitoring systems and university staff consultation. For more information see: (Wesson, 1991).

▶ The use of curriculum-based measurement (CBM) by special education teachers was compared to the use of conventional monitoring systems used by special education teachers and general education teachers. Specifically, teachers' willingness to make adaptations in math was explored. A total of 25 general education and 37 special education teachers participated in this study. Results showed that special education teachers who used CBM adapted their students' programs more frequently and relied on more objective databases than special and general education teachers who used conventional monitoring systems. For more information see: (Fuchs, Fuchs, & Bishop, 1992).

▶ The effect of differential implementation of curriculum-based measurement (CBM) on the math computation achievement of students with mild disabilities was investigated in a study involving 29 special education teachers. Each teacher monitored the performance of two students over a 4-month period. Students whose teachers implemented CBM more accurately in terms of frequency of measurement, timing of instructional changes, and ambitiousness of goals made significantly greater gains in math computation than did students whose teachers implemented CBM less accurately. Students whose teachers implemented CBM more accurately also made significantly greater gains in math computation than did students whose teachers did not use CBM at all. For more information see: (Allinder, 1996).

tings, and *(d)* evaluation in the mainstream. During the first phase, *environmental assessment*, special and general education teachers collaborate to determine the specific skills and behaviors required for success in the general education setting. This information is used to plan instruction in a special education setting that will get students ready for the general education class. The information also is used to plan instructional modifications for the general education setting. During the second phase, *intervention and preparation*, the special education teacher teaches the skills identified in phase one. During the third phase, *promoting transfer across settings*, the student returns to the general education setting and both teachers help ensure that the student uses the newly acquired skills. During the fourth phase, *evaluation in the mainstream*, data are collected to determine how well the student has adjusted to the new setting (Fuchs, Fuchs, & Fernstrom, 1992; Fuchs et al., 1996; see Validation Box 8.3).

CBM also has been used to evaluate and compare the academic achievement of students with learning disabilities in various settings. Specifically, the Basic Academic Skills Samples (BASS) (Espin, Deno, Maruyama, & Cohen, 1989), a curriculum-

VALIDATION BOX
8.3

Curriculum-Based Measurement and Transenvironmental Programming

▶ In a study involving 11 special education teachers, 21 general education teachers, and 44 students with disabilities (i.e., 41 with learning disabilities and 3 with behavior disorders), curriculum-based measurement (CBM) and transenvironmental programming (TP) were used to help integrate students with disabilities back into general education classes for math instruction. Structured interviews, self-report measures, report card grades, and behavior rating scales were used to evaluate the effectiveness of the CBM and TP. After 3 months in the general education setting, students who received CBM and TP believed they had learned more, were perceived by their teachers as better students, and worried less about math than peers who were low achievers but not in jeopardy of being referred for special education services. Teacher-assigned grades corroborated these student perceptions. Neither the special nor the general educators perceived differences between the behavior of the students who received CBM and TP and those who did not (i.e., control group students). For more information see: (Fuchs, Fuchs, & Fernstrom, 1992).

▶ In another study, 27 special educators from 21 elementary and middle schools and their 47 students with learning disabilities were assigned to one of four groups. Some students received transenvironmental programming only, some received curriculum-based measurement only, some received both transenvironmental programming and curriculum-based measurement, and the remaining students formed a control group receiving none of these treatments. Teachers who used transenvironmental programming and curriculum-based measurement were more successful at moving students from resource room settings to general education settings, fostering math achievement, and promoting positive attitude changes among the students. Math achievement, however, was slower in the general education classrooms than in the resource rooms. For more information see: (Fuchs, Roberts, Fuchs, & Bowers, 1996).

based measure, has been used to assess reading and mathematics progress among elementary students with mild learning disabilities and students with severe learning disabilities in both resource and general education classrooms. Research suggests that students with mild or severe learning disabilities who were included full-time in general education classes made significantly more progress on the BASS reading measure than students with learning disabilities who were taught in resource rooms. There was no difference between the students with learning disabilities in the two placements on math performance. Additionally, significantly more of the students with mild learning disabilities in general education settings made progress comparable to typical peers than did the students with mild learning disabilities who were educated in resource rooms. The students with severe learning disabilities performed similarly on the CBM in both settings (Waldron and McLeskey, 1998).

In addition to using CBM to help students transition into general education classes and to compare students' performance in different settings, CBM also can be used to form instructional reading groups at the beginning of the year. Once the groups are formed, students with reading difficulties can be assessed through CBM on a weekly basis to determine whether the reading program is working (Hasbrouck, Woldbeck, Ihnot, & Parker, 1999). Research has shown that CBM reading probes are effective predictors of current reading group instruction for normally achieving students and students with disabilities. Thus, some support exists for using CBM rather than more invasive, time-consuming standardized tests. One of the advantages of using CBM rather than individually administered achievement tests is that the special education support personnel who typically administer the lengthy standardized assessments would have more time for consultation with teachers and parents (Schendel & Binder-Reschly, 1989; see Validation Box 8.4).

VALIDATION BOX 8.4

Curriculum-Based Measurement and Reading Group Instruction

In a study involving 1,223 students in grades one through eight in eight school districts, the criterion validity of CBM reading measures was examined in three ways: the relationship between teacher perceptions and student performance; the relationship between CBM scores and reading performance on the Iowa Tests of Basic Skills; and the ability of CBM to differentiate between general education students, Chapter 1 students, and students with mild disabilities. Results showed that teacher perceptions via a rating scale, the Iowa Test of Basic Skills, and CBM predicted instructional reading groups equally well. Specifically, these three nontraditional assessment methods were able to stratify the 1,223 students into Chapter 1, resource room, or regular education reading groups with 76 percent accuracy. For more information see: (Schendel & Binder-Reschly, 1989).

So, although CBM is typically used to monitor student performance using classroom curricula, it also can be used to assist in making placement decisions, to compare and evaluate the effectiveness of alternative placements, and to help make instructional decisions regarding reading groups and the need for additional reading services. The benefits obtained from implementing CBM are particularly helpful when teaching diverse groups of students.

Benefits of Curriculum-Based Measurement

A variety of benefits result when teachers use curriculum-based measurement to assist in their instructional endeavors. Included among these benefits are:

- Increased sensitivity to student progress (Deno, 1985);
- Improved communication with parents, teachers, and students regarding instructional goals and progress toward the goals;
- Quicker recognition regarding the effectiveness of the instructional methods being used;
- Increased use of instructional adaptations (Fuchs, Fuchs, & Bishop, 1992);
- Increased motivation among students; and
- Decreased implementation time and cost as compared to standardized tests (Deno, 1985).

Each of these benefits ultimately has the potential to increase teacher effectiveness and thus increase student achievement.

Portfolio Assessment

Another system for monitoring student progress is portfolio assessment. Portfolio assessment involves teachers and students working collaboratively to collect and analyze a variety of student products over a period of time (e.g., grading period or school year). This purposeful and systematic collection of student work reflects progress toward specific instructional goals (Pierce & O'Malley, 1992). There are five basic steps involved in portfolio assessment: *(a)* identify the portfolio purpose, *(b)* select the portfolio type, *(c)* plan the portfolio assessment procedures, *(d)* collect and organize student products, and *(e)* evaluate student performance. Duffy, Jones, and Thomas (1999); Nolet (1992); Olson and Platt (2000); Salend (1998a); Salend (1998b); Swicegood (1994); and Wesson and King (1996) have summarized guidelines for implementing these steps.

Identify the Portfolio Purpose

Portfolios are used in a variety of settings for different purposes. It is important to identify the purpose for the portfolio prior to initiating the process of portfolio assessment. The purpose for the portfolio influences what items are included, who selects the items, how the items are organized, and how the portfolio is evaluated. Potential purposes for portfolios include the following:

- ▶ Monitor progress of student knowledge and skills over time;
- ▶ Document student performance on tasks routinely performed in natural or authentic contexts (e.g., videotape or observation notes of student purchasing items from school store);
- ▶ Monitor progress toward IEP goals;
- ▶ Monitor student attitudes over time;
- ▶ Showcase students' best work;
- ▶ Document school experiences and accomplishments;
- ▶ Involve students in self-evaluation of affective and cognitive growth;
- ▶ Foster independent thinking;
- ▶ Increase collaboration and communication between teacher and student;
- ▶ Assist with goal setting;
- ▶ Provide a product for students to use when applying for jobs or college admission;
- ▶ Identify curriculum needs; and
- ▶ Assist in communicating with parents and/or other teachers about student performance.

Select the Portfolio Type

Once the purposes of the portfolio are identified, the various types of portfolios are considered. The type that best addresses the identified purposes is selected. Nolet (1992) identified two major types of portfolios: assessment and instructional. *Assessment* portfolios contain systematically collected items to help teachers evaluate their teaching methodology and the effectiveness of their instruction. *Instructional* portfolios, on the other hand, which are used for motivating students, facilitating discussions, and/or promoting reflection, help students improve their performance. It is not uncommon for teachers to use one portfolio to address the purposes of both assessment and instructional portfolios.

Other common types of portfolios are cumulative, goal-based, showcase, activity-based, process, and product (Duffy, Jones, & Thomas, 1999; Reetz, 1995; Swicegood, 1994). Cumulative portfolios include ongoing evidence of student work and are created to monitor changes in student performance within the class curriculum over the course of the school year. For example, writing samples may be collected the first week of school and intermittently throughout the year. These work samples are then used to evaluate student progress with regard to the technical and mechanical aspects of writing, as well as the creative process used in writing. Goal-based portfolios include evidence of student progress on predetermined goals. Specific curricular-associated goals, IEP goals, or goals agreed upon among student, teacher, and parents are used. Work samples that reflect progress toward the identified goals are collected for inclusion in the portfolio throughout a designated period of time (e.g., year, semester). Showcase portfolios include samples of students' best work. These portfolios frequently are used to help students obtain employment, gain admittance to postsecondary training programs, or gain admittance to college. Activity-based portfolios include evidence related to the range of learning experiences or activities in which students participate. These portfolios are used to document the breadth and depth of student learning experiences and to ensure that students are exposed to variety within the curriculum. Process portfolios include documentation related to the specific steps or process a student uses to complete an assignment. For example, if a student is completing a science paper, the portfolio could contain products that relate to the substeps involved in writing the paper (e.g., note cards, bibliography, printouts of information obtained from the Internet, first draft of paper). Product portfolios include examples of student work that relate to specific topics. The teacher provides the student with a table of contents that outlines the required topics or products. The student is responsible for generating and including work samples for everything listed on the table of contents.

Additional types of portfolios can be designed to meet other purposes and needs that arise. It also is possible to combine characteristics from the different types of portfolios to address special circumstances.

Plan the Portfolio Assessment Procedures

After identifying goals and selecting the type of portfolio to use, a variety of decisions must be made regarding the specific portfolio assessment procedures. The following questions help guide the planning of these procedures:

- Who will select and collect items to include in the portfolio (i.e., student, teacher, student and teacher)?
- When will the items be collected?
- How will the portfolio be organized?
- What container will be used (e.g., accordion folder, hanging file crate, notebook)?
- Will families of students be involved in any way?
- Will portfolios be shared with others (e.g., students, parents, administrators, other teachers, IEP team)?
- Where will the portfolios be kept?

In addition to answering these questions, decisions must be made related to portfolio evaluation. This is one of the most challenging and yet most important aspects of portfolio assessment. No set rules exist for evaluating the contents of a portfolio; therefore it is helpful to establish scoring guidelines before implementing this type of assessment. These scoring guidelines are called rubrics. Rubrics have three main features: criteria, levels of quality, and indicators (Olson & Platt, 2000). The *criteria* are the major dimensions or components that will be evaluated (e.g., grammar usage and writing mechanics, organization, creativity, neatness). A total of three to five criteria is recommended (Popham, 1997). The *levels of quality* are the evaluative terms or descriptors used to report the degree to which the student's performance meets the criteria (e.g., excellent, proficient, acceptable, below expectations; exceeds expectations, meets expectations, below expectations; highly acceptable, acceptable, not acceptable). The *indicators* specify the specific requirements for each criteria and level of quality. For example, indicators for *highly accept-*

able (level of quality) in *organization* (criteria) might be *includes table of contents that is easy to follow, all materials are in sequential order, tabbed sections are used to differentiate types of assignments.* Figure 8.5 illustrates a sample portfolio rubric. In addition to assessing the level of quality for each established criteria, it is possible to determine an overall impression of the student's performance. In such cases, it is important to consider whether or not each criterion is equally important. If some criteria are more important than others and points or rating systems are being used, then weighting or giving more value to certain criteria makes sense.

Once the rubric for evaluating student portfolios is established, other planning decisions must be made. Included among these are:

▶ Who will review and evaluate the portfolio?
▶ How often will the portfolio be evaluated?

	Grammar and Writing Mechanics	Creativity	Spelling and Vocabulary	Neatness
Exceeds expectations	▶ Uses three different sentence structures (i.e., simple, compound, complex) ▶ Uses correct grammar, punctuation, and capitalization ▶ Organizes writing well	▶ Uses many sources to acquire information ▶ Creates tables to summarize ▶ Includes illustrations ▶ Includes unique examples for interest and clarification	▶ Spells all words correctly ▶ Uses challenging words and spells them correctly	▶ Typed with fewer than three typos ▶ Clean margins ▶ Title page ▶ Page numbers included
Meets expectations	▶ Uses two different sentence structures ▶ Fewer than five grammatical, punctuation, and capitalization errors	▶ Uses multiple sources to acquire information for paper ▶ Uses variety to promote reader interest	▶ Fewer than five spelling errors in paper ▶ Uses a few challenging vocabulary words	▶ Typed but with three to ten typographical errors ▶ Handwritten and easy to read
Below expectations	▶ Uses one type of sentence structure throughout paper ▶ More than four grammatical, punctuation, and capitalization errors	▶ Uses one source to acquire information ▶ Little evidence of creativity	▶ More than four spelling errors ▶ Uses only very basic vocabulary (primarily one-syllable words)	▶ Handwritten and illegible in parts ▶ Crumpled paper ▶ Stray marks in margins

FIGURE 8.5

Sample Rubric for Portfolio Assessment.

▶ Who will receive feedback regarding student performance?
▶ When will follow-up conferences occur to discuss student performance?

Collect and Organize Student Products

The portfolio purpose and type will influence how the student products are organized. Table of contents and dividers are helpful organizers. Also, within each designated section of the portfolio, it usually makes sense to organize the work in sequential order according to the date it was completed. Portfolios need an organizational framework to prevent them from becoming a hodgepodge of student work without meaningful implications.

Portfolio assessment typically involves two types of data: raw data and summarizing data (Valencia, 1990). The raw data are the actual student work samples. Based on these work samples, teachers generate summarizing data related to the student's performance. The summarizing data may include checklists, rating scales, curriculum-based measurements, and/or anecdotal notes from the teacher. Great variety exists with regard to potential items for student portfolios. Again, the portfolio purpose and type will influence the selection of appropriate products. Table 8.3 lists potential portfolio products.

TABLE 8.3

Potential Portfolio Products

Content Area	Potential Products
Reading	▶ Audio tape of oral reading
	▶ Video tape of oral reading
	▶ Book reports
	▶ Log of books read
	▶ Book critiques
	▶ Representative assignments/work samples
	▶ Curriculum-based measurement graphs
	▶ Informal reading inventories
	▶ Criterion-based reading assessments
	▶ Student self-evaluations
	▶ Reading results from standardized assessments
	▶ Records/progress charts related to mastery of reading strategies
Math	▶ Permanent products related to problem solving
	▶ Evidence of solving real-life problems using math
	▶ Math projects
	▶ Representative assignments/work samples
	▶ Curriculum-based measurement graphs
	▶ Criterion-based math assessments
	▶ Student self-evaluations
	▶ Math results from standardized assessments
	▶ Records/progress charts related to mastery of math strategies

(*continued*)

TABLE 8.3

Potential Portfolio Products (*continued*)

Content Area	Potential Products
Written Expression	▶ Prewriting activities/semantic maps ▶ Stories ▶ Reports ▶ Illustrations ▶ Articles for school paper ▶ Letters ▶ Journal entries ▶ Applications (e.g., job, college, loan) ▶ Résumé ▶ Disks containing word processing assignments ▶ Representative assignments/work samples ▶ Curriculum-based measurement graphs ▶ Criterion-based writing assessments ▶ Student self-evaluations ▶ Written expression results from standardized assessments ▶ Records/progress charts related to mastery of writing strategies
Science	▶ Science projects ▶ Science reports ▶ Lab reports ▶ Scientific experiment ▶ Video tape of experiment ▶ Evidence of investigations related to local problems ▶ Science-related photographs/diagrams ▶ Applications of the scientific method ▶ Representative assignments/work samples ▶ Curriculum-based measurement graphs ▶ Criterion-based science assessments ▶ Student self-evaluations ▶ Science results from standardized assessments
Social Studies	▶ Maps ▶ Reports ▶ Artifacts from various cultures ▶ Projects ▶ Video tapes of community projects ▶ Exhibits related to social studies ▶ Evidence of involvement in political campaigns ▶ Documentation of student government participation ▶ Curriculum-based measurement graphs ▶ Criterion-based social studies assessments ▶ Student self-evaluations ▶ Social studies results from standardized assessments

Regardless of what items are selected for inclusion in the portfolio, caption statements should be created. Caption statements are concise, written statements in which students and/or teachers explain what the item is and why it was selected for inclusion in the portfolio. Table 8.4 lists sample portfolio caption statements. Getting students involved in writing caption statements provides a structure for self-reflection. In order to write captions, students must think about why a particular item is significant enough to include in their portfolio. If students have difficulty writing captions, written or verbal prompts may be provided to assist them. Written prompts that address improvements, pride, special efforts, IEP objectives, content areas, thematic units, projects, difficulties, and strategy use include:

Improvements
    This piece shows my improvement in _____ .
    I used to _____ , but now I _____ .
Pride
    I am proud of this work because _____ .
    In this piece, notice how I _____ .

TABLE 8.4

Sample Portfolio Caption Statements

Portfolio Products	Possible Caption Statements
Science Report	This science report is organized well and includes information from ten sources!
Writing Sample	This writing sample includes complete sentences and accurate punctuation. Spelling is accurate and creative ideas are used.
Math Exam	This exam assessed understanding of fractions, decimals, and percentages. The grade on this exam reflects a thorough understanding of the content.
Social Studies Map	This map was a challenge to complete. As you can see, state names, major rivers, major cities, and state capitals are included. Next time, a legend will be included and a larger drawing will be made to allow for more writing space.
Curriculum-Based Assessment Graph for Reading	Oral reading rates have doubled in two weeks! Errors have reduced to three or fewer! This is great progress.
Letter from Penpal	This letter made my day. I've made a very good friend.

Special Efforts

This piece shows something that is hard for me. As you can see, I have worked hard to _____ .

IEP Objectives

This work shows my progress on _____ .

I have learned to _____ .

I will continue to _____ .

Content Areas

In (content area) I have been working on _____ .

I selected this piece because _____ .

My goal in (content area) is _____ .

Thematic Units

I have been working on a unit relating to the theme of _____ .

As part of this unit, I selected the following pieces: _____ .

These pieces show that I _____ .

Projects

I have been working on a project about _____ .

In this project, I learned _____ .

The project shows I can _____ .

Difficulties

This piece shows the trouble I have with _____ .

Strategy Use

This piece shows that I used the following method: _____ .

The steps I used were: _____ , _____ , and _____ .

(Reetz, 1995; Countryman & Schroeder, as cited in Salend, 1998a, pp. 443–444).

Included among possible verbal prompts are questions such as: "What did you learn from this?" "What could you do next time to make this even better?" "Why did you select this piece?" "How is this piece different from your previous work?" "What was challenging about this?" "How did you go about completing this assignment?" (Salend, 1998a). Questions such as these help students think about their portfolio work and their academic progress. In addition to writing caption statements for portfolio work, it is very important to date each item. This allows students and teachers to monitor progress over time.

Adequate time must be provided for collecting and organizing student products and for reflecting on what the products suggest regarding student performance. Without designating time for these organizational tasks, the portfolio will simply become a collection of products without much meaning.

Evaluate Student Performance

After collecting and organizing items for the portfolio, student performance evaluation occurs. Systematic, ongoing evaluation is critical to the success of portfolio assessment. As was discussed earlier, the use of rubrics is particularly helpful for evaluating portfolios. Rubrics help teachers establish standards for excellence, communicate their expectations, evaluate student work in a fair and consistent manner, and provide better feedback. Moreover, rubrics help students learn to monitor the quality of their own work (Goodrich, 1996-1997; Salend, 1998a). Rubrics are helpful for evaluating individual items within a portfolio and for determining an overall impression of student performance taking into consideration all of the items in the portfolio. In addition to using predetermined rubrics, summative data provided by the teacher and/or student also are helpful in the evaluation process.

General consensus exists with regard to the importance of students self-assessing their portfolio work (Duffy, Jones, & Thomas, 1999; Wesson & King, 1996). Students with disabilities, however, may have problems with this type of metacognitive task. Thus, it is important to spend time teaching them how to evaluate their work. Providing students with questions to think about and answer can be very helpful (Olson & Platt, 2000). Sample questions that may be helpful include:

- Why did I include this work in my portfolio?
- What is good about this item? Is there something I need to improve?
- Is this better than previous work? What's better about it?
- What do I know now that I didn't know last year?
- What do I still need to do?
- What is my favorite part of the portfolio?
- What is unique about my portfolio?
- What do I want my mom and dad to understand about my portfolio?

Another important aspect of portfolio evaluation is having periodic conferences with students to discuss their performance as reflected in the portfolio and to set future goals. During these conferences, students should have an opportunity to express their thoughts about their work and to identify areas that need improvement (Lovitt, 1995).

Some concern has been expressed related to the potential for bias and lack of consistency when evaluating student portfolios (Nolet, 1992; Salvia & Ysseldyke, 1995). The use of clearly written and understood rubrics with clearly articulated criteria helps address this concern. Investigators have shown that consistency is possible among multiple evaluators (Herman & Winters, 1994; see Validation Box 8.5).

VALIDATION BOX 8.5

Portfolio Assessment and Evaluation Consistency

Three elementary school teachers and three raters participated in a study to determine whether portfolios can be scored reliably (i.e., consistently) across evaluators. Each teacher contributed the portfolios of two high-ability, two medium-ability, and two low-ability students for three raters to evaluate. The raters also were teachers and were experienced in using the district's rubric for scoring writing sample assessments. These same rubrics were used to evaluate the portfolios. Percent agreement among the three raters ranged from 0.89 to 1.00, indicating high levels of evaluation consistency. For more information see: (Herman, Gearhart, & Baker, 1993).

Ms. Martin is using Kim's portfolio to point out how much progress has been made in written expression. At the beginning of the year, Kim had difficulty writing single sentences. Now she writes multiple-paragraph stories. These reflection sessions are meaningful for both Ms. Martin and Kim. They realize their hard work has been worthwhile!

Benefits of Portfolio Assessment

A variety of benefits can result when teachers use portfolio assessment to assist in their instructional endeavors. Included among these benefits are:

- Modifying instructional practices based on student needs (Herman & Winters, 1994);
- Gaining insight regarding how students learn and think about their work (Richter, 1997);
- Teaching students to evaluate their own performance;
- Providing more useful information than traditional assessment in terms of developing specific instructional plans (Garcia, Rasmussen, Stobbe, & Garcia, 1990; Rueda & Garcia, 1997);
- Communicating with parents and other teachers (Carpenter, Ray, & Bloom, 1995; Toyne & Bundgaard, 1997);
- Comparing current student performance to previous student performance on content that doesn't lend itself to timed tasks (i.e., curriculum-based measurement) (Nolet, 1992);
- Fostering independent thinking among students (Duffy, Jones, & Thomas, 1999).

Each of these benefits ultimately has the potential to improve the teaching and learning process. Data-based studies examining the effectiveness of portfolio assessment are limited, but interest among educators and researchers seems to be high (Herman & Winters, 1994). It is, therefore, anticipated that additional research is forthcoming (see Validation Box 8.6).

Technology-Assisted Assessment

Clearly, ongoing monitoring of student progress through systems such as curriculum-based measurement and portfolio assessment are very important. These assessment procedures supplement grading systems and provide teachers, students, and parents with more detailed information regarding student progress. This information results in better teaching and consequently better learning. There is, however, a time investment involved in organizing and implementing these assessment systems. Technological applications are being developed to assist with the efficiency of using ongoing assessment systems.

Technology and Curriculum-Based Measurement

Fuchs and Fuchs and their colleagues at Peabody College of Vanderbilt University have developed and refined software programs to facilitate the use of curriculum-based measurement in reading, spelling, and math. Their software automatically generates CBM tests, administers those tests to students at the computer, scores the

VALIDATION BOX 8.6

Portfolio Assessment

- Twelve teachers from two elementary schools participated in a study designed to compare the use of portfolio data to the use of traditional assessment data when planning instruction for students with limited English. Specifically, teachers' abilities to identify students' strengths and weaknesses were investigated. Additionally, the teachers' abilities to design educational interventions were explored. Teachers who received portfolio data were able to design specific instructional strategies for the students as well as teachers who had worked with the students for a year. Teachers who received traditional assessment data, however, requested additional information about the students and were unable to recommend specific instructional strategies. For more information see: (Garcia, Rasmussen, Stobbe, & Garcia, 1990).
- In another study, 21 special education teachers, 21 teachers with bilingual credentials, and 21 school psychologists evaluated traditional and portfolio assessment data from a case study involving a bilingual student. Results indicated that portfolio data led to a greater number of specific recommendations and judgments from the respondents than traditional data. The portfolio data also led to the identification of more student strengths than traditional data. For more information see: (Rueda & Garcia, 1997).

tests, provides feedback to the students, and stores student data for future analysis. The software capabilities include *skills analysis*, *expert systems*, and *group data analysis*.

Skills analysis involves item-by-item analysis across several recent tests to determine which skills the student has mastered and which skills need additional work. Each CBM test includes samples of all the skills in the year's curriculum. Thus, in addition to a total test score indicating overall proficiency in the year's curriculum, the student's performance on each of the individual skills in the curriculum also is measured. Using the computer software for this type of detailed analysis is much faster than analyzing student tests by hand.

Expert systems within the software programs generate recommendations for what and how to teach students whose CBM data indicate inadequate academic progress. Specifically, expert systems identify which skills should be taught, what instructional strategies should be used for acquisition of new skills and retention of mastered skills, and what motivational strategies should be used. Expert systems help teachers break away from their standard instructional routines and use alternative strategies with students who are having difficulty learning.

Group analysis capabilities provide four types of descriptive information about the performance of an entire class. First, a classwide graph is provided that illustrates the overall progress of the group. Students needing additional assistance (i.e., performing below the twenty-fifth percentile of the group) are listed. Second, a monthly report is generated that indicates the skills on which the class has improved, deteriorated, or stayed the same. Third, a classwide skills analysis shows every student's mastery status on skills practiced during the past half month. Fourth, a rank ordering of all the students in the class is provided (i.e., highest to lowest CBM median scores for the past half month).

The software capabilities related to skills analysis, expert systems, and group analysis were designed to improve the instructional decision making that results from the CBM process. Programmatic evaluation of these various components confirms the importance of providing teachers with detailed information with specifically stated recommendations (Fuchs, Fuchs, & Hamlett, 1993) (see Validation Box 8.7 on p. 369 and Validation Box 8.8 on p. 370).

Technology and Portfolio Assessment

The notion of technology-based portfolios is gaining interest among educators (Duckworth & Taylor, 1995; Male, 1997; Niguidula, 1997). Digital portfolio software is used to create multimedia collections of student work. For example, the Electronic Portfolio[1] (published by Scholastic, 2931 East McCarty St., Jefferson City, MO 65102; telephone: [800] 724-6527) allows students and teachers to scan student work samples and/or student art samples and save them on a diskette or laser disk. The program also provides a means for including sound and video clips of student presentations and performances. Using this software, portfolios are organized by subject, theme, or project and student work samples are linked to national stan-

---

[1]Electronic Portfolio is a registered trademark of Scholastic Inc.

VALIDATION BOX

8.7

Skills Analysis Technology and Curriculum-Based Measurement (CBM)

▶ The use of CBM technology capable of skills analysis was explored in a 15-week study involving 30 special education teachers from 16 schools and 91 students with mild and moderate disabilities in grades 1 to 9. CBM with graphed performance and skills analysis was compared to CBM with graphed performance only and a control group with no systematic monitoring system. Results showed that CBM with graphed performance and skills analysis resulted in more specific instructional changes and higher student achievement than both the CBM with graphed performance only and the control group. For more information see: (Fuchs, Fuchs, Hamlett, & Stecker, 1990).

▶ In a similar study, the use of CBM technology capable of graphing performance and skills analysis was compared to CBM with graphed performance only, CBM with graphed performance and ordered lists of student spelling errors, and a control group. Again, the study was 15 weeks and involved 30 special education teachers from 16 schools. Teachers who used CBM with graphed performance and skills analysis effected higher student achievement than the control group and the CBM with graphed performance only. For more information see: (Fuchs, Fuchs, Hamlett, & Allinder, 1991).

dards, districtwide standards, rubrics, and/or individualized lesson plans. The Grady Profile Portfolio Assessment[2] (published by Aurbach & Associates, 9378 Olive Street Road, Suite 102, St. Louis, MO 63132; telephone: [800] 774-7239 or [314] 432-7577 [outside U.S.]; fax: [314] 432-7072; e-mail: www.aurbach.com/) is another software program that helps students and teachers (preK to college) create technology-based portfolios. The Grady Profile Portfolio Assessment allows entry of sound (e.g., oral reading, oral report), video (e.g., student acting in a play), graphics (e.g., student artwork, tables), text (e.g. student-authored story), and computer-generated work (e.g., spreadsheet program). Student demographic and educational data also are entered (e.g., gender, birth date, ethnicity, special services, scholastic history, attendance record). The program provides a place for students to self-assess and reflect on their work. Links to school, district, state, and national standards are available. Teachers and students opt to use the components of these programs that help meet the predetermined purpose of the portfolio.

There are two primary advantages for using technology-based portfolios over traditional portfolio files. First, technology-based portfolios have greater flexibility. Word processing, database, and spreadsheet software (e.g., Microsoft Office 2000[3])

[2]The Grady Portfolio Assessment is a registered trademark of Aurbach & Associates.
[3]Microsoft Office 2000 is a registered trademark of Microsoft Corporation.

Expert System Technology and Curriculum-Based Measurement (CBM)

▶ The effects of expert system technology and CBM on teacher planning and student achievement in math were explored in a 20-week study involving 33 teachers in 15 schools. CBM software with expert system instructional consultation, CBM software without an expert system component, and a control group (i.e., no CBM) were compared. Both CBM groups revised their students' instructional programs more frequently than the control group, but the CBM group with the expert system resulted in the highest student achievement. For more information see: (Fuchs, Fuchs, Hamlett, & Stecker, 1991).

▶ In a similar study, the effects of expert system technology and CBM on teacher planning and student achievement in reading were explored. Again, 33 teachers in 15 schools participated in the study. The students of these teachers had mild to moderate disabilities and ranged from first to ninth grade. CBM software with expert system consultation, CBM software without expert system consultation, and a control group with no CBM were compared. Both CBM groups outperformed the control group on several reading measures assessing fluency and comprehension. The CBM group with the expert system consultation, however, planned more diverse instructional programs and their students outperformed the other two groups on an outcome measure requiring written recall. For more information see: (Fuchs, Fuchs, Hamlett, & Ferguson, 1992).

▶ In another study, involving 40 general educators, the effectiveness of CBM classwide decision-making structures was explored. Each of the 40 teachers had at least one student with a learning disability in math. CBM software with classwide reports and instructional recommendations, CBM software with classwide reports without instructional recommendations, and a control group without CBM were compared. Teachers who received CBM with instructional recommendations designed better instructional programs that resulted in greater math achievement among the students than teachers in the other two groups. For more information see: (Fuchs, Fuchs, Hamlett, Phillips, & Bentz, 1994).

can be used in conjunction with interactive hypermedia and audio and video clips to create a variety of products to include in the digital portfolio. For example, students might collect, organize, and analyze marketing data using spreadsheet software. Based on the analysis of data, students might compose a report using a word processing program. Finally, students may present their reports to the class. The spreadsheet data, report, and videotape of the presentation all can be stored in the students' digital portfolios. A second advantage of using digital portfolios is that they take up less storage space than traditional paper portfolios. Large amounts of

These students are working on a class report that will become a part of their digital portfolios.

information can be stored on laser disks. The information is easy to access. Additionally, it is easy to add new information (Campbell, 1992).

Technical support is helpful when using electronic portfolios for the first time. It also is important to remember the important components of effective portfolio assessment. As with traditional paper portfolios, the purpose for the portfolio is identified, the type of portfolio is selected, assessment procedures are planned, student products are organized and collected, and student performance is evaluated. Additionally, the assessment data included in the portfolios are used to make instructional decisions.

Support for using digital portfolios is available primarily through anecdotal reports from individual schools and/or classrooms (Male, 1997; Niguidula, 1997). Experimental research needs to be conducted to further evaluate and explore the potential uses and benefits of digital portfolios.

Practice Activities

▶ Select one of the alternative grading systems and develop a detailed plan outlining how you would use it.

▶ Administer one-minute timings to a student with disabilities and determine appropriate CBM goals using one of the methods discussed in this chapter.

▶ Develop curriculum-based assessment probes and collect student data for at least two weeks. Display the data in graph format. Use these data to develop appropriate lesson plans for the student.

▶ Identify a student with special learning needs and implement portfolio assessment procedures.

▶ Select one subject area and create related rubrics to assess student portfolio products.

POST ORGANIZER

Monitoring student progress is one of the most important aspects of being a teacher. A variety of grading systems have been used to communicate how well a student is doing in school. There appears to be general agreement that alternative or modified grading systems are sometimes appropriate for students with special learning needs. Moreover, specific monitoring systems such as curriculum-based measurement and portfolio assessment are needed. These systems help teachers make important instructional decisions and communicate student progress in a detailed and meaningful way. Technological tools can help teachers manage ongoing monitoring of student progress.

References

Afflerbach, P. (1993). Report cards and reading. *The Reading Teacher, 46,* 458–465.

Allinder, R. M. (1996). When some is not better than none: Effects of differential implementation of curriculum-based measurement. *Exceptional Children, 62,* 525–535.

Brookhart, S. M. (1994). Teachers' grading: Practice and theory. *Applied Measurement in Education, 7*(4), 279–301.

Bursuck, W. D., Munk, D. D., Olson, M. M. (1999). The fairness of report card grading adaptations. *Remedial and Special Education, 20,* 84–92, 105.

Bursuck, W., Polloway, E. A., Plante, L., Epstein, M. H., Jayanthi, M., & McConeghy, J. (1996). Report card grading and adaptations: A national survey of classroom practices. *Exceptional Children, I62,* 301–318.

Campbell, J. (1992). Laser disk portfolios: Total child assessment. *Educational Leadership, 49*(8), 69–70.

Carpenter, C. D., Ray, M. S., & Bloom, L. A. (1995). Portfolio assessment: Opportunities and challenges. *Intervention in School and Clinic, 31,* 34–41.

Christiansen, J., & Vogel, J. R. (1998). A decision model for grading students with disabilities. *Teaching Exceptional Children, 31*(2), 30–35.

Cohen, S. B. (1983). Assigning report card grades to the mainstreamed child. *Teaching Exceptional Children, 15,* 86–89.

Colby, S. A. (1999). Grading in a standards-based system. *Educational Leadership, 56*(6), 52–55.

Deno, S. (1985). Curriculum-based measurement: The emerging alternative. *Exceptional Children, 52,* 219–232.

Deno, S. L., Mirkin, P., & Wesson, C. (1984). How to write effective data based IEPs. *Teaching Exceptional Children, 16*(2), 99–104.

Duckworth, S., & Taylor, R. (1995). Creating and assessing literacy in at-risk students through hypermedia portfolios. *Reading Improvement, 32*(1), 26–31.

Duffy, M. L., Jones, J., & Thomas, S. W. (1999). Using portfolios to foster independent thinking. *Intervention in School and Clinic, 35,* 34–37.

Duke, D. L. (1989). School policies and educational opportunities for minority students. *Peabody Journal of Education, 66*(4), 17–29.

Ellett, L. (1993). Instructional practices in mainstreamed secondary classrooms. *Journal of Learning Disabilities, 26,* 57–64.

Espin, C., Deno, S., Maruyama, G., & Cohen, C. (1989). *Basic academic skills samples (BASS)* . Minneapolis: University of Minnesota Learning Disability/Mildly Handicapped Research Project.

Evans, S. S., Evans, W. H., & Mercer, C. D. (1986). *Assessment for instruction.* Boston: Allyn & Bacon.

Fuchs, L. S., Deno, S. L., & Mirkin, P. K. (1984). The effects of frequent curriculum-based measurement and evaluation on pedagogy, student achievement, and student awareness of learning. *American Educational Research Journal, 21,* 449–460.

Fuchs, L., & Fuchs, D. (1986). Effects of systematic formative evaluation: A meta-analysis. *Exceptional Children, 53,* 199–208.

Fuchs, L. S., Fuchs, D., & Bishop, N. (1992). Teacher planning for students with learning disabilities: Differences between general and special educators. *Learning Disabilities Research & Practice, 7,* 120–128.

Fuchs, D., Fuchs, L., & Fernstrom, P. (1992). Case-by-case reintegration of students with learning disabilities. *The Elementary School Journal, 92,* 261–281.

Fuchs, L. S., Fuchs, D., & Hamlett, C. L. (1993). Technological advances linking the assessment of students' academic proficiency to instructional planning. *Journal of Special Education Technology, XII*(1), 49–62.

Fuchs, L. S., Fuchs, D., Hamlett, C. L., & Allinder, R. M. (1991). The contribution of skills analysis to curriculum-based measurement in spelling. *Exceptional Children, 57,* 443–452.

Fuchs, L. S., Fuchs, D., Hamlett, C. L., & Ferguson, C. (1992). Effects of expert system consultation within curriculum-based measurement, using a reading maze task. *Exceptional Children, 58,* 436–450.

Fuchs, L. S., Fuchs, D., Hamlett, C. L., Phillips, N. B., & Bentz, J. (1994). Classwide curriculum-based measurement: Helping general educators meet the challenge of student diversity. *Exceptional Children, 60,* 518–537.

Fuchs, L. S., Fuchs, D., Hamlett, C. L., & Stecker, P. M. (1990). The role of skills analysis in curriculum-based measurement in math. *School Psychology Review, 19,* 6–22.

Fuchs, L. S., Fuchs, D., Hamlett, C. L., & Stecker, P. M. (1991). Effects of curriculum-based measurement and consultation on teacher planning and student achievement in mathematics operations. *American Educational Research Journal, 28,* 617–641.

Fuchs, D., Roberts, P. H., Fuchs, L. S., & Bowers, J. (1996). Reintegrating students with learning disabilities into the mainstream: A two-year study. *Learning Disabilities Research & Practice, 11*, 214–229.

Garcia, E., Rasmussen, B., Stobbe, C., & Garcia, E. (1990). Portfolios: An assessment tool in support of instruction. *International Journal of Educational Research, 14*, 431–436.

Gersten, R., Vaughn, S., & Brengelman, S. U. (1996). Grading and academic feedback for special education students and students with learning difficulties. In T. R. Guskey (Ed.), *ASCD 1996 yearbook: Communicating student learning* (pp. 13–24). Alexandria, VA: Association for Supervision and Curriculum Development.

Gliszczinski, C., & Wesson, C. L. (1989). Curriculum-based measurement. *LD Forum, 15*(1), 47–49.

Goodrich, H. (1996–1997). Understanding rubrics. *Educational Leadership, 54*(4), 14–17.

Guskey, T. R. (1994). Making the grade: What benefits students? *Educational Leadership, 52*(2), 14–20.

Hasbrouck, J. E., & Tindal, G. (1992). Curriculum-based oral reading fluency norms for students in grades 2 through 5. *Teaching Exceptional Children, 24*(3), 41–44.

Hasbrouck, J. E., & Woldbeck, T., Ihnot, C., & Parker, R. I. (1999). One teacher's use of curriculum-based measurement: A changed opinion. *Learning Disabilities Research & Practice, 14*, 118–126.

Herman, J. L., Gearhart, M., & Baker, E. L. (1993). Assessing writing portfolios: Issues in the validity and meaning of scores. *Educational Assessment, 13*, 201–224.

Herman, J. L., & Winters, L. (1994). Portfolio research: A slim collection. *Educational Leadership, 52*(2), 48–55.

Koorland, M. A., Keel, M. C., & Ueberhorst, P. (1990). Setting aims for precision learning. *Teaching Exceptional Children, 22*(3), 64–68.

Lovitt, T. C. (1995). *Tactics for teaching.* Englewood Cliffs, NJ: Merrill, an imprint of Prentice-Hall.

Male, M. (1997). *Technology for inclusion* (3rd ed.). Boston: Allyn and Bacon.

Marston, D., Dement, K., Allen, D., & Allen, L. (1992). Monitoring pupil progress in reading. *Preventing School Failure, 36*(2), 21–25.

Mercer, C. D., & Mercer, A. R. (1998). *Teaching students with learning problems* (5th ed.). Upper Saddle River, NJ: Merrill, an imprint of Prentice-Hall.

Mercer, C. D., & Miller, S. P. (1991–1994). *Strategic math series.* Lawrence, KS: Edge Enterprises.

Munk, D., & Bursuck, W. D. (1998). Report card grading adaptations for students with disabilities: Types and acceptability. *Intervention in School and Clinic, 33*, 306–308.

Niguidula, D. (1997). Picturing performance with digital portfolios. *Educational Leadership, 55*(3), 26–29.

Nolet, V. (1992). Classroom-based measurement and portfolio assessment. *Diagnostique, 18*(1), 5–26.

Olson, J. L., & Platt, J. M. (2000). *Teaching children and adolescents with special needs* (3rd ed.). Upper Saddle River, NJ: Merrill, an imprint of Prentice-Hall.

Ornstein, A. C. (1994). Grading practices and policies: An overview and some suggestions. *NASSP Bulletin, 78*(561) 55–64.

Pierce, L. V., & O'Malley, J. M. (1992). *Performance and portfolio assessment for language minority students.* Washington, DC: National Clearinghouse for Bilingual Education.

Polloway, E. A., Epstein, M. H., Bursuck, W. D., Roderique, T. W., McConeghy, J. L., & Jayanthi, M. (1994). Classroom grading: A national survey of policies. *Remedial and Special Education, 15*, 162–170.

Popham, W. J. (1997). What's wrong and what's right with rubrics. *Educational Leadership, 55*(2), 72–75.

Reetz, L. J. (1995, April). *Portfolio assessment in inclusion settings: A shared responsibility.* Paper presented at the annual meeting of The Council for Exceptional Children, Indianapolis, IN.

Richter, S. E. (1997). Using portfolios as an additional means of assessing written language in a special education classroom. *Teaching and Change, 5*(1), 58–70.

Rojewski, J. W., Pollard, R. R., & Meers, G. D. (1990). Grading mainstreamed special needs students: Determining practices and attitudes of secondary vocational educators using a qualitative approach. *Remedial and Special Education, 12*(1), 7–15, 28.

Rojewski, J. W., Pollard, R. R., & Meers, G. D. (1992). Grading secondary vocational special education students with disabilities: A national perspective. *Exceptional Children, 59*, 68–76.

Rueda, R., & Garcia, E. (1997). Do portfolios make a difference for diverse students? The influence of type of data on making instructional decisions. *Learning Disabilities Research & Practice, 12*, 114–122.

Salend, S. J. (1998a). *Effective mainstreaming: Creating inclusive classrooms* (3rd ed.). Upper Saddle River, NJ: Merrill, an imprint of Prentice-Hall.

Salend, S. J. (1998b). Using portfolios to assess student performance. *Teaching Exceptional Children, 31*(2), 36–43.

Salvia, J., & Hughes, C. (1990). *Curriculum-based assessment: Testing what is taught.* New York: Macmillan.

Salvia, J., & Ysseldyke, J. E. (1995). *Assessment* (6th ed.). Boston: Houghton Mifflin.

Schendel, J., & Binder-Reschly, M. (1989). *Criterion validity of curriculum based assessment and correlation with teacher ratings and ITBS scores* (Report No. EC 230 554). Des Moines, IA: Iowa State Department of Education, Bureau of Special Education. (ERIC Document Reproduction Service No. ED 318 152)

Smith, D. D., & Lovitt, T. C. (1982). *The computational arithmetic program.* Austin, TX: PRO-ED.

Swicegood, P. (1994). Portfolio-based assessment practices. *Intervention in School and Clinic, 30*, 6–15.

Toyne, J., & Bundgaard, K. (1997). Using portfolio assessment for accountability in a fully integrated classroom. Research in the Classroom. *Tenth Annual Report of Research Projects Conducted by Educators in Their Classrooms 1995–1996* (Report No. SP 037 385). Denver, CO: Colorado Department of Education, Special Education Services Unit. (ERIC Document Reproduction Service No. ED 408 285)

Valencia, S. (1990). A portfolio approach to classroom reading assessment: The whys, whats, and hows. *The Reading Teacher, 43*, 338–340.

Vasa, S. F. (1981). Alternative procedures for grading handicapped students in the secondary schools. *Education Unlimited, 3*(1), 16–23.

Waldron, N. L., & McLesky, J. (1998). The effects of an inclusive school program on students with mild and severe learning disabilities. *Exceptional Children, 64*, 395–405.

Wesson, C. L. (1991). Curriculum-based measurement and two models of follow-up consultation. *Exceptional Children, 57*, 246–256.

Wesson, C. L., & King, R. P. (1996). Portfolio assessment and special education students. *Teaching Exceptional Children, 28*(2), 44–48.

Wood, J. W. (1998). *Adapting instruction to accommodate students in inclusive settings.* Upper Saddle River, NJ: Merrill, an imprint of Prentice-Hall.

Engaging in Professional Growth and Development

Creating a profession of teaching in which teachers have the opportunity for continual learning is the likeliest way to inspire greater achievement for children, especially those for whom education is the only pathway to survival and success.

—Linda Darling-Hammond

ADVANCE ORGANIZER

The importance of monitoring student progress and various methodologies for doing so were discussed in Chapter 8. Clearly, ongoing monitoring systems are needed to ensure that student learning is taking place and to provide teachers with feedback regarding the effectiveness of their instruction. In addition to monitoring the performance of students, teachers must monitor their own professional growth and development. The process of learning to teach is a career-long endeavor that is far from over at the completion of a teacher-preparation program. As diversity among student populations increases and knowledge about validated instructional practices expands, it becomes more and more important for teachers to view themselves as continuous learners. The purpose of this chapter is to present a variety of processes that teachers use to promote ongoing professional development. Included among these processes are induction and mentoring programs, partnership learning, collegial learning, action research, and teacher portfolios.

It is becoming increasingly evident that ongoing professional development is a critical component for successful teaching. The challenges that teachers face while addressing the needs of their students vary from one day to the next. No two days of teaching are exactly alike. Thus, the "one size fits all" approach to teaching is rarely effective. Teachers must constantly think about and analyze their teaching. They must continuously ask questions such as "How can I make this lesson better?" "What does the literature say about teaching math?" "What can I try next if this doesn't work?" "What can I do to increase student learning?" "What made that lesson go well?" "Did I cover too much or too little?" "What were the strengths and weaknesses of the lesson?" "How can I promote student motivation?" "Are new field-tested materials available?" "Am I taking advantage of all available resources?" "How can I do my job better?" and/or "What are my professional goals for this semester?" The list of potential self-reflection questions is, of course, endless. Such questions help teachers study and monitor their teaching practices. It is so important for teachers to slow down long enough to think about what they're doing and why they're doing it. They also must invest time in learning about new validated methods and curricula as they become available.

A variety of approaches are available to promote ongoing professional development among teachers. Most of these approaches emphasize the importance of teachers working with other teachers. Collegiality among peers provides opportunities for new ideas, a sense of community, objective opinions, and ongoing support.

Induction and Mentoring Programs

Typically, the most challenging time for a teacher is when he or she first enters the profession. The first year of teaching is particularly challenging. In addition to limited teaching experience, first-year teachers typically have more lessons to develop and fewer resources from which to obtain ideas for the lessons than more experienced teachers. Additionally, beginning teachers are learning how to best meet the behavioral needs of their students. Concurrent to these issues and concerns, beginning teachers are becoming acquainted with the culture of the school in which they have been hired. Learning about required paper work, extracurricular responsibilities, and district policies and procedures adds to the demands placed on beginning teachers. In recognition of the challenges involved in starting a career as a teacher, many school districts offer induction programs. The induction program functions as a logical extension of the preservice program (e.g., teacher-preparation program typically at a university or college) and as the forerunner to a more comprehensive, career-long professional-development program (Huling-Austin, 1990; Odell, Huling, & Sweeny, 2000). Induction programs are designed to provide systematic and sustained assistance to teachers during their initial years (i.e., 1 to 3 years) in the profession. In some districts, experienced teachers who are new to the district also are included in these programs.

Induction programs vary from one school district to the next, but most programs are developed with the following five goals in mind (Huling-Austin, 1990):

1. Improve teaching performance;
2. Increase the retention of promising beginning teachers during the induction years;
3. Promote the personal and professional well-being of beginning teachers by improving teachers' attitudes toward themselves and the profession;
4. Satisfy mandated requirements related to induction and certification; and
5. Transmit the culture of the system to beginning teachers. (p. 539)

A variety of methods and program components are used to meet these goals. Staff development personnel typically are involved in determining which methods and/or program components will work best for their teachers (Huling-Austin, 1986). Included among the possibilities are:

- Printed materials of employment conditions and school regulations;
- Orientation meetings and visits;
- Seminars on curriculum and effective teaching topics for beginning teachers;
- Training sessions for mentor teachers and other support personnel;
- Observations by supervisors/peers/assessment teams and/or videotaping of the beginning teacher in the classroom;
- Follow-up conferences with observers;
- Consultation with experienced teachers;
- Support (helping/buddy/mentor teachers);
- Opportunities to observe other teachers (in person or through subject-specific videotapes);
- Released time/load reduction for beginning teachers and/or support teachers;
- Group meetings of beginning teachers (for emotional support);

▶ Assignment to a team teaching situation;

▶ Credit courses for beginning teachers (university and/or local credit); and

▶ Beginning teacher newsletters and other publications designed to provide helpful teaching tips for the novice teacher. (p. 2)

One of the most promising components of teacher-induction programs is mentoring. Mentoring is defined as "a professional practice that occurs in the context of teaching whenever an experienced teacher supports, challenges, and guides novice teachers in their teaching practice" (Odell & Huling, 2000, p. xii). A wide variety of attributes are associated with mentoring relationships. Included among these are teaching, nurturing, modeling, supporting, refining, sponsoring, advising, coaching, reflecting, protecting, encouraging, befriending, and counseling (Anderson & Shannon, 1988; Brennan, Thames, & Roberts, 1999; Odell, 1990; Wasley, 1999).

There appears to be consensus among educators and researchers that learning to teach "involves the gradual acquisition of professional expertise over an extended

Supportive relationships between beginning and experienced teachers represent a win-win-win approach to improving instructional practice. The beginning teacher benefits from the support and guidance of the experienced teacher; the experienced teacher frequently improves her own practice while sharing ideas and gains a strong sense of contributing to the profession in a meaningful way; and the students in both teachers' classes benefit from the improved instructional practices.

period of time" (Morine-Dershimer, 1992, p. xiii), and that mentor teachers play a significant role in helping novices acquire this expertise. The mentoring process typically involves four phases: *(a)* developing the relationship, *(b)* determining the mentoring content, *(c)* applying effective styles and strategies, and *(d)* disengaging the relationship (Odell, 1990). During the first phase, mentors and novice teachers become acquainted and begin to establish a positive rapport. Several informal meetings help in terms of getting the relationship started. The initial rapport helps set the stage for building a strong professional relationship. The primary goal during the first phase of the mentoring process is to establish an atmosphere of support and trust. During the second phase of the mentoring process, decisions are made regarding the type of support that will benefit the novice. The novice takes the lead in terms of identifying the support that is needed. Clearly, the type of support (e.g., systems information, instructional, emotional) varies over time; it also varies from one novice to another. Thus, mentoring must be tailor-made for the specific individuals involved. During the third phase of the mentoring process, decisions are made with regard to the specific methods for helping the novice (e.g., discussion, reflection, observations, peer coaching). Regardless of what methods are used, it is important for mentors to communicate support rather than take on an evaluative role. During the fourth and final phase, the mentoring relationship reaches culmination. To facilitate the transition from mentor–novice support to colleague–colleague support, novices should be informed about available resources for continued professional development activities. They also should be encouraged to participate in the activities.

The specific nuances of each of these phases differ among various mentoring programs, but consensus exists among educators and researchers that mentors are key to the success of the programs. Thus, mentors must be selected carefully. They must receive quality preparation and training and should have opportunities to participate in the development of the mentoring program (Odell, Huling, & Sweeney, 2000). Rowley (1999) identified six essential qualities of a good mentor. He indicated that a good mentor is *(a)* committed to the role of mentoring, *(b)* accepting of the beginning teacher, *(c)* skilled at providing instructional support, *(d)* effective in different interpersonal contexts, *(e)* a model of a continuous learner, and *(f)* able to communicate hope and optimism. Mentoring programs that include mentors with these qualities are likely to be of benefit to beginning teachers (see Validation Box 9.1 on p. 382).

Partnership Learning

One of the most common approaches to promote professional development among teachers is to offer a variety of workshops on teaching-related topics. Typically, these workshops are offered before or after the school day or on several designated inservice days interspersed throughout the school year. In some cases workshop leaders or "experts" are invited to the school or school district to present information to groups of teachers. In other cases, teachers are given opportunities to attend pro-

Induction and Mentoring Programs

▶ Seventeen studies were included in a review of literature related to induction programs. Only data-based studies published between 1977 and 1988 were included in this review. Agreement among researchers emerged regarding *(a)* the needs and concerns of beginning teachers (e.g., classroom management, student evaluation, individual student differences, dealing with parents), as well as the need for induction programs to help beginning teachers with these issues; *(b)* the need for flexibility within induction programs (i.e., context-specific needs should be addressed as beginning teachers experience them); *(c)* the importance of having support (e.g., mentor teacher); *(d)* the need for various stakeholders (e.g., institutions of higher education, state education agencies, local education agencies, professional organizations, service agencies) to become involved in providing support to beginning teachers, and *(e)* the need for beginning teachers to be placed in assignments that are likely to result in success, rather than extremely difficult placements. For more information see: (Huling-Austin, 1990).

▶ A study involving 19 first-year teachers was conducted to explore the effects of a two-year induction program on teaching performance. The program incorporated clinical supervision from university faculty and school district personnel and school-based support systems (i.e., mentor teachers and weekly seminar meetings). Quantitative and qualitative analyses revealed that teachers who participated in the induction program made significant gains in their level of teaching skills during the two-year program. During participants' first year of teaching, they significantly decreased inefficient use of class time and increased instructional time. During participants' second year of teaching, they improved their classroom organization and behavior management skills. Consequently, time spent in academically related activities increased. For more information see: (Schaffer, Stringfield, & Wolfe, 1992).

▶ A survey study was conducted to determine whether elementary teachers who received yearlong structured support from mentor teachers in a collaborative university/school system teacher mentor program were still teaching four years after their initial teaching year. The overall attrition rate for four years was 4 percent and the attrition rate for females was higher than for males. Teachers were asked to rate how helpful seven categories of mentoring support had been in their first year of teaching: emotional, instructional, resources, discipline, parental, management, and system. Emotional support received during their first year of teaching was most valued. Support in using instructional strategies and obtaining resources for the classroom was valued second highest. Less value was placed on support received in disciplining students and working with parents and the least amount of value was attributed to managing the school day and functioning within the school system. For more information see: (Odell & Ferraro, 1992).

fessional conferences. When teachers receive support to attend conferences or workshops away from their schools, they typically are expected to bring the information back to their colleagues. Thus, it is not uncommon for teachers to provide inservices for other teachers. Regardless of who is designated as the staff development leader, the use of partnership learning enhances the inservice process. Partnership learning involves presenting information in ways that promote equal partnerships among the staff development leader and the teachers attending the workshop or training session (Knight, 1997a). Dialogue among participants is a major component of partnership learning and various points of view are valued. Partnership learning is based on the following nine guiding principles:

1. *Equality.* Partnership learning is based on conversations between inservice participants. All participants are recognized as equal partners, and consequently no view is more important or more valuable than any other.
2. *Reflection.* In partnership learning, reflection plays an important role in the learning process. Numerous opportunities for participants to reflect on the practical implications of the inservice are provided.
3. *Choice.* In partnership learning, a participant's choice during communication about the content is recognized and valued. Coercion is avoided.
4. *Dialogue.* Partnership learning is built on dialogue, rather than on lecture. Presenters do not dominate, impose, or control the conversation. Instead, they engage participants in conversation about content and encourage everyone to think and learn together.
5. *Expertise.* Inservice leaders, using partnership learning, believe that other participants' knowledge and expertise are as important as their own. They encourage participants to invent useful applications of the content.
6. *Learning with Participants.* In partnership learning, the leader's goal is to learn along with the participants. Multiple perspectives about the content are beneficial to everyone. It is important for the leader to learn how the inservice content will fit within the participants' particular environments.
7. *Voice.* In partnership learning, all participants are encouraged to voice their opinions about the inservice content. Staff development leaders recognize, value, and encourage different ways of perceiving the content.
8. *Engagement.* Partnership learning is based on the belief that effective instructional practices must be used to ensure that all participants learn the inservice content. To encourage efficient and effective learning for all participants, strategies that ensure participant engagement in content are used (e.g., questioning, small-group discussions).
9. *Interactive.* Partnership learning involves a minimal amount of lecturing. Most of the inservice time is spent in interactive dialogue with many opportunities for participants to voice their ideas and concerns (Knight, 1997a).

In partnership learning, teachers and/or visiting experts use these guiding principles to conduct their workshops or training sessions. Getting all participants actively involved in the learning process is an important goal of partnership learning.

Knight (1997a) identified six strategies that staff development leaders use to promote the principles of partnership learning: *(a)* question recipes, *(b)* thinking devices, *(c)* cooperative learning, *(d)* reflective learning, *(e)* experiential learning, and *(f)* effective stories. Each of these strategies enhances the quality of inservice sessions and results in outcomes that are superior to traditional lecture methods (Knight 1997a; Knight, 1997b). The strategies can be used in isolation or together (see Validation Box 9.2).

Question Recipes

Question recipes are simple questions that staff development leaders use to encourage conversation during training sessions. These questions are open-ended and nonjudgmental to promote participation from all participants. Question recipes are worded carefully to accomplish a variety of purposes. For example, when the dialogue needs to shift to a realistic discussion of potential success and challenges with a new program, a question recipe such as, "How do you see this working with your students?" is used. When multiple perspectives are needed to enrich the dialogue, a question recipe such as, "What are some other ways of viewing this?" is appropriate. When the emotional sides of an issue need to be explored, a question recipe such as, "How does this make you feel?" is helpful. In addition to asking these questions, it is important for the staff development leader to demonstrate empathetic listening to the various responses.

**VALIDATION BOX
9.2**

Partnership Learning

In a study involving 74 teachers, staff development that used partnership learning structures (e.g., thinking device, cooperative learning, question recipes) was compared to traditional staff development (lecture with periodic summary statements and question-answer periods every 10 minutes). The study participants were taught two strategies from the University of Kansas Learning Strategy Curriculum. Findings revealed that when teachers were taught using partnership learning they were more engaged in the learning process and remembered more of the content than when traditional staff development techniques were used. Additionally, teachers enjoyed partnership learning more than traditional staff development and indicated they were more likely to implement the strategies that were taught using partnership learning. For more information see: (Knight, 1998).

Thinking Devices

Thinking devices are items specifically used to elicit analysis, conversation, ideas, and reflection from participants. The devices serve as springboards for further thinking about the content within the inservice. One example of a commonly used thinking device is a two- to three-paragraph narrative (i.e., vignette) that summarizes or illustrates a particular issue of concern to teachers (Knight, 2000a). Typically, vignettes are read aloud during inservice sessions and then question recipes are used to promote meaningful dialogue. One of the best ways to create vignettes that directly relate to the inservice participants' needs is to interview the participants prior to the inservice session. Pre-inservice interviews provide specific information about teacher challenges, student needs, and cultural norms within the school or school district. This information is very helpful for creating relevant vignettes (Knight, 2000b). Other examples of thinking devices include film clips, case studies, pictures, and/or songs. Each of these items can be used to promote productive thinking and dialogue. Regardless of which device is used, participants' views, reactions, and ideas are accepted and valued.

Cooperative Learning

Cooperative learning is an interactive process whereby learners work in groups to teach themselves specific content. Members of the groups take on various roles (e.g., quality checker, recorder, facilitator, researcher) to ensure that the learning task is accomplished in an effective and efficient manner. The use of cooperative learning with school-aged students was discussed extensively in Chapter 6. For staff development purposes, the same general principles apply. Teachers work together to promote positive interdependence and interactions within the groups. Moreover, they help one another meet the group goals. Specifically, cooperative learning helps teachers understand new content, solve problems, share ideas, and create new programs.

Reflective Learning

Reflective learning involves activities that prompt learners to consider how the content being covered can be generalized to their personal or professional lives. Typically, reflective learning involves small-group discussion related to a specific problem. The group explores how the content of the workshop or training session might be applied to solve the identified problem. For example, if the workshop topic is "methods for improving reading comprehension" and three strategies have been covered, a reflective learning activity might be to determine how to integrate instruction on these strategies into the existing literature-based curriculum. In small groups, the teachers can discuss issues related to scheduling the instruction, availability of needed materials, involvement of parents, and who will teach which strategies.

Experiential Learning

Another type of learning that teachers use during staff development activities is experiential learning. Experiential learning involves simulations related to the practice being studied. In other words, experiences are created that allow the learners to actively engage in what is being taught. For example, if teachers are learning a particular teaching routine, they can take turns demonstrating the routine with their peers acting as school-aged students. Another example is teachers completing an assignment that they've created for their students. Experiential learning provides invaluable insight related to the cognitive and emotional elements involved in the activity.

Effective Stories

The final strategy for partnership learning is using effective stories. Stories are entertaining and engaging and help learners understand and remember content. They offer background information, illustrate key concepts, interject humor, and/or provide valuable examples. Teachers who use stories during staff development activities should select topics to which the participants will relate. Stories that touch human emotions work well.

These six partnership learning strategies are tools teachers can use to enrich their staff development activities particularly when serving as leader or facilitator of learning endeavors for other teachers. These strategies also are appropriate for teachers who serve in other leadership roles such as team leader or department chairperson. Although schools traditionally are viewed as learning environments for students, many benefits emerge when schools are viewed as learning environments for teachers as well. The active engagement of teachers in inservice activities (i.e., planning and implementation) is supported in the literature. Specifically, research suggests that successful inservices are based on teachers' expressed needs and have immediate applicability to the classroom. Additionally, research suggests teachers prefer to interact with colleagues at the same grade level and prefer inservices with themes continued over time (Berman & Friederwitzer, 1981).

Collegial Learning

Relationships among teachers typically are structured in one of three ways: (a) competitively, (b) individualistically, or (c) cooperatively (Johnson & Johnson, 1987). In *competitive structures*, teachers work against each other to achieve a goal that only one or a few can attain. Personal gain is maximized at colleagues' expense (e.g., merit pay systems). In *individualistic structures*, teachers work by themselves to accomplish goals unrelated to the goals of their colleagues. They generally believe that the success or failure of their colleagues has little effect on their professional lives. In *cooperative structures*, teachers work together to achieve joint goals. They

VALIDATION BOX
9.3

Competitive, Individualistic, and Cooperative Structures

A meta-analysis of 133 studies that compared the effectiveness of competitive, individualistic, and cooperative structures was conducted. Each of these studies involved adult participants. Findings revealed that cooperation promoted higher achievement than either competitive or individualistic learning. Cooperation also promoted more positive interpersonal relationships, greater social support, and higher self-esteem among adults than competitive or individualistic efforts. For more information see: (Johnson & Johnson, 1987).

seek outcomes that benefit both themselves and their colleagues. Fortunately, school personnel are recognizing the value of cooperation and are adopting practices that promote collegiality among teachers (see Validation Box 9.3).

A variety of collegiality learning approaches are available to facilitate professional growth and to assist teachers in solving critical problems. These approaches typically involve small groups of colleagues (i.e., peers) who view one another as equals and use nonhierarchical methods of communication to solve school-based problems. Participation in such groups promotes professional development and helps teachers make important educational decisions. Included among the validated collegial processes are structured dialogue, collaborative problem solving, collaborative consultation, specialist consultation, intervention assistance teams, peer coaching, and teacher study groups.

Structured Dialogue

Johnson and Pugach (1991) developed a four-step structured dialogue process for teachers to use when attempting to solve problems. The four steps in their dialogue process are *(a)* clarifying questions, *(b)* summary, *(c)* interventions and predictions, and *(d)* evaluation. These steps are designed to foster teachers' development and implementation of alternative interventions for students with learning and behavior problems:

> *Step 1.* During the first step, *clarifying questions*, the teacher who has a problem initiates a meeting with a partner teacher. The initiating teacher brings a written description of the problem to the meeting and provides an overview of the problem. The initiating teacher then generates and answers questions in an attempt to clarify all aspects of the problem. The partner teacher prompts the initiating teacher, as needed, to ensure that who, what, and where aspects of the situation are explored. For example, the partner teacher might say, "Is there a question you can ask and answer regarding when Billy loses his temper?" When

the initiating teacher feels the relevant issues have been identified, the teachers progress to step two.

Step 2. Summary has three parts: *(a)* a revised description of the concern, *(b)* the teacher's feelings about and response to the situation, and *(c)* aspects of the situation over which the teacher has control. The initiating teacher summarizes these three parts and begins to think about potential solutions to the problem.

Step 3. During *interventions and predictions*, the initiating teacher generates at least three potential interventions or solutions to the problem. The initiating teacher predicts the potential results of each intervention. Both benefits and hazards are considered for each intervention.

Step 4. During *evaluation*, the initiating teacher develops an evaluation plan that includes data collection to monitor both the implementation and outcomes of the selected interventions. A follow-up meeting is scheduled for two weeks in the future to discuss the effectiveness of the plan.

The structured dialogue process is designed to promote reflective problem solving. The "listening" teacher avoids the role of expert consultant. Instead, the individual seeking assistance is guided through the process and ultimately decides which solutions or interventions to try (Welch, Brownell, & Sheridan, 1999). Thus, the identified solutions are comfortable for the teacher seeking assistance and likely to be implemented in a timely manner (see Validation Box 9.4).

Collaborative Problem Solving

Knackendoffel, Robinson, Deshler, and Schumaker (1992) developed a collaborative problem-solving process for school personnel to use to address the complex needs of students who present special challenges. The purpose of the process is to draw on expertise from more than one person to find solutions to student-related problems. The Problem-Solving Worksheet is used to guide individuals through the thirteen-step process (see Fig. 9.1 on p. 390).

Step 1. Define the Problem

The first step in the collaborative problem-solving process is to clearly define the problem. Much of the success of the collaborative problem-solving process is contingent on having a clear understanding of the problem. Specificity is important when defining the problem. In some cases, numerous problems are discussed, but ultimately the most important problem (i.e., the one that needs to be addressed first) should be agreed upon. Questioning techniques are used to help colleagues define the problem (e.g., "What does Terry need to do to pass your class?" "What type of assignments does she fail to turn in?"). Once the problem is defined, paraphrasing the problem statement ensures that both teachers understand the problem (e.g., "So, in other words, the problem is . . ."). The clearly defined problem is recorded on the Problem-Solving Worksheet.

VALIDATION BOX
9.4

Four-Step Structured Dialogue Process

▶ A study was conducted to investigate the effectiveness of using a 4-step structured dialogue process (i.e., clarifying questions, summary, interventions and predictions, and evaluation) to solve classroom problems involving students with learning or behavioral difficulties. There were 91 teachers in the study, 4 junior high school teachers and 87 elementary school teachers. Teachers who used the 4-step peer collaboration process demonstrated less restrictiveness and greater tolerance for the range of cognitive abilities among students. Comparison teachers who did not use the 4-step process became more restrictive and less tolerant of the range of cognitive abilities. Additionally, 86 pecent of the teachers who used the 4-step process reported improvement or much improvement regarding the status of the interventions selected through peer collaboration. For more information see: (Johnson & Pugach, 1991).

▶ There were 191 teachers in a second study designed to evaluate this 4-step dialogue process. This study was a replication of the Johnson and Pugach (1991) study with additional outcome measures. At the completion of this yearlong study, the group of teachers who used the 4-step dialogue process showed a 50 percent decrease in referrals to special education, while the group of teachers who did not use the 4-step process demonstrated a slight increase in referrals. The teachers who used peer collaboration increased their confidence in handling classroom problems, increased positive teacher affect toward the class, and demonstrated more tolerance toward cognitive deficits. Additionally, 88 percent of the teachers who used the peer collaboration reported that their problem was solved after engaging in the 4-step process. For more information see: (Pugach & Johnson, 1995).

Step 2. Gather Specific Information about the Problem

The second step in the collaborative problem-solving process is to gather as much information as possible to clarify the problem. Again, asking specific questions is helpful. If answers to the following questions are not known, further discussion is needed (Knackendoffel et al., 1992).

▶ Do I know precisely what the student is or is not doing?
▶ Do I know when the behavior is or is not occurring?
▶ Do I know in what settings the behavior is or is not occurring?
▶ Do I know what is expected of the student?
▶ Do I know whether the student has the skills to do what is expected?
▶ Do I know what solutions have already been tried? (p. 24)

Once information has been gathered, it should be summarized. The colleague who initiated the problem-solving session needs to be assured that his or her concern is understood. Without this assurance, there is little motivation to continue the process.

Problem-Solving Worksheet

Problem-Solving Team Members: _____ Role: _____

Student _____ Date: _____

Problem: _____

Details: _____

Alternative Solutions: _____ Ratings: _____

Problem Solving Worksheet (*continued*)

Solution to Be Tried First: _____

Implementation Steps: _____ When: _____ Who: _____

How Will the Plan Be Monitored? _____

What Are the Criteria for Success? _____

Date and Time of Next Appointment: _____

FIGURE 9.1

Problem-Solving Worksheet. (From *Collaborative Problem Solving* [pp. 53–54], by E. A. Knackendoffel, S. M. Robinson, D. D. Deshler, and J. B. Schumaker, 1992, Lawrence, KS: Edge Enterprises. Copyright 1992 by E. A. Knackendoffel, S. M. Robinson, D. D. Deshler, and J. B. Schumaker. Reprinted with permission. *Note: Collaborative Problem Solving* may be ordered through Edge Enterprises, P.O. Box 1304, Lawrence, KS 66045; telephone: [785] 749-1473; fax: [785] 749-0207.)

Step 3. Explain the Problem-Solving Process, and State Its Usefulness

If any participant is using the collaborative problem-solving process for the first time, the sequential steps should be explained. Individuals tend to be more comfortable when they know what is coming. Explanations allow the process to proceed with efficiency and reduce the likelihood of problems emerging. If everyone involved in the collaborative problem-solving process has used the method before, then a quick review of what will be done is sufficient.

Step 4. Identify Alternative Solutions

The fourth step in the collaborative problem-solving process is to identify possible solutions to the problem. Both collaborative partners should participate in brainstorming possible solutions. It's a good idea for the teacher who initially sought help for the problem to begin the brainstorming process. When he or she begins to run out of ideas, the partners take turns coming up with additional possibilities. During this step, positive or negative evaluations of the potential solutions are avoided. Even ideas that don't seem feasible are valuable because they sometimes trigger new ideas. Additionally, the process of teachers working together to find solutions is facilitated when all ideas are accepted without criticism. The alternative solutions or potential solutions are recorded on the Problem-Solving Worksheet (see Fig. 9.1).

Step 5. Summarize Solutions

The fifth step in the collaborative problem-solving process is to verbally summarize the alternative solutions. This summary allows both teachers to make additional comments and ensures that both are ready to begin analyzing the alternative solutions.

Step 6. Analyze Possible Consequences

The sixth step involves analyzing the possible consequences of each potential solution. This analysis helps ensure that the best of the brainstormed solutions is selected. The analysis takes into consideration four factors: *(a)* benefits for the student, teacher, and anyone else involved; *(b)* problems for individuals involved; *(c)* practicality of the idea; and *(d)* amount of time and effort involved in implementing the solution. It is important for both teachers to be very honest about their feelings during this stage. Extensive discussion is helpful and ensures that each solution on the list is considered carefully.

Step 7. Rate Each Solution

After discussion about each solution, a rating system is used to help determine which idea to try first. Rating descriptors such as "Excellent," "Good," and "Fair" can be used or a numeric system of "1," "2," and "3" with "1" being best can be used. The teacher responsible for implementing the solution takes leadership in the rating. If both teachers are going to implement the solution, then consensus between the two is needed.

Step 8. Select the Best Solution

The preceding steps typically result in the emergence of one clearly superior solution. That solution now is identified. Additional discussion occurs, if needed. The purpose of the eighth step in the collaborative problem-solving process is to reach a final decision about which solution to try first. This solution is recorded on the Problem-Solving Worksheet.

Step 9. Determine Satisfaction with the Chosen Solution

The ninth step is included to ensure that both teachers are happy with the selected solution. Without high levels of satisfaction, it is unlikely that the solution will be implemented. If either person has reservations about the selected solution, it may be helpful to brainstorm further and come up with something else.

Step 10. State Support for the Decision

During the tenth step, teachers acknowledge their support for one another and the decision that has been made. Conveying confidence in the decision and the process used to make the decision, as well as communicating a willingness to support one another during the implementation of the solution, is important.

Step 11. Develop a Plan of Action

The eleventh step involves developing a plan of action. Decisions are made regarding all the necessary steps for implementing the plan. Specifically, agreements need to occur regarding who is responsible for each step. Time lines for completing these implementation steps also are determined. These steps and target completion dates are recorded on the Problem-Solving Worksheet (see Fig. 9.1).

Step 12. Develop a Monitoring System and Specify Criteria for Success

It is very important to discuss and record how the selected solution will be monitored and evaluated. A system needs to be developed to determine whether the solution is a good one, whether modifications need to be made, or whether a totally different solution needs to be tried. Time lines for monitoring the effectiveness of the solution ensure that an ineffective solution won't continue too long. Both teachers need to agree on the criteria for success to avoid differences of opinion regarding the effectiveness of the solution.

Step 13. Schedule the Next Appointment

The final step in the collaborative problem-solving process simply involves setting a date and time to meet again. There are several advantages for scheduling a follow-up meeting. First, this communicates that support from one another is going to continue and reduces feelings of being alone with the problem. Second, having a set time to get back together encourages people to get started with the solution without unnecessary procrastination. Third, setting a follow-up time while both individuals are together prevents the hassle of coordinating calendars at another point in time. Follow-up meetings to discuss how things are going continue until both teachers agree they are no longer needed.

The thirteen steps in this problem-solving process promote a sense of "we're in this together." It may be helpful to have a list of the steps available during the collaborative meeting. The Problem-Solving Worksheet (see Fig. 9.1) also is helpful in terms of ensuring that the process steps are followed.

Undoubtedly, structured procedures assist with the technical aspects of collaboration. There are, however, other aspects of collaboration that are equally important. Interpersonal skills and relationships between collaborators affect the success of problem-solving efforts. The tone of collaborative meetings also is very important. Positive collaborative relationships develop across several problem-solving sessions as trust, respect, and open communication between individuals emerges (Knackendoffel, 1996).

Peer collaboration works best when the individuals involved share the following beliefs:

1. All participants in the collaborative relationship have equal status.
2. All educators can learn better ways to teach all students.
3. Educators should be involved continuously in creating and delivering instructional innovations.
4. Education improves when educators work together rather than in isolation. Effective collaborative relationships involve people who see themselves on the same side, working toward positive outcomes for students (p. 582) (see Validation Box 9.5)

VALIDATION BOX

9.5

Collaborative Problem Solving

▶ In a study involving eight secondary special education teachers, collaborative problem-solving skills were assessed before and after a workshop designed to teach the steps in the Collaborative Problem-Solving Strategy. The training involved one workshop that lasted a little over 1 hour. Prior to the workshop, teachers, on average, used only 41.5 percent of the targeted problem-solving skills. After the workshop, teachers used 94.4 percent of the skills. For more information see: (Knackendoffel, 1989).

▶ In another study, involving eight secondary special education teachers and 22 general education content teachers, factors related to implementing teaming strategies (including the Collaborative Problem-Solving Strategy) were investigated. Both special and general education teachers ranked the set of skills included in the teaming strategies as being very important. Special education teachers' self-ratings on teaming skills and general education teachers' ratings of special education teachers' teaming skills revealed positive increases in problem-solving abilities. The general education teachers rated the special-education teachers higher than the special education teachers rated themselves. Both general and special education teachers reported improvement in their collaborative relationships with one another after receiving training in the teaming strategies. Moreover, both groups of teachers were satisfied with the procedures in the strategies and described the outcomes of their consultation sessions as positive. For more information see: (Knackendoffel, 1989).

Collaborative Consultation

Idol, Nevin, and Paolucci-Whitcomb (1994) describe a similar process (i.e., collaborative consultation) that results in professional growth and development while simultaneously helping students. They define *collaborative consultation* as "an interactive process that enables groups of people with diverse expertise to generate creative solutions to mutually defined problems" (p. 1). Typically, the group solution or outcome is better than what individuals would produce independently. This makes the time and energy invested in the process worthwhile.

Principles of Collaborative Consultation

Specific principles are followed throughout the collaborative consultative process (Nevin, Thousand, Paolucci-Whitcomb, & Villa, 1990). These principles are:

1. Group members view one another and their students as possessing unique and needed expertise.
2. Group members frequently participate in face-to-face interactions.
3. Group members share leadership roles and responsibilities and hold one another accountable for agreed-on tasks.
4. Group members understand the importance of reciprocity (i.e., give and take).
5. Group members agree to use consensus building to increase social interaction and meet group goals.

These principles increase the likelihood that the collaborative process will result in positive outcomes for everyone involved. In addition to following these principles, group members need expertise in three areas: *(a)* knowledge about validated teaching practices, behavior management, curricula, and successful teaching strategies; *(b)* interpersonal communicative, interactive, and problem-solving skills to enhance and facilitate the group process; and *(c)* intrapersonal attitudes that promote collaboration (e.g., face fear, share a sense of humor, take risks, respond proactively; Idol et al., 1994).

Problem-Solving Stages

The six stages in the collaborative consultation process are gaining entry and establishing team goals, problem identification, intervention recommendations, implementation of recommendations, evaluation, and follow-up (Idol et al., 1994). These stages are used to facilitate a series of decision-making steps. The previously mentioned principles and areas of expertise are used throughout these six stages.

The purpose of Stage 1, *gaining entry and establishing team goals*, is to establish rapport among all group members so that everyone feels valued, accepted, and a part of the group. To assist with this, group members define and agree on what their roles and responsibilities will be throughout the collaborative consultative process. They also agree on the group goals. A variety of collaborative behaviors help individuals gain entry and acceptance from the group. Included among these are:

▶ Treat others with respect (i.e., listen, maintain confidentiality, use manners);

▶ Share relevant information about own skills so others can determine how to use expertise of group members;

▶ Use appropriate language that group members will understand;

▶ Listen to others;

▶ Model the use of interview skills to receive information, share information, explore feelings, and plan future directions;

▶ Demonstrate a willingness to learn from others;

▶ Give and receive feedback with patience and mutual respect;

▶ Manage conflict and confrontation appropriately (i.e., seek win-win methods for resolving conflicts); and

▶ Adapt situational leadership to collaborative consultation (i.e., adjust collaboration style to match the needs of group members.

In addition to helping gain entry into the group, using these behaviors helps the group reach its goals in a positive manner.

The purpose of Stage 2 is to *identify the problem*. Assessment data are needed to identify the problem accurately. These data may come from a variety of sources (e.g., classroom observations, curriculum-based assessment, portfolio assessment, standardized tests, parent and teacher reports). Once data are collected and shared, the collaborative group reaches consensus regarding the nature of the problem. It is helpful to compose a problem statement that includes specific examples (e.g., "Clifford has difficulty getting along with peers. From November 1 to 15, he ate lunch alone every day, he was involved in two fistfights in physical education class, and was sent to the dean twice for threatening to harm other students. Clifford doesn't appear to have any friends.") Once the problem statement is agreed upon, the team begins developing goals and objectives to address the problem. It is important to spend the necessary time to ensure that the problem is clearly identified because the remaining steps in the collaborative consultation process are based on the identified problem.

The purpose of Stage 3, *intervention recommendations*, is for the group collaborators to explore possible solutions for the problem. Brainstorming techniques are helpful for acquiring a variety of ideas from the group. The combination of everyone's good thinking results in a richer collection of options. Clearly, knowledge about validated practices is important during this stage. Such knowledge enhances the overall quality of the suggestions that emerge. Once the options are identified, collaborators explore the advantages and disadvantages of the suggested interventions. At this point in the collaborative process, it is important to view the options as belonging to the group, rather than the individuals who initially suggested them. Thus, the advantages and disadvantages can be explored more freely, without individuals feeling as though the team is evaluating them. Gradually, the list of options is narrowed down until consensus is reached on a final solution to the problem.

The purpose of Stage 4, *implementation of recommendations*, is to devise a plan of action for carrying out the agreed-on solution. Specifically, the team specifies what will be done, including all the substeps involved in implementing the plan.

Additionally, decisions are made regarding time lines for the substeps. The team agrees on who is responsible for each step. Finally, the team decides how to evaluate the effectiveness of the intervention. Each of these decisions is recorded in written format to ensure that everyone understands what will take place. The Plan of Action form may be used for recording purposes (see Fig. 9.2).

The purpose of Stage 5 is for the collaboration team to *evaluate* their work. In addition to evaluating the effectiveness of the implemented intervention, the team evaluates the collaborative consultation process and the impact of the process on the school, school system, and community. Feedback from all participants (i.e., teachers, parents, students) in the process is helpful. During Stage 5, the collaborative consultation team establishes criteria and standards for evaluating program effectiveness, identifies components of the program to evaluate, and creates measurement systems that are objective, reliable, and easy to implement. A variety of decisions are made in preparation for the evaluation process. Included among these are: *(a)* when data will be collected, *(b)* how data will be collected, and *(c)* how data

Collaborative Consultation Team Plan of Action

Student Name: _____   Team Members: _____
Date: _____   _____
                                                     _____

Primary Goal(s):

Related Objectives:

Decision of the Team:
☐ Modify Interventions   ☐ Develop New Interventions   ☐ Refer for Multidisciplinary   ☐ Discontinue Intervention
☐ Continue Interventions to   Relevant to the New Goal(s)   Team Evaluation   (Explain Below)
   Maintain Progress

Date	Selected Intervention to Be Implemented (Enumerate each substep necessary to carry out the plan)	Person(s) Responsible for Intervention	Target Date for Implementation	Review Date	Evaluation

FIGURE 9.2

Collaborative Consultation Recording Form. (From *Collaborative Consultation* [p. 215] by L. Idol, A. Nevin, and P. Paolucci-Whitcomb, 2000, Austin, TX: PRO-ED. Copyright 2000 by PRO-ED. Reprinted with permission.)

will be analyzed and disseminated. Additionally, decisions need to be made regarding who will conduct the evaluation. Members of the team, individuals not on the team, or a combination of the two may conduct the evaluation.

The purpose of Stage 6, *follow-up*, is to use the evaluation data to make decisions regarding next steps for the team to take. Program successes are celebrated and needed modifications are discussed. Interventions that are partially successful or not successful at all are redesigned or discontinued. Similarly, if the collaborative process needs to be refined, the team develops a plan for doing so. In some cases, the plan includes expanding the membership of the team to elicit additional expertise.

These six stages provide a framework for two or more individuals to use when collaborating to solve educational challenges. The stages, although presented in a logical sequence, are not mutually exclusive. Sometimes stages overlap. For example, the information gathering that occurs in Stage 2 may continue throughout the subsequent stages. The six-stage collaborative consultation process is flexible and may be used to solve a variety of problems (Idol, Nevin, & Paolucci-Whitcomb, 1994). Teachers who participate in collaborative consultation learn and benefit from others' expertise and ideas (see Validation Box 9.6).

Specialist Consultation

Specialist consultation is a process for providing indirect services to students with special needs. This approach to consultation typically involves a specialist (e.g., special education teacher, school psychologist, mental health worker, social worker) and one or more concerned persons (e.g., general education teachers, parents) who come together to address individual student or whole-class problems (Sheridan, Welch, & Orme, 1996). The specialist takes a lead role in facili-

VALIDATION BOX

9.6

Collaborative Consultation

A review of literature included 12 studies that were published between 1989 and 1992. The effectiveness of collaborative consultation was investigated in each study. Some studies evaluated the effects of collaborative consultation on students (preschool, elementary, and high school) and other studies evaluated the effects of collaborative consultation on teachers. Findings from the review revealed that *(a)* students with special education needs can be served effectively when their teachers collaborate to generate appropriate interventions, *(b)* school personnel can learn to collaborate with one another, and *(c)* collaborators can expect positive changes in schools, themselves, and students as a result of collaborative consultation. For more information see: (Idol, Nevin, & Paolucci-Whitcomb, 1994).

tating the problem-solving process and shares ideas and suggestions for the individuals seeking assistance. Even though the specialist takes a leadership role in this type of consultation, collegiality among professionals still is very important. Without a sense of camaraderie, teachers are less likely to value input from the specialist.

As in collaborative consultation, specialist consultation emphasizes the identification of objectives or desired outcomes and potential processes for achieving them. Step-by-step consultation procedures and relationship-building skills similar to those discussed in the preceding section are very helpful for achieving successful consultation sessions. In some specialist-consultation models, the specialist selects a target behavior related to the IEP goals of the student involved and then facilitates a problem-solving process in which the teacher generates and evaluates possible strategies for teaching the student (Peck, Killen, & Baumgart, 1989). Regardless of the specific process used, the true measure regarding the benefit of specialist consultation is whether or not the teacher receiving the assistance actually implements the new ideas and whether this implementation leads to student success (Noell & Witt, 1999; see Validation Box 9.7).

VALIDATION BOX 9.7

Specialist Consultation

▶ In a review of literature (1989 to 1998), six studies were identified that investigated the relationship between specialist consultation and intervention implementation. Positive outcomes were achieved in all six studies. In four of the studies, however, it was noted that performance feedback from the consultant increased the implementation rate. Thus, ongoing feedback that extends beyond the initial consultation session is very important. For more information see: (Noell & Witt, 1999).

▶ Another review of literature included 46 studies involving specialist consultation. The studies in this review were published from 1985 to 1995. Each of the 46 studies was categorized as "behavioral consultation," "mental health consultation," or "other consultation model." The most consistently positive results were obtained for the behavioral consultation model. Of all outcomes reported in the 21 behavioral consultation studies, 89 percent were considered positive and 11 percent were considered neutral. No negative outcomes were reported. Of all outcomes reported in the 5 mental health consultation studies, 57 percent were considered positive and 43 percent were considered neutral. Again, no negative outcomes were reported. Of all outcomes reported in the 13 studies categorized as other consultation models, 29 percent were considered positive, 65 percent were considered neutral, and 6 percent were considered negative. For more information see: (Sheridan, Welch, & Orme, 1996).

Intervention Assistance Teams

Many school districts use intervention assistance teams to facilitate problem solving related to general education students who are experiencing school difficulties. Intervention assistance teams work collaboratively to assist teachers with challenging students prior to considering a referral for special education services (Whitten & Dieker, 1995). On average, intervention assistance teams meet once a week and include general-education teachers and support personnel (e.g., counselor, learning disability specialist, consultant) (Whitten & Dieker, 1993). It also is important to have professionals on the team who have expertise and experience working with culturally and linguistically diverse students (Harris, 1995). Intervention assistance teams provide a positive forum for educators to become more culturally competent. Specifically, team members help one another consider the role culture plays in the teaching–learning process (Craig, Hull, Haggart, & Perez-Selles, 2000). It is important to determine whether a student's difficulties are due to sociocultural factors rather than specific learning or behavioral deficits. This determination is needed to avoid overreferring non-Anglo students for special education services and to determine strategies that are appropriate given the students' background experiences. Special care must be given to ensure that students' language acquisition and acculturation needs are met (Hoover & Collier, 1991).

Intervention assistance team meetings typically begin with the general education teacher sharing information regarding the student of concern. The student's strengths and weaknesses are discussed and the teacher's objectives for the student are shared. The team then brainstorms strategies and supports that are available to help the student. The team brainstorming encourages collaboration among the professionals and takes advantage of their varied expertise. The ultimate goal of the team is to identify interventions that will allow the student to succeed in the general education classroom and thus avoid the need for a special education referral. Some of the typical supports provided by intervention assistance teams include (a) suggesting specific strategies, adaptations, and accommodations; (b) scheduling modifications; (c) conducting observations; (d) sharing materials; (e) conferencing with parents; (f) identifying potential support personnel; and (g) charting student behavior (Murdick & Petch-Hogan, 1996; Whitten & Dieker, 1993). Once decisions are made regarding interventions to try, a plan for follow-up is devised. It is important for the team to come back together at a later date to determine whether the interventions were successful. If they were, great! If they weren't, then a referral for formal evaluation is advisable. Based on the outcome of this evaluation, decisions are made regarding the student's eligibility for special education services.

A variety of benefits emerge when intervention assistance teams are used. Included among these are:

- Students remain in the least restrictive environment with their peers and special education stigma is avoided (Chalfant, Pysh, & Moultrie, 1979; Graden, Casey, & Bonstrom, 1985; Nelson, Smith, Taylor, Dodd, & Reavis, 1991);

▶ Student performance improves based on team-generated interventions (Chalfant & Pysh, 1989);

▶ Student behavior problems are reduced (Fuchs et al., 1990; Sindelar, Griffin, Smith, & Watanabe, 1992);

▶ The number of special education referrals is reduced; referrals occur only after other interventions have failed; time and money typically spent on the referral process are saved and can be used to support students in general education settings (Evans, 1990; Fuchs, Fuchs, Bahr, Fernstrom, & Stecker, 1990; Sindelar et al., 1992);

▶ General education teachers receive support for addressing the needs of diverse groups of students (Chalfant, Pysh, & Moultrie, 1979);

▶ Data are gathered that are helpful if a special education referral ultimately is made (Bay, Bryan, & O'Connor, 1994); and

▶ Teachers learn from one another and increase their knowledge regarding instructional alternatives (Bay et al., 1994; Chalfant & Pysh, 1989).

As the amount of diversity among students increases, the need for collaboration among educators becomes critical. Intervention assistance teams provide a forum for teachers to work together to meet students' diverse needs. Pooling professional expertise and working together enhance the potential for success and promotes growth and development for both students and their teachers (see Validation Box 9.8).

VALIDATION BOX
9.8

Intervention Assistance Teams

▶ The prereferral intervention practices used in 49 school districts in Michigan were assessed through a survey study. Findings revealed that most districts either recommend (N = 28) or require (N = 19) prereferral interventions. Only two districts did not recommend or require a prereferral intervention process. Intervention teams primarily used prereferral strategies with students suspected of having mild disabilities. The prevalence of academic and behavioral strategies was equivalent. For more information see: (Bahr, 1994).

▶ In a survey study involving responses from 83 schools, information was acquired related to the use of intervention assistance teams. Findings revealed that 54 percent of the schools used intervention assistance teams and 45 percent had no formal teaming process. In some of the latter schools informal processes were used (e.g., principal met with general education teacher) or teachers simply documented prereferral activities without collaborating with other professionals. Findings also revealed that intervention assistance teams met the needs of 59 percent of the students referred to them, while 41 percent ultimately were referred for a formal evaluation to determine eligibility for special education services. Most of the teams (74 percent) used a collaborative approach to problem solving and attempted to reach consensus among team members. The teams found that a wide spectrum of teaching strategies were effective with students who had special needs. For more information see: (Whitten and Dieker, 1993).

▶ Sixteen studies involving prereferral intervention approaches and/or factors associated with prereferral intervention were included in a review of literature. Findings revealed that prereferral intervention approaches (a) have a positive effect on special education service delivery practices, (b) increase the abilities of teachers to educate students who are experiencing difficulty, (c) improve the attitudes of teachers toward such students, and (d) decrease the overidentification of students as having disabilities. For more information see: (Nelson, Smith, Taylor, Dodd, & Reavis, 1991).

▶ State Directors of Special Education for each of the 50 states and the District of Columbia participated in a 4-item telephone survey designed to determine the status of the state's prereferral procedure (i.e., required, recommended, or not required) and to identify provisions being made to implement prereferral strategies. Findings revealed that 19 of the state education agencies required a prereferral intervention process (PIP), 15 recommended PIP, 9 did not require PIP, and 8 reported using other intervention methods. In 84 percent of the states requiring PIP and 53 percent of the states recommending PIP, general education teachers were responsible for ensuring that the interventions were implemented. Fourteen of the 19 states that required PIP and 11 of the 15 states that recommended PIP reported that teachers received training on specific prereferral intervention strategies prior to initiating referrals for special education. Most of this training was provided by state, local, or division educational agencies. For more information see Wood, Lazzari, Davis, Sugai, & Carter, 1990).

▶ Five descriptive studies were conducted with 96 teacher assistance teams in seven states. Data from these studies revealed that team consultation (a) improves student performance, (b) results in appropriate strategies for students without disabilities, (c) assists teachers in meeting the needs of students with disabilities in general education classes, and (d) helps identify students who should be evaluated for special education services. The assistance teams in these studies were effective in reducing the total number of students evaluated for special education, improving teacher morale, facilitating faculty communication, and expediting the process for evaluating students with possible disabilities. Assistance teams were perceived as effective because of three primary factors: principal support, teacher support, and the professional and interpersonal skills of team members. For more information see: (Chalfant & Pysh, 1989).

Peer Coaching

Peer coaching is another collegial learning process that teachers use to improve their teaching. Typically, peer coaching models involve teams of two to three teachers who work together to learn new curricula, identify specific ways to improve teaching skills, and/or solve various classroom challenges. One of the major purposes of peer coaching is to "build communities of teachers who continuously engage in the study of their craft" (Showers, 1985, p. 43). Another major purpose of peer coaching is to help teachers transfer newly learned innovations into their classrooms. For example, after attending a staff development workshop on a validated reading program, peer coaching can be used to help teachers implement the new program. An underlying premise of peer coaching is that the process of teaching and learning can always improve and that peers who support one another can facilitate the improvement. Peer coaching processes provide a framework for bridging gaps in knowledge and skill among colleagues.

There are two primary coaching models: expert coaching and reciprocal coaching (Ackland, 1991). Expert coaching involves professionals with specific expertise working with teachers who want to acquire expertise in the same area. Typically, the coaches in this model are specially trained teachers who already have expertise in the area being coached. In some cases, veteran teachers serve as mentors to coach novice teachers. In other instances, select teachers are asked to attend workshops on some specific instructional innovation. These teachers then return to their schools and share their newly acquired expertise with other teachers. Additionally, the coaches observe and work with teachers in their classrooms. The reciprocal coaching model, on the other hand, involves teachers learning instructional techniques together. The teachers help one another implement the new techniques in their classrooms (Ackland, 1991; Vail, Tschantz, & Bevill, 1997; see Validation Box 9.9 on pp. 402–403 and Validation Box 9.10 on p. 404).

Expert and reciprocal coaching processes both involve a coaching-feedback cycle that usually includes a preobservation conference, classroom observation, and postobservation conference. During the preobservation conference, the coach and

---

VALIDATION BOX 9.9

Peer Coaching: Expert Model

▶ In a study involving 21 teachers and 6 peer coaches, the expert coaching model was evaluated. Peer coaches were teachers who had previous experience in training and were viewed as successful teachers by their principals. The peer coaches trained the 21 teachers in new teaching models and then provided peer coaching (weekly observations and conferences) to 15 of the 21 teachers. The coached teachers transferred the teaching models into their repertoires at greater rates than uncoached teachers. Additionally, students of the coached teachers performed better on a concept attainment measure than students of the uncoached teachers. For more information see: (Showers, 1984).

▶ A year-long study was conducted to determine whether trained teacher coaches could help other teachers improve their instructional practices in reading. There were eight teacher coaches and eight teacher coachees (i.e., teachers who received the coaching). After receiving training, the teacher coaches met with their coachees a minimum of one hour per week to discuss reading instruction, observe in other classes together, or demonstrate teaching strategies. After receiving coaching, teachers increased the amount of formal reading instruction in their classes and provided their students with more appropriate reading level materials. Additionally, time spent in noninstructional or transitional activities was decreased. For more information see: (Kurth, 1985).

▶ In another expert coaching study, two special education teachers served as coaches for 12 general education teachers over a two-year period of time. The coaching occurred in a large, inner-city elementary school where 99 percent of the student population was nonwhite and 42 percent were classified as limited English proficient. Over 97 percent of the students qualified for free or reduced-cost lunch programs. The coaches observed the teachers and then presented one or two suggestions for improving the learning environment. Next, the coaches and teachers developed an action plan for implementing the suggestion(s). This cycle was repeated throughout the study. Findings revealed: *(a)* implementation of the suggestions proceeded in an irregular fashion, reflecting how hard it was to change ingrained patterns of teaching behavior, *(b)* general and special education teachers approached instruction differently (discovery approaches versus systematic instruction), *(c)* general education teachers' perceptions regarding student performance revealed more specificity, more responsibility, and more understanding of students' needs as the study progressed, and *(d)* general education teachers realized they could promote student learning through a variety of teaching strategies and techniques. For more information see: (Gersten, Morvant, & Brengelman, 1995).

▶ In another study involving expert coaching, there were four elementary teachers and one coach (i.e., a retired teacher with 32 years of experience). The teachers received inservice on an integrated instructional approach and the direct instruction teaching model. Each teacher participated in seven collaborative sessions with the coach. The teacher and the coach participated in implementation of the new teaching approach and then met to evaluate the lesson and generate ideas for improvement in future lessons. Findings indicated that teaching refinements are more likely to occur when teachers collaborate with a coach than when they work independently. The four teachers in this study refined and improved their teaching after collaborating with the coach. The students in the four teachers' classes increased their active engagement in the lessons. For more information see: (Kohler, Crilley, & Shearer, 1997).

coachee (i.e., teacher being coached) form a collaborative partnership. The purpose for the coaching is clarified, goals are set, and the coachee identifies what assistance he or she wants from the coach. The focus of the coaching observation is agreed on during the preobservation conference. A variety of options are available for classroom observations. Most coaching models involve the coach observing the coachee, but alternatives to this are available. For example, the coach and coachee

Peer Coaching: Reciprocal Model

▶ A yearlong study was conducted with 41 high school teachers to investigate the use of reciprocal peer coaching. The teachers developed action plans to improve their teaching and selected a colleague to form a peer-coaching pair. Throughout the year, teachers participated in two coaching observations and follow-up conferences each month. Interviews and questionnaires were used to evaluate the peer-coaching program. Interviews revealed that the frequency of observations and high comfort level with peers lead to a much higher rate of instructional growth than working with supervisors. Several teachers stated that one or two visits per year by an administrator had no impact on their teaching. Questionnaire findings revealed that 97 percent of the teachers met their action plan goals and 88 percent indicated that peer coaching made a significant difference in their instruction compared to previous years. For more information see: (Munro & Elliott, 1987).

▶ Another reciprocal peer-coaching study involving preobservation conferences, classroom observations, and postobservation conferences was conducted with 22 elementary teachers. Teachers selected a peer-coaching partner and determined who would be coach and who would be coachee. After two cycles of the peer-coaching process, the roles switched to provide all participants opportunities to be a coach. Results indicated that after participating in the coaching process, teachers significantly increased conceptual levels involved in thinking about their teaching (indicated through responses to open-ended statements). Additionally, 3 of the 5 teacher pairs showed a gain in their use of discourse on a Reflective Teaching Index. Of the 22 teachers, 18 reported that the peer-coaching process changed their teaching in positive ways. For more information see: (Phillips & Glickman, 1991).

▶ The effectiveness of reciprocal peer coaching was investigated in a study involving three kindergarten teachers and their classes. The teachers' goal in this study was to improve their ability to implement student-pair activities (i.e., students working together to apply what was taught in a lesson). The teachers were particularly concerned with enhancing the participation of students with social and behavioral needs. The teachers took turns observing one another and the target students. Follow-up conferences were held to discuss and jointly assess the observed lessons. The coaching resulted in the teachers increasing their use of suggestions, prompts, questions, and related talk to facilitate students' social interaction with classmates. Additionally, the teachers learned to employ spontaneous adaptations in academic materials, skills, and/or social interaction processes among the student pairs. Several of the target students improved their social interaction skills. For more information see: (Kohler, Ezell, & Paluselli, 1999).

may decide to observe together in classrooms other than their own to obtain new ideas to help the coachee (Kurth, 1985). Another option is for teachers to reverse the typical coaching roles. With this option, the teacher doing the teaching is considered the coach and the teacher observing is the coachee. The teacher who is observing is doing so to learn from his or her colleague (Showers & Joyce, 1996). The postobservation conference is used to reflect on the observed lesson. Self-reflection and support from peers are important components of the follow-up conference. Judgmental comments are avoided to promote positive collaborative relationships.

In addition to using the coaching feedback cycle, many coaching models include teacher support groups. These groups consist of three or four coaching teams. The support groups meet on a regular basis to discuss the instructional techniques they're learning and to assist one another with challenges they're facing. These groups provide additional support beyond the immediate coaching team.

Peer coaching is a flexible staff-development process that helps teachers think about and improve their instructional performance. The process is adaptable and allows teachers to meet a variety of goals. Specifically, peer coaching has been used to help teachers:

- Improve student learning through improved instruction
- Translate theory to practice
- Implement what is learned in workshops and inservice training sessions
- Refine and master new teaching models
- Reflect on teaching
- Provide professional support to colleagues
- Learn from one another
- Build positive school communities
- Challenge themselves
- Try new innovations
- Alleviate burnout and isolation
- Foster communication and trust
- Exchange knowledge and materials
- Receive ongoing, positive feedback

Regardless of the purpose for the coaching or which of the two models (i.e., expert or reciprocal) is used, there are some general recommendations that apply to implementing peer coaching. Following these suggestions increases the likelihood that peer coaching processes will result in success. First, participation in peer coaching should be voluntary and teachers should collaborate with individuals with whom they feel comfortable. Initially, some teachers are uncomfortable with the idea of another adult coming into their classroom and watching them teach; thus it is important for teachers to be paired with peers they trust and enjoy. Collaborative relationships emerge more quickly if teachers have a voice regarding their partners. Coercing someone to participate in peer coaching and/or to participate with particular peers is not likely to result in genuine collaboration. Second, teachers who want to participate in peer coaching should be supported to do so. Training should be provided to ensure that everyone understands the coaching objectives and designated procedures. Additionally, there needs to be support related to the logistics involved in coaching. For example, there needs to be time for pre- and postconferences. The logistics of the classroom observations also need to be worked out (e.g., coverage of the observing teacher's class). Third, every effort should be made to avoid "evaluative tones" during the coaching process. Teachers need to feel safe and supported, not judged; otherwise, the collaborative nature of coaching breaks down. A variety of strategies are used to avoid evaluative tones. Specifically, the coach uses supportive rather than judgmental language (see Table 9.1). The coachee demonstrates leadership in identifying areas needing support and determines the coach's role in providing the support (see Table 9.2). The coach asks questions to help the coachee reflect on his or her performance (see Table 9.3) and assists the coachee in a variety of ways (e.g., coplanning, sharing materials and ideas, listening to concerns, seeking additional resources).

TABLE 9.1

Supportive Versus Judgmental Coaching Language

Supportive Coaching Language	Judgmental Coaching Language
What would you like help with?	I think you should work on behavior management.
I noticed Sydney answered only one question during the lesson. Is this typical?	Why don't you engage Sydney in the lesson instead of calling on the same students all the time?
How do you feel about the lesson?	I think the first part of the lesson was great, but things started falling apart midway through. Wouldn't you agree?
Would you like to come watch my math lesson tomorrow? I'm going to teach the students how to represent multiplication problems using manipulative devices.	Remember to give the students a few minutes to experiment with the manipulative devices, tell them to put the manipulative devices aside while you are giving directions, or give them the manipulative devices after the directions. Then you won't have half the class playing around.
What would you like me to do when I come into your classroom?	I'll count the number of times you use specific praise statements and the number of times you could have used praise statements, but didn't. Genuine-sounding praise is really important, you know.

TABLE 9.2

Dialogue Example and Nonexample of Coachee Leadership

Coachee Leadership	Lack of Coachee Leadership
Coach: What would you like help with?	Coach: What would you like help with?
Coachee: I really want to get better at managing math lessons that involve the use of manipulative devices. Would you come and observe one of these lessons?	Coachee: I don't know. Maybe you could just come in and see what you see and we can go from there.
Coach: Sure. Is there something in particular you're concerned about?	Coach: Are you feeling stressed about any particular curricular area or any classroom procedure?
Coachee: I don't feel that I have the students' full attention during these lessons. I'm particularly concerned about Ray. I'm going to try to engage him through questioning techniques at the beginning of the lesson and then I'm going to have him work with Bobby to solve some addition problems. Maybe you can record his on- and off-task behaviors in both parts of the lesson and then we can compare the two.	Coachee: No, I don't let the stress get to me. I just tell myself that stress is part of the job.
	Coach: Are there any students in your class that you're particularly concerned about?
Coach: Sounds good to me. Is there anything else I can help with?	Coachee: I don't play favorites. I'm concerned about all of them. Why don't you just come in and maybe you can see something that I should work on. I think Mr. Coercion (the principal) really wants us to do this coaching thing, so if you come in and watch me, and then I go in and watch you, we can say we did it. Extra brownie points never hurt, you know.
Coachee: No, not that I can think of.	
Coach: OK. Thanks for inviting me into your class. This will be fun.	

TABLE 9.3

Prompting Questions That Help the Coachee Identify Strengths of the Lesson as Well as Things to Do Differently in the Future

1. What was the best thing about that lesson?
2. Is there anything about the lesson you'd change next time? If so, what and why?
3. Did things go as you planned? If not, why not?
4. Were there any surprises?
5. What did you learn from preparing and teaching this lesson?
6. What did the students learn?
7. Were the objectives for the lesson met?
8. Were students' needs addressed?
9. Were you comfortable with the pacing?
10. Overall, how do you think the lesson went?

Teacher Study Groups

Collegial learning also is promoted through teacher study groups. Study groups provide a forum for teachers to engage in professional growth and development. The three major functions of study groups are *(a)* to help teachers implement curricular and instructional innovations, *(b)* to plan school improvement, and *(c)* to study research on teaching and learning (Murphy, 1992). Involvement in study groups promotes a sense of community among colleagues. Specifically, a study group is defined by Birchak and colleagues as a group of people who:

> come together to talk and create theoretical and practical understandings with each other. This talk integrates theory and practice, sharing and dialogue in powerful ways. It is not an inservice or staff meeting but it supports these other professional meetings. It is a place where educators push their thinking and support others, but it is not a place where change is imposed on its members or where certain members decide on the needs of other members. (p. 28)

There are different types of study groups: whole-faculty groups, job-alike groups, topic-centered groups, teacher research groups, professional literature groups, and special-project groups (Birchak et al., 1998; Murphy & Lick, 1998). These groups are used in a variety of ways to meet different purposes and promote new learning.

Whole-faculty study groups consist of teachers who teach at the same school. Through a consensus process, the faculty at a specific school agree that every teacher will participate in a study group that meets regularly to support whole-school improvement. These groups have an organizational focus. They address shared issues and concerns and promote positive staff relationships. Their primary goal is to get the entire faculty to implement and integrate effective teaching and learning practices into school programs so that student learning increases. The collective energy and synergy of the whole faculty helps move the school forward. Improvement within individual classrooms ultimately results in an improved school. Whole-faculty study groups are most successful when all teachers understand the group process, when at least 75 percent of the faculty endorse the process, and when the whole faculty is involved in analyzing student data and identifying student needs that the study groups can address (Murphy & Lick, 1998).

Job-alike groups include individuals who share the same type positions (e.g., principals' study group, first grade teachers' study group; curriculum coordinators' study group). Thus, group members share many similar concerns. Job-alike groups typically have members from different schools who come together to study common issues and concerns.

Topic-centered groups are composed of individuals who are interested in the same topic. These groups frequently are smaller interest groups within a larger organization. These groups may meet for brief periods of time to pursue a particular topic and then disband when members are ready to move on to new areas of interest.

Research groups consist of teachers interested in collecting data within their classrooms. In some groups, the research projects are collaborative and, in others, each member is involved in an individual research project. The group provides a forum for teachers to share their findings, obtain support, and receive suggestions from other teacher researchers.

One of the most popular study group formats involves reading and discussing professional literature. Members of the study group read a professional book, journal articles, and/or research reports about teaching and then discuss the material with one another (Birchak et al., 1998; Fishbaugh & Hecimovic, 1994; Makibbin & Sprague, 1991; Powell, Berliner, & Casanova, 1992; Sparks & Hirsh, 1997). This process helps teachers translate research into their own classroom practices. Discussion typically focuses on understanding the research, evaluating the credibility of the research, and implementing the research.

Study groups also are used to work on special projects. For example, some groups consist of teachers who want to develop, expand, or learn new curricula; other groups meet to create meaningful unit and lesson plans (Glatthorn, 1987; Makibbin & Sprague, 1991). Study-group formats also provide adult learning experiences. For example, teachers read and discuss novels written for adults or practice creative writing. These adult learning experiences are then discussed with an emphasis on implications for their own classroom teaching practices (Birchak et al., 1998).

Although most study groups meet face-to-face, it also is possible for teachers to use technology such as the Internet to communicate and learn together. E-mail and listservs allow an individual teacher to send messages to everyone in the group simultaneously. This technology provides opportunities for study group membership to extend beyond the local school district. Teachers from all parts of the country share ideas, pose and respond to questions, and benefit from others' expertise. Moreover, teachers may subscribe to electronic journals, read them online, and then join a discussion group with other teachers interested in the same topic. Online continuing education classes and online professional development conferences also are available. Teachers who participate in these online learning opportunities may subsequently form an online study group to discuss the newly acquired information (Herner & Higgins, 2000).

Rich (1995) surveyed teacher groups in the United States and Canada and found that study groups emerge in a variety of ways. In some cases, teachers initiate the study group process because they want to get together with other teachers to share ideas and concerns. New curricular innovations sometimes are the impetus behind the formation of these study groups. Teacher-initiated study groups also address issues related to professional knowledge, political action, and professional problem solving. They frequently meet social development needs of professionals as well. Friendships emerge, trust develops, and teachers acquire a sense of belonging.

Sometimes study groups emerge as a result of participation in other groups. For example, teachers who attend a particular workshop or training session may decide to continue meeting at their respective schools or within group members' homes. The meeting agendas are created to promote the continuation of learning among the teachers. Members of these groups tend to focus on professional reading and sharing classroom ideas. As members become confident with their knowledge and ideas, they begin to think about ways to share their information with other groups of teachers.

Another way that teacher groups emerge is through the efforts of school district administrators, consultants, and/or staff developers. These individuals initiate "voluntary" group meetings. Rich's (1995) survey study revealed that teachers sometimes felt obligated to participate even though the groups were promoted as being voluntary. The agendas for these meetings sometimes are controlled by the school district administrators and sometimes controlled by the teachers. The typical agendas for these groups is implementation of new curricula. Social support for teachers seems to be less evident in groups that emerge due to administrative efforts.

Regardless of how teacher groups emerge, the role of teacher talk is critical to the group process. Without free-flowing talk, teachers remain isolated in their own classrooms and miss opportunities to reflect on their practices and beliefs with the support of others. The quality of the free-flowing talk is, of course, influenced by the amount of trust among members of the group. As time progresses and trust increases, the group process matures and becomes more meaningful.

Educators and researchers have identified important characteristics of effective study groups. These experts agree that study groups are likely to result in positive outcomes when members:

- Select the topics to be studied (Murphy, 1992; Powell, Berliner, & Casanova, 1992; Rich, 1995);
- Select the materials to be used (Powell et al., 1992);
- Set the agenda for the study group and develop an action plan (Murphy & Lick, 1998; Rich, 1995; Zins, Maher, Murphy, & Wess, 1988);
- Establish nonthreatening, supportive environment and norms that encourage participation (Murphy & Lick, 1998; Zins et al., 1988);
- Share ideas openly and precisely and reflect on their practice (Makibbin & Sprague, 1991);
- Direct the meetings (Rich, 1995);
- Recognize that each individual in the group has equal status (Murphy & Lick, 1998);
- Evaluate the effectiveness of the group (Murphy & Lick, 1998);
- Facilitate networking processes that continue outside the group meetings (Murphy & Lick, 1998; Zins et al., 1988);
- Meet on a regular basis (e.g., once a week for about an hour) (Makibbin & Sprague, 1991; Murphy, 1992; Murphy & Lick, 1998; Sparks & Hirsh, 1997);
- Rotate leadership (Murphy & Lick, 1998; Zins et al., 1988);
- Keep the groups small (i.e., two to eight teachers) (Glatthorn, 1987; Murphy, 1992; Murphy & Lick, 1998; Sparks & Hirsh, 1997); and
- Keep logs to summarize group activities (Murphy & Lick, 1998).

Although there is much consensus among experts regarding these characteristics, there are differing opinions with regard to whether participation should be voluntary or mandatory. Those who believe participation should be voluntary (Birchak et al., 1998; Paquette, 1987) indicate that teachers will benefit only if they *want* to be a part of the group. Murphy (1992), on the other hand, suggests that participation should not be voluntary. She says:

> It is not optional that student learning improve and that schools get better. Volunteerism supports individual, not organizational, development. I understand that there is a fine line between individual rights and the rights of the organization. While I support the individual in selecting development activities that meet personal needs, those individual rights should not hinder the organization's progress. (p. 73)

Regardless of whether participation is voluntary or mandatory, it is helpful to have someone serve as facilitator of the study group. This person may be from the school where the group meets or from outside the school. Some groups use the same facilitator for each meeting; others rotate the responsibility. The primary role of the facilitator is to enact the structures that the group has agreed on and to promote productive talk during the meetings. Specifically, the facilitator:

▶ Develops strategies and language to support others in sharing their experience;

▶ Helps participants establish credibility (i.e., supports their connections between theory and practice);

▶ Creates a trusting environment (i.e., mediates personal conflicts, reflects on the group process, discusses personal interrelationships, and relates personal issues to a broader context of education);

▶ Negotiates individual agendas and develops a shared group agenda;

▶ Encourages and acknowledges the contributions of a variety of voices to avoid domination of group "talk time";

▶ Keeps the conversation flowing and helps members reflect by asking questions and summarizing comments;

▶ Reinforces and monitors the structure and focus of discussion, particularly at the beginning and ending of sessions;

▶ Makes resources available to enhance the conversation;

▶ Steps back from participating in the discussion but knows when to share. (Birchak et al., 1998)

Study groups that are organized well with a clear purpose offer support for teacher learning. These groups provide a forum for teachers to acquire new information about teaching and learning through interactions with peers while simultaneously receiving personal and professional support. Members of study groups get to know one another well and develop a genuine sense of community and professionalism. Study groups stimulate both individual and collective growth, which results in overall school improvement (Sanacore, 1993; see Validation Box 9.11 on p. 412).

Study Groups

▶ Survey research involving 26 teacher study/support groups in the United States and Canada was conducted to investigate study groups and how they evolve. Study groups that evolved because of exposure to other groups used similar procedures as spontaneous, teacher-initiated study groups. It was noted, however, that study groups that evolved because of exposure to other groups confined their learning to topics related to the initial group purpose (e.g., workshop topic), whereas teacher-initiated groups explored a broader range of topics. Findings also revealed that special care must be taken when groups are formed by school district administrators because contrived support doesn't meet teachers' needs. These groups function best when the teachers set the agendas to ensure that their personal and professional needs are addressed. For more information see: (Rich, 1995).

▶ The use of study groups within a high school was investigated. There were 15 heterogeneous study groups with four to six instructional staff members in each group. The groups met for one hour once a week to study curricula, assessment, and school climate issues in order to improve student performance. This school ranked second lowest in the district in grade point average and had the second highest course failure rate. After implementing teacher study groups, this high school's cumulative grade point average was third highest in the district and the course failure rate dropped by 40 percent overall and 62 percent for students identified as limited English proficient. For more information see: (Charles & Clark, 1995).

▶ In another study involving 20 school psychologists, interviews and a survey were used to obtain information related to experience as a participant in an ongoing study group. Ninety percent of the respondents believed their job enthusiasm increased because of their group participation and 95 percent reported a substantial increase in the number of times they contacted one another to consult about specific cases. All respondents reported increased familiarity with other psychological services programs and 90 percent reported they increased the range of services they offered. Respondents also reported increased involvement in professional organizations, increased "intellectual curiosity," and increased knowledge and skills as a result of study group participation. For more information see: (Zins, Maher, Murphy, & Wess, 1988).

Benefits of Peer Collegiality

Clearly, peer collegiality comes in many forms. Each of the processes discussed in this section (i.e., structured dialogue, collaborative problem solving, collaborative consultation, specialist consultation, intervention assistance teams, peer coaching, and teacher study groups) promotes professional growth and development among teachers. Each provides a forum for teachers to work together to improve their teaching and consequently improve student learning.

Teaching is a challenging profession with many demands. Peer collegiality helps teachers meet these demands. The sense of "we're in this together" is fostered when colleagues work together, share ideas, and support one another (see Validation Box 9.12).

Action Research

Action research is another staff development method that teachers use to improve their practice and develop their professional skills. Action research is research conducted by teachers to answer educational questions of significant interest. The goal

---

VALIDATION BOX
9.12

Peer Collegiality

▸ In a study involving 15 teachers in six schools, retrospective interviews were used to investigate collegiality in the workplace. The teachers in this study successfully implemented a new approach (i.e., the process approach) for teaching reading and writing. The interviews were used to investigate the ways teachers had used collegial relations when they made the instructional changes. Findings revealed that collegial talk was a critical component in the gradual process of learning to teach reading and writing in a different manner. Some talk was planned and scheduled (e.g., workshops, class), but much of the talk occurred on an informal basis. All 15 teachers named at least one colleague with whom they talked on a daily basis about concrete issues related to the new instructional approach. More experienced teachers talked about the theoretical underpinnings of the approach; less experienced teachers talked in more concrete terms and were more prone to backsliding in their implementation. For more information see: (Ellis, 1993).

▸ In a study involving 105 teachers and 14 administrators, organizational characteristics conducive to continued "learning on the job" were studied. Four relatively successful schools and two relatively unsuccessful schools were selected for the study. Interviews supplemented by observation were used to collect data. The successful and unsuccessful schools differed in their norms of interaction among staff. In successful schools, more than in unsuccessful schools, teachers pursued a greater range of professional interactions with colleagues and/or administrators. These interactions included talk about instruction, structured observations, and collaborative planning. Collegial interactions in successful schools occurred in more locations and with greater frequency than interactions in unsuccessful schools. Additionally, in the successful schools, a greater number of teachers were involved in collegial interactions, and these teachers used a more precise, shared language than teachers in the unsuccessful schools. For more information see: (Little, 1982).

of the research is to improve teaching and learning. Action research typically follows six sequential steps: *(a)* formulate research question, topic to explore, or problem statement; *(b)* plan for data collection; *(c)* collect data; *(d)* analyze data; *(e)* report results; and *(f)* take action (Sagor, 1992).

The first step involves selecting a question to answer or a topic to explore. The question or topic is something about which the teacher cares deeply. It relates to teaching and learning and is within the teacher's sphere of influence (e.g., ways to motivate students) (Sagor, 1997). Teachers select meaningful topics that focus on student learning (Calhoun, 1994). To be meaningful, teachers need to be able to put the findings from their research into action. Once the topic of research is selected, decisions are made related to data collection. What data will help answer the question or address the problem? Who should collect the data? How and when should data collection take place? Are there existing sources of data (e.g., student cumulative files)? In some cases, it is helpful to seek input from others (e.g., other teachers, research facilitators, administrators, university researchers) when planning how to collect the data. After these decisions are made, the data are collected and analyzed to determine what has been learned. It is typically helpful to obtain data from multiple sources to develop an accurate picture of how students are performing and of what students are experiencing. Multiple sources of data result in greater knowledge and understanding of the learner and the learning environment (Calhoun, 1994). School personnel who participate in action research frequently have opportunities to share their findings. On-site sharing sessions with other teachers involved in action research and/or districtwide conferences are potential places for teachers to share what they've learned with others. The final step in the research process is to put the findings into action. This, of course, is the heart of the process because it results in improved practice. Some teachers find it helpful to use study groups (discussed earlier) along with action research. When this is done, teachers combine information from professional reading with findings from their action research projects to make informed decisions about their practice (Joyce, Wolf, & Calhoun, 1993). One of the nice things about action research is it frequently leads to additional questions and serves as a trigger for another round of investigation (Sparks & Hirsh, 1997). Thus, an evolutionary process of improved practice occurs.

Action research is conducted by individual teachers or teams of teachers who share similar interests and/or concerns. The research question or problem frequently dictates whether an individual or team approach is used. The basic strategies for conducting action research are the same for individual and team approaches. Team research, however, requires cooperation among teachers and administrators, whereas individual research does not (McLean, 1995). Both individual and team approaches result in useful information that can be used to solve educational problems. When teams of teachers get involved in action research, within a culture that supports such investigation, schoolwide issues can be investigated and teachers benefit from the collective wisdom of the team. It has been noted that schools with organizational cultures that support action research are more productive and more satisfying places to work than are schools void of teacher inquiry (Rosenholtz, 1989).

Sagor (1997) reported numerous characteristics of successful action research programs based on work that he completed in two high schools. Specifically, he identified four cultural markers that predicted whether or not action research would be a positive force for educational change within a school: *(a)* common focus, *(b)* collective locus of control (efficacy), *(c)* common cultural perceptions, and *(d)* appreciation of leadership. In other words, action research is most successful in schools where faculty members have common and clear understandings of the school's goals and are quick to protect these goals. Additionally, action research is likely to succeed in schools where teachers feel that change is within their collective power, where teachers perceive their school culture in very similar ways, and where teachers view leadership from teachers and/or administrators as supportive, but with high expectations. Miller and Pine (1990) also commented on the conditions that are needed for action research to succeed. They indicated that teachers need *(a)* time (as part of their regular load) for discussion, reflection, and investigation; *(b)* an atmosphere with freedom to experiment; *(c)* technical assistance and consulting services; *(c)* reasonable material and financial support; *(c)* university credit or staff development credit; *(f)* opportunities to share their work (e.g., in-house publications, conferences, workshops); and *(g)* support from administrators. When these factors are in place, action research tends to be an ongoing process that promotes healthy, self-renewing school environments (see Validation Box 9.13).

Teacher Portfolios

In Chapter 8, portfolios were discussed as a tool for monitoring student progress. The use of portfolio assessment no longer exists only for students. Teachers now use portfolios to monitor their own professional development. "A teaching portfolio is a structured collection of teacher and student work created across diverse contexts

---

VALIDATION BOX
9.13

Action Research

Two elementary teachers and four middle school teachers participated in a study designed to examine their beliefs about using action research to redesign instruction to meet new state standards of learning. Qualitative data were gathered from action research projects, participants' written reflections, focus groups, and a six-month follow-up survey. The results revealed that the students of these six teachers gained a more explicit understanding of the connection between learning and assessment, took responsibility for their learning, and received improved instruction. The teachers gained autonomy and confidence for redesigning instruction, improved their problem-solving abilities, and learned to use classroom data more effectively. For more information see: (Neapolitan, 1999).

At the end of a busy week, Ms. Campbell enjoys working on her portfolio. It gives her a chance to reflect on her teaching. She thinks about her successes and identifies areas in which she would like to improve. This quiet time helps Ms. Campbell maintain a positive perspective related to her teaching.

over time, framed by reflection and enriched through collaboration, that has as its ultimate aim the advancement of teacher and student learning" (Wolf & Dietz, 1998, p. 13). In other words, portfolios provide teachers with opportunities for self-reflection and collegial interactions based on documented episodes of their own teaching experiences (Wolf, 1996).

Teaching portfolios include information about a teacher's practice and carefully and thoughtfully document a set of accomplishments over an extended period of time. Portfolios help teachers *(a)* think about their teaching, *(b)* identify areas in which they'd like to improve, and *(c)* create an individualized professional development plan. Portfolios primarily are used to help teachers advance their own learning. Some state departments of education require teachers to maintain portfolios to complete beginning teacher programs and/or to renew professional teaching licenses (Golomb, 1996). Additionally, in some school districts, teachers use portfolios to become eligible for salary bonuses. Portfolios also are used to earn national recognition and/or advanced certification from professional education organizations (e.g., National Board for Professional Teaching Standards) (Wolf, 1996). Thus, portfolios serve a variety of purposes and can be used over the course of one's career (Bartell, Kaye, & Morin, 1998).

Portfolios typically contain a combination of teaching artifacts (e.g., unit overviews, lesson plans, student projects, assessment tools, maps of classroom environments, class newsletters, annual evaluations, videotapes, letters of commendation, student case studies) and written reflections (Athanases, 1993; Wagenen & Hibbard, 1998; Wolf, 1996). If the purpose of the portfolio is to improve one's teaching, then evidence of less-than-perfect lessons are included along with the improved versions. Materials are included that demonstrate learning from one's own instruction. Materials also are included that show the positive impact that teacher learning has on student performance (Wagenen & Hibbard, 1998). This type of portfolio provides opportunities for teachers to think about their lessons and identify the critical components that are needed to improve them.

Regardless of what materials are included in the portfolio, it is important to organize them in a logical, useful manner. Some portfolios include a table of contents and three sections: background information, teaching artifacts and reflections, and professional information. The first section, background information, includes a résumé, description of the teaching context, educational philosophy, and teaching goals. The second section in the portfolio includes the artifacts along with written statements describing the significance of the selected items. The final section, professional information, includes formal evaluations, letters of commendation, and a list of professional activities (Wolf, 1996). Portfolios also can be organized around a philosophy-of-teaching statement. This statement is the first item in the portfolio. Next, a curriculum unit that reflects the teaching philosophy is included. Finally, an assessment of the unit is designed and placed in the portfolio. This type of portfolio illustrates the interconnectedness of the teacher's beliefs, instruction, and assessment (Kelly, 1999). Another way to organize portfolios is to have three sections: What? So What? and Now What? The *What?* section includes a collection of assignment, assessments, and student work samples. The *So What?* section includes an analysis of the quality of the student work and the connections between the teaching activities and the students' performance. The *Now What?* section includes recommendations for improving instructional materials and strategies to help students perform even better (Wagenen & Hibbard, 1998). Finally, portfolios can be organized using professional standards or school goals (Wolf & Dietz, 1998).

As was discussed in Chapter 8, digital portfolios also are an option. Software programs (e.g., *Electronic Portfolio, Grady Profile Portfolio Assessment*) are available that allow teachers to organize artifacts that represent their teaching endeavors. These programs have the capability of integrating sound, video, graphics, and text into the portfolio. Digital portfolios can be upgraded and reorganized easily. Moreover, the contents can be cross-referenced in many ways (Martin, 1999). A certain degree of technical expertise and support is needed to develop digital portfolios.

Both paper-based and digital portfolios provide opportunities for teachers to think about their successes as well as areas in which they'd like to improve. They are useful when collaborating with and learning from other teachers, and, perhaps most importantly, they promote career-long learning among teachers through self-evaluation and self-regulation. This type of professional development process is meaningful for many teachers (see Validation Box 9.14 on p. 418).

VALIDATION BOX

9.14

Teacher Portfolios

▶ A survey study was conducted to determine implications of using portfolios during job searches and for ongoing staff development. The participants in this study were 45 recent graduates who were just beginning their careers as teachers. Results indicated that these beginning teachers used portfolios created in their teacher preparation program during 83 percent of their job interviews. Over half of the participants reported that they updated their professional portfolios on an ongoing basis. They also noted that portfolios were a useful tool for reflecting on the professional and personal growth during their first years in the classroom. For more information see: (Jonson & Hodges, 1998).

▶ A longitudinal study investigated the use of portfolios among three cohort groups: undergraduates who were preparing to enter a year-long internship program; post-baccalaureate interns taking part in the year-long intensive, internship program; and graduates of the program in their first or second years of teaching. Data from ten case studies were reviewed to investigate the use of portfolios over time. Findings revealed that *(a)* teacher reflection became more elaborated over time, *(b)* conversation about portfolio entries supports teacher awareness of the knowledge of practice, *(c)* the reflective process reveals significant aspects of one's teaching practice that ultimately are identified as part on one's teaching philosophy, and *(d)* the process of reflection that emerges from public, collaborative inquiry results in learning about oneself, and about the values one holds for teaching and learning. For more information see: (Lyons, 1998).

Practice Activities

▶ Attend a teacher inservice or training session and look for evidence of partnership learning techniques. Evaluate the effectiveness of these techniques.

▶ Role-play a structured dialogue process.

▶ Role-play the collaborative problem-solving process.

▶ Outline a plan for developing special expertise to share with other teachers.

▶ Interview school personnel to learn about various problem-solving approaches used in nearby schools.

▶ Conduct coaching sessions with peers.

▶ Develop a study group to acquire in-depth knowledge about one of the topics in this text.

▶ Outline a plan for an action research study.

▶ Conduct an action research study.

▶ Organize a portfolio related to current teaching experiences.

```
 ┌─────────────┐
 │ P O S T │ ORGANIZER
 └─────────────┘
```

Engaging in professional growth and development is very important for all teachers. Learning to teach is a career-long endeavor, an ongoing process of improving educational practice. Teachers must constantly add to their instructional repertoire in order to meet the needs of diverse groups of students. Ongoing professional development serves as nourishment for teachers who are hungry to make a difference in the lives of their students. A variety of methods are available to improve teaching and consequently the learning of students. The professional development practices discussed in this chapter are beneficial for veteran teachers as well as novices. Moreover, they can be used alone or combined with other practices.

References

Ackland, R. (1991). A review of the peer coaching literature. Journal of Staff *Development, 12,* 22–27.

Anderson, E. M., & Shannon, A. L. (1988). Toward a conceptualization of mentoring. *Journal of Teacher Education, 39*(1), 38–42.

Athanases, S. Z. (1993). Adapting and tailoring lessons: Fostering teacher reflection to meet varied student needs. *Teacher Education Quarterly, 20*(1), 71–81.

Bahr, M. W. (1994). The status and impact of prereferral intervention: "We need a better way to determine success." *Psychology in the Schools, 31*, 309–318.

Bartell, C. A., Kaye, C., & Morin, J. A. (1998). Portfolio conversation: A mentored journey. *Teacher Education Quarterly, 25*(1), 129–139.

Bay, M., Bryan, T., & O'Connor, R. (1994). Teachers assisting teachers: A prereferral model for urban educators. *Teacher Education and Special Education, 17*(1), 10–21.

Berman, B., & Friederwitzer, F. (1981). A pragmatic approach to inservice education. *Action in Teacher Education, 3*(1), 51–58.

Birchak, B., Connor, C., Crawford, K. M., Kahn, L. H., Kaser, S., Turner, S. & Short, K. G. (1998). *Teacher study groups: Building community through dialogue and reflection*. Urbana, IL: National Council of Teachers of English.

Brennan, S., Thames, W., & Roberts, R. (1999). Mentoring with a mission. *Educational Leadership, 56*(8), 49–52.

Calhoun, E. F. (1994). *How to use action research in the self-renewing school*. Alexandria, VA: Association for Supervision and Curriculum Development.

Chalfant, J. C., & Pysh, M. V. (1989). Teacher assistance teams: Five descriptive studies on 96 teams. *Remedial and Special Education, 10*(6), 49–58.

Chalfant, J. C., Pysh, M. V., & Moultrie, R. (1979). Teacher assistance teams: A model for within-building problem solving. *Learning Disability Quarterly, 2*, 85–96.

Charles, L. & Clark, P. (1995). Study groups in practice: Whole-faculty study groups at Sweetwater Union High School. *Journal of Staff Development, 16*(3), 49–50.

Craig, S., Hull, K., Haggart, A. G., & Perez-Selles, M. (2000). Promoting cultural competence through teacher assistance teams. *Teaching Exceptional Children, 32* (3), 6–12.

Ellis, N. E. (1993). Collegiality from the teacher's perspective: Social contexts for professional development. *Action in Teacher Education, 25*(1),42–47.

Evans, R. (1990). Making mainstreaming work through prereferral consultation. *Educational Leadership, 48*(1), 73–77.

Fishbaugh, M. S. E., & Hecimovic, T. (1994). *Teacher study groups as a means of rural professional development* (Report No. RC 019 570). Austin, TX: Paper presented at the Annual National Conference of the American Council on Rural Special Education. (ERIC Document Reproduction Service No. ED 369 600)

Fuchs, D., Fuchs, L. S., Bahr, M. W., Fernstrom, P., & Stecker, P. M. (1990). Prereferral intervention: A perspective approach. *Exceptional Children, 56*, 493–513.

Fuchs, D., Fuchs, L., Gilman, S., Reeder, P., Bahr, M., Fernstrom, P., & Roberts, H. (1990). Prereferral intervention through teacher consultation: Mainstream assistance teams. *Academic Therapy, 25*, 263–276.

Gersten, R., Morvant, M., & Brengelman, S. (1995). Close to the classroom is close to the bone: Coaching as a means to translate research into classroom practice. *Exceptional Children, 62*, 52–66.

Glatthorn, A. A. (1987). Cooperative professional development: Peer-centered options for teacher growth. *Educational Leadership, 45*(3), 31–35.

Golomb, K. G. (1996). A work in progress. *Learning, 25*(3), 50–52.

Graden, J. L., Casey, A., & Bonstrom, O. (1985). Implementing a prereferral intervention system. Part I. The model. *Exceptional Children, 51*, 377–384.

Harris, K. C. (1995). School-based bilingual special education teacher assistance teams. *Remedial and Special Education, 16*(6), 337–343.

Herner, L. M., & Higgins, K. (2000). Forming and benefiting from educator study groups. *Teaching Exceptional Children, 32*(5), 30–37.

Hoover, J. J., & Collier, C. (1991). Meeting the needs of culturally and linguistically diverse exceptional learners: Prereferral to mainstreaming. *Teacher Education and Special Education, 14*(1), 30–34.

Huling-Austin, L. (1986). What can and cannot reasonably be expected from teacher induction programs. *Journal of Teacher Education, 37*(1), 2–5.

Huling-Austin, L. (1990). Teacher induction programs and internships. In W. R. Houston (Ed.), M. Haberman, & J. Sikula (Associate Eds.), *Handbook of research on teacher education* (pp. 535–548). New York: Macmillan.

Idol, L., Nevin, A., & Paolucci-Whitcomb, P. (1994). *Collaborative consultation* (2nd ed.). Austin, TX: PRO-ED.

Johnson, D. W., & Johnson, R. T. (1987). Research shows the benefits of adult cooperation. *Educational Leadership, 45*(3), 27–30.

Johnson, L. J. & Pugach, M. C. (1991). Peer collaboration: Accommodating students with mild learning and behavior problems. *Exceptional Children, 57*, 454–461.

Jonson, K., & Hodges, C. (1998). *Developing professional portfolios in a teacher education program.* (Report No. SP 037 860). New Orleans: Paper presented at the Annual Meeting of the American Association of Colleges for Teacher Education. (ERIC Document Reproduction Service No. ED 418 070)

Joyce, B., Wolf, J., & Calhoun, E. (1993). *The self-renewing school.* Alexandria, VA: Association for Supervision and Curriculum Development.

Kelly, L. (1999, March). Teacher portfolios: Tools for successful evaluations. *Education Update, 41*(2), 4.

Knackendoffel, E. A. (1989). *Development and validation of a set of teaming strategies for enhancing collaboration between secondary resource and content teachers.* Unpublished doctoral dissertation, University of Kansas, Lawrence.

Knackendoffel, E. A. (1996). Collaborative teaming in the secondary school. In D. D. Deshler, E. S. Ellis, & B. K. Lenz (Eds.), *Teaching adolescents with learning disabilities* (2nd ed.) (pp. 579–616). Denver: Love.

Knackendoffel, E. A., Robinson, S. M., Deshler, D. D., & Schumaker, J. B. (1992). *Collaborative problem solving.* Lawrence, KS: Edge Enterprises.

Knight, J. (1997a). Open conversations: The art & practice of partnership learning. *Stratenotes, 6*(3), 1–4.

Knight, J. (1997b). *Partnership learning training packet.* Lawrence, KS: Center for Research on Learning, University of Kansas.

Knight, J. (1998). *The effectiveness of partnership learning: A dialogical methodology for staff development.* Unpublished doctoral dissertation, University of Kansas, Lawrence.

Knight, J. (2000a). Seeking first to understand. Part 2. Reporting back on interviews to make professional development sessions more successful. *Stratenotes, 8*(7), 1–4.

Knight, J. (2000b). Seeking first to understand: Using interviews to make professional development sessions more successful. *Stratenotes, 8*(6), 1–3.

Kohler, F. W., Crilley, K. M., & Shearer, D. D. (1997). Effects of peer coaching on teaching and student outcomes. *Journal of Educational Research 90*(4), 240–250.

Kohler, F. W., Ezell, H. K., & Paluselli, M. (1999). Promoting changes in teachers' conduct of student pair activities: An examination of reciprocal peer coaching. *The Journal of Special Education, 33*, 154–165, 188.

Kurth, R. J. (1985). *Training peer teachers to improve comprehension instruction.* (Report No. SP 025 994). Chicago, IL: Paper presented at the Annual Meeting of the American Educational Research Association. (ERIC Document Reproduction Service No. ED 256 733)

Little, J. W. (1982). Norms of collegiality and experimentation: Workplace conditions of school success. *American Educational Research Journal, 19*, 325–340.

Lyons, N. (1998). Reflection in teaching: Can it be developmental? A portfolio perspective. *Teacher Education Quarterly, 25*(1), 115–127.

Makibbin, S. S., & Sprague, M. M. (1991). *Study groups: Conduit for reform.* (Report No. SP 035 146). St. Louis, MO: Paper presented at the Meeting of the National Staff Development Council. (ERIC Document Reproduction Service No. ED 370 893)

Martin, D. B. (1999). *The portfolio planner: Making professional portfolios work for you.* Upper Saddle River, NJ: Merrill, an imprint of Prentice-Hall.

McLean, J. E. (1995). *Improving education through action research: A guide for administrators and teachers.* Thousand Oaks, CA: Corwin Press.

Miller, D. M., & Pine, G. J. (1990). Advancing professional inquiry for educational improvement through action research. *Journal of Staff Development, 11*(3), 56–61.

Morine-Dershimer, G. (1992). Foreword. In G. P. DeBolt (Ed.), *Teacher induction and mentoring: School-based collaborative programs* (xiii–xvi). Albany, NY: State University of New York Press.

Munro, P., & Elliott, J. (1987). Instructional growth through peer coaching. *Journal of Staff Development, 8*(1), 25–28.

Murdick, N. L., & Petch-Hogan, B. (1996). Inclusive classroom management: Using preintervention strategies. *Intervention in School and Clinic, 31*(3), 172–176.

Murphy, C. (1992). Study groups foster schoolwide learning. *Educational Leadership, 50*(3), 71–74.

Murphy, C., & Lick, D. W. (1998). *Whole-faculty study groups.* Thousand Oaks, CA: Corwin Press.

Neapolitan, J. E. (1999). *Teachers' beliefs about redesigning instruction to meet new standards through action research.* (Report No. SP 038 561). Chicago, IL: Paper presented at the Annual Meeting of the Association of Teacher Educators. (ERIC Document Reproduction Service No. ED 430 975)

Nelson, J. R., Smith, D. J., Taylor, L., Dodd, J. M., & Reavis, K. (1991). Prereferral intervention: A review of the research. *Education and Treatment of Children, 14*, 243–253.

Nevin, A., Thousand, J., Paolucci-Whitcomb, P., & Villa, R. (1990). Collaborative consultation: Empowering public school personnel to provide heterogeneous schooling for all or, Who rang that bell? *Journal of Educational and Psychological Consultation, 1*(1), 41–67.

Noell, G. H., & Witt, J. C. (1999). When does consultation lead to intervention implementation? Critical issues for research and practice. *The Journal of Special Education, 33*, 29–35.

Odell, S. J. (1990). *Mentor teacher programs*. Washington, DC: National Education Association.

Odell, S. J., & Ferraro, D. P. (1992). Teacher mentoring and teacher retention. *Journal of Teacher Education, 43*(3), 200–204.

Odell, S. J., & Huling, L. (2000). Introduction: Leading the teaching profession toward quality mentoring. In S. J. Odell & L. Huling (Eds.), *Quality mentoring for novice teachers* (pp. xi–xvi). Indianapolis, IN: Kappa Delta Pi.

Odell, S. J., & Huling, L., & Sweeny (2000). Conceptualizing quality mentoring—background information. In S. J. Odell & L. Huling (Eds.), *Quality mentoring for novice teachers* (pp. 3–14). Indianapolis, IN: Kappa Delta Pi.

Paquette, M. (1987). Voluntary collegial support groups for teachers. *Educational Leadership, 45*(3), 36–39.

Peck, C. A., Killen, C. C., & Baumgart, D. (1989). Increasing implementation of special education instruction in mainstream preschools: Direct and generalized effects of nondirective consultation. *Journal of Applied Behavior Analysis, 22*, 197–210.

Phillips, M. D., & Glickman, C. D. (1991). Peer coaching: Developmental approach to enhancing teacher thinking. *Journal of Staff Development, 12*(2), 20–25.

Powell, J. H., Berliner, D. C., & Casanova, U. (1992). Empowerment through collegial study groups. *Contemporary Education, 63*, 281–284.

Pugach, M. C., & Johnson, L. J. (1995). Unlocking expertise among classroom teachers through structured dialogue: Extending research on peer collaboration. *Exceptional Children, 62*, 101–110.

Rich, S. J. (1995). Teacher support groups: Why they emerge and the role they play. *Education Canada, 35*(3), 15–21.

Rosenholtz, S. J. (1989). *Teachers' workplace: The social organization of schools*. New York: Longman.

Rowley, J. B. (1999). The good mentor. *Educational Leadership, 56*(8), 20–22.

Sagor, R. (1992). *How to conduct collaborative action research*. Alexandria, VA: Association for Supervision and Curriculum Development.

Sagor, R. (1997). Collaborative action research for educational change. In A. Hargreaves (Ed.), *ASCD yearbook: Rethinking educational change with heart and mind* (pp. 169–191). Alexandria, VA: Association for Supervision and Curriculum Development.

Sanacore, J. (1993). Using study groups to create a professional community. *Journal of Reading, 37*(1), 62–66.

Schaffer, E., Stringfield, S., & Wolfe, D. (1992). An innovative beginning teacher induction program: A two-year analysis of classsroom interactions. *Journal of Teacher Education, 43*(3), 181–192.

Sheridan, S. M., Welch, M., & Orme, S. F. (1996). Is consultation effective? A review of outcome research. *Remedial and Special Education, 17*(6), 341–354.

Showers, B. (1984). *Peer coaching: A strategy for facilitating transfer of training*. (Report No. EA 018 629). Eugene, OR: Center for Educational Policy and Management. (ERIC Document Reproduction Service No. ED 272 849)

Showers, B. (1985). Teachers coaching teachers. *Educational Leadership, 42*(7),43–48.

Showers, B., & Joyce, B. (1996). The evolution of peer coaching. *Educational Leadership, 53*(6), 12–16.

Sindelar, P. T., Griffin, C. C., Smith, S. W., & Watanabe, A. K. (1992). Prereferral intervention: Encouraging notes on preliminary findings. *The Elementary School Journal, 92*, 245–259.

Sparks, D., & Hirsh, S. (1997). *A new vision for staff development*. Alexandria, VA: Association for Supervision and Curriculum Development.

Vail, C. O., Tschantz, J. M., Bevill, A. (1997). Dyads and data in peer coaching: Early childhood educators in action. *Teaching Exceptional Children, 30*(2), 11–15.

Wagenen, L. V., & Hibbard, K. M. (1998). Building teacher portfolios. *Educational Leadership, 55*(5), 26–29.

Wasley, P. (1999). Teaching worth celebrating. *Educational Leadership, 56*(8), 8–13.

Welch, M., Brownell, K., Sheridan, S. M. (1999). What's the score and game plan on teaming in schools? A review of the literature on team teaching and school-based problem-solving teams. *Remedial and Special Education, 20*(1), 36–49.

Whitten, E., & Dieker, L. (1993). Intervention assistance teams: A collaborative process to meet the needs of students at-risk. *B. C. Journal of Special Education, 17*, 275–283.

Whitten, E., & Dieker, L. (1995). Intervention assistance teams: A broader vision. *Preventing School Failure, 40*(1), 41–45.

Wolf, K. (1996). Developing an effective teaching portfolio. *Educational Leadership, 53*(6), 34–37.

Wolf, K., & Dietz, M. (1998). Teaching portfolios: Purposes and possibilities. *Teacher Education Quarterly, 25*(1), 9–22.

Wood, J. W., Lazzari, A., Davis, E. H., Sugai, G., & Carter, J. (1990). National status of the prereferral process: An issue for regular education. *Action in Teacher Education, XII*(3), 50–56.

Zins, J. E., Maher, C. A., Murphy, J. J., & Wess, B. P. (1988). The peer support group: A means to facilitate professional development. *School Psychology Review, 17*(1), 138–146.

Maintaining a Positive Focus

*Fifty years from now it will not matter what kind of
car you drove, what kind of house you lived in, how
much you had in your bank account, or what your
clothes looked like. But the world may be a little better
because you were important in the life of a child.*
—Anonymous

┊A D V A N C E┊ ORGANIZER

The previous chapters in this text contain information on validated practices for planning, delivering, and evaluating educational practices. Using validated practices increases the likelihood that both students and teachers will experience success in the classroom. It is important to remember that teaching is both an art and a science. In addition to becoming technically sound and mastering the science of effective practices, it is important for teachers to view themselves as artists who integrate creativity into the classroom to enhance teaching and learning. Teaching requires a constant search for new ways to capture and maintain student interest. Inspiring students to become the best they can be while simultaneously treating one another with dignity and respect is a constant goal and perhaps the greatest contribution a teacher can make. The content in this chapter reminds us of the tremendous influence teachers have on their students. Those who enter this profession must do so with an open heart, an open mind, and a willingness to continue the learning process throughout their careers.

Teachers are, without a doubt, among the most special human beings on this planet. Their concern for students along with their strong commitment to excellence in teaching ultimately makes the world a better place to live. In essence, teachers are creators of the future. The knowledge they share and the example they set on a daily basis are orchestrated to truly make a difference in the lives of their students and future generations. To use Henry Adams's words, "A teacher affects eternity; he can never tell where his influence stops."

The ways in which teachers create positive futures are endless. Teachers create positive futures when they continue to update their knowledge and skills, when they spend a little extra time with a student who needs help, when they visit a student in the hospital, and when they pat a student on the back and say, "I'm so proud of you." Teachers create positive futures when they stay up late grading papers, when they try to figure out why their last lesson didn't work, and when they stand in the shower thinking about how to help a troubled student. Teachers create positive futures when they spend their own money on materials for their classrooms, when they make home visits, when they lie awake thinking about their students, and when they share their best ideas with other teachers. Teachers create positive futures when they expect great things from their students (Miller, 1999). Teachers frequently extend themselves above and beyond the call of duty because they want to make a difference in the lives of their students and want to contribute to the creation of a better society. Teachers believe that education is the best vehicle for accomplishing this challenging task.

Stories about Teachers Who Made a Difference

Students remember and value the caring and competence of dedicated teachers for many years and sometimes a lifetime. Most of us have memories of special teachers who made a difference in our lives. Some of these memories have been shared in the form of stories and others remain imprinted in our hearts. As teachers, it's important to realize and remember that what we do on a daily basis really does matter. The following stories from students and teachers have been selected for inclusion in this chapter to help remind us of the tremendous role teachers play in the creation of positive futures. Read, enjoy, and think about the importance of teaching as a profession.

Stories from Students

Student Story Number 1 by Leo Buscaglia

I certainly couldn't have done it without her. Though there have been many individuals in my life who have had a strong effect upon my view of the world and

Mr. Reynolds has excellent rapport with his students. He focuses on their positive accomplishments. High-five celebrations are enjoyed in his class.

who have served as mentors, none have shaped my future more than an elementary-school special-education teacher, Miss Hunt.

I was the youngest son of a very large Italian immigrant family. We spoke Italian in the home and English was a second language to me. My parents carried their Italian heritage across the sea, and in many ways I was different. I preferred opera to popular music. I knew Italian fairy tales rather than those read by my neighbors. Our food was different. Our view of life was more full of joy of the moment, passionate behaviors, and deep family ties.

Though I saw all of these things as decided advantages, I fear that our school psychologist saw me through different eyes. My English language skills were low and my view of the world was radically unrealistic. He classified me, after the usual tests, as mentally deficient and recommended special class placement.

It was in the special class setting that I encountered Miss Hunt. She was caring, warm and wonderful. She paid little, if any, attention to labels such as "retarded." She saw us all as children with rich possibilities and unlimited potentials. She helped me to love learning and created an unforgettable loving, accepting environment for us all. I was soon blossoming: reading, writing, sharing and expressing my uniqueness in a myriad of positive ways. She nurtured my mind and my psyche and encouraged me to be proud of who I was.

After several months in her class, she insisted that I be retested. Much to her joy and my despair, I tested out of her class and into a regular classroom. But Miss Hunt's door remained forever open to me. She continued to encourage me and to convince me that there was a wondrous life ahead of me.

I cannot help wonder what might have become of me if I had not encountered Miss Hunt. What she taught me in a short period of time has remained with me all my life, especially my professional life as a teacher. For years I attempted to find her, but to no avail. I wanted very much to thank her and to express the wonder in the life knowledge she shared with me. But I know that with Miss Hunt, it didn't matter. She was a lover, and love is certainly its own reward.

Leo F. Buscaglia, Ph.D., Author, Glenbrook, Nevada (Bluestein, 1995, pp. 14–15)
(Reprinted with permission. *Mentors, Masters and Mrs. MacGregor: Stories of Teachers Making a Difference*, Dearfield Beach, FL: Health Communications, Inc. Copyright 1995, Jane Bluestein.)

Student Story Number 2 by Lee Mirabal

I came from a background of verbal abuse and had very low self-esteem. I was very withdrawn as a child and do not remember most of my teachers. I felt that they did not like me. The one teacher I had who really does stand out was Mrs. Keener, my tenth-grade English teacher. I remember looking up at her at the beginning of the school year, and looking at her long beautiful fingernails and her perfect hair, and thinking about how someday I would like to have fingernails and hair like Mrs. Keener.

But as I grew to appreciate this teacher in other ways, I realized that she noticed something in me that no one else did—that I spoke English very well. I was raised in the South in an area where sometimes people did not speak properly. But for some reason, my pronunciation, my accent, and my grammar were always better than average, and she took an interest in me because of that.

Nobody ever told me I was good at anything, and she did! She used to say, "Oh, I love the way you pronounce that," or she would tell the class, "Listen to the way Rosalee pronounces that word." She pointed me out in a positive way, and was actually the first person in my life to ever do that. This was the only high school course I took that, when I left, I felt that I had really learned something, that I was really interested in the subject—all because a teacher took a special interest in me, because she saw something in me. She gave me something for the first time in my life that I felt I was good at.

And look what I became—a radio talk-show host! Who could imagine the amount of influence she had on what I became!

Lee Mirabal, "Ageless," Nationally Syndicated Radio Talk-Show Host, Entrepreneur, Mother and Wife, Chicago, Illinois (Bluestein, 1995, pp. 16–17) (Reprinted with permission. *Mentors, Masters and Mrs. MacGregor: Stories of Teachers Making a Difference*, Dearfield Beach, FL: Health Communications, Inc. Copyright 1995, Jane Bluestein.)

Student Story Number 3 by Bob Moawad

I graduated from a high school so small that if you wanted to be in the top 10 percent you had to be first or second—there were only 23 students in my graduating class. Leona Friermood was our longstanding English teacher and debate coach. Even though we were small in numbers, year after year, Kalama High School in Kalama, Washington, was formidable opposition for any school of any size in the state. It wasn't because of our natural abilities. It was because a teacher understood what the word "educate" means—seeing us not for what we were but for what we were capable of becoming.

Mrs. Friermood constantly affirmed her belief in us. I was very active in high school. I remember her asking me to compose a speech for a United Nations speech contest. I responded, "I'm involved in student government, in band, in sports and in the play. I can't." Her response: "Yes, you can. And you will." And I did! She said, "I'll help you. You need to write a fifteen-minute speech on 'What the United Nations means to me.'" She said, "Bobby, you have great interpretative reading skills. You just need to read your speech in this competition."

So I wrote the speech. She helped me fine-tune it. Then Mrs. Friermood said, "You know all the other students will just be reading their speeches." I said, "Well that's all you *need* to do." She said, "Well that's all you need to do, but what an edge you would have if you memorized yours." I said, "Mrs. Friermood . . ." She said, "You can. And you will." And I did!

She was an amazing person. She reminded me a little bit of Listerine—it didn't taste good but you knew it was good for you. She understood that *educate* meant to "pull from within" and not to simply transmit information. She was an inspiration to all of us. Many students weren't sure what to think of her because she could be very stern. But after graduating, they'd look back with great admiration. She always had that twinkle in her eyes and was our greatest cheerleader. She'd say, "You beat Castle Rock in football and I'll climb the flagpole." After the win, she'd be sitting on a ladder next to the flagpole for ten minutes during lunch break.

Years later, she was dying of cancer. One of my personal highlights was being asked to be master of ceremonies for "This is Your Life, Leona Friermood." Her students filled the auditorium to honor this amazing teacher. I'll always remember her. She was a great educator, but most of all, she educared!

Bob Moawad, 53, Educator, CEO, Edge Learning Institute,
Tacoma, Washington (Bluestein, 1995, pp. 261–262)
(Reprinted with permission. *Mentors, Masters and Mrs. MacGregor: Stories of Teachers Making
a Difference*, Dearfield Beach, FL: Health Communications, Inc. Copyright 1995, Jane Bluestein.)

Student Story Number 4 by Chuck Glover

One of the most memorable teachers in my life was Clyde Alford, or "Coach" as we knew him. Coach didn't run a big-time outreach program or teach in an inner-city environment. He spent his life helping working-class eighth-graders better understand math—and life—in the small town of St. Albans, West Virginia. Coach must have loved a challenge.

How do you teach algebra to a kid who knows everything about everything important (and math wasn't important); who had emotional problems about which space and time do not allow elaboration; and who had a physical predisposition to weight gain that contributed to his obesity (over 200 pounds at age 13)? Being fat and in middle school is an instant recipe for ostracism a la carte. This was me, floundering and fluctuating, discouraged and uncertain.

I did finally begin to catch on to the algebra, thanks to Coach's persistence. But not before I began to catch on to some other lessons. Coach taught me three lessons. First, I learned that I needed to have something in life compelling me forward. "Let the future pull you forward instead of letting the past push you forward," Coach would say. Second, he taught me that a job is what you make of it. You can enjoy it or dread it—the choice is yours. And finally, I learned to never, never quit. "You will not discover your unrealized resources unless you are tested in some way."

The lessons were not easily learned. But somehow I think that Coach didn't choose his line of work because it was easy. And maybe that's lesson number four: The recipe for happiness doesn't always include happiness as an ingredient. What Coach taught me I imagine he taught to every boy and girl in eighth-grade algebra over the years. By doing so he gave us a foundation for a more successful life. Do you remember this saying: "We can count the number of seeds in an apple, but who can know how many apples are in a seed"?

What I am now in large part is due to Coach. Because of him, all the lives across this country and abroad that I have been privileged to touch have been touched by Coach as well. Thanks, Coach, wherever you are.

Chuck Glover, International Speaker, Instructional Specialist,
Chesterfield, Virginia (Bluestein, 1995, pp. 263–264)
(Reprinted with permission. *Mentors, Masters and Mrs. MacGregor: Stories of Teachers Making
a Difference*, Dearfield Beach, FL: Health Communications, Inc. Copyright 1995, Jane Bluestein.)

Student Story Number 5: "Purple" (author unknown)

In first grade, Mr. Lohr said my purple tepee wasn't realistic enough, that purple was no color for a tent, that purple was a color for people who died, that my drawing wasn't good enough to hang with the others. I walked back to my seat counting the swish, swish, swishes of my baggy corduroy trousers. With a black crayon, nightfall came to my purple tent in the middle of an afternoon.

In second grade, Mr. Barta said, "Draw anything." He didn't care what. I left my paper blank and when he came around to my desk, my heart beat like a tom-

tom while he touched my head with his big hand and in a soft voice said, "The snowfall. How clean and white and beautiful." (Canfield & Hansen, 1995, p. 211).

Stories from Teachers

Teacher Story Number 1: "We're the Retards" by Janice Anderson Connolly

On my first day of teaching, all my classes were going well. Being a teacher was going to be a cinch, I decided. Then came period seven, the last class of the day.

As I walked toward the room, I heard furniture crash. Rounding the corner, I saw one boy pinning another to the floor. "Listen, you retard!" yelled the one on the bottom. "I don't give a damn about your sister!"

"You keep your hands off her, you hear me?" the boy on top threatened.

I drew up my short frame and asked them to stop fighting. Suddenly, 14 pairs of eyes were riveted on my face. I knew I did not look convincing. Glaring at each other and me, the two boys slowly took their seats. At that moment, the teacher from across the hall stuck his head in the door and shouted at my students to sit down, shut up, and do what I said. I was left feeling powerless.

I tried to teach the lesson I had prepared but was met with a sea of guarded faces. As the class was leaving, I detained the boy who had instigated the fight. I'll call him Mark. "Lady, don't waste your time," he told me. "We're the retards." Then Mark strolled out of the room.

Dumbstruck, I slumped into my chair and wondered if I should have become a teacher. Was the only cure for problems like this to get out? I told myself I'd suffer for one year, and after my marriage that next summer I'd do something more rewarding.

"They got to you, didn't they?" It was my colleague who had come into my classroom earlier. I nodded.

"Don't worry," he said. "I taught many of them in summer school. There are only 14 of them, and most won't graduate anyway. Don't waste your time with those kids."

"What do you mean?"

"They live in shacks in the fields. They're migratory labor, pickers' kids. They come to school only when they feel like it. The boy on the floor had pestered Mark's sister while they were picking beans together. I had to tell them to shut up at lunch today. Just keep them busy and quiet. If they cause any trouble, send them to me."

As I gathered my things to go home, I couldn't forget the look on Mark's face as he said, "We're the retards." *Retards*. That word clattered in my brain. I knew I had to do something drastic.

The next afternoon I asked my colleague not to come into my class again. I needed to handle the kids in my own way. I returned to my room and made eye contact with each student. Then I went to the board and wrote *ECINAJ*.

"That's my first name," I said. "Can you tell me what it is?"

They told me my name was "weird" and that they had never seen it before. I went to the board again and this time wrote JANICE. Several of them blurted the word, then gave me a funny look.

"You're right, my name is Janice," I said. "I'm learning-impaired, something called dyslexia. When I began school I couldn't write my own name correctly. I couldn't spell words, and numbers swam in my head. I was labeled 'retarded.'

That's right—I was a 'retard.' I can still hear those awful voices and feel the shame."

"So how'd you become a teacher?" someone asked.

"Because I hate labels and I'm not stupid and I love to learn. That's what this class is going to be about. If you like the label 'retard,' then you don't belong here. Change classes. There are no retarded people in this room.

"I'm not going to be easy on you," I continued. "We're going to work and work until you catch up. You *will* graduate, and I hope some of you will go on to college. That's not a joke—it's a promise. I don't *ever* want to hear the word 'retard' in this room again. Do you understand?"

They seemed to sit up a little straighter.

We did work hard, and I soon caught glimpses of promise. Mark, especially, was very bright. I heard him tell a boy in the hall, "This book's real good. We don't read baby books in there." He was holding a copy of *To Kill a Mockingbird*.

Months flew by, and the improvement was wonderful. Then one day Mark said, "But people still think we're stupid 'cause we don't talk right." It was the moment I had been waiting for. Now we could begin an intensive study of grammar, because they wanted it.

I was sorry to see the month of June approach; they wanted to learn so much. All my students knew I was getting married and moving out of state. The students in my last-period class were visibly agitated whenever I mentioned it. I was glad they had become fond of me, but what was wrong? Were they angry I was leaving the school?

On my final day of classes, the principal greeted me as I entered the building. "Will you come with me, please?" he said sternly. "There's a problem with your room." He looked straight ahead as he led me down the hall. *What now?* I wondered.

It was amazing! There were sprays of flowers in each corner, bouquets on the students' desks and filing cabinets, and a huge blanket of flowers lying on my desk. *How could they have done this?* I wondered. Most of them were so poor that they relied on the school assistance program for warm clothing and decent meals.

I started to cry, and they joined me.

Later I learned how they had pulled it off. Mark, who worked in the local flower shop on weekends, had seen orders from several of my other classes. He mentioned them to his classmates. Too proud to ever again wear an insulting label like "poor," Mark had asked the florist for all the "tired" flowers in the shop. Then he called funeral parlors and explained that his class needed flowers for a teacher who was leaving. They agreed to give him bouquets saved after each funeral.

That was not the only tribute they paid me, though. Two years later, all 14 students graduated, and six earned college scholarships.

Twenty-eight years later, I'm teaching in an academically strong school not too far from where I began my career. I learned that Mark married his college sweetheart and is a successful businessman. And, coincidentally, three years ago Mark's son was in my sophomore honors English class.

Sometimes I laugh when I recall the end of my first day as a teacher. To think I considered quitting to do something *rewarding!*

Janice Anderson Connolly (Canfield & Hansen, 1995, pp. 194–197)
Condensed from "Don't Waste Your Time With Those Kids," by J. A. Connolly. In P. R. Cane (Ed.), from *The First Year of Teaching*, 1999, NY: Walker and Company. Copyright 1999 by Pearl Rock Cane. Reprinted with permission from Walker and Company, 435 Hudson St., New York, NY 10014: 1-800-289-2553. All rights reserved.

Teacher Story Number 2: "Three Letters from Teddy" by Elizabeth Silance Ballard

Teddy's letter came today and now that I've read it, I will place it in my cedar chest with the other things that are important in my life. "I wanted you to be the first to know." I smiled as I read the words he had written and my heart swelled with a pride that I had no right to feel.

I have not seen Teddy Stallard since he was a student in my 5th-grade class, 15 years ago. It was early in my career, and I had only been teaching for 2 years. From the first day he stepped into my classroom, I disliked Teddy. Teachers (although everyone knows differently) are not supposed to have favorites in a class, but most especially they are not to show dislike for a child, any child. Nevertheless, every year there are one or two children that one cannot help be attracted to, for teachers are human and it is human nature to like bright, pretty, intelligent people, whether they are 10 years old or 25. And sometimes, not too often, fortunately, there will be one or two students to whom the teacher just can't seem to relate.

I had thought myself quite capable of handling my personal feelings along that line until Teddy walked into my life. There wasn't a child I particularly liked that year, but Teddy was most assuredly one I disliked. He was dirty. Not just occasionally, but all the time. His hair hung low over his ears, and he actually had to hold it out of his eyes as he wrote his papers in class. (And this was before it was fashionable to do so!) Too, he had a peculiar odor about him which I could never identify.

His physical faults were many, and his intellect left a lot to be desired, also. By the end of the first week I knew he was hopelessly behind the others. Not only was he behind; he was just plain slow. I began to withdraw from him immediately.

Any teacher will tell you that it's more of a pleasure to teach a bright child. It is definitely more rewarding for one's ego. But any teacher worth her credentials can channel work to the bright child, keeping him challenged and learning, while she puts her major effort in the slower ones. Any teacher can do this. Most teachers do it, but I didn't, not that year.

In fact, I concentrated on my best students and let the others follow along as best they could. Ashamed as I am to admit it, I took perverse pleasure in using my red pen; and each time I came to Teddy's papers, the cross marks (and they were many) were always a little larger and a little redder than necessary.

While I did not actually ridicule the boy, my attitude was obviously quite apparent to the class, for he quickly became the class "goat," the outcast, the unlovable, the unloved. He knew I didn't like him but he didn't know why. Nor did I know then or now why I felt such an intense dislike for him. All I know is that he was a little boy no one cared about, and I made no effort on his behalf. The days rolled on. We made it through the Fall Festival and the Thanksgiving holidays, and I continued marking happily with my red pen. And as the Christmas holidays approached, I knew that Teddy would never catch up in time to be promoted to the sixth-grade level. He would be a repeater.

To justify myself, I went to his cumulative folder from time to time. He had very low grades for the first 4 years, but no grade failure. How he had made it, I didn't know. I closed my mind to the personal remarks. First Grade: Teddy shows promise by work and attitude, but has poor home situation. Second Grade: Teddy could do better. Mother terminally ill. He receives little help at home. Third Grade: Teddy is a pleasant boy. Helpful, but too serious. Slow learner. Mother passed away end of the year. Fourth Grade: Very slow, but well behaved. Father shows no interest. Well, they passed him four times, but he will certainly repeat the fifth grade! Do him good! I said to myself.

And then the last day before the holiday arrived, our little tree on the reading table sported paper and popcorn chains. Many gifts were heaped underneath, waiting for the big moment. Teachers always get several gifts at Christmas, but mine that year seemed bigger and more elaborate than ever. There was not a student who had not brought me one. Each unwrapping brought squeals of delight, and the proud giver would receive effusive thank yous. His gift wasn't the last one I picked up: in fact, it was in the middle of the pile. Its wrapping was a brown paper bag, and he had colored Christmas trees and red bells all over it. It was stuck together with masking tape. "For Miss Thompson from Teddy," it read. The group was completely silent, and for the first time I felt conspicuous—embarrassed because they all stood watching me unwrap that gift. As I removed the last bit of masking tape, two items fell to my desk: a gaudy rhinestone bracelet with several stones missing and a small bottle of dime-store cologne, half empty. I could hear the snickers and whispers, and I wasn't sure I could look at Teddy. "Isn't this lovely," I said as I tried to place the bracelet on my arm. Would you help me fasten it?" He smiled shyly as he fixed the clasp, and I held up my wrist for all of them to admire. There were a few hesitant oohs and ahhs, but as I dabbed the cologne behind my ears, all the little girls lined up for a dab behind their ears.

I continued to open the gifts until I reached the bottom of the pile. We ate our refreshments, and the bell rang.

The children filed out with shouts of "See you next year!" and "Merry Christmas!" but Teddy waited at his desk. When they had all left, he walked toward me, clutching his gift and books to his chest. "You smell just like Mom," he said softly. "Her bracelet looks real pretty on you, too. I'm glad you liked it." He left quickly. I locked the door, sat down at my desk and wept, resolving to give Teddy what I had deliberately deprived him of—a teacher who cared.

I stayed every afternoon with Teddy from the end of the Christmas holidays until the last day of school. Sometimes we worked together. Sometimes he worked alone while I drew up lesson plans or graded papers.

Slowly, but surely, he caught up with the rest of the class. Gradually, there was a definite upward curve in his grades. He did not have to repeat the fifth grade. In fact, his final averages were among the highest in the class, and although I knew he would be moving out of the state when school was out, I was not worried for him. Teddy had reached a level that would stand him in a good stead the following year, no matter where he went. He had enjoyed a measure of success, and as we were taught in our teacher training courses, "Success builds success."

I did not hear from Teddy until seven years later, when his first letter appeared in my mailbox.

Dear Miss Thompson,

I just wanted you to be the first to know. I will be graduating second in my class next month.

Very truly yours,

Teddy Stallard

I sent him a card of congratulations and a small package—a pen and pencil gift set. I wondered what he would do after graduation. Four years later Teddy's second letter came.

Dear Miss Thompson,

I wanted you to be the first to know. I was just informed that I'll be graduating first in my class. The university has not been easy, but I liked it.
Very truly yours,
Teddy Stallard

I sent him a good pair of sterling-silver monogrammed cuff links and a card, so proud of him I could burst! And now today, Teddy's third letter.

Dear Miss Thompson,

I wanted you to be the first to know. As of today I am Theodore J. Stallard, M.D. How about that!!

I'm going to be married in July, the 7th, to be exact. I wanted to ask if you could come and sit where Mom would sit if she was here. I'll have no family there as Dad died last year.
Very truly yours,
Teddy Stallard

I'm not sure what kind of gift one sends to a doctor on completion of medical school and state boards. Maybe I'll just wait and take a wedding gift, but my note can't wait.

Dear Ted,

Congratulations! You made it, and you did it yourself! In spite of those like me, and not because of us, this day has come for you. God bless you. I'll be at the wedding with bells on!

Students with Learning Disabilities, 5/e by Mercer © 1997.
Reprinted by permission of Pearson Education, Inc. Upper Saddle River, New Jersey 07458

There are many, many stories about teachers and the meaningful work they do. Talk to anyone and, undoubtedly, they too will have a story to share about a special teacher who made a difference in their lives. The themes of the stories vary. Some revolve around a year of competent teaching skills that ultimately resulted in loving specific content, and others revolve around a single statement on a particular day that changed a life forever. Regardless of the details of the story, the conclusions tend to be the same: teachers matter and they matter in a BIG way.

Many intrinsic rewards result from being a successful teacher. It is particularly rewarding to help students discover their talents, to watch "the light bulb come on" when something new is understood for the first time, and to inspire students to want to learn and do their best work. Much satisfaction is gained from influencing students to become more humane and from helping them to feel better about themselves and their capabilities. It also is very rewarding to watch students transform into happy, successful citizens who will make it in the "real world."

Some students show appreciation for their teachers immediately through smiles, "high fives," handshakes, hugs, letters, small gifts, giggles of joy, or verbal expressions; some come back years later to visit and say thanks; and others keep outward expressions hidden but carry warm memories in their hearts. Regardless of whether or not appreciation is outwardly expressed, teachers know when they've made a connection, when they've made a difference, when they've contributed to the creation of a positive future. What a terrific feeling this is! Perhaps the primary motivation for becoming a teacher is the meaningful nature of the work. Teachers have the opportunity to share their gifts, talents, creativity, skills, knowledge, and personalities and, in many cases, directly observe the fruits of their labor. Watching students grow and develop and realizing that one's efforts as a teacher were part of the process is a wonderful experience. Perhaps Martin Haberman (1995b) said it best: "Life's greatest gift is the opportunity to throw oneself into a job that puts meaning and hope into the lives of other people. Seizing this opportunity is the surest way to put meaning and hope into one's own life" (p. xii).

What It Takes to Be a Successful Teacher

Undoubtedly, those who enter the profession of teaching do so with the intent of becoming a successful teacher and consequently achieving a sense of pride and purpose through their life's work. Teaching, however, is not a profession for everyone. It takes a special kind of person to become a successful teacher and it takes a lot of hard work. Thus far in this chapter, the focus has been on the positive influence that teachers have on students. Unfortunately, the antithesis also is true. Teachers who don't enjoy their work or who lack the skills and disposition required to be a successful teacher can have a negative influence on their students. Thus, it is very important to carefully consider what it takes to be a successful teacher when making decisions about entering or remaining in the profession.

Use Validated Practices

One of the most important things that teachers can do to enhance the likelihood of success in their chosen profession is to learn about and then implement validated practices. There have been significant advances in educational research over the past few decades; consequently, more is known about effective practices now than ever before. Thus, teachers have the opportunity to implement practices that have been validated through research, rather than simply using a trial-and-error approach to teaching. Naturally, the outcomes are better and both students and teachers enjoy the resulting success.

Some educators and researchers have expressed concern and offered explanations for the gap between what is known about good practice and the time it takes to actually see this knowledge implemented in classrooms (see Warby, Greene, Higgins, & Lovitt, 1999); while others (Klingner, Vaughn, Hughes, & Arguelles, 1999; Vaughn, Klingner, & Hughes, 2000) have noted that we should be impressed with the extent to which complex instructional practices are maintained by teachers in spite of great difficulty (e.g., time required for implementation; high-stakes testing and accompanying pressure to prepare students for standardized achievement tests; lack of support). Regardless of which position one takes, the bottom line remains that to be a successful teacher, one must implement practices that work. It is important to be a wise consumer and constantly seek educational practices that have been validated (i.e., research-based) and instructional materials that have been field-tested (i.e., used and improved with students and teachers prior to being published). Teachers who use research-based practices and programs increase the likelihood of achieving success with their students. Additionally, precious instructional time is preserved and the learning process is more efficient when teachers implement validated practices. The importance of this, particularly when teaching students who have diverse learning challenges, cannot be overemphasized.

A variety of approaches are used to facilitate ongoing efforts to implement validated practices. Two of these approaches (i.e., peer coaching and teacher study groups) were discussed in Chapter 9 as collegial learning processes that promote professional development among teachers. Both peer coaching and teacher study groups also have been used to help teachers translate research into their classroom practices (Gersten, Morvant, & Brengelman, 1995; Sanacore, 1993). In addition to peer coaching and teacher study groups, several step-by-step processes are available to help teachers understand and implement validated practices.

Translating Research Articles

Research articles from professional journals are an excellent resource for teachers who want to stay current with regard to educational practices. It has been noted, however, that teachers benefit from a step-by-step process for identifying appropriate research articles and then translating the article's content into their classroom practices (Warby et al., 1999; Warby, 1998). This process includes the following seven steps:

1. Identify the problem or concern. Assess instructional needs and prioritize topics to research.
2. Seek a variety of sources. Look for journal articles that address the selected topic. These frequently are found in university, public, or school libraries. The Internet also can be used to locate relevant research articles. The most commonly used database is Educational Resources Information Center (ERIC), Web site: www.ed.gov.
3. Read, review, and evaluate the information found. Once potential sources of relevant information are located, conduct specific searches to determine how much research is available on the topic of interest. If a great deal of research is available, the search can be limited to the most recent studies.
4. Select primary sources. When possible, locate original sources of research. In other words, find articles in which researchers describe their own experimental studies. This information is apt to be accurate and detailed.
5. Distinguish between theory and opinion. Locate articles that report experimental studies. The articles typically have a methods or procedures section that includes a discussion of the research design, variables that were manipulated to assess change, and descriptions of data collection and analysis.

6. Review the parts of a research article (e.g., title, abstract, methodology). Read the article and decide whether the research adequately addresses the problem or concern identified in step 1. Also decide whether the research is potentially a good "fit" within the context that it will be used.
7. Translate the research into practice. After deciding that the research might be helpful, identify the sequential steps for implementation and write them down. Identify modifications needed for particular classes or individual students. Record the article reference (i.e., author[s], publication date, title of article, journal name, volume, number, and pages) in case revisiting the information becomes necessary.

This translation process represents a systematic way for educators to acquire and ultimately integrate research-based practices into their daily work with students. Although a certain amount of time and effort are required in this process, there also are direct payoffs for both teachers and students (see Validation Box 10.1).

Using Workshop–Implementation–Follow-up Routines

Another approach for integrating research into classrooms involves a three-step process known as the Consumer-Validated-Research Approach (CVRA) (Eaker & Huffman, 1984). In step 1, researchers conduct workshops for teachers and provide research summaries on topics of interest. In step 2, the teachers participating in the workshop generate a plan for implementing the research-based practices in their classrooms. In step 3, the teachers reconvene (a few weeks after the original workshop) and report on their implementation progress.

In a similar approach, six steps are used to help integrate research-based practices (e.g., self-management strategies) into classroom settings (Lovitt & Higgins, 1996). These steps are: *(a)* identify a topic, *(b)* present and interpret research, *(c)* provide follow-up, *(d)* reconvene, *(e)* continue with one teacher, and *(f)* meet with the district administrator. In the first step, a research-based practice is selected and relevant research is gathered. In the second step, an all-day meeting is held with teachers. Research on the selected topic is presented. Rationales for using the practice are emphasized and steps for implementation are shared. Teachers select stu-

VALIDATION BOX

10.1

Translating Research Articles

In a study involving 37 graduate students, the effectiveness of using the step-by-step process for translating research articles into a plan for practice was evaluated. The experimental group who received training in the step-by-step process outperformed the control group in their ability to translate research articles into a plan for classroom implementation. Both groups revealed positive perceptions regarding the benefits of research-based knowledge. For more information see: (Warby, 1998).

VALIDATION BOX

10.2

Workshop–Implementation–Follow-up Routines

A 7-step workshop–implementation–follow-up routine was used with 10 experienced secondary teachers of youth with mild disabilities. After attending a workshop to learn about self-management strategies, they implemented a variety of self-management projects in a variety of classroom settings. The workshop presenters provided follow-up support to the teachers, and teachers reconvened 4 months later to share their results with one another. All 10 teachers stayed with the project and implemented self-management strategies with at least one student. The students benefited and the teachers indicated they would continue using the validated self-management strategies even after the study ended. For more information see: (Lovitt & Higgins, 1996).

dents with whom they will use the practice. In the third step, the teachers implement the practice and researchers and/or project staff provide ongoing support through phone calls and classroom visits. Ways to improve the practice and/or extend it to more students are discussed during these calls and visits. In the fourth step, the teachers come back together for another all-day meeting. This time the teachers describe their experience implementing the practice and share data illustrating the progress of their students. They also discuss how they plan to use the practice in the future. In the fifth step, one teacher is selected to assist in training additional teachers to use the research-based practice. During the sixth and final step, a meeting is held with district administrators to plan additional inservice sessions on research-based practices (see Validation Box 10.2).

Be Persistent and Continually Preserve Student Learning

In addition to using validated practices, successful teachers are persistent and continually seek to preserve student learning. They constantly seek solutions to the many challenges that emerge while teaching diverse groups of students. Moreover, successful teachers believe it is their responsibility to find ways to keep students engaged in learning (Haberman, 1995b). This isn't as easy as it sounds. As has been mentioned throughout this text, there is great diversity among and between students in today's schools. Regardless of individual student characteristics (e.g., learning disabilities, behavioral disorders, mental retardation, mental health problems, limited English proficiency) and life experiences (e.g. abusive home life, poverty, affluence, routine transience, gang exposure) teachers are responsible for managing, teaching, and providing positive learning experiences for *all* of their students. Successful teachers avoid blaming students, families, or neighborhoods for poor student performance in school. They recognize that factors outside of school influence

Ms. Paulsen is a warm and caring teacher who continually looks for ways to ensure student learning. Her lessons are meaningful and thought-provoking and require active student involvement. Consequently, student motivation is high and everyone puts forth maximum effort most of the time.

student performance, but they also realize that regardless of the life conditions of their students, it is their job to engage students in the learning process. Thus, successful teachers focus their time and energy on creating meaningful lessons that will motivate their students and result in positive learning experiences. This requires a great deal of commitment and a willingness to continually ask, "What can I try next?" or "How can I do this better?" Successful teachers guard against complacency and continually look for positive ways to meet the academic, social, and emotional needs of their students. When one thing doesn't work, they try something else. Simply put, they refuse to "give up."

In addition to great persistence, successful teachers continually protect and preserve the learning of their students (Haberman, 1995b). This protection and preservation come in various forms. At times, teachers find themselves in advocacy roles. Advocacy for special services, curricula, and instructional approaches is sometimes needed to ensure that students get what they need and succeed in school. This type of advocacy sometimes requires teachers to take an unpopular stance among colleagues and administrators. It is, of course, important for teachers to handle these "delicate" situations in a professional and humane manner. It is imperative, how-

Ms. Jones never gives up on her students. She resists complacency and always brings enthusiasm to her teaching. She loves teaching and her students know it!

ever, for teachers to preserve and protect their students' learning even if this means "going against the grain" or standing up against "loud, influential voices." Successful teachers keep the best interests of their students at the forefront of their thinking and find ways to break through learning barriers. They persist on behalf of students' learning in positive ways.

Recognize the Potential for Burnout and Activate Strategies to Prevent It

The challenges that teachers face at times can cause even the "best of the best" to feel discouraged and tired. Large caseloads and class sizes, lack of resources and support, conflicting rules and policies, number of class interruptions, excessive paperwork, and lack of time to accomplish goals are potential contributors to teacher stress and burnout (Brownell & Smith, 1993; Haberman, 1995a; Wisniewski & Gargiulo, 1997). Required attendance in meetings that lack meaningful information also contributes to teacher stress. This is especially true when the meetings require excessive amounts of time, lack organization, or fail to address teacher concerns and needs. Robert Fulghum (1993) shared the following story about one of his faculty meeting experiences:

> Faculty meetings are black holes that suck intelligence out of nice people's minds. I hated them so much I always sat on the floor in the back of the room and concentrated on sleeping with my eyes open. Sometimes I survived by imagining what everybody in the room looked like sitting there in their underwear.
>
> Once I almost died in a faculty meeting. I had taken a paring knife to school to sharpen in the school shop and had put the paring knife in the outside pocket of my book satchel, which was next to me on the floor when I fell over laughing at some absurd thing. I drove the knife through the fleshy part of the back side of my right arm and into my rib cage. It wasn't as serious a wound as it seems, but I passed out from shock and lay there on the floor. Nobody paid me any attention until blood started seeping out onto the rug.
>
> An ambulance was called, and I was hauled away to be stitched up.
>
> The event entered into the mythology of faculty life. "Fulghum hated faculty meetings so much he tried to kill himself during one."
>
> It took a while for the chairman of the meeting, the young assistant headmaster, to believe I wasn't faking when I did my hara-kiri act and fell over. He believed I would do anything to get out of a faculty meeting, and here was proof. His suspicion was well founded. It was true. (pp. 139–140)

School personnel sometimes miss the mark when it comes to wise use of professional time. The complex nature of a teacher's job requires the development of effective time-management skills. In Stephen R. Covey's books, *The 7 Habits of Highly Effective People* and *First Things First*, he discusses a time-management model that involves four types of activities in which people spend their time. The first type involves crises, pressing problems, and deadline-driven projects. These activities are *important and urgent* and need immediate attention. The second type involves building relationships, planning, preventing future crises or problems, and recognizing new opportunities. These activities are *important, but not urgent*. The third type involves interruptions, some mail, some calls, some reports, some meetings, and popular endeavors. These activities are *not important, but urgent*. Finally, the fourth type involves trivia, busywork, some mail, some phone calls, time wasters, and pleasant endeavors. These activities are *not important and not urgent*. Covey's model suggests that stress and burnout occur when too much time is spent involved in the first type of activities (those that are important and urgent) and that the best way to prevent this stress and burnout is to devote more time to the second type of activities (those that are important, but not urgent). In other words, to reduce the amount of time spent dealing with crises, more time should be spent in building relationships, planning, thinking, and preventing stressful events. In order to do this, the amount of time spent in the third and fourth type of activities (not important, but urgent; not important, not urgent) must be reduced (Covey, 1989).

In addition to poor decisions regarding the use of time, another factor that contributes to teacher stress is the organizational structure found within some schools. Educational institutions tend to be bureaucratic systems that sometimes get in the way of effective teaching and learning (Haberman, 1995b). In bureaucratic systems, authority frequently is communicated through policy statements, rules, and job descriptions. Moreover, politics sometimes influences the decisions that are made regarding the operation of a school. At times, this results in educational barriers that teachers must work around. If too much time and energy is spent dealing with the bureaucracy, teachers may begin to experience burnout.

Successful teachers recognize the potential for burnout and develop active strategies to prevent it. Specifically, they figure out how to "work the system," establish support networks with colleagues, demonstrate high levels of personal commitment to their students (Brownell, Smith, McNellis, & Lenk, 1994–1995), and simultaneously take good care of themselves.

Work the System

One of the best ways to prevent teacher burnout is to develop coping strategies for dealing with the bureaucracy of "the system." Successful teachers "learn as much as possible about the informal structure of the school as quickly and as well as possible, in order to avoid falling victim to the formal organization of the school. They know which janitor, which secretary, which safety guard, which other teachers will help them do what they want with the least paperwork, permissions, or hassle. Stars are experts at using this informal structure to make the system work for their children" (Haberman, 1995b, p. 66). Successful teachers who stay in the profession figure out what they need from the system to make instruction work for their students. They also figure out which rules and policies must be followed and which can be bent to benefit students (Brownell et al., 1994–1995). In other words, they figure out how to gain the widest discretion for themselves and their students without having the system "punish" them (Haberman, 1995a). Making these determinations is challenging for novice teachers, but over time it becomes easier.

Establish Support Networks with Colleagues

Another strategy for preventing teacher burnout is to develop supportive working relationships with colleagues. As was discussed in Chapter 9, induction and mentoring programs; partnership learning; and collegial learning processes such as structured dialogue, collaborative problem solving, collaborative consultation, specialist consultation, intervention assistance teams, peer coaching, and teacher study groups facilitate problem solving and promote professional development. Another positive outcome that frequently occurs when teachers get involved in collegial professional development processes is a sense of support among colleagues. This support is helpful in terms of preventing burnout. Some teachers who think similarly and therefore find it easy to support one another form informal support networks. Regular, positive contacts with colleagues results in a sense of "we're all in this together." These contacts also help teachers realize that the challenges they face in

Teachers benefit from establishing positive relationships with their colleagues. These relationships help keep teachers energized and provide mutual support when challenges arise.

their classrooms are not solely the result of their own inadequacies (Brownell & Smith, 1993). The emotional sustenance that emerges when colleagues spend time together and support one another is quite valuable.

Maintain a Personal Commitment to Students without Neglecting Yourself

Maintaining a personal commitment to students also helps teachers prevent burnout. It is helpful to remember that student learning and development is the top priority and as Goethe so aptly stated, "Things which matter most must never be at the mercy of things which matter least." Keeping this in mind helps teachers decide how to spend their professional time and energy. It is easier to say "no" to nonpurposeful requests and/or time wasters when students clearly are the first priority.

Although commitment to students is very important, this doesn't mean total involvement in work to the exclusion of everything else in life. The most successful professionals learn to strike a balance between their careers and the noncareer aspects of their lives (e.g., family, friends, leisure pursuits) (Cherniss, 1995). Stephen Covey (1989), in his national best seller *The 7 Habits of Highly Effective People*, discussed the importance of developing a personal mission statement (i.e., philosophy, creed, or constitution by which one lives). Personal mission statements focus on what a person wants to be (character), what a person wants to do (contributions and achievements), and the values and principles that will be followed during the process of being and doing. In other words, the mission statement becomes the criterion by which everything else in life is measured. Writing a mission statement requires individuals to think deeply about the meaning of their lives. They must consider the various roles they play and related goals for these roles. Writing a mission statement promotes proactivity and a sense of balance. Once one's mission is clarified, it becomes easier to make personal and professional decisions. When faced with life challenges, reflection on one's mission statement frequently brings clarity regarding how to respond to the challenges.

Acknowledge Mistakes and Learn from Them

Another important characteristic of successful teachers is the ability to recognize one's own mistakes and then take responsibility for them. It is particularly important for teachers to recognize mistakes that have to do with human relations with their students (e.g., misjudging a student, embarrassing a student, hurting a student's feelings). Successful teachers realize the importance of apologizing when these types of mistakes are made. If the mistake was made in front of the students' peers, then the apology should be public as well (Haberman, 1995a; Haberman, 1995b). In addition to apologizing for recognized mistakes, teachers must try to learn from them. The goal, of course, is to avoid making the same mistake multiple times. *Learning from mistakes* is an important message to communicate to students. Students need to realize that mistakes are a necessary part of learning. Communicating and modeling this message helps students accept their own fallibility (Haberman, 1995b; see Validation Box 10.3).

VALIDATION BOX

10.3

Successful Teachers

The correlation between the Urban Teacher Selection Interview (UTSI) and successful teacher practice was evaluated in a study involving 38 teachers. The UTSI was used to assess teacher dispositions including persistence, protection of students and student learning, approach to at-risk students, approach to teacher burnout, and fallibility. Results of the interview were used to rank prospective teachers related to their predicted success as teachers in urban schools. Approximately 9 months later, half of the teachers were ranked based on principals' evaluations of their performance as teachers; approximately 2-1/2 years later, the remaining teachers were ranked based on principals' evaluations of their performance as teachers. The findings were the same for both groups of teachers. With only a couple of exceptions, those who ranked in the top half on their interview also ranked in the top half based on performance evaluations. Those who ranked in the bottom half on their interview also ranked in the bottom half of the performance evaluations. Thus, the dispositions assessed during the interview were good predictors of success as teachers. For more information see: (Haberman, 1993).

The content presented in this text emphasizes the critical importance of being fundamentally sound and technically proficient in efforts to plan, deliver, and evaluate instructional practices. The importance of this is without contradiction. Teaching, however, cannot be reduced to technique alone. Heart and soul must also be brought into the classroom. It is important to remember that one of the primary missions of schooling is to help students become good people who feel a sense of connection to others and who display a sense of decency in their journey through life. Robert Fulghum (1996) said that all he needed to know about *how to live* and *what to do* and *how to be* was learned in kindergarten. Teachers must help students learn and remember Fulghum's important life lessons. They are:

Share everything.
Play fair.
Don't hit people.
Put things back where you found them.
Clean up your own mess.
Don't take things that aren't yours.
Say you're sorry when you hurt somebody.
Wash your hands before you eat.
Flush.
Warm cookies and cold milk are good for you.
Live a balanced life—learn some and think some and draw and paint and sing and dance and play and work every day some.
Take a nap every afternoon.
When you go out into the world, watch out for traffic, hold hands, and stick together.
Be aware of wonder. Remember the little seed in the Styrofoam cup: The roots go down and the plant goes up and nobody really knows how or why, but we are all like that.
Goldfish and hamsters and white mice and even the little seed in the Styrofoam cup—they all die. So do we.
And then remember the Dick-and-Jane books and the first word you learned—the biggest word of all—LOOK. (pp. 6–7)

Clearly, teaching is challenging work. The rewards, however, make the challenging journey worthwhile. Perhaps the most important aspect of teaching is maintaining a positive focus toward oneself and one's students. With regard to oneself, it is important to take pride in both large and small accomplishments and to resist negative thinking. Cognitive theorists Dr. Albert Ellis and Dr. Aaron Beck, as well as the Nobel Prize winner and spiritual leader of Tibet, the Dalai Lama, have discussed the importance of training the mind to counteract negative thoughts (His Holiness The Dalai Lama & Cutler, 1998). Doing so increases one's personal happiness and enhances professional accomplishments. In addition to maintaining a positive focus toward oneself, it also is important to maintain a positive focus toward the students. Teachers must never lose sight of the potential that exists within each of their stu-

Perhaps the greatest reward for teaching is watching students succeed and realizing that you contributed to that success. Teachers are in the business of creating a positive future one student and/or one class at a time. Enjoy the journey.

dents. Moreover, teachers must continue to remember that student learning is of utmost importance and the role they play in their students' lives is very significant. The example teachers set, the care that they share, and the expertise they develop over the course of their careers truly make a difference. Perhaps the thank yous from students communicate this best:

Thank you, teacher, for seeing me. (Age 5)

Thank you, teacher, for my "at-home" reading books. (Age 5)

Thank you, teacher, for the happy faces. (Age 6)

Thank you, teacher, for loving me. (Age 6)

Thank you, teacher, for showing us all the things that we could do. (Age 6)

Thank you, teacher, for helping me with my work and keeping me safe at school. (Age 8)

Thank you, teacher, for teaching me all the things you know. (Age 9)

Thank you, teacher, for being patient and not yelling all the time. (Age 10)

Thank you, teacher, for helping me with stuff I get stuck on. (Age 11)

Thank you, teacher, for being the best teacher I know. If you were to fall down a well the whole world would feel sorrow. (Age 11)

Thank you, teacher, for telling me never to eat a jalapeno burger. My friend did once and she couldn't talk for ten minutes. (Age 11)
Thank you, teacher, for encouraging us to ask questions. (Age 12)
Thank you, teacher, for giving me the courage to speak in public. (Age 13)
Thank you, teacher, for having tolerance and listening when we have something to say. (Age 15)
Thank you, teacher, for giving me the benefit of the doubt. (Age 16)
Thank you, teacher, for caring enough about me to not accept anything but my best. (Age 17)
Thank you, teacher, for caring enough to make sure I succeeded. (Age 17)
Thank you, teacher, for giving me chances to get my act together. (Age 18)

(Morrow, 1999, pp. 84, 86, 87, 93, 96, 98, 99, 101, 104, 106, 109, 111, 113, 115, 116)

Practice Activities

▶ Think about one of your all-time favorite teachers. Identify the characteristics of that teacher that made him or her special.
▶ Locate a research-based journal article that describes a study conducted with students in grades K through 12. Use the seven-step process, outlined in this chapter, to translate the research into a plan for classroom practice.
▶ Identify a list of things you can do as a teacher to preserve student learning.
▶ Talk to several practicing teachers about their strategies for preventing teacher burnout.
▶ Develop a mission statement that reflects a balance between the personal and professional aspects of your life.

Review of Chapters 8 to 10

Chapters 8 through 10 addressed issues related to evaluating student and teacher performance. Procedures for monitoring student progress, various structures for engaging in professional growth and development, and the importance of maintaining a positive focus were emphasized. The following questions are designed to provide review and promote integration of information from Chapters 8 to 10. While reviewing, it is important to remember that careful monitoring of student progress is necessary for effective and efficient learning to take place. Moreover, teachers' knowledge, skills, and dispositions greatly influence the quality and quantity of student learning. Thus, in addition to monitoring student performance, teachers must monitor their own performance and continually seek ways to improve their professional practice. Before closing the final chapter in this book, consider the following questions:

1. What are the advantages and disadvantages of using alternative grading systems for students with disabilities?
2. For what purposes should curriculum-based assessment be used?
3. How do teachers determine whether adequate progress is being made when implementing curriculum-based assessment?
4. Why should curriculum-based assessment data be displayed in graph format?
5. For what purposes should portfolio assessment be used?
6. How do teachers determine whether adequate progress is being made when implementing portfolio assessment?
7. How can technology be used to assist with ongoing monitoring of student progress?
8. How do partnership learning strategies enhance teacher workshops?
9. Why is collegial learning important for professional growth and development?
10. Which collegial learning processes have the greatest appeal to you? Why?
11. What potential benefits are associated with action research?
12. How can teacher portfolios result in improved practice?
13. Should teacher success be measured? If so, how should it be measured?
14. What constitutes a successful teacher?

T E X T REVIEW AND POST-ORGANIZER

The validated practices described throughout this text will make the job of teaching easier and more fulfilling. The importance of educational planning was emphasized in the first three chapters. In Chapter 1, the recent school reform movements and the extensive diversity found among the students in today's schools were discussed. It is important to understand school context and student characteristics when planning appropriate instructional programs. As this understanding begins to emerge, the validated planning processes described in Chapter 2 and the suggestions for classroom organization in Chapter 3 become meaningful. The quality and quantity of preparation that takes place prior to instruction play a major role in teachers' success or lack thereof. Planning and classroom organization are ongoing processes that continue throughout each school year. Teachers continually refine these processes and, over time, determine what works best for their particular teaching situation.

Along with the intricacies of instructional planning and organization, teachers select particular instructional models to provide a framework for their teaching. The Explicit Instruction, Direct Instruction, and Strategy Instructional models were presented in Chapter 4. Each of these models has been used successfully to provide instruction to diverse groups of students. Explicit and Direct Instruction are used to deliver content and teach specific academic and behavioral skills, whereas strategy instructional models are designed to teach students *how* to learn and perform. Thus, teachers can use more than one instructional model depending on the content being taught and the needs of the students. Regardless of what instructional model or combination of models a teacher uses, specific effective teaching behaviors are used to promote student achievement. These effective teacher behaviors were reviewed in Chapter 5. Specifically, validated practices for beginning a lesson, continuing a lesson, and ending a lesson were discussed. The point was made that in addition to technical expertise, teachers need to communicate a sense of caring to their students. Additional information regarding effective methods for delivering instruction was addressed in Chapters 6 and 7. A variety of instructional arrangements (e.g., peer tutoring, cooperative learning, computer-based instruction) have been validated as have numerous methods for modifying curriculum and instruction (e.g., accommodations, adaptations, assistive technology). This is particularly important when facilitating the success of students with special needs in general education curricula.

After planning and delivering instruction, validated practices are used to monitor student performance and thus make judgments about the instructional program. In Chapter 8, a variety of grading practices and several supplemental monitoring procedures (e.g., curriculum-based measurement, portfolio assessment) were discussed. Undoubtedly, careful monitoring of student progress is needed to provide effective and efficient instruction. Lack of student progress is a clear indicator that something related to the instructional process needs to change. Thus, when students struggle with their learning, teachers must examine their instructional decisions and practices to determine what can be done differently to promote better student progress. Teachers are responsible for promoting student learning. This cannot be done adequately without carefully monitoring student performance.

In addition to planning, delivering, and evaluating instructional practices, teachers must engage in professional growth activities. Learning to teach is a career-long endeavor that can be facilitated through the processes discussed in Chapter 9. It's really important to resist complacency in teaching. No two groups of students are the same; therefore, new challenges emerge each and every school year. Teachers must continuously seek better ways to do their work, better ways to reach their students, better ways to make a difference. New discoveries, new research, new programs continually emerge that affect the potential for success in the classroom. The students deserve our best work. Let's teach them well!

References

Bluestein, J. (1995). *Mentors, masters and Mrs. MacGregor: Stories of teachers making a difference.* Deerfield Beach, FL: Health Communications, Inc.

Brownell, M. T., & Smith, S. W. (1993). Understanding special education teacher attrition: A conceptual model and implications for teacher educators. *Teacher Education and Special Education, 16,* 270–282.

Brownell, M. T., Smith, S. W., McNellis, J., & Lenk, L. (1994–1995). Career decisions in special education: Current and former teachers' personal views. *Exceptionality, 5,* 83–102.

Canfield, J., & Hansen, M. V. (1995). *A 2nd helping of chicken soup for the soul: 101 more stories to open the heart and rekindle the spirit.* Deerfield Beach, FL: Health Communications, Inc.

Cherniss, C. (1995). *Beyond burnout: Helping teachers, nurses, therapists, and lawyers recover from stress and disillusionment.* New York: Routledge.

Covey, S. R. (1989). *The 7 habits of highly effective people.* New York: Simon & Schuster.

Eaker, R., & Huffman, J. (1984). Linking research and practice: The consumer validation approach. *Roeper Review, 6,* 236–237.

Fulghum, R. (1988). *All I really need to know I learned in kindergarten: Uncommon thoughts on common things.* New York: Villard Books.

Fulghum, R. (1993). *Maybe (maybe not): Second thoughts from a secret life.* New York: Ballantine Books.

Gersten, R., Morvant, M., & Brengelman, S. (1995). Close to the classroom is close to the bone: Coaching as a means to translate research into classroom practice. *Exceptional Children, 62,* 52–66.

Haberman, M. (1993). Predicting the success of urban teachers (the Milwaukee trials). *Action in Teacher Education, 15*(3), 1–5.

Haberman, M. (1995a). Selecting 'star' teachers for children and youth in urban poverty. *Phi Delta Kappan, 76,* 777–781.

Haberman, M. (1995b). *Star teachers of children in poverty.* Lafayette, IN: Kappa Delta Pi.

His Holiness The Dalai Lama & Cutler, H. C. (1998). *The art of happiness.* New York: Riverhead Books.

Klingner, J. K., Vaughn, S., Hughes, M. T., & Arguelles, M. E. (1999). Sustaining research-based practices in reading: A three year follow-up. *Remedial and Special Education, 20,* 263–274, 287.

Lovitt, T. C., & Higgins, A. K. (1996). The gap: Research into practice. *Teaching Exceptional Children, 28*(2), 64–68.

Miller, S. P. (1999). Teachers create positive futures. In D. Barwood, D. Greaves, & P. Jeffery (Eds.), *Teaching Numeracy and Literacy: Interventions and Strategies for "At Risk" Students* (pp. 1–16). Lilydale, Victoria, Australia: Australia Resource Educators' Association.

Morrow, J. G. (1999). *The best thing about my teacher: Notes of appreciation from students.* Nashville, TN: Broadman & Holman.

Sanacore, J. (1993). Using study groups to create a professional community. *Journal of Reading 37*(1), 62–66.

Vaughn, S., Klingner, J., & Hughes, M. (2000). Sustainability of research-based practices. *Exceptional Children, 66,* 163–171.

Warby, D. (1998). *Formative evaluation: An instrument to measure the effects of using the universal format.* Unpublished doctoral dissertation, University of Nevada, Las Vegas.

Warby, D. B., Greene, M. T., Higgins, K., & Lovitt, T. C. (1999). Suggestions for translating research into classroom practices. *Intervention in School and Clinic, 34,* 205–211, 223).

Wisniewski, L., & Gargiulo, R. M. (1997). Occupational stress and burnout among special educators: A review of the literature. *The Journal of Special Education, 31,* 325–346.

Photo Credits

INDEX